CRIMINOLOGY

LITTLE, BROWN AND COMPANY   Boston/Toronto

CRIMINOLOGY
Analysis and Critique of Crime in America

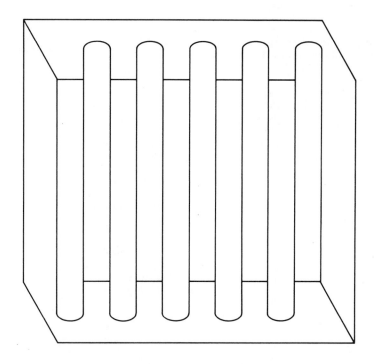

RICHARD QUINNEY City University of New York

Library of Congress Catalog Card No. 75-1584

FOURTH PRINTING

*Published simultaneously in Canada
by Little, Brown & Company (Canada) Limited*

Printed in the United States of America

Portions of this book were previously published in Richard Quinney, *The Social Reality of Crime* (Boston: Little, Brown, 1970). Part of Chapter 2 is a revision and expansion of pp. 108–123 in Richard Quinney, *The Problem of Crime* (New York: Dodd, Mead, 1970).

Parts of Chapters 7, 8, and 9 are drawn from Marshall B. Clinard and Richard Quinney, *Criminal Behavior Systems: A Typology*, 2nd ed. Copyright © 1967, 1973 by Holt, Rinehart and Winston, Publishers. Reprinted by permission of The Dryden Press.

Acknowledgments

Chapter opening illustrations: Pages 2, 32, 116, and 278 The Bettmann Archive. *Pages 14 and 66* Frank Siteman. *Page 42* George Skadding, Time/Life Agency. *Page 94* Marshall Henrichs. *Page 130* Copyright © 1972 by Paramount Pictures Corporation. *Page 146* Wide World Photos. *Page 164* Christopher W. Morrow, Stock, Boston. *Page 196* Margaret Bourke-White, Time/Life Agency. *Pages 224 and 292* Cary S. Wolinsky, Stock, Boston. *Page 240* Jeff Albertson, Stock, Boston.

The following authors and publishers have granted permission to include material from their publications. Page numbers for specific citations appear in the Notes.

Ronald L. Akers. Excerpts from "The Professional Association and Legal Regulation of Practice," *Law and Society Review*, 2, no. 3 (May 1968): 465, 466, and 476. *Law and Society Review* is the official publication of the Law and Society Association, the copyright holders. Reprinted by permission.

Abraham S. Blumberg. Excerpts from *Criminal Justice*, copyright © 1967 by Abraham S. Blumberg. First New Viewpoints edition, published 1974 by Franklin Watts, Inc.

Robert M. Carter and Leslie T. Wilkins. Table from "Some Factors in Sentencing Policy." Reprinted by special permission of the *Journal of Criminal Law, Criminology and Police Science*. Copyright © 1967, by Northwestern University School of Law, Vol. 58, No. 4, p. 512.

Morris Cobern. Excerpts from "Some Manpower Aspects of the Criminal Justice System." Reprinted, with permission of the National Council on Crime and Delinquency, from *Crime and Delinquency*, April 1973, pp. 198–199.

Congressional Quarterly Almanac. Excerpts from *Congressional Quarterly Almanac*, 1972, Vol. 28 (Washington, D.C.: Congressional Quarterly, Inc.), p. 91. Reprinted by permission.

Donald R. Cressey. *Criminal Organization* (New York: Harper & Row, 1972). Copyright © 1972 by Donald R. Cressey. Reprinted by permission.

Walter Dennis, Erich Goode, Lester Grinspoon, Aryeh Neier, and Norman Zinberg. "Letters to the Editor," *The New York Times*, April 24, 1973. © 1973 The New York Times Company. Reprinted by permission.

Kai Erikson. Excerpts from *Wayward Puritans: A Study in the Sociology of Deviance.* Copyright © 1966 John Wiley & Sons. Reprinted by permission of John Wiley & Sons, Inc.

Robert E. Esser, Henry Clay Frick, 2d, Albert Greenwood, William M. Manger, Gabriel G. Nahas, and Philip Zeidenberg. "Letters to the Editor," *The New York Times*, May 31, 1973. © 1973

Preface

Our lives, our view of the world, and our way of knowing about crime have undergone considerable change in the last few years. *Criminology: Analysis and Critique of Crime in America,* which began as a revision of an earlier book, *The Social Reality of Crime,* reflects the vast changes that have taken place. In *Social Reality,* published in 1970, I tried to provide a reorientation to criminology, basing the study on revised assumptions about American society and our relation to it. The purpose of *Criminology* continues to be a new understanding of crime.

Crime has acquired a different meaning for us as the events of recent years forced a reconsideration of the nature of crime in American society. A perspective based on a constructionist view of reality, in relation to social conflict, no longer seems appropriate. Rather, our understanding of contemporary experience depends on a critical analysis of reality. The discussion in *Criminology* examines crime in terms of the social, political, and economic forces in the United States. Crime is ultimately related to the political economy of the nation.

The constituent elements of the criminal system are covered, including the law, the offender, the types of crime, the enforcement and judicial administrations, custody and punishment, and treatment and corrections. Interspersed throughout the text are "Documents" and "Viewpoints"—items from various sources to amplify the discussion. These are drawn from official publications and from statements by authorities and practitioners in the field of criminal justice.

I have tried to present my critical understanding of crime in one book in order to inform, to share ideas that aim toward a better society. Our understanding contributes to a way of life, a politics of being in the world.

Contents

III PATTERNS OF CRIMINAL BEHAVIOR

IV ENFORCING AND ADMINISTERING CRIMINAL LAW

V THE POLITICAL ECONOMY OF CRIME

CRIMINOLOGY

INTRODUCTION

1
The Study of Crime

Can you imagine a world without crime? What would our lives be like without criminals? With all the crime policies and programs, the political words and deeds, the rhetoric on law and order, completely eliminating crime would remove part of our experience. Crime is basic to the American way of life and to civilization in the Western world, which depends on the idea of crime and on the idea of suppressing it.

Why shouldn't we begin to study the world's old and great problem, crime, with some anticipation? Here is a chance to learn about a subject close to our imaginations throughout our lives. Our eagerness increases when we apply critical intelligence to some of our conventional wisdom about crime in America. Stripping away superficial layers, we find that sometimes that which is apparent is not always real. Myths about crimes have obscured truth and reality.

First we should see just what it is about crime that interests us. For some of us crime may have taken concrete form — we may have been the object of criminal laws and the system that administers criminal justice. Or we may have been victims of violent or exploitative acts. Then too, crime has entered our imagina-tions in one way or another all our lives. We have grown up in a world of crime.

We understand crime, then, as we begin to understand ourselves; we cannot adequately understand crime in America unless we *do* examine ourselves. To know any phenomena of this world, and crime in particular, we need to relate our biographies to the past and to present experiences of the age.

We grow up in a world of shared meanings. The most consequential meanings form everyday folklore and are spread today by the mass media — the radio, comic books, the movies, or television. At an impressionable age (and, in fact, all through our lives) we are drawn into a fictional world, a commercialized fiction that for us becomes a reality. Crime, criminals, and the law are probably the commonest and most vivid images that we mold into our lives as we grow up. Even as adults we are faced with portrayals of crime in the movies, in the newspapers, and on television. Crime is big business in commercial communications.

What ideas and characters have shaped the

way your mind and imagination handle crime? The differences, of course, have a lot to do with your generation. But whether your views on law and crime are shaped by a Lone Ranger, a Perry Mason, or a Colombo, you have been developing a typically American version of crime. Whether you grew up on Dick Tracy, Gangbusters, Dragnet, or Mod Squad, you have been creating your own world of crime, helped along by others.

Before going further you might give some thought to your own conception of crime. You are likely to find both a self and a conception of crime that have been partly obscure in your mind. For me, growing up in the forties and fifties, the Lone Ranger was a screen through which I viewed the world. Three nights a week we sat by the radio listening to the latest adventures of the masked man in his pursuit of badmen and criminals. We waited anxiously for good to triumph over evil. My world was made real by this frontier character. Now, confronting this earlier world, I am able to gain a better understanding of crime in America.[1]

Development of Criminology

Criminology as the "scientific" study of crime grew in reaction to turmoil and disorder in the European countries. The early theorists in criminology and the social sciences in general were disturbed by the many rebellions and revolutions in the eighteenth and nineteenth centuries. It was their hope that the new sciences could discover the natural laws on which society had grown and provide a program for social tranquillity.

Criminology began with a conservative ideology. Looking for the laws of social order, criminologists have favored social arrangements as they are. Anything that appears to threaten the social order, such as crime, is regarded as violating the natural laws of society. Instead of looking upon crime as a form of rebellion or as a force for creative change, it has been seen as a pathology that must be controlled or eliminated. We can trace criminology's theoretical development by following its attempts to explain crime as it affects social order.[2]

The most important ideas in criminology before the nineteenth century came from thinkers in the group commonly called the "classical school." It was the culmination of eighteenth-century humanitarian rationalism, and came along just before scientific methods were first used in studying human behavior. Such writers as Cesare Beccaria, Jeremy Bentham, and Samuel Romilly studied the relationship of citizens to the state's legal structure.[3] Reacting against contemporary legal practices, these writers objected to the inconsistencies in the way criminal law was administered, proposing reforms that were more in keeping with their conception of human life. Bentham's slogan, "the greatest happiness of the greatest number," proposed utility as the measure of all goodness. In practice, however, the society's good was placed before the individual's rights.

Modern criminology, says William A. Bonger, began in the 1830s when crime was first studied as a social phenomenon.[4] During the early and middle parts of the nineteenth century, scholars in Europe gathered and analyzed criminal statistics. Alexander von Oettingen of Germany devoted his *Moralstatistik* to the problem of measuring crime. In Belgium, statisticians such as Adolphe Quetelet studied the social nature of crime as reflected in criminal statistics. A. M. Guerry, in charge of judicial statistics for Paris, analyzed rates of crime for the regions of France. Several Italian socialists also actively observed crime. During this period, journals were established for publishing these studies and an international criminological association was founded.

English interest in the ecological distribution of crime was very active between 1830 and 1860.[5] Industrialization and the growing cities led several English writers to examine the social problems brought about by these changes, especially crime. Rawson W. Rawson published a paper entitled "An Inquiry into the Statistics of Crime in England and Wales" in the *Journal of the Statistical Society of London*. Joseph Fletcher, Rawson's successor as honorary secretary of the Statistical Society of London, reported on the crime rates of England in relation to social characteristics of geographical areas. Henry Mayhew, one of the founders of *Punch*, made detailed ecological analyses of crime in London, published as *London Labour and London Poor.*

A large study was done later in the century by Charles Booth, *Life and Labour of the People of London*. Booth was a merchant, shipowner, and manufacturer who, though he benefited from industrialization, was aware that the social conditions it brought about were not ideal. His biographers observe that "Booth appears to be a true Victorian insofar as he acclaimed the positive values of industrial and commercial enterprise, but sought at the same time to devise methods of combating the evils that had resulted from it."[6] A practical man, Booth believed that social policy should be guided by facts, and he set out to gather them. He used scientific inquiry to improve understanding of social problems.

Americans were inclined to equate crime with sin, pauperism, and immorality. Even when they recognized crime as a distinct phenomenon, they usually thought of it as an ill that should not be a part of social life. Crime therefore was one of the problems that fell into the embrace of nineteenth-century reformism in America.

Many persons in positions of authority saw the need for knowledge that would guide their endeavors and supply them with rational grounds for implementing reform — that was the strongest stimulus behind the social science movement in the second half of the century. That social science could supply knowledge to be used for reform became an important idea in the American academic community.[7] Criminology became one of the first courses in the curriculum of the newly established social science departments.

Crime also was studied as a social phenomenon by people engaged in prison and welfare work. Among these early criminologists were Z. B. Brockway, superintendent of Elmira Reformatory; Michael Cassidy, prison administrator; E. C. Wines, secretary of the Prison Association of New York; Franklin B. Sanborn, chairman of the Massachusetts Board of State Charities; and Richard Vaux, president of the Board of Inspectors of Eastern State Penitentiary. They saw crime as produced by "disharmony" in the way in which social forces or institutions of society worked. Their viewpoint

has been summarized as follows: "When these institutions were not soundly constructed, or when their functions were not realized competently and responsibly, and when the patterns of behavior characteristic of groups of people differed from predominating standards, crime was a natural consequence."[8]

Crime grew rapidly along with the growing American cities. Several authors in the latter half of the nineteenth century have written about the urban crime problem. For example, Charles Loring Brace, devoting his life to organizing charities, found the causes of crime in the way of life led by a significant portion of the urban population. In *The Dangerous Classes of New York,* Brace described in great detail the conditions of life among various groups. At the same time, Edward Crapsey described several types of crime in his book, *The Nether Side of New York*. His underlying theory was that crime had developed in the city because community integration was lacking and because of corruption permeating the political structure.

Other writers added to American writings the religious ideas of the social gospel movement. Several Protestant leaders, such as Washington Gladden in *Applied Christianity* and Walter Rauschenbusch in *Christianity and the Social Order*, argued for a religion that would adjust Christianity to the world's problems. This movement, like others during the century, helped to shape American ideas about social problems, including crime.

Another European system of ideas has greatly molded criminology's development. These ideas culminated in the "positive school" of criminology. Particularly among Italian criminologists, it utilized the point of view and methodology of the natural sciences, and emphasized determinism of conduct.

Cesare Lombroso's *L'uomo delinquente,* published in 1876, was the synthesis of this line of thought. Lombroso presented in vivid form his theory of the criminal's physical inferiority — the criminal was *born* that way, a throwback to a more primitive and savage man. In a speech at the Congress of Criminal Anthropology at Turin in 1906, Lombroso recalled his discovery:

In 1870 I was carrying on for several months researches in the prisons and asylums of

Pavia upon cadavers and living persons, in order to determine upon substantial differences between the insane and criminals, without succeeding very well. Suddenly the morning of a gloomy day in December, I found in the skull of a brigand a very long series of atavistic anomalies, above all an enormous middle occipital fossa and a hypertrophy of the vermis, analogous to those that are found in inferior invertebrates. At the sight of these strange anomalies, as a large plain appears under an inflamed horizon, the problem of the nature and of the origin of the criminal seemed to be resolved; the characters of primitive men and of inferior animals must be reproduced in our time.[9]

Lombroso later modified his thoughts on the born criminal, including many diverse environmental factors in his theory on the causes of crime. Other Italian positivists, especially Enrico Ferri and Raffaele Garofalo, also began to emphasize various kinds of related factors.

In addition to their theories, the positivists proposed a kind of criminal responsibility based on the needs of society rather than on the free will and moral guilt of the offender. The position on the responsibility of the individual to society was stated clearly by Ferri: "Man is always responsible for every one of his acts, for the sole reason that he lives in society, and for as long as he does so."[10] It was thus the individual's duty to adjust to the state's demands.

Later in their careers, both Ferri and Garofalo adapted themselves to Mussolini's Fascist regime. Their political alignment may not have been accidental or a matter of practical compromise; Vold writes that positivism's general orientation is consistent with totalitarianism:

The end of Ferri's career, assent to Fascism highlights one of the implications of positivistic theory, namely, the ease with which it fits into totalitarian patterns of government. It is centered on the core idea of the superior knowledge and wisdom of the scientific expert, who, on the basis of his studies, decides what kind of human beings his fellow men are who commit crime, and who, on the basis of this knowledge and scientific insight, prescribes appropriate treatment without consent from the person so diagnosed [i.e., the criminal]. There is an obvious similarity in conception of the control of power in society between positivism and the political reality of centralized control of the life of the citizen by government bureaucracy indifferent to democratic public opinion.[11]

The first decades of the twentieth century brought many explanations of crime based on many diverse factors. The early theorists felt that the individual offender's characteristics were most important. In the United States the writings of the Italian positivists were being translated, directly influencing a number of American criminologists.[12] Lombroso's influence continued to appear in works throughout the first half of the century.[13] As criminology developed in the United States, most of Lombroso's biological emphasis was discarded, though his positivism was accepted. Gustav Aschaffenburg's *Crime and Its Repression* presented to American criminologists a severe criticism of Lombroso's biological theory. Using data from Germany, Aschaffenburg considered many individual and social factors as causes of crime.

The most crucial blow to Lombrosian theory was the evidence Charles Goring presented in his statistical study of 3,000 male convicts, published under the title *The English Convict*. With data he collected as a medical officer at Parkhurst Prison, Goring sought "to clear from the ground the remains of the old criminology, based upon conjecture, prejudice, and questionable observations," and "to found a new knowledge of the criminal upon facts scientifically acquired, and upon inferences scientifically verified; such facts and inferences yielding, by virtue of their own established accuracy, unimpeachable conclusions."[14] In concluding that there was no born criminal type and that crime was not inherited, Goring turned criminologists to the study of psychological characteristics, especially defective intelligence, as a cause of criminal behavior.[15]

Criminologists, reacting against the practice of explaining crime as caused by just one factor, now looked for multiple causes. Searching for factors or variables, measuring and correlating them to criminal behavior, also reflected the trend toward empiricism in the social sciences. One of the first empirical studies was William Healy's *The Individual Delinquent*, in which he considered a large variety and combination of factors. The multiple factor approach was also used by Cyril Burt in *The Young Delinquent*, attributing a percentage of causative importance to each of the factors. The multiple-factor approach is still found today in such works as the Gluecks' *Unraveling Juvenile Delinquency*.

The most recent individualistic emphasis in the study of crime is found in psychiatry. In most of the psychoanalytic theories, crime is a form of substitute behavior.[16] Such works include Karpman's *The Individual Criminal*, Lindner's *Rebel Without a Cause*, Abrahamsen's *Who Are the Guilty?*, and Alexander and Staub's *The Criminal, the Judge, and the Public*.

The *sociological* study of crime moved very slowly in the United States during the first part of the century. With today's hindsight, we can see that the study of crime by early sociologists was filled with questionable assumptions and was not specifically aimed at social matters. One of the first works on crime by a sociologist, Frances A. Kellor's *Experimental Sociology*, was actually a study of the physical differences (according to height of forehead, length of ears, mouth width, nasal index) between women criminals and women students. The introduction to that book, by C. R. Henderson, one of the first members of the sociology department at the University of Chicago, expressed a social moralism tempered by relativism, hinting too at the adventure the early sociologists felt in the new social science: "The university cannot neglect any phase of social life. As in astronomy the study of perturbations in the movements of known bodies leads to the discovery of new worlds, so in social science the investigation of evil brings us nearer to an understanding of the good and helps us on the path upward."[17]

The study of crime as a social phenomenon during this period was also affected by evolutionary theory, particularly social Darwinism. This theoretical orientation to crime was best displayed in Arthur C. Hall's *Crime and Its Relation to Social Progress*. In the introduction Franklin H. Giddings, first professor of sociol-

ogy at Columbia University, set the tone by suggesting that as civilization evolves it is necessary to define some behaviors as criminal, adding that "this process of connecting immoralities into positive crimes is one of the most powerful means by which society in the long run eliminates the socially unfit, and gives an advantage in the struggles for existence to the thoughtful, the considerate, the far-seeing, the compassionate; so lifting its members to higher planes of character and conduct."[18]

Maurice Parmelee, perhaps more than any other person at the beginning of the century, brought about the union of sociology and criminology. Parmelee, in *The Principles of Anthropology and Sociology in Their Relations to Criminal Procedure*, at places drawing favorably upon Lombroso's theory, suggested a sociological criminology. Later, in 1918, in the first American attempt at a comprehensive exposition of criminological knowledge, Parmelee in his *Criminology* analyzed the social sources of crime. Nevertheless, he found it necessary to discuss evolution, the physical environment, "criminal traits," and the "organic basis of criminality." His work, despite these faults, represents the transition in the United States from an eclectic study of crime to a sociological kind of explanation.

During the twenties and thirties a truly sociological criminology was achieved by sociologists at the University of Chicago. Albion W. Small, as founder and head of the first university sociology department in the United States, gathered a distinguished group of colleagues at the University of Chicago. Persons with broad ability and scope created a sociological tradition with the study of crime as one of its principal goals. Their underlying theme was that criminal behavior is similar to any other social behavior.

A major influence on the students of crime at the University of Chicago was the work of Robert E. Park. Park, with a colleague, E. W. Burgess, suggested studying the spatial distribution of social phenomena within the city.[19] Students of Park and Burgess examined the relationship of various deviant behaviors to urban growth and ecological patterns. Frederick M. Thrasher, in his study of 1,313 gangs in Chicago, argued that groups of boys in "interstitial areas" of the city could, by participation, become unified delinquent groups.[20]

Clifford R. Shaw and his collaborators, studying the distribution of delinquency rates, found, among other things, that delinquency was concentrated in deteriorated areas of the city and that the areas of high delinquency consistently had high rates in spite of population changes.[21] In a number of case studies, including *The Jack-Roller, Natural History of a Delinquent Career,* and *Brothers in Crime,* Shaw shifted from physical factors in the environment to the cultural environment and social participation. Slum youth were seen as participating in a culture that prescribed or encouraged delinquent behavior.

By the late thirties, three distinct conceptions of crime had been developed. These were formulated into three theories: differential association, social structure and anomie, and cultural conflict. The first was presented by Edwin H. Sutherland in the 1939 revision of his popular criminology textbook, *Principles of Criminology.* In his "theory of differential association," Sutherland offered an explanation of crime that would replace the multiple-factor approach and go beyond the simple enculturation explanation of crime.[22] He provided an integrative theory for criminology, assuming that the many diverse factors and correlates of crime are important as far as they affect an individual's associations and learning experiences. Postulating that criminal behavior is learned in primary association with others, in relative isolation from opposing values, it continues to serve as one of the major theoretical perspectives in criminology.

At the same time that Sutherland was presenting his theory, Robert K. Merton published his now famous article, "Social Structure and Anomie."[23] Elaborating upon Emile Durkheim's description of how aspiration appears and regulatory norms break down, Merton sought to explain the kinds and amounts of deviation in society. An explanation for crime will be found in society's social and cultural structure rather than in the individual. He went beyond other conceptions of social disorganization, suggesting that there are different "modes of adaptation" to society. With his theory he tried to explain both the behavior of individuals and the rates of crime.

A third theory, based on the idea of cultural conflict, was presented by Thorsten Sellin in his monograph, *Culture Conflict and Crime.* Recognizing how important criminal law is in studying crime, Sellin argued:

> Among the various instrumentalities which social groups have evolved to secure conformity in the conduct of their members, the criminal law occupies an important place, for its norms are binding upon all who live within the political boundaries of a state and are enforced through the coercive power of the state. The criminal law may be regarded as a part of the body of rules, which prohibit specific forms of conduct and indicate punishments for violations. The character of these rules, the kind or type of conduct they prohibit, the nature of the sanction attached to their violation, etc., depend upon the character and interests of those groups in the population which influence legislation. In some states, these groups may comprise the majority, in others a minority, but the social values which receive the protection of the criminal law are ultimately those which are treasured by dominant interest groups.[24]

Sellin believed that culture conflict could arise in several ways, each of its forms being potentially related to crime. One conflict develops in the growth of a civilization and another from the contact between the norms of divergent cultural codes. Sellin gave support to his theory by reviewing research on criminal behavior among immigrants, the foreign-born, and second-generation immigrants. In all cases, crime was viewed as a matter of conflict between norms of conduct, and legal norms are one form of conduct norms.

Theoretical developments in criminology since World War II have primarily extended the perspectives formulated at the end of the thirties.[25] But perhaps the most significant change in recent years is the attention that has been given to the legal process. As people have learned to see crime as a legal construct imposed on some persons by others, criminology has expanded. Such current subjects as the formulation of criminal law, law enforcement, administration of criminal justice, criminal behavior patterns, and social reaction to crime are built on the thesis that crime is a socially and legally defined phenomenon.[26] Crime is being viewed as part of the process of conflict and change, in relation to the underlying social, political, and economic structure of society.

Research Methods and Modes of Inquiry

Criminologists examining their methodology in studying crime try to make their work less complex by splitting it into general categories. These are the traditional "research methods" of criminology. They provide us with a very general summary of the kinds of methodologies used in studying crime: (1) statistics on crimes, (2) statistics on traits and conditions of criminals, (3) the individual case study, (4) the limited case study, (5) the study of the criminal "in the open," and (6) the experimental method.[27]

Actual research is much more complicated than these categorical methods indicate. All research is essentially a *process*, in which choices are made at many stages during the research. The methods are many and are combined in various ways during the research. Methodological decisions are made on such diverse matters as the kind of research case to be used, the type of research population and sample, the sources of data collection, the techniques of gathering data, and the methods of analyzing the research findings.

The research design is just the first problem in criminological research; research findings must be related to a body of theory. At all stages there is an interplay between theory and research. In fact, it is often the theory of crime chosen by the researcher that determines which methods will be used in the research.

Ultimately, however, the student of crime has to work with much broader assumptions about ontology and epistemology. That is, the criminologist is constantly faced with assumptions (consciously recognized or not) about reality and the grounds of knowledge, which shape the accumulating knowledge about crime. What we know as criminology is formed more by such assumptions, including our own values and ideology, than by the concrete methods of research: the research methods are inextricably linked to the criminologist's notions about the world.

When we discuss research on crime, we should divide the different approaches into more general forms. These *modes of inquiry* contain assumptions about research and reality. Furthermore, each mode of inquiry is specifically related to the American order. They are: (1) the positivistic, (2) the social constructionist, (3) the phenomenological, and (4) the critical. From the last we will develop a critical theory of crime.[28]

Positivism

The positivistic mode of inquiry begins with the realist's assumptions about existence: the primary objective is to "discover" the laws of the real world. The larger philosophical problems of explanation are generally set aside.

The positivist follows a simple epistemology that absolutely separates the knower from the known, assuming that objectivity is possible because he believes that an order exists independent of the observer. The observer's cognitive apparatus ideally does not affect the nature of what is known. With enough knowledge, accumulated systematically, the scientist could predict future events and control their occurrence. An orderly universe could be established by knowledge and by manipulating the external world.

With their mechanistic conception about how social facts are related, positivists usually present their explanations as governed by causality. They do not examine, nor are they even aware of, the philosophical assumptions by which the observer operates.[29] Nor do they recognize that the explanation depends upon the kinds of things investigated, or that it requires describing the unique context in which events occur. Likewise, the positivist refuses to recognize that to assess and make statements about human actions is to engage in a moral endeavor; he sees his activity as "value free."

The intellectual failure of positivism is that it is not reflexive — the positivist makes little or no attempt to examine or even question the metaphysics of inquiry, to turn the activity of explanation back upon itself, to be introspective.

Positivist thought has also failed politically because it accepts the status quo. Positivists do not question the established order, just as they do not examine scientific assumptions. The official reality is the one within which the positivist operates and which he accepts and supports. The positivist takes for granted the ideology that emphasizes bureaucratic rationality, modern technology, centralized authority, and scientific control.[30]

Criminologists, therefore, have consequently devoted almost all their efforts to established interests. Traditionally they have concentrated on the violator of criminal law, rather than on the legal system itself.[31] They usually try to solve the crime problem by changing the lawbreaker, not the legal system. Just recently some criminologists, realizing that law itself is problematic, have turned to study the law. But for the most part these studies have been based on the positivistic mode of thought.

Following the positivistic mode of inquiry, criminologists have developed their own wisdom about social and political life, but their research and theory have done little more than provide a rationale for the established order. A social theory that would allow for human liberation was not developed. It now seems that positivistic thought cannot provide liberating conceptions of human existence. Instead, we must turn to some alternative modes of inquiry.

Social Constructionism

Social constructionist thought begins with a recognition of philosophical idealism. Social constructionists work with an ontology that questions the existence of an objective reality apart from the individual's imagination. They assume that objects cannot exist *independently* of our minds, that any reality is important only as long as it can be perceived. The epistemological assumption is that observations are based on mental *constructions*, rather than on raw apprehension of the physical world. The social constructionist is interested primarily not in the correspondence between "objective reality" and observation, but in that between observation and the utility of such observation in understanding our own subjective, multiple worlds.

Following these assumptions, the social scientist's constructs have to be founded upon the world created by social actors. Alfred Schutz conceptualized the problem: "The constructs of the social sciences are, so to speak, constructs of the second degree, that is constructs of the constructs made by the actors

on the social scene, whose behavior the social scientist has to observe and explain in accordance with the procedural rules of his science."[32] The world that is important to the social constructionist, then, is the one created by the social actions of human beings, by interaction and communication with others. This *social reality* involves the social meanings and the products of the subjective world of everyday life.[33]

The social constructionist mode of inquiry is a major advance over positivistic thought in the crucial area of reflexivity. The social constructionist questions the process by which he knows, instead of taking it for granted. The social constructionist reflects on his activity as observer, using to advantage the social and personal character of his observation. But this reflexivity does not extend to a political position, and possible political action — a shortcoming inherent in this mode of inquiry.

Moreover, social constructionist thought generally concentrates on the world of meanings created by social actors. It emphasizes, especially in ethnomethodological studies (which are meant to describe the actual world of social actors), the construction of social order. Such concentration often ignores a world of events and structures independent of the social actor's consciousness. This is the conservative side of social constructionist thought, making it inadequate for a critical perspective. Lichtman says that "It is overly subjective and voluntaristic, lacks an awareness of historical concreteness, is naive in its accounts of mutual typification and ultimately abandons the sense of human beings in struggle with an alien reality which they both master and to which they are subordinate. It is a view which tends to dissolve the concept of 'ideology' or 'false consciousness' and leaves us, often against the will of its advocates, without a critical posture toward the present inhuman reality."[34]

Therefore, it is often necessary to revise or reject the world as some social actors conceive it. Social constructionists do give us the beginnings for examining multiple realities, which might allow us to transcend the official reality, and ultimately, our current existence. But they fail to provide a yardstick for judging whether one reality has more good in it than another.

Social relativism prevents a critical understanding of the social world.

The social constructionist perspective, however, has given new vitality to the study of crime. Departing significantly from positivistic studies, social constructionists have turned to the problematic nature of the legal order. Crime and other stigmatized behaviors are examined first as categories created and imposed upon some persons by others.[35] Crime exists because the society constructs and applies the label *crime*. Criminal law, too, is not separate from society, but is itself a construction, created by those who are in power. The administration of justice is a human social activity that is constructed as various legal agents interpret and impose their order on those they select for processing.

Social constructionist thought stops here, although, to be sure, it has critical implications. It offers the libertarian ideal that individuals should not be controlled by others, that people must be free to pursue their potential, that social order is created for political purposes. Nevertheless it does not show what a new world should look like, and without such an image our understanding of reality lacks a critical perspective.

Phenomenology

Phenomenological inquiry departs markedly from a positivistic and social constructionist inquiry in its basic intention. The other modes of thought are aimed at explaining social life, but phenomenological thought begins by examining how we understand the world. Explanation as a form of thought is itself examined. The phenomenologist is most interested in the philosophical problems of epistemology and ontology.

Phenomenologists, though they differ considerably among themselves, generally agree that our knowledge of the physical world comes from our experiences. But, they continue, when we talk about the physical world we are not limited by our actual experiences; we are able to talk about *possible* experiences, and so we alter our perception of things in the world. As long as a physical object exists in the world, it is possible to perceive it. We are capable of perceiving the essence of things.

The phenomenologist may proceed by "bracketing" the question of objective reality in order to turn attention to the reality that manifests itself immediately in consciousness. Following Kant's distinctions, the phenomenologist is primarily interested in the *phenomenon*, or the appearance of reality in itself.[36] Yet, it is possible to think about what is not known, the "thing-in-itself," or the *noumenon*, of which the phenomenon is the known aspect. Our knowledge of phenomena is always subject to revision.

From consciousness itself we get our understanding of the world. Knowledge about the world cannot stand apart from our sense of things. Any understanding of an objective thing can come about only through our consciousness of the thing; reality is to be found in our consciousness of it. Essence, or the essential, is thus what the human mind understands through its consciousness, during its experiences in the world. Any objectivity is to be achieved by means of our own subjectivity — that is, through our consciousness.

Phenomenological thought is thought in its purest form. Following Kant's distinction between thinking and knowing, phenomenologists are engaged in thinking beyond the limitations of knowledge.[37] There is the urge to think and understand in contrast to solely construct-verifiable knowledge. Knowledge is not denied, but room is made for thinking about the possibilities, and about such otherwise unthinkable topics as the meaning of our existence.

The urge to think forces us to transcend our conventional knowledge about the world and our place in it. It allows us to remove ourselves momentarily from our concrete experiences. Heidegger describes this kind of thought: "Meditative thinking demands of us not to cling one-sidedly to a single idea, nor to run down a one-track course of ideas. Meditative thinking demands of us that we engage ourselves with what at first sight does not go together at all."[38] A comportment that enables us to keep open the meaning hidden in the world, in the arrangements of modern society, is described by Heidegger as "openness to the mystery." By this openness and a "releasement toward things," in meditative thinking, we seek our true nature. And, Heidegger writes, "They grant us the possibility of dwelling in the world in a totally different way. They promise us a new ground and foundation upon which we can stand and endure in the world of technology without being imperiled by it."[39]

It is in the transcendental thinking of the phenomenologists that we find the inspiration for moving beyond the conventional wisdom of the age, including our contemporary knowledge of crime and the legal order. Instead of reifying the social order (treating it as if it had concrete existence), or giving an account of ordered existence, the movement is toward transcending our experience. This is a necessary step as we begin to act in a way that will demystify the social world. The primary interest is not in developing a new social science (still a reified science) but in creating a new existence, free of all reifications.

Phenomenological thought by itself, however, is incomplete for attaining our objectives. Although it provides a drastic and necessary move beyond the other modes of thought, it lacks the critical edge that would allow us to truly transcend the present, in life as in mind. Phenomenology does make us question the assumptions by which we know and by which we live. This is its major achievement. But we need a philosophy that will allow us to actively transcend the existing order, and will allow us to be committed. We thus turn to the development of a critical philosophy.

A Critical Mode of Inquiry

A critical mode of inquiry is a radical philosophy — one that goes to the roots of our lives, to the foundations and the fundamentals, to the essentials of consciousness.[40] In rooting out presuppositions we are able to assess every actual and possible experience. The operation is one of demystification, removing the myths — the false consciousness — created by the official reality. Conventional experience is revealed as a reification of the social order, exposing the underside of official reality. The liberating force of radical criticism is the movement from revelation to the development of a new consciousness and an active life in which we transcend the established existence.

Thinking is the beginning of a critical philosophy. For in the act of thought we engage in a reflective life that liberates us from preconceptions. Such theorizing, Blum contends,

expresses self, is a display of mind. Furthermore: "This 'calling to mind,' following an interpretation of Wittgenstein, is a way of recovering what one has all along, it is a way of seeing and as such it is inextricably tied to a way of living. More than this, it is to reconstitute or re-create out of one's life and history of a society another possibility for seeing. To theorize is to re-formulate one's self."[41] The theorist thus shows another possibility for seeing and living. Such theorizing has the potential of allowing us to comprehend a version of a possible society.

The classic philosophical tradition holds the attitude that ideas are to inform actions, that life is to be enlightened by thought. A critical philosophy, as Habermas has suggested, is one that destroys the illusion of objectivism (the illusion of a reality apart from consciousness).[42] Conceived in this way, thought itself is necessarily critical. In demystifying our lives our attention is directed to a critique of our current existence.

The chief characteristic of thinking, Hannah Arendt writes in an essay on thinking and moral considerations, is that it interrupts all doing, all ordinary activity.[43] We are momentarily removed from our worldly associations; it is as though we entered into a different existence. Arendt adds that "thinking, the quest for meaning — rather than the scientist's thirst for knowledge for its own sake — can be felt to be 'unnatural,' as though men, when they begin to think, engage in some activity contrary to the human condition."[44] She concludes that only with thought that is aimed toward ideals (with the desiring of love, wisdom, beauty, and justice) are we prepared with a kind of thought that promotes a moral existence. Only when we are filled with what Socrates called *eros*, a love that desires what is not, can we find what is good.

Without critical thought we are bound to the only form of social life we know — the current one. We are not then free to choose a better life; our only activity further supports the system in which we are bound. Our current cultural and social arrangements, supported as they are by a bureaucratic-technological system of production and distribution, are a threat to individual freedom — including the freedom to know that this system is imperfect and may be altered. Such a system can keep an opposition from growing within it. In aspiring to the rewards that the system holds out to us, we are unable to consider an alternative existence. Such is the message of Marcuse in his discussion of the "one-dimensional" character of our present reality.[45] Only by negation of the present can we experience something else.

A critical philosophy lets us break with the ideology of the age, for built into critical thinking is the ability to think negatively. This *dialectical* form of thought allows us to question current experience.[46] By being able to entertain an alternative, we can better understand what exists. Instead of merely looking for an objective reality, we are interested in negating the established order, which will make us better able to understand what we experience. By applying this dialectic in our thought we can comprehend and surpass the present.

Moreover, dialectical thinking moves us to a reconstruction of our lives. In order to reject something we must have some idea of what things could be like.

Toward a New Criminology

Contemporary criminology is closely tied to the state's interests. In the name of developing knowledge about crime, some criminologists support the institutions at the expense of human freedoms. The needs of the people are identified with the social policies of the American state. And instead of understanding crime as created by the political authority that defines behavior as criminal, it has been understood in terms of the offender's behavior. Seeking a critical understanding and questioning the legal system have traditionally fallen outside the dominant ideological and scientific interests of most criminologists.

The liberal ideology underlies most research and theory in contemporary criminology. Although it is by no means monolithic or consistent, as Anthony Platt has observed, most of its assumptions are shared by criminologists today.[47] Following this ideology, criminologists (1) follow a legalistic definition of crime, accepting the state's definitions, (2) support reformist measures in rehabilitating "criminals"

and amelioristic reforms of society, (3) reject general theory and macroscopic historical analysis, favoring pragmatism and social behaviorism, and (4) are susceptible to cynicism and a lack of passion, ignoring the possibility of far-ranging changes in society. These liberal values are translated into the kinds of research criminologists conduct, the theories they construct, and the way in which they are ideologically tied to the state.

Criminologists then are the ancillary agents of political power. They provide the kinds of information that governing elites use to manipulate and control those who threaten the system.[48] As "experts," criminologists inform the managers of the state. This alliance between criminology and the state, however, is far from being an explicit conspiracy; rather, the relationship is much more natural and subtle. That is, criminologists automatically serve the interests of the state by following their own unexamined assumptions about the world and their understanding of it. By pursuing a narrow scientific model, supported by a liberal ideology, criminologists find their interests tied to those of the state.

My purpose in this book is to work toward developing a new criminology. We will gain an understanding of crime in American society by a presentation that moves back and forth between the conventional wisdom about crime and the new conceptions that negate traditional ideas. We will, accordingly, cover the diverse facets of crime: from the legal system in theory to the law in action, from the theories of criminologists to the public's social reality, from the "criminal's" world to that of legal authority, from the traditional approaches of crime control to the radical notions of social existence. We can do all this by recognizing the nature of the society in which we live, the character of our times, and our own place in the past, present, and future history of American society.

The success of this venture will be in our ability, yours and mine, to examine our common experiences critically. Our understanding will be realized as we start to act in ways that give meaning to our experience. Our imaginations will be altered as we change our ways of thinking and our ways of living. In this manner we all begin to create a critical life.

2

Criminal Statistics and Crime Rates

Statistics that cover the number of times each kind of crime occurs in our country are collected by innumerable agencies of the government for their own purposes. These statistics have traditionally served as the primary data for criminological research. But how the statistics are collected and used arouses unending controversy among criminologists, and they have questioned the meaning of the statistics.[1]

Sources of Criminal Statistics

Most of the criminal statistics available to criminologists, on which they rely in their research and from which they derive their generalizations, come from official sources, that is, from the statistics gathered by agencies of government.[2] In fact, criminologists often equate criminal statistics with official statistics. Keeping the source of these statistics in mind, we have the following definition:

> By criminal statistics we mean (a) uniform data on offenses or offenders expressed in numerical terms: (b) derived by official agencies (police, prosecutors, courts, penal institutions, etc.) from their records; (c) classified, tabulated and analyzed in order to establish relationships between or among the classes of items tabulated; and (d) published — preferably annually — in a uniform manner.[3]

The regular collection of official criminal statistics by governmental agencies has not had a noteworthy history. The state of New York started to collect judicial statistics in 1829. Eventually, during the nineteenth century, twenty-four other states adopted the practice. The statistics were derived from reports sent by state attorneys or clerks of criminal courts to state officials; the results of this collection are summarized here:

> To sum up the situation existing at the end of the period 1829 to 1908, twenty-five states were collecting judicial statistics and twenty-three states statistics of prisoners, an impressive total were it not that with rare exceptions both kinds of statistics were of very doubtful value, serving no scientific purpose. Police statistics were mentioned occasionally in laws but that is about as far

as they got. The Federal Government had tried from time to time in a half-hearted way to collect judicial criminal statistics, also police statistics, but failed in each attempt. Its efforts to collect statistics of prisoners had, however, met with reasonable success. In the 1904 report, the earlier mistake of making the statistics relate solely to a point of time was rectified but the length of time intervening between the statistical inquiries was discouragingly long.[4]

The official statistics available for use in criminological research are collected by federal, state, and local governments, and the sources may be further divided according to the administrative stages at which the statistics are compiled. The criminal statistics criminologists most commonly use are based on the reports of local police departments, gathered by the federal government. In 1927, at a convention of the International Association of Chiefs of Police, a Committee on Uniform Crime Reports was appointed. Two years later the committee published a guide for collecting police statistics titled *Crime Reporting: A Complete Manual for Police*. In 1930, the Federal Bureau of Investigation took over the system of reporting police statistics and issued the first bulletin of the *Uniform Crime Reports*, which was published monthly at first, then quarterly until 1944, and semiannually until 1957. Since 1958 the *Uniform Crime Reports* have been issued annually, with quarterly preliminary reports.

Judicial statistics are compiled and published from prosecutions, dismissals, acquittals, convictions, prison sentences, fines, and probation. In 1932, the United States Bureau of the Census began to publish such statistics for state courts, but discontinued the task in 1947. Some states continue to collect their own court statistics, but the great variations in collection procedures make state comparisons nearly impossible. On the federal level, the Administrative Office of the United States Courts publishes an *Annual Report* compiling the judicial statistics of the federal courts. Figures on juvenile delinquency appear as judicial statistics on youth who appear before selected local courts and have been published since 1946, under the direction of the Children's Bureau of the United States Department of Health, Edu-

cation, and Welfare, in a series known as *Juvenile Court Statistics*.

Statistics on prisoners have been published annually since 1926 in *National Prisoner Statistics*. Presently under the direction of the Federal Bureau of Prisons of the United States Department of Justice, this report includes information on the number of commitments to state and federal penal institutions as well as information on prison populations and discharges. The Federal Bureau of Prisons also issues an annual report entitled *Federal Prisons*, which provides statistical data on persons convicted of violating federal laws. Several state departments of correction issue periodic reports on prisoners within their jurisdictions.

Still other sources of criminal statistics include the reports of a number of other governmental and private agencies, such as: *Vital Statistics in the United States*, which incorporates the reports of homicide submitted by local coroners; special reports occasionally published by the United States Treasury Department; reports of special offenses against the Federal Deposit Insurance Corporation; information on certain federal violations reported in the *Annual Report of the Attorney General of the United States*; records of burglaries and robberies committed against member banks of the American Bankers Association; reports of state departments of public welfare; and special surveys and reports of historical interest, such as *Criminal Justice in Cleveland* of 1922, *The Missouri Crime Survey* of 1926, *The Illinois Crime Survey* of 1929, the *Survey of the Administration of Justice in Oregon* of 1932, and the series of reports in the state of New York in the late twenties by the Commission on the Administration of Criminal Justice.[5]

Criminal Statistics as Measures of Crime

Most collections of criminal statistics have been gathered for purposes other than those explicitly intended in a specific criminological research project, so that the appropriate use of criminal statistics by the criminologist is an important issue. All criminal statistics, of course, represent the operations of agencies charged with administering criminal law. Most criminologists, and the general public for that matter, have attempted to use criminal statistics as measures of the "actual amount of criminality" in any geographical area or in the country as a whole.

When criminal statistics are used in assessing the "true" incidence of criminality, valid criticisms may indeed be raised about the methods of collecting criminal statistics. Pessimistic appraisals like the following are relevant *if* criminal statistics are used to indicate actual criminality:

> Since around 1920, a great deal of effort has been put forth in different parts of the United States, and at various levels of government, toward the production of useful criminal statistics. But despite all of this work, there has not been produced in the United States any systematic collection of information on crime which furnishes the factual information desired, or which is comparable to the criminal statistics of many other countries.[6]

> The statistics about crime and delinquency are probably the most unreliable and most difficult of all social statistics. It is impossible to determine with accuracy the amount of crime in any given jurisdiction at any particular time. Some behavior is labeled "delinquency" or "crime" by one observer but not by another. Obviously a large proportion of all law violations goes undetected. Other crimes are detected but not reported, and still others are reported but not officially recorded. Consequently any record of crimes, such as crimes known to the police, arrests, convictions, or commitments to prison, can at most be considered an "index" of the crimes committed. But these "indexes" of crime do not maintain a constant ratio with the true rate, whatever it may be. We measure the extent of crime with elastic rulers whose units of measurement are not defined.[7]

Such criticisms have led to numerous suggestions and recommendations to improve the collection of criminal statistics, especially to improve the procedures used in the *Uniform Crime Reports*.[8] One great difficulty in using available criminal statistics as indexes of criminality is the obvious lack of uniform reporting. Because of our political organization, each of the fifty states represents a separate political jurisdiction. Each state has its own constitutional provisions, penal codes, courts, criminal procedures, and systems of law enforcement. Furthermore, in each state criminal law is not centrally administered but is, instead, a local activity. These political facts throw unpredictable variation into the recording of criminal offenses and the comparability of information on criminal offenses from state to state and from one locality to another within states.[9]

Sellin pointed out some time ago that "the value of a crime rate for index purposes decreases as the distance from the crime itself in terms of procedure increases."[10] That is, police records are more reliable measures of the actual incidence of criminal offenses than arrest statistics, arrest statistics are more reliable than court statistics, and court statistics are more reliable than prison statistics. The implication is that many offenses are "lost" between the records of police and prosecution. Aware of these discrepancies, criminologists usually use the records of police rather than other sources to make inferences about the extent of criminality. The principal source of such information is in the statistics designated as "crimes known to the public." These statistics, as contained in the annual *Uniform Crime Reports*, consist of the offenses that are recorded by the police departments of approximately 8,000 jurisdictions in the United States. For the annual report, the offense records of the local police departments are grouped into twenty-nine offense categories. Seven of the categories (murder and nonnegligent manslaughter, forcible rape, robbery, aggravated assault, burglary, larceny of fifty dollars and over, and auto theft) are combined and designated by the Federal Bureau of Investigation as the "Index of Crime" (Table 2.1).

We can see how criminal statistics are reduced as they move from one criminal procedure to another in the difference between "crimes known to the police" and "crimes cleared by arrest." Furthermore, the discrepancy between crimes known to have occurred and arrests made in connection with the known crimes varies widely from one category

Table 2.1. Index of Crime, United States, 1972

Area	Population[a]	Total crime index	Violent[b] crime	Property[b] crime	Murder and non-negligent manslaughter	Forcible rape	Robbery	Aggravated assault	Burglary	Larceny $50 and over	Auto theft
United States total	208,232,000	5,891,924	828,151	5,063,773	18,515	46,431	374,555	388,650	2,344,991	1,837,799	880,983
Rate per 100,000 inhabitants		2,829.5	397.7	2,431.8	8.9	22.3	179.9	186.6	1,126.1	882.6	423.1
Standard Metropolitan Statistical Area	147,640,000										
Area actually reporting[c]	97.9%	4,980,123	720,626	4,259,497	14,391	39,237	358,018	308,980	1,955,027	1,496,620	807,850
Estimated total	100.0%	5,038,715	726,587	4,312,128	14,596	39,718	359,493	312,780	1,979,377	1,517,216	815,535
Rate per 100,000 inhabitants		3,412.8	492.1	2,920.7	9.9	26.9	243.5	211.9	1,340.7	1,027.6	552.4
Other cities	23,547,000										
Area actually reporting	91.0%	412,345	43,212	369,133	1,041	2,353	8,309	31,509	161,931	170,927	36,275
Estimated total	100.0%	451,470	48,357	403,113	1,195	2,581	9,104	35,477	177,618	185,873	39,622
Rate per 100,000 inhabitants		1,917.3	205.4	1,711.9	5.1	11.0	38.7	150.7	754.3	789.4	168.3
Rural	37,047,000										
Area actually reporting	75.5%	320,530	36,732	283,798	1,826	3,136	4,426	27,344	154,034	109,131	20,633
Estimated total	100.0%	401,739	53,207	348,532	2,724	4,132	5,958	40,393	187,996	134,710	25,826
Rate per 100,000 inhabitants		1,084.4	143.6	940.8	7.4	11.2	16.1	109.0	507.5	363.6	69.7

[a] Population is Bureau of the Census provisional estimate as of July 1, 1972.
[b] Violent crime is offenses of murder, forcible rape, robbery and aggravated assault; property crime is offenses of burglary, larceny $50 and over and auto theft.
[c] The percentage representing area actually reporting will not coincide with the ratio between reported and estimated crime totals since these data represent the sum of the calculations for individual states which have varying populations, portions reporting and crime rates.
Source: Federal Bureau of Investigation, *Uniform Crime Reports — 1972* (Washington, D.C.: U.S. Government Printing Office, 1973), p. 61.

Figure 2.1   Crimes Cleared by Arrest, 1972

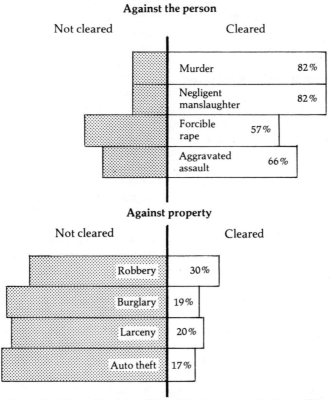

Against the person

Not cleared   Cleared

Murder	82%
Negligent manslaughter	82%
Forcible rape	57%
Aggravated assault	66%

Against property

Not cleared   Cleared

Robbery	30%
Burglary	19%
Larceny	20%
Auto theft	17%

Source: Federal Bureau of Investigation, *Uniform Crime Reports — 1972* (Washington, D.C.: U.S. Government Printing Office, 1973), p. 32.

of offenses to another. As shown in Figure 2.1, police departments cleared by arrest 82 per cent of the murders, 82 per cent of the negligent manslaughters, 57 per cent of the forcible rapes, 66 per cent of the aggravated assaults, 30 per cent of the robberies, 19 per cent of the burglaries, 20 per cent of the larcenies, and 17 per cent of the auto thefts. The police count a clearance when they have identified someone whom they believe to be the offender of a known offense, have sufficient evidence to charge the person, and actually take him or her into custody. Arresting one person can conceivably clear several crimes, or, on the other hand, *several* persons may be arrested in clearing one known offense.

How much the criminal statistics may be reduced between known crimes and convicted persons received in prisons was discussed by

Van Vechten in analyzing "criminal case mortality" in several jurisdictions.[11] Distinguishing seven levels of criminal procedure, he found that, for all the crimes known in the District of Columbia, 35.7 per cent resulted in offenses cleared, 10.0 per cent in persons charged, 7.5 per cent in judicial prosecutions, 5.9 per cent in convictions, 3.7 per cent in sentences to prison, and 3.6 per cent in prisoners received from courts. The clear decrease from the first procedural level to the last demonstrates the difficulty of using criminal statistics far removed from the offense itself to measure the "actual" amount of criminality.

Perhaps the most critical problem in using official criminal statistics as indicators giving the incidence of criminality, even when "offenses known to the police" are employed, is that an unknown amount of criminality never becomes a part of the public record. For various reasons many criminal offenses are never reported to the police, or when reported are not recorded by them. Any violation of the criminal law carries with it some probability that it will come to the attention of law-enforcement agencies. The probability that an offense will not be reported or recorded is controlled by several factors: (1) Some offenses are known only to the offender and are not likely to be reported. (2) Because they lack knowledge of the criminal law, victims and witnesses may not report criminal violations. (3) Witnesses to an offense may not want to report the offense because of inconvenience, embarrassment, fear, or lack of interest in law enforcement. (4) The victim or witness may be afraid of being implicated in the violation or in other violations if investigated. (5) The victim or witness may fear reprisal if the criminal offense is reported. (6) Friends and relatives may try to protect the offender and, therefore, will not report the offense. (7) The victim may fear unfavorable publicity and embarrassment. (8) Social values and public opinion do not favor full enforcement of some criminal laws. (9) Some criminal offenses are not readily visible to the general public or law-enforcement agencies. (10) Law-enforcement agencies may wish to conceal some criminal offenses.[12]

The existence of "hidden criminality" has been demonstrated in a number of studies in criminology. While she was examining how official statistics measure juvenile delinquency, Robison found that about a third of the behavior problems known to New York City agencies did not become court cases.[13] Other researchers found in studying boys in a special counseling program that many were "unofficial delinquents." The juvenile offenses were known by some authorities but were handled informally.[14] In a study of the delinquent behavior reported by Texas college students committed in their high school days and college years, Porterfield found that they had engaged in amounts and forms of delinquent behavior similar to those for which the juveniles had been officially processed in court.[15] The college students, because of their advantageous backgrounds, had not been refered to court for their illegal acts; the other

juveniles, however, had been officially handled.

In a more recent investigation, Short and Nye compared the self-reported juvenile behavior of students in three midwestern high schools and three western high schools to the reported delinquency of juveniles in a western training school.[16] Among the things they found was that delinquent conduct among the non-institutional students was extensive and that there were similarities between the institutionalized and noninstitutionalized students in self-reported delinquent conduct. Other recent studies using the self-reporting techniques of measuring delinquency have investigated differences according to social class, sex, race, religion, family relations, and rural-urban residence.[17]

Adult criminality also is much more widespread than the official criminal statistics show. Wallerstein and Wyle published in 1947 the responses New York residents gave to a questionnaire containing 49 offense categories.[18] The respondents, 1,020 men and 678 women, were asked to check the offenses they had committed. Ninety-one per cent of the sample admitted that they had committed one or more of the offenses. The men had on the average committed 18 of the offenses and the women averaged 11 offenses each. Of the men, 89 per cent admitted to larceny, 85 per cent to disorderly conduct, 49 per cent to assault, and 35 per cent to concealed weapons. Among the women, 83 per cent admitted to larceny, 81 per cent to malicious mischief, 76 per cent to disorderly conduct, 74 per cent to indecency, and 39 per cent to auto misdemeanors.

Many special forms of reported offenses are not collected in the traditional sources of criminal statistics.[19] Some of these occur in commerce and industry, management-labor relations, union management, income-tax reporting, and social security and public administration. Most of these offenses are dealt with by state and federal regulatory agencies; the statistics covering them are in the files and reports of the respective agencies. Such criminal records do not usually become a part of official criminal statistics. If we rely on the traditionally collected criminal statistics we obscure these and other prevalent crimes. We can say then that official statistics serve better as indicators of society's reaction to specific kinds of offenses than as a way of measuring the amount of criminality in society.

The most recent evidence that official statistics indicate only part of the real number of crimes is contained in surveys conducted for the President's Commission on Law Enforcement and Administration of Justice. A sample of national households was surveyed, asking whether anyone living in the household had been a victim of a crime during the preceding twelve months. It was found that "the actual amount of crime in the United States today is several times that reported in the *Uniform Crime Reports.*"[20]

A national survey conducted for the President's Commission by the National Opinion Research Center (NORC) estimated the rate of crimes against the person to be twice as high as that of the *Uniform Crime Reports* (UCR) and more than three times as high for property crimes.[21] An even more dramatic survey of unreported crime was reported in three Washington precincts. As Figure 2.2 shows, for offenses against individuals the number reported in the survey, depending on the offense, was from three to ten times greater than the number in police statistics. If we are looking for the actual rates of crime in American society, we are not likely to find them in the statistics gathered by government agencies.

What Do the Crime Rates Mean?

Using the official criminal statistics to measure the incidence of criminality is a questionable practice. Furthermore, if we criticize the criminal statistics and advocate better crime-reporting procedures, we accept the assumption that official statistics can serve as indexes of the actual amount of crime. Nevertheless, these official statistics are still used as indicators of criminality in society. Numerous studies have drawn upon official statistics in the attempt to draw conclusions about the *extent* of crime and delinquency and the *characteristics* of offenders.[22]

Two conclusions are often reached by those who use official statistics: (1) the crime rate is higher than it "should be," and (2) the crime

rate has continued to increase since World War II. The student of crime, and the entire public, will continue to be reminded periodically that the crime rate for the current year is higher than that of previous years. Newspapers report as news the releases of the annual *Uniform Crime Reports*. We are reminded by the FBI that our crime rate continues to increase sharply. Figure 2.3 from the *Uniform Crime Reports* is typical of the kind of graphic description regularly presented to the public. Once we know that the crime rate is increasing, we are expected to experience collective alarm. The reader is not usually, however, given the additional information that no one is certain what the criminal statistics mean. They may mean only that law-enforcement procedures change from year to year. The crime rate may not reflect the actual amount of crime so much as it does the way in which police departments operate and change their operations.

In other words, it may well be that the wrong question is being asked of our criminal statistics. Official statistics, first, represent only a fraction of some unknown amount of offensive behavior in a geographical area. In this use of statistics is much "hidden criminality," and the statistics are "dark figures." Second, because most human behavior can at some time be labeled as criminal at one stage or another of criminal procedure by those with the authority to do the labeling, the statistics reflect the policies and behaviors of the agencies administering criminal law.

Let us broaden our conception of official criminal statistics to include the fact that criminal statistics also represent the labeling of behavior as criminal. Then, instead of assuming that criminal statistics indicate only the *incidence of criminal behavior* in a population, we will assume as well that criminal statistics reflect differentials in the *administration of criminal law.*[23] These two conceptions of criminal statistics may not necessarily be regarded as mutually exclusive. A third meaning of the statistics is that they reflect a combination of the first two conceptions, a mixture of the *incidence of criminality and the administration of criminal law*.

A fourth meaning of criminal statistics is

Figure 2.2   Estimated Rates of Offense:[a] Comparison of Police[b] and Bureau of Social Sciences Research Survey Data for Three Washington, D.C., Precincts (Rates per 1,000 Residents 18 Years or Over)

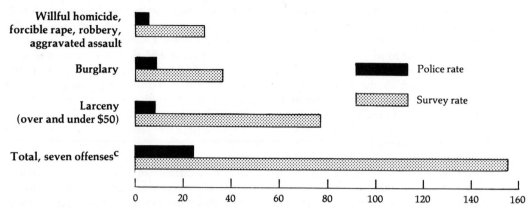

[a]Incidents involving more than one victim adjusted to count as only one offense. A victimization rate would count the incidence for each individual.

[b]Police statistics adjusted to eliminate nonresident and commercial victims and victims under 18 years of age.

[c]Willful homicide, forcible rape, robbery, aggravated assault, burglary, larceny (over and under $50), and motor vehicle theft.

Source: President's Commission on Law Enforcement and Administration of Justice, *The Challenge of Crime in a Free Society* (Washington, D.C.: U.S. Government Printing Office, 1967), p. 21.

Figure 2.3   Increase in the Crime Rate, 1968–1973

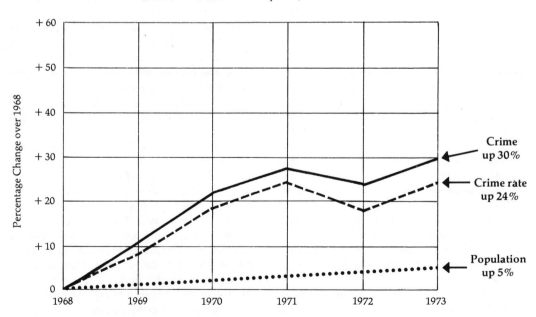

Crime = crime index offenses
Crime rate = number of offenses per 100,000 inhabitants

Source: Federal Bureau of Investigation, *Uniform Crime Reports—1973* (Washington, D.C.: U.S. Government Printing Office, 1974. p. 3.

that they indicate the *socially recognized volume of crime*. They are the society's production figures. Whether there is more or less "actual" criminality, strict or lenient administration of criminal law, or some combination of criminality and administration, is not the issue. The crucial question is why societies and their agencies report, manufacture, or produce the volume of crime that they do.

With a similar notion in mind, Cressey has suggested that the kind of reporting system that is devised in a society is useful for the varying personnel engaged in controlling, treating, and preventing crime. A vagueness in criminal statistics is useful because it decreases the wide range of ideological and theoretical commitments of the many persons dealing with criminals. He suggests a "sociology of crime reporting":

> The kind and amount of statistics compiled on crime and delinquency are, in a very real sense, an index of social concern about crime and delinquency. Why do we report and compile what we do? What pressures are there on workers in the field to report some deviations and not others? What pressures are there for and against establishment of uniform categories for reporting and compilation? Why do we ask the personnel who are in direct contact with criminals to look at what they look at?[24]

For us, then, the meaning of criminal statistics is clear: they represent the nature and extent of crime recognized in the society at a particular time.

The Politics of Crime Rates

In the final analysis crime rates have to be understood as *political* devices. It is for political purposes that criminal statistics are gathered. And likewise it is according to political needs that criminal statistics are recorded and interpreted. For that reason, American crime rates are subject to great manipulation, from their inception to their use. It is impossible to know from any statistic the "true" rate of crime. Whether crime is increasing or decreasing in American society is a question that can never

be answered objectively without considering the politics of the times.

Crime rates, therefore, are used to justify or instigate a multitude of political (including social and economic) interests. High crime rates are used by the police to rationalize the need for more personnel and equipment. But they cannot drastically reduce the rates without jeopardizing further appropriations. The police have an interest in maintaining both a high and a low rate of crime.

Politicians often have made crime rates an issue in their political campaigns, promising to reduce the crime rate. Barry Goldwater, the Republican presidential candidate, introduced "law and order" into the 1964 campaign. The rhetoric was escalated by the candidates in the 1968 presidential campaign. Each candidate developed his own version of law and order as a battle cry in the campaign. Richard Nixon, then the Republican candidate, touched it off in his acceptance speech at Miami, charging that "some of our courts in their decisions have gone too far in weakening the peace forces as against the criminal."[25] In even greater detail, Nixon presented his position on law and order in a paper, "Toward Freedom from Fear." His position was made clear: "Just as justice dictates that innocent men go free, it also means that guilty men must pay the penalty for their crimes. It is this second part of justice to which the nation must begin to address itself in earnest. . . . By now Americans, I believe, have learned the hard way that a society that is lenient and permissive for criminals is a society that is neither safe nor secure for innocent men and women."[26]

The 1964 Democratic candidate, Hubert Humphrey, responded by promising to halt "rioting, burning, sniping, mugging, traffic in narcotics and disregard for law." But he added that "the answer lies in reasoned effective action by our authorities, not in attacks on our courts, our laws or our Attorney General."

The former governor of Alabama, George Wallace, running as an independent candidate, took the extreme position on the law and order issue. His solution was simple: free the police of all restraint. Wallace repeated his position everywhere he went, usually bringing the house down with the message: "If you walk

DOCUMENT

AMERICAN CRIME RATES: AS UNDERSTOOD BY THE BUSINESS WORLD

Crime — Signs That the Worst Is Over

Suddenly, a break in the years-long crime wave. Reports from cities that succeeded in reversing the trend tell why — and suggest hope for the future.*

With spring came good news:

For the first time in 17 years, there has been a downturn — instead of a rise — in crime in this country.

The number of serious crimes reported in the United States in 1972 was 3 per cent less than in the year before.

This downturn was disclosed in preliminary statistics compiled by the Federal Bureau of Investigation, based on Uniform Crime Reports from local, State and county law-enforcement agencies all across the nation.

Announcing the figures on March 28, U. S. Attorney General Richard G. Kleindienst acknowledged that "crime is still unacceptably high." There is especial concern over the fact that crimes of violence, such as murder, rape and aggravated assault, continued to increase slightly last year — up 1 per cent — even while crimes against property were on the decline.

By Government officials — and by many private citizens — however, the figures were hailed as signs that the worst of the long crime wave may be over.

President Richard Nixon, who stressed demands for "law and order" in both of his presidential election campaigns, described the FBI report as "very heartening." He said:

> These results are a tribute to the men and women in the front lines of the war against crime — our law-enforcement officers. Public opinion is untying their hands and they are once again being given the public support they deserve. . . .
>
> We can turn the tide of crime in America. These statistics demonstrate that we are well on our way. Now we must have the tools we need to finish the job.

Among the "tools" sought by Mr. Nixon are laws to restore the death penalty for certain federal crimes and stiffen penalties for trafficking in "hard" drugs — heroin and morphine.

On March 28, he announced a reorganization to consolidate antidrug programs in a single new agency inside the Department of Justice.

Attorney General Kleindienst said of the crime downturn: "This is a day that we have been looking forward to for many years. It is an important milestone in the fight to reduce crime. . . ."

STEPS TOWARD ACHIEVEMENT

How was that "milestone" achieved? What did law-enforcement officials do that helped curb crime in 1972?

Source: Reprinted from *U. S. News & World Report,* April 9, 1973, pp. 26–28.

*A report from this same publication, however, released as this book went to press dimmed this hope of a decrease in crime. Crime went up 6 per cent in 1973 and an even greater increase was projected for 1974.

DOCUMENT (Continued)_____

Downturn in Serious Crime[a] after Sixteen Years

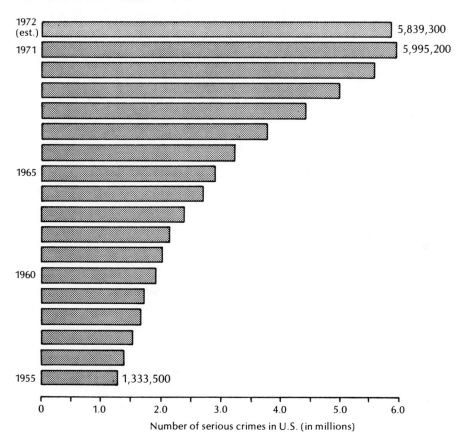

a Serious crimes include murder, forcible rape, robbery, aggravated assault, burglary, larceny over $50, and auto theft.

A survey by editors of *U. S. News & World Report* provides some clues.

In almost every city surveyed where crime declined, officials reported that police forces had been enlarged. More patrolmen were put on the beat, with forces concentrated in high-crime areas.

Improved equipment was described as a big help in some cities. Communication between police units and headquarters was speeded by radio systems. Computers provided instant access to criminal records. Helicopters were employed increasingly for aerial patrols.

Expanded programs of treating drug addicts were cited for helping to turn many addicts away from crime.

In a few cities, officials say that the courts are speeding their disposition of criminal cases and thus helping to keep "repeaters" off the streets.

Not all the credit is given to law-enforcement and other official agencies, however. Improving conditions in some trouble areas of big cities were reported

DOCUMENT (Continued) _____

to be helping to change the attitudes of people. Citizen co-operation with police was praised by many officials.

Americans, it seems, are increasingly concerned about the rise of crime and more and more willing to help do something about it.

Before last year's downturn, there had been 16 years of steady — and often large — increases in serious crimes. Between 1955 and 1971, their number had multiplied more than fourfold, as shown in the chart on page [25].

The peak of the spiral was reached in 1968, when the annual rise was 17 per cent. The increase was 11 per cent in 1969 and again in 1970, then slowed to 6 per cent in 1971.

Especially encouraging to officials was this: Nationwide, serious crime declined 8 per cent in the final three months of last year, after increasing by 1 per cent in the first nine months. This spurs hope for a continued decline this year.

The violent-crime increase of 1 per cent in 1972 was small compared with that of 9 per cent in 1971. Robberies, which make up a large proportion of the violent crime, actually decreased last year by 4 per cent.

Declines of 2 to 7 per cent were reported in burglary, larceny and auto theft, as shown [below].

Crimes That Are Decreasing	Number in 1972 (Prelim.)	Change from 1971	**Some Violent Crimes Are Increasing**	Number in 1972 (Prelim.)	Change from 1971
Auto theft	875,000	down 7%	Forcible rape	46,400	up 11%
Robbery	372,000	down 4	Aggravated assault	384,700	up 6
Larceny, $50 and over	1,821,900	down 3	Murder	18,300	up 4
Burglary	2,321,000	down 2			

Source: Federal Bureau of Investigation.

BIG CITIES LEAD

The 1972 decline of crime was most marked in the worst crime centers — the big cities. In the six U. S. cities of a million or more population, the combined decrease was 12 per cent; in cities of 500,000 to a million, it was 7 per cent; in cities of 100,000 to 500,000, it was 2 per cent.

Of the 154 cities in the nation having 100,000 or more population, 94 cities reported a decline in serious crime. This compared with decreases reported by 53 cities the year before, 22 cities in 1970 and 17 cities in 1969.

The record of the nation's 50 largest cities for 1972 is shown in the chart on page [27].

In contrast with major cities, crime rose slightly in smaller cities—up 1 per cent in those of 25,000 to 100,000, up 4 per cent in those with 10,000 to 25,000 inhabitants, and up 5 per cent in towns of less than 10,000.

DOCUMENT (Continued)

**The Crime Picture in 50 Biggest Cities: Percentage Change
in Number of Crimes in 1972, Compared with 1971**

Washington, D.C.	down 27%	Los Angeles	down 4%
San Francisco	down 19	Milwaukee	down 4
Nashville	down 18	Philadelphia	down 4
New York	down 18	St. Louis	down 4
Norfolk	down 18	Seattle	down 4
El Paso	down 17	Dallas	down 3
Detroit	down 16	Oakland	down 3
Indianapolis	down 16	Birmingham	no change
Honolulu	down 15	Portland, Oreg.	no change
New Orleans	down 15	Memphis	up 23
Kansas City, Mo.	down 13	Omaha	up 16
Cleveland	down 11	San Jose	up 13
Louisville	down 11	Atlanta	up 11
Pittsburgh	down 11	San Diego	up 10
Columbus, Ohio	down 10	Long Beach, Calif.	up 9
Miami	down 10	Phoenix	up 9
Newark	down 10	Tampa	up 6
Boston	down 9	Toledo	up 6
Rochester, N.Y.	down 9	Denver	up 3
Buffalo	down 7	Houston	up 3
Baltimore	down 6	San Antonio	up 3
Fort Worth	down 6	Minneapolis	up 2
Cincinnati	down 5	Oklahoma City	up 2
Jacksonville	down 5	St. Paul	up 2
Chicago	down 4	Tulsa	up 1

Source: Federal Bureau of Investigation.

Suburban areas reported a crime increase of 2 per cent, and crime rose 4 per cent in rural areas.

By geographical regions, this was the 1972 picture: Crime down 8 per cent in the Northeastern States, down 3 per cent in North Central States, down 2 per cent in Southern States, up only in the Western States, where it rose 2 per cent.

"TO REDUCE ... ERROR"

Defending the accuracy of the FBI's figures against charges that crime statistics are being "politicized" and "used to support Mr. Nixon's claims of progress," Mr. Kleindienst said in a speech at Scottsdale, Ariz., March 28:

"Every human effort is made to make these reports as accurate as possible.

"Of course, the rise of data processing has greatly aided this effort. The FBI has helped individual States to adopt standard requirements for crime reporting, and the number of such States continues to increase. This means that control factors are being applied to reduce human error or bias. . . . So the truth is that the proportion of crimes reported continues to increase — a trend which makes the latest figures showing a crime reduction even more remarkable."

DOCUMENT (Continued) _____

Mr. Kleindienst claimed a share of the credit for anticrime programs initiated by the Nixon Administration, including more than 2 billion dollars of federal aid to State and local law-enforcement agencies.

THE CAPITAL'S STORY

It is the nation's capital — Washington, D.C. — that the Nixon Administration points to with greatest pride.

Serious crime in Washington declined 27 per cent last year — the steepest drop of any big city in the country, according to the FBI report.

Washington, only a few years ago, was widely known as the "crime capital" of the nation. Richard Nixon vowed in his 1968 campaign that if elected President he would restore the city to "freedom from fear."

In his first year in the White House, Mr. Nixon proposed — and Congress enacted — a tough anticrime law for the federally governed District of Columbia.

Crime soon began to drop. By 1971, the city had 18.5 per cent fewer crimes than in 1969. The decline accelerated last year.

D.C. Police Chief Jerry Wilson lists the following as prime factors in the improvement:

A sharp increase in the police force — up from 3,100 to 5,100 officers.

An expanded program of methadone treatment for drug addicts.

Improved street lighting in high-crime neighborhoods.

A court reorganization that "has cut sharply the backlog of criminal cases awaiting trial."

An improvement in relations between the police and the community.

"There is a clear determination that crime must be stopped," Chief Wilson says. "You don't hear that antipolice rhetoric any more."

NEW YORK'S EFFORT

New York is another major city with a sharp drop in crime — down 18 per cent last year. Mayor John Lindsay told *U. S. News & World Report:*

"We think that among our most effective and important efforts have been improved management and employment of police manpower, new police equipment, citizen involvement and drug-treatment programs now involving more than 50,000 addicts.

"We have a special police platoon that operates only during the high crime hours — 6 P.M. to 2 A.M. We've moved men out from behind desks and onto the streets. We've created anticrime patrols — men in civilian clothes who blend into the street scene until they suddenly emerge to arrest criminals in the middle of a crime.

"We've given New York's police the most modern, high-speed communication system in the world, and a computerized dispatch system.

"We've increased the police auxiliary — that is, citizen volunteers who wear uniforms and perform non-law-enforcement duties — from a few hundred to 5,000. And we've just announced a new 5-million-dollar block-security program that will give citizen groups money and technical assistance to make their homes, stores and neighborhoods safer.

"We think we've passed the peak of the drug-crime problem in the city. Statistics indicate a drop in the number of crimes that are generally drug-related."

DOCUMENT (Continued)_____

"REFLECTS NEW PRIDE"

In San Francisco, where crime went down 19 per cent last year, Mayor Joseph Alioto attributed the improvement to the addition of more policemen on the streets and to the successful operation of the city's social programs.

"Our so-called ghetto areas are building themselves into neighborhoods," he said. "The improved crime picture reflects a sense of new pride and hope in our neighborhoods, which are rebuilding and casting aside the despair- and disillusionment of the 1960s."

San Francisco Police Chief Donald M. Scott cited as other factors: a computer network, financed in part by federal aid; communications equipment, including walkie-talkie radios; antidrug educational programs, and police participation in youth programs.

"Kids are not hostile to police when they know them through activities," the chief said.

An antiburglary program, financed by federal funds, is credited with cutting burglaries 25 per cent in the Mission district of San Francisco.

What he needs most now, Chief Scott said, is more manpower.

The importance of manpower is also stressed by police chiefs of two cities in Tennessee.

Nashville Chief Hugh B. Mott credits the addition of 200 street patrolmen for that city's 18 per cent reduction in serious crimes. Memphis Chief Bill Price says crime went up 23 per cent there because he had too few policemen.

In Topeka, Kans., Chief of Police Dana L. Hummer said that city's 15 per cent reduction in crime resulted from an enlarged police force and the use of new helicopters as "observation posts in the sky."

Topeka voters approved a half-cent local sales tax to finance the expansion of the police force.

In Indianapolis, where the crime drop was 16 per cent, *U. S. News & World Report* was told by Assistant Police Chief Donald Schaedel: "We have pushed citizen involvement in the fight against crime, and it's paying off."

Citizens are encouraged to buy and use police radio receivers, ride in patrol cars and visit police headquarters.

Police are permitted to take their patrol cars home at night, with the result that off-duty arrests have increased.

THE "STRESS" PLAN

Detroit has a program called STRESS, which stands for "stop the robberies, enjoy safe streets." Its officers, operating in plain clothes, are described by police officials as a significant factor in the city's 16 per cent drop in serious crimes last year.

Also, a reorganization of the police department has put more patrolmen into high-crime areas and a city-sponsored methadone program is credited with cutting crime by narcotic addicts.

Hartford, Conn., reported a 20 per cent reduction in crime. Mayor George Athanson attributes it to a "multiple approach," including:

Better trained policemen.

Reorganization of the police department to provide maximum manpower during hours of peak criminal activity.

DOCUMENT (Continued)_____

Specially trained squads to deal with burglaries, robberies, car thefts.
Improved co-operation with neighboring police departments.
Involvement of the business community in job training, recreational and other social programs.

New York's Mayor Lindsay summed up an attitude expressed by officials in several other cities when he said:
"We still have a long way to go. But we believe that efforts like these and others can and will make a real dent in the crime problem."

out of this hotel tonight and someone knocks you on the head, *he'll* be out of jail before *you're* out of the hospital, and on Monday morning they'll try the policeman instead of the criminal. That's right, we're going to have a *police* state for folks who burn the cities down. They aren't going to burn any more cities." The law and order issue was becoming a racist euphemism for suppressing the demands of blacks in the urban ghettoes.

The law and order issue, with its own variations, was repeated in the presidential election of 1972. This time, Richard Nixon, the incumbent, explicitly used criminal statistics to bolster his position, but this time he argued that the crime rates were actually *decreasing* during his administration. George McGovern, the Democratic candidate, refuted Nixon's use of criminal statistics. A "numbers game" was being played with the American crime rates. McGovern nevertheless found it necessary to offer similar law and order programs to control crime. Crime control now was clearly a means for keeping the established order from being destroyed.

The ultimate use of criminal statistics for political ends is currently being planned and implemented. By improving the techniques of national surveys, as first used in research for the President's Crime Commission, the government is developing a system for continuously monitoring crime. The objective, however, is not merely to get a more complete record of otherwise unreported crime, but to gather information that can be used to devise more effective means of law enforcement. An administrative official of the Information and Statistics Service (of the Law Enforcement Assistance Administration) observed about these new statistical methods: "Actually, under-reporting is only of marginal interest to our study. We are attempting to design a statistical methodology that will allow us to continuously monitor the characteristics of crime in the country; who are the victims; what is the genesis of a certain type of crime; where, how and when does it occur. These are the questions we want answers to, to provide tools for planning responses by police and other social agencies."[27]

We are well on the road to a national crime data reporting system. A national data bank, from which information can be retrieved instantly, will provide the most rational and political device for the authoritarian control of the population. The use of criminal statistics has progressed to its ultimate purpose, to protect the interests of the American social and economic order.

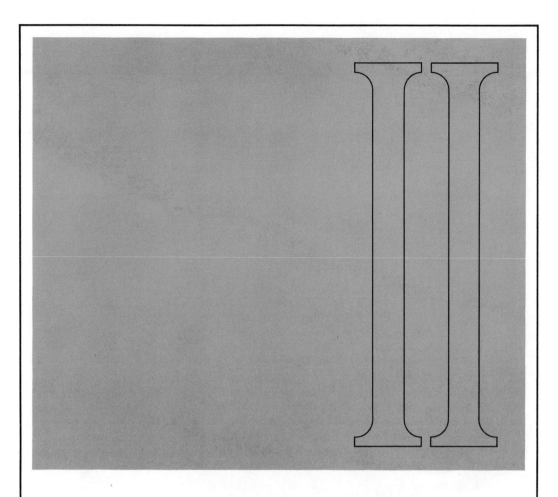

CRIMINAL LAW

3

Sociology of Criminal Law

We begin to survey and analyze the theories of criminology by going over those which deal directly with the criminal law. Because the law gives behavior its criminal definition, it is our starting point, as it must be in any discussion of crime. The early studies were on sociological jurisprudence; as we move from those to more recent theories on the criminal process, we will understand how the criminal law is formulated and administered. Then, criticizing these theories, we will have a foundation on which we can construct a new theory giving crime a social reality. That theory will be based on our critical understanding of criminal law in the United States.

Sociological Jurisprudence

Today's study of criminal law had its origin in a legal philosophy known as "sociological jurisprudence." Around the turn of this century several legal scholars began to consider the social nature of law. An Austrian, Eugen Ehrlich, in particular, distinguished between the "positive law" and the "living law."[1] The positive law can be effective only when it corresponds to the living law: that is, when legal codes are based on underlying social norms, or real life. In other words, law is to be understood as part of the social order.

Similar thoughts were developing a little later in the United States. The early American sociologists incorporated law into their theoretical frameworks. E. A. Ross referred to law as "the most specialized and highly furnished engine of control employed by society."[2] Lester F. Ward, an advocate of government control and social planning, foresaw a day when legislation would undertake to solve "questions of social improvement, the amelioration of the condition of all the people, the removal of whatever privations may still remain, and the adoption of means to the positive increase of the social welfare, in short the organization of human happiness."[3] The possibility of social reform, by legal means available to the state, was also emphasized by Albion W. Small.[4]

The early sociologists' ideas directly influenced the school of legal philosophy that developed into a major force in American legal thought — sociological jurisprudence. Roscoe Pound, its principal figure, drew from those sociologists when he asserted that law should be studied as a social institution.[5] Pound thought of law as a specialized form of social control that brings pressure to bear on each man "in order to constrain him to do his part in upholding civilized society and to deter him from anti-social conduct, that is, conduct at variance with the postulates of social order."[6]

Pound argued that law is not merely a complex of rules and procedures, and called for the study of "law in action," not law in the books. For some purposes it may be useful to view law as separate from society, developing according to its own internal logic and proceeding along its own lines. But law also simultaneously reflects society and influences it. In a social sense, law is both social product and social force. Pound's juristic approach, however, took law as both a product and a force in a very special way. In jurisprudence, law as a social product reflects the consciousness of the whole society. This *consensus* model, in criminal law, is described here: "The state of criminal law continues to be — as it should — a decisive reflection of the social consciousness of a society. What kind of conduct an organized community considers, at a given time, sufficiently condemnable to impose official sanctions, impairing the life, liberty, or property of the offender, is a barometer of the moral and social thinking of a community."[7]

At the heart of Pound's sociological jurisprudence was his theory of interests, according to which the law functions for socially worthwhile purposes. In this theory, he looked upon law as reflecting the needs of the well-ordered society:

> For the purpose of understanding the law of today I am content to think of law as a social institution to satisfy social wants — the claims and demands involved in the existence of civilized society — by giving effect to as much as we may with the least sacrifice, so far as such wants may be satisfied or such claims given effect by an ordering of human conduct through politically organized society. For present purposes I am content to see in legal history the record of a continually wider recognizing and satisfying of human wants or desires through social control; a more embracing and more effective securing of social interests; a continually more complete and effective elimination of waste and precluding of friction in human enjoyment of the goods of existence — in short, a continually more efficacious social engineering.[8]

The interests Pound had in mind would maintain and, ultimately, improve the social order. His was a teleological as well as a consensus theory: some interests must be fulfilled for the good of the whole society, and these are to be achieved through law; only the right law could develop in a civilized society.

Sociological jurisprudence has generally used a *pluralistic* model for law as a social force. Accordingly, law regulates social behavior and establishes social organization. It puts order into human relations by restraining individual actions and by settling disputes in social relations. In recent juristic language, law functions "first, to establish the general framework, the rules of the game so to speak, within and by which individual and group life shall be carried on, and secondly, to adjust the conflicting claims which different individuals and groups of individuals seek to satisfy in society."[9] And Pound says:

> Looked at functionally, the law is an attempt to satisfy, to reconcile, to harmonize, to adjust these overlapping and often conflicting claims and demands, either through securing them directly and immediately, or through securing certain individual interests, or through delimitations or compromises of individual interests, so as to give effect to the greatest total of interest or to the interests that weigh most in our civilization, with the least sacrifice of the scheme of interests as a whole.[10]

In the theory of interests, therefore, the legal order is created in society to regulate and adjust the conflicting desires and claims. Law provides the framework within which individual and group life is carried on, according to the postulates of social order. A legal historian has written, "The law defines the extent to which it will give effect to the interests which it recognizes, in the light of other interests and of the possibilities of effectively securing them through law; it also devises means for securing those that are recognized and prescribes the limits within which those means may be employed."[11] The law is an instrument that controls interests according to the requirements of social order.

Pound's theory included three classes of interests: individual, public, and social:

> Individual interests are claims or demands or desires involved immediately in the individual life and asserted in the title of that life. Public interests are claims or demands or desires involved in life in a politically organized society and asserted in the title of that organization. They are commonly treated as the claims of a politically organized society thought of as a legal entity. Social interests are claims or demands or desires involved in social life in a civilized society and asserted in the title of that life. It is not uncommon to treat them as the claims of the whole social group as such.[12]

Pound warned that the three types are overlapping and interdependent and that most claims, demands, or desires can be placed in all the categories, depending on one's purpose. He argued, however, that it is often expedient to put claims, demands, and desires in their most general form; that is, into the category of social interests.

Surveying the claims, demands, and desires found in legal proceedings and in legislative proposals, Pound suggested that the most important social interest appears to be security against actions that threaten the social group. Others are the security of social institutions, including domestic, religious, economic, and political; morals; conserving social resources; general progress, including the development of human powers and control over nature for the satisfaction of human wants; and individual life, especially the freedom of self-assertion. According to Pound, any legal system depends upon the way in which these interests are incorporated into law.

Pound's thought changed legal philosophy, and his assumptions have been accepted by sociologists, but few have attempted to revise his theory of interests. Any revision would have to move beyond these pluralist assumptions, critically examining how the power elite imposes its interests on the society, in spite of some diversity of interests among elite groups. Then too, we would have to consider law as a consequence of interests, not merely an instrument that functions outside of interests to resolve conflicts between them.

Legalistic Criminology

Naturalistic (nonlegal) definitions of crime have dominated American criminology, but a legalistic theory has been growing steadily. The need for returning to this legal notion was dramatized in the early thirties in a report by Michael and Adler of the state of knowledge in criminology.[13] Critical of past research on the etiology (causes) of criminal behavior, they suggested that it was the criminal law that defined criminology's scope and boundaries:

> If crime is merely an instance of conduct which is proscribed by the criminal code it follows that the criminal law is the formal cause of crime. That does not mean that the law produces the behavior which it prohibits, although, as we shall see, the enforcement or administration of the criminal law may be one of the factors which influence human behavior, it means only that the criminal law gives behavior its quality of criminality.[14]

Michael and Adler observed that "the most precise and least ambiguous definition of crime is that which defines it as behavior which is prohibited by the criminal code" and, further, that "this is the only possible definition of crime."[15]

A strong adherent of legally defining crime was a sociologist trained in the law, Paul W. Tappan. Though he advocated explaining an offender's behavior, Tappan warned, "Our definitions of crime cannot be rooted in epithets, in minority value judgments or prejudice, or in loose abstractions."[16] He recognized that a person is a criminal only because his behavior has been defined as criminal by the state. Answering his own question, "Who is the criminal?" Tappan went so far as to propose that "only those are criminals who have been adjudicated as such by the courts."[17]

Several criminologists have since called for a legalistic conception of crime. C. Ray Jeffery, reviewing diverse definitions of crime, suggested that it should be studied within the framework of the criminal law, from which we could ascertain under what conditions behavior becomes defined as criminal and how legal codes interact with other normative systems.[18] Jeffery called for a sociology of criminal law, following a legalistic theory:

> The sociology of criminal law would provide us with a framework for the study of crime, and at the same time it would enable us to differentiate between the criminal and the non-criminal. The legal criterion is the only standard that differentiates the two groups. Further studies of the personality makeup of the offender, of the type engaged in for the past fifty years, are never going to furnish a differential. An explanation of criminal behavior is going to depend upon an explanation of behavior. Such an explanation necessarily involves many non-sociological factors. It is to be questioned at this time whether the sociologist would do better to be more concerned with group reactions to certain types of behavior. The study of social structure is sociological; the study of human motivation is only quasi-sociological. A study of social systems in relation to the topic "law and society" would eventually lead to a theory of crime.[19]

Vold illustrated how important criminal law is to the study of crime, observing the dual problem of explanation in criminology:

> Crime always involves both human behavior (acts) and the judgment or definitions (laws, customs, mores) of fellow human beings as to whether specific behavior is appropriate and permissible, or is improper and forbidden. Crime and criminality lie in the area of behavior that is considered improper and forbidden. There is, therefore, always a dual problem of explanation — that of accounting for the behavior, *as behavior*, and equally important, accounting for *the definitions* by which specific behavior comes to be considered as crime or non-crime.[20]

Considering this dual question further, Turk wrote that the distinctly criminological problem is the study of criminality.[21] He argued that the criminal law determines the criminal status of people and behavior, and an explanation of such criminality is the only explanation of crime. Because the legal definition of behavior determines what is regarded as criminal, the criminologist has to study how criminal law is formulated and administered.[22]

Sociology of Criminal Law

Sociologists and other social scientists have become interested in making the law a subject for empirical research. Social science and law have converged in a movement that defines and combines their mutual interests.[23] To ensure the exchange of ideas between the disciplines attending to legal matters, the Law and Society Association was formed in 1964. In the first issue of the association's journal, the editor described the new convergence:

> During the past decade, each of the social sciences has found it necessary to face legal policy issues of highest relevance to the disciplines themselves and to the society as a whole. In political science, the decision process in the courts and administrative agencies has been explored to an extent which parallels earlier and continuing work on the legislatures. Political scientists have also turned their attention to the implementation of legal decisions, especially where the institutions of government have been seen as an important determinant of the impact of law. Sociologists, too, are showing increasing interest in the legal process. Their studies have been concerned with the manner in which the population is affected by law in such areas as civil rights, poverty, and crime. Both professions have joined with the anthropologists in studying the relationship between society and culture on the one hand and the nature and operation of legal institutions on the other. In addition, other professional groups — notably economists, social workers, clinical and social psychologists, and psychiatrists — are increasingly called upon for information thought to be of value in the formulation of legal policy. Above all, the legal profession has moved from a position of reluctant consumer of such information to an active participant in the research process.[24]

The research resulting from this convergence and from recent research in criminology form the basis for the sociology of criminal law, which has gathered a body of empirical research in a relatively short time. Most of the research is dominated by the positivistic mode of thought. The legal system is taken for granted, and research is aimed at explaining how the system operates, with studies on how laws are formulated, enforced, and administered.[25] Few ask why law exists, whether law is indeed necessary, or what a just system would look like. If they consider the value of justice, it is the equitability of the system that interests them, not whether the system's very existence is just. They may suggest changes in particular laws, but the legal system itself is to remain intact.[26] And they may point to inadequacies in the administration of justice, but their prescriptions for change are more technical and efficient procedures.

Even the research that departs from the positivistic mode avoids critically analyzing the present system. Social constructionist thought, as found in ethnomethodological studies, may suggest that the administration of criminal law requires that those in positions of power construct a reality.[27] But this research fails to help us reach a position from which we could analyze reality by holding up to it a higher ideal of human justice. A critique of the legal order in advanced capitalist society is missing from the sociology of criminal law. Without an image of what could be, that sociology has no possibility of understanding even the current reality.

The theoretical perspective that sociology does have accepts the legal order, and treats law as the realization of rationality. Furthermore, the legal order can be strengthened and made more efficient by applying scientific methods. In an essay on the sociology of law, Selznick writes that "legal reasoning cannot but accept the authority of scientifically validated conclusions regarding the nature of man and his institutions. Therefore, inevitably, sociology and every other social science have a part in the legal order."[28] This sociology — narrowly construed as the scientific study of law — not only studies law but supports the legal order; their fates are tied together.

As presently conceived and practiced, a sociology of criminal law cannot break out of the ideology of the age and ask critical questions about the legal order. It can only confirm the existing order and exacerbate the problems of the age.

The Social Reality of Crime

A theory that helps us begin to examine the legal order critically is the one I call the *social reality of crime*. Applying this theory, we think of crime as it is affected by the dynamics that mold the society's social, economic, and political structure. First, we recognize how criminal law fits into capitalist society. The legal order gives reality to the crime problem in the United States. Everything that makes up crime's social reality, including the application of criminal law, the behavior patterns of those who are defined as criminal, and the construction of an ideology of crime, is related to the established legal order. The social reality of crime is constructed on conflict in our society.

The theory of the social reality of crime is formulated as follows.[29]

I. THE OFFICIAL DEFINITION OF CRIME: *Crime as a legal definition of human conduct is created by agents of the dominant class in a politically organized society.*

The essential starting point is a definition of crime that itself is based on the legal definition. Crime, as *officially* determined, is a *definition* of behavior that is conferred on some people by those in power. Agents of the law (such as legislators, police, prosecutors, and judges) are responsible for formulating and administering criminal law. Upon *formulation* and *application* of these definitions of crime, persons and behaviors become criminal.

Crime, according to this first proposition, is not inherent in behavior, but is a judgment made by some about the actions and characteristics of others. This proposition allows us to focus on the formulation and administration of the criminal law as it applies to the behaviors that become defined as criminal. Crime is seen as a result of the class-dynamic processes that culminate in defining persons and behaviors as criminal. It follows, then, that the greater the number of definitions of crime that are formulated and applied, the greater the amount of crime.

II. FORMULATING DEFINITIONS OF CRIME: *Definitions of crime are composed of behaviors that conflict with the interests of the dominant class.*

Definitions of crime are formulated according to the interests of those who have the power to translate their interests into public policy. Those definitions are ultimately incorporated into the criminal law.[30] Furthermore, definitions of crime in a society change as the interests of the dominant class change. In other words, those who are able to have their interests represented in public policy regulate the formulation of definitions of crime.

The powerful interests are reflected not only in the definitions of crime and the kinds of penal sanctions attached to them, but also in the *legal policies* on handling those defined as criminals. Procedural rules are created for enforcing and administering the criminal law. Policies are also established on programs for treating and punishing the criminally defined and programs for controlling and preventing crime. From the initial definitions of crime to the subsequent procedures, correctional and penal programs, and policies for controlling and preventing crime, those who have the power regulate the behavior of those without power.[31]

III. APPLYING DEFINITIONS OF CRIME: *Definitions of crime are applied by the class that has the power to shape the enforcement and administration of criminal law.*

The dominant interests intervene in all the stages at which definitions of crime are created. Because class interests cannot be effectively protected merely by formulating criminal law, the law must be enforced and administered. The interests of the powerful, therefore, also operate where the definitions of crime reach the *application* stage. As Vold has argued, crime is "political behavior and the criminal becomes in fact a member of a 'minority group' without sufficient public support to

dominate the control of the police power of the state."[32] Those whose interests conflict with the ones represented in the law must either change their behavior or possibly find it defined as criminal.

The probability that definitions of crime will be applied varies according to how much the behaviors of the powerless conflict with the interests of those in power. Law enforcement efforts and judicial activity are likely to increase when the interests of the dominant class are threatened. Fluctuations and variations in applying definitions of crime reflect shifts in class relations.

Obviously, the criminal law is not applied directly by those in power; its enforcement and administration are delegated to authorized *legal agents.* Because the groups responsible for creating the definitions of crime are physically separated from the groups that have the authority to enforce and administer law, local conditions determine how the definitions will be applied.[33] In particular, communities vary in their expectations of law enforcement and the administration of justice. The application of definitions is also influenced by the visibility of offenses in a community and by the public's norms about reporting possible violations. And especially important in enforcing and administering the criminal law are the legal agents' occupational organization and ideology.[34]

The probability that these definitions will be applied depends on the actions of the legal agents who have the authority to enforce and administer the law. A definition of crime is applied depending on their evaluation. Turk has argued that during "criminalization," a criminal label may be affixed to people because of real or fancied attributes: "Indeed, a person is evaluated, either favorably or unfavorably, not because he *does* something, or even because he *is* something, but because others react to their perceptions of him as offensive or inoffensive."[35] Evaluation by the definers is affected by the way in which the suspect handles the situation, but ultimately the legal agents' evaluations and subsequent decisions are the crucial factors in determining the criminality of human acts. As legal agents evaluate more behaviors and persons as worthy of being defined as crimes, the probability that definitions of crime will be applied grows.

IV. How Behavior Patterns Develop in Relation to Definitions of Crime: *Behavior patterns are structured in relation to definitions of crime, and within this context people engage in actions that have relative probabilities of being defined as criminal.*

Although behavior varies, all behaviors are similar in that they represent patterns within the society. All persons — whether they create definitions of crime or are the objects of these definitions — act in reference to *normative systems* learned in relative social and cultural settings.[36] Because it is not the quality of the behavior but the action taken against the behavior that gives it the character of criminality, that which is defined as criminal is relative to the behavior patterns of the class that formulates and applies definitions. Consequently, people whose behavior patterns are not represented when the definitions of crime are formulated and applied are more likely to act in ways that will be defined as criminal than those who formulate and apply the definitions.

Once behavior patterns become established with some regularity within the segments of society, individuals have a framework for creating *personal action patterns*. These continually develop for each person as he moves from one experience to another. Specific action patterns give behavior an individual substance in relation to the definitions of crime.

People construct their own patterns of action in participating with others. It follows, then, that the probability that persons will develop action patterns with a high potential for being defined as criminal depends on (1) structured opportunities, (2) learning experiences, (3) interpersonal associations and identifications, and (4) self-conceptions. Throughout the experiences, each person creates a conception of self as a human social being. Thus prepared, he behaves according to the anticipated consequences of his actions.[37]

In the experiences shared by the definers of crime and the criminally defined, personal-action patterns develop among the latter because

they are so defined. After they have had continued experience in being defined as criminal, they learn to manipulate the application of criminal definitions.[38]

Furthermore, those who have been defined as criminal begin to conceive of themselves as criminal. As they adjust to the definitions imposed upon them, they learn to play the criminal role.[39] As a result of others' reactions, therefore, people may develop personal-action patterns that increase the likelihood of their being defined as criminal in the future. That is, increased experience with definitions of crime increases the probability of their developing actions that may be subsequently defined as criminal.

Thus, both the definers of crime and the criminally defined are involved in reciprocal action patterns. The personal-action patterns of both the definers and the defined are shaped by their common, continued, and related experiences. The fate of each is bound to that of the other.

V. Constructing an Ideology of Crime: *An ideology of crime is constructed and diffused by the dominant class to secure its hegemony.*

This ideology is created in the kinds of ideas people are exposed to, the manner in which they select information to fit the world they are shaping, and their way of interpreting this information.[40] People behave in reference to the *social meanings* they attach to their experiences.

Among the conceptions that develop in a society are those relating to what people regard as crime. The concept of crime must of course be accompanied by ideas about the nature of crime. Images develop about the relevance of crime, the offender's characteristics, the appropriate reaction to crime, and the relation of crime to the social order.[41] These conceptions are constructed by communication, and, in fact, an ideology of crime depends on the portrayal of crime in all personal and mass communication. This ideology is thus diffused throughout the society.

One of the most concrete ways by which an ideology of crime is formed and transmitted is

Figure 3.1   The Social Reality of Crime

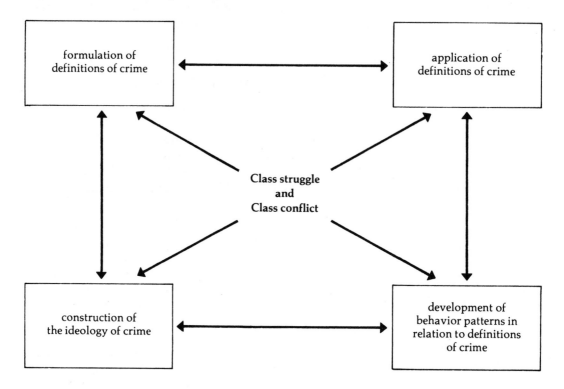

the official investigation of crime. The President's Commission on Law Enforcement and Administration of Justice is the best contemporary example of the state's role in shaping an ideology of crime.[42] Not only are we as citizens more aware of crime today because of the President's commission, but official policy on crime has been established in a crime bill, the Omnibus Crime Control and Safe Streets Act of 1968. The crime bill, itself a reaction to the growing fears of class conflict in American society, creates an image of a severe crime problem and, in so doing, threatens to negate some of our basic constitutional guarantees in the name of controlling crime.

Consequently, the conceptions that are most critical in actually formulating and applying the definitions of crime are those held by the dominant class. These conceptions are certain to be incorporated into the social reality of crime. The more the government acts in reference to crime, the more probable it is that defi-

nitions of crime will be created and that behavior patterns will develop in opposition to those definitions. The formulation of definitions of crime, their application, and the development of behavior patterns in relation to the definitions, are thus joined in full circle by the construction of an ideological hegemony toward crime.

VI. CONSTRUCTING THE SOCIAL REALITY OF CRIME: *The social reality of crime is constructed by the formulation and application of definitions of crime, the development of behavior patterns in relation to these definitions, and the construction of an ideology of crime.*

The first five propositions are collected here into a final composition proposition. The theory of the social reality of crime, accordingly, postulates creating a series of phenomena that increase the probability of crime. The result, holistically, is the social reality of crime.

Because the first proposition of the theory is a definition and the sixth is a composite, the body of the theory consists of the four middle propositions. These form a model of crime's social reality. The model, as diagrammed, relates the proposition units into a theoretical system (Figure 3.1). Each unit is related to the others. The theory is thus a system of interacting developmental propositions. The phenomena denoted in the propositions and their relationships culminate in what is regarded as the amount and character of crime at any time — that is, in the social reality of crime.

The theory of the social reality of crime as I have formulated it is inspired by a change that is occurring in our view of the world. This change, pervading all levels of society, pertains to the world that we all construct and from which, at the same time, we pretend to separate ourselves in our human experiences. For the study of crime, a revision in thought has directed attention to the criminal process: all relevant phenomena contribute to creating definitions of crime, development of behaviors by those involved in criminal-defining situations, and constructing an ideology of crime. The result is the social reality of crime that is constantly being constructed in society.

4

Legal Order and Crime Control

We now turn to the legal order, which determines what is criminal in America. Without criminal law there would be no crime, in the official sense. Moreover, the legal order provides the context for enforcing and administering criminal law. Composed of statutes, court opinions, and administrative rulings, law is also a process. It includes the making of legal decisions by agents of the state. In substance and in process, criminal law in the modern state consists of the regulation of human conduct by those invested with the authority to act in the name of the society.

The Legal Tradition

Conventional wisdom is built on the belief in the necessity of the state and inevitability of law. These assumptions are so ingrained in us that we rarely, if ever, consciously think about them. Yet, the state and its legal order intimately shape the reality of our lives.

> More than ever before men now live in the shadow of the state. What they want to achieve, individually or in groups, now mainly depends on the state's sanction and support. . . . It is possible not to be interested in what the state does; but it is not possible to be unaffected by it. The point has acquired a new and ultimate dimension in the present epoch: if large parts of the planet should one day be laid waste in a nuclear war, it is because men, acting in the name of their state and invested with its power, will have so decided, or miscalculated.[1]

Our failure to recognize how deeply the state influences our lives has kept us from understanding why the legal order exists and how it continues to survive. An unquestioning belief in the state prevents an analysis that would allow us to view the state as a sometimes coercive instrument used by an economically dominant class.[2] Such an examination would raise critical questions about the state and the legal order.

The state and the legal order are inseparable; to understand one is to understand the other. The common assumption is that the state's legal order has progressed naturally from the customary patterns in prepolitical societies. Yet, as anthropologist Stanley Diamond has observed, custom and law are related by contradiction rather than continuity. Law, instead of being an embodiment of custom, is symptomatic of the state's emergence. Diamond writes:

> Law is the instrument of civilization, of political society sanctioned by organized force, presumably above society at large, and buttressing a new set of social interests. Law and custom both involve the regulation of behavior but their characters are entirely distinct; no evolutionary balance has been struck between developing law and custom, whether traditional or emergent.[3]

Law is thus a mark of "civilization." A legal order was necessary only when the state broke down communal solidarity and divided the group into conflicting factions. In the early states, crimes were invented to serve the state's needs; that is, legal sanctions were needed to protect its new interests. Rather than healing breaches of custom, the laws protected the sovereign. In other words, crime and the laws that served it were possible only when the state came into being.[4] It broke up customary patterns to gain economic and political dominance, and established a legal system to enforce its sovereignty.

With this understanding of the legal order, we begin to see that law may be the antonym rather than the synonym for order. Law has its origins in the pathological social relations brought about by the state itself. Diamond writes: "Law arises in the breach of a prior customary order and increases in force with the conflicts that divide political societies internally and among themselves. Law *and* order is the historical illusion; law versus order is the historical reality."[5] Diamond concludes that modern Western civilization, with its state and legal order, is the one least likely to serve as a guide for building a human society.

Criminal Law

Throughout history, criminal law has been a political phenomenon. It began at the same time as the political state was created. In early societies custom prevailed, and injuries to wronged people were handled by the family and the community. The concept of criminal law developed only when the custom of private or community wrong was replaced by the principle that the state is injured when one of its subjects is harmed. The community's right to deal with wrongdoing was taken over by the state as the "representative" of the people; the state could now act by means of the criminal law to protect its own interests.

Criminal law as we know it today in the Western world came into being in several political contexts, the most important of which were Greece, Rome, England, and early America. We can follow its development in the political and economic structure of the new states.

Criminal Law and Democracy in Ancient Greece

The decisive step in forming criminal law was taken in Athens at the beginning of the sixth century B.C. Solon, after being appointed *nomothete* (lawgiver or legislator), with dictatorial powers, instituted formal enactments giving every citizen the right of action in the prosecution applying to some offenses. Greek society was in the throes of a political crisis. Solon's enactments, which formed the basis for the developing criminal law in Greece, were part of an attempt to solve the crisis and rehabilitate Greek government.

A number of facts about the Athenian political struggle have been established.[6] All functions of government were exclusively in the hands of the *eupatrids*, a hereditary class of Athenian aristocrats. The inferior orders of citizens, the peasant proprietors (the *georgi*) and the artisans (the *demiurgi*), could have no part in government except by attaching themselves to a member of the aristocracy. Below this level was the lowest class of freemen, the propertyless population (variously named *thetes, hectemori,* and *pelatae*), whose members had few rights and many of whom were no better off than serfs. Still lower were the slaves, without rights of any kind.

The class and political structure in Athens consisted of an oligarchy of the wealthy and

VIEWPOINT

LEGITIMACY AND THE RULE OF LAW

Public order in a free society does not and cannot rest solely on applications or threats of force by the authorities. It must also rest on the people's sense of the legitimacy of the rule-making institutions of the political and social order and of the rules these institutions make. Persons obey the rules of society when the groups with which they identify approve those who abide by the rules and disapprove those who violate them. Such expressions of approval and disapproval are forthcoming only if the group believes that the rule-making institutions are in fact entitled to rule — that is, are "legitimate."

The income tax laws, for example, make this point clear. In a way, these laws represent consensual taxation. True, some potential violators are deterred by the strong probability of detection and punishment, but detection and punishment remain possible only because the great majority voluntarily obey the law. Unless the great majority of citizens voluntarily maintained accurate records and filed accurate returns, the tax structure would collapse. No amount of investigation or force could insure the success of our tax laws as presently written. Regardless of the popular folklore, however, most Americans are apparently more honest in reporting their incomes voluntarily than the citizens of many other nations with far less violent crime than we have. They do so because they recognize, albeit grudgingly, the legitimacy of the rule-making institution itself. But if this kind of episode occurs too frequently or persists for too long without change — as in the case of prohibition or the decision to wage war in Vietnam — the institution itself will soon begin to suffer a loss of legitimacy.

This concept of acceptance of rules based upon legitimacy may be termed the "rule of law." The phrase is useful to describe the willingness of a people to accept and order their behavior according to the rules and procedures which are prescribed by political and social institutions — such as legislatures and universities — and enforced, where necessary, either by those bodies or by other institutions — such as governors, police, and courts. The "rule of law" expresses the idea that people recognize the legitimacy of the law as a means of ordering and controlling the behavior of *all* people in a society, the governors and the governed, the rich and the poor, the contented and the discontented.

Source: National Commission on the Causes and Prevention of Violence, *Law and Order Reconsidered* (New York: Bantam Books, 1970), pp. 8–9.

---

privileged that ruled over a large proletariat. The lower classes were politically subjugated and were subjected to merciless economic exploitation. This oppressiveness, accompanied by the proletariat's increasing economic strength, eventually produced discontent among those excluded from government. The ruling aristocrats reacted with compromise:

In such a situation the alternative to revolution and perhaps tyranny was compromise,

and this the ruling class, or some of them, were wise enough to see. And we must believe that these wiser men were keenly alive to the menace which confronted them in the presence of a prosperous alien population, chafing under the denial of the political rights to which their economic strength entitled them, ready at the first opportunity to fan into the flame of revolution the smouldering discontent of the native proletariat.[7]

The political compromise that arose from

the class conflict in ancient Greece provided the beginnings for the criminal law of the Western world. The step toward criminal law gave citizens some protection from one another and sometimes from government itself. By legal reform, as an alternative to possible revolution, Solon and his council established popular courts, provided for appeal from the decisions of magistrates, and gave citizens the right to initiate prosecutions. The foundations of democratic government and criminal law occurred together in a mutually supportive relationship.

The victory for the people of Athens was far from complete, however.

> The democratic republic itself operated as a social dictatorship. It was the domination of a citizen minority who alone exercised political rights over the noncitizen majority of women, slaves and foreigners. And even within the boundaries of the citizen body, the wealthier elements dominated.[8]

A ruling class composed of slaveholders and rich merchants governed this early political democracy. The new criminal law served the interests of the dominant class in the democratic state.

Criminal Law in the Roman Empire

Criminal law developed slowly among the Romans. Although eventually they distinguished between *civilis* and *criminalis,* law in Rome was devoted primarily to private legal matters and civil procedure. When a criminal law did develop, its principal business was offenses against the state and punishing such offenders. The Romans were efficient administrators of their empire, rather than students and practitioners of justice.

The law of the Twelve Tables in the middle of the fifth century B.C. was based on the idea of the injured party's right to private vengeance. Punishment was inflicted by the state, however, for crimes committed directly against the commonwealth. Although most of the provisions in the Twelve Tables, as codifications of Roman customary law, rested on the concept of private law, the Twelve Tables were originally created as a safeguard for part of the population. In effect the Twelve Tables pro-

tected the plebeians against unfair treatment by the patricians.[9]

As Rome grew from a rural community to a powerful city-state, the "private criminal law" of the Twelve Tables proved increasingly inadequate.

> The "private criminal law" of the Twelve Tables reflected the conditions of a primitive commonwealth of modest dimensions and rustic character. It was bound to prove increasingly inadequate as Rome developed into a metropolis dominated by powerful social tensions; and the growth of the urban proletariat and of the slave population was certainly accompanied by a rise in criminality which demanded vigorous measures for the maintenance of public security.[10]

During the third century B.C. and the beginning of the second century, a criminal jurisdiction with tribunals and courts was established to control those engaged in such politically threatening activities as violence, treason, arson, poisoning, carrying weapons, and stealing state property.[11]

The criminal law that appeared late in the Roman Republic was created mainly to protect the state itself. Protection of the individual's rights was not a vital part of Roman law. Criminal law in Rome was created by the interests that could be best satisfied by maintaining a strongly controlled political regime.

Criminal Law in England

Criminal law could develop only as the state achieved political domination, allowing law to be established and administered in the name of a centralized governmental authority. For Anglo-American law, this occurred in England during the latter part of the eleventh century and continued throughout the twelfth.[12] With the Norman invasion of England in 1066 and the strong rule of the Norman kings, the old tribal-feudal system of law was replaced by a criminal law that lay in the hands of a central authority, the Crown. Before that the territory we now know as England was divided into separate units with their own laws. These legal systems could not foster a criminal law.

The Anglo-Saxons' law was originally a system of tribal justice. Each tribe, as a group of kinsmen, was controlled by its own chief and armed warriors who met and, along with other duties, passed laws. Any wrong was regarded as against or by the family; and the family atoned or carried out the blood feud if an offense occurred between kinship groups.

By the tenth century, England was divided into six or eight large kingdoms. Civil wars among local tribes had brought some political consolidation. The leaders accepted Christianity, which provided not only a spiritual unit but, as in the Roman Catholic Church, centralized control. In the reorganization, tribal chiefs were replaced by kings who became both military leaders and landlords. As feudalism changed the organization of Saxon society, between the eighth and eleventh centuries, the blood feud was replaced by a system of compensations. Eventually the kinship group's collective responsibility was absorbed by the kingdom. Compensation for offenses became the domain of the king, lord, or bishop, rather than the kinship group. One of King Aethelred's laws made it a breach of the king's peace to resort to the feud before compensation had been demanded from the offender or his family.[13]

With the Norman invasion of England and the reign of the Norman kings the old tribal-feudal system of law disappeared and a new system appeared in England. When William conquered England in 1066, he proclaimed himself the "supreme landlord" of all England. By this move, implemented by the Domesday Survey, he redistributed the land, with the Norman nobles at the top, and placed all social relationships on land tenure, under his control. William took another important step, separating state law from canon (church) law. But the most important move taken in William's time toward a criminal law was unifying England under one head, the "King of England."

The administratively able Norman kings developed centralized legal institutions, creating several courts to place law under the jurisdiction of the king's government. Writs (orders written by the courts) were devised by which cases could be carried out of baronial courts into the king's courts. Itinerant judges were sent into the various "hundreds" and "shires" to administer the king's laws. By the end of Henry II's reign (1154–1189), the law of England was in the Crown's hands. A court of "common law" was established to give justice to all men. A new procedure and a new conception of offenses had been created.[14] Now for the first time some offenses were regarded as clearly violating the peace of king and country. England had a criminal law.

English criminal law came about to protect particular interests, primarily those of the king. The criminal law placed the affairs of his subjects under his jurisdiction. The powerful landholders and the church could no longer freely create and administer law in their own courts. Law that affected the nation was now the king's law; the nation's interests were those of the king.

Eventually the English monarch's power diminished and finally vanished when parliamentary government was created. Today, because of the political unification in the eleventh and twelfth centuries and the creation of a criminal law at the same time, a common law survives. Its justice continues to be more common for some people than for others.

Law for the New Propertied Class

Laws to protect private property were soon established in England. The movement from an agricultural economy to a new order based on industry and trade required legal structure to protect the new economic class's interests. Before the fifteenth century the Western world had no legal conception of theft. During that century, in England, the modern law of theft was officially formulated into criminal law. It was shaped by changing social conditions, and especially by pressing economic interests. Defining theft as a crime solved a legal problem that arose within a particular historical context.

The English decision that resulted in the legal concept of theft occurred in 1473, in the Carrier's Case, documented and interpreted by Jerome Hall in his book *Theft, Law and Society*.[15] The facts of the case are these: the defendant was hired to carry bales of goods to Southampton; instead of fulfilling his obligation, he carried the bales to another place, broke them open, and took the contents. The man was apprehended and charged with felony.

The most illustrious judges of the time discussed the case at length. Although the defendant was finally held guilty by a majority of the judges, a portentous legal problem developed during the proceedings. Before the case arose, the common law recognized no criminality in a person who came legally into possession of something and "converted" it to his own use. The reasoning followed in the common law was that the owner of transported goods was responsible for protecting himself by employing trustworthy persons. There was, in the Carrier's Case, a legal problem of *stare decisis* ("following previous decisions") in which the judges regarded themselves as bound by the common law.

Until the Carrier's Case it had been agreed that although trespass (taking property from one who is in possession of it) was an essential element of larceny, a person in possession of property could not commit a trespass upon that property. Because a bailee (an employee who is trusted with property) had possession, larceny could not technically be committed by such an employee. The judges, however, departed from precedent by introducing a new concept that could be neither found among the legal rules nor logically derived from them. For the judges held that "breaking bulk" terminated the bailment, that such property at once reverted to the bailor's possession, and that removing it from the bales supplied the trespass. Hall observes: "By this refinement the door was opened to admit into the law of larceny a whole series of acts which had up to that time been purely civil wrongs."[16] Law was being made by judges in the Carrier's Case by departing from and renouncing precedents of the common law.

An important question is which forces were active in creating a new legal concept. Hall outlines the changes that were occurring in fifteenth-century England. These changes, coupled with the social conditions and the institutions of the period, made a change in the law of theft convenient. To begin with, in the political realm, the courts were subservient to the wishes of Edward IV. This meant that the special interests of the Crown were protected by the courts. Among the king's interests that

received the favor of the courts were the royal commercial activities, including trade with merchants on the Continent. Edward was himself a merchant and carried on many private ventures.

Economic conditions were especially important for the decision reached in the Carrier's Case: a commercial revolution was taking place in England and Europe. The old feudal structure resting on an agricultural economy was giving way to a new order based on industry and trade. Also, "(1) the complainant was an alien merchant; (2) he had a covenant with the kings which provided safe passage for him and his goods; (3) the property taken is described as being within bales, and weighing twenty pounds; (4) the defendant was a carrier; (5) and he was to deliver the merchandise at Southampton."[17]

Hall contends that the complainant was a foreign merchant (probably Italian) whose trade was desired by the Crown. Such foreign merchants were subject to special risks: local merchants were naturally hostile toward foreign trade. Moreover, foreign merchants were handicapped in transporting goods because they were uncertain of finding trustworthy carriers who would not abscond with the goods. The king attempted to relieve the situation by issuing covenants of safe-conduct through the country.

The merchandise taken by the bailee in the Carrier's Case was probably wool or cloth, or both, usually transported in bales. Also, Southampton was a principal port for shipping these goods, for trade with Latin countries in particular. All these deductions mean that "the interests of the most important industry in England were involved in the case."[18]

Conditions in fifteenth-century England directly affected the decision in the Carrier's Case:

We are now in a position to visualize the case and the problem presented to the judges as a result of the legal, political and economic conditions described above. On the one hand, the whole complex aggregate of political and economic conditions described above thrusts itself upon the court. The more powerful forces of the time were interrelated very intimately and at many points: the New Monarchy and the *nouveau riche* — the mercantile class; the business interests of both and the consequent need for a secure carrying trade; the wool and textile industry, the most valuable, by far, in all the realm; wool and cloth, the most important exports; these exports and the foreign trade, this trade and Southampton, chief trading city with the Latin countries for centuries; the numerous and very influential Italian merchants who bought English wool and cloth inland and shipped them from Southampton. The great forces of an emerging modern world, represented in the above phenomena, necessitated the elimination of a formula which had outgrown its usefulness. A new set of major institutions required a new rule. The law, lagging behind the needs of the times, was brought into more harmonious relationship with the other institutions by the decision rendered in the Carrier's Case.[19]

The Carrier's Case of 1473 vividly demonstrates how changing social conditions and new class interests bring about the formulation of a criminal law. The decision provided the framework for further developing the law of theft. Eventually, with the growth in banking and the use of paper currency, the law was expanded to include the act of embezzlement by clerks, officers, and the like. A parliament in the eighteenth century passed an embezzlement statute to protect mercantile interests.

The legal protection of property continues to be to the interest of the propertied class. Protecting private property became a basic purpose of criminal law in the new American state. To this day a large portion of American criminal law is devoted to protecting the property of the dominant economic class.

English Common Law
in the American Colonies

The early criminal laws of the American colonies developed within the tradition of the English common law. The English charters for founding settlements in the New World provided that the laws established in the settlements should not be contrary to the laws of England. During the American colonial period,

colonial statutes that were counter to the English common law could be disallowed by the Crown's Privy Council. In addition, the decisions of the provincial courts were subject to appeal by the Privy Council where any radical departure from the common law could be corrected.[20] But in spite of these provisions for controlling the American colonies in accord with the political and economic interest of the Crown and stockholders, local interests shaped the early American criminal laws.

Some local conditions in America made irrelevant or impractical the English legal practices. Even the vast differences in settlement and development within colonies would foster divergences in their legal systems.[21] Except for England's primary political interest in controlling its colonies, they were relatively free to develop their own legal systems.

The criminal laws that developed in America, however, did not depart substantially from English common law.[22] The interests embodied in it became the ones that were instrumental in formulating American criminal law. Several forces were at work, beyond the standards set by the Crown, which ensured the continuance of English common law in America. One important force was in the fact that the early settlers, coming from the mother country, were deeply imbued with the ideas and traditions of the common law. Another force was adherence to the liberal ideal of democracy. The natural law conception of man's inherent rights as a human being inspired the Declaration of Independence (1776) as it had the British Bill of Rights (1689).[23] John Locke's formula, "life, liberty, and property" (later broadened to include the pursuit of happiness), was an underlying value for American law. The English common law was exalted and perpetuated in nineteenth-century America by the popularity of such codifications as Sir Edward Coke's *Institutes* and Sir William Blackstone's *Commentaries on the Laws of England*. One more force made the interests of English common law the same as those of American law: the attempts by American lawyers to adapt the common law to American conditions.[24] Although they ran into much conflict with their colleagues, American lawyers were generally successful in asserting England's legal heritage against provincial interests.

All these forces combined to produce an American law incorporating the class interests of English common law. Political independence did not signify new beginnings in law. Class interests in a new setting best describes early America's legal development.

Law and Order on the Frontier

As the American frontier expanded, two legal problems developed naturally. One was the legal status and control of the native Americans, the Indians. The second problem, at times related to the first, was legal regulation in territories that did not yet have their own law.

The Crown did not recognize the sovereign right of the native Indians and acknowledged only their right of occupancy in the land.[25] In other words, because no law was there, any law established in America was to be imposed by the Crown or by the colonial settlers according to standards set by the Crown. As the law developed, any offense against the colony by Indians outside colonial territory was administered by tribal leaders. But for Indians within the territory, cases were tried in colonial courts. The Indians subject to colonial law were judged not by their own customary law but according to the English settlers' interests.

Later a new problem arose in formulating and administering law in the western Indian territory. The United States federal government sent agents and legal officers into the expanding territories. Troops of the United States Infantry first brought "law" to the western Indian territory, carrying out the treaties and the government policy — moving the Indians from their land. Courts were established to settle disputes between the white men and Indians.

When the United States Court for the Western District of Arkansas was created at Fort Smith, and Judge Isaac C. Parker was appointed, a new phase of law and order arrived on the frontier. On May 2, 1875, Judge Parker arrived in Fort Smith to take over the Federal District Court of the territory. His task was to control the Indians who were against the white man and to put an end to the "outlawry" of the breed of men who have since become the western folk heros. Judge Parker quickly acquired his reputation as "the hanging judge." In his twenty-one years on the bench at Fort Smith, Judge Parker heard 13,490 cases and convicted 9,454 persons, of whom 344 were tried for offenses punishable by death. Of the 344 cases, 165 were convicted and 160 of these were sentenced to the gallows. Seventy-nine persons were eventually hanged, two were killed attempting to escape and two more died in jail awaiting execution. Judge Parker saw this as his mission:

> During the twenty years that I have engaged in administering the law here, the contest has been one between civilization and savagery, the savagery being represented by the intruding criminal class. The United States government, in its treaties from the days of Andrew Jackson, stipulated that this criminal element should be kept out of the country, but the treaties have only been made to be broken. . . . Thus this class keeps on increasing; its members marry, and the criminal population keeps ever growing larger. . . . At the present time there seems to be a criminal wave sweeping over the country, the like of which I have not yet seen before.[26]

Judge Parker, according to his sympathetic biographer, "had taken pardonable pride in eradicating lawlessness from his jurisdiction. He had taught the criminal class to fear the law and respect the rights and property of peaceful citizens, and had helped the Indian advance to a higher civilization."[27]

In the fast-growing western mining camps some kind of order was needed to resolve the conflicts between miners and the disputes over land and mining rights. There were as yet no territorial or state governments to create and administer law. In this void a "local law" developed among the miners to regulate their own interests.[28] In other words, a popular sovereignty was created in the mining territory to formulate and administer its own form of law. The miners' customs, or local laws, spread throughout the western territories. Eventually, when states were formally established, the miners' local laws were enacted into statute law or incorporated into the legal precedents of court decisions. The economic interests of miners in the nineteenth century were formulated into laws that continue to operate in the twentieth century.

Legislating Crime Control

During the sixties in the United States the legal order entered a new stage of development.[29] Beginning early in the decade the nation's problems were simply and conveniently concentrated into one domestic enemy — crime. Crime and fear of it were crucial in political campaigns. The federal government assumed a new role, launching the "war on crime." In a presidential message to the 89th Congress in 1965, Lyndon Johnson declared that "we must arrest and reverse the trend toward lawlessness."[30] Suggesting that "crime has become a malignant enemy in America's midst," the president charted a course of action that would use legal control and law enforcement: "This active combat against crime calls for a fair and efficient system of law enforcement to deal with those who break the law. It means new priority to the methods and institutions of law enforcement."

The problem was conceived to be a national one, and crime prevention and crime fighting were to be intensified at all levels of government. The federal effort, Johnson continued, would consist of "(1) increased federal law enforcement efforts, (2) assistance to local enforcement efforts, and (3) a comprehensive, penetrating analysis of the origins and nature of crime in modern America." The president appointed a commission — the President's Commission on Law Enforcement and Administration of Justice — to study the crime problem and to make recommendations for action. Hearings were held by the Senate Judiciary Committee, and crime control legislation was subsequently enacted.

Crime control today is accomplished by a variety of laws and enforcement agencies on the national level. The federal government, especially through its legislative bodies, establishes official policies of control. In the last decade Congress has enacted many crime bills. This legislation reveals that Congress felt the established order was being challenged, as in the statement that opens one of the crime bills:

Congress finds that the high incidence of crime in the United States threatens the peace, security and general welfare of the Nation and its citizens. To prevent crime and to insure the greater safety of the people, law enforcement efforts must be better coordinated, intensified, and made more effective at all levels of government.

Congress finds further that crime is essentially a local problem that must be dealt with by State and local governments if it is to be controlled effectively.

It is therefore the declared policy of the Congress to assist State and local governments in strengthening and improving law enforcement at every level by national assistance. It is the purpose of this title to (1) encourage States and units of general local government to prepare and adopt comprehensive plans based upon their evaluation of State and local problems of law enforcement; (2) authorize grants to States and units of local government in order to improve and strengthen law enforcement; and (3) encourage research and development directed toward the improvement of law enforcement and the development of new methods for the prevention and reduction of crime and the detection and apprehension of criminals.[31]

Not only was the war on crime intensified by this legislation, but the federal government stimulated local governments to engage in the battle by creating the Law Enforcement Assistance Administration, with large amounts of financing and guidance.

President Johnson sounded the call in a message to Congress in 1967, warning the legislators that "crime — and the fear of crime — has become a public malady," and reminded them of their "duty to seek its cure."[32] Johnson's legislative proposals gave Congress the opportunity to further define the crime problem. Hearings were held by the Senate Subcommittee on Criminal Laws and Procedures and by the House Judiciary Committee, providing the framework for defining the crime problem in modern words, and suggesting stricter law enforcement, more limited rights for defendants, and use of the most recent technology in the war on crime. The Senate Committee's chairman, John McClellan, opened the hearings on March 7, 1967, by stating that "It is quite probable that these hearings and the bills we will be considering will mark the turning point in the struggle against lawlessness in this nation."[33] The survival of the state and the social and economic order (the "society") seemed to be at stake: "The rate of increase in crime cannot continue if our society is to remain safe and secure and our people protected against the ravages of crime."

These efforts culminated in the Omnibus Crime Control and Safe Streets Act of 1968. The new crime legislation initially assisted state and local governments by making law enforcement and criminal administration more effective — in trying to more effectively ensure domestic order. By the time the bill was passed it carried several amendments in a deliberate attempt to overturn Supreme Court decisions that supposedly "coddled criminals" and "handcuffed the police." All voluntary confessions and eyewitness identifications — regardless of whether a defendant had been informed of his rights to counsel — could be admitted in federal trials. State and local law enforcement agencies were given broad license to tap telephones and engage in other forms of eavesdropping. Law enforcement officials were permitted these practices without a court order. Anyone convicted of "inciting a riot or civil disorder," "organizing, promoting, encouraging, or participating in a riot or civil disorder," or "aiding and abetting any person in committing" such offenses would be disqualified for employment by the federal government for five years.

The government has continued enacting crime-control legislation. The Congress and the presidency have worked together to construct a comprehensive program of crime control.[34] Several congressional committees — including four Senate committees, five House committees, and two appropriations committees — are actively formulating crime control policies. Coming from these efforts is a crime bill

for the District of Columbia, drug control legislation, an organized crime bill, and proposals for future legislation. There is no sign that the administration and the Congress will cease their crime control interests and activities.

In July of 1970, President Nixon signed into law the District of Columbia crime bill. Crime there had become a symbolic issue for president and Congress, deserving an exemplary crime control program. The bill has new laws of regulation and these potentially repressive measures:

Authorization for "no-knock" searches, under which a policeman with a warrant could force his way into a building without announcing his presence or identifying himself if there was reason to believe evidence inside would otherwise be destroyed.

Preventive, or pretrial, detention, under which a defendant could be jailed without bail for up to 60 days if a hearing established that he might commit further crimes if he were released.

Establishment of a mandatory five-year sentence upon a second conviction for a crime of violence in which the defendant was carrying a gun.

Authorization for wiretaps by the police with court approval, but restricting their use when the communication involved was between physician and patient; attorney and client; clergyman and parishioner; or husband and wife.[35]

The bill not only regulates crime in the District of Columbia, but serves, as Attorney General Mitchell suggested, as a model for all the states.

The government's crime control was further advanced in October of 1970 by the Organized Crime Control Act. Although labeled as an "organized crime" bill, its provisions apply to a wide range of offenses.[36] Fundamental procedural policies cover such matters as grand jury powers, illegally obtained evidence, long-term sentencing, self-incrimination, and due process of law. Grand juries are instructed to issue reports on noncriminal misconduct by an appointed public official, with little safeguard for the accused against reports made by the grand jury. Federal judges are authorized to impose an additional sentence of up to 25 years on a class of so-called "dangerous special offenders." The sentence can be imposed upon a convicted person in a hearing before a judge rather than in a jury trial. The bill also revises the laws dealing with the immunity of a witness from prosecution and other procedural safeguards, to overcome some of the problems in gathering evidence.

Soon to follow the organized crime bill was the Comprehensive Drug Abuse Prevention and Control Act. Like the organized crime bill, the new law covered activities only superficially related to drug control and suspended some constitutional rights. Witnesses could be forced to testify in almost any federal case; new provisions were made for admitting wiretapping evidence; grand jury powers were extended; search and seizure without warrant were expanded; and special offenders could be given extended sentences by judges. Drug control, like control over other criminal activities, had become an excuse for Congress and the presidency to control anything that seemed to threaten the existing order.

The government continues to expand its crime control program. As the seventies began, the Senate could praise itself for passing a good share of legislation for the crime control program. Of twenty proposed anticrime measures, thirteen had already been passed by the Senate by January of 1970. The Senate majority leader, Senator Mansfield, could state: "After the passage of these bills, we may then direct ourselves to the more difficult tasks of identifying and addressing ourselves to the task of eradicating the causes of criminal behavior."[37] Even if the government were to turn its attention to the conditions that underlie criminally defined behavior, it is unlikely that the system that makes crime possible would get a critical examination.

National Law Enforcement

The enforcing and administering of criminal law consists of much more than the efforts at control made by local police departments and criminal courts. Indeed, the control of crime is being determined increasingly by the federal government. The middle sixties began a great change in law enforcement and administration of justice. Responding to the threats against American institutions, the federal government took the leadership in controlling crime. Pursuing its war on crime, it created an apparatus for controlling crime unparalleled in world history. To understand crime control today, we must examine this rationalized, coordinated, and scientifically advanced national system of crime control.

The modern state creates a complex of bureaucratic agencies as it establishes control over the population. These agencies carry out the objectives of state authority, and also solidify and protect the economic interests that underpin the state. An adequate picture of the state control of crime must therefore take into account what these bureaucratic agencies do. The state bureaucracies and the people who function within them reinforce the state's political and economic objectives.

The United States federal government had long shied away from interfering in local law enforcement activities, but the time was ripe by the mid-sixties for a program that would give national direction to law enforcement. At President Johnson's urging, in a special message to Congress on February 6, 1967, greater federal efforts and expenditures for law enforcement were suggested "to strengthen the system and to encourage the kind of innovations needed to respond to the problems of crime in America."[38] Congress responded by creating the Office of Law Enforcement Assistance, within the Department of Justice. The new agency, operating from 1965 to 1968, supported nearly 400 projects aimed at "helping local governments improve their overall criminal justice systems." These projects included "training, research and demonstration efforts to prevent and control crime; to improve law enforcement, corrections, courts and other criminal justice agencies; and to assist these agencies in recruiting and upgrading personnel."[39]

But this was only the beginning. By 1968 Congress had passed the Omnibus Crime Control and Safe Streets Act, in which a major provision (Title I) created the Law Enforcement Assistance Administration (LEAA). As an

DOCUMENT_____

HOW LEAA OPERATES

Congress established LEAA to channel funds to states for improving their law enforcement capabilities. It also directed LEAA to undertake certain other activities. Descriptions of the major areas of activity of LEAA follow.

COMPREHENSIVE PLANS

LEAA serves 55 jurisdictions — the 50 States and American Samoa, the District of Columbia, Guam, Puerto Rico and the Virgin Islands. Each jurisdiction has a State Planning Agency (SPA) which is required by law to be the recipient of LEAA planning, block action and discretionary funds.

Before an SPA can receive its block action funds, it must develop a comprehensive state plan for improving law enforcement. It is awarded a planning grant (based on its population) to support the SPA and underwrite its development of the comprehensive plan. Except as noted below, it must pass on 40 percent of its planning grant to units of local government to assist them in developing the plan.

Most states have a number of Regional Planning Councils which combine local units of government for more effective use of resources. There are presently more than 450 such councils. Congress in FY [fiscal year] 1971 required that representation on the Regional Planning Councils include public agencies maintaining crime control or reduction programs, in addition to representation from law enforcement agencies and units of local government as required by the 1968 Act. The SPAs themselves are also required to maintain this representation.

Congress also required SPAs to assure that major cities and counties receive funds to develop plans and coordinate local activities. However the law now allows LEAA to waive the requirement that 40 percent of each state planning grant be passed on to units of local government, if the requirement is inconsistent with the development of a state comprehensive plan.

State planning requires not only the preparation and updating of plans for improving criminal justice systems during the fiscal year, but also the projection of funding commitments 4 years beyond that year. Total planning grant awards increased from $20.9 million in FY 1970 to $25.8 million in FY 1971.

GRANTS

When LEAA approves the comprehensive plan, it then awards each state a block action grant to put the plan into effect. The grants are called "block" because they are awarded as a lump sum. They are called "action" because they intended to carry out Part C of the Act, the action section.

LEAA also awards discretionary grants directly to states, cities, counties, and other units of government. Congress authorized LEAA to award 15 percent of its total action funds at its discretion for promising projects. A major portion of these funds has gone to the nation's largest cities to help them deal with crime problems.

The Federal share for most action programs is 75 percent, with the states providing the remaining 25 percent; the breakdown is 50–50 for construction proj-

---

Source: *Third Annual Report of the Law Enforcement Assistance Administration*, Fiscal Year 1971 (Washington, D.C.: U.S. Government Printing Office, 1972), pp. 3–5.

DOCUMENT (Continued)_____

Distribution of LEAA Funds (FY 1971 Budget: $529,000,000) [a]

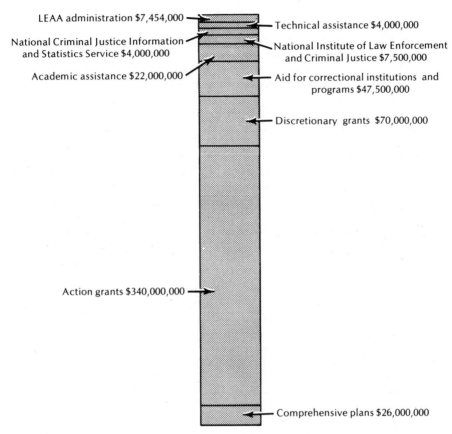

LEAA administration $7,454,000

Technical assistance $4,000,000

National Criminal Justice Information and Statistics Service $4,000,000

National Institute of Law Enforcement and Criminal Justice $7,500,000

Academic assistance $22,000,000

Aid for correctional institutions and programs $47,500,000

Discretionary grants $70,000,000

Action grants $340,000,000

Comprehensive plans $26,000,000

[a] Includes supplemental appropriation.

ects; and the Federal share for correctional facility construction (Part E grants) may be up to 75 percent.

During FY 1971, the states were required by law to pass on at least 75 percent of their block action grants to local governments. Beginning July 1, 1972, states will pass on the percentage of action funds equal to the total local government expenditures in relationship to the total state and local government expenditures for law enforcement during the preceding fiscal year. . . .

Block action grant awards increased from $182.7 million in FY 1970 to $340 million in FY 1971. Discretionary grants increased from $32 million in FY 1970 to $70 million in FY 1971.

RESEARCH

The National Institute of Law Enforcement and Criminal Justice is the research arm of the agency and carries out programs of research and development to

DOCUMENT (Continued)_____

advance the state of the art of law enforcement and criminal justice. The Institute awards funds for innovative projects in crime control, new equipment and techniques.

EDUCATION

Under the Law Enforcement Education Program (LEEP), LEAA awards funds to colleges and universities which, in turn, provide grants and loans for college study by law enforcement professionals and students preparing for careers in criminal justice. About 10 percent of the nation's uniformed police have attended college courses through this program, and thousands of preservice students have received tuition loans under the program. LEAA obligated $20.9 million for LEEP in FY 1971, up from $17.9 million in FY 1970.

STATISTICS AND SYSTEMS ANALYSIS

During FY 1971, LEAA carried out research and development programs in statistics and systems analysis. These programs were designed to strengthen statistics research and make statistics on crime and criminal justice more available to the criminal justice community, and to apply new concepts of systems analysis both to LEAA operations and to criminal justice operations at the state and local level.

OTHER PROGRAMS

LEAA made plans in FY 1971 to establish a National Criminal Justice Reference Service. This is intended to be an information service for the entire law enforcement and criminal justice community. Its staff will collect relevant research and development reports and will document action project results sponsored by LEAA, by other Federal agencies, and by state and local criminal justice agencies, universities, private and community organizations, and individuals.

---

agency within the Department of Justice, to replace and supersede the Office of Law Enforcement Assistance, LEAA assumed a broader and more pervasive plan of federal involvement in law enforcement and crime control. Support for the enlarged program came from all quarters, because domestic security was the name of the game.

The LEAA has grown steadily. During its first years it received a congressional appropriation of $63 million. The budget increased sharply to $268 million in 1970, and was further increased to $529 million in 1971. The Senate authorized $1.15 billion for 1972 and $1.75 billion for 1973. In preparing the annual report, the administrator of LEAA, citing the generous appropriations, advised the president and the

Congress on the mission and success of his agency:

The mission of LEAA is to reduce crime and delinquency by channeling Federal financial aid to state and local governments, to conduct research in methods of improving law enforcement and criminal justice, to fund efforts to upgrade the educational level of law enforcement personnel, to develop applications of statistical research and applied systems analysis in law enforcement, and to develop broad policy guidelines for both the short and long-range improvement of the nation's Criminal Justice System as a whole.[40]

Most of LEAA's budget goes to states and localities for the fight against crime. Officially, this is the objective:

State and local governments receive the bulk of LEAA aid. To be effective, law enforcement planning and action programs must be broad and comprehensive. Congress recognized the most meaningful primary unit to accomplish improvements is the state. Within this framework, the state and its cities can increase cooperation; there can be greater coordination among police, courts, and corrections. The bulk of the LEAA budget therefore goes in block grants to the 50 states, which in turn re-allocate most of those funds to their city and county governments.[41]

Nevertheless, though the states are the units for receiving block grants, "the goal of the LEAA program is across-the-board improvement of the Nation's criminal justice system." Thus, we are told, "For the first time in our history, all levels of government and all parts of the criminal justice system are working together in a coordinated, nationwide approach to the urgent problems of crime and criminal justice."[42]

To carry out its program "more effectively and efficiently," LEAA has gone through several bureaucratic reorganizations. The function of the agency's headquarters in Washington now "is largely to develop and implement policy guidelines, to channel Federal funds to the states, to undertake research, to provide special assistance to states in such areas as applied systems analysis, and to provide technical assistance."[43] In other words, LEAA seems to be trying to maximize the possibility of building a comprehensive national crime control program, under the guise of decentralization. Each state, however, in order to receive the grants and technical assistance of LEAA, has had to set up a comprehensive law enforcement agency. And to be eligible for federal funds, each state agency must annually draw up a law enforcement plan, which must in turn be approved by LEAA, for "comprehensive state-wide law enforcement improvements in police, courts, and corrections."

Along with encouraging, or forcing, state governments to develop law enforcement plans, LEAA awards federal funds to state and local governments for developing programs to improve and strengthen law enforcement, gives funds for training law enforcement agents, and supports research and the development of methods for improving law enforcement and the reduction of crime. These programs are administered in the three operating divisions of LEAA: the Office of Criminal Justice Assistance, the National Institute of Law Enforcement and Criminal Justice, and the Office of Operations Support (Figure 4.1). All of this means, in other words, that a nationally sponsored program of crime control has been created.

At the same time, a huge bureaucracy devoted to crime control is being created not only in Washington but in each of the states. And LEAA has ten regional offices, each with its own director, deputy director, administrative services, technical assistance staff, and operations division. Much of the federal support of LEAA must go to these bureaucratic state and regional agencies. It gives some encouragement to those who fear governmental repression that much of the funds and energies of LEAA are being used up merely to keep these bureaucracies going. The potential effectiveness of LEAA is necessarily limited by its bureaucracy.[44]

But the aims of LEAA are specific and of lasting consequence. In testimony before the Legal and Monetary Affairs Subcommittee of Congress, the administrator of LEAA at that time, Jerris Leonard, made clear the government's objectives in the war on crime:

> For the future, reducing crime nationally will not be an easy job. It will not be cheap, in either labor or money. But it can be done, and the present LEAA program must be the major vehicle for doing it.
> For those without blinders, unmistakable signs of progress already are evident. Many more will become apparent if we can have unmatched dedication by local, state, and federal officials; responsible assistance from the public; and continued support from the Congress, whose Judiciary Committees gave LEAA a remarkably sound bill of health following extended hearings last year.
> In many ways, American citizens are safer now than they were three years ago. A year from now, they will be safer than they are today. The decade of the 1960s ended as the most lawless in our history. The decade of the 1970s can end with crime long since

Figure 4.1   Law Enforcement Assistance Administration

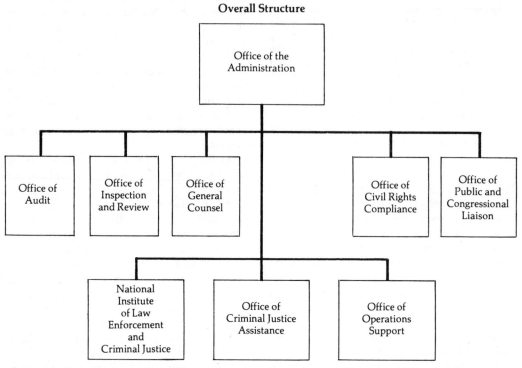

Overall Structure

Office of the
Administration

Office of
Audit

Office of
Inspection
and Review

Office of
General
Counsel

Office of
Civil Rights
Compliance

Office of
Public and
Congressional
Liaison

National
Institute
of Law
Enforcement
and
Criminal Justice

Office of
Criminal Justice
Assistance

Office of
Operations
Support

Source : Annual Report of the Attorney General of the United States, 1971 (Washington, D.C.: U.S. Government Printing Office, 1972), p. 143.

under control, if we are not diverted from our task by phantoms.[45]

Crime Control by the Department of Justice

The federal government today is concentrating its crime control efforts within the agencies in the Department of Justice (Figure 4.2). With the principal forces of crime control now centralized in the Justice Department, the possibility of controlling the citizenry is considerable. Not only is the Justice Department engaged in law enforcement for the government, but it is establishing the policies for controlling crime as well.

Surveillance by the FBI

The control of crime in the American state has traditionally been handled by the Justice Department's Federal Bureau of Investigation. Since its creation by a secret executive order in

the administration of Theodore Roosevelt, the FBI has developed into a national police and investigative force with 9,000 special agents, a clerical staff of 10,000, 59 regional offices, and hundreds of local "resident offices."[46] But more important than these figures is the FBI's involvement in more than simply investigating violations of federal law; it specializes in gathering domestic intelligence and protecting internal security. Its history is one of controlling "domestic subversion," from investigating spy activities in wartime, to pursuing communists, to suppressing radical political action in recent years. Under its long-time former director, J. Edgar Hoover, the FBI has developed into a self-perpetuating bureaucracy that, though occasionally subject to criticism, sometimes operates beyond public control for the benefit of itself and the government.[47] To expect that the FBI will change (Hoover died in 1972) is to ignore the nature of the FBI's bureaucracy and the service it performs for the state in maintaining domestic security.

Figure 4.2   Department of Justice

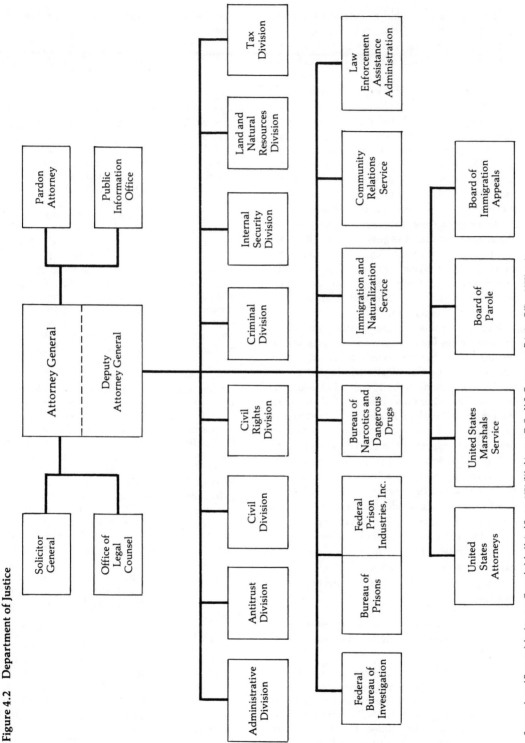

Source: Annual Report of the Attorney General of the United States, 1971 (Washington, D.C.: U.S. Government Printing Office, 1972), p. iv.

The FBI has been able to extend its surveillance activities over the years by legislative enactments overturning Supreme Court decisions. Since the mid-sixties the FBI has freely engaged in electronic eavesdropping, court-ordered and otherwise.[48] Each year the telephones of tens of thousands of citizens are wiretapped, at a cost of about $5 million for these operations alone. Using the title "national security," the FBI legally and illegally justifies this operation. Defending the government's inherent right to wiretap dissident domestic groups, then Deputy Attorney General Richard Kleindienst maintained that no distinction can be made between Americans and foreigners when the aim is to destroy the government: "It would be silly to say that an American citizen, because he is an American, could subvert the government by actions of violence or revolution and be immune from, first, identification, and second, prosecution."[49]

It came as a shock to many Americans in the early seventies that the government was spying on them. In a Senate investigation led by the Subcommittee on Constitutional Rights (chaired by Sam J. Ervin, Jr.), it was disclosed that several government agencies, the FBI included, were heavily involved in obtaining intelligence information on hundreds of thousands of law-abiding yet suspect citizens. With the justification that domestic security is in jeopardy, the government is building a "national data bank," or "criminal justice information center," for instantly retrievable intelligence information on "persons of interest." The government's purpose is to avert internal subversion and threats to the domestic order. Upon discovering the existence and extensiveness of such surveillance, *The New York Times* reported to its readers:

The Government is gathering information on its citizens in the following reservoirs of facts:

A Secret Service computer, one of the newest and most sophisticated in Government. In its memory the names and dossiers of activists, "malcontents," persistent seekers of redress, and those who would "embarrass" the President or other Government leaders are filed with those of potential as-

sassins and persons convicted of "threats against the President."

A data bank compiled by the Justice Department's civil disturbance group. It produces a weekly printout of national tension points on racial, class and political issues and the individuals and groups involved in them. Intelligence on peace rallies, welfare protests and the like provide the "data base" against which the computer measures the mood of the nation and the militancy of its citizens. Judgments are made; subjects are listed as "radical" or "moderate."

A huge file of microfilmed intelligence reports, clippings and other materials on civilian activity maintained by the Army's Counterintelligence Analysis Division in Alexandria, Va. Its purpose is to help prepare deployment estimates for troop commands on alert to respond to civil disturbances in 25 American cities. Army intelligence was ordered earlier this year to destroy a larger data bank and to stop assigning agents to "penetrate" peace groups and civil rights organizations. But complaints persist that both are being continued. Civilian officials of the Army say they "assume" they are not.

Computer files intended to catch criminal suspects — the oldest and most advanced type with the longest success record — maintained by the Federal Bureau of Investigation's National Crime Information Center and recently installed by the Customs Bureau. The crime center's computer provides 40,000 instant, automatic teletype printouts each day on wanted persons and stolen property to 49 states and Canada and it also "talks" to 24 other computers operated by state and local police departments for themselves and a total of 2,500 police jurisdictions. The center says its information is all "from the public record," based on local and Federal warrants and complaints, but the sum product is available only to the police.

A growing number of data banks on other kinds of human behavior, including, for example, a cumulative computer file on 300,000 children of migrant farm workers kept by the Department of Health, Education and Welfare. The object is to speed the distribution of their scholastic records, including such teacher judgments as "negative attitude," to school districts with larger itinerant student enrollments. There is no stat-

DOCUMENT_____

NATIONAL CRIME INFORMATION CENTER (NCIC)

The National Crime Information Center is now in its sixth year of service providing computerized information on crime and criminals to local, State and Federal law enforcement agencies in all 50 States and the District of Columbia, as well as to the Royal Canadian Mounted Police. All FBI offices are linked to the NCIC except for the office at San Juan, P.R., which is scheduled to be included during 1972.

The nationwide system includes 45 individual State and metropolitan area computer systems which in turn provide the capability for an estimated 6,000 local law enforcement agencies to enter their own records into the NCIC and make inquiries directly to the main NCIC computer.

The dynamic development of the entire NCIC system can be attributed greatly to the free exchange of constructive ideas and suggestions channeled through the NCIC Advisory Policy Board. The 23-member Board consists of 18 State law enforcement administrators, two sheriffs, two major city chiefs of police and one FBI representative. From the beginning the NCIC has been developed by local, State and Federal law enforcement representatives comprising the NCIC Working Committee. This is made up of local law enforcement representatives from each State. Several meetings a year are held at regional and national levels.

This chart [omitted] which I hand to the Chairman depicts the NCIC network. The shaded sections represent areas having direct access to the NCIC computer through State and metropolitan computer systems. Also shown on the chart is the division of the country into the four NCIC Policy Board Regions.

(Discussion off the record.)

Mr. Rooney. We shall insert this chart on the NCIC network at this point in the record.

Mr. Hoover. The central computer, located at FBI Headquarters in Washington, D.C., operates 24 hours a day, 7 days a week, as it handles an average of over 90,000 transactions a day. On January 18, 1972, for the first time in the NCIC history, over 100,000 transactions were completed in a single day. The new high was 100,620 transactions representing an average of more than one transaction each second of the day. Law enforcement agencies are averaging over 725 "hits" a day. These positive responses result in the apprehension of wanted persons, the solution of crime and the recovery of stolen property.

The records stored in the NCIC files consist of six categories of stolen property, a category on wanted persons and another on criminal histories. As of February 1, 1972, a total of 3,273,142 records were stored in the NCIC with 93 percent of these relating to the six stolen property categories and only 7 percent dealing with wanted persons and criminal histories. I hand to the Chairman a chart showing a breakdown of the records in the computer.

Mr. Rooney. We shall insert this chart at this point in the record.

COMPUTERIZED CRIMINAL HISTORY PROGRAM

Mr. Hoover. The NCIC's Computerized Criminal History program became operational on November 29, 1971. The FBI, under this program, eventually will

Source: From the testimony of John Edgar Hoover before the House Subcommittee on Appropriations, Federal Bureau of Investigation, *Appropriation 1973* (Washington, D.C., 1972), pp. 34–36.

DOCUMENT (Continued)

Breakdown of Records in NCIC Computer as of February 1, 1972

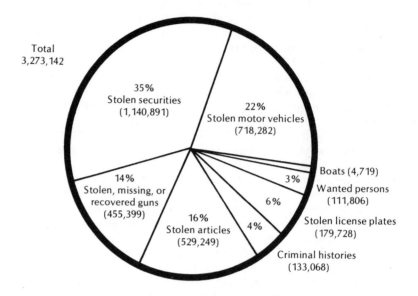

Total
3,273,142

35% Stolen securities (1,140,891)

22% Stolen motor vehicles (718,282)

14% Stolen, missing, or recovered guns (455,399)

16% Stolen articles (529,249)

3%

Boats (4,719)

Wanted persons (111,806)

6%

4%

Stolen license plates (179,728)

Criminal histories (133,068)

provide computerized criminal history information through an expanded NCIC communications network to the entire criminal justice community. This much-needed service will be available to the Nation's courts, corrections agencies, and prosecutors, as well as to the law enforcement agencies.

The many complex policy and operational considerations involved in developing the program are being worked out with the local, State and Federal agencies through the NCIC Working Committee and the NCIC Advisory Policy Board. The Attorney General has approved the general policies established to safeguard the security and confidentiality of the Computerized Criminal History files.

The local, State and Federal agencies participating in the Computerized Criminal History program will be charged with the responsibility of upgrading their capabilities in the fields of identification, communications and information handling. The Law Enforcement Assistance Administration is providing financial assistance to the local and State agencies to aid in their improvement efforts.

utory control over distribution of the data by its local recipients — to prospective employers, for example.[50]

The war is at home; domestic security is at stake.

Controlling Domestic Order

The war began as a governmental attack on "crime in the streets." The presidential and congressional elections of 1964 and 1968 capitalized on the rising crime rate in America.

Each candidate blamed the crime problem on the other candidates. Richard Nixon, in the election of 1968, committed himself to a full-scale attack on the problem. Blaming the rising crime rate on the incumbent administration, he had to deal with lawlessness as soon as he entered the White House. The greatest threat to law and order now seemed to be the protests against the war in Vietnam, the draft system, and racial injustice. With his newly appointed attorney general, John Mitchell, and the ready assistance of Hoover and the FBI, he turned public attention to these politically dissident actions as the really serious crimes facing the nation.

Shortly after the president took office, the attorney general announced that he intended to prosecute "hard-line militants," such as those who crossed state lines "to incite riots" on college campuses. The attorney general told the nation, citing evidence collected by the FBI, that "a great deal of evidence has been collected on this aspect of campus disorders," and that "I would say this is a very serious component."[51] A few days later, the assistant attorney general announced to the public that he was prepared to prosecute such militants under the newly enacted antiriot law. "These statements," Richard Harris writes in his study of the early years of Nixon's Department of Justice, "on top of a promise by Deputy Attorney General Kleindienst to go after 'radical, revolutionary, anarchistic kids,' suggested that the Department now fully shared Hoover's conviction that most of the trouble in the country was caused by a few radicals and that if they were locked up everything would be fine again."[52]

The government was thus prepared to launch a concerted drive against political dissent, whether it was expressed in thought, word, or deed. Political dissent was now defined as criminal by a legal structure created for that purpose and meant to provide for its control. Attacks began to be carried out by the government. A trial was held against the "Boston Five" for conspiring to interfere with the operations of the Selective Service System by organizing public rallies, writing and circulating dissident statements, and encouraging draft-age men to resist the draft.[53] Similarly, the government prosecuted the "Chicago Eight" for conspiring to cross state lines, during the 1968 Democratic Convention, with the intent of inciting a riot and committing some illegal act. The "Oakland Seven" were charged with conspiracy to commit the misdemeanors of trespass and resisting arrest in a stop-the-draft demonstration. The "Harrisburg Seven" were tried for, among other things, a plot to kidnap presidential advisor Henry Kissinger. Daniel Ellsberg was tried for passing Pentagon documents to the press. And Black Panther groups were harassed in various ways, including being raided and killed by local and federal agents. Political action against the government, or against its policies, had been defined as such a threat to the regime that dubious criminal charges and repressive acts had to be undertaken.

The government has continued to use a host of legal weapons in attempting to secure domestic order. Although the conspiracy law has not been upheld in higher appeals courts, the law with its ensuing trials has nevertheless served to stifle dissent. In addition to the conspiracy prosecutions, false raids on private premises, and invasions of human rights, the government has resorted to tactics available in the legal system. A "preventive detention" law has been enacted to detain "dangerous" persons. As a pretrial detention measure, defendants can be confined to a jail by a judge's decision, being denied the right to bail. And the mass arrest has been used to detain large numbers of political demonstrators. In the May Day demonstration of 1971 in Washington, nearly 13,000 persons were rounded up and confined in jails and special camps. Although most of the charges were later dropped, the government had stopped a protest against itself. These tactics do not usually result in successful prosecutions, however, and often are judged unconstitutional.

The new use of the grand jury symbolizes the administration's initiative in crime control: "The nationwide grand jury network is emerging as a 'chosen instrument' of an Administration strategy to curb dissent and to intimidate and demoralize radicals. This strategy is so effective because federal prosecuting officials — who themselves have no power of subpoena —

are using the coercive powers of the grant jury for police and intelligence purposes."[54] The federal grand jury operation is being directed and coordinated by the Internal Security Division (ISD) of the Department of Justice. It reviews thousands of FBI reports about radical activities, determining violations of statutes. Further information is provided by the Justice Department's Interdivisional Intelligence Unit (IDIU), now a broad intelligence system that observes and collects data on many radical and antiwar activities. With this information, grand juries are activated by the government to hold secret sessions on suspected criminal or subversive activities. Thus, the grand jury has been reformed from a "people's panel" sometimes used to curb prosecutions to a tool for prosecuting political behavior.[55] Further intelligence information is secured by these grand juries from testimony by subpoenaed witnesses. And this testimony, without the protection of counsel, may subject witnesses to jail sentences for contempt or for a crime.

The new enemy today in the American state is the "criminal." Crime threatens the domestic order of its society.

5

Criminal Laws in America

Within the general framework that is our legal order the specific laws on crime control are formulated, enforced, and administered. The criminal laws have been shaped within the religious, political, economical, and social foundations of the United States. The result is a code of criminal laws with the purpose of preserving and controlling the American social order.

Religious Foundations

Along the shores and tidewater basin later called Boston Harbor, a Puritan community was established in 1630. Although the Massachusetts Bay Colony was chartered as a commercial enterprise, the objectives of its settlers were clearly religious and social. From the time the Puritans landed, their chief aim was, Governor John Winthrop said, to build "a City upon a Hill," a society that would be an example of godliness to the world. Religious interests were to be predominant in creating a social and legal order in early Massachusetts.

The colony carried on political traditions of England, from which the settlers had come. Among these were the belief that government is made to regulate imperfect man, that political leaders must be obeyed, and that the welfare of the whole is more important than that of the individual. Puritanism drew as well from the medieval imagery of piety, doom, and sin.[1] Out of these older ideas the Puritans developed a conception of the covenant: government had originated in a compact among the people. But more than this, the power of the state was legitimate because it was a government conforming to God's decree. "Thus, in subjecting themselves to a state that was divinely approved, the people also subjected themselves to obedience to God."[2]

The Puritans, adhering to the covenant, took the word of God as a basis for establishing government and society in Massachusetts Bay. They saw themselves as an elite chosen by God to represent Him on earth. But most important for government, they considered the positions to which the leaders were elected in the colony as ordained by God. Once elected, the governor and the magistrates were granted power by divine authority. As "Gods upon earth," the leaders must be obeyed for the covenant to be kept. Winthrop forcefully expressed this idea to the Puritans: "The determination of law belongs properly to God: He is the only lawgiver, but He hath given power and gifts to man to interpret his laws; and this belongs principally to the highest authority in a commonwealth, and subordinately to other magistrates and judges according to their several places."[3] The covenant's logical conclusion was rule by a few for the interests they deemed appropriate: "The government of Massachusetts was thus a dictatorship of a small minority who were unhesitantly prepared to coerce the unwilling to serve the purposes of society as they conceived it."[4]

The early history of Massachusetts Bay Colony shows a continuing problem about the place of law in a religious community.[5] The early settlers resolved the problem by constructing a legal structure on biblical authority. The Scriptures were a most appropriate source for establishing a government according to God's word. In 1635 the General Court of the colony ordered work to begin on a legal code. By 1641 a brief bill of rights, known since as the Body of Liberties, was passed. Finally, in 1648, a comprehensive code of law, known as "Laws and Liberties," was adopted. The code — the first of its kind in the English-speaking world — was a compilation of constitutional guarantees, provisions for the conduct of government, trade, military affairs, and the relations between church and state, as well as the substantive law of crime, tort, property, and domestic relations. At the beginning of the code was the Epistle that dramatically related the laws of the colony to the religious principles of the Old Testament Scriptures:

> So soon as God had set up Political Government among his people Israel he gave them a body of laws for judgment both in civil and criminal causes. These were brief and fundamental principles, yet withall so full and comprehensive as out of them clear deductions were to be drawn to all particular cases in future times.[6]

The code was a unique effort to order life and conduct in accordance with the ideals of Puritanism.

The biblical influence in the law formulated for the colony is most clearly observed in the criminal (or capital) laws of the code. All punishable by death, they included idolatry, witchcraft, blasphemy, bestiality, sodomy, adultery, rape, man stealing, treason, false witness with intent to take life, cursing or smiting a parent, stubbornness or rebelliousness on the part of a son against his parents, and homicide committed with malice aforethought, by guile or poisoning, or in anger or passion. Most of the provisions, as well as other enactments, were annotated by some chapter and verse from the Old Testament, and several incorporated biblical phraseology. Compare this provision from the law with its counterpart in the Old Testament on rebellion of the son:

> *Code of 1648:* If a man have a stubborn or REBELLIOUS SON, of sufficient years and understanding (*viz*) sixteen years of age, which will not obey the voice of his Father, or the voice of his Mother, and that when they have chastened him will not harken unto them: then shall his Father and Mother being his natural parents, lay hold on him, and bring him to the Magistrates assembled in Court and testifie unto them, that their Son is stubborn and rebellious and will not obey their voice and chastisement, but lives in sundry notorious crimes, such a son shall be put to death.

> *Deuteronomy 21:18–21:* If a man have a stubborn and rebellious son, which will not obey the voice of his father, or the voice of his mother, and that, when they have chastened him, will not harken unto them: Then shall his father and his mother lay hold on him, and bring him out unto the elders of his city, and unto the gate of his place; And they shall say unto the elders of his city, This our son is stubborn and rebellious, he will not obey our voice; he is a glutton, and a drunkard. And all of the men of his city shall stone him with stones, that he die. . . .[7]

Other capital laws contain words, clauses, or phrases taken directly from the Old Testament:

> Thus, the witchcraft provision defined a witch as one that "hath or consulteth with a familiar spirit" in terms of Leviticus 20:27 and Deuteronomy 18:11, which speak respectively of one "that hath a familiar spirit" and of "a consulter with familiar spirits."

Again, it is prescribed in Leviticus 20:15 and 16 that "if a man lie with a beast, he shall surely be put to death: and ye shall slay the beast," and a similar punishment was provided "if a woman approach unto any beast, and lie down thereto"; by comparison, the bestiality law of Massachusetts states that "If any man or woman shall LYE WITH ANY BEAST, or bruit creature, by carnal copulation; they shall surely be put to death: and the beast shall be slain, and buried, and not eaten." In the same chapter of Leviticus, 20:13, it is stated that "If a man also lie with mankind, as he lieth with a woman, both of them have committed an abomination"; the colony law against sodomy prescribes that "if any man LYETH WITH MAN-KINDE as he lieth with a woman, both of them have committed abomination. . . ." In Exodus 21:16 it is declared that "he that stealeth a man, and selleth him, or if he be found in his hand, he shall surely be put to death"; in Massachusetts law, "If any man STEALETH A MAN, or Man-kinde, he shall surely be put to death." Finally, the colonial provision that "if any child, or children . . . shall CURSE, or SMITE their natural FATHER, or MOTHER: he or they shall be put to death," is paralleled by Exodus 21:15 and 17, to the effect that "he that smitteth his father, or his mother . . . And he that curseth his father, or his mother, shall surely be put to death."[8]

There can be no doubt that the religious principles of the Old Testament were one of the cornerstones for the Puritans' criminal law. The Bible's authority served as a justification for the law's provisions. The law was God's word enacted on earth.

The purpose of law for the Puritans was the accomplishment of God's will in a society bound by a religious and political covenant. The state's authority was thus religiously condoned. Carrying that theory to its conclusion, the state's welfare, rather than that of the individual, was the state's chief interest. Law and government, therefore, have the power to coerce individuals according to the interests of those who hold power: "The end of law as viewed by the colonists was less alien to our own conceptions than a first impression might suggest. In politically organized society, law operates as a restraint on individual action for the benefit of some other individual or of the group as a whole."[9] The state's authority now had a religious and moral basis.

Protecting the Political Order

The early criminal codes in America, primarily religious, equated sin with crime. The laws punished religious offenses, such as idolatry, blasphemy, and witchcraft. Infractions against persons or property were declared to be offenses against God. Prosecutions for religious infractions practically disappeared, however, after the Revolution, but prosecutions for economic and disorderly offenses increased.

The pre-Revolutionary notion that the function of criminal law was to enforce the community's morals and religion shifted dramatically to the post-Revolutionary view that criminal law is to protect property and physical security. The state became actively involved, using the criminal law, in promoting stability of the social order.[10] Political acts against the state and its economy also were controlled by the criminal law. No longer worried about sinners, the new state elite "feared organized groups of malcontents bent upon reconstruction of society. . . . In short, their fear was that the economically underprivileged would seek material gain by banding together to deprive more privileged persons of their wealth and standing."[11] Criminal law had a single purpose: to promote order in a new society.

Protecting the political order has become a primary characteristic of the American state. In creating criminal laws, those in power preserve the system as it is. The struggles and conflicts between power holders, their foes, and the contenders for political power take many forms. Criminal laws are formulated in the attempt to control or eliminate the political foe from competition.[12] As political weapons, these laws limit the political action of those who appear to jeopardize the established order's stability and survival.

The American state, in its claim to be a political democracy, maintains a paradox with two opposing ideals. The state claims the power to govern but grants the freedom that may result in words and actions against the state. The opposing ideals can coexist because of the unspoken agreement that "the majority agrees to tolerate the criticism and dissent of the minority (or minorities), while the minority agrees to seek power only through persuasion and political activity, not through violence."[13] In the abstract, the majority is not to persecute the minority and the minority is not to express dissent by revolution.

The boundaries and definitions of political freedom are by no means constant in any society, however. The latitude of dissent that may be regarded as legitimate varies from one time to another. During some periods extensive and loud dissent may be tolerated, but in other periods it may be suppressed by the criminal law.

Political expression is especially restricted during periods of tension and conflict. Expecting a political emergency, the government is likely to take actions to protect the political order. The events that led to the American Revolution illustrate the ways in which criminal law may be used to maintain the desired political order. England as the imperial nation naturally tried to hold its political control over the colonies. At the same time the British government was faced with other problems, including administration of its territorial acquisitions elsewhere in North America and a mounting debt at home. To organize a more efficient administration, Britain made several demands on the colonies, such as the trade and revenue acts passed in Parliament, which tightened control over the colonies. At the same time, however, the colonies were developing a revolutionary ideology and a new nationalist spirit. Britain's attempt to demand more of the colonies and the Americans' growing desire for freedom of political action produced a sharp clash of interests.[14] After insurrections and a war, the colonies won independence in 1783.

One of the devices the British government used to establish and preserve its own political order in the colonies was substantive criminal law. The law of treason applied against the colonists began in a statute enacted in the time of Edward III, making it a crime to plot or imagine the death of the king, to adhere to the king's enemies, to give them aid and comfort, or to levy war against the king. The law of seditious libel was also used to control public criticism of British efforts, though how much they resorted to it to control dissent is debated.[15] But ironically, each of the colonies formulated similar laws to protect its own political interests. These political criminal laws were almost identical to the English laws that were being imposed on them.

The English common law on political crime was eventually adopted by the states and the federal government. It seemed oppressive in the hands of the British but it was now a law for Americans to impose on those who appeared to endanger their government. The federal government in 1798 enacted the Sedition Act to punish anyone who uttered or published statements against the government of the United States.[16] The law, curtailing loyalty to the British, was an instrument with which the Federalists tried to suppress the activities (considered as pro-French) of the opposition Republican party.[17]

The law of treason was shaped by American fears of British Loyalists during and immediately after the Revolution. Drawing upon English common law once again, the Americans formulated and utilized treason laws against those who aided the British or fled to the enemy.[18] After the Declaration of Independence, the state legislatures enacted antiloyalist laws. "Test acts" compelled a declaration of loyalty from those who appeared to be indifferent or enemies of the Revolution. They also had laws (1) disfranchising the Loyalists or removing them from office, (2) suppressing, quarantining, and exiling Loyalists, (3) providing for the crime of adhering to Great Britain, and (4) amercing (subjecting to arbitrary punishment), taxing, or confiscating the property and estates of Loyalists.[19] In most states Loyalists were legally defined as traitors.

All the states today have criminal laws to prevent subversion of the political order, which, however, is not always clearly defined in the state laws, although most agree on which kinds of behavior are subversive:

There can no doubt be general agreement that, at the very least, subversive activities include (1) the use of violent or otherwise unconstitutional means to change this country's political or economic institutions; (2) the commission of espionage, sabotage, and other crimes of stealth in behalf of foreign enemies or domestic cliques; (3) the bearing of arms against the United States, and other affirmative behavior in aid of hostile forces; and (4) the entry into a conspiracy to perform these acts or the actual though unsuccessful attempt to do them. Conduct of these types is unquestionably within the reach of criminal laws in every American state.[20]

Numerous federal statutes also have been created to control subversive activity. The Espionage Act of 1917 made it a crime to "willfully make or convey false reports or false statements with intent to interfere with the operations or success of the military or naval forces of the United States." A 1918 amendment to the Espionage Act broadened the proscriptions in words reminiscent of the Sedition Act of 1798. The Voorhis Act of 1940 required persons and organizations that act as agents of foreign powers to register with the government. The Smith Act of 1940 forbade advocating the overthrow of the government. The Internal Security Act of 1950 (McCarran Act) required communist and communist-front organizations to register and strengthened other legislation on subversion. The Immigration and Nationality Act of 1952 (McCarran-Walter Act) provided for deporting resident aliens because of disloyal beliefs and associates. The Communist Control Act of 1954 required Communist party members to register with the attorney general. Loyalty and security programs have been initiated and blacklist procedures have been established as well.

Political expression is an especially delicate matter in the United States. Americans, compared to other peoples in representative governments, seem particularly intolerant of social and political differences.[21] This intolerance is expressed by withholding civil rights for some social and political minority groups, religious groups, racial and ethnic groups, and political dissenters. Criminal laws and rulings have been formulated to handle these differences. Specific behaviors that political minorities may

commit out of conscience have been made illegal. Along with the many acts that have been defined as subversive (by the groups in power), attempts to express dissatisfaction with nuclear testing, civil defense, racial discrimination, and war have been subject to criminal action. Volumes of laws have been used in suppressing dissent and protest. Demonstrators for racial civil rights and other causes have been arrested on such charges as disorderly conduct, breach of peace, parading without a permit, trespassing, loitering, and violating fire ordinances. Under other laws, persons have been arrested for refusing to pay income taxes used for military purposes, for picketing military bases, for engaging in student protests, and for refusing to register for the draft.

The criminal laws that have been established to control perceived threats to the state are patently political. The political regime is to be protected from any internal or external dangers. The law upholds the state. Even when certain procedural guarantees such as due process and the right of civil disobedience are recognized, the law can be qualified at every point to maintain the status quo.

Nowhere is this qualification of law better illustrated than in the military conscription laws. The involvement of the United States in Southeast Asia brought new light to this matter. Those of draft age who could show absolute pacifism on religious grounds could avoid military servitude. There may well be constitutional grounds to support selective conscientious objection, but until such a right is legally recognized, those who claim it are defined as criminal.[22]

Conspiracy and related laws are among the best examples of the government's attempt to ensure its own survival. Legal cases, especially ones like the Boston Five (a "conspiracy" to aid in violating the Selective Service law) and the Chicago Eight (concerning the demonstrations during the 1968 Democratic Convention), have shown how far the government will use the criminal law to ward off apparent political dangers. In these cases dubious charges have been made, the most questionable being that of "conspiracy." As a political weapon, the conspiracy law requires that the prosecution merely show that the defendants conspired, or rather, communicated in some way about a demonstration, draft resistance, or whatever. The prosecution need not show that the defendants actually engaged in overt acts, but merely that they said something. Among other things, whether or not the defendants are convicted, the conspiracy law is an effective form of political harassment whereby those who threaten the system can be detained for long periods of time at great personal expense.

The so-called antiriot laws accomplish similar objectives for the state. Six of the eight Chicago defendants were prosecuted under 18 U.S. Code 2101 and 2102, the newest federal antiriot act. The act makes it a felony to travel in interstate commerce with the intent to incite or participate in a riot. "Riot" is defined in the statute as any assemblage of three or more persons, in which at least one person threatens injury to another person or property, or actually does injure another person or property. The act was conceived in response to the ghetto riots of the sixties. Speaking for an earlier version of the law, a statement by a congressman from Georgia illustrates that the act was a simplistic attempt to solve urban disorders by striking at the "outside agitators" who supposedly were behind the outbreaks of civil disorder:

> There is impressive evidence that many of the riots which have been plaguing our cities have been incited by persons who have been traveling from one city to another, deliberately stirring up trouble. We have all heard that in so many instances, preceding a riot, an outside agitator has appeared in the community to harangue an audience concerning the grievances. Sometimes those grievances have been real, sometimes they have not. But real or not, often the speeches of these agitators have been criminally inflammatory, and often in clear violation of our laws against inciting to riot.[23]

Such thinking gets laws of consequence enacted.

The most insidious, yet blatant, tactic used by the government against its citizens (including its political offenders) is the refusal to publicly and legally recognize the concept of political crime. Its reason lies in the Anglo-American doctrine of legalism: obedience to the law is a moral absolute.[24] Because opposition to the government could not be legally *and* morally recognized in this tradition, political crime could not be incorporated into the law. Political offenders have usually been dealt with under "nonpolitical" laws. The political offender has been officially handled in the same way as the conventional offender. To admit political crime into domestic jurisprudence would be to recognize the limitations of liberal democracy (that is, democratic elitism).

Promoting American Business: Antitrust Laws

Toward the end of the nineteenth century an antimonopoly movement gathered in response to new economic conditions. It was accompanied by a body of doctrine regarding the problem of monopoly as soluble only by government intervention. Subsequent action by the federal government brought an innovation in criminal law, that is, the concept that the state is responsible for protecting the national economic order from private interests within that order. This departure from the traditional scope and purpose of the criminal law meant that the criminal law not only protected private property but also assisted in maintaining a specific kind of national economy. American capitalism was secured, not threatened, by the new legal regulations.

A tradition for antitrust legislation was already in the common law of England and America.[25] The common law precedents had established that specific commercial activities were to be restricted by law. Yet the common law doctrine as applied by the individual states was not effective in controlling the monopolies growing in the United States. Broad interpretation by state courts of the interstate commerce clause of the Constitution and the first article of the Fourteenth Amendment allowed many corporations to expand greatly beyond state borders and to receive the federal government's protection. Because no federal common law regulated monopolies, the need for federal antitrust legislation was clear.

Opposition to trusts and monopolies was aroused in several segments of American society. Diverse groups, not always with compatible ideologies, agitated for antimonopoly legislation.[26] Some groups were gravely worried about the corporations that were ruthlessly exploiting national resources for their own profit-making ventures. Labor was hostile to powerful corporations, finding itself at a distinct disadvantage in bargaining with them. Small businessmen feared possible surrender or ruin because of the wealth and facilities concentrated in gigantic corporations. Declining farm prices were attributed to the growth of large corporations. The Populist party actively supported agrarian antagonism toward big business. A Granger expressed the antimonopoly spirit of the period, relating monopoly to the question of progress:

Progress which the possessors of the good things of earth call innovation, progress the cardinal principle of this democracy of the people, will go on as all history shows. It must be through continual strife, for progress is but a contest still going on in spite of the death chants, the impenetrable armor, and the resisting spirit of self; a contest which has been going on through earth's long day, and will still go on until evening — until the mighty purposes of creation are accomplished, and the many are entitled to preeminence over the few in the view of the earth as they are now entitled in the eye of heaven. This is what the great democracy of the people demands. That is what the antimonopoly movement means.[27]

In the 1880s, monopolies were attacked in the name of the theory and practice of laissez-faire economics. A challenge was presented to the long-ingrained classical economics. Individual radicals were influential also, such as Wendell Phillips and Peter Cooper, and the writings of Henry George, Edward Bellamy, and Henry Demarest Lloyd reached wide audiences. President Cleveland brought the issue to the front in a tariff message of 1887 and stressed it with even greater urgency in the following year: "As we view the achievements of aggregated capital we discover the existence of trusts, combinations and monopolies, while the citizen is struggling far in the rear or is trampled to death beneath an iron heel. Corporations which should be carefully restrained creatures of the law and servants of the people, are fast becoming the people's masters."[28] That year the platforms of both major political parties pledged to oppose trusts and monopolies.

The widespread opposition to monopolies brought on the Sherman Act of 1890. The law, drafted primarily by Senator John Sherman of Ohio, declared that "(1) Every contract, combination in the form of trust or otherwise, or conspiracy, in restraint of trade or commerce among the several States, or with foreign nations is hereby declared to be illegal . . . (2) Every person who shall monopolize, or attempt to monopolize . . . any part of the trade or commerce among the several States or with foreign nations, shall be deemed guilty of a misdemeanor. . . ." To combine in restraint of trade and to monopolize became public offenses. The federal government was empowered to proceed against violations of the law by criminal action.

Broadly, the interest to be protected in the law was the nation's economic order. Supporters of antitrust legislation did not, for the most part, aim to alter the economic order, but to protect the free-enterprise system. "The interest to be protected was the maintenance of a competitive economy based on private enterprise. The State did not mean to become owner or entrepreneur, but it felt compelled to use its legislative, administrative, and judicial machinery for the protection of the economic well-being of the community as a whole — as conceived by a liberal economic philosophy — and to defend it against powerful industrial and commercial interests."[29]

Further legislation and measures for more strictly enforcing antitrust laws followed. During the administration of Theodore Roosevelt particular attention was given to regulating corporations. Roosevelt's intentions were clear, to work within the capitalistic system:

In dealing with the big corporations we call trusts, we must resolutely purpose to proceed by evolution and not by revolution. . . . Our aim is not to do away with corporations; on the contrary these big aggregations are an inevitable development of modern industrialism. . . . We can do nothing of good in the way of regulating and supervising these corporations until we fix clearly in our minds that we are not attacking the corporations, but endeavoring to do away with any evil in them. We are not hostile to them; we are merely determined that they shall be so handled as to subserve the public good."[30]

The legislation and court rulings during the "progressive era," the first fifteen or twenty years of this century, actually protected and strengthened business in America. In that period, with the establishment of new laws, big business triumphed.

> There were any number of options involving government and economics abstractly available to national political leaders during the period 1900–1916, and in virtually every case they chose those solutions to problems advocated by the representatives of concerned business and financial interests. Such proposals were motivated by the needs of the interested businesses, and political intervention into the economy was frequently merely a response to the demands of particular businessmen. In brief, conservative solutions to the emerging problems of an industrial society were almost uniformly applied. The result was a conservative triumph in the sense that there was an effort to preserve the basic social and economic relations essential to a capitalist society, an effort that was frequently consciously as well as functionally conservative.[31]

The crowning achievement for corporate business was the Federal Trade Commission, which ruled out "unfair methods of competition." Business and politics became one. "The business community knew what it wanted from the commission, and what it wanted was almost precisely what the commission sought to do. No distinction between government and business was possible simply because the commission absorbed and reflected the predominant values of the business community."[32]

The legislation and actions of the New Deal, in Franklin D. Roosevelt's administration, added much governmental planning and protection for the capitalist economy. Yet in spite of the antitrust legislation and enforcement since the Sherman Act of 1890, the purpose was clearly to protect the capitalistic system from abuse, not to create a new type of economic order. Franklin Roosevelt was not the socialist the public thought and feared, but was indeed a conservative:

> It would be a mistake to assume that this socialization was developed entirely at the expense of private enterprise. Indeed it is certain that the New Deal did more to strengthen and to save the capitalist economy than it did to weaken or destroy it. That economy had broken down in many nations abroad, and its collapse contributed to the rise of totalitarian governments which completely subordinated business to the state. The system was on the verge of collapse in the United States during the Hoover administration, and it is at least conceivable that had that collapse been permitted to occur, it might have been followed by the establishment of an economy very different from that to which Americans were accustomed. Historically Franklin Roosevelt's administration did for twentieth-century American capitalism what Theodore Roosevelt's and Wilson's had done for nineteenth-century business enterprise: it saved the system by ridding it of its grosser abuses and forcing it to accommodate itself to larger public interests. History may eventually record Franklin D. Roosevelt as the greatest American conservative since Hamilton.[33]

The attack upon corporations, beginning in the latter part of the nineteenth century and continuing to the present, has not been against business but has been inspired and led by the business interest itself.

The Health Industry: Pure Food and Drug Laws

The legal processes which protect the public's health are similar to those found in corporate legislation. Government has established more and more controls on the manufacture and sale of food and drugs. Criminal laws and commissions have been created to protect our health. The food and drug industry interests, however, receive more protection from these controls than does the public interest.

Through the first half of the nineteenth century the United States was chiefly an agricultural nation and watching purity of food and safeness of drugs depended on the family. During this period the principle of *caveat emptor* ("let the buyer beware") prevailed. Beginning in the industrial era after the Civil War, the economy grew in complexity. Many new products were introduced and the consumer became further removed from the producer. The standards for judgment became uncertain. *Caveat emptor* was eventually replaced by another attitude that favored protecting the consumer and put the blame for poor food and drug standards on the manufacturer or distributor. The new value, *caveat vendor* ("let the seller beware") was reinforced in legislation, making the producer and distributor responsible for the quality of food and drugs.

With food and drugs being produced and shipped in ever larger amounts, the possibilities for spoilage, adulteration, and misrepresentation grew. The public gradually was made aware of the problem of adulteration through bulletins and reports, purchasing the products, and reading popular books, articles, and newspaper editorials. The Division of Chemistry of the Department of Agriculture, under the direction of Dr. Harvey W. Wiley, was especially effective in defining the abuses as a threat to public welfare. His dramatic "poison squad" experiments showed that some food preservatives were harmful and dangerous. The division also showed that a thriving interstate business was developing in patent (nonprescription) medicines, some of which were of questionable value.

After the public became aware of dangers in the foods and drugs they were consuming, conflicts arose over a solution.[34] State and federal legislative measures were proposed, but there was strong opposition because of value conflicts between interest groups, usually between consumer and producer. The first attempts to gain passage of legislation were instigated by the interest groups desiring to protect their products from what they thought was unfair competition. Consequently, the early bills that were passed dealt with one or two products and did not apply to the basic problem of adulteration and misrepresentation in food and drugs.

Not until the 1880s was the first federal pure food and drug legislation introduced that would benefit the public. These measures, however, were defeated: "It and other efforts like it were defeated by a durable alliance of quacks, ruthless crooks, pious frauds, scoundrels, high-priced lawyer-lobbyists, vested interests, liars, corrupt members of Congress, venal publishers, cowards in high office, the stupid, the apathetic, and the duped."[35] With opposing interests like these not much could be hoped for in defense of the public's interest.

More than one hundred fifty pure food and drug bills were introduced in Congress from 1880 to 1906. Most were never heard of after their introduction, and the few that were approved were of minor significance.[36] But continued pressure from the popular press and opinions from congressional constituents overcame the apathy, and in 1906, the Federal Food and Drug Act was passed by both the House and Senate. The act declared it unlawful to manufacture in any territory, or to introduce into any state, any adulterated or misbranded food or drug. Offending products were to be seized, and criminal penalties were provided for anyone found guilty of violating the act's provisions.

The need for revising the act, however, became apparent shortly after its passage. The absence of control over advertising was an especially serious loophole for evading the spirit of the law, and the law's labeling requirements permitted extravagant and unwarranted therapeutic claims for a product. Also, the 1906 act contained no provisions applying to cosmetics or to safe and effective health devices. In spite of amendments in 1912 (the Sherley amendment) and 1919 (the New Weight Act), impure and unsafe foods and drugs had not been effectively controlled by law.

A renewed effort was made to regulate food and drugs. Further awareness of the problem was provided in such popular works as Kallet and Schlink's *100,000,000 Guinea Pigs* and Lamb's *American Chamber of Horrors*.[37] Consumer organizations were formed and consumer research groups were established. After Franklin D. Roosevelt took office in 1933 a committee was appointed to draft new legislation.

A bill to correct the deficiencies in the 1906 law was introduced in 1933. As expected, attacks were launched against the bill. Particularly active in opposing it was the organization representing the patent medicine interests, the United Medicine Manufacturers of America. The organization tried to block the bill with a drive involving "7 plans." The plans would:

(1) secure cooperation of newspapers in spreading favorable publicity; (2) enlist all manufacturers and wholesalers to instruct customers through their salesmen; (3) secure the pledge of manufacturers, wholesalers, advertising agencies, and all other interested affiliates to address letters to Senators to gain their promise to vote against the bill; (4) line up with other organizations, such as the Drug Institute, Proprietary Association, National Association of Retail Druggists, to make a mass attack on the bill; (5) enlist the help of carton, tube, bottle, and box manufacturers; (6) ridicule organizations favoring the bill; and (7) convey by every means available — radio, newspapers, mail, and personal contact — the alarming fact that if the bill is adopted, the public will be deprived of the right of self-diagnosis and self-medication.[38]

But the public interest succeeded, at least in theory. The Federal Food, Drug, and Cosmetic Act was enacted in 1938, requiring, among other things, more effective methods for controlling false labeling and advertising. Informative, specific labeling was definitely required. False advertising of foods, drugs, and cosmetics was prohibited, with more severe penalties for violating the law. And authority was established for setting standards for the identity, quality, strength, and purity of drugs. In 1951, the Durham-Humphrey Amendment to the act was passed placing stricter controls on the dispensing of drugs.

Other special federal laws were enacted to govern the manufacture and marketing of some classes of drugs (narcotics, marijuana, biological products). Still other laws regulated such activities as weighing, measuring, and mailing foods and drugs.[39] The federal laws were complemented by state laws also regulating manufacturing, labeling, and advertising, but in addition overseeing pharmacy.[40]

Continued interest in providing the public with safe and pure foods can be seen in the federal government's inquiry into the drug industry at the beginning of the sixties. Presumably interested in the broad problem of administered prices, the Senate Subcommittee on Antitrust and Monopoly under Chairman Estes Kefauver touched on such topics as the high cost of drugs, the flood of new drugs released each year, the multiple names for identical chemicals and compounds, advertising and promotion of drugs, safeness and efficacy of drugs, and violation of antitrust laws by drug manufacturers.[41] The hearings were highly critical of the amount of money drug manufacturers spend on advertising and promotion in comparison to what they spend for research. After the hearings, amid strong opposing pressure from the large pharmaceutical houses and their lobbying organizations, Congress passed in 1962 the Kefauver-Hart Drug Act. The act, however, was not successful in regulating drug prices, but it did secure provisions for stricter control of drug testing, labeling, and advertising.

Although the drug act of 1962 corrected many abuses in the drug industry, the problems remain. The federal agency that is supposed to regulate the food and drug industry, the Food and Drug Administration (FDA), is more closely tied to the industry's interests than to the general public's needs. In fact, the public is kept insulated from the activities of the FDA, which has the benign attitude "that the public is primarily an ignorant and hysterical mob from whom any suggestions of danger must be kept at all cost."[42] The attitude is fostered by the FDA's general faith in the food industry, assuming that the industry voluntarily ensures the safety and quality of food it produces and distributes. Because of this mistaken belief, the FDA is not able to advance the public interest:

In the place of sustained action to advance health by helping to improve the American diet, the FDA substitutes a naive faith that the way American food is produced, preserved, and distributed is exceptionally fine. It maintains this faith in the face of increasing scientific evidence that chemical additives can be extremely dangerous, that the vitamin content of the American diet is deteriorating, that saturated fat in food may be a contributing factor to more than 70 percent of all American deaths, and that American food is getting filthier. Faith has a way of withstanding fact. But while the FDA goes through the ritualistic exercise that it passes off as regulation, it is the food consumer who is injured.[43]

In other words, the FDA is not able to effectively enforce the laws on consumer protection. Not only does it lack the inclination, but it does not have the knowledge and techniques to detect and enforce violations. It is far behind the advances made by the food industry.

As a result, between 1950 and 1965 the food industry went through its period of fastest growth almost completely unmonitored. In that time a brand new series of problems — including the hazards involved with the chemical environment through the use of food additives, the threat of food contamination becoming nationwide through a modern mass-distribution system, the monitoring of dangerous pesticide residues in widely distributed foods, the introduction of brand new synthetic foods made up entirely of chemicals — developed without serious and effective attention from the FDA.[44]

Clearly the food and drug industry is regulated to the advantage of the industry itself. To assume that such criminal laws protect the public's welfare is to misunderstand criminal law in American society. Regulatory criminal law protects the national economy, not the public.

Regulating Occupational Practice

Legal regulation of occupations has a long and uneven history. The beginnings are to be found among the medieval guilds. Their licensing practices sought to protect the members' economic interests and the community from harmful economic and trade activities. By the beginning of the nineteenth century, professional and occupational licensing was well established in America, especially for law and medicine. Later in the century the laws were greatly modified, and many were repealed, following the laissez-faire philosophy. But with the eventual founding of national and state occupational associations, regulations were once again established.

These associations were meant mostly to promote the interests of the occupations, often to protect one occupation from encroachment by another. In research on the regulation of health professions, Ronald L. Akers writes:

> The foundings of state associations were often for the express purpose of promoting occupational legislation, sometimes in a defensive move to prevent other, already established, professions from regulating them. The New Jersey Pharmaceutical Association (1870), for instance, was formed only after steps were undertaken by the medical society of New Jersey to force legislative measures on "all dispensers of medicines" in the state. Within a week of the formation of the New York Optical Society (1896), a bill to regulate the practice of refracting opticians (the early denotation of optometrists) was introduced in the New York legislature. Securing passage of a medical practice act was one of the main reasons for the organization of the Virginia Medical Society. The initial organization of each of the five professions in Kentucky was shortly followed by the enactment of a practice act. Since its organization, each association has been the driving force in legislation regulating practice in its own field.[45]

By 1900 all the established professions had their own laws, reacting to pressure from their associations. The occupational associations, not the general public, have been responsible for the laws that regulate the occupations. To this day, the statutes and administrative codes that regulate occupations and professions are made by themselves, representing their own parochial interests. Especially through their associations, they have a monopoly on the lawmaking that affects their operations.

> The state association, in conjunction with the examining board, initiates moves for legislation, decides what provisions should be added, deleted, or changed, drafts preliminary and final proposed bills, persuades a legislator to introduce the bill, and works

for its passage throughout the time it is being considered. If proposed practice legislation comes from any other direction, the association will oppose it and work for its defeat.[46]

Each occupation attempts to protect itself from competition by other occupations. Of the relationship among five health professions in one state, this was observed:

> The general picture of the context of conflict among the five professions in Kentucky can be summarized as follows: Chiropractic and optometry generally do not oppose one another but have not made any apparent efforts to cooperate with and support one another. Medicine, dentistry, and pharmacy in recent times have not actively opposed one another and, in fact, are members of an allied group of health professions. Medicine and chiropractic consistently oppose each other, and sometimes optometry and medicine engage in political combat. Medicine, dentistry, and pharmacy occasionally all oppose certain aspects of chiropractic's legislation. Secondarily, they may be politically opposed to optometry. Medicine and dentistry seem to cooperate more closely than any other two groups, and they seldom oppose pharmaceutical legislation, although not always wholeheartedly supporting it. Finally, each profession experiences conflict with additional groups besides the other four health professions.[47]

The professions with the greatest organizational resources and cohesive structures are the most successful in gaining legislation that favors their own interests. The power of some occupations to overwhelm other groups is a basic fact in legislative politics. All this passes under the guise of maintaining high standards of service for the public good.

The enforcing and administering of occupational laws depend on especially created agencies rather than on police and prosecutors. The administrative hearing of cases, rather than trial procedures, closely approximates juvenile court procedures. The actions are more often remedial, using injunctions, rather than direct punishment of the offender by fine or imprisonment. All this becomes apparent when we consider that an apprehended burglar or robber is punished by a jail sentence, a fine, or probation, whereas a doctor may be punished by revoking his license, a lawyer by disbarment, or a businessman by a government warning or injunction, levying civil damages, or suspending his license to do business.

Regulation of the medical profession is an excellent example of the way in which occupational laws are enforced and administered. Most states have a special administration agency for regulating medical practice laws. In New York, a board of examiners is appointed by the regents of the state, composed of medical practitioners, appointed by the governor with the consent of the state senate. It issues licenses and is responsible for disciplining members, which may consist of revoking licenses after a hearing. Only as a last resort are cases turned over to the state's attorney general for criminal prosecution.

This means that the physician is almost a free agent. His license is a lifetime certificate to practice mostly at his own discretion. When violations of laws on medical practice are detected, the state board is not fast to act. Self-discipline among doctors is more illusory than real.

> Within the profession itself the disciplining of colleagues has little support; physicians do not like to police their fellows, and this reluctance is reflected at every level of organized medicine. At that, the strongest penalty a medical society or hospital staff can levy is expulsion. But removal from a society or hospital has no bearing on the doctor's license; though unacceptable to his peers, the offender retains his legal privilege to treat patients. Moreover, just as the profession is slow to prosecute violators within its own ranks, so also is it loath to pursue the cause of more effective laws. As a result, the inadequate statutes currently on the books are likely to remain unamended for the foreseeable future.[48]

Yet malpractice suits and other cases do arise in the medical profession and sometimes reach the courts. At least 2,000 professional-liability claims are brought against doctors for malpractice each year in the United States. The Law Department of the American Medical Association estimates that at least one malpractice claim has been filed against 18 per cent of the doctors in private practice. The judgments and settlements in malpractice cases total about $50 million each year.[49]

But the malpractice plaintiff meets strong resistance when he or she takes a case before the court.[50] Many courts actually obstruct the plaintiff by requiring testimony by medical witnesses. According to this procedure, the doctors who testify are very likely to sympathize with their fellow doctors. Doctors and hospital staffs are known to tamper with medical records, if such tampering will reflect favorably on the defendant's case. Just as false or biased testimony may be given in malpractice suits, so too may records be altered.

Because occupations and professions are an integral part of the American economy, it is to be expected that they, as well as their practitioners, will receive favorable treatment under the criminal law. Not only does the law protect these groups, it makes their activity possible. The criminal law promotes the welfare of these groups more than it protects the public that is subject to their activities. The political economy of the United States is secured in the legal regulation of occupations and professions.

From Religion to Economics: Sunday Law

Since Sunday became different from other days of the week, interests have been effective in guarding it by criminal law. Until fairly recent times religious interests determined the legal meaning of the Sabbath. Today, however, Sunday is protected by the law because of the influence that social and economic interests have.

Sunday law, or "blue law," started with the command from Mount Sinai: "Ye shall keep the Sabbath therefore; for it is holy unto you: every one that defileth it shall surely be put to death" (Exodus 31:14). The command gained legal character in A.D. 321 when Emperor Constantine, after his own conversion to Christianity, issued an edict requiring all work to cease on the day that was settled by law to be the Sabbath.[51] Numerous statutes regulating activities on Sunday were later enacted in England. In 1237, Henry III forbade

attendance at markets on Sunday; the Sunday showing of wools at the staple was banned by Edward III in 1354; in 1409, Henry IV prohibited some games on Sunday; Henry VI proscribed Sunday fairs in churchyards in 1444 and four years later made unlawful all fairs and markets and all showings of goods or merchandise; Sunday bodily labor was disallowed by Edward VI in the mid-sixteenth century; and Sunday sports and amusements were restricted in 1625 by Charles I. The early English Sunday laws were aimed at frequenting markets, participating in commercial activity, laboring, and engaging in amusements on Sunday.

The American colonies wasted little time in enacting Sunday laws. The colonial Sunday laws, however, were similar to the later English statute of Charles II (29 Charles II, c. 7, 1677). The law stated:

> For the better observation and keeping holy the Lord's day, commonly called Sunday; be it enacted . . . that all the laws enacted and in force concerning the observation of the day, and repairing to church thereon, be carefully put in execution; and that all and every person and persons whatsoever shall upon every Lord's day apply themselves to the observation of the same, by exercising themselves thereon in the duties of piety and true religion, publicly and privately; and that no tradesman, artificer, and workman, laborer, or other person whatsoever, shall do or exercise any worldly labor or business or work of their ordinary callings upon the Lord's day, or any part thereof (works of necessity and charity only excepted) . . . and that no person or persons whatsoever shall publicly cry, show forth, or expose for sale any wares, merchandise, fruit herbs, goods, or chattels, whatsoever, upon the Lord's day, or any part thereof. . . .

This law added to the earlier statutes the concept of compulsory worship and church attendance on Sunday. The idea was evident in the 1610 statute of the colony of Virginia, which made church attendance compulsory, for both the morning and afternoon services.[52] Such laws were to benefit the churches of the colonies, just as they had been meant to protect the established church in England.

Most states today have Sunday laws among

their statutes. Their substance no longer relates to church attendance, but to other diver-
sions that are likely to occur on Sunday, such
as labor, amusement, and sales. The change in
the substance of Sunday law is indicated in
the statutes of New York State. The first Sabbath law of New York, included in conditions
of the Burgomaster of New Amsterdam of
1656, required the Scriptures to be read in
public by a hired schoolmaster. Shortly after,
in 1664, the "Duke of York laws" were issued
to regulate worship on Sunday. The forerunner
of the present Sunday law, however, was an
act of 1695 that forbade labor on Sunday. The
act continued in effect until 1788, when it was
adopted as part of the laws under the state
constitution. Revisions were made in 1813,
1830, and 1909, but the body of the act remained. Today the statute prohibits on Sunday
acts "which are serious interruptions of the
repose and religious liberty of the community."
Thus, in New York, as in other states, the law
of church attendance has shifted to a law restricting work on Sunday. Sunday law has
become "closing" law.

The enforcement of Sunday law, needless to
say, is not usually taken seriously. The laws
are sporadically enforced, and then only with
discretion in local settings. However obsolete
these laws may seem, the formulation and
administration of Sunday law has recently
been revived:

> The Sunday blue laws are unfair and seem
> to serve no useful function in our society
> today. However, due to their antiquity, they
> are well established and widespread, al-
> though seldom enforced. In addition to their
> ages, their widespread incorporation and
> continuation are due to a large degree to
> various pressure groups. Their incorpora-
> tion probably had its basis in the religious
> pressure elements, and their continuance, in
> the pressure groups representing the retail
> sellers' associations.[53]

New pressure groups with other than religious
interests have been effective in renewing Sunday laws. Secular and economic rather than
religious interests are in control, accompanied
by such rationales as relaxation, leisure, and
recreation.

The action of pressure groups on Sunday

legislation can be seen in recent amendments
to the statutes, changing the wording to include the private interests of specific groups.[54]
In 1957 the Massachusetts Sunday law was
amended to allow frozen custard stands to
operate on Sunday. The frozen custard lobby
got the ice cream sales clause expanded to permit the sale on Sunday of "frozen dessert
mixes." Likewise, local pressure groups in
Massachusetts were active in changing the
Sunday statute to permit the selling of fishing
bait on Sunday. Pressure groups in New York
were also able to have the Sunday law expanded, allowing roadside stands to sell farm
products.

The Automobile Dealers Association has
moved several states to amend their Sunday
laws on selling automobiles on Sunday. The
action was inspired by the combination of the
traditional Sunday pleasure drive with Sunday
shopping on the superhighway. Sunday drivers
were finding it convenient to purchase autos
from the automobile dealers on the highways.
This meant that auto dealers within the city
limits, beyond the highways, could not com-
pete with the highway auto dealers. Into this
crisis stepped the Automobile Dealers Association, dominated by downtown dealers, successfully lobbying to prohibit the sale of autos on
Sunday. A similar phenomenon has put restrictions on the sale of other kinds of
merchandise in the large discount stores also
on the superhighways. Downtown businesses
have been successful in local areas in having
statutes amended or enforced to curb the competition of businesses with easy access to the
affluent Sunday driver.

The United States Supreme Court in 1960
heard an appeal from the Maryland Court of
Appeals. The Maryland State Court had convicted and fined employees of a large department store on a highway in Anne Arundel
County for selling on Sunday a looseleaf
binder, a can of floor wax, a stapler, staples,
and a toy. The Maryland State Court had ruled
that the conduct of the employees violated a
Maryland statute forbidding the sale on Sunday of all merchandise, except the retail sales
of tobacco products, confectioneries, milk,
bread, fruit, gasoline, oils, greases, drugs,
medicines, newspapers, and periodicals. After

hearing the case the Supreme Court upheld (on May 29, 1961), in *McGowan* v. *Maryland*, the conviction of the Maryland State Court.

The Supreme Court's principal argument in *McGowan* v. *Maryland* was that although Sunday law originated for religious purposes, today the law is maintained for secular purposes:

> In the light of the evolution of our Sunday Closing Laws through the centuries, and of their more or less recent emphasis upon secular considerations, it is concluded that, as presently written and administered, most of them, at least, are of a secular rather than of a religious character, and that presently they bear no relationship to establishment of religion, as those words are used in the constitution of the United States.[55]

Furthermore, the opinion continues, secular interests may be served on Sunday: "The present purpose and effect of most of our Sunday Closing Laws is to provide a uniform day of rest for all citizens; and the fact that this day is Sunday, a day of particular significance for the dominant Christian sects, does not bar the State from achieving its secular goals." It was argued too that "the present purpose and effect of the statute here involved is not aid to religion but to set aside a day of rest and recreation." Finally, on the issue of religious liberty, Chief Justice Warren, in writing the majority opinion, observed that Sunday law does not violate constitutional rights: "People of all religions and people with no religion regard Sunday as a time for family activity, for visiting friends and relatives, for late sleeping, for passive and active entertainments, for dining out, and the like."[56]

The Supreme Court in its decision has therefore recognized that "Sunday closing legislation no longer exclusively represents religious interests."[57] That it now represents economic interests is recognized in the court's decision, in the remark that the recent Sunday laws of such states as New Jersey were reformulated because of pressure from labor groups and trade associations. The Court said too that modern Sunday legislation in England was promoted by such interest groups as the National Federation of Grocers, the National Chamber of Trade, the Drapers' Chamber of Trade, and the National Union of Shop Assistants.

The conclusion, therefore, is that a criminal law may be intended for a particular interest at one time and then amended and implemented at another time for some other class interests. Sunday law, in existence for hundreds of years for religious reasons, was never officially negated, nor ever much enforced. But with changes in social conditions and with a shift in economic interests, it lives once again.

Criminalization: Sexual Psychopath Laws

Some criminal laws, not unlike our other social passions and conveniences, have times of increased popularity. The formulation of "sexual psychopath" laws is an instance of fashion in law. Beginning in the late thirties and extending into the fifties, more than half the states enacted sexual psychopath laws. The statutes varied somewhat from one state to another, but generally defined the sexual psychopath as "one lacking the power to control his sexual impulses or having criminal propensities toward the commission of sex offenses."[58] The laws provided that a person diagnosed as a sexual psychopath be confined for an indefinite period in a state hospital for the insane. Why were these laws enacted then, and what social interests were involved in their formulation?

Sexual psychopath laws responded in part to public anxiety about serious sex crimes. Like the earlier and somewhat comparable "habitual offender" laws that also swept the country, the sexual psychopath laws were a partial solution to a condition that was being defined as a social problem.[59] Consequently, as the American legal system characteristically does, it created a new law to solve a problem.

The problem of the sex offender, as defined by the public, was based on propositions most of which were false or at least questionable:

> Namely, that the present danger to women and children from serious sex crimes is very great, for the number of sex crimes is large and is increasing more rapidly than any other crime; that most sex crimes are committed by "sexual psychopaths" and that

these persons persist in their sexual crimes throughout life; that they always give warning that they are dangerous by first committing minor offenses; that any psychiatrist can diagnose them with a high degree of precision at an early age, before they have committed serious sex crimes; and that sexual psychopaths who are diagnosed and identified should be confined as irresponsible persons until they are pronounced by psychiatrists to be completely and permanently cured of their malady.[60]

But once the public has been aroused, partly by press coverage of a few spectacular sex crimes, and partly by a misinformed conception of the sex offender, sexual psychopath legislation followed as the answer to the problem.

Yet the public's concern about sex offenses could not be effective in formulating criminal law without organizing action groups within the community. Concrete pressure for sexual psychopath legislation was provided in most states by committees, most of which were guided by psychiatrists. These committees presented sexual psychopath bills to the public and to the legislatures as the most scientific and enlightened method of protecting society against dangerous sex criminals; it has been pointed out that "the psychiatrists, more than any others, have been the interest group back of the laws."[61] A committee of psychiatrists and neurologists in Chicago wrote the bill that became the sexual psychopath law of Illinois. In Minnesota all the members of the governor's committee except one were psychiatrists.

That the sexual psychopath laws were predominantly formulated by psychiatrists accounts for most of their substance. Because a common assertion among psychiatrists is that serious sex crimes are the result of emotional or mental pathology, or that all psychological defectives have actual or potential sexual abnormalities, it is little wonder that the laws stipulated that sex offenders be handled as psychologically disturbed and treated as patients. But the psychiatric interest in formulating the laws was also a matter of private economics.

Their interest in the legislation was, nevertheless, reinforced by the more general movement promoting the treatment of all offenders. Also, many professionally trained persons employed in corrections have believed that emotional traits are the explanation for crime. Treating the criminal as a patient, therefore, was consistent with the aims of those engaged in applying the sexual psychopath laws.

In spite of the rush to enact sexual psychopath laws, there has been a tendency not to enforce them, for several reasons:

One is that the laws were passed in a period of panic and were forgotten after the emotion was relieved by this action. A second reason is that the state has no facilities for the care and custody of sexual psychopaths; the state hospitals are already crowded with psychotic patients. A third reason is that the prosecutor and judge, anxious to make records as vigorous and aggressive defenders of the community, favor the most severe penalty available and are unwilling to look upon serious sex criminals as patients. They use the sexual psychopath laws only when their evidence is so weak that conviction under the criminal law is improbable. Finally, it is reported that defense attorneys have learned that they can stop the proceedings under this law by advising their clients to refuse to talk to the psychiatrists. The psychiatrists can make no diagnosis if those who are being investigated refuse to talk.[62]

But perhaps "the greatest saving grace has been the almost uniform lack of enforcement that has followed their enactment."[63] The sexual psychopath laws depart from some of the most fundamental conceptions of criminal law. Most important, the Anglo-American legal doctrine of *nulla crimen sine lege*, prohibiting prosecution without clearly specified substantive norms, is denied by most of the sexual psychopath statutes. Because the individual may be adjudged either without a criminal charge or without a finding of guilt, merely by diagnosis that he or she is a sexual psychopath, due process considerations are ignored. Furthermore, the concept of "sexual psychopath" is so vaguely and variously defined by psychiatrists that there is a great deal of variation in diagnoses and much discretion in the administration of the law.

There appears to be no agreement as to the syndromes of aberration that justify special treatment. Indeed, hospital authorities handling cases of alleged sex psychopaths committed to them by the courts discover a wide spread of psychological types — many who are normal, along with neurotics, psychotics, epileptics, feeble-minded, alcoholics, and constitutional types. Agreement among authorities is often difficult enough to attain for purposes of classifying individuals where traditional and fairly precise clinical categories are involved; consensus is impossible in the no man's land of psychopathic personality. The hazard inherent in the substantive definitions of these statutes is manifest upon inspection; the psychopathology is defined by such nondiscriminating terminology as "impulsiveness of behavior," "lack of customary standards of good judgment," "emotional instability," or "inability to control impulse." The cases adjudicated under these criteria display varied forms of personality organization and a widely assorted sexual symptomatology, a significant proportion of which is in fact normal behavior viewed from either a biological or statistical point of view.[64]

And in some jurisdictions persons may be adjudicated without having a criminal charge placed against them and without it being established that a crime has been committed. "Thus individuals who are nonpsychotic and nondefective, against whom no charge has been laid, may be confined for long periods in hospitals that lack both the space and the treatment facilities to handle them. By the simple expedient of shifting jurisdiction to civil courts, these legislators have made it possible to commit minor deviates who are not insane to psychiatric institutions where they do not belong."[65]

We have no reason to believe that rashes of such legislation will not recur. Law has its element of fashion. The drug addiction control law created in New York State may become an example for other states. More people could be adjudicated and confined for a long time in institutions without the safeguards of due process. The establishment of official policies in the name of the common good, and under the guise of scientific knowledge, is always a force in formulating some types of criminal law.

Controlling Morality and the Social Order

When morality is controlled, at the same time the more material aspects of society will be controlled. That is, laws on private and (sometimes) public morality reflect the desire to preserve all aspects of life. If the moral base of social and economic life should be threatened, then the social and economic order itself might give way. Laws regulating sexual activities, drinking, drug use, and the like are enacted to control the whole environment, even the most intimate aspects of one's life, so that the established order can be secured and perpetuated according to its own interests.

A great many American laws are meant to control personal behaviors contrary to the morals that some in the community hold. Many of these criminal laws are kept on the books, without serious or uniform enforcement, because they reflect a popular sense of reprobation. The behaviors they prohibit are regarded, at least by some, as wrong and unworthy of the society. The criminal laws meant to protect morality and public order include those which regulate some kinds of sexual conduct, prostitution, homosexuality, abortion, drinking, the use of drugs, and public behaviors defined by such names as "public nuisance," "loitering," "trespassing," and "vagrancy."

Regulating Sexual Conduct

Much of the anxiety about public order has to do with controlling sexual conduct, which in Anglo-American society at least, is based on a fairly rigid conception of appropriate sexual expression. Our moral sense carries strong Puritan overtones. To be moral in America is to be *sexually* discreet. Likewise, a sex bias is evident in the laws that regulate sexual conduct in favor of males.

The range of sexual conduct covered by law is so extensive that the law makes potential criminals of most of the adolescent and adult population.[66] One of the principal reasons for such complete control over sexual behavior is to protect a specific kind of family system that preserves the institutions in our society. A great number of state laws seek to control acts that might otherwise endanger the chastity of women before marriage, such as the many laws on rape (statutory and forcible), fornication, incest, and sexual deviance of juveniles. The criminal laws on adultery also are intended to protect the family by preventing sexual relations outside the marriage bond.[67] The Puritans of Massachusetts Bay Colony gave sexual relations within the family so much importance that they made adultery a crime punishable by death. Other criminal laws today as in the past regulate sexual relations of family members. These laws help preserve the cherished monogamous family pattern.

Some of our criminal laws on sexual behavior were formulated to protect specific aspects of marriage and family life in relation to the larger social order. Several southern states enacted laws to prevent marriages between blacks and whites. In 1967, however, the Supreme Court ruled that an antimiscegenation statute of Virginia was unconstitutional. Such "slavery laws," held over from a bygone era, had been formulated originally to ensure the slavery status of blacks and in more recent times have been used to maintain segregation of the races.

Another type of criminal law, also enacted early in Virginia, pertained to bastardy among women of the lower ranks. It was instituted not only for a moral purpose but was to ensure the maximum work from domestic servants.

> Having paid a very high price for their labor, their masters, not unnaturally, were opposed to their entering a relationship which was quite certain to lead to interruptions in their field work, perhaps, at the very time their part in that work would be most valuable, if not wholly indispensable. Not only would the birth of children make it necessary for them to lie by for a month or more, but it might even result in their deaths, and the complete loss of the money invested by the planter in their purchase.[68]

Also, the blame for the offense could be placed on the servant woman overpowered by the advances of her masters.

Criminal law has also been formulated to prevent exposing members of the society to that which is regarded by some as lewd or obscene. The Comstock Act of 1873 stands in American criminal law as a landmark in the control of obscenity. Before that time the common law was not clear on the issue. In fact, obscenity was not considered to be a problem before the nineteenth century, but by the middle of that century it had been given an identity by the Victorian Age.[69] Several segments of the population became interested in protecting women and the young. Finally, in 1873, under pressure for a statutory law, the Comstock Law was enacted, providing for censorship of literature and other printed matter that might come into the hands of the innocent.

Today well-organized groups, such as the National Organization for Decent Literature, continue to pressure courts and legislatures for statutes and decisions regulating obscenity. Countering this move are recommendations for relaxing the legal controls over obscene materials in this country.[70] These, in turn, meet severe reactions, with the president of the United States suggesting that proposals condoning pornography "would increase the threat to our social order as well as to our moral principles."[71]

The interest in controlling "obscene" materials was supported in the 1973 Supreme Court decision, *Miller* v. *California*, establishing new standards for judging the content of books, magazines, plays, and movies. This new decision abandons the 1957 ruling, in *Roth* v. *United States*, which had allowed sexual materials that were of "redeeming social value." The new decision gives local communities and states the power to determine what is obscene, without reference to a national standard. State and local courts may now punish the printing or sale of works that appeal to the "prurient interest in sex." Such judgment is to be based on "contemporary community standards." Giving new direction to obscenity law, the Supreme Court is allowing the power structure within the community to establish standards that will protect its own established order.

Prostitution, Homosexuality, and Abortion

The laws on prostitution vary greatly throughout the country. In most states solicitation is a misdemeanor punished by a fine or a jail sentence of one year. Repeated apprehensions, however, may result in a charge of felony. In some states laws control not only solicitation by prostitutes but also those who exploit and patronize prostitutes. Prostitution may be defined as a crime, but the conduct is frequent in all societies. The laws remain, however, as a representation of what some in the society expect in the ideal moral order. The Wolfenden Report of England perhaps best expressed the reasons for the continued legal regulation of prostitution:

> If it were the law's intention to punish prostitution per se, on the ground that it is immoral conduct, then it would be right that it should provide for the punishment of the man as well as the woman. But that is not the function of the law. It should confine itself to those activities which offend against public order and decency or expose the ordinary citizen to what is offensive or injurious; and the simple fact is that prostitutes do parade themselves more habitually and openly than their prospective customers, and do by their continual presence affront the sense of decency of the ordinary citizen. In so doing they create a nuisance which, in our view, the law is entitled to recognize and deal with.[72]

There are moves in the United States to revise the prostitution laws. Supposedly to make the statutes less discriminatory toward women, some suggest reducing the penalties and including the male patrons in the law. But some groups, especially community leaders and law-enforcement agents, would like to "clean up" some areas of the cities. Pamela Roby, studying the revision of the New York State law on prostitution, documents that the final law is written by the groups that have the most power and resources to shape public policy.[73] In the end it is not the class interests of the prostitute that are being considered in the law, but the interests of those who make the law. Their order prevails through the criminal law.

Criminal penalties for homosexual acts in the United States have been severe. Some states provide penalties of ten or more years of imprisonment. In actuality, however, relatively few are arrested for homosexual acts

and when penalties are administered they usually are lenient. A moral connotation is still attached to homosexuality by many people, though the trend may be toward removing some homosexual acts from the list of crimes. In 1955 the American Law Institute concluded that homosexual behavior between consenting adults in private should be removed from the criminal law.[74] The state of Illinois, revising its penal code in 1961, adopted the institute's recommendation. Similar legal reforms are currently under consideration, although other states have been reluctant to revise their homosexual statutes.

Abortion has long been defined as a crime. Though a few states today allow pregnancy to be terminated on broad medical grounds, most prohibit abortion except when the mother's life is in danger. Taking a life is a moral offense, but the question of whether or not life is taken when an abortion is performed is subject to debate. Various groups have exerted pressure to have their views represented in an appropriate abortion law.[75] Legal reform has taken place in England in part through the well-organized activities of the Abortion Law Reform Association. Similar reform proposals have been advanced in the United States. The Planned Parenthood Federation called for a law that would recognize therapeutic abortion for psychological, eugenic, and humanitarian purposes. The American Law Institute proposed a model abortion code with similar provisions. Such legalization schemes have been opposed primarily by the Roman Catholic Church.[76]

The legal solution to the abortion controversy was reached at the beginning of 1973, when the United States Supreme Court handed down its landmark ruling on abortion.[77] States may prohibit abortions only during the last ten weeks of pregnancy, after the fetus has become "viable" or likely to survive on its own if prematurely delivered. The court's decision in effect repeals most of the abortion laws in the United States.

Drinking and Drunkenness

Although drinking itself is not a crime, being drunk in public view may result in a criminal arrest. Criminal laws have been formulated to handle persons who openly disturb the public order.[78] The person who drinks excessively may be apprehended simply because he or she is disturbing a community's sense of propriety or because being intoxicated may lead to other acts of public nuisance or disturbance. To become intoxicated and exuberant in one's own home is proper middle-class behavior, but to be drunk in public is to violate the Puritanical standards of moral strength and personal discipline.

It is likely that public drunkenness will not be treated as crime in the future. A legal change has occurred already. In 1966 the United States Court of Appeals for the District of Columbia ruled that a chronic alcoholic cannot be convicted of the crime of public drunkenness. Because the defendant under a drunkenness charge "has lost the power of self-control in the use of intoxicating beverages," the court held, the defendant lacks necessary criminal intent to be guilty of a crime and cannot therefore be punished under the criminal law. Similar rulings and legislative measures may eventually eliminate a vast number of criminal offenses.

The current trend in the law associated with drinking and drunkenness in part extends the forces that repealed the Eighteenth Amendment to the Constitution in 1933. That was the end of the "great experiment" known as Prohibition, which had been established by the Volstead Act and ratified by the Eighteenth Amendment in 1920. It has been observed that the movement to ban drinking and the liquor trade was an assertion of the rural Protestant mind against the urban culture that grew up at the end of the nineteenth century and the beginning of the twentieth.[79] For a significant portion of the population Prohibition meant stamping out sin in an evil society. The rural element was temporarily successful in enacting Prohibition legislation, but succumbed within thirteen years to the inevitable.

Amid resentment against drinking and what it represented, specific interest groups were active in the movement that led to legislation. The Prohibition party was founded in 1869 as a third political party to deal with the problem of drinking. Later, such organizations as the Anti-Saloon League and the Women's Christian Temperance Union crusaded against alcohol and the saloon. The lobbying efforts of these groups were effective in bringing about state and local temperance legislation. The "dry" lobby groups exerted great pressure against legislators. The Anti-Saloon League could "With the menace of thousands of votes cast at the next election against any legislator who dared to vote against a dry measure . . . make the representatives of the people vote against their personal wet convictions."[80] The dry interest groups, with other forces in American society at the time, brought about formal enactment of Prohibition:

In this way, the Eighteenth Amendment and the Volstead Act became the law of the land. Through the many roots of prohibition — rural mythology, the psychology of excess, the exploited fears of the mass of the people, the findings of science and medicine, the temper of reform, the efficiency of the dry pressure groups, their mastery of propaganda, the stupidity and self-interest of the brewers and distillers, the necessary trimming of politicians, and the weakness of the elected representatives of the people — through all these channels the sap of the dry tree rose until the legal prohibition of the liquor trade burst out new and green in the first month of 1920. The roots had been separate; yet they were all part of a common American seed. They combined and contributed to the strength of the whole. The Anti-Saloon League, bent on its particular reform, was the heir and beneficiary of many interactions in American life. As the drys stood on the threshold of victory at the opening of the twenties, they could see manifest destiny in the success of their cause. They seemed to be the darling army of the Lord. Behind them appeared to lie one mighty pattern and purpose. Before them hung the sweet fruits of victory.[81]

But Prohibition was to fail both as law and as a noble experiment. An outdated morality could not be enforced by criminal law. Rural interests were replaced by the interests of a new social order.

The old order of the country gave way to the new order of the cities. Rural morality was replaced by urban morality, rural voices by urban voices, rural votes by urban votes.

A novel culture of skyscrapers and suburbs grew up to oust the civilization of the general store and Main Street. A technological revolution broadcast a common culture over the various folkways of the land. It is only in context of this immense social change, the metamorphosis of Abraham Lincoln's America into the America of Franklin Roosevelt, that the phenomenon of national prohibition can be seen and understood. It was part of the whole process, the last hope of the declining village. It was less of a farce than a tragedy, less of a mistake than a proof of changing times.[82]

Law of Vagrancy

Vagrancy has been a crime in nearly every one of the United States. Because the state statutes had their heritage in English law, the common law meaning of "vagrancy" is either stated or implied in the statutes: a vagrant is an idle person, beggar, or person wandering without being able to give a good account of himself. Most important is the nature of the person: "Vagrancy is the principal crime in which the offense consists of being a certain kind of person rather than in having done or failed to do certain acts."[83]

Vagrancy laws are widely used on the community level to detain questionable and suspicious persons. They and their enforcement are aimed at potential criminals, are used sometimes in lieu of other charges, and often are the means for ridding the community of those who do not meet the standards set by the respectable members.

The crime of vagrancy derives from early English laws that came into existence during the fourteenth century in response to changing social conditions.[84] The first full-fledged vagrancy law was enacted in 1349, making it a crime to give alms to able-bodied, unemployed persons and establishing that such persons would be criminally punished. The law and supplementary statutes were formulated, after the Black Death and the flight of workers from landowners, to supply needed labor: "There is little question that these statutes were designed for one express purpose: to force laborers (whether personally free or unfree) to accept employment at a low wage in order to insure

the landowner an adequate supply of labor at a price he could afford to pay."[85]

Changing social conditions in England made it unnecessary to enforce the vagrancy statutes. But by the sixteenth century, with increased emphasis on commerce and industry, vagrancy law was revived. Because of changes in the social structure, the law shifted from regulating labor to controlling criminal activities. This paragraph summarizes the law's development in early English society:

These laws were a legislative innovation which reflected the socially perceived necessity of providing an abundance of cheap labor to landowners during a period when serfdom was breaking down and when the pool of available labor was depleted. With the eventual breakup of feudalism the need for such laws eventually disappeared and the increased dependence of the economy upon industry and commerce rendered the former use of the vagrancy statutes unnecessary. As a result, for a substantial period the vagrancy statutes were dormant, undergoing only minor changes and, presumably, being applied infrequently. Finally, the vagrancy laws were subjected to considerable alteration through a shift in the focal concern of the statutes. Whereas in their inception the laws focused upon the "idle" and "those refusing to labor" after the turn of the sixteenth century an emphasis came to be upon "rogues," "vagabonds," and others who were suspected of being engaged in criminal activities. During this period the focus was particularly upon "roadmen" who preyed upon citizens who transported goods from one place to another. The increased importance of commerce to England during this period made it necessary that some protection be given persons engaged in this enterprise and the vagrancy statutes provided one source for such protection by re-focusing the acts to be included under these statutes.[86]

In other words, the formulations and changes in the vagrancy statutes were made by powerful interest groups.

With only minor variations the vagrancy statutes remained the same through the seventeenth and eighteenth centuries. They were adopted by American colonies and states to serve the same purposes they were performing

VIEWPOINT

DECRIMINALIZATION

On Chasing the Marijuana Smoker

On March 11, President Nixon reiterated his long-standing opposition to eliminating the criminal penalties for use, possession or sale of marijuana. In so doing, he ignored the findings of every major study and official inquiry about marijuana, and disregarded the conclusions of the National Commission on Marijuana and Drug Abuse, which he appointed. We can only conclude that the President, like many Americans, stubbornly subscribes to the myths of marijuana rather than realistically assessing the costs to both the individual and society of continued criminal prohibition.

With the President we can agree on one point: Illicit drug use in the United States today has reached frightening proportions. We firmly disagree, however, with the President's continued reliance on the criminal approach. Decriminalizing private possession and use of marijuana would be a sensible step in ameliorating the drug problem. We can no longer pay the price of ruined lives, wasted resources and ineffective drug education by chasing marijuana smokers.

Since the 1930's the dangers of marijuana have been grossly exaggerated, a fact increasing numbers of young people have discovered from first-hand experience. As a result, warnings about heroin, amphetamines, methaqualone and barbiturates are ignored. Removing the criminal penalties for the personal use of marijuana would demonstrate a willingness to deal honestly with marijuana, and afford the opportunity to enhance our now-impoverished credibility as drug educators.

Enforcement of the marijuana laws is diverting valuable law enforcement resources away from the areas where they are critically needed. The American Bar Association has estimated there were 226,000 marijuana-related arrests in this country last year. While law enforcement officials often tell us they now concentrate on the commercial trafficker, and not the user, the Marijuana Commission found otherwise. Only 7 per cent of the state arrests were against the seller, while 93 per cent were for possession and use. Our society can ill afford to burden the country's police forces with the impossible task of trying to pursue and arrest the 26 million people in the U.S. who have now used marijuana.

The President has chosen to apply the infamous "domino theory" to drugs, and is in essence asking, "If we change the laws relating to marijuana, where do we draw the line?" It is clear that marijuana smoking is a firm fact of life and no conceivable law enforcement program can eradicate its use. We must draw the line where the harmful aspects of enforcement exceed the drug's potential for harm, and for marijuana the line is drawn away from the criminal law.

Our drug laws should be in accord with the most accurate information available, and based on the possibility of harm presented by a particular drug; not on prejudice, fear, emotionalism or moral fervor. We support a policy of discouragement for all recreational drug use, but we can no longer continue to make criminals out of those who choose to ignore our advice.

Walter Dennis, Erich Goode, Lester Grinspoon, M.D.,
Aryeh Neier, Norman Zinberg, M.D.   Washington, April 13, 1973

Source: "Letters to the Editor," The New York Times, April 24, 1973. The writers are advisory board members of the National Organization for the Reform of Marijuana Laws.

VIEWPOINT_____

A RESPONSE TO DECRIMINALIZATION

What Marijuana Can Do to You

The spokesmen for Normal (National Organization for the Reform of Marijuana Laws) in their efforts to obtain the commercial availability of marijuana in the United States [letter April 24] ignore the following:

1. Marijuana contains toxic substances (THC and its metabolites) which are only soluble in fat and stored in body tissues, including brain, for weeks and months, like DDT. The storage capacity of tissues for these substances is enormous — which explains their slow deleterious effects in habitual smokers. Anyone using these substances more than once a week cannot be drug free. Moderate usage is difficult to achieve because of one of the most serious hazards of cannabis usage: the development of tolerance, i.e., the necessity of increasing dosage in order to obtain the initial effect. As a result of this tolerance, a significant number of habitual users of marijuana will require increased dosages of stronger preparations (hashish) or escalate to more potent drugs. The National Commission has reported that there are already 500,000 heavy marijuana users in the U.S. How did they get there and what happens to them?

Marijuana smoke induces cancer in tissue cultures of human lung; samples of the lung removed from American soldiers in Germany who used hashish daily presented squamous metaplasia, a lesion statistically and anatomically linked with carcinoma of the lung. Marijuana usage leads to cellular damage in man: the cellular mediated immune response (white blood cells) is impaired in marijuana smokers. This impairment of lymphocyte function is associated with chromosome breakage observed in casual as well as chronic marijuana users. If such breakage occurs in the gonads (germ cells) where the by-products of marijuana accumulate electively because of their high fat content, birth defects will result. Such defects have been produced in animals treated with marijuana.

2. Since 1924 all international conventions of scientific and legal experts have recommended that cannabis derivatives as well as opium and coca leaves be classified among the "stupefying drugs" which may only be used for medical purposes and that private possession or use of any of these drugs be considered an offense. As marijuana has no therapeutic value, the Single Convention of the United Nations on Stupefying Drugs (1961), of which the U.S. is a party, recommends that cultivation of the plant (drug type) be eliminated over a 25-year period. These recommendations were taken at the initiative of the representatives from Asia and Africa who claim that the widespread usage of marijuana is associated with physical and mental morbidity of a large section of their people and with social stagnation.

In the view of the foregoing, should the United States and its President unilaterally denounce the Single Convention by removing all penalties "for use, possession, or sale of marijuana"?

Robert E. Esser, Henry Clay Frick 2d, Albert Greenwood
William M. Manger, Gabriel G. Nahas, Philip Zeidenberg
New York, May 25, 1973

Source: "Letters to the Editor," _The New York Times,_ May 31, 1973. _The signers are all medical doctors at the College of Physicians and Surgeons, Columbia University._

in English society. Today the vagrancy laws continue to provide a way of controlling persons and activities regarded as undesirable in the community, particularly those who might endanger private property and threaten order.

The vagrancy laws are currently being evaluated and questioned, however. One writer has stated, "The time is surely at hand to modernize the vagrancy concept or, better yet, to abandon it altogether for statutes which will harmonize with notions of a decent, fair, and just administration of criminal justice, and which will at the same time make it possible for police departments to discharge their responsibilities in a reasonable manner."[87] A significant change in the law has been made in the state of New York. In 1967 the New York Court of Appeals ruled unconstitutional a statute of 1788 that provided for arresting people with no visible means of support.[88] The court ruled that the law "constitutes an overreaching of the proper limitations of the police power." Furthermore, the court said that the statute has little use "other than, perhaps, as a means of harassing, punishing or apprehending suspected criminals in an unconstitutional fashion." The old statute was declared unconstitutional on the ground that it interfered with a citizen's liberty to conduct himself as he sees fit as long as he does not interfere with the rights of others. Such repeal, which is occurring in other states as well, will end the use of laws of the vagrancy type to enforce community order. Perhaps other means of maintaining public order, legal or extralegal, will be substituted for vagrancy law.

Controlling Drugs

Before the turn of this century there was no significant legislation on manufacturing or distributing narcotic drugs. But states and the federal government soon enacted laws to control them. This legislation of morality required a shift in the conception of drug use and a different manner of handling the problem. Drug users were moved from one category to another, from a problem shared by the general population to one in the lower classes, the "unrespectable" part of society.[89]

The Harrison Act passed by Congress in 1914 defined users of specific drugs as criminals. In technical language it required that all drug-handlers be registered and that the fact of securing drugs be made a matter of record.[90] But in the act's interpretation, court rulings in specific cases, and supplementary laws, criminal sanctions were provided for the unauthorized possession, sale, or transfer of drugs. The states too have enacted antinarcotic laws. In the United States, penalties for violating drug laws have become more severe in recent years. Possessing narcotics is now a felony instead of a misdemeanor.

Drug laws have not only defined users as criminals but have created public suspicion and fear of drug users and addicts. Today the use of any type of drug — addictive or not, a narcotic, marijuana, or a psychedelic — produces a public response that will almost certainly result in the call for legislation. Much of this atmosphere has been created by the Federal Bureau of Narcotics. The bureau has been responsible for administrative decisions that are the basis for most of the drug legislation.[91] The Bureau of Narcotics has defined its interests as total restriction of drugs and complete enforcement of the law. These interests have become the standards by which the public now views and officially acts upon the use of drugs.

Great Britain's policy on drugs is sharply different from ours. In England drug addiction is considered a medical rather than a legal problem; the addict is not regarded as a criminal. The Dangerous Drug Act of 1920 defined the addict as a patient who may receive drugs upon the medical discretion of a physician.[92] As a result, drug addicts in England do not have to resort to criminal activities to maintain a drug supply. Because of the British approach to drug addiction, it is now being argued, primarily by academicians, that the American policy on drug use is unsound and that to deal more effectively with the problem official policy should be changed. Lindesmith has made several proposals: (1) anti-narcotic laws should be written so that addicts do not have to violate them solely because they are addicts; (2) drug users are admittedly handicapped by their habits but they should nevertheless be encouraged to engage in productive labor even when they are using drugs; (3) cures should not be imposed upon narcotics victims by force but should be voluntary; (4) police officers should be prevented from exploiting drug addicts as stool pigeons just because they are addicts; and (5) heroin and morphine addicts should be handled according to the same principles and moral precepts applied to barbiturate and alcohol addicts because these three forms of addiction are similar.[93]

Other policies are being instituted to control the "drug problem." There is a trend to handle drug addiction as a disease — the addict is a "sick" person. Substitute drugs, such as methadone, are being administered to addicts. The federal government is establishing new laws, such as the Comprehensive Drug Control Act of 1970. Drug use, according to the president, has "assumed the dimensions of a national emergency."[94]

The state, defining drug use and addiction as a problem, has conditioned the public to respond by condemning the drug user, rather than questioning the kind of social order that makes drug use a viable alternative to everyday reality. Being taught to believe that the problem is in the drug user's morality or physical condition, rather than in the social order's pathology, those who rule maintain order without any threatening changes. The existing order is secured by legislating morality. The moral order and the social-economic order are inseparable; they serve each other.

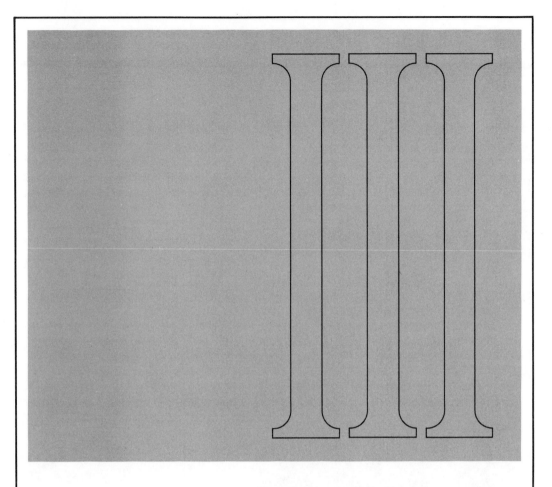

PATTERNS OF
CRIMINAL BEHAVIOR

6

Sociology of Criminal Behavior

All behavior may be understood if we know the social, economic, and political organization in which it occurs. It is the organization of society that gives behavior its source and its meaning.

Social theorists have traditionally divided societies into polar (extreme) types commonly based on the relative amount of consensus or conflict in the society. The two models of society contrast sharply. Moreover, the theories of behavior (particularly criminal behavior) based on these models differ markedly.

The consensus model, also referred to as "the functional model," describes the societal organization as a functionally integrated system held together in equilibrium. In the conflict model, on the other hand, societies are assumed to be shaped by diversity, coercion, and change.[1] The functional model assumes consensus on the major values, even among pluralistic groups; the conflict model suggests that society is held together by force. Power, as the ability of persons, groups, and classes to determine the conduct of others, is the heart of the conflict model.[2] Those who have the power to shape and enforce public policy determine the fate of those who lack this power.

The conflict model is incomplete if it stops here. If a critical perspective is to be developed, and if a theory of crime in American society is to be built from the model, we must recognize the economic structure of the society and its *class* conflict. In other words, then, what began as a conflict analysis must be turned into a class analysis. That America is a capitalist society is a crucial fact in analyzing its crime and criminal behavior.

We thus proceed with the recognition that American society is class-divided.[3] All parts of our life are affected by the fact that the means of production are owned and controlled by the few. Crime and criminal behavior are closely tied to society's organization into classes.

Criminal Behavior in a Class Society

All of us, whether or not we are at times defined as criminal, act in reference to normative patterns learned in our social and cultural settings. In a class society, we have normative systems as points of reference for personal behavior. Because we are differentially located in the society according to social classes, we learn behavior selectively. The content of our learning depends greatly on our position in the society. Therefore, learning of behavior is structured and selective; a class-divided society has *differential learning structures*.

In his search for understanding of criminal behavior, Edwin H. Sutherland may be credited with the most systematic formulation of how behavior patterns are learned.[4] His argument was that people acquire patterns of criminal behavior in the same way in which they acquire patterns of lawful behavior — by interacting with others in communication. The learning includes techniques of committing offenses as well as the specific direction of motives, attitudes, and rationalizations. The motives and rationalizations, in turn, are learned from favorable or unfavorable definitions of the law. It follows, from Sutherland's proposition of "differential association," that you become delinquent or criminal because you learn more definitions favorable to violating the law than those unfavorable to violating it.

Criminal behavior patterns are not learned randomly, but are structured according to a person's selective exposure to situations in which both criminal and anticriminal behavior patterns are present. *Rates* of criminal behavior can thus be explained by Sutherland's concept of "differential social organization."

> In a multi-group type of social organization, alternative and inconsistent standards of conduct are possessed by various groups, so that an individual who is a member of one group has a high probability of learning to use legal means for achieving success, while an individual in another group learns to accept the importance of success and to achieve it by illegal means. Stated in another way, there are alternative educational processes in operation, varying with groups, so that a person may be educated in either conventional or criminal means of achieving success.[5]

Therefore, the likelihood that a person will engage in criminal behavior depends on the relative exposure to various kinds of norms and, similarly, the extent to which *categories* of people engage in criminal behavior is related to the society's criminal and anticriminal behavior patterns.

This theory about how criminal behavior is learned has been described more recently as differences in access to types of "opportunity" structures. Moreover, persons are located in two opportunity structures — legitimate and illegitimate. Such opportunities are conceived of as both learning and performance:

> Our use of the term "opportunities," legitimate or illegitimate, implies access to both learning and performance structures. That is, the individual must have access to appropriate environments for the acquisition of the values and skills associated with the performance of a particular role, and he must be supported in the performance of the role once he has learned it.[6]

Accordingly, the learning and performance of the criminal role, as of the conventional role, depends upon patterned relationships through which values and skills are transmitted.

Whenever criminal behavior has been viewed according to learning structures, whether in the theory of differential association or in the reformulations, it has been assumed that some behavior patterns are objectively "criminal." Such an assumption is fallacious; the social reality of crime tells us that behaviors are neither criminal nor noncriminal. All behaviors are commonly *social*, and they become criminal when they have been officially defined as such by authorized agents of the state. Without such defining, all behaviors are in a sense "criminal," because all could conceivably be prosecuted under some law.

Because American society is class-divided, because criminal laws represent the values of the dominant class, and because learning structures differ in the content of behavior patterns, persons and behaviors are subject to different probabilities of being defined as criminal. A probability terminology allows us to speculate about the likelihood that specific persons or behaviors will become criminal — that is, will be defined as criminal. People who learn

VIEWPOINT

EDWIN H. SUTHERLAND'S THEORY OF
DIFFERENTIAL ASSOCIATION

The following statement refers to the process by which a particular person comes to engage in criminal behavior.

1. *Criminal behavior is learned.* Negatively, this means that criminal behavior is not inherited, as such; also, the person who is not already trained in crime does not invent criminal behavior, just as a person does not make mechanical inventions unless he has had training in mechanics.

2. *Criminal behavior is learned in interaction with other persons in a process of communication.* This communication is verbal in many respects but includes also "the communication of gestures."

3. *The principal part of the learning of criminal behavior occurs within intimate personal groups.* Negatively, this means that the impersonal agencies of communication, such as picture shows and newspapers, play a relatively unimportant part in the genesis of criminal behavior.

4. *When criminal behavior is learned, the learning includes (a) techniques of committing the crime, which are sometimes very complicated, sometimes very simple; (b) the specific direction of motives, drives, rationalizations, and attitudes.*

5. *The specific direction of motives and drives is learned from definitions of the legal codes as favorable or unfavorable.* In some societies an individual is surrounded by persons who invariably define the legal codes as rules to be observed, while in others he is surrounded by persons whose definitions are favorable to the violation of the legal codes. In our American society these definitions are almost always mixed and consequently we have culture conflict in relation to the legal codes.

6. *A person becomes delinquent because of an excess of definitions favorable to violation of law over definitions unfavorable to violation of law.* This is the principle of differential association. It refers to both criminal and anti-criminal associations and has to do with counteracting forces. When persons become criminal, they do so because of contacts with criminal patterns and also because of isolation from anti-criminal patterns. Any person inevitably assimilates the surrounding culture unless other patterns are in conflict; a Southerner does not pronounce "r" because other Southerners do not pronounce "r." Negatively, this proposition of differential association means that associations which are neutral so far as crime is concerned have little or no effect on the genesis of criminal behavior. Much of the experience of a person is neutral in this sense, e.g., learning to brush one's teeth. This behavior has no negative or positive effect on criminal behavior except as it may be related to associations which are concerned with the legal codes. This neutral behavior is important especially as an occupier of the time of a child so that he is not in contact with criminal behavior during the time he is so engaged in the neutral behavior.

7. *Differential associations may vary in frequency, duration, priority, and intensity.* This means that associations with criminal behavior and also associations

---

Source: From Edwin H. Sutherland, *Principles of Criminology*, 4th ed. (Philadelphia: J. B. Lippincott, 1947), pp. 6–8.

VIEWPOINT (Continued)_____

with anti-criminal behavior vary in those respects. "Frequency" and "duration" as modalities of associations are obvious and need no explanation. "Priority" is assumed to be important in the sense that lawful behavior developed in early childhood may persist throughout life, and also that delinquent behavior developed in early childhood may persist throughout life. This tendency, however, has not been adequately demonstrated, and priority seems to be important principally through its selective influence. "Intensity" is not precisely defined but it has to do with such things as the prestige of the source of a criminal or anti-criminal pattern and with emotional reactions related to the associations. In a precise description of the criminal behavior of a person these modalities would be stated in quantitative form and a mathematical ratio be reached. A formula in this sense has not been developed and the development of such a formula would be extremely difficult.

8. *The process of learning criminal behavior by association with criminal and anti-criminal patterns involves all of the mechanisms that are involved in any other learning.* Negatively, this means that the learning of criminal behavior is not restricted to the process of imitation. A person who is seduced, for instance, learns criminal behavior by association but this process would not ordinarily be described as imitation.

9. *While criminal behavior is an expression of general needs and values, it is not explained by those general needs and values since non-criminal behavior is an expression of the same needs and values.* Thieves generally steal in order to secure money, but likewise honest laborers work in order to secure money. The attempts by many scholars to explain criminal behavior by general drives and values, such as the happiness principle, striving for social status, the money motive, or frustration, have been and must continue to be futile since they explain lawful behavior as completely as they explain criminal behavior. They are similar to respiration, which is necessary for any behavior but which does not differentiate criminal from non-criminal behavior.

It is not necessary, at this level of explanation, to explain why a person has the associations which he has; this certainly involves a complex of many things. In an area where the delinquency rate is high a boy who is sociable, gregarious, active, and athletic is very likely to come in contact with the other boys in the neighborhood, learn delinquent behavior from them, and become a gangster; in the same neighborhood the psychopathic boy who is isolated, introvert, and inert may remain at home, not become acquainted with the other boys in the neighborhood, and not become delinquent. In another situation, the sociable, athletic, aggressive boy may become a member of a scout troop and not become involved in delinquent behavior. The person's associations are determined in a general context of social organization. A child is ordinarily reared in a family; the place of residence of the family is determined largely by family income; and the delinquency rate is in many respects related to the rental value of the houses. Many other factors enter into this social organization, including many of the small personal group relationships.

the behavior patterns of the class not represented in the formulating and applying of criminal laws are more likely to act in ways that will be defined as criminal than those who learn the behavior patterns of the class that formulates and applies criminal definitions. All behaviors are *social*, with varying probabilities that they will become defined as criminal, depending on their location in a class of society.

Where Do These Behavior Patterns Come From?

The problem is not one of explaining "criminal behavior," but explaining the development of behavior patterns that have relative possibilities of being defined as criminal. The question raised by the problem is: What are the structural sources of such behaviors? Generally, all structural sources are important, depending on how much the criminal definitions will be imposed on the behaviors produced by the sources.

The bulk of criminology consists of research and writing on the causes of "criminal behavior." This material can be reinterpreted as the *structural sources of the behaviors that may become defined as criminal.* Various sources might be considered; however, I will concentrate on three general types of social structures that serve as the basis for patterning criminally defined behavior: (1) the age-sex structure, (2) the social class structure, and (3) the ethnic-racial structure. All three are related to the organization of society. The probability that a behavior will both exist and be defined as criminal depends on where the people are in the various structures of society.

Age-Sex Structure

In the official statistics on crime, contact with agents of the law follows a fairly consistent pattern according to the age and sex of those who are defined as criminal. These questions may be asked: What are the behavioral variations according to age and sex status? How do behaviors become structured according to age and sex? And how are criminal definitions related to these behaviors?

For all categories of criminal offenses, taken collectively, the age of maximum criminality is later adolescence and young adulthood. Most people arrested by the police are between the ages of 18 and 24. Males become involved in offenses several times as often as females.[7] The risk of being defined as criminal is much higher for young persons and for males.

The differences in criminal liability according to age and sex can be viewed as the behavioral variations of those defined as criminal. Those under 25 years of age, when arrested, tend to be charged with vandalism, auto theft, burglary, arson, larceny, liquor law violations, robbery, buying and receiving stolen property, and forcible rape. Arrests for drunkenness, gambling, driving under the influence of alcohol, fraud, embezzlement, and vagrancy occur most often among those over 25 years of age. The percentage under 25 who are arrested thus varies considerably from one offense charge to another. For the year 1972, 86.6 per cent of the arrests for vandalism involved persons under 25, but only 15.2 per cent of the arrests for gambling consisted of persons under 25.[8]

The difference in criminal liability according to sex is similarly striking when we consider the kinds of offenses. Some are disproportionately male and others are much less likely to involve males. In accordance with the arrest figures for offenses in general, for 1972, 84.9 per cent of those arrested were males. For specific offenses, males were arrested for 84.6 per cent of the murders, 93.5 per cent of the robberies, 86.8 per cent of the aggravated assaults, 94.8 per cent of the burglaries, and 94.3 per cent of the auto thefts.[9]

How closely can we assume that these arrest situations reflect behavioral variations according to differences in age and sex? Do official criminal statistics reflect the behavioral variations of the age groups and the sexes, or are the statistics only indicators of selective law enforcement? Studies of self-reported behavior provide a partial answer. Of juveniles, it has been found that (1) self-reported delinquency is extensive and variable, (2) the variations in the kinds of reported delinquencies are similar to variations in the official arrest figures, (3) boys report a much higher proportion of delinquencies than girls, and (4) institutionalized juvenile delinquents rank much higher than high school students in seriousness of involvement in delinquent behavior.[10] Similarly, studies of self-reported behavior among adults indicate that the general population is engaged in activities that could be defined as criminal and that, in addition, men are involved in behaviors that could be criminally defined more than are women.[11] The issue, therefore, is understanding how behavior varies according to age and sex. Then we have the ultimate matter of explaining why the behaviors are defined as criminal according to age and sex in American society.

The behavioral patterns of youth are strongly influenced by youth's place in the age structure. Though social class accounts for the major variations in behavior among youths, growing up in relation to elders has much influence on the kinds of behavior pursued by youths. Adolescent gangs, which engage in many activities that may be defined as delinquent or criminal, can be explained as an attempt by adolescents to gain the status not granted them by adults.[12] Age grading in the larger society leads to gang membership and associated activities to fill the status gap between childhood and adulthood. Delinquent activity naturally results when a society does not provide meaningful functions for adolescents.[13] Activities that have a high probability of being defined as delinquent or criminal are to be expected when an age group is not provided with any other meaningful ways of involvement and fulfillment.

Because adolescence is a time for experimentation, for establishing an identity, activities with high delinquency or criminal potential may be the only solution for gaining that identity.[14] Although such problems of identity are critical for both sexes, they are qualitatively different for boys and girls. Some adolescent version of the adult male role must be achieved by the young male adolescent, and girls must attempt some kind of a solution that corresponds to the adult female role. Both the male and female attempts at identity result in different patterns of adolescent behavior. Boys therefore tend to steal, destroy property, or engage in fighting in an attempt to achieve

power, prestige, and wealth. On the other hand, girls tend to become involved in activities that are possible within the traditional female role.[15] The sex roles of the adult world thus serve as general models for creating youthful activities that may, in turn, become defined as delinquent or criminal by adults.

As juveniles advance in the age structure of society, they learn to behave in more "adult" ways. The behavior patterns learned and pursued in adulthood have varying probabilities of being defined as criminal. The extent to which the behaviors are in fact so defined depends greatly on the careers developed by the adults. Criminal careers develop in part according to personal experiences in contact with agents of the law.

A good part of the difference between adult male and female involvement in criminally defined activity is a consequence of the conventional adult sex roles in our society. Men are expected to be active and aggressive; women are expected to be more passive. Each role leads to differing kinds and amounts of behavior that may be criminally defined. Men traditionally have had greater opportunity to engage in the forms of activity — including making a gainful living — which may result in behaviors that have high potentials of being defined as criminal.

Whatever the kind or amount of specific behaviors, they are criminal because they are so defined by others. The behaviors that provide the objects for criminal definition can be explained by position in the age-sex structure of society, but the application of criminal definitions must be explained by the place of the persons and behaviors as they compare with the expectations of those who enforce and administer the criminal law. Behaviors that violate the sensibilities and interests of the dominant class are the ones that have a high probability of being defined as criminal in American society.

Social Class Structure

The official statistics on crime consistently indicate an overrepresentation of persons from the lower class. And studies of American communities have shown that the lower class is most vulnerable to law enforcement and judicial action. In one New England town the lower classes accounted for about 90 per cent of the arrests over a seven-year period.[16] We have many such figures, and we can conclude that members of the lower class, in comparison to members of the middle and upper classes, have the greatest probability of being arrested and convicted for their behaviors.

Some recent evidence qualifies, among juveniles at least, what illegal activity is like in the class structure. In one study comparing institutionalized juveniles and self-reported behavior among high school students, 50 per cent of the boys in a training school for delinquents were from the lowest of four categories of socioeconomic status; however, when the high school boys reported their behaviors, only 13 per cent of delinquent activities were reported among boys of the lowest socioeconomic status.[17] Such studies show that behavior that may be defined as criminal is more evenly distributed throughout the class structure than is indicated by the official statistics on juvenile delinquency.

It may be argued, therefore, that such conduct is distributed throughout the social class structure, but that the lower class nevertheless has the greatest *risk* of officially being defined as delinquent or criminal. Furthermore, lower-class members, compared with members of the other classes, are involved in behavior patterns that automatically have a greater probability of being officially handled as criminal. Lower-class people are more likely to engage in activities that result in charges of drunkenness, assault, disorderly conduct, burglary, and robbery. Middle- and upper-class people, on the other hand, tend to be involved in activities that, although they may conceivably be defined as criminal, are not traditionally dealt with by criminal sanction. Although criminal laws cover such middle-class behaviors as fraud, falsification of records, evasion of taxes, misuse of funds, and malpractice, these behaviors are not usually handled by traditional criminal procedures. We can conclude that the behavior patterns of the social classes are qualitatively different and that these patterns are subject to differing probabilities of being defined as criminal. How, then, can we explain the varying behavior patterns of the social classes in relation to criminal definitions?

The behavior patterns of each social class are learned during childhood. In addition to the behaviors associated with each class, the members of some social classes develop behaviors in response to the problems of growing up in a class structure. Some, depending upon their experiences in early life, their later circumstances, and their confrontation with the law, continue in a style of life that includes behaviors that have a high probability of being defined as criminal. For some others, a criminal career may be the culmination of a personal history that took shape in the class structure.

For the *lower-class* child, especially for the boy, growing into adulthood involves gradually learning the cultural traditions of the lower class. It has been suggested, at least by research conducted in Boston in the fifties, that the problem for the boy in the "hard-core" lower class is that as he matures he has to cope with a female-dominated household.[18] The adolescent street gang, accordingly, is the social mechanism for becoming a male adult in the lower class. Learning the lower-class structure emphasizes the "focal concerns" of trouble, toughness, smartness, excitement, fate, and autonomy. In following these cultural patterns within the adolescent gang, lower-class boys engage in activities that may well become defined as delinquent or criminal. Thus, lower-class behavior readily and automatically becomes criminal under the legal standards that embody the cultural patterns of another class.

Growing up in the *working class*, a cut above the lower class, presents its own problems for the boy who is faced with the problem of adjusting to middle-class standards.[19] Working-class boys have learned the cultural patterns of one class but are assessed, particularly in the schools, by middle-class standards that emphasize ambition, self-reliance, postponing immediate satisfaction, good manners, wholesome recreation, controlling physical aggression, and respect for property. Because working-class boys do not fare well when assessed according to the "middle-class measuring rod," they seek a solution by creating a "delinquent subculture." The "subculture" that they form or join may be opposed to middle-class values.[20] The solution for the working-class boy then consists of a way of life that, being opposed to the standards of the middle class, prescribes behaviors that have a good probability of being defined as delinquent or criminal.

For *middle-class* youths, activity that can be defined as delinquent or criminal may result from following the practices of the middle class itself. Some of the behaviors of middle-class youths, which may be in conflict with the law, are in fact a logical extension of values held by most middle-class adults. Some middle-class youths make use of the "subterranean values" of the middle class, allowing these to serve as a code for everyday behavior instead of reserving them for leisure-time activity.[21] For most people growing up in the middle class, its values need not necessarily be rejected to permit their violation. Rather, "techniques of neutralization" may be learned as motivation and rationalization for behavior that is at odds with middle-class (and usually legal) standards.[22] At any rate, middle-class youths, and also youths of the upper class, engage in behaviors that may be defined as delinquent or criminal, but the probability that such behavior will ever appear in the official statistics on delinquency and crime is relatively slight.

The conclusion we must come to about how social class, structuring of behavior patterns, and criminal definitions interact is clear. Each social class has or develops its own behavior patterns, many of which may be defined as delinquent or criminal. But, because the formulating, enforcing, and administering of criminal law are based on a definite conception of appropriate behavior, primarily the standards of the middle class, official rates of delinquency and crime differ widely from one social class to another. The probability that a person will be defined as criminal, therefore, is greatly affected by his location in the class structure.

Racial-Ethnic Structure

The statistics on race and crime indicate that, for their proportion in the population, blacks are arrested between three and four times as frequently as whites. Although blacks comprise about one-ninth of the population in the United States, they account for more than a quarter of the arrests for all offenses.[23] Similarly, judicial and prison statistics show that blacks have higher rates of conviction and imprisonment than whites. The status of being a black, then, compared with being white, involves a much greater risk of being arrested, convicted, and imprisoned. The probability of being defined as criminal thus varies according to one's location in the racial structure.

There are differences, too, in the kinds of behavior for which blacks and whites are arrested. Of the arrests in 1972 for all the offense categories, blacks outnumbered whites in arrests for murder, forcible rape, robbery, carrying and possessing weapons, prostitution, and gambling.[24] Whites, on the other hand, outnumbered blacks in arrests for such offenses as negligent manslaughter, fraud, embezzlement, vandalism, drunkenness, drunken driving, disorderly conduct, and vagrancy. The variations between blacks and whites in the offenses for which they are arrested are extensive.

Differences in the crime rates of ethnic, nationality, and Third-World groups are also evident.[25] And, as with the variations according to race, differences in the rates of crime are found in the types of offenses among different ethnic groups. Italian immigrants in the United States have traditionally had high rates of homicide and low rates of drunkenness, whereas Irish immigrants have had lower rates of homicide and much higher offense rates for drunkenness. Also, though the immigrants themselves have offense patterns similar to those of the home country, their children have most often been arrested for offenses characteristic of the areas in which they have settled. Also, the extent to which the crime rate of the ethnic and nationality groups conforms to that of the native whites varies with the time the groups have been in the United States.[26] Finally, younger members of ethnic and racial groups take on the crime rates of the native whites more than do the older members.

Location in the racial-ethnic structure, therefore, presents a person with the behavior patterns of an ethnic, nationality, or racial group. Especially among blacks, behavior may be

VIEWPOINT_____

DELINQUENCY AND DRIFT

An alternative image of the delinquent can be developed by accepting the implications of soft rather than hard determinism. One effect of restoring choice to man is to render feasible a joining of classical with positivist assumptions. I wish to maintain the spirit of positive inquiry but to suggest certain modifications of its picture of the delinquent. These modifications consistently follow lines implicit in the classic criminological view.

Some men are freer than others. Most men, including delinquents, are neither wholly free nor completely constrained but fall somewhere between. The general conditions underlying various positions along a continuum from freedom to constraint may be described. Viewed in this way, determinism loses none of its heuristic value. We may still act as if all were knowable, but we refrain at least temporarily from an image of the delinquent that is tailored to suit social science. The image of the delinquent I wish to convey is one of drift; an actor neither compelled nor committed to deeds nor freely choosing them; neither different in any simple or fundamental sense from the law abiding, nor the same; conforming to certain traditions in American life while partially unreceptive to other more conventional traditions; and finally, an actor whose motivational system may be explored along lines explicitly commended by classical criminology — his peculiar relation to legal institutions.

The delinquent is casually, intermittently, and transiently immersed in a pattern of illegal action. His investment of affect in the delinquent enterprise is sufficient so as to allow an eliciting of prestige and satisfaction but not so large as to "become more or less unavailable for other lines of action." In point of fact, the delinquent is available even during the period of optimum involvement for many lines of legal and conventional action. Not only is he available but a moment's reflection tells us that, concomitant with his illegal involvement, he actively participates in a wide variety of conventional activity. If commitment implies, as it does, rendering oneself presently and in the future unavailable for other lines of action, then the delinquent is uncommitted. He is committed to neither delinquent nor conventional enterprise. Neither, by the canons of his ideology or the makeup of his personality, is precluded.

Drift stands midway between freedom and control. Its basis is an area of the social structure in which control has been loosened, coupled with the abortiveness of adolescent endeavor to organize an autonomous subculture, and thus an independent source of control, around illegal action. The delinquent *transiently* exists in a limbo between convention and crime, responding in turn to the demands of each, flirting now with one, now the other, but postponing commitment, evading decision. Thus, he drifts between criminal and conventional action.

To be loosened from control, conventional or delinquent, is not equivalent to freedom, and, thus, I do not propose a free or calculating actor as an alternative to constraint. Freedom is not only the loosening of controls. It is a sense of command over one's destiny, a capacity to formulate programs or projects, a feeling of being an agent in one's own behalf. Freedom is self-control. If so, the delinquent has clearly not achieved that state. The sense of self-control, irrespec-

_____
Source: From David Matza, *Delinquency and Drift* (New York: John Wiley & Sons, 1964), pp. 27–30.

VIEWPOINT (Continued)_____

tive of whether it is well founded, exists to varying degrees in modern man. Those who have been granted the potentiality for freedom through the loosening of social controls but who lack the position, capacity, or inclination to become agents in their own behalf, I call drifters, and it is in this category that I place the juvenile delinquent.

Drift is motion guided gently by underlying influences. The guidance is gentle and not constraining. The drift may be initiated or deflected by events so numerous as to defy codification. But underlying influences are operative nonetheless in that they make initiation to delinquency more probable, and they reduce the chances that an event will deflect the drifter from his delinquent path. Drift is a gradual process of movement, unperceived by the actor, in which the first stage may be accidental or unpredictable from the point of view of any theoretic frame of reference, and deflection from the delinquent path may be similarly accidental or unpredictable. This does not preclude a general theory of delinquency. However, the major purpose of such a theory is a description of the conditions that make delinquent drift possible and probable, and not a specification of invariant conditions of delinquency.

In developing an alternative picture, it should be obvious that not all delinquents correspond to the drifter here depicted. By hypothesis, most delinquents, although perhaps not most criminals, approximate the model. The delinquent as drifter more approximates the substantial majority of juvenile delinquents who do not become adult criminals than the minority who do. Some delinquents are neurotically compulsive and some in the course of their enterprise develop commitment. These flank the more ordinary delinquent on either side, and during situations of crisis perhaps play crucial leadership roles. Partially because he is more sensational and dramatic, the extraordinary delinquent has received greater attention in both mass media and criminological theory. The mundane delinquent is the exemplary delinquent in that he personifies, more fully than the compulsive or the committed, the spirit of the enterprise. The delinquent drifter is less likely to command our attention and we have partially ignored him. However, the drifter is not less a problem than the compulsive or committed delinquent even though he is far less likely to become an adult criminal. Though his tenure is short, his replacements are legion. Though his ideology does not make violations of personal and property rights mandatory, under certain conditions it condones them. Thus, what follows is not a plea for the delinquent but a plea for a reassessment of his enterprise.

_____

shaped too by reaction to the position to which people have been assigned. Much of their behavior represents a reaction to subordination, social-class position, economic insecurity, denial of employment opportunities, restricted participation, and discrimination.[27] That which becomes defined as criminal may be an attempt to create an existence that,

ideally, is ensured in the American dream. And more recently, attempts by blacks to overthrow the oppression imposed by their subordinate position in American society have been defined as criminal by the white power elite.

Each group, then, develops its own behavior patterns in reference to its position in the ethnic-racial structure of society.[28] The behavior patterns consequently differ from one group to another, but their criminality is determined by the fact that persons of the class in power, using the legal resources of the American state, define the behavior as criminal. Behaviors that threaten the social order have a high probability of being defined as criminal.

Ecological Structuring of Crime

When we look at rates of crime and delinquency according to their geographical or ecological distribution, regularities become apparent. In general, despite variations from one offense category to another, crime rates in the United States are higher in some states than in others, higher in urban areas than in rural areas, higher in larger cities than in smaller cities, and higher in the center of cities than in the areas farther from the center.[29] Moreover, the high rates of crime and delinquency are found in areas characterized by lower-class, nonwhite populations living in substandard physical conditions.

Though such regularities can be explained in any number of ways, ecological areas serve as structures for learning behavior patterns and for pursuing particular behaviors. Whether or not these behaviors are criminal, however, depends on decisions by others. Therefore, crime rates are ecologically distributed in accordance with the probability that specific behaviors, learned and pursued within the respective areas, will be criminally defined. The geographic variations in offense rates may thus be investigated according to the ecology of behavior patterns and criminal definitions.

Regional Variations

The amounts and types of crime vary broadly from one region to another. An early study found that some offenses displayed a gradient pattern throughout the country.[30] Murder was concentrated in the southeastern states, with a gradient to the north and west, and robbery was concentrated in the mid-central states, with decreasing rates on either side of a line running through the center of the United States. Essentially the same patterning of offenses was found several years later; some offenses showed more of a regional concentration.[31]

The regional variation in crime rates can be readily observed in the annual reports of offenses known to the police in the United States. In the 1972 report, the East South Central region had the lowest total crime rate, and the Pacific region had the highest.[32] In the specific offense categories, the South Atlantic region had the highest murder rate (13.4 per 100,000 population) and the highest aggravated assault rate (263.8). The Pacific region had the highest rate of forcible rape (35.8) and burglary (1,809.0), the Middle Atlantic region had the highest robbery rate (315.2), and New England had the highest auto theft rate (681.8). On the other hand, New England had the lowest rates in the country for murder (3.3) and forcible rape (10.9); the West North Central region had the lowest rate (105.8) of aggravated assault; and the East South Central region had the lowest rates of burglary (740.0), larceny (543.4), and auto theft (236.6).

These variations can be explained by different behavior patterns, with relative probabilities of being defined as criminal, according to regions of the country. There are, first, regional variations in normative systems and behavior patterns. In the South a tradition of violence, including prescriptions on the use of weapons, accompanied by a code of personal honor, provides the background for behavior patterns that have a good chance of being defined as criminal.[33] The relationship of whites and blacks in the South leads to personal conflict both within the two groups and between them.

Second, opportunity for some activities varies according to region. The high rate of property offenses in the West is in part a result of the casual style of living, the openness of the region, and the availability of property.[34] Opportunities for activities that may be defined as burglary, robbery, larceny, and theft thus vary from one region to another. Finally, regions differ in expectations of enforcement and administration of criminal law. Behavior patterns vary regionally, therefore, in both the conduct that may be criminally defined and the behaviors that result in getting the conduct defined as criminal.

Community Variations

One of the most consistent findings in the ecology of crime is that overall crime rates are higher for urban than rural areas and that they increase with size of city.[35] Urban areas usually have higher rates for all major offenses, except for murder: the greatest differences in rates between rural and urban areas are for crimes against property, and the differences are less apparent for crimes against the person. The rates for all categories of offenses increase progressively with each category of city size.

Differences in offense rates between rural and urban areas can be accounted for by basic differences in the learning and opportunity structures of the two areas. Rural areas have a comparative absence of behavioral norms and social processes that are conducive to behaviors that may be defined as criminal.[36] Gang activity in rural areas is relatively limited. The possibilities for learning techniques and motivations for committing criminally defined activities are not as readily available in rural areas as in urban areas.

Opportunities for carrying out such property offenses as robbery, burglary, larceny, and auto theft are much greater in urban than in rural areas, and they become even more prevalent in large cities. In such ways, then, urban areas (especially the larger cities) provide the cultural and structural environments for developing behavior patterns that may result in criminally defined activities.

Variations within Cities

Studies over several decades have documented fairly consistent patterns in crime and delinquency rates in American cities. Research by members of the "Chicago school" established that the highest offense rates generally occur in the low-rent areas near the center of the city and that the rates decrease farther from the city center.[37] Such studies have shown too that the relative rates of crime and delinquency are maintained within the areas of the city in spite of changes in population.

The distribution of offense rates is related to social characteristics of areas within cities. From several sources we conclude that offense rates of areas are related to their economic, family, and racial composition. In Baltimore, delinquency rates of census tract areas were associated with the percentage of owner-occupied housing and the ratio of nonwhites to whites.[38] Similar findings appear in the distribution of offense rates in Washington, D.C., Detroit, and Indianapolis.[39] Using somewhat different modes of analysis and theoretical assumptions, others have found that similar variables are related to the ecology of crime and delinquency in Seattle, San Diego, and Lexington, Kentucky.[40] Such findings continue to accumulate, but it is important to account for the relationships between social characteristics of areas and their offense rates. One meaningful explanation may be the different kinds of learning and opportunities in the areas. The learning of behaviors and the opportunity to engage in behavior patterns differ.

Behavior patterns that may conflict with legal definitions necessarily develop within ecological areas of the city. Initially such behavior among adolescents may be inspired by no more insidious purpose than adventure and recreation. Thrasher found some time ago in his classic studies of gangs in parts of Chicago that children, in forming play groups, engage in activities that may be defined as illegal.[41] In time, conflict with other groups in the neighborhood and contact with other values may bring the members into activities such as stealing from stores, robbery, and aggressive acts against other gangs.[42] Violent gang activity may become a collective response of adolescents in lower-class slums to the problems of living in such areas of the city.

The diversity of cultural traditions within ecological areas, and the juxtaposition of the traditions, appears to be important in developing the types and amounts of criminally defined activities. Where adult activity is fairly stable and organized, adolescent behavior usually takes on the same qualities.[43] Where adult patterns are not so integrated, juvenile activities (some of which may be defined as delinquent) are unorganized and more violent.

Extending this formulation, it has been suggested that different types of adolescent "subcultures" appear in relation to the "criminal" and "noncriminal" patterns integrated in the neighborhood.[44] Where adult patterns are integrated, the subcultures of adolescents will be "criminal" and the gangs will engage in theft, extortion, and similar activities to achieve status and income. In unintegrated areas, characterized by transiency and instability, "conflict" subcultures develop. Where neither criminal nor noncriminal traditions are available to youth, a "retreatist" subculture relying on drug use and sensual experiences will appear. Whatever the utility of such a conceptualization, different behavior patterns develop in areas of the city according to the social and cultural structure there.[45]

Areas within the city differ in their way of structuring behavior patterns and in the opportunities they offer for engaging in behaviors that may be criminally defined. Crime rates vary from neighborhood to neighborhood, depending on the opportunities for pursuing particular activities.[46] The opportunities for committing each type of crime depend on the availability of such targets as safes, cash registers, personal possessions, and other persons, and are reflected in the rates for each type of offense. Rates for burglary, robbery, and larceny are highest in areas that have much business and commercial activity. Rates of auto theft are highest where a great deal of space is devoted to parking. Rates of forcible rape are highest where the proportion of resident females is high, and rates of murder and assault are highest where many personal victims are available.

All behavior patterns, then, develop within definite ecological areas. The patterns, though, are related not only in content but also in the probability that they will be defined as criminal. According to the perspective provided here, the forms and amounts of crime in any community are the product of the conflict between the behavior patterns of the community and the patterns represented by those who are formulating and applying criminal definitions. Because the kind and extent of this conflict vary ecologically, rates of crime are differentially distributed according to ecological areas.

Personal Action and Social Conditions

To understand crime we need also to see the personal side of criminal behavior. The criminal's social psychology has been of special interest to theoretical criminologists. In fact, much of the theory and research in criminology is devoted to studying "the criminal." We will analyze the human construction of meaningful social action. The social psychology of the criminal is important in analyzing how people create action patterns that provide a source of personal identity and a basis for social behavior. In short, personal action patterns are the essence of a life that is both human and social.

The assumption in social psychology that is consistent with our analysis of society begins by asserting that human actions are purposive and meaningful. This humanistic conception suggests that people develop an awareness of self by being members of society, and subsequently engage in personal actions, of breaking from the established order.[47] Conformity is very much a matter of self-control; and nonconformity may be consciously pursued in finding personal identity. It is thus *against* something that the self can appear.[48]

By conceiving of the person as able to reason and choose courses of action, we may see human life as changing and becoming, rather than merely being.[49] The kind of culture that we develop shapes our ability to be creative. Our culture may help us develop the capacity for greater freedom of action. Not only are we shaped by our physical, social, and cultural experiences, but we are able to select what we are to experience and develop. The belief in realizing human potential is growing and is being incorporated into a contemporary conception of human behavior.

The *social action* frame of reference that serves as the basis for the humanistic conception is drawn from the work of several writers.[50] Max Weber originally suggested that "Action is social insofar as, by virtue of the subjective meaning attached to it by the acting individual (or individuals), it takes account of the behavior of others and is thereby oriented in its own course."[51] Human behavior is *intentional*, has *meaning* for the actors, is *goal-*

oriented, and takes place with an *awareness* of behavior's consequences.

Because people engage in social action, a *social reality* is created: interacting with others, we construct a meaningful world of everyday life.

> It is the world of cultural objects and social institutions into which we are all born, within which we have to find our bearings, and with which we have to come to terms. From the outset, we, the actors on the social scene, experience the world we live in as a world both of nature and of culture, not as a private but as an intersubjective one, that is, as a world common to all of us, either actually given or potentially accessible to everyone; and this involves intercommunication and language.[52]

Social reality consists of both our social meanings and the products of our subjective world. We construct activities and patterns of actions as we attach meaning to everyday existence.[53] Social reality is thus both a *conceptual reality* and a *phenomenal reality*. Having constructed social reality, we find a world of meanings and events that is real to us as conscious social beings.

Marxian theory, however, may allow us to understand the relationship between human action and social conditions. In an often quoted line, Karl Marx observed: "Men make their own history, but they do not make it as they please; they do not make it under circumstances chosen by themselves, but under circumstances directly encountered, given, and transmitted from the past."[54] Instead of assuming that human beings are, on the one hand, the products of external conditions or, on the other, totally free agents, this theory proposes a dynamic and dialectical interplay between social circumstances and our ability to act independently. We are, in a sense, the products of our own product, but we are also historical agents who shape the circumstances that we encounter.[55] Our consciousness and our actions come out of a historical struggle to realize ourselves within our social relationships. We make our history and initiate our actions, but we do all this in a social and historical environment that conditions our immediate possibilities.

In this context each person seeks a meaningful existence. In the abstract, the paths to salvation are many. But each of us is bound by the social space we occupy in our own time in history. The alternatives at our command are limited. Our horizons are set by what we see as the possibilities of being human and by the opportunities that are structured around us.

The action patterns that people develop for themselves are solutions to the problems of being socially human. Each person's actions, including a patterning of self-images and overt behaviors, are shaped by relationships with others. In a socially structured environment, with the help of our friends (and others), we create a meaningful life.

The substance of a person's action is problematic. Though the content of the actions is shaped by our social and cultural location in society, actions are ultimately the product of each individual.[56] But the name that will be given the behavior is also an enterprise of others. And the names are often simplistic — "good" or "bad," "virtuous" or "sinful," "law-abiding" or "criminal." Personal actions are thus constructed in part by the reactions of other people. The person may develop a way of behaving — including a supporting style of life — that takes its reference from criminal definitions. Criminal definitions not only provide behavior with the quality of criminality, but also assist in living a life.

Achieving Self through Criminal Behavior

Each of us has a conception of the self, communicates with that self, and acts toward that self.[57] By regarding yourself as a separate and distinct entity, you can act in a world that is simultaneously created, confronted, and interpreted. We thus act according to our way of experiencing the world. Action, then, is conduct that is personally constructed by the actor. For each person, action is pursued according to the personal meaning attached to that action and, furthermore, according to the personal interpretation of others' actions.

A person's self-conception is always being formed. People place themselves or are placed into categories with which they can identify, such as age, sex, occupation, ethnic group, and social class.[58] Actions themselves give us an identity. Based on our own constructions and decisions, the self is ever becoming.

Achieving a sense of self, however temporary, is crucial to human beings. But the ease with which self-conceptions can be formed varies from one time to another and from one social situation to another. For people in some situations at specific times, achieving self-identity is especially problematic.

> In every age men ask in some form the questions: Who am I? Where do I belong? The degree of awareness and the kind of emphasis with which these questions are asked vary at different periods. Times of swift change and social dislocation bring them to the fore, against the background of whatever personal hopes and social harmonies an earlier period has cultivated.[59]

The achievement of self is critical for people confronted with external environments that defy ready interpretation. Similarly, situations that frustrate expectations and aspirations promote a crisis in self-identity. But each person seeks a meaningful existence, so that some solution must be achieved.

Situations that people find undesirable or difficult to interpret may lead to self-conceptions in opposition to the established order. It may not be unusual, therefore, to find that actions that result from such attitudes are defined by those in power as criminal. A great deal of the traditionally defined criminal behavior has been a response by individuals and groups to situations considered inadequate for attaining specific aspirations.[60] Calculated violation of the law may be a rational solution to socially structured and perceived problems. Protest and resistance against unjust conditions and policies may be most appropriately pursued in activities that violate criminal laws.

Today, especially, violating the law is more than mere social deviance.[61] Criminally defined activity is actually *political* behavior. Actions against the law are becoming ideological in orientation, directed toward restructuring the social and political order. When persons and groups of persons try to reach the goals they want by means of actions against the established order, the representatives of that order are likely to respond by formulating and applying criminal definitions.

Actions are a part of developing a self, and they become patterned. For many, these action patterns have a fairly high probability of being defined by others (and perhaps by self) as criminal. But in expressing such actions, people develop self-conceptions. Criminally defined behavior, like any other behavior, has meaning to the actors and is pursued in achieving self.

The role of the self in developing action patterns that may be defined as criminal or delinquent was explored in an investigation lasting several years, mostly under the direction of Walter C. Reckless. The researchers examined the *self-concepts* of teen-age boys to determine whether or not variations in conceptions of self account for specific patterns of behavior. The initial study explored and described the responses of 125 "good" boys, nominated by their teachers and substantiated by official records as nondelinquent, to a battery of self-evaluation items. The researchers reported that the 125 boys portrayed themselves as law-abiding and obedient.

> Specifically, the vast majority defined themselves as being stricter about right and wrong than most people, indicated that they attempted to keep out of trouble at all costs and further indicated that they tried to conform to the expectations of their parents, teachers, and others. The nominees did not conceive of themselves as prospects for juvenile court action or detention, and they stated that their participation in such activities as stealing had been minimal and that their friends were either entirely or almost completely free of police and juvenile court contact.[62]

In subsequent research the authors reported that the "bad" boys' self-concepts consisted of perceptions of getting into trouble, having friends who were in trouble, disliking school, expecting to go to jail, and so on.[63] Follow-up studies of the "good" and "bad" boys indicated that the earlier self-conceptions were predictive of later behavior, a much greater proportion of boys with "poor" concepts of self having juvenile court records than boys with "good" self-conceptions.[64] The authors have proposed that the concept of self can insulate youths in high delinquency areas from involvement in delinquency.

In our quest to discover what insulates a boy against delinquency in a high delinquency area, we believe we have some tangible evidence that a good self-concept, undoubtedly a product of favorable socialization, veers slum boys away from delinquency, while a poor self-concept, a product of unfavorable socialization, gives the slum boy no resistance to deviancy, delinquent companions, or delinquent subculture. We feel that components of the self-strength, such as a favorable concept of self, act as an inner buffer or inner containment against deviancy, distraction, lure, and pressures.[65]

Such research clearly supports the position that self-conceptions and action patterns are interdependent.[66] Yet, this research requires some reinterpretation to take into account the theory of the social reality of crime. I argue that *both* those who engage in behavior that is not usually defined as criminal or delinquent ("good" boys) and those who engage in behavior that has a high probability of being defined as criminal or delinquent ("bad" boys) are involved in meaningful social actions. Their respective self-conceptions and actions are personally appropriate. Only from the perspective of others' standards can self-conceptions and actions be evaluated positively or negatively, as "appropriate" or "inappropriate," "good" or "bad." A boy's affirmative answer to a question about the possibility that he will appear in juvenile court does not necessarily show an "inappropriate" or "poor" self-concept, but is more a personal prediction of future events based on past experience.[67] From each person's perspective, all action patterns, no matter how others evaluate them, are personally meaningful. Behavior that may be defined as criminal by others is behavior that is pursued in achieving self.

Association, Learning, Identification, and Commitment

Each person constructs a "reality world," one's own view of the self and all that is about the self. Only as we participate in others' worlds, however, are we able to develop our own world. In other words, by occupying space with others in a social setting, we share a symbolic environment.[68]

Shared meanings are provided for most persons by membership in some kind of social group. According to *reference group* terminology, social groups furnish members with a frame of reference to organize perceptions and experiences.[69] People act, then, in reference to the perspectives of their groups. Furthermore, their actions are in part an attempt to preserve and enhance social status within their groups. Consequently, we can look for an explanation for variations in people's behavior in their group experiences.

The theory of *differential association*, as first formulated by Edwin H. Sutherland, provides such an explanation of "criminal" behavior.[70] All persons acquire their behavior during associations with others. Some, however, become criminal because their associations involve an excess of definitions favorable to violating the law. The theory of differential association extends the theoretical perspective of the socialization that occurs in primary groups.[71] The learning of "criminal" behavior patterns is not fundamentally different from other socialization, during which the individual is differentially exposed to various norms about some socially significant form of behavior.

The problem in the theory of differential association, however, has been not so much theoretical as empirical. Few systematic guides are provided for empirically verifying the theory. The theory was formulated at such a high level of abstraction that it has not been possible to test it with empirical data. At best, it has been subject only to partial testing by research on the variables of association, including the frequency, duration, priority, and intensity of association. These limited studies, nevertheless, have shown that people who associate with delinquents (however defined) report more or engage in more alleged delinquent behavior than those who associate with others.[72]

Although the general principle of differential association probably holds for much behavior that is defined as delinquent and criminal, variations in the theory can be expected in concrete situations. To explore and explain these variations, the theory can be reformulated according to the logical and explanatory relations of such conceptual units as "criminal behavior," "symbolic interaction," "primary groups," "selective pattern of exposure," "crime-related learning," and others.[73] In turn, if the theory is to be empirically tested, each unit must be divided into further subclasses of elements. Testable hypotheses can then be derived from the possible relations between the subclasses of the conceptual units. That is, separate hypotheses of differential association can be derived and tested on such matters as the kind of offense, the kind of interaction, the characteristics of the primary groups, and the type of normative exposure. When some of the derived hypotheses are empirically tested, the role of association in developing personal action patterns in relation to criminal definitions is likely not only to be supported, but to be strengthened by specification according to different types of social situations.

This strategy tells us that there is more to learning criminally defined behavior than simple association with other people. Not only are other processes involved, but association itself is complex. The theory has been reconceptualized by Daniel Glaser according to an imagery of role playing.[74] The concept of differential association is first replaced by that of *differential identification*. All persons, accordingly, identify with others, that is, view their own behavior from the perspective of other people. Moreover, most identify with both "criminal" and "noncriminal" persons, by direct association, by reference to criminal roles portrayed in mass media, or as a negative reaction to forces opposed to crime. "The theory of differential identification, in essence, is that a person pursues criminal behavior to the extent that he identifies himself with real or imaginary persons from whose perspective his criminal behavior seems acceptable."[75] Thus, people who engage in criminally defined behavior identify with and consequently direct their actions toward those who are behaving similarly. All factors are important in the theory of differential identification, depending on how much they affect the choice of the others from whose perspective one views his

or her own behavior. Our choices vary, and so accordingly do our behaviors.

According to the perspective we have developed thus far, the individual engages in behavior, some of which may be defined as criminal or delinquent, rationally and voluntarily. In any situation the individual acts according to his own evaluation of the situation and according to his reference to others. In the language of learning theory, social actions may be conceptualized as *operant* behavior, that is, behavior emitted in the presence of specified conditions and maintained by its consequences. In other words, the behavior is stimulated by expecting a specific response. Most social behaviors are operant, ranging from such forms as handshaking and sexual behavior to wearing clothing and driving a car. Social relations are maintained by the consequences they produce for the interacting parties. Thus it has been argued that criminally defined behavior is also operant behavior: "Criminal behavior is maintained by its consequences, both material and social."[76] The criminally defined behaves in order to produce a personally desired effect, whether it is acquiring money, sexual gratification, or removing another person.

The concept of operant behavior as it applies to criminally defined behavior has been employed in a thorough revision of the theory of differential association.[77] Each proposition of the theory was reformulated by Burgess and Akers on the principle that behavior is a function of its past and current environmental consequences. The authors used the related idea of *reinforcement* — actions are repeated according to the behavior's consequences to the actor. They suggest, among other things, that criminal behavior is learned according to the principles of operant conditioning and that a person engages in the behaviors that have been most highly reinforced in the past. Consequently, some people engage in criminally defined behavior because it has been more highly reinforced than other behavior. Personal action patterns, some of which may be defined as criminal, thus develop in reference to others' responses. Actions are utilitarian, being pursued and repeated for their personal consequences.

The decision of whether or not to engage in behavior that has a high probability of being defined as criminal is based on what the person considers the consequences a course of action will bring. When confronted with a situation that may be resolved by actions that may be criminally defined, a person may evaluate the consequences of one form of action over another. Among the considerations that affect a decision to act in a specific way is your *commitment* to contingency interests.[78] That is, you may consider the consequences of some line of action for interests no more than indirectly associated with the present situation. Acting persons may have "commitments to conformity: not only fear of the material deprivations and punishments which might result from being discovered as an offender but also apprehension about the deleterious consequences of such a discovery on one's attempts to maintain a consistent self-image, to sustain valued relationships, and to preserve current and future statuses and activities."[79] Those who have strong commitments to law-abiding behavior are not likely to engage in actions that have a high probability of being defined as criminal. The consequences would not be to their advantage.[80]

But for most, commitment to the legal code and its specific laws is not a stable and constant matter. People vary in their commitments during their lives and, furthermore, qualify their commitments according to the immediate context of their actions. Delinquents *drift*, as David Matza suggests, between standards of conduct. "The delinquent transiently exists in a limbo between convention and crime, responding in turn to the demands of each, flirting now with one, now the other, but postponing commitment, evading decision. Thus, he drifts between criminal and conventional action."[81] Flexibility in their commitment to legal standards is used temporarily by delinquents, especially, to lessen the control of legal norms on their actions.[82] Persons violating the law are thus able at the same time to maintain some commitment to the standards of the law. Actions defined as either criminal or delinquent do not necessarily represent commitment to violation itself, but are more likely to be

episodic actions calculated to produce specific consequences for the actors.

According to a social control theory, delinquent and criminal acts generally occur when a person's "bond" to society is weak or broken. The conforming individual maintains an allegiance to conventional norms and practices, but the deviant is likely not to be attached to conventional ways.[83] Those who do not share in the rewards of the system, including those engaged in rejecting these "rewards," will behave in ways that will be defined as criminal by those who uphold the system. Many of those who aspire to a new life tomorrow are the deviants and criminals of today.

Persons may behave, then, looking ahead to the consequences of their actions. The consequences they desire are socially learned. They act in the context of group association and identification. Their commitments to one group rather than others, and their shifts in such commitments, are always problematic. But with one's past behavior, present interests, and future hopes, actions are considered for their possible ramifications. Whether the actions will be defined as criminal by others may or may not be one of the things one considers when acting in a concrete situation.

Action Patterns and Criminal Definition

Personal actions are symbolic both for the actors and the respondents. As interaction continues between parties, or as the actor confronts similar situations, the meanings of personal actions become more firmly established. Eventually we develop patterns of actions in reference to our interactions with others. *Social reactions* of others are important in developing such patterns. In the reactions of others we learn to regard ourselves in a specific way. What we become, including how we behave, will depend very much on the way we have been and continue to be assessed and defined by others.

Most reactions of others are directed toward controlling personal actions.[84] These social reactions to behavior come from various sources. Generally, social reaction is found in the informal judgments of others in face-to-face encounters, and also in the organized formal control of private or public agencies. Both forms of reaction provide social definitions of a situation. The actions of some persons are singled out for special consideration by others during social reaction.

Although social reaction operates as social control, it is at the same time a means of *conferring* definitions on persons, probably producing the actions that are the object of control. That is to say, as others react negatively to your actions, you begin to accept the definitions others have conferred on you. This self-definition according to the definitions of others was pointed out some time ago in a discussion of how a community may react to a juvenile's adventurous behavior by eventually defining the child as bad. He or she responds by accepting the definition and acting in reference to it.

> From the community's point of view, the individual who used to do bad and mischievous things has now become a bad and unredeemable human being. From the individual's point of view there has taken place a similar change. He has gone slowly from a sense of grievance and injustice, of being unduly mistreated and punished, to a recognition that the definition of him as a human being is different from that of other boys in his neighborhood, his school, street, community. This recognition on his part becomes a process of self-identification and integration with the group which shares his activities. It becomes, in part, a process of rationalization; in part, a simple response to a specialized type of stimulus. The young delinquent becomes bad because he is defined as bad and because he is not believed if he is good. There is a persistent demand for consistency in character. The community cannot deal with people whom it cannot define. Reputation is this sort of public definition.[85]

You are likely to become the thing you are described as being.

Defining a person negatively, therefore, affects the person's definition of himself and his subsequent actions. People may channel their efforts toward behaviors that have a high potential of criminality because they have been defined as being deviant in some way. Accordingly, much of the research and writing on of-

fenders' physical characteristics can be reinterpreted as social definitions. The physical stereotypes of the criminal may often characterize specific offenders, but the relationship is not so much genetic as it is a self-fulfillment of others' perceptions and definitions. It may well be that some offenders conform to Lombroso's "stigmata" of overly small or large head, asymmetry of face, ears of unusual size, receding chin, and so forth.[86] People with such characteristics are not savage "throwbacks," however, but they are people who are endowed with human characteristics, defined by others as deviant (both physically and socially); to be officially defined as criminal; and to engage in the behaviors consistent with the status they have been assigned.

Similarly, many of the notorious outlaws of the West may have had red hair.[87] Yet, being redheaded did not genetically make such men and women criminals. Rather the social definitions of others prescribed redheaded people as deviant, thus making the consequence true. In the same way we may accept the finding that delinquents usually are mesomorphs (muscular, athletic, and aggressive).[88] Boys of such appearance and temperament are probably more likely than other boys to be recruited into juvenile gangs and to engage in behaviors that may readily be defined as delinquent. Physical characteristics are first socially defined, then self-defined in relation to social reactions, and subsequently shape the patterning of personal actions. The interaction of physical characteristics, social reactions, and personal action is dramatically illustrated by Richard Speck, slayer of eight Chicago nurses in the summer of 1966. When finally arrested, Speck, who had been described as physically and personally unattractive, was identified by the tattoo on his arm — which read, "Born to raise hell."

The extent to which personal action patterns develop in response to others' social reactions depends on how much the person accepts and adjusts to his assigned role. "Secondary deviation," as proposed by Edwin M. Lemert, is useful in conceptualizing the transition that may occur in a person's self-conception and behavior as he is confronted with social reactions. The deviance imputed to a person remains "primary deviation" to that person as long as it is rationalized or otherwise dealt with as a socially acceptable role. As a person continues to act, and as social reactions are repeated and strengthened, deviation becomes secondary. Lemert writes:

> Secondary deviation refers to a special class of socially defined responses which people make to problems created by the societal reaction to their deviance. These problems are essentially moral problems which revolve around stigmatization, punishments, segregation, and social control. Their general effect is to differentiate the symbolic and interactional environment to which the person responds, so that early or adult socialization is categorically affected. They become central facts of existence for those experiencing them, altering psychic structure, producing specialized organization of social roles and self-regarding attitudes. Actions which have these roles and self attitudes as their referents make up secondary deviance.[89]

People develop such a position toward themselves and others because their identity and actions are organized around the deviance that others have imputed to them.

Defining a person as "criminal" is the extreme form of stigmatization. Criminal conviction — even confrontation with the police and judicial prosecution — modifies a person's identity and actions. The "criminalization of deviance" may thus force those engaged in specific kinds of behavior to redefine themselves and their actions.[90] Such public branding can lead a person to new situations and activities. The development of a new style of life, in turn, increases the probability of further criminal definition. By social reaction, then, in the form of criminal definition, crime is again created and perpetuated.

7

Conventional Crime in American Society

What is criminal behavior like in American society? To further understand crime in the United States, we need to examine the patterns of crime, and then relate them to the whole cultural and structural context of our society.[1]

A large portion of crime is regulated by the traditional criminal laws that cover person, property, and public order. These "conventional" crimes are typical of a system that emphasizes personal safety, protects private property, and maintains a sense of appropriate conduct in the community. Conventional crime consists of many offenses, including murder, assault, forcible rape, robbery, burglary, larceny, vandalism, auto theft, prostitution, homosexuality, drunkenness, drug use, shoplifting, and forgery. Each kind of offense varies along with the offender's characteristics, the context in which the offense happens, and how the offense pattern relates to American society.

Accepting the naturalness of these crimes in American society is our starting point in understanding crime patterns. The structure of the social, economic, and political institutions fundamentally shapes behavior in the society. The class structure of that society provides both the opportunities and barriers for specific kinds of conduct and life style.

A society based on competitive social and economic relations produces its own forms of criminal behavior.[2] Crime is the isolated individual expressing himself against the society's alienating conditions. Much criminal behavior in this country can be called a means of *survival*, an attempt to exist in a society within which survival is not ensured by other, collective, means. Conventional crime, therefore, is basic in American society.

Crimes of Violence

Violence in American Society

Violence is abstractly prohibited by the criminal law as well as by the society's moral values. It is commonly assumed that all violence is antithetical to organized society. In practice, however, violence against other human beings is an idea subject to many qualifications. Killing is a tactic in time of war, as long as the state has people it can define as the "enemy"; those killed or injured under wartime conditions exceed by millions the numbers killed by civilian murder and assault. For a civilian to kill a fellow human being willfully may warrant the death penalty or life imprisonment; for a soldier to do the same to the enemy warrants a medal for heroism. Far more people are killed or injured for reasons of state than by criminal violence.

The United States has a violent history. During the sixties, with conflicts brought on by racial discrimination, war, and other violence, Americans may have been more violent toward one another than in the recent past but probably less violent than in the latter half of the nineteenth century. With such a diverse population and economic structure, immigrant and racial groups were thrown into fierce competition with each other and with the dominant Anglo-American group in their quest for economic security.[3] Built into American society, with class and ethnic divisions, is the practice of violence.

Violence is unevenly used to solve personal and interpersonal problems throughout American society. Violent crimes are closely linked to males, particularly young men; for many people maleness is equated with physical aggression. Male aggression can be a device to maintain supremacy over women, as it seems to be with forcible rape.[4]

That cultural definitions of violence are important is revealed in the wide regional differences in criminal homicide. Homicide rates have consistently been highest in the southern region of the United States. There, cultural definitions promote personal violence in some situations and weapons are carried more in some areas than in others. The pattern of violence in the South, one writer has suggested, lies in historical factors such as the influence of slavery as a repressive system on the culture, the type of immigration (Scotch-Irish and fundamentalist) and, above all, "the development of a Southern world view that defines the social, political and physical environment as hostile."[5]

Possessing weapons is a part of the culture of violence in the United States. A 1969 survey found that Americans have in their possession 90,000,000 firearms, including 24,000,000 hand guns, 35,000,000 rifles, and 31,000,000 shotguns.[6] Forty-nine per cent of the 60.4 million American households reported owning firearms, or 2.2 firearms per household. Such ownership is highest in the South (59 per cent) and lowest in the East (33 per cent). Whereas rifle ownership declines sharply with the size of the community, handgun ownership is slightly higher in large cities than in rural areas or in the suburbs.

Firearms, usually handguns, are commonly used in the United States in crimes involving violence. In the ten years up to 1974, the number of homicides involving firearms increased by about 50 per cent. Firearms permit greater range, more concealment, and attacks by people either unwilling or unable to overpower a victim by other means. When a gun is used the chances of death are five times greater than with a knife. The percentage of homicides and aggravated assaults involving firearms parallels that of firearm ownership; a Detroit study showed that firearms violence increased after an increase in handgun acquisition.[7] In the United States today about one in five serious assaults is committed with a firearm. More than 65 per cent of murder victims are killed by a gun.

The conventional forms of violence — murder, aggravated assault, armed robbery, and forcible rape — are found almost exclusively in the lower class. Nine out of ten criminal homicides in Philadelphia were committed by persons in the lower-class occupations such as laborers. Very few homicides were committed by those in white-collar occupations.[8] The norms of the lower class include violence as a means of resolving conflicts. And in the larger social structure, people of the lower class are constantly confronted with problems that demand solutions in which violence has a rational part.

Social Relationships

Most murders and aggravated assaults are concrete responses, growing out of social interaction between one or more parties, to situations which come to be defined as requiring that violence be used. Violence may result from one argument or dispute or from a series of arguments, sometimes extending over years, between husband and wife, lovers, neighbors, or fellow employees. Verbalization in these arguments declines, and emotional reactions increase, until, in a final argument, a climax is built up, and one of the parties is injured or killed with a weapon.

Because of the interplay between persons in a situation leading to violence, the victim often "causes" his or her own death or serious injury. A Philadelphia study showed that more than one in four criminal homicides were precipitated by the victim, who first showed or used a deadly weapon or struck a blow in an altercation.[9] Victim-precipitated homicides were found to be significantly associated with blacks, victim-offender relationships involving male victims of female offenders, mate slaying, alcohol in the homicide situation or in the victim, and victims with a record of assault or arrest. Other homicides, not included in this figure, involved infidelity of a mate or lover, failure of the victim to pay a debt, and use of vile names by the victim in such a manner that the victim contributes to the homicide.

Homicide and assault are similar in that they both often involve interaction between relatives, friends, or acquaintances. Moreover: "The ostensible motives in homicide and assault are often relatively trivial, usually involving spontaneous altercations, family quarrels, jealous rages, and the like. The two crimes are similar; there is often no reason to believe that the person guilty of homicide sets out with any more intention to harm than the one who commits an aggravated assault. Except for the seriousness of the final outcomes, the major distinction is that homicides most often involve handguns while knives are most common in assault."[10] Although people in American cities often worry about physical assaults by strangers on the streets, personal violence is far less likely to come from a stranger. According to a survey, about 70 per cent of willful killings, nearly two-thirds of aggravated assaults, and high percentages of forcible rapes are committed by family members and others previously known to the victims.[11]

A government survey involving a 10 per cent random sample of offense and arrest reports in seventeen large cities found that only a fifth of assaults involved strangers, which was considerably higher even than the figure for homicide.[12] This study also found that one in four of 668 criminal homicides was between family members and 9 per cent involved other primary group relationships, 15.4 per cent involved an acquaintance, and only 15.6 per cent were committed by strangers. Forcible rape, however, was found slightly more likely to be committed by a stranger (53 per cent), with the balance by people with whom the victim had some acquaintance.

Likewise, many crimes of violence are *intraracial*, carried out against persons of one's own racial group: most homicide, aggravated assault, and forcible rape consists of whites victimizing whites and blacks victimizing blacks. In the study of seventeen large cities, it was found that 24 per cent of the homicides were between whites and 66 per cent between blacks (Table 7.1).[13] Six per cent involved blacks killing whites and 4 per cent whites killing blacks. In a Houston study 97 per cent of the black victims were killed by blacks, 91 per cent of the white victims were killed by whites. Eighty-six per cent of the Latin-Americans were killed by other Latin-Americans.[14] In Chicago only 6.6 per cent of the criminal homicides were interracial, and of this small number 80 per cent involved the killing of whites by non-whites.[15] A larger government survey of 1,493 aggravated assault cases in seventeen large cities found that one-fourth of the assaults were between whites, 66 per cent between blacks, 8 per cent involved blacks attacking whites, and 2 per cent involved whites attacking blacks.[16] The study also found that 90 per cent of the forcible rapes were intraracial; of these 30 per cent were both white, 60 per cent were both black, 10 per cent were whites raping blacks, and less than 1 per cent were blacks raping whites. It is finally in the interpersonal relations of people that the conditions and forces of American society are made manifest.

Crimes against Property

Property Crimes in American Society

Property crimes — especially larceny and burglary — are among the most important crimes

Table 7.1.   Characteristics of the Victim and the Offender by Sex, Race, and Age, Criminal Homicide in 17 Cities, 1967 (in percentages)[a]

	Sex of Victim			Total (Victims)[b]	
Sex of Offender	*Male*	*Female*			
Male	62.3%	17.5%		79.8%	(455)[c]
Female	16.4	3.8		20.2	(115)
Total (offenders)[b]	78.7	(449)	21.3	(121)	100.0	(570)

	Race of Victim			Total (Victims)[b]	
Race of Offender	*White*	*Negro*			
White	24.0%	3.8%		27.8%	(159)[c]
Negro	6.5	65.7		72.2	(412)
Total (offenders)[b]	30.5	(174)	69.5	(397)	100.0	(571)

	Age of Victim				Total (Victims)[b]	
Age of Offender	*0–17*	*18–25*	*26 and over*			
0–17	3.3%	1.6%	4.2%		9.1%	(49)[c]
18–25	3.6	10.3	19.8		33.5	(182)
26 and over	3.5	6.7	47.0		57.4	(311)
Total (offenders)[b]	10.4	(56)	18.6	(101)	71.0	(385)	100.0	(542)

[a] Total number of known criminal homicide victim-offender interactions, by sex, 570; by race, 571; by age, 542. Frequencies weighted according to total reported violent crimes for 1967, by type, in the 17 cities surveyed.
[b] Total row and column percentages may not exactly equal 100.0 per cent because of the weighting procedure and rounding.
[c] Numbers are given in parentheses.
Source: Crimes of Violence, Vol. 11, A Staff Report Submitted to the National Commission on the Causes and Prevention of Violence, Donald J. Mulvihill and Melvin M. Tumin, Co-Directors (Washington, D.C.: U.S. Government Printing Office, 1969), p. 210.

in American society because they violate the value placed on private property. A value system that emphasizes property, however, contains its own contradictions about the violation of that property. Although property is cherished and protected, the desire to acquire it, by whatever means necessary, is great too. The same normative system that protects the property stimulates the need to gain more of it. It is in this contradiction that crimes against property must be understood.

Those who engage in property crimes (probably a good portion of the population) differ from one another in the extent to which they violate the criminal law in acquiring property. Property crimes also make up different proportions of their livelihood. And the offenders vary in their skills and techniques for committing property offenses. Some offenders violate the law occasionally and others make a career of it. All of them share the belief in the importance of private property, their difference is in the frequency and degree to which they will violate the law to achieve that goal.

Most offenders who occasionally commit property crimes are relatively committed to the values of society. Naive check forgers "appear to have acquired normal attitudes and habits of law observance."[17] Adult department store pilferers are generally "respectable" citizens who have little or no contact with criminal groups.[18] Juveniles involved in joyriding (involving auto theft) either have no criminal record or none other than for auto theft and are likely to come from conventional middle-class neighborhoods.[19]

Occasional property crime as a rejection of the dominant behavior patterns is open to question in other forms of property crime. Much destruction of property by vandalism seems to be a way of challenging the values placed on private property in our society. Evidence is increasing that middle-class behavior patterns are not internalized by all persons and groups and that many law violators are involved in a world of their own relatively isolated from the dominant class of American society.[20]

The tentative and sporadic commitment to the dominant culture is evident among those who more regularly engage in property crimes, especially among juveniles. Delinquents do not completely reject the dominant values and norms of the larger society but neutralize them in violating the law. Such delinquents also make use of the "subterranean values" of the dominant society, using these as a code of behavior instead of reserving them for leisure-time activities. Being uncommitted, the delinquent "drifts" between a delinquent and a nondelinquent way of life.[21]

In a society that values the acquisition of property but is structured with economic inequality, property crime is inevitable. Criminal patterns may develop as solutions to the problem of acquiring that which is valued. Property crime is an integral part of a society that both values property and limits the possibility for obtaining it.

Careers of Property Offenders

The conventional property offender is generally a product of the areas of poverty in which juvenile gangs are active. Some indication of this is the fact that the fifty-seven largest cities with populations of more than 250,000 account for nearly three out of four robberies committed annually in the United States. Violent personal offenders come out of these areas, and also offenders who commit robbery and burglary. A government report concluded that "Study after study in city after city in all regions of the country have traced the variations in the rates for these crimes. The results, with monotonous regularity, show that the

offenses, the *victims*, and the *offenders* are found most frequently in the poorest, and most deteriorated and socially disorganized areas of cities."[22]

Thus, it is common for property offenders to begin their careers early in life as juvenile delinquents in a class-divided society. People from fifteen to seventeen years of age are the group most frequently arrested for burglaries, larcenies, and auto theft. In 1972, 51 per cent of those arrested for burglary were under eighteen, and 19.8 per cent were under twenty-one. For auto theft, 53.6 per cent were under eighteen and 71.5 per cent were under twenty-one. Comparable figures for robbery were 31.9 per cent under eighteen and 54 per cent under twenty-one.[23] A Philadelphia study found that the highest arrest rates in the population for robbery were for ages 15 to 19 and 20 to 24.[24] The early life histories of these offenders show a pattern of truancy, destruction of property, street fighting, and delinquent gang membership. By the time they are young adults, they have an extensive history of contact with the law, and may have had some experience in an institution.

As juvenile offenders progress into conventional career crime, they become more committed to crime as a way of life and develop a criminal self-conception. Because of repeated offenses and subsequent arrests and convictions, conventional offenders eventually identify with crime. Occasional property offenders who pursue criminal activity only sporadically experience vacillating self-conceptions. But for conventional criminals who regularly commit offenses, a criminal self-conception is almost inescapable. And because property offenders are dealt with rather severely before the law, by arrest and sentencing, such offenders readily come to regard themselves as criminals. The criminal record is a constant reminder that the person has been stigmatized by the society, and may construct a vicious circle in which the offender continues in a life of crime.

Conventional property criminals are likely to have a diversified offense record, committing a number of offenses that may include theft, larceny, robbery, and burglary. The amount of money involved in each offense is relatively small, the offenses provide a part of the offenders' livelihood, and must be repeated regularly. Many people arrested for robbery have records in theft rather than in acts of violence. A Boston study of robbery suspects apprehended during the first six months of 1968 found that among juveniles five times as many had been previously arrested for theft as for violent crimes.[25] National figures show that for suspects under seventeen the ratio is about 7 to 1. A Philadelphia study of arrests for robbery reported:

> Using different types of indexes of prior police arrest record, our study reveals that when an offender has a previous record, he is much more likely to have a criminal profile of offenses against property than against the person. For example, only 4 percent of the offenders have a past profile of assault, but 45 percent have a pattern of robbery, larceny or burglary. There is no significant difference between Negro and white offenders in this respect; neither is there a difference in criminal background between the violent and non-violent robbers of our study. Robbers, thus, are not a special class, but are primarily thieves who occasionally, though rarely, use force to achieve their objects. The display of violence in this context is on the whole an isolated episode. It is general persistence in crime, not a widespread specialization in crimes of violence, which is the main characteristic of robbers.[26]

Because of their relative lack of skill and organization, property offenders, compared with organized and professional criminals, are more likely to be eventually arrested and imprisoned. Consequently, conventional property offenders form a large portion of the prison population — perhaps as many as half the inmates.[27] With similar offenders in mind, Gibbons said this about the career of these criminals:

> Many semiprofessionals spend a considerable part of their early adult years in penal institutions where they are likely to be identified as "right guys" or antiadministration inmates. It does not appear that conventional treatment efforts are successful in deflecting many of these persons away from continuation in crime. On the other hand, many of them ultimately do withdraw from crime careers upon reaching the early middle-age period.[28]

When crime is pursued as a way of life, as it is by conventional property offenders, other ways of living are not readily available. Furthermore, the excitement and notoriety of a criminal career may seem more rewarding to the criminal than the hard work, mediocrity, and monotony provided by a respectable, law-abiding career. A group consciousness among criminals makes movement to a law-abiding life less comprehensible and desirable. By their early thirties, most conventional offenders, however, feel that a law-abiding career holds greater possibility than a criminal career that has not been particularly successful. A relatively small number continue on to make professional careers of conventional crime.

A few juvenile gang delinquents continue to engage in illegal activities as adults, particularly as adult conventional career criminals, but it is unclear why many of them discontinue criminal behavior in their mid-twenties or early thirties. One writer has pointed out that "it is much easier to determine why offenders continue in criminal careers than it is to understand what makes them quit."[29] As they grow older, they lose touch with deviant and criminal associates because of marriage and family responsibilities. Such a change in life style is more important in breaking a criminal pattern than are attempts at rehabilitation in correctional institutions.

Property Crime as a Profession

Some people engage in highly specialized property crimes explicitly for economic gain. By skill and sometimes by elaborate techniques, many of these professional criminals are able to acquire large sums of money without being arrested or prosecuted. Their activities include pickpocketing, shoplifting, sneak-thieving from stores, stealing from jewelry stores by substituting articles, stealing from hotel rooms, and miscellaneous rackets, such as passing illegal checks and extorting money from others engaged in illegal behavior.

Professional criminals come from better economic backgrounds than do other conventional property offenders. A person entering a career of professional crime may continue to engage in legitimate employment until he is successful in crime. Professional criminals are also likely to begin their careers at a relatively late age. Furthermore, once in professional crime, they continue in it for the rest of their lives. The confidence man's career has been summarized as follows:

> The con man begins his special career at a much older age than other criminals, or perhaps it is better said that he continues his criminal career at a time when others may be relinquishing theirs. Unemployment occasioned by old age does not seem to be a problem of con men; age ripens their skills, insight, and wit, and it also increases the confidence they inspire in their victims. With age the con man may give up the position of the roper and shift to being an inside man, but even this may not be absolutely necessary. It is possible that cultural changes outmode the particular con games older men have been accustomed to playing and thereby decrease their earnings somewhat, but this seems unlikely. We know of one con man who is seventy years of age and has a bad heart, but he is still as effective as he ever was.[30]

Longevity in crime is attributable in part, of course, to the fact that very few professional criminals are ever arrested, brought to trial, convicted, or serve time in prison.

Professional offenders develop a philosophy of life to justify their actions and to enhance their self-images. They believe that all men are actually dishonest, and justify their behavior by believing that all persons would violate the law if they had the skill and opportunity. Joseph "Yellow Kid" Weil, a successful confidence man, said of himself:

> The men I fleeced were basically no more honest than I was. One of the motivating factors in my action was, of course, the desire to acquire money. The other motive was a lust for adventure. The men I swindled were also motivated by a desire to acquire money, and they didn't care at whose expense they got it. I was particular. I took money only from those who could afford it and were willing to go in with me in schemes they fancied would fleece others.[31]

Professional offenders can thus justify their own behavior by the conduct of their victims, who, after all, have been willing to participate in an illegal act. Such rationalizations are shared and supported by professional offenders in their associations with one another.

Group associations are important among professional offenders, as we see by the way in which people are recruited into the world of professional theft: recognition by other professional thieves is the essential quality.[32] Without that recognition, no amount of knowledge and experience can provide the offender with the qualifications for a successful career built around the social role of the professional offender.

To be recognized by established professional thieves, two elements are necessary: selection and tutelage. Selection takes place as professional offenders come in contact with other offenders (amateur thieves, burglars), with those on the fringes of crime (pimps, "fences"), or with people in legitimate occupations. The contacts are made in places where professional offenders are working, in jails, or in places of leisure-time activities. Selection, which must be by mutual agreement between established and prospective professionals, is followed by a probationary period in which the neophyte learns the skills, techniques, attitudes, and values of the professional offender. The person assimilates standards of group morality, such as honesty among professionals and not informing on others. Gradually they become acquainted with other professional thieves. They eventually acquire the special language or argot by which members communicate.[33] With such knowledge and expertise, the person develops a life in a world that is shared with other professional offenders.

The social nature of other forms of professional crime is somewhat different from that of professional theft. Some professional criminals may work alone, and some are self-taught, requiring little tutelage or recognition. For fraudulent check writing, little training is necessary; the skills required are elementary. One professional offender's learning has been described:

> He was first a check writer, which is a craft requiring little or no tutelage. It takes no great flash of wisdom to realize that people will give you money for a slice of paper

or to realize that if you are going to depend on that for your livelihood, it might be more pleasant to use names other than your own. Highly skilled craft aspects, such as check raising, are now fairly rare. The problem in check passing is handling the person with the money you want, and that is dependent on personal style rather than technical skill. Check writing is a solitary profession, it is better done alone, it is one in which the worst thing that can happen is to become well-known. Check writers do not socialize very well; they may meet in jail, but they do not tend to hang around together outside.[34]

Check writing is not the only professional crime that can be successfully executed alone and without a great deal of training. Although professional shoplifters sometimes work in small troupes, many prefer to work alone.[35] Lemert found in his study of check forgers that these offenders carefully avoid contacts and interaction with other criminals:

> Moreover, their preference for solitude and their secretiveness give every appearance of a highly generalized reaction; they avoid not only cooperative crime but also any other kinds of association with criminals. They are equally selective and cautious in their contacts and associations with the noncriminal population, preferring not to become involved in any enduring personal relationships.[36]

And in armed robbery, when career offenders do have social organization, it is usually in the form of a partnership. Not a permanent association of offenders, group activity is smaller and more flexible:

> Hence there is little evidence in the social organization of robbers of group cohesion during periods of stress in the manner described by Sutherland. The robber's organization is a more fluid arrangement taking into account existing conditions; it is not conceived by those involved as a permanent group but more or less a loose confederation of individuals joined together for a specific purpose on a short-term basis. Among certain types of robbers specific role relationships do develop; however, these always are assumed to be temporary by the robbery participants even though the association is

of some duration. When this type of social organization exists no provision need be made for incapacitated members; each member considers himself on his own.[37]

Professional property crime, nevertheless, continues to exist because the activity is related to other patterns in the society. Not only are professional criminals engaged in a full-time economic activity, but they provide services for other people. Many forms of professional crime, especially the confidence game, depend on cooperation by normally law-abiding people who serve as accomplices. Also involved are those who assist in "fixing" cases, including police, attorneys, and judges. And the "fences" assist in distributing stolen property.[38]

The close association between professional crime and the dominant society is finally evident in the patterns of professional crime, and the changes in these patterns. A task force report by the President's Crime Commission found these associations and changes:

> As conditions in society change, certain criminal occupations become relatively unprofitable, and other opportunities develop. The nature of crime will tend to change accordingly. Criminal activity like legitimate business activity may respond to the market, to supply and demand curves, and to technological developments. Professional crime, guided by the profit motive, can be expected to be particularly responsive to such factors. One example is the reported decline in safecracking. This is apparently due in part to such factors as increased law enforcement surveillance and mobility, and improvements in the design of safes. Undoubtedly the fact that safes no longer play an important role has also contributed to the decline — modern economic transactions involve the transfer of credits much more than the transfer of cash. Thus it may have become both more difficult and riskier to rob safes, and also less profitable. At the same time, more promising opportunities for crime have arisen. One of these is check-passing. The Commission's study learned that nearly every burglar nowadays is also in the check business. One professional burglar said that in one period of several weeks between burglaries he passed over $20,000 of stolen

checks. A generation ago burglars did not even look for checks to steal.[39]

Other changes in professional crime, influenced by social and economic changes, include crimes related to the automobile, such as auto theft, auto stripping, and stealing from parked cars. There has also been a rapid increase in frauds related to home improvement and insurance. In general, professional criminals are turning from picking pockets, confidence games, and bank robbery to other economic opportunities. Professional crime, like legitimate activities, must alter its enterprises, diversify, or reorganize to remain solvent.

Crimes of the Public Order

Public Order Crimes in America

The largest proportion of officially defined crimes are violations against public order. Included among these offenses, defined as criminal in various ways, are prostitution, homosexuality, drunkenness, selling and using narcotics, gambling, traffic violations, disorderly conduct, and vagrancy. Although there are striking differences in the various behaviors, all the offenses violate in some way the sense of public order held by the dominant class.

Yet, much of the behavior of public order offenders is consistent with the behavior patterns dominant in the society. Users of drugs, prostitutes, homosexuals, traffic violators, excessive drinkers, and so on are not much different in their attitudes toward the society's general goals from those who are engaged in legitimate behaviors. The prostitute's behavior is a response to the female role, representing the further exploitation of women.

> Prostitution is a blatant example of the sexual oppression of women. The sexual ideology and economic exploitation which force poorer women into criminal prostitution are pressures to which all women in our society are subject. . . . The socio-economic structure of our society has in fact served to perpetuate the profession and the ideology that women exist only to serve the pleasures and needs of men.[40]

Prostitution thus becomes a commercial enterprise with the same goals as many other occupations in our society.

Those who engage in homosexual behavior are taking part in a widely practiced sex behavior. The homosexual is involved in a community of friendships, some of which are as lasting as heterosexual marriages.

The use of drugs such as heroin and marijuana, though disapproved, has its counterparts in the frequent use of alcohol, cigarettes, tranquilizers for relaxation, barbiturates for sleeping and relaxation, and other minor drugs such as aspirin. In a sense coffee and tea are also drug stimulants that can have strong effects when consumed regularly in large quantities. Some idea of the wide use of the more accepted drugs is indicated by the manufacture each year of more than a million pounds of barbiturate derivatives in the United States, or the equivalent of 24 half-grain doses for each person in the country, enough to kill each of us twice.[41] In 1957 it was estimated that 7 per cent of the adult population was regularly using tranquilizers, sedatives, and drug stimulants; in 1967 one out of four, or 27 per cent, were doing so.[42]

The economic considerations in many public-order offenses are readily apparent. Much of the behavior involved in these offenses provides an economic commodity for both those who offer the service or product and the dominant culture that receives it. Prostitution is closely allied to regular economic forces: "Our laissez-faire economy and its integration through a price system allows the relatively free operation of supply and demand whether it be commerce in grain futures or sex service."[43] The general male chauvinistic culture makes sexual exploitation possible.

The largest financial gains from public-order crimes, however, are currently made in manufacturing and selling narcotics. The addiction of a large portion of the population provides a lucrative business for those engaged in one way or another with narcotic drugs. Those who profit from the addiction of others are many, ranging from the manufacturers and sellers of narcotics to those involved in controlling narcotics. In the last category is the vast organizational apparatus created to define, process, harass, confine, and "rehabilitate" the drug addict.[44] Criminal syndicates, politicians, the police, agency bureaucrats, and correctional workers have a symbiotic relationship. The relationship has been vividly described:

> The real drug problem in America is that government narcotics bureaucracies and organized crime have had a status quo working relationship for decades. This arrangement denies legitimate opiate addicts reasonable access to their specific medicines. The black market for opiates consequently created serves to increase the number of addicts, not decrease it, serves only to increase the social disorientation of addiction, not cure it, serves to discredit helpless sick citizens, not minister to them. This arrangement increases the pain of addiction. This arrangement profits only Narcotics Control Agencies and Organized Crime Networks. Both depend on continued criminalization of addicts to maintain their complementary parasitic existences. Both groups have grown with the growth of the black market they have created. In this situation the medically sick junkie is a victim, treated like a Jew under Hitler, driven mad in the streets to seek relief from unendurable pain and social degradation imposed on him by police bureaucracy and organized crime.[45]

Public-order offenses, like other kinds of crimes in American society, are deeply embedded in the society's organization and operation. These are produced by the contradiction in society: if a society cannot provide a humane, unalienating existence, it must contend with activities that are defined as criminal. These crimes are at the same time a threat to the society and furnish needed services and commodities for those dominating the society.

Social Context of Public Order Crimes

Crimes such as prostitution, homosexual behavior, and drug use grow out of, and are supported by, rather clearly defined normative patterns in the larger society. Within these social contexts people engage in acts that the dominant society regards as public-order crimes.

Prostitution. Women who engage in acts of prostitution develop attitudes and behavior patterns that are part of the role of being a prostitute: a special language, ways of bartering with customers, impersonal relationships with them, as well as a large number of rationalizations for their activities.[46] The earnings of most prostitutes, even allowing for payments to a pimp or for "protection" from the police, are higher than most working women get.

Prostitutes are generally classified according to methods of operation.[47] There are individual prostitutes, organized houses of prostitution, call-girl and similar arrangements, and "high-class," independent prostitutes. One type is the woman who works in an organized house or brothel. New women are "broken in" to the rules and regulations and each new prostitute soon learns techniques. They learn how to handle a large number of customers without running the risk of losing them as patrons, how to deal with types of men, and how to protect themselves against venereal disease. Another type of prostitute is the call girl, who has contributed greatly to eliminating street soliciting and red-light houses. The call girl often depends on some organization for recruiting her patrons, although she may operate independently and have her own list of patrons who call upon her directly. Patrons are secured more often through an intermediary, such as a bellhop, a hotel desk clerk, or a taxi driver, who, for a fee, will give the patron the telephone number used by the women or arrange for a hotel or motel room. Prostitution is usually associated with panderers or pimps who solicit for the women and often live off their earnings.

Much prostitution is knowingly permitted and may even be encouraged through legitimate, but shady, businesses, such as burlesque shows, night clubs, or amusement parks. Taxi dance halls, particularly, afford opportunities for the dancers to make engagements with their patrons, either in a room hired for the occasion or in the dancer's own room or apartment. Managers and performers in go-go places, cabarets, or burlesque shows have techniques for recruiting patrons for later dates.

Many prostitutes are able to leave the occupation. A few others achieve and maintain a high standard of living. Arrest records, however, make leaving the profession difficult. For many of them, eventually affected by venereal disease, alcoholism, and drug addiction, the end is a derelict life, punctuated more or less regularly by arrests and jail sentences. The illegality of prostitution forces the prostitute into a world of police, courts, and correctional institutions. Her contacts with legal authorities often become complicated by arrests for alcoholism, drugs, and petty theft. Her position makes her vulnerable to blackmail by the police and to other political and legal corruption. Often she is forced by the police to be an informer on thefts and drug use.

Homosexual Behavior. Sex is but one aspect of a total life pattern, generally not independent of it and seldom dominant in it. Labeling a person a "homosexual" is somewhat misleading, making one aspect of life cover the entire pattern; we are not likely to speak of a nonhomosexual and a "heterosexual." There are homosexuals in business and the professions and in lower and upper classes. Some are married, and, like the heterosexual person, have many interests and avocations. But legal definition and harassment by the dominant society have caused homosexuals to be thought distinct from the rest of the population. Homosexuality thus becomes a part of one's self-conception.

Homosexuality also involves learning a social role. This identity grows out of participating in a homosexual subculture. In a small community, homosexuals may be bound by sex and friendship, often cutting across class and occupational lines, relieving anxiety and furnishing social acceptance. Within such groups, narrating sexual experiences and gossip about sexual exploits of others give some unity to the group, and provide a situation that can dramatize adherence to homosexual values.

The homosexual community thus consists of a large number of distinctive groups within which friendship binds the members together in a strong and relatively enduring bond and between which the members are linked by tenuous but repeated sexual contacts. The result is that homosexuals within the city tend to know of each other, to recognize a number of common interests and common moral norms, and to interact on the basis of antagonistic cooperation. This community is in turn linked with other homosexual communities in Canada and the United States, chiefly through the geographical mobility of its members.[48]

The subcultural world of the homosexual has its own special vocabulary, with words such as "gay," "straight," and "queen," and is "similar in some respects to that of the underworld; in others to that of the theater."[49] There are also subculturally defined ways of establishing homosexual relations. In many communities homosexuals gather in special meeting places, usually at street corners, parks, bars, clubs, or lavatories.[50] Recognition by other homosexuals appears to involve specific gestures, clothes, a way of walking, and a special vocabulary. A homosexual group as a subcommunity comes to have its "own status symbols and mythology, and may provide the same kind of social and psychological support that a family group provides for other people."[51]

Those who are involved in homosexual behavior, and the style of life traditionally associated with it, are currently seeking their own liberation.[52] "Coming out" is not only a self-liberating act, but is political as well. Members of the dominant society — which embodies the heterosexual ethos — are being told that a person's sexual life cannot be dictated by the standards of others. Nevertheless, the law stands ready to define as criminal behaviors that violate the moral sense of the dominant members of the community. Sexual liberation is part of the larger movement toward liberating all minority groups.

Drug Use. Most drug users, whether of the hard drugs or marijuana, do not think of themselves as criminals, for they deny the validity of drug laws and consider inhumane and cruel the punishment of what should be a matter of individual choice. Widespread support for their views is found among fellow users of drugs and even among segments of the population of nonusers, particularly for marijuana. Persons who use the opiates seldom think of themselves as real criminals because they see themselves as in a unique situation whenever they are "hooked" on a drug. They feel it is because of necessity that they violate the law by using the drugs or by committing offenses to "support" their habit. Some indication that drug addiction need not be associated with self-regarding criminal attitudes is the fact that in almost all capitalist countries the incidence of drug addiction among doctors is high and, less often, among nurses.[53] The use of drugs is becoming common among a large portion of the population.

People learn to use drugs primarily by associating with others who are users. Most are started by friends and marital partners. They not only learn how to use drugs and appreciate them but they learn positive beliefs about the benefits of drugs, which others help to reinforce constantly.[54] The new user learns about the sources of supply and that he must remain part of the group to ensure this supply.

Marijuana, in particular, is used as a group activity, lending itself to friendship and participation in a group setting. It is smoked in intimate groups, which determines how it affects the individual:

(1) It is characteristically participated in in a group setting; (2) the others with whom one smokes marijuana are usually intimates, intimates of intimates, or potential intimates, rather than strangers; (3) one generally has long-term continuing social relations with the others; (4) a certain degree of value consensus will obtain within the group; (5) a value convergence will occur as a result of progressive group involvement; (6) the activity maintains the circle's cohesion, reaffirms its social bonds by acting them out; (7) participants view the activity as a legitimate basis for identity — they define themselves, as well as others, partly on the basis of whether they have participated in the activity or not.[55]

Drug addiction involves participating in an elaborate subculture supported by group norms, which one writer has called a "survival system."[56] This involves justifying the ideology for drug usage and the "reproductive" system: that addicted persons must continually recruit new members in order to sell them drugs to support their habit. There is also defensive communication, with its own argot for drugs, suppliers, and drug users, which must be learned by the initiates, and the "neighborhood warning systems," in which addicts are protected by others. Supporting the habit requires a complex distribution network of the illegal drugs, a "circulatory" system that teaches addicts how to secure illegal drugs. Drugs are imported and wholesale distribution is made mostly by crime syndicates or other highly organized groups.

Once addicted to a narcotic drug like morphine or heroin, an individual depends on a continuous supply, and this demand usually becomes the most important aspect of his daily life. Although originally these addicts took the drug for pleasure or an effect, most soon take it to ward off the painful withdrawal symptoms. As they build up tolerance and need larger and more frequent dosages, the cost of supporting the addiction may be as high as $15 to $40 or more a day. That is generally more than the addict earns, forcing him to engage in theft or other illegal activities simply to get an adequate supply.

Addicts therefore may engage in petty thefts or prostitution to support their habit. Even when criminal activities become associated with securing funds to maintain the drug habit, crime does not become an end in itself. Addicts, juvenile or adult, who engage in other crime do so chiefly to obtain funds with which to purchase illicit drugs. They may go in for stealing, burglary, or "rolling drunks," occasionally even robbery, to get enough money to buy their drugs. They may break into hospitals and doctors' offices to steal drugs, turn to prostitution, or sell drugs and become drug "pushers" to get enough drugs for their own needs.

The widespread popularity of drugs in the United States supports a criminal population here and a whole class of speculators and growers in the drug-producing countries, but devours our capital and our productivity. Until we devise alternatives to our social, economic, and political ways, a less harmful panacea for life's oppressiveness, drugs will be with us.[57]

Victims of Crime

All crimes have a victim. Specific acts, in fact, are defined as criminal because someone or something is conceived of as a victim. In this sense, then, the victim *precedes* the official definition of an act as criminal. If a victim cannot be related to a specific act, a criminal law is neither created nor enforced. A "victimless" crime can only be one that is defined after the fact by an outside observer.[58]

That every crime has a victim is recognized in the legal definitions of crime. One legal scholar described a crime as "any social harm defined and punishable by law."[59] The "social harm," of course, can be a physical injury to an individual, *if* the state feels that such an injury also threatens its social order, to the most diffuse harm that in some way is regarded as hurting the body social.

Obviously, not all conduct that could conceivably result in social harm is regulated by law. Only acts that cause harm to those who are able to make and enforce the law officially become crimes. And, similarly, when the social harms that are a part of the written law cease to be regarded by those in power as a harm to their interests, these laws are no longer enforced. Every act may conceivably involve a victim, but only the acts that threaten the welfare of the ruling class become crimes. Social harm, no matter how abstract, is a reality decided upon by those who rule.

The presence of a victim, then, the one *officially* designated, is an indication that the social order has been challenged. The victim, a concrete one, apart from the state itself, is held up as a defense of the social order.

Therefore, according to the criminal law and the traditional conception of victimization, *the victim* is the object of *conventional* crime. Someone is a victim when his property is stolen; murder is against another person in particular; and some crimes are committed against the community, or "public order." In all these crimes a victim is the rationale for the law that regulates conventional crime.

Even for conventional crimes, the victims are those who are already oppressed in the society. Except for auto theft, the victims of all the major conventional crimes are disproportionately in the lower income levels.[60] The highest victimization rates for murder, rape, robbery, aggravated assault, burglary, and larceny are in the $0–$2,999 and $3,000–$5,999 income brackets. Except for larceny, the highest rates of victimization are for blacks. The lower class and blacks, in particular, are major victims of conventional crimes.

Why we conceive of some persons as victims and others not as victims is thus a consequence of our common sense assumptions. Our own character is indicated by the kinds of persons we single out as the victims of crime. Those who make proposals for compensating victims are writing as much about themselves as they are about specific programs. And whenever the criminologist confronts the victim, a particular view of reality is being presented.

Thus, it comes as no surprise that other contenders for the category of victim are usually excluded from criminological attention, because it would take an alternative world view to conceive of them. Breaking out of the theory of reality that has dominated conventional thought, we would revise or at least expand our image of victimization and begin to conceive of other victims: those who suffer police force, war, the "correctional" system, state violence, racism and sexism, and oppression of any kind.

To regard one class of persons as victims and another not as victims is therefore an appeal to one's own morality. To argue that abortion is victimless is to exclude the living fetus as a victim. To regard the person who loses property as a victim is to value the sanctity of private property. To conceive of the person who is assaulted as a victim is to hold a view of proper social conduct. And to regard prisoners as criminals rather than as victims of an imperfect system that places them there to begin with and sometimes brutalizes them once they are there is to accept a particular notion of law and order.

8

Crimes of Business in the American Economy

The economic structure of a society generates its own forms of crime. A society that is based on accumulating capital gives rise to criminal conduct also bent on acquiring property and wealth. Pecuniary success is the measure of worth in American society.

Our economy, based on competition and on success at that game, promotes a form of life emphasizing the rightness of any activity pursued in the interest of one's business or occupation. Consequently, "respectable" members of society engage in criminal activities, crimes usually not considered by them or most of the public as criminal. Such business and occupational activities as misrepresentation in advertising, fraudulent financial manipulations, illegal rebates, misappropriating public funds, splitting fees, and fraudulent damage claims are regarded as little more than the American way of doing business. Even organized crime has developed as a form of business in the United States. That which is done in the name of business and gainful employment is usually beyond the reach of law, and it costs much more in social harms than the conventional crimes that receive most of the publicity in our society.

Crimes in Occupations and Professions

Alienation and Survival in Work

Most crime consists of both exploiting others and surviving within the system. People in many occupations survive in their work by taking part, in small ways or massively, in criminal activities, some of them harming those who receive their services. The small businessman who shortchanges the customer is committing an illegal and harmful act against the public. The failing lawyer who arranges to fix a case engages in a criminal act in attempting to survive in the profession.

In less-skilled occupations, people engaging in criminal activity reflect the alienation they suffer in their work. The American worker feels alienated in many ways: powerlessness within the bureaucratic organization of work; work that is meaningless because it is fragmented and impersonal; isolation from other workers; and estrangement from the act of

131

work itself.[1] Marx observed, "The *alienation* of the worker in his product means not only that his labor becomes an object, assumes an *external* existence, but that it exists independently, *outside himself,* and alien to him, and that it stands opposed to him as an autonomous power. The life which he has given to the object sets itself against him as an alien and hostile force."[2] The worker's activity, therefore, is for someone else's benefit and profit, not to satisfy his own social and psychological needs. Being alienated from control of the work means he can get little satisfaction from work itself; work is only to earn wages.

Worker alienation sometimes impels the worker to commit crimes against the system. In the factory he may remove property. Such "pilfering," however, is very selective, indicating moral compunction even in crimes against the alienating bureaucracy.[3] To take property from the company, at least, is to gain some control over the product of one's work.

Crimes against the work situation reflect a struggle, conscious or not, against the exploitation that the worker's life and activity are subjected to. Political actions against employers are fairly common:

On the assembly lines of the American automobile industry, this revolt extends as far as clandestine acts of sabotage against a product (the automobile body) which appears to the worker as the detestable materialization of the social uselessness and individual absurdity of his toil. Along the same lines is the less extreme and more complex example of miners fighting with admirable perseverance against the closing of the mines where they are exploited under inferior human and economic conditions — but who, individually, have no difficulty in recognizing that even if the coal they produced were not so bad and so expensive, their job, under the prevailing conditions, would still be abominable.[4]

These defensive actions could become more politically motivated and organized in the future. For built into the American political economy is the contradiction that ever-increasing economic growth necessitates the kind of labor that further alienates workers from their needs. We may yet see further economic expansion increasing the crimes of survival.

Occupational and Professional Crime

Crimes in occupations and professions must be understood as part of the economic system's structure and culture. The norms and values that prevail in the pursuit of economic gain also regulate the activity of occupational and professional members. Many activities defined as criminal, some of them just recently made criminal, follow closely the dominant patterns of legitimate behavior. A popular ideology supports such crimes as embezzlement:

"Honesty is the best policy, but business is business"; "It is all right to steal a loaf of bread when you are starving"; "All people steal when they get in a tight spot." Once these verbalizations have been assimilated and internalized by individuals, they take a form such as: "I'm only going to use the money temporarily, so I am borrowing, not stealing," or "I have tried to live an honest life but I've had nothing but troubles, so to hell with it."[5]

A symbiotic relationship connects occupational crime and the society's organization. This has been brought to our attention by the discovery that doctors are committing offenses regularly, using the medical insurance system.[6] Not only are they obtaining money excessively and probably illegally for services supposedly rendered, but they are violating income tax laws in doing it. A Treasury official told Congress that more than one doctor out of every three who receives substantial income from treating patients under the Medicare and Medicaid programs is cheating on his income tax. Figures on this tax evasion came out in an investigation of tax returns from 11,000 doctors who received $25,000 or more in Medicare and Medicaid payments in 1968. Because about 65 per cent of the income received by doctors in the United States (estimated as $11.6 billion in 1968) comes from health plans, the violations amount to a sizable sum. Needless to say, without the health plans doctors would have to find money elsewhere if they wanted to maintain their large incomes. The American Medical Association continues to lobby for such programs, rather than support an extensive medical program that would assure care to everyone, possibly at the expense of reducing the doctor's yearly income.

The relationship of occupational crime to the dominant culture is found in most other occupational and professional activities as well. The automobile industry, a key part of the American economy, is a classic example. Criminal conduct in selling and servicing automobiles is built into the market structure of the automobile manufacturing industry. Much of the auto dealer's fraudulent behavior is a result of the forces placed on him by the manufacturer. This is the relationship that sets up the possibility of criminal behavior:

> While only four domestic manufacturers of cars remain, their products are distributed through 30,000 dealers with facilities scattered throughout the United States. Technically, the dealer is an independent businessman. Rarely, however, does he have the capital to acquire more than a fraction of the value of property involved in the dealership. The rest is supplied by the manufacturer, and although the dealer may increase his ownership, rising costs of real estate, equipment and facilities, plus expansion of the dealership, may keep him dependent on the manufacturer for a long time. Further, he operates under restrictive agreement, terms of which are set by the manufacturer.[7]

The auto dealer must meet minimum sales responsibilities, which often leads to fraudulent warranties. He also engages in unscrupulous sales tactics and other behaviors of questionable legality, including high finance charges, parts pushing, service gouging, forcing accessories, and phony repairs.

Thus we can see that occupational and professional crime are closely allied to the dominant patterns in the American social and economic order. Schur discusses "our criminal society":

> Of course, this undercurrent of values conducive to business crimes and related offenses is not surprising, given the extensive influence of the "business spirit" in our society. Indeed, certain of the values that help promote criminality in America are far from being subterranean in character. Thus, sociologist Donald Taft has cited the following "characteristics of American society" as having possible significance in the causation of crime: "its dynamic quality, complexity, materialism, growing impersonality, individualism, insistence upon the importance of status, restricted group loyalties, survivals of frontier traditions, race discrimination, lack of scientific orientation in the social field, tolerance of political corruption, general faith in law, disrespect for some law, and acceptance of quasi-criminal exploitation." While this list is something of a hodgepodge (including some subterranean values, some more dominant ones, and also a few behaviors that are more a result of certain values than values in their own right), the first few items — dynamism, complexity, materialism, impersonality, and individualism — may be especially noteworthy. These are clearly dominant values or characteristics of American life, and they seem in some sense to have very real bearing on at least some types of criminality.[8]

Occupational and Professional Offenders

Offenders in occupations and professions usually regard themselves as respectable citizens, not as criminals. Because the offender is a member of a legitimate occupation, it is difficult to conceive that any activity in that occupation could be a crime. In fact, a noncriminal self-conception is one of the essential elements in this form of crime. Those who violate financial trust, such as embezzlers, are able to engage in such behavior only when they can apply to their own conduct verbalizations allowing them to adjust their opinion of themselves as trusted persons with their concepts of themselves as users of entrusted funds or property.[9] These violators thus define their situations by rationalizations enabling them to regard their violations as essentially noncriminal. They think of their behavior as merely "borrowing," justified by unusual circumstances or a nonsharable problem that can be resolved by violating their position of trust.

Likewise, the life organization of the occupational or professional offender is not built around a criminal role. That person has many roles, the most prominent one being that of respected citizen. The reputations of occupational offenders have been observed in several studies. In an examination of the most flagrant price and rationing violations during World War II in which criminal prosecution was instituted, less than one violator .in ten was reported to have had any criminal record.[10] In studies of other occupational offenders, it has been found that by far the majority of the offenders reside in the most desirable areas of the city.[11] In career and life style, the occupational offender can hardly be distinguished from the nonoffender.

Since Sutherland introduced the idea of white-collar crime, most studies of occupational crime have observed the behavior of occupational offenders in their group associations.[12] Occupational crimes have been explained according to the principle of differential association: criminal behavior is learned from others who define the behavior favorably and in isolation from those who do not. In some occupations members may even learn specific techniques by which the law can be violated, and build up such rationalizations as "business is business," or "good business demands it." This diffusion of illegal practices is spread from someone already in the occupation to new people, and from one business establishment, political machine, or white-collar group to another. The majority of black-market violations in the United States by businessmen appear to have their origins in behavior learned in association with others.[13] Unethical and illegal practices are circulated in the trade as part of a definition of the situation, and rationalizations to support these violations of law are transmitted by this differential association. Types of violations are picked up in conversations with businessmen and from descriptions in trade journals and the press.

Each occupation or profession has its own group norms about the possibility of illegal behavior. Moreover, occupational crimes are related to the structure of the occupation in which the offender is engaged and to the roles the offender plays within the occupation. The importance of the occupation's structure and the offender's role has been shown in a study of violations in filling prescriptions among retail pharmacists.[14] Because retail pharmacy does consist of two divergent occupational role expectations, professional and business, pharmacists experience the problem of adapting to one of several "occupational role organizations," which produce different tendencies toward prescription violation. Pharmacists with an occupational role organization that includes an orientation to the professional role are bound by a system of occupational control that includes guides for compounding and dispensing prescriptions. Pharmacists who lack the professional orientation to pharmacy are not bound by the occupational controls. The business-oriented pharmacists are interested in the general business goal, monetary gain. They subscribe to the popular belief in business that self-employment carries with it independence and freedom from control. The professional norms, as incorporated in the prescription laws, exercise little control over the occupational behavior of the pharmacists who are oriented to the business role. Other occupations and professions probably have their own norms and structures for violating criminal law.

Corporate Crime

Crime in the American Corporate Economy
The problem of crime in America finds its ultimate expression and source in the country's corporate economy. Even under criminal law, much of it enacted just recently, the corporation and its officials are liable for a whole range of harms committed against the people. We recognize today that some parts of our lives and our environment are being victimized by corporations. Both public reaction and criminal law are defining many corporate activities as criminal.

Crimes by corporations must be understood by knowing first their political economy. In modern times, in the United States, "economic power is concentrated in the hands of a relatively few supercorporations that are now moving toward a dominance in the world economy to match their position in the domestic economy."[15] Not only does the economy seem to be determined by corporate power, but the state finds itself increasingly serving the corporate interest.

Our nation is being poisoned with the ultimate threat of extinction by pollution and destruction of our environment, the main factor in which is the plunder of our natural resources. Everybody appears agreed on this. There is a widespread tendency to blame this dangerous situation on science and technology. But the real source of the problem must be sought elsewhere. It lies in the very nature of the social system under which we are forced to live.

The main impulse of our social system is the quest for profit. The result is unplanned, anarchic production, which allows the pollution and indiscriminate plunder of our natural resources. The ones responsible are the monopolies, the corporations, who have made enormous profits while they pollute and destroy our environment. It is estimated that hundreds of billions of dollars will be needed just to remedy the pollution and destruction wrought by the monopolies and their predecessors.

The major victims are the working people, who suffer from the effects of pollution every minute of their lives.[16]

In the United States our existence has been taken for granted. The dominant ideology has consisted of a firm belief that economic growth and technological application are the surest way to progress. The crimes resulting from this ideology and practice are many, including pollution of air, water, and land, adulteration and poisoning of food, and frauds against the consumer. Another of these crimes is the high accident rate and hazardous conditions in factories and mines:

This mass murder, because it takes place within the industrial processes, has always been acceptable to capitalist society as nec-essary and normal. Workers' lives have always been expendable for the corporations. Sixty die from industrial accidents every day. Thousands are maimed and crippled. This, industry cannot deny. In spite of the overwhelming evidence to the contrary, the coal companies still try to deny that the black lung disease, from which hundreds of thousands of coal miners have died, is related to the unhealthy conditions in their coal mines. Corporations in other industries are no different. On the scale of profits, human lives are worthless.[17]

The relationship of corporate crime to the economy is obvious in still other ways, such as the fraudulent methods corporations use to promote their products to the consumer. Corporate advertising is one of the most sophisticated forms of fraud, an integral part of the production and distribution system. Moreover, "any sensitive observer of the American scene recognizes that modern mass advertising at its heart represents a kind of institutionalization of deception and misrepresentation. Indeed many perceptive social critics insist it is nothing less than an enormous swindle — albeit a somewhat genteel one."[18] The prevalence of these violations is indicated in the report that a third of the nation's manufacturers of prescription drugs are violating federal laws prohibiting false and misleading advertising.[19] The drug companies spend approximately $2.4 billion producing drugs and between $600 and $800 million on advertising and promotion. Among the violations are the extending or distorting of claims for usefulness beyond that approved in the product's final printed labeling; quotes from studies used to imply improperly that the study represents a much larger and general experience with the drug; data from papers that report no side effects, ignoring contrary evidence from much better research; and ads constructed from data once valid but rendered obsolete or false by more recent research. Not only is the promotion criminal, but the health and safety of the public are endangered. Many American products, as prescribed in the advertisements, cause thousands of injuries and deaths to consumers each year.[20]

Strong legal actions are not usually taken

against these corporations or their officers. When they are initiated, it is usually by administrative agencies, and they are not a significant problem for the corporation. For often, even after long litigation, the only penalty is a modest fine against the corporation or an insignificant sentence for an official. But companies are usually given advance notice of their violations; they may be asked simply to modify their advertising claims, or to alter or withdraw their product. Court action may be only a last resort. Only fundamental change in our political economy will make a solution to corporate crime possible.

Systematic Crimes

When corporations and their officials violate the criminal law they have appropriate rationalizations for their conduct. They are able to maintain a noncriminal self-conception, as this testimony by a Westinghouse executive in the heavy electrical equipment industry antitrust case illustrates:

> *Committee Attorney:* Did you know that these meetings with competitors were illegal?
> *Witness:* Illegal? Yes, but not criminal. I didn't find that out until I read the indictment. . . . I assumed that criminal action meant damaging someone, and we did not do that. . . . I thought that we were more or less working on a survival basis in order to try to make enough to keep our plant and our employees.[21]

An official of the Ingersoll-Rand Corporation said, "It is against the law." But he added, "I do not know that it is against public welfare because I am not certain that the consumer was actually injured by this operation."

Considering the testimony of the corporate offenders in the electrical equipment cases, Geis offers an explanation that says much about the offenders' rational character and their decision to violate the law:

> For the conspirators there had necessarily to be a conjunction of factors before they could participate in the violations. First, of course, they had to perceive that there would be gains accruing from their behavior. Such gains might be personal and professional, in

terms of corporate advancement toward prestige and power, and they might be vocational, in terms of a more expedient and secure method of carrying out assigned tasks. The offenders also apparently had to be able to neutralize or rationalize their behavior in a manner in keeping with their image of themselves as law-abiding, decent, and respectable persons. The ebb and flow of the price-fixing conspiracy also clearly indicates the relationship, often overlooked in explanations of criminal behavior, between extrinsic conditions and illegal acts. When the market behaved in a manner the executives thought satisfactory, or when enforcement agencies seemed particularly threatening, the conspiracy desisted. When market conditions deteriorated, while corporate pressures for achieving attractive profit-and-loss statements remained constant, and enforcement activity abated, the price-fixing agreements flourished.[22]

Corporate crimes are now being recognized, and the character of the corporation itself as an offender is being understood. The nation's leading corporations appear to be committing destructive criminal acts systematically and repeatedly; not randomly and occasionally, but as a standard operating procedure. To ensure profits at a minimum of expense, these corporations are willfully engaging in crime. As legal entities, they, and some of the corporate officials who make decisions, are criminal.

Crime by corporations receives strong support from similar and even competing individuals and businesses. Lawbreaking becomes a normative pattern in some corporations, and violation norms are shared among corporations and their executives. Corporate officials learn the necessary values, motives, rationalizations, and techniques favorable to specific kinds of crime. Many businessmen may even, for a large part of their day, be isolated from law-abiding definitions of business conduct. Further, businessmen are often shielded from criticism, and may find some support for their activities in the mass media. Then too, business executives associate chiefly with other businessmen, both at work and in their social activities, so that the implications of corporate crime are removed from personal scrutiny.

Corporate crime involves organization among the participants. It may range from the comparatively simple reciprocal relationships in a business transaction to the more complex procedures in the illegal activities among several large corporations. The latter may not only include another corporation, but may extend to many corporations and subsidiaries. The illegal activity may be quite informally organized, as in false advertising, it may be simply organized, though deliberate, as in black market activities, or it may be complex and involved, as in antitrust violations.

The extent of group involvement and rational planning in corporate crime is indicated in the antitrust crimes of the electrical equipment corporations:

> The offenders hid behind a camouflage of fictitious names and conspiratorial codes. The attendance roster for the meetings was known as the "Christmas card list" and the gatherings, interestingly enough, as "choir practice." The offenders used public telephones for much of their communication, and they met either at trade association conventions, where their relationship would appear reasonable, or at sites selected for their anonymity. It is quite noteworthy, in this respect, that while some of the men filed false travel claims, so as to mislead their superiors regarding the city they had visited, they never asked for expense money to places more distant than those they had actually gone to — on the theory, apparently, that whatever else was occurring, it would not do to cheat the company.[23]

The corporate officials would even draw lots to determine who would submit the pricing bids. Promotions within the corporation depended on the officials' willingness to go along with these schemes. Price-fixing, in other words, has become an established way of corporate life.

Operations in the food industry, finally, dramatically illustrate how much corporate support goes to criminal practices.[24] This is the largest retail industry in the United States; the corporations in it are moving toward monopoly of some products. Ninety-five per cent of the prepared soups are sold by Campbell Soup, and 85 per cent of the breakfast food is produced by four firms (Kellogg, General Foods, General Mills, Quaker Oats). Other large corporations are becoming a part of the food conglomerates: the Greyhound Corporation has taken over Armour Foods, International Telephone and Telegraph has taken over Continental Bakery, and so forth. The food business is, of course, a giant industry whose goal is making a profit rather than promoting the consumer's health. And the governmental agency, the Food and Drug Administration, is a defender of the industry's interests, more than an advocate for the public.

The food industry then is relatively free to engage in wholesale deception, misrepresentation in advertising, misbranding, and selling dangerous foods. Hazardous chemicals can be added to foods with inadequate research on their effects. Food preservatives and additives are used to enhance the profits of the industry, possibly harming the consumer's health. Crimes by corporations are crimes against the people.

The Business of Organized Crime

Organized Crime in the American Economy

The economy of American society not only creates and perpetuates criminal activity in business and corporate enterprise, but fosters a kind of crime organized for the explicit purpose of making economic gain by criminal activities. More concretely, "Organized crime is a continuing conspiracy to gain money and power without regard for law by utilizing economic and physical force, public and private corruption, in an extension of the free-enterprise system."[25]

The principal feature that differentiates organized crime from other crimes of business is the degree to which the objective to profit from crime is itself rationalized.[26] Organized crime's objective is to serve the interests of the thousands who have organized themselves into criminal enterprise. Criminal organizations, with their divisions of labor, their permanence, and their ability to escape the law, are businesses that make crime profitable in the American economy.

Organized crime in the United States is a phenomenon of the twentieth century. During the frontier period, outlawed activities were carried out on a modest scale by roving criminal groups. In the cities, criminal groups gained control of illegal activities in their localities, such as gambling, prostitution, distribution of beer and liquor, and rackets. After the turn of the century, organized crime expanded into more activities and extended over larger geographical areas.

One event brought about the greatest change in organized crime: Prohibition, forbidding by law the sale and distribution of alcoholic beverages. Because of the Eighteenth Amendment, adopted in 1920, and the supporting Volstead Act, organized crime was able to provide the illegal services and commodities demanded by millions of citizens. Conflict between organized adult gangs and widespread violence were inevitable as rival groups competed to serve the public. A number of the strongest gangs finally won dominance. These organized groups, because of the large sums of money they amassed and the elaborate organization they achieved, continued in illegal activity after Prohibition was repealed.

The modern era of organized crime is represented by the crime syndicate. Organized crime has expanded so much that leaders coordinate illegal activities across state and regional boundaries. Now organized crime has expanded into many legitimate businesses and occupations. Contrary to popular belief, the national crime syndicate is not limited to Italians in the Mafia.[27] The national crime syndicate, as organized in 1934, is still today a "combination," the Mafia being a minor part of the syndicate. The leader and genius behind the syndicate, in fact, is Meyer Lansky, a man of Jewish background. The history of the syndicate consists of the combined efforts of Irish, German, Jewish, and, more recently, Cuban exile elements. The syndicate today is in control of the drug market and gambling, but is expanding into an international organization of crime.

The character of the American political economy does not stop organized crime from continuing its expansion. Organized crime, like legitimate business, attempts to achieve maximum returns with a minimum of expenditure by efficient organization and skilled management. The difference is that legitimate business operates within the law (most of the time) and organized crime operates outside the law. Organized crime seems to be more significantly affected by economic facts of supply and demand, and the fads in consumer habits, than by legislation and sporadic attempts at formal control.

We are left with the impression that organized crime receives a great deal of toleration in the United States. The reason could be a close relationship to legitimate business. A criminologist concluded that

> . . . organized crime must be thought of as a natural growth, or as a developmental adjunct to our general system of private profit economy. Business, industry, and finance all are competitive enterprises within the area of legal operations. But there is also an area of genuine economic demand for things and services not permitted under our legal and social codes. Organized crime is the system of business functioning in the area. It, too, is competitive, and hence must organize for its self-protection and for control of the market.[28]

Organized crime thus provides illegal services and products to business, government and the public. It continues without undergoing a great deal of legal action against it because of its relationship to the political economy.

Control of Criminal and Legitimate Business

Organized crime has traditionally operated in areas of illicit behavior, such as gambling, prostitution, loan sharking, extortion and racketeering, and narcotics, but gambling has been the largest source of revenue. It includes lotteries, off-track horse-betting, numbers games, large dice games, and illegal casinos. Few organized gambling operations in large cities are not tied to such operations. Bets may vary from a quarter to very large sums and the profits for organized crime are enormous, ranging into the hundreds of millions of dollars. Gambling operations are very complex.

DOCUMENT_____

A PARTIAL CHRONOLOGY OF EVENTS IMPORTANT TO THE DEVELOPMENT OF ORGANIZED CRIME IN THE UNITED STATES

1898 Arnold Rothstein becomes a high-school dropout in New York City.

1900 Immigrants continue to arrive in great numbers.

1902 Big Jim Colosimo marries a Chicago madam and organizes a white-slave ring.

1903 Nicola Gentile arrives illegally from Sicily and becomes a Mafia trouble-shooter.

1908 The Bureau of Investigation, later famous as the FBI, is formed.

1910 Mann Act intended to end white slavery becomes law and sets precedent for federal police action in matters involving interstate commerce.

1912 Owney "the Killer" Madden becomes boss of the Gophers in New York.

1913 Arthur "Mickey" McBride becomes newspaper "circulator" in Cleveland as newspaper wars provide training for future gangsters.

1917 United States enters World War I and J. Edgar Hoover becomes a clerk in the Justice Department.

1919 Gamblers advised by Arnold Rothstein "fix" the World Series.

1920 Volstead Act to enforce constitutional ban on liquor becomes effective . . . John "the Fox" Torrio takes charge of murdered Colosimo's empire in Chicago . . . Rothstein experiments with rumrunning in New York . . . Warren Harding elected President as voters seek "normalcy."

1921 "Ohio Gang" goes to Washington with Harding and era of corruption begins . . . George Remus becomes "King of the Bootleggers" as first phase of Prohibition begins.

1923 President Harding dies suddenly but pursuit of the fast buck continues as public and private policy.

1924 J. Edgar Hoover promoted to boss of Bureau of Investigation . . . Al Capone conquers Cicero, Illinois, when Torrio's peaceful penetration fails . . . Bugs and Meyer Mob operates in New York under leadership of Meyer Lansky.

1925 Al Capone takes charge in Chicago as Torrio quits in disgust . . . Pioneer rumrunner "Big Bill" Dwyer convicted in New York, but Frank Costello goes free.

1926 Moe Dalitz quits Detroit Purple Gang to join with Morris Kleinman, Samuel Tucker, and Louis Rothkopf to form the Cleveland Syndicate.

1928 Mafia civil war results in abortive "Grand Council" meeting in Cleveland.

1929 St. Valentine's Day Massacre fails in its purpose but gives Chicago something to brag about . . . Torrio helps create alliance of bootleggers known as "Big Seven" at Atlantic City meeting . . . Stock Market crash on October 29 marks beginning of economic depression which gives organized crime its big chance to get roots down.

1931 Joe "the Boss" Masseria murdered by Lucky Luciano on April 15 as Mafia civil war ends . . . Salvatore Maranzano murdered by the Bugs and Meyer Mob on behalf of the "Combination" on September 11 as Mafia is "Americanized" and given a secondary role in crime . . . Capone convicted.

Source: Hank Messick and Burt Goldblatt, *The Mobs and the Mafia* (New York: Thomas Y. Crowell Company, 1972), pp. 205–208.

DOCUMENT (Continued)_____

1932 Franklin D. Roosevelt's election is defeat of big-city political bosses.

1933 Banks close, forcing businessmen to turn to gangsters . . . Molaska, Inc., formed on November 25, a few days before Prohibition ends. Torrio forms Prendergast-Davies to sell liquor legally.

1934 National Crime Syndicate formed along NRA lines and "Murder, Inc.," created as enforcement arm.

1935 Thomas E. Dewey appointed special prosecutor in New York . . . Dutch Schultz, last of the independents, murdered by the National Crime Syndicate.

1936 Dewey sends Charles "Lucky" Luciano to prison, but Lansky promises to get him out.

1937 "Big Heat" begins as Louis "Lepke" Buchalter becomes most wanted man and The Mob discovers America. Lansky goes to Cuba and Benjamin "Bugsy" Siegel goes to California.

1939 Torrio, like Capone, convicted on tax charges . . . Lepke surrenders, ending Big Heat . . . Germany invades Poland, closing Havana gambling joints . . . Sir Stafford Sands creates legal machinery to permit gambling in the Bahamas . . . Moses Annenberg, father of the bookie wire service, pleads guilty to tax evasion and turns his empire over to Mickey McBride who reorganizes it as Continental Press.

1940 Cleveland Syndicate expands into Kentucky at Newport . . . Abe Reles sings about Murder, Inc., fingers Lepke, Siegel, others.

1941 Lepke is sentenced to die . . . Reles, under guard, is murdered and Siegel beats the rap.

1942 Thomas E. Dewey becomes governor of New York.

1943 Leaders of the Chicago Syndicate are indicted on March 18 in movie-extortion plot. Nitti kills himself the same day, but others eventually win quick parole . . . Operation Underworld features Lansky and Luciano helping Naval Intelligence win the war and making Lansky acting boss of the Mafia.

1944 Gangsters get rich in black market activity and prepare for postwar expansion . . . Batista flees Cuba after free election and comes to Florida.

1945 Casino era begins as Lansky operates in Florida, New York, Louisiana, Nevada, New Jersey, and elsewhere.

1947 Bugsy Siegel opens his dream casino, the Flamingo, and then is murdered on June 20. Nevada gambling boom begins.

1948 Fuller Warren elected governor of Florida in prologue to attempt by Chicago Syndicate to muscle in on S & G Syndicate in Miami Beach . . . Cleveland Syndicate invests in Desert Inn on Las Vegas "Strip."

1950 Kefauver Committee begins hearings, Florida casinos closed.

1951 Kefauver Committee puts finger on Frank Costello in pioneer television spectacular in New York. Goes out of business after exposing links between crime, business, and politics . . . Senator Joseph McCarthy sees Red.

1952 McCarthy hysteria diverts public interest from real gangsters to alleged Reds . . . The country likes Ike and elects Dwight D. Eisenhower President . . . Batista regains power in Cuba with help from Lansky.

1953 Lansky spends three months in prison in New York, then moves to Hollywood, Florida . . . Joe Adonis ordered deported.

DOCUMENT (Continued)_____

1954   Lansky begins building new gambling empire in Cuba.

1955   Hawksbill Creek Act makes ex-convict Wallace Groves the "King of Grand Bahama" Island.

1957   Frank Costello wounded and deposed . . . Albert Anastasia challenges Lansky in Cuba and is murdered . . . Mafia meeting at Apalachin, N.Y., is a fiasco . . . "Special Group" created in Justice Department to fight organized crime . . . James R. Hoffa replaces David Beck as boss of the Teamsters Union and its pension funds.

1959   Batista and Lansky flee Cuba as Fidel Castro takes over and closes casinos . . . Abner "Longie" Zwillman dies mysteriously.

1960   "Special Group" in Justice Department is disbanded . . . John F. Kennedy defeats Vice-President Richard M. Nixon . . . Lansky shows his hand in the Bahamas.

1961   Robert F. Kennedy becomes Attorney General and begins a "coordinated" war on crime . . . FBI begins mass bugging of Mafia telephones . . . George Ratterman survives frame to close down Newport . . . Bay of Pigs disaster ends Mafia hopes for Cuban gambling revival.

1962   "Trigger Mike" Coppola, boss of numbers racket in Harlem, pleads guilty to tax charges in Miami after his wife tells all to IRS agents Richard Jaffe and Joseph Wanderschied.

1963   Joseph Valachi sings Nicola Gentile's old, sad song and the FBI "discovers" La Cosa Nostra . . . President Kennedy is murdered in Dallas.

1964   First gambling casino opens on Grand Bahama Island with Lansky's men in control . . . Crime war falters as FBI concentrates on gangsters with Italian names.

1967   Bay Street Boys defeated in Bahama election but gambling remains essential industry . . . James R. Hoffa goes to prison . . . Howard Hughes buys Desert Inn and other Las Vegas casinos but remains invisible.

1968   Paradise Island Casino opens in Nassau with Richard M. Nixon as guest of honor and Thomas E. Dewey a secret stockholder . . . Robert F. Kennedy assassinated while campaigning for presidential nomination . . . Nixon elected President.

1969   John Mitchell becomes Attorney General . . . Mary Carter Paint Company becomes Resorts International . . . "Cuban Mafia" begins peaceful takeover of narcotics traffic.

1970   Drive to establish legal gambling casinos defeated in Miami Beach . . . Lansky escapes to Israel well in advance of indictment and declares plans to become Israeli citizen.

1971   Joe Colombo, latest Mafia leader, seriously wounded in New York. . . Joe Adonis dies in exile . . . President Nixon commutes Hoffa's sentence and sends him home for Christmas.

Most large-city gambling is established or controlled by organized crime members through elaborate hierarchies. Money is filtered from the small operator who takes the customer's bet, through persons who pick up money and slips, to second-echelon figures in charge of particular districts, and then into one of several main offices. The profits that eventually accrue to organization leaders move through channels so complex that even persons who work in the betting operation do not know or cannot prove the identity of the leader. Increasing use of the telephone for lottery and sports betting has facilitated systems in which the bookmaker may not know the identity of the second-echelon person to whom he calls in the day's bets. Organization not only creates greater efficiency and enlarges markets, it also provides a systematized method of corrupting the law enforcement process by centralizing procedures for the payment of graft.[29]

Loan sharking, lending money at rates higher than the legally prescribed limit, is another major area of profit. Much of the money for lending comes from gambling operations. Loans are made to small businessmen whose channels of credit are closed, gamblers, narcotics users, politicians, and others who need money to cover their expenses or debts.

Narcotics sales are organized like a legitimate importing-retailing business, distributing drugs through several levels to the street peddler. Because of severe penalties, organized crime is less involved at the retail level, leaving that to individual pushers.

The large amounts of cash and the international connections necessary for large, long-term heroin supplies can be provided only by organized crime. Conservative estimates of the number of addicts in the nation and the average daily expenditure for heroin indicate that the gross heroin trade is $350 million annually, of which $21 million are probably profits to the importer and distributor. Most of this profit goes to organized crime groups in those few cities in which almost all heroin consumption occurs.[30]

Organized crime groups extend their operations to control many other kinds of products and services. The wholesaling of perishable products, such as fruit, vegetables, and fish, is often an area of racketeering operations. Racketeering, the systematic extorting of money from individuals or organizations, is prevalent in laundry businesses, cleaning establishments, trucking, loading businesses, and among such workers as motion picture operators, bartenders, waiters, truck drivers, and retail clerks. These organizations are especially vulnerable to the rackets. One of the simplest forms of this type of racketeering is the protection racket: individuals or organizations are "protected," by payment of regular fees, for the privilege of operating without being injured, damaged, or destroyed by the organized criminals. This kind of operation is not exclusive of other forms of racketeering, but may be used as one means of maintaining control over services and commodities.

Racketeering has operated successfully in controlling some groups of organized labor. It uses schemes such as infiltrating labor unions, extorting money from employees for union cooperation, and cheating the members of the union by not paying them union wages or misusing union welfare and pension funds. Workers may be forced to pay high fees and dues to find and hold jobs. Union leadership may be taken over by organized criminals. A large part of union operating funds may go to organized crime. Furthermore, money may be extorted from employers; strikes are often threatened as a means of controlling them. The building trades are particularly vulnerable to racketeering because they need to purchase materials at crucial times and to complete projects by a scheduled date.

To its control of criminal activities, organized crime has added infiltration into legitimate businesses by illegal means and by investing large financial resources. Organized crime has at times, of course, used legitimate business as a front for other criminal activities. More recently, however, it has found in legitimate business a major source of income. Organized crime has a vested monopoly in some legitimate enterprises, such as cigarette-vending machines and jukeboxes. They own many enterprises, such as real estate, retail firms, restaurants and bars, hotels, automobile agencies, trucking companies, food companies, linen supply outlets, garbage collection routes, and other such services. The Kefauver Committee found that organized crime had infiltrated about fifty areas of legitimate business, including advertising, the amusement industry, the automobile industry, banking, insurance, jukebox distribution, the liquor industry, loan businesses, the oil industry, radio stations, real estate, and scrap surplus sales.[31]

Organized crime invests some of its profits from illegal services in legitimate businesses, giving it a legitimate source of profits and also helping to avoid prosecution. The organizational arrangement involves full-time business consultants, accountants, and attorneys. Control of businesses is secured by (1) investing concealed profits acquired from gambling and other illegal activities, (2) accepting business interests as payments for the owner's gambling debts, (3) foreclosing on usurious loans, and (4) using various forms of extortion. A favorite operation is placing a business it has acquired into fraudulent bankruptcy after taking its assets.[32]

Structure of Organized Crime

Like any other large business enterprise, organized crime requires a structure of positions with a hierarchy of command. At the top of the pyramid are powerful leaders, the "lords," who make the important decisions and run the organization. They maintain a master-serf relationship over others in the feudal structure. A middle echelon of gangsters, henchmen, and lieutenants carry out the leaders' demands. At the bottom of the structure are those marginally associated with organized crime — narcotics peddlers, prostitutes, bookies, runners — who deal directly with the public. The structure is held together by a chain of command, personal loyalties, a moral code, alliances with rival groups, and hostility toward conventional society.

The hierarchic structure of organized crime makes generalizing about its members' careers difficult. Some have specialized training, as in law and accounting, and are directly recruited, and others, as young men, are given university training with the idea that they will join the syndicate. "Cosa Nostra members occupying the higher echelons of organized crime are orienting their sons to the value of education, if only as a part of the general move toward respectability. . . . they are sending their sons to college to learn business skills, on the assumption that these sons will soon be eligible for 'family' membership."[33] Many organized criminals, especially those lower in the hierarchy, have careers like that of the conventional offender, associating with young gang members and a long series of delinquencies and crimes. Instead of ending their careers in their early twenties, however, they continue their criminal activities in association with organized criminals.

Organized crime may thus provide a person with the opportunity for a lifetime career in crime. Selecting a career in organized crime, rather than one of the other criminal careers, apparently depends on the social conditions in the area in which the person lives.[34] Little is known, however, about the criminal's specific mobility from one position to another once he is a part of the hierarchy of organized crime. Their career histories are not usually available because of the secrecy in their work. There are indications, however, that as organized crime has moved from the bootlegging and prostitution rackets of the twenties and thirties into gambling, usury, and the control of legitimate businesses, the need for expertise in management operations grows and security and secrecy are needed less because the new operations are more in the open. Organized crime syndicates, therefore, are becoming more loose, flexible, and creative, rewarding those in the organization who display the ability to make profits.

Progression into organized crime increasingly isolates the offender from conventional society. Despite variations according to the person's location within the hierarchy, most organized offenders are committed to the world of crime. Most of their activities continuously violate the law. But by self-justification, based in part on a contempt for the rest of society, they are able to maintain an appropriate self-image. Underworld leaders may, however, choose to live segmented lives, retiring to seclusion and pseudorespectability.[35] Their commitment, nevertheless, remains with the world of crime, where they receive their prestige and power, and are provided with a luxurious style of life.

Throughout their careers those in organized crime associate regularly with other offenders. These associations and the support they give are provided by the very characteristics of organized crime. The crime syndicate, organized to maintain a large-scale business enterprise for coordinating and controlling products and services, ensures the association of persons involved in similar illegal activities.

All organized criminals observe more or less a code of behavior. The code is highly developed and extends into areas such as maintaining internal discipline and power of leadership. It involves "(1) *intense loyalty* to the organization and its governing elite, (2) *honesty* in relationships with members, (3) *secrecy* regarding the organization's structure and activities, and (4) *honorable behavior* which sets members off as morally superior to those outsiders who would govern them."[36] Loyalty, respect, honor, and absolute obedience are expected of all members. Compliance is helped by custom, material rewards, and violence, through either beatings or executions. No subordinates should interfere with the leader's interests, they should not inform the police, and, if necessary, subordinates should go to prison to protect those in power in the organization.

Although the code of organized criminals is purportedly for the protection of "the people," it is administered and enforced for the protection of each boss. Since the boss of a "family" has the most to lose if the organization is weakened through an attack by outsiders, he enthusiastically promotes the notion that an offense against one is an offense against all. Moreover, this same principle protects the boss from his own underlings. The principle gets transformed so that it deals with matters of safety rather than matters of offense — the safety of all depends upon the safety of each. Since each conforming member is guaranteed a livelihood without fear of encroachment by other members or by nonmembers, each member must be "protected." This transformation, of course, authorizes the boss to take extreme measures to insure his own safety by crushing any plot or potential plot against

him by his underlings. The principle also encourages informing. Despite the code's admonition to be tight-lipped, one is guilty by association if he does not report that a member has injured him or another member. By promulgating the idea that "We are all equals in matters of defense," the boss makes lower-status workers his "boys," who henceforth are dependent upon his paternalism. Organized criminals frequently refer to some subordinate, who might be fifty years old, as "the kid." A boss who can establish that he will assist his followers when they have been offended or when they are in need has gained control over these men. They become indebted to him. They are obligated to reciprocate, in the name of "honor" and "loyalty," thus enhancing his privileged position. The saying is, "If you don't respect the boss, no one will respect you."

Those aspects of the code which prohibit appealing to outside authorities for help and justice also serve to concentrate power in the hands of the few and, hence, to enable leaders to exploit followers. The ruler of an organized-crime unit, whether it be an entire Cosa Nostra "family" or a thirty-man lottery enterprise, has three classes of enemies — law-enforcement officers, outsiders who want his profits, and underlings. The code protects him from all of them.[37]

The continued existence of organized crime depends on maintaining permanent immunity from interference by law-enforcement agencies. It is achieved in several ways.[38] First, the leaders of organized crime are not usually arrested and prosecuted, because they stay behind the scenes of operation — gangland activity cannot be readily traced to its leaders. Second, persons lower in the hierarchy of organized crime, if arrested, are likely to be released by action from their superiors. Such release and avoidance of prosecution and punishment are ensured by what is popularly known as the "fix." People not directly involved in criminal activity sometimes contribute to the protection of organized criminals. Law-enforcement officials, judges, doctors, businessmen, and others may at times provide services needed to protect organized criminals.

Another way of acquiring immunity is by

gaining political power with contributions to political organizations. Elected officials may owe their election to organized criminals. Regular "payoffs" to officials provide protection for organized crime, which may be permanently immune to law enforcement because of political graft and corruption. Fourth, because it provides the public with illicit and desired services, such as prostitution, gambling, and narcotics, it gets some immunity from arrest and prosecution from public toleration.

Immunity can also be found in the functioning of the law itself. Laws and enforcement procedures have not been especially successful in coping with organized crime. Its survival and continuance are possible because legal action is kept at a minimum. Lack of effective legislation and weak law enforcement also reflect public toleration of organized crime.

Finally, by infiltrating legitimate business,

organized crime is able to evade the law. It often operates behind a legitimate facade obscuring its operation and making its detection difficult. Also, racketeering escapes the law because intimidated businessmen must contend with reprisal if they report it. And organized crime and legitimate business may mutually assist one another, as in regulating prices of commodities or enforcing labor contracts. Interdependence between the underworld of crime and the upperworld of business ensures that both systems will be maintained. Mutual assistance, accompanied by the profit motive, provides assured immunity.

Organized crime has grown into a huge business in the United States and is an integral part of the political economy. Enormous amounts of illegitimate money are passed annually into socially acceptable endeavors. An elaborate corporate and financial structure is now tied to organized crime.

9

Crime in the American State

The major crimes that occur in the United States are bound to the political organization of our society. The state, which establishes and manages the system of social control, sometimes violates its own laws in securing this control. It may infringe the criminal code for reasons of state, and it occasionally goes further, violating laws of higher jurisdiction and even basic human rights.

These acts can be called crimes, though unlike ordinary crime, if they are uncovered, they often escape penalty. But their frequency and profound importance, and even their presence, have become marked in recent years. Any of these acts can be called criminal, whether found at the top of government or in any of its agencies.

Crimes against Human Rights

Violating Civil Liberties

The state has been accused of crimes in several areas of life. The civil rights movement showed how government officials will violate the law to keep the system intact. Court decisions and legislative acts have made some of the behaviors illegal, even when committed by officials of the state. We have come to realize that many of our civil liberties are being narrowed by those who are supposed to guarantee these rights. In the name of "law and order," legal agents have slighted laws that are to protect such rights as free speech, assembly, and due process. Federal agents have violated the law in their surveillance and in their quest for evidence usable in criminal prosecution. Local police, too, have been accused of blatantly violating human rights, as well as the conventional laws of murder and assault, in running the affairs of state.[1]

The United States Constitution guarantees some rights that are not to be infringed upon. Governmental surveillance, according to Supreme Court rulings, is illegal in most situations. Such techniques as unreasonable search and seizure, interrogation, wiretapping, and various forms of electronic surveillance have been declared unconstitutional except in specified cases. Nevertheless, government agents continue to use these forms of surveillance, a fact which was dramatically brought to public attention by the disclosure that the Army was obtaining information on 18,000 civilians.[2]

It has been disclosed that several government agencies, including the FBI, also are heavily engaged in obtaining information about law-abiding citizens by these means.[3] The investigations on the Watergate crimes have uncovered the extent to which citizens are being denied their civil liberties in the name of "national security," and the many criminal techniques (including burglary) the government uses to obtain information. Agencies of the state, including the presidency, may also resort to espionage and sabotage against citizens, obtaining information illegally and even falsifying records and documents. Among the disclosures was the plan approved by President Nixon for gathering domestic intelligence. Blackmail and extortion have been used against individuals and organizations, as in the threat of income tax prosecutions if funds were not provided for campaign and other expenses. Some of these activities, such as burglary by agents of the FBI in gathering information for the presidency, have been going on for many years. These may be not only unconstitutional but may violate criminal codes. It is always problematical, however, whether these crimes will be prosecuted, because the government itself would have to do the prosecuting.

A classical strategy used by a state to promote its own security is the criminal law, which it wields against those who appear to threaten the state's existence. The state traditionally responds by establishing a legal system that defines as "criminal" any conduct that threatens it, and denying the citizen's rights of dissent. These "political crimes" form a significant part of legal history, especially in recent years.[4] This use of criminal law is usually illegal; the laws are illegal in formulation and inevitably result in criminal means of enforcement.

In the last decade the American state has gone through many political trials to promote its own interests. Those who objected to war in Southeast Asia were sometimes harassed and prosecuted. "Rioters" in the ghettoes, rebelling against the abuses they suffer, have been subjected to various laws by the state, which has used many old laws, or created new laws, to control dissent. Law enforcement agencies and the judiciary have tried to prosecute those who apparently threaten the state, but the government's strategy is not working. Trials pending for years are being thrown out of court because of the means the government used to prosecute them. Charges against such groups as the Chicago Seven, the Harrisburg Seven (the Berrigan case), the Daniel Ellsberg and Anthony J. Russo, Jr., case, and the Gainesville Eight were dropped because the police, the prosecution, or the court used criminal techniques in conducting them.[5]

Crimes in Law Enforcement

Conventional Crimes by Agents of the Law

The police have traditionally been the governmental agents most exposed to opportunities for committing conventional felonies and misdemeanors while enforcing the law; crimes by the police have been documented throughout the history of law enforcement in American communities. A study of police operations in Washington, Boston, and Chicago reported that "27 percent of all the officers were either observed in misconduct situations or admitted to observers that they had engaged in misconduct."[6] The forms of crime included shaking down traffic violators, accepting payoffs to alter sworn testimony, stealing from burglarized establishments, and planting weapons on suspects. Documented elsewhere are illegal raids against innocent persons, participating in narcotics traffic, and extorting money from the prostitution business.[7] The Knapp Commission of New York City found that well over half the police force in that city are engaged in some form of crime and corruption.[8] The activities range from accepting bribes to selling stolen articles, from selling heroin to tapping telephones illegally, from blackmail to murder.

Violence is part of police work, and brutality in making an arrest is often claimed. Investigating police abuses in New York City, Paul Chevigny found that the police will make an arrest to cover up an assault committed against the suspect, concealing their own violence by arresting and charging the citizens with some offense.[9]

Crimes by the police can be understood if we look closely at police work. The police recruit, during his training, adopts a very definite outlook on his work and develops a justification for using specific procedures in the line of "duty." He learns an ideology that later affects his work:

> The policeman finds his most pressing problem in his relationships to the public. His is a service occupation but of an incongruous kind, since he must discipline those whom he serves. He is regarded as corrupt and inefficient by, and meets with hostility and criticism from, the public. He regards the public as his enemy, feels his occupation to be in conflict with the community, and regards himself to be a pariah. The experience and the feeling give rise to a collective emphasis on secrecy, an attempt to coerce respect from the public, and a belief that almost any means are legitimate in completing an important arrest. These are for the policeman basic occupational values. They arise from his experience, take precedence over his legal responsibilities, are central to an understanding of his conduct, and form the occupational concepts within which violence gains its meaning.[10]

Many of the illegal activities of the ordinary policeman are prescribed and supported by group norms of law enforcement. Research has shown that criminal practices of police are patterned by an informal "code": "It was found that the new recruits were socialized into 'code' participation by 'old timers' and group acceptance was withheld from those who attempted to remain completely honest and not be implicated. When formal police regulations were in conflict with 'code' demands among its practitioners, the latter took precedence."[11]

In fact, the policeman may give little thought to the legality of his own actions when he is enforcing other laws. The law that is meant to protect the citizen from abuses by government authorities is more likely to be regarded by the policeman as an obstacle to law enforcement. "For him, due process of law is, therefore, not merely a set of constitutional guarantees for the defendant, but also a set of working conditions which, under increasingly liberal opinions by the courts, are likewise becoming increasingly arduous."[12] From the policeman's standpoint, the public's civil liberties impede his performance on the job. That is how the law is sometimes broken by its enforcers.

The opportunity for unlawful behavior among the police is especially acute in the black community and in political protests. Here the police already have their own group norms prescribing some illegal behavior and providing support for it. Several studies have shown that the majority of policemen are hostile and prejudiced toward blacks,[13] which can impair their ability to always keep their behavior lawful. In the ghetto riots of the late sixties, police violence was reportedly common.

Police handling of political protesters also has often been violent and illegal. The police response to the demonstrations at the 1968 Democratic National Convention in Chicago has been described as "unrestrained and indiscriminate police violence."[14] These confrontations increase the chances for violence because of the views the police share about protesters. That is, "organized protest tends to be viewed as the conspiratorial product of authoritarian agitators — usually 'Communists' — who mislead otherwise contented people."[15] Such ideas, combined with frustration and anger, provide ready support for harsh police actions. And because the police look on most people they find in these situations as already guilty, they think their own methods of control and apprehension are appropriate — no matter how criminal these methods may be.

Other agents of the law, such as the officials who guard and "correct" conventional offenders, violate the law in their work. These crimes correspond closely to the objectives of security and punishment. Prison guards, in particular, are to do whatever is necessary to maintain security in the prison.

These crimes are documented only when a crisis happens. Several crimes committed by correctional workers became known to the public following prison riots in New York City jails.[16] The inmates were responding to the harsh conditions in the jails, including excessive bail, overcrowding, and months of being confined without indictment or trial. After the revolt had been ended peacefully by negotiations between the inmates and the mayor's office, correctional officers systematically beat the prisoners in the courtyard of one of the jails. The beatings were recorded in photographs and eyewitness accounts. A reporter for the *Daily News* described what he saw:

> It was a gruesome scene. About 250 prisoners were sitting on the grass. Behind them, 30 Correction Department guards were lined up, all of them holding weapons — ax handles, baseball bats, and night sticks. One inmate was dragged out a doorway onto a loading platform and five guards attacked him with their clubs. They battered his head and blood flowed over his face and body. He was kicked off the platform and several other guards pounded him again with their clubs. His limp form then was lifted off the ground and thrown into a bus as another prisoner was hauled out and belted across the back with a club. Then more clubs rained down on him until he was motionless and bloodsoaked. He too was thrown into the bus. Another man was pushed out, his hands above his head. A bat caught him in the stomach and he doubled over. More clubs came down on his spine. Eight guards were slugging away at one time. A fourth prisoner emerged but the guards seemed to let go of him. He began running but the guards caught him and one put a knee into his groin. He toppled over and more guards kicked him over and over. Some more prisoners got the same treatment.[17]

As it often turns out with such incidents, three weeks after the beatings the district attorney announced the indictment of eight inmates, exonerating all the guards.

The results of crimes committed by agents of the law are usually predictable: the charges are dropped, the defendants are cleared, or, at most, an official may be dismissed. Although three students were killed and several more injured at Orangeburg State College in 1968, the South Carolina highway patrolmen who fired the shots were cleared of any wrongdoing. Similar events and results were to occur later at Jackson State College in Mississippi.

Likewise, at Kent State University in 1970, National Guardsmen killed four students, and then were exonerated of any blame. Instead, a state grand jury indicted twenty-five persons in connection with campus protests. The grand jury did not indict any guardsmen because they "fired their weapons in the honest and sincere belief and under circumstances which would have logically caused them to believe that they would suffer serious bodily injury had they not done so." (No evidence of the sniper fire that they feared could be found.) The "major responsibility" for the events at Kent State, the grand jury continued, "rests clearly with those persons who are charged with the administration of the university." The university administration, the report asserted, had fostered "an attitude of laxity, over-indulgence and permissiveness," and faculty members had placed an "over-emphasis" on "the right to dissent."[18] The idea that the government could be at fault was never entertained by the grand jury.

The killings at Attica prison in New York State demonstrate violence by the state. In September of 1971, more than forty were killed by state troopers when the prisoners demanded prison reforms. Fearing that the rebellion was a threat to law and order, Governor Rockefeller ordered in the state troopers.[19] Actions such as these are beginning to be understood by the public; crime by the state is becoming a part of the public consciousness.

Crimes of Provocation

The ideology of the American state promotes the myth that law enforcement is a neutral force that is intended to maintain the democratic process. However:

> The history of America contradicts this official image of neutrality and equal justice. The pattern is clear: when women tried to vote and Labor claimed its right to organize, at the beginning of this century, police were used as poll-watchers, as strike-breakers, and as shock troops by those who held industrial power; in the 1950's as black people began a new round in their centuries-old struggle for equal protection, police were once again used to defy the Constitution in the name of states' rights and public order; in the 1960's police again and again were sent in to disperse hundreds of thousands of citizens peacefully exercising their First

Amendment rights to protest an unconstitutional war in Southeast Asia. All this time, on a day to day, face to face level the typical law enforcement slogan "to protect and to serve" meant one thing to the powerful or the passive and another to the powerless or the dissident.[20]

The practice in which a law-enforcement agency uses a policeman or an informer to encourage or plan actions that violate the law is itself a crime. Yet, we are now realizing this practice may be common. How widespread is this crime of informers becoming agents provocateurs and encouraging or committing illegal acts? The list of suspected instances includes these:

One of the people most involved in encouraging the violence that accompanied the Chicago Democratic Party Convention was actually an undercover police officer; two members of a national peace committee who always tried to push the group into confrontations with the police were both police provocateurs; a young man who provided a bomb to blow up a Seattle U.S. Post Office was an FBI and city police informer; another FBI informer burned buildings at the University of Alabama; police agents tried to incite violence at Yale University during the demonstrations of May 1971; a Chicano activist in Los Angeles who attempted to provoke his group into terrible acts of violence was an informer for the Treasury Department; the Weatherman group in Ohio was infiltrated by an informer who won a position for himself through advocacy of the most extreme forms of violence; the Black Panther Party "Minister of Defense" in Los Angeles, who helped bring about a shootout with the police, was actually a police informer; a New York City undercover police officer tried to convince a veterans' peace group that it should use violent tactics; another police provocateur, who had vandalized a state college campus, attempted to convert a San Diego peace march into a pitched battle with police; in upstate New York, an informer, who was on the FBI payroll, tried to set up a class to teach students at Hobart University how to make and use bombs; informers working for the FBI and local police set up a bombing attempt in Mississippi in an effort to kill two KKK members; a Chicago police informer provided the false tip which led to the killing of two Panther leaders there; a police informer led an illegal SDS sit-in at an Illinois college and later — claiming he was a Weatherman — helped to hurl the president of the college off the stage; a police informer attempted to force a militant Seattle group into taking on violent activities; two men who had led the shutting of a massive gate at Ohio State University and set off a violent confrontation with the police, were officers of the state highway patrol; and the false report claiming guns were stored in the Black Muslim Temple in Los Angeles came from a paid police informer, who claims he was instructed to make the report so that the police who employed him would have an excuse to raid the temple.[21]

Such accounts appear to be endless, making us realize that the state systematically engages in acts of provocation in attempting to protect itself. Persons and groups thought to be threats to the system have found themselves harassed by surveillance. Law enforcement agents have raided the homes of blacks, probably in response to acts of provocation by agents provocateurs among the Black Panthers.[22] Acts like these may be systematically practiced to eliminate any group that does not accept the state's legitimacy; it is, after all, supposed to be guardian of the national interest.

How far will the state go to protect its own interests? Recently revealed plans might have imposed martial law in the United States if a plot involving the 1972 Republican Convention, which was to be held in San Diego, had come off:

The plan entailed planting a number of agents-provocateurs both inside and outside the 1972 Republican Convention in San Diego. Agents were to infiltrate the groups planning demonstrations against the war and poverty. At the time of the demonstrations these agents were to provoke street battles with the police surrounding the convention hall; meanwhile, agents inside the convention hall were to have planted explosives, timed to blow up simultaneously with the "riot in the streets." The result, he [Louis E. Tackwood] claimed, would be to create a nation-wide hysteria that would then provide President Richard M. Nixon with the popular support necessary to declare a state of national emergency; the government could then arrest all "radicals," "militants," and "left-wing revolutionaries."[23]

In the Watergate crimes we recognize the full authoritarian possibilities in the modern state. The break-in at the Democratic National Convention headquarters (in the Watergate apartment complex) consisted of much more than a mere burglary and the installation of electronic listening devices. The invading team was discovered putting forged documents *into* the files. They also had incendiary and bomb manufacturing devices and implements.

> One thing was perfectly clear: this espionage mission was involved with far more than eavesdropping. As the investigation of the event unfolded during the 1972 presidential campaign, it became clear that Watergate was but the tip of the iceberg. Hundreds of thousands of dollars and scores of men were revealed as part of a national network for political espionage, sabotage and provocation. The contacts for the provocateurs who were recruited turned out to be men from the White House, some of the President's closest advisors.[24]

Crimes of provocation now come from the highest sources; this could be a design for our country's future.

Crimes of War

Criminologists, content to study criminal acts by individuals against society or the government, have neglected international incidents that could also be called criminal, in which the government itself or its agents are implicated. One of these is war, today entirely a governmental function. War is, obviously, violence. Many violent acts that are forbidden without question in peacetime are accepted as necessary in wartime and as a natural part of that unnatural business. Some acts of this kind, though, go beyond even the laws that nations have accepted as governing their behavior at war. These are war crimes.

Sociologists, confronted with these acts, conveniently ignore them, suggesting that they are not "crimes" as they define them, that these acts are not a system of behavior, or that only history can determine which acts are crimes. They fail to realize that these acts (1) are covered by the criminal laws, (2) can be systematic, integral parts of a political and economic system, and (3) are crucial in a nation's history. If we do not consider such crimes, we abdicate both our integrity as scholars and our responsibilities as human beings.

An elaborate body of international laws covers the crimes of war. The laws of war are of ancient origin, and up to the eighteenth century were mostly preserved by unwritten tradition.[25] Gradually the laws were codified and courts were established to try violations of the laws. In the last hundred years international laws and treaties have firmly codified an international law of war. The United States is party to twelve conventions pertinent to land warfare, including the detailed Geneva Conventions of 1949. The most authoritative and encompassing statement of war crimes is found in the Chapter of the International Military Tribunal at Nuremberg, where war crimes are defined as

> Violations of the laws or customs of war which include, but are not limited to, murder, ill-treatment or deportation to slave-labour or for any other purpose of civilian population of or in occupied territory, murder, or ill-treatment of prisoners of war or persons on the high seas, killing of hostages, plunder of public or private property, wanton destruction of cities, towns or villages, or devastation not justified by military necessity.[26]

"The laws of warfare are part of American law, enforceable in American courts, not only because the United States is party to most of the major multilateral conventions on the conduct of military hostilities but also because the laws of warfare are incorporated in international customary law, which under the Constitution is part of American law."[27] The United States also recognizes that the laws of war apply to us in the *Field Manual* of the Department of the Army. The Manual makes it clear that the international laws are also "the supreme law of the land," and that "the law of war is binding not only upon States as such but also upon individuals and, in particular, the members of their armed forces."[28] The international laws of war are part of American law, and may be enforced against both civilians and soldiers, by national or international courts.

Now, let us see how international law can be applied to a country accused of monstrous acts in a long war: the United States in Vietnam. We assume that the government and its representatives discussed here are guilty of these crimes. How are they guilty, and how can the international courts prove their guilt and bring the guilty to trial?

At the Nuremberg war crimes trials, Chief Prosecutor Justice Jackson of the United States Supreme Court declared: "If certain acts and violations of treaties are crimes, they are crimes whether the United States does them or whether Germany does them. We are not prepared to lay down a rule of criminal conduct against others which we would not be willing to have invoked against us." Years later many believed the United States had put itself in the respondent's position. But those who level the charge of war crimes against the United States are not the obvious victors. The countries in Southeast Asia, though continually advancing their own condition, are not yet in a position to conduct a war crimes trial. And other nations have not been inclined to convene an international trial. Nevertheless, the words of Justice Jackson are coming back to haunt many Americans.

Our century has been dominated by a single view of reality: the liberal view, which may have been the source of both our problems as a nation and our inability to understand these problems. So it is that the war in Southeast Asia and the crimes associated with it may be made understandable by another theory of reality, a socialist theory. What did liberals predict about our involvement in Southeast Asia?

Did they predict that the American government, continuously advised by university professors, would persist for several years in methods of warfare and of pacification that are criminal in international law and custom, and that are modeled on communist methods? Did they predict that the American government, in pursuit of its presumed strategic interests, would prop up, by firepower and money, any puppet, however repressive, provided only that he would not have dealings with Russia and China? Did they anticipate that the principles of the Nuremberg trials and pledges to international order would be brought into contempt so soon and by a democracy?[29]

The liberal theory always held that the Vietnam war was, at most, a mistake. The socialist theory, scoffed at by most intellectuals in the late fifties and early sixties, suggested another meaning. Rather than viewing the war as an accident or miscalculation, an event that would cease with immediate American withdrawal, that theory predicted the United States would extend the war.

What the United States did, and continues to do in various ways, in Southeast Asia is a logical outcome of policies that have long existed. That the United States has intervened in the affairs of other nations has been taken for granted. Its right to interfere in the development of these countries, including the right to suppress national revolts, has been patently accepted. To overthrow revolutionary governments and to replace them with military dictatorships has been recognized as good foreign policy. Instead of questioning a foreign policy that is guided by corporate capitalism, in which national interests are defined as business interests, liberals have proclaimed this arrangement. And these arrangements and ideas helped bring about the Vietnam war.

The dramatic disclosure of a massacre involving more than 500 civilians in the My Lai #4 hamlet of Son My village raised the first serious consideration of war crimes by the United States in the Vietnam war. That disclosure, not made until several months after the March 16, 1968 massacre, suggested a series of war crimes over a long time:

The official policies developed for the pursuit of belligerent objectives in Vietnam appear to violate the same basic and minimum constraints on the conduct of war as were violated at Songmy. B-52 pattern raids against undefended villages and populated areas, "free bomb zones," forcible removal of civilian populations, defoliation and crop destruction and "search and destroy" missions have been sanctioned as official tactical policies of the United States government. Each of these tactical policies appears to violate the international laws of war binding upon the United States by international treaties ratified by the U.S. Government with the advice and consent of the Senate. The overall conduct of the war in Vietnam by the U.S. armed forces involves a refusal to differentiate between combatants and non-combatants and between military and non-military targets.[30]

The implications of Son My are far-reaching. The United States government seems to have pursued official policies of warfare that constitute war crimes: "It would, therefore, be misleading to isolate the awful happening at Songmy from the overall conduct of the war. It is certainly true that the perpetrators of the massacre at Songmy are, if the allegations prove correct, guilty of the commission of war crimes, but it is also true that their responsibility is mitigated to the extent that they were executing superior orders or were even carrying out the general line of official policy that established a moral climate in which the welfare of Vietnamese civilians is totally disregarded."[31]

Let us, then, examine some of the specific acts by the United States government in Southeast Asia that are defined as criminal in the international laws of war.

Murder and Ill-treatment of Civilians

The Son My massacre of civilian men, women, and children took place in a standard American military operation. Trying to trap a Vietcong unit, an American brigade (C Company of Task Force Barker) appear to have killed almost every villager they could lay hands on, although no opposition or hostile behavior was encountered.

The tragedy of Son My cannot obscure the fact that the killing of civilians by American forces became an everyday occurrence in Vietnam. Estimates have suggested that American or South Vietnamese forces killed or wounded

ten civilians for every Vietcong.[32] Civilian casualties in South Vietnam ran into the hundreds of thousands. The Kennedy Subcommittee on Refugees estimated that there were about 300,000 casualties in 1968. According to a conservative estimate for the years 1965 to 1969, 1,116,000 South Vietnamese civilians were killed and 2,232,000 were wounded: between a fifth and a quarter of the population was killed or wounded by military operations in the war. Not included in these figures are the unknown number of casualties from disease and malnutrition brought on by the war. Likewise, these figures do not include the casualties suffered by the civilians of North Vietnam, many as a result of massive bombing. Thousands of other civilians were killed as the war was "wound down."

Destruction of Nonmilitary Targets

The United States engaged in heavy aerial bombardment in Vietnam. The bomb tonnage exceeded that delivered in all the allied bombing in Europe and Asia during World War II. By February of 1969, 3,200,000 tons of bombs had been dropped on an agricultural country slightly larger than New York State: 180 pounds of bombs for every man, woman, and child in Vietnam, or 25 tons of bombs for every square mile of North and South Vietnam.[33]

The strictly legal question is whether or not these bombs fell on military objectives:

> Under the traditional approach to the war-crimes concept, no legal issue is presented with respect to the bombing of genuinely strategic military targets such as factories, ammunition depots, oil refineries, airports, and — particularly in the Vietnam context — roads, bridges, viaducts, railroad tracks, trucks, trains, tunnels, and any other transportation facilities. Furthermore, we assume that accidental and incidental damage to nonmilitary and non-strategic targets is not a war crime.[34]

But the kind of bombing carried out by the United States government appears to have been quite different; it is accused of carrying out a deliberate, nonaccidental bombardment of nonmilitary targets. In North Vietnam, B-52 bombers were said to have continuously attacked schools, churches, hospitals, private homes, dikes, and dams.[35]

In South Vietnam, bombing of rural villages was a standard military policy. Any area could be more or less indiscriminately bombed. "While such strategy violates all international law regarding warfare and is inherently genocidal, it also adjusts to the political reality in South Vietnam that the N.L.F. is and can be anywhere and that virtually the entire people is America's enemy."[36] Military policy, the accusation says, turned an entire nation into a target.

Murder and Ill-treatment of Prisoners of War

The laws of war concerning the treatment of prisoners of war are precise: it is a war crime to murder or torture prisoners. "According to the Nuremberg precedents, captors may not shoot prisoners even though they are in a combat zone, require a guard, consume supplies, slow up troop movements, and appear certain to be set free by their own forces in an imminent invasion. The Hague Conventions of 1907 require that prisoners be humanely treated, and the Geneva Convention of 1949 prohibits 'causing death or seriously endangering the health of a prisoner of war.' In particular it stipulates that 'no physical or mental torture, nor any other form of coercion, may be inflicted on prisoners of war to secure from them information of any kind whatever.' "[37]

Yet there are numerous reports of the murder and ill-treatment of prisoners by American military forces as well as by the American trained and supported South Vietnamese Army.[38] Detailed accounts have been given of the beheading and shooting of wounded prisoners and of torture. Instead of incarcerating prisoners, execution is often carried out at the time of capture. Some combat soldiers characterized these actions as "everyday things," "expected" combat behavior, and "standard operating policy." Violations of the international laws of war became an issue of American military policy in Southeast Asia.

Other Crimes

American armed forces, working with the Army of South Vietnam, sprayed more than 100 million pounds of herbicidal chemicals on about half (5 million acres) of the arable land in South Vietnam. The object was "to defoliate trees affording cover for enemy forces and to kill certain plants, including rice, which furnish food for Vietcong forces and their civilian supporters.[39] In addition, 14 million pounds of CS gas, which incapacitates combatants and civilians, was used. In other words, the United States relied extensively on chemical warfare in Vietnam and later in Cambodia.

The Geneva Gas Protocol of 1925 states that the "use in war of asphyxiating, poisonous or other gases, and of all analogous liquids, materials, or devices, has been justly condemned by the general opinion of the civilized world," and prohibits the use of such weapons. Even with the most limited interpretation of the protocol, as lethal devices, the liquids and sprays used by the United States in Southeast Asia were in violation of international law.[40] Napalm too was widely used in Vietnam and surrounding countries.

In officially conducting a war against the population of Vietnam, the United States and some of its leaders could be charged with genocide, a crime again humanity, a crime covered by international treaties and for which all but two of the defendants at Nuremberg were convicted.

"The case for these stark accusations is based on the conclusions that both South Vietnam and the United States violated the Geneva Declaration of 1954 by hostile acts against the North, unlawful rearmament, and refusal to carry out the 1965 national elections provided for in the Declaration, and that the United States likewise violated the United Nations Charter by bombing North Vietnam."[41] The United States attempted to legitimize its war by claiming that self-defense measures were required in response to documented armed attacks.

But whether or not the sweeping accusations of genocide and aggression are invoked, the United States position before the traditional laws of war is open to one question: how can these violations be understood and what legal or moral recourse is there for the people of Southeast Asia and for the world community?

World Justice

Only a few war crime violations have been prosecuted — and these by military courts. Lieutenant William Calley stood a court-martial trial for his part in killing civilians at Son My. It became clear at the trial that Calley was being used as a scapegoat for decisions made by others at higher levels of command. But crucial questions about individual responsibility were raised during the trial.[42] According to the Nuremberg principles and the Army's *Field Manual*, members of the armed forces are bound to obey only *lawful* orders; orders violating international law are not to be obeyed. Moreover, questions were raised about war crimes by the United States, and according to international law, those who make and administer these policies must be held responsible. In the Tokyo War Crimes Trial, the defendant, General Yamashita, was convicted and executed for failing to restrain his troops from committing crimes against civilians in the Philippines during the closing months of World War II. That trial established for international law that "A leader must take affirmative acts to prevent war crimes or dissociate himself from the Government. If he fails to do one or the other, then by the very act of remaining in a government of a state guilty of war crimes, he becomes a war criminal."[43]

There are considerable grounds, therefore, for regarding policy-makers and those who administer policy as war criminals. One noted legal scholar, Telford Taylor, who was chief counsel for the prosecution at Nuremberg, has suggested that with the precedents in international law, several civilian leaders and military officers could be held criminally responsible for their acts.[44] The Rusks, McNamaras, Bundys, and Rostows, as well as the military leaders, such as the Joint Chiefs of Staff (especially General Westmoreland), should have borne responsibility for the war crimes in Southeast Asia.

To invoke the law, if it could be done beyond the manipulations of the regime themselves, is probably to expect too much of legal institutions. The war crimes of the United States cannot be probed adequately in a court-martial proceeding when the responsibility lies higher. It seems more critical to develop a moral judgment on our recent history.

A national or international board of inquiry may be the most appropriate way to deal with war crimes. The main objective of this approach, as Richard Falk argues, is to achieve a measure of rectitude as a result of *moral clarification*. Moreover:

> Such a focus is not punitive, the idea is not to catch, convict and punish individuals, but to expose, clarify, and repudiate their conduct. Such an enterprise can only be effective if it represents as authoritative a collective judgment of mankind as a whole reached in a proceeding that was fair, but honest. Americans concerned at once with avoiding any deepening polarization at home, and with renouncing crimes committed on their behalf, should join together in calling for an *external* process of inquiry and judgment, perhaps in the form of a specially constituted U.N. Commission of Inquiry. For Americans of conscience this is the time for neither insurgency, nor silence.[45]

In the end, everyone is responsible for the acts of government. It is the responsibility of all peoples of the world to remove the oppression of national empires and to achieve world justice and human liberation.

Crime, Business, and American Politics

Crime as an economic enterprise depends on the symbiotic alliance between politics and business, which in turn enhances all three realms. In fact, in many areas of the American political economy the distinctions between criminal and legitimate activity are becoming obsolete. Criminal politics and criminal business, corrupt politicians and political officials serving business, threaten to become an institutional arrangement. Crime is reaching into the highest levels of politics and business; it is becoming nationalized.

Roughly since Prohibition, an unseen alliance has gradually developed in the United States, entangling organized crime, politicians, public officials, and agencies of law enforcement and administration of justice. Organized crime has become a part of politics, and politics has infiltrated organized crime. Organized criminals have found it necessary to get into politics to protect their operations from governmental interference. Their liaison with public officials is a passport to immunity from the law, preventing interruptions to their business, which is amassing large economic gains. People in politics discover that involvement in organized crime furnishes lucrative financial rewards. Collaboration with organized crime also gives the political system a way of controlling the country's social and economic organization. The political, economic, and criminal realms are increasingly becoming rolled into one.

The known examples illustrating how deeply business and politics are involved in crime are overwhelming. Small cities as well as large ones have their own cases of systematic crime. A few documented cases will show this tainted, self-sustaining relationship. In Reading, Pennsylvania, we can see how a syndicate controlled an entire community:

Operating in conjunction with a local underworld figure, most of the municipal administration from the mayor on down was corrupted. As a result, the biggest illegal still since Prohibition was tied into the city water supply, the biggest red-light district on the East Coast was set up, and the biggest dice game east of the Mississippi, within an easy drive of either Philadelphia or New York, was launched. Nothing was done for the city. Industry started leaving; downtown Reading became an eyesore. When murmurs of public discontent grew too loud, mob-controlled "reformers" were promptly whisked on the scene. As the city steadily began to wither, a Justice Department task force noticed that the only sign of civic improvement was new parking meters. The company involved in the installation of these meters had a history of kicking back to municipal governments to get the business. It was this thread that eventually unraveled the whole mess, but until outside aid arrived, the local citizenry was truly helpless.[46]

The case in which New York City official James L. Marcus was involved shows how organized crime can infiltrate city politics and economics:

The manner in which organized crime may effectively sink its claws into public officials can be seen in the case of James L. Marcus, former Commissioner of Water Supply, Gas and Electricity, in New York City and a close advisor and member of Mayor Lindsay's inner circle. Deeply in debt from business investments and Wall Street plunges, Marcus was referred by a business associate to Anthony Corallo, a reputed lieutenant in the Thomas Lucchese Cosa Nostra "family" with a reputation as a labor racketeer and loan shark. Paying interest to Corallo on cash loans said to be at an annual rate of 104 per cent, Marcus sank further in debt, and was finally pressured into doing business "favors" to the Cosa Nostra loan shark and his associates. The result was a tangled web of rigged municipal contracts, bribes, and illegal real-estate deals. In 1968, Marcus pleaded guilty to taking a $16,000 kickback in return for awarding a $835,000 city contract to clean a Bronx reservoir and received a fifteen-month sentence for his part in this and several other conspiracies.[47]

Collusion is further illustrated in Newark, New Jersey:

Illustrative of this wide scope of political corruption is perhaps the city of Newark, New Jersey, which in 1969 was rocked by a major scandal involving public officials, law-enforcement agents, and organized crime. In the first of two mass indictments, a federal grand jury charged the mayor, Hugh Addonizio, with income-tax evasion and sixty-six counts of extortion involving a share in payoffs totaling $253,000 from a business firm that had contracts with the city. Also included in the indictments were eleven current or former city officials and a reputed prominent member of the Cosa Nostra. Barely a day before this action by the grand jury, a series of gambling raids by some 100 FBI agents (apparently sparked by information derived from wiretaps) in Newark and surrounding suburbs resulted in scores of arrests and led to another mass indictment of fifty-five persons. Almost a dozen of those indicted were reported to be Cosa Nostra members, including Simone Rizzo Decavalcante, alleged boss of one of the six Cosa Nostra "families" in the New York metropolitan area. (This huge interstate operation, extending as far as Troy, New York, reportedly brought the syndicate $20 million a year.) The indictments of these gambling figures also charged that some of them had "solicited and obtained" tipoffs from Newark city police on any impending gambling raids.[48]

Lasting control over an American city by organized crime, involving a relationship between local politicians and business, is documented in a study of "Wincanton," pseudonym for an Eastern industrial city controlled by a crime syndicate for the last fifty years. The Stern syndicate, operating gambling enterprises in the city, was able "to put cooperative politicians in office, to buy off those who occupied strategic enforcement positions, and to implicate most city officials in various forms of corruption so completely that they would be unable to turn upon him."[49] City officials have added to their syndicate payoffs by demanding bribes from individuals and companies doing business with the city. Many city, state, and federal laws were violated, and the law enforcement apparatus was under illegal control. Only those not involved in the established politics and business of the community, namely, the majority of the citizens, were excluded from this arrangement. The city had a local ruling class, deeply involved in and dependent on crime.

Similar associations between city officials, members of organized crime, and business leaders were found in a western city. Investigating corruption there, William Chambliss observed that the arrangement has become institutionalized in the city.

I have argued, and I think the data demonstrate quite convincingly, that the people who run the organizations which supply the vices in American cities are members of the business, political, and law enforcement communities — not simply members of a criminal society. Furthermore, it is also clear

from this study that corruption of political-legal organizations is a critical part of the life-blood of the crime cabal. The study of organized crime is thus a misnomer; the study should consider corruption, bureaucracy, and power. By relying on governmental agencies for their information on vice and the rackets, social scientists and lawyers have inadvertently contributed to the miscasting of the issue in terms that are descriptively biased and theoretically sterile. Further, they have been diverted from sociologically interesting and important issues raised by the persistence of crime cabals. As a consequence, the real significance of the existence of syndicates has been overlooked; for instead of seeing these social entities as intimately tied to, and in symbiosis with, the legal and political bureaucracies of the state, they have emphasized the criminality of only a portion of those involved. Such a view contributes little to our knowledge of crime and even less to attempts at crime control.[50]

That the intimacy binding crime, economics, and politics has reached the national level is dramatically shown in events of recent years. Resignation by a vice president of the United States is startling evidence of how high the infection has climbed. Vice President Spiro T. Agnew resigned from that office after pleading no contest — the equivalent in law of a guilty plea — to a charge of income tax evasion, and permitted the court to publish evidence that he had extorted bribes for a decade.[51] From the time he was county executive in suburban Baltimore until he reached the second highest national office, Agnew received cash in kickbacks and payments from engineers who wanted government business.

In return for his bargained plea, Mr. Agnew was assured that the government would drop all other prosecution against him.[52] He was free to proclaim his innocence of any wrongdoing, and the court settled for a sentence of three years of unsupervised probation and a fine of $10,000. Now a convicted felon, he was also (unlike most felons) free to pursue his private life, which undoubtedly would include business as well as pleasure. The state once again remained relatively exempt from a searching examination. The public, however, had one more indication — this time from the top — about the close relationship among crime, economics, and American politics.

Investigations have uncovered other instances of collusion: organized crime's part in policies toward revolutionary Cuba.[53] Distressed that Fidel Castro tossed organized crime operations out of Cuba, closing down gambling casinos and brothels, syndicate figures and Cuban rightwing exiles cooperated with the CIA in planning and executing the attempted Bay of Pigs invasion and the subsequent attempts to assassinate Castro. Some of these same people and forces were later to surface in the crimes related to Watergate.

The connection between organized crime and government has been covered up by the federal government's law enforcement agencies. The FBI has long tried to perpetuate the idea that organized crime is limited to a few persons of Italian descent and that there is no such thing as a national crime syndicate.[54] To disclose a nationwide criminal conspiracy would have required the FBI, then under J. Edgar Hoover's direction, to investigate and expose gangster friends and supporters who were deeply involved in business and politics. We now have better evidence, however, on how far organized crime reaches in the United States: "The gray area between crime and business and politics deepened and widened until in the 1970's it is impossible to say where one ends and the other begins."[55] We need realistic understanding of this kind to start looking for thoughts and actions that will provide an alternative to a future built on the association of crime, business, and politics.

Watergate — Beneath and Beyond

From the time the offices of the Democratic National Committee in the Watergate buildings in Washington, D.C., were broken into in June of 1972, Americans gradually became aware of crimes committed by the state, its leaders and officials, and those hired to commit criminal acts. Acts of spying and sabotage were directed from the White House, whose purpose (as former President Nixon said) was to "stop security leaks and to investigate other sensitive matters."[56] As the disclosures multiplied, crimes far beyond Watergate were exposed.

Still more crimes were committed as the investigations went forward, to cover up the criminal world that made Watergate possible or necessary. The name "Watergate" came to include not only a plot within the president's reelection committee and the coverup activities, but all the schemes the state and its leaders resorted to.

Watergate uncovered a "second government" in the United States, or perhaps better, a previously unsuspected form of influence and control spreading through the government. Watergate was but the tip of a coolly rational bureaucratic iceberg; the real forces lay in the political depths below.

Beneath Watergate is a government with "a combination of vast and complicated interlocking forces, pulling in the CIA here and organized crime there, using politicians one time and émigré thugs the next, which seems to regard government as a tool for financial enrichment."[57] These operations are usually beyond the reach of citizens. "Other scandals — whether called by that name in the press or not, as with the Watergate 'caper' — are also sure to follow, for it seems obvious that the kind of milieu in which the President has chosen to immerse himself will continue to produce policies self-serving at best, shady at average, and downright illegal at worst, and that at least some of this will break through to public attention."[58] This power will not be washed away by investigations, prosecutions, or the new administration; the underside of the United States is likely to reign for some time, until politics and economics can be changed.

The secret government's clandestine operations tell us of some forces involved in established politics and economics. These operations are connected with government and business agencies; when discovered they are covered by lies. A pattern visible in these spy and sabotage operations consists of the agents who reappear in many of the same assignments. This listing of the men indicted in the Watergate break-in reveals some of the complex criminal operations in the American state, and the key roles played by the CIA and the FBI.

Bernard L. Barker (alias Frank or Fran Carter). Half-Cuban American who lived in Cuba for a number of years and left after Castro's revolution. Former employee of the Central Intelligence Agency and reported to have had a role in the abortive Bay of Pigs invasion of Cuba. Founded Barker Associates, a Miami real estate firm, in 1971.

Virgilio R. Gonzalez (alias Raul or Raoul Godoy or Goboy). Cuban who emigrated to United States at time of Castro's rise. Employed as locksmith.

Eugenio R. Martinez (alias Gene or Jene Valdes). Former pre-Castro Cuban legislator. Exile reportedly active in anti-Castro movement. Said to have been associated with CIA. Member of Barker's real estate firm.

James W. McCord Jr. (alias Edward J. Warren and Edward J. Martin). Former FBI agent. CIA employee for 19 years until retirement in 1970. Salaried security coordinator for the Republican National Committee and Nixon's re-election committee until day after his arrest.

Frank A. Sturgis (alias Frank Angelo Fiorini, Edward J. Hamilton and Joseph DiAlberto or D'Alberto). Reportedly former American gun-smuggler for Castro, later active in anti-Castro Cuban exile activities, including Bay of Pigs invasion. Said to have had extensive links with CIA. Described as an associate of Barker.

E. Howard Hunt Jr. CIA employee, 1949–70. Reportedly had key role in 1961 Bay of Pigs invasion. Writer of spy novels. Part-time consultant to White House counsel Charles W. Colson from 1970 until March 29, 1972. Consultant projects included declassification of the Pentagon Papers and intelligence work in narcotics enforcement.

G. Gordon Liddy. Former FBI agent. Special assistant to assistant Treasury secretary, 1969–71, when he was reportedly fired for unauthorized activities. Joined White House staff in July 1971 and said to have suggested bugging *The New York Times* during Pentagon Papers controversy. Joined Nixon re-election committee in late 1971, where he was finance counsel at time of Watergate break-in. Dismissed by Mitchell for refusing to answer FBI's questions.[59]

As the Watergate investigation proceeded, it seemed clear that these men were agents for criminals much higher in the American business and political establishment. This and other events of recent years suggest not a series of isolated incidents, but a conspiracy led by powers within the United States. An observer with close ties to the intelligence establishment said: "A look at the power and history of the 15 years lying behind Watergate — at the CIA and the espionage establishment tied to Gordon Liddy's bungling burglars and the bright young men who proposed Gestapo-like plans for the White House — suggests that there was indeed a conspiracy — possibly one whose reach extended beyond CREEP [Committee to Re-elect the President] and even the White House itself."[60] Other events, involving United States foreign as well as domestic operations, may be similarly connected.

Inquiries into Watergate and the subsequent coverup disclosed many other alliances and related criminal operations, connecting the United States government, organized crime, and clandestine intelligence networks. Not the least of these discoveries is the possible connection of some of the Watergate figures, agencies, and operations to past political assassinations: John Kennedy, Martin Luther King, Robert Kennedy, and the attempted assassination of George Wallace were conspiratorial plots to maintain control over the established political and economic system in the United States by those groups, persons, and forces which arranged Watergate.[61] From the assassination of John Kennedy in Dallas to the Watergate burglary in Washington, a single path appeared to be traceable.

The path of crime, it seemed, led finally to the highest level of the United States government, the presidency itself. Politics, business, and organized crime appeared tightly intertwined in the circle of people and events around the career of Richard Nixon. In an extensive investigation, a researcher uncovered hints about Nixon's business and organized crime dealings in Florida and the Caribbean since the late forties:

> Nixon visited Miami numerous times in the late Forties, contrary to all of his official biographies. While there, he yachted with Richard Danner, Bebe Rebozo, and Tatum "Chubby" Wofford of the syndicate-con-

trolled Wofford Hotel. Danner also had mob connections at that time.

Nixon has invested in two southern Florida land deals; others involved in both projects have had links with organized crime. Two men in particular — Leonard Bursten and Nathan Ratner — have had business connections with organized crime.

Nixon concealed his ownership of a Key Biscayne lot for four years until a mortgage held by another Lansky associate, Arthur Desser, was paid off.

Nixon's closest friend, Bebe Rebozo, was a war profiteer in the early Forties in the tire recapping business. Three of his associates served on the Dade County tire allocation board, in clear violation of OPA regulation No. 3C-118. At the same time Nixon was working in the legal interpretations unit of the OPA in Washington, D.C.

Nixon technically concealed his employment with the OPA until he was President.

Nixon is linked to the "Havana Connection" — a funnel for organized crime and reactionary Cuban politics. Indictees in the Watergate case also figure in this connection.

Nixon has received campaign contributions from two men who have had direct connections to organized crime.

Nixon has appointed a number of men, including John Connally, William Rogers, and Will Wilson, who have indirect ties to organized crime.

The mob-favored Miami National Bank was the chief creditor in a bankruptcy case which led to a $300,000,000 suit, still pending, against Nixon and other members of his New York law firm for their alleged part in skimming over $5,000,000 off the bankrupt firm's accounts.

Nixon's rise to wealth and power has required the silent loyalty of a wide range of personalities whose names only occasionally surface in the glare of scandal — with good reason. Richard Nixon would not be where he is today were it not for his uncanny ability to thrive on political crisis. As much as anything else it is his self-proclaimed poker-playing instincts — the cautious, calculating, close-mouthed style and the ability to keep a stone face in rough as well as smooth times — that has carried Nixon to the Presidency.[62]

The full extent of crime in the American state is just beginning to surface; some of the criminal associations and dealings were revealed by Watergate. The Nixon administration's operations this time overstepped the bounds of trickery and deceit acceptable in American politics, and the administration was called to account for *some* of its criminal acts.

ENFORCING
AND ADMINISTERING
CRIMINAL LAW

10

Police in the Community

The substantive criminal law is just one aspect of the legal order. The state creates a complex of judicial bureaucracies and law enforcement agencies to enforce and administer the law, carrying out the objectives of state authority, protecting and securing its interests. Law enforcement is crucial in maintaining the established social and economic order in the United States; its agencies, especially local police departments, are bureaucracies that protect the existing order.

Law Enforcement in America

Rise of the Police

The police rose to influence and power in the nineteenth century because they were needed to preserve the established social order. They were a separate agency that could respond to attacks that were being made on domestic order in London, Paris, and the growing American cities. The propertied classes feared the threat they felt from the "dangerous classes," the "agglomeration of the criminal, vicious, and violent — the rapidly multiplying poor of cities whose size had no precedent in history."[1]

The policed society relieved the propertied class of coercing the population by themselves. Police were a domestic force outside the military that would maintain domestic order. Mobs and riots, whether in reacting to oppressive conditions or other impulses, could be contained by a separate police force, performing for the propertied classes.

The new police bureaucracy could penetrate society in a way impossible for military forces. Diffused throughout society, they could work at preventing crime by detecting and apprehending criminals. The convenience was more than technical: "The replacement of intermittent military intervention in largely unpoliced society by continuous professional bureaucratic policing meant that the benefits of police organization — continual pervasive moral display and lower long-term costs of official coercion for the state and propertied classes — absolutely required the moral cooperation of civil society."[2] The police had become an integral part of society, to be morally accepted by everyone. They were a garrison force, used constantly against the internal enemy.

The movement to a policed society can be traced from the constabulary system to the modern professional police.[3] In early England, citizens were mutually responsible, through the "pledge" system, for maintaining law and order. Eventually local noblemen appointed constables to enforce the law. When the local areas, known as "hundreds," were grouped to form "shires," the office of the "shire-reeve" (later "sheriff") came into being. During the reign of Edward I (1272–1307) the first official forces were formed in the large towns of England. These "watch and ward" officers were charged with protecting property and arresting offenders between sunset and daybreak. In 1326 Edward II created the justices of the peace to assist the sheriff in policing the country, but the constable remained the primary law enforcement officer in all the English towns.

As long as England was rural these law-enforcement offices were adequate. But by the middle of the eighteenth century, towns and cities had grown fairly large, and innovations in law enforcement were needed. One of the most important experiments was the appointment by Henry Fielding (he wrote *Tom Jones*) of a foot patrol, later known as the "Bow Street Runners," in the Bow Street magistracy of London. Such a small force could not, however, keep order in the city, and conditions were so critical that as the eighteenth century ended, committees in the House of Commons called for a better system of protecting the public. Finally a committee of the Commons issued a report on the increase in crime and urged a change in the method of policing the metropolis. Sir Robert Peel introduced a police reform bill that was passed by Parliament in 1829.[4] The Metropolitan Police Act established for London a police force separate from the old constabulary system and served as the model for other cities in Great Britain.

The American colonies adopted the English law enforcement offices.[5] American villages and rural areas had their night watchmen, constables, sheriffs, and justices of the peace. In the early nineteenth century, American cities too established their own forces. London's police plan was adopted by New York in 1844,

and in the next ten years similar police systems were organized in Chicago, Boston, and Philadelphia. By the early 1900s most cities in the United States had unified police forces.

The professional police force in American cities was an attempt to control the behavior of those who rebelled against oppressive urban conditions. In Boston, for example, the problem of mob violence "soon compelled the municipality to take a more significant step, to create a new class of permanent professional officers with new standards of performance."[6] The new police force in American cities served to maintain the desired order.

The police were now to prevent disorder, according to a preventive conception of law enforcement: "the police take the initiative and seek out those engaged in violating the law — those engaged in specific behaviors that are designated as illegal."[7] Preventing crime seemed a rational way of keeping public order.[8] The objectives of the police force are the same today, only now the methods of law enforcement are aided by the latest in scientific and technological developments, plus bureaucratic management and the science of social behavior.

Forms of Law Enforcement

Law enforcement in the United States today, with half a million employed in approximately 40,000 law-enforcement agencies, cannot be treated as a unitary system. The duties vary, with at least five types of public law-enforcement systems, conforming roughly to the major levels of government: (1) the police agencies of the federal government; (2) the state police forces and criminal investigation agencies of the fifty states; (3) the sheriffs in more than 3,000 counties, plus a few county police forces that either duplicate the sheriff's police jurisdiction or displace it; (4) the police of a thousand cities and more than 20,000 townships or New England towns, to which must be added an unknown number of magisterial districts and county districts in the South and West; and (5) the police of 15,000 villages, boroughs, and incorporated towns, together with a small number of special-purpose forces serving public quasi-corporations and ad hoc districts.[9] Add to these the law-enforcement activities of private police agencies and you have a great many systems of law enforce-

DOCUMENT_____

RECENT DEVELOPMENTS IN POLICE MANPOWER

EMPLOYMENT

Total full-time local police department employment, which increased at a rate of 4.7 per cent annually between 1966 and 1969, grew 7.1 per cent annually from 1969 to 1971, to about 420,000. Civilian employment rose to 60,000, a 14 per cent annual change, while sworn personnel rose 6 per cent per year to 360,000. If the 1969–71 rates of change continue, almost 560,000 workers — 460,000 sworn personnel and 100,000 civilians — will be employed in local police agencies in 1975. With a shift toward the greater use of civilian workers, the mix could conceivably be 425,000 sworn and 135,000 civilians.

EXPENDITURES

In fiscal year 1969–70, $4.5 billion was spent by state and local governments for police departments, a 14 per cent increase from the previous year and about the same rate of change as in the 1967–69 period. In 1970–71 local police agencies spent $4.4 billion — $3.6 billion on compensation and $835 million on supplies and equipment. The rapid increase in supplies and equipment from $276 million in 1969 reflects the impact of Law Enforcement Assistance Administration grants.

On the basis of these more recent changes, projections for 1975 expenditures total $7 billion for a model reflecting current employment practices and $6.7 billion for an estimate emphasizing more civilian employment. The table presents these updated projections.

Local Police Department Employment and Associated Costs (1971 and 1975)[a]

| | | 1975 | |
Category	1971	Current trends of employment policy	Shift toward civilian employment
Employment (in thousands)			
Policemen and detectives	360	460	425
Civilian personnel	60	100	135
Total	420	560	560
Expenditures (in millions of current dollars)			
Employee compensation[b]	$3,595	$5,970	$5,640
Other	835	1,050	1,100
Total	$4,430	$7,020	$6,740

[a]Sources of this information are U.S. Bureau of the Census, *Government Finances in 1970–71* (Washington, D.C.: U.S. Government Printing Office, 1972); *Public Employment in 1971* (Washington, D.C.: U.S. Government Printing Office, 1972).
[b]Employee compensation includes salaries, pensions, and costs of other fringe benefits.

Source: From Morris Cobern, "Some Manpower Aspects of the Criminal Justice System," *Crime and Delinquency,* 19 (April 1973), pp. 198–199.

DOCUMENT (Continued)_____

From 1969 to 1970, expenditures for correction increased by $233 million to $1,624 million, a 17 per cent increase. Between 1967 and 1969 the annual increase was 10.5 per cent and from 1962 to 1969, 8.4 per cent. The high rate of inflation in recent years has modified the purchasing power of these expenditures.

CONCLUSIONS

In recent years there has been a more equal distribution of resources among the various segments of the law-enforcement–criminal-justice–rehabilitation system. However, a serious shortage of knowledge concerning the economics and cost-effectiveness of the law enforcement system remains, while the incidence of crime and the resources to deal with it continue to grow.

---

ment, related in their functions and at times overlapping in their jurisdictions.

And within the systems are specific police agencies. Some federal agencies have law-enforcement powers, such as the Federal Bureau of Investigation, the Secret Service, the Bureau of Narcotics, Post Office Inspectors, the Bureau of Internal Revenue, the Bureau of Customs, the Immigration Border Patrol, and the Alcohol Tax Unit of the Department of the Treasury. The federal government also maintains the United States Marshal as a law enforcement agent whose duty it is to preserve order in the courtrooms, handle subpoenas and summonses, seize goods, transport prisoners, and serve as a disbursing officer.[10]

Law enforcement on the state level was not established in the United States until the first part of this century. In 1905, Pennsylvania organized the first state police force; by World War II, all the states had followed. Today the state police forces perform such varied functions as patrolling highways, investigating fires, inspecting liquor, arresting juvenile offenders, and inspecting property.[11] They also provide services to local police forces, including criminal identification, laboratory services, and communication services.

Outside public law enforcement is a type usually obscured from public view: *private police*. Private agencies such as Pinkerton's, Inc., came into being in the middle of the last century when private companies desired protection that civil police could not give them. Railroads, coal companies, and iron ore com-

panies employed their own police forces to control theft and robbery, and in some cases to prevent and break strikes of workers against the companies.[12] Today numerous kinds of businesses, industries, and institutions use them to guard property, apprehend thieves, investigate offenses, and to detect fraud and embezzlement.

More than 3,000 private police agencies are engaged in privately enforcing criminal law, providing detective and protective services.[13] More than a billion dollars is spent annually on these services. The Pinkerton agency alone has a staff of nearly 30,000. Although private police do not usually make arrests, suspects they apprehend may be turned over to public police for official arrest and prosecution.

Legal and Discretionary Law Enforcement

Legal Regulation of the Police

Law enforcement takes place within a very tenuous framework of social control and legal regulation. In fact, contrary to popular belief, few activities of the police are regulated by the law. Any regulation that does apply to them comes mainly from decisions made in recent years by the courts. They developed independently of the other judicial agencies, so that most of their behavior falls outside legal control.

Most of the law regulating police behavior has developed awkwardly and indirectly from specific cases in which defendants have ques-

VIEWPOINT_____

PROFILE OF A PRIVATE POLICE AGENCY:
PINKERTON'S, INC.

Pinkerton's, Inc., is the oldest and largest firm providing contract guard and investigative services in the United States.* The firm's total revenues in 1969 were $120.5 million, with net earnings of 3.5 per cent of revenues; the annual compound growth rate in revenues in the 1965–1969 period was 15.8 per cent. In 1967, the last year for which reliable data on the contract crime-protection industry are available, Pinkerton's had 18.6 per cent of the total "detective agency and protective service" industry revenues. Growth is achieved primarily internally, rather than by extensive acquisitions. Total employment in 1969 was 27,000, of which 17,000 were full-time and 10 per cent were unionized.

The firm was founded in 1850 by Allan Pinkerton, who emigrated from Scotland in 1842 and became the Chicago Police Department's first detective. Eight years later, at the age of 31, he founded his own detective agency with nine men. For more than half a century, Pinkerton's was the only investigative force that crossed state borders and operated in all parts of the country. Pinkerton men were called upon for service by local, state, and federal agencies, as well as by private interests. Their colorful adventures included hunting down such notorious outlaws as Jesse James, and averting an assassination attempt on Abraham Lincoln. At the start of the Civil War, Pinkerton put his detective force at the disposal of the Union. This led to the first organized Secret Service, headed by Pinkerton himself. With the organization of the FBI in 1924 and the subsequent growth of effective public police investigative forces, Pinkerton's has concentrated on serving private business and industry. Since 1883, they have been the official detective arm of the Jewelers Security Alliance, and in connection with that assignment, they maintain information files on 1.5 million known criminals. The term "private eye" grew out of the unblinking eye that was Pinkerton's trademark for many years.

Over the years Pinkerton's has developed policies on the type of business it does and does not accept. Today, the company will not accept investigative business regarding labor organizing activities for either labor or management; domestic or marital problems; political personalities or situations; or the defense of persons under prosecution by the public police. Also, the company will not provide guard services in a strike, unless the firm being struck is a permanent client. Pinkerton's will not keep its guards in a struck plant unless both union and management agree.

The two prohibitions involving labor/management problems stem from two periods in Pinkerton's history that earned the agency the hatred of labor unions and the distrust of many persons outside organized labor. The first was its role

---

Source: From James S. Kakalik and Sorrel Wildhorn, *The Private Police Industry: Its Nature and Extent,* vol. II (Washington, D.C.: Law Enforcement Assistance Administration, 1972), pp. 45–46.

    * Material drawn from personal interviews with Pinkerton's, Inc., executives; 1969 Pinkerton's, Inc., Annual Report; Prospectus for sale of Class B common stock in Pinkerton's, Inc., Ernst & Ernst, February 26, 1969; *The Pinkerton's, The Detective Dynasty that Made History,* by J. D. Horan, Crown Publishers, 1967; 1967 Census of Business; 1968 Bear, Stearns, and Co., report, *Crime Protection, A Growth Industry;* 1970 Predicasts, Inc., Special Study 56, *Security Systems;* 1970 Burnham and Co. report on investment opportunities in the Security, Protection, and Investigation Services Industry; "Last of the Pinkerton's Keeps Watch," *Business Week,* March 5, 1960.

VIEWPOINT (Continued)_____

in the infamous Homestead massacre of 1892, when Pinkerton guards were used to reopen a struck steel mill. After that incident, Congress decided that such agencies could not work directly for the federal government and passed the Pinkerton's Law. Pinkerton's also decided to eschew guarding struck plants unless both sides agreed. The second event occurred in 1936, when a Senate subcommittee, headed by Senator Robert La Follette, Jr., investigating labor espionage called in Pinkerton's executives. In that period, this work accounted for up to 30 per cent of the agency's business. The work involved offering companies confidential reports on labor unrest in their plants and on the work of union organizers. La Follette's investigation produced much bitter questioning of Pinkerton's activities, and when it was over Congress passed a resolution saying that "the industrial spy system breeds fear, suspicion, and animosity, tends to cause strikes and industrial warfare, and is contrary to sound public policy." Simultaneously, Pinkerton's quit its labor espionage.

Today the primary source of Pinkerton's business is furnishing uniformed security personnel (90 per cent of total revenues in 1969). They provide security personnel for industrial plants, institutions (especially hospitals and campuses), high-rise buildings, special events (the largest force ever supplied to a special event was 800 for a college football game), and race tracks. The largest single contract was for security at the New York World's Fair in 1964–65, when up to 4,500 personnel were on duty at one time. Investigation has declined relative to other services and accounted for only about $7 million in 1969. The firm does not operate central station alarm systems but does manufacture security devices such as watchmen's clocks and anti-intrusion alarms. In 1969 they initiated a Patrol and Inspection Service. Security consulting and survey services are also offered.

The corporation is currently headquartered in New York City and maintains offices in 93 North American cities.

---

tioned the procedures used in their criminal convictions. Primarily by default, the Supreme Court has sought to provide a few legal guarantees to protect the person against actions by the state. The court has ruled on a number of issues directly related to law enforcement, such as arrest warrants, search and seizure, interrogation, confessions, wiretapping and eavesdropping, the use of informers, and the right of counsel. The assumption is that controlling police *mis*conduct will somehow regulate police behavior.

The Supreme Court decisions on law enforcement are generally founded on three provisions in the Constitution. The Fourth Amendment provides: "The right of the people to be secure in their persons, houses, papers, and effects, against unreasonable searches and seizures, shall not be violated, and no warrants shall issue but upon probable cause, supported by oath or affirmation, and particularly describing the place to be searched, and the persons or things to be seized." The Fifth Amendment provides that "no person . . . shall be compelled in any criminal case to be a witness against himself, nor be deprived of life, liberty, or property, without due process of law." And the Fourteenth Amendment provides that "no state shall . . . deprive any person of life, liberty, or property without due process of law, nor deny to any person within its jurisdiction the equal protection of the laws." Several recent Supreme Court decisions have resulted from the review of criminal cases in which these constitutional guarantees have been jeopardized.[14]

One of the first constitutional tests of law-enforcement practices confronted by the Supreme Court was in the *Weeks* v. *United States* case of 1914. In establishing the "exclusionary rule" in that case, the court ruled that evidence obtained by illegal means must be excluded from criminal procedure. With the *McNabb* v. *United States* case in 1943, the Supreme Court ruled that confessions are inadmissible if obtained by federal officers during an unlawful detention. The McNabb decision was elaborated upon in 1957 in *Mallory* v. *United States*. The court ruled that confessions are inadmissible when they are obtained from an arrestee who has not been properly brought before a magistrate. In 1961 the court ruled in *Mapp* v. *Ohio* that evidence obtained by unreasonable searches and seizures must be excluded from state and federal criminal trials. The *Gideon* v. *Wainwright* decision of 1963 ensured the right of counsel for defendants, which was further specified in 1964 in *Massiah* v. *United States* and *Escobedo* v. *Illinois*. The decisions of 1964 provide that the accused in custody may not be questioned until the request for legal counsel has been complied with. Specific guidelines for law enforcement and minimum procedural safeguards were established in 1966 in *Miranda* v. *Arizona.*

More recently, however, the courts have retreated from some of these decisions. In *Harris* v. *New York,* the Supreme Court withdrew some provisions of the Miranda decision, on the illegal obtaining of incriminating statements from the defendant. Likewise, recent crime bills have in effect overturned some of the earlier court rulings. And in the lawless void, day-to-day police behavior is almost unlimited.

But no matter what the extent of judicial regulation of police conduct, the court's influence on law enforcement is of little consequence. Even when the court rulings touch local police departments, there is hardly any effect on arrest practices. As in the Miranda case, data on the police interrogation of suspects show that the police always have evidence apart from the interrogation itself.[15] And restrictions on interrogation, when they are observed by the police, do not limit them in making an arrest and charging the suspect with a crime.

In the end, then, we cannot expect the court

to have much effect on police conduct, other than perhaps on their handling of a few major offenses. Egon Bittner observes that there are reasons for limiting the court's influence on the police:

> First, it generally does not touch the vast domain of charges involving disorderly conduct and other minor offenses. This is so because in such cases the merits of the police decision ordinarily are not questioned by either the defendants or the judges. Second, because the police are often exposed to strong pressures to take some action against conditions that offend the public, they sometimes have to proceed in ways that could not be sustained on grounds of legality. Police officials are quite frank about it, referring to public opinion as one source of their authority. Third, policemen in many jurisdictions proceed against some types of illegal activity — notably those involving the so-called sumptuary crimes — with deliberate neglect of rules of legal restraint. In most of these cases arrests are made without intent to prosecute and primarily for harassment purposes. By such means they hope to make plying some unsavory occupation more hazardous and less profitable. Fourth, judicial influence is totally irrelevant for the immense variety of activities that have nothing to do with law enforcement or legality but is primarily oriented to easing some social strains. For instance, no court has thus far presumed to inquire whether police service should be authorized and made available for helping to settle marital disputes.[16]

The result is that the police are almost totally free to pursue their own course of action. They are bound mainly by the rules of their own occupation and the interests of those they serve.

Police Discretion

Contrary to any framework of legal control, then, much police behavior is a matter of *discretion*: how they act is determined by their own standards combined with the general objective of preserving domestic order. Still it is commonly assumed that the police are operating entirely according to a body of legal prescriptions. Police discretion is relatively unknown to the public, which is not aware that no legal code provides specific instructions for enforcing the law.

DOCUMENT_____

THE MIRANDA WARNING

The U.S. Supreme Court, in Miranda v. Arizona, 384 U.S. 436 (1966), established procedural safeguards for police interrogation of accused persons in police custody. "A suspect being questioned is *in custody when he is under arrest or is deprived of his freedom of action in any significant way.*" If the police propose to interrogate a person in police custody, he must first be warned and advised that:

1. He has the right to remain silent.
2. Anything he says can be used against him in a court of law.
3. He has the right to consult with an attorney and to have an attorney present during questioning.
4. If he cannot afford an attorney, one will be appointed for him prior to any questioning if he so desires.

A suspect may waive such rights after the warning has been given and the opportunity to exercise his rights has been afforded him, but the waiver by the accused must be made knowingly and intelligently. After a waiver, opportunity to exercise these rights must be afforded the suspect throughout all subsequent interrogation. Unless and until such warning and waiver are demonstrated by the prosecution at trial, no evidence obtained as a result of interrogation can be used against the person questioned. The burden of demonstrating that the defendant knowingly and intelligently waived his privilege against self-incrimination and his right to counsel rests on the prosecution.

A standard way to demonstrate this waiver by the suspect is a signature on a copy of the Miranda Warning (see figure) or a signed statement equally extensive. The investigator must offer affirmative evidence of the willingness of the suspect to waive his privileges and participate in the interrogation and of the fact that at no time before or during the resultant interrogation did the suspect indicate in any manner that he wished to remain silent or state that he wanted an attorney.

The Miranda Warning. The U.S. Supreme Court decision in *Miranda v. Arizona* established this warning as a prerequisite to any police interrogation of a suspect once a case has focused and the suspect has been taken into custody.

MIRANDA WARNING

1. YOU HAVE THE RIGHT TO REMAIN SILENT.

2. ANYTHING YOU SAY CAN AND WILL BE USED AGAINST YOU IN A COURT OF LAW.

3. YOU HAVE THE RIGHT TO TALK TO A LAWYER AND HAVE HIM PRESENT WITH YOU WHILE YOU ARE BEING QUESTIONED.

4. IF YOU CANNOT AFFORD TO HIRE A LAWYER, ONE WILL BE APPOINTED TO REPRESENT YOU BEFORE ANY QUESTIONING, IF YOU WISH ONE.

Source: From Paul B. Weston and Kenneth M. Wells, *Elements of Criminal Investigation* (Englewood Cliffs, N.J.: Prentice-Hall, 1971), pp. 62–63.

DOCUMENT (Continued)

> ### WAIVER
>
> AFTER THE WARNING AND IN ORDER TO SECURE A WAIVER, THE FOLLOWING QUESTIONS
> SHOULD BE ASKED AND AN AFFIRMATIVE REPLY SECURED TO EACH QUESTION:
>
> 1. DO YOU UNDERSTAND EACH OF THESE RIGHTS I HAVE EXPLAINED TO YOU?
>
> 2. HAVING THESE RIGHTS IN MIND, DO YOU WISH TO TALK TO US NOW?

Many assume too that the police fully enforce the criminal law by arresting all who violate the law. The ideal of *full enforcement* of the law is, in fact, preserved officially in formal law as well as in popular conception.[17] Criminal statutes are so stated as to imply that the duty of the police is to faithfully enforce all the laws, against everyone, in all circumstances, at all times. The stereotype of the policeman shows him as the ministerial officer whose function it is to detect crime, gather evidence, and make arrests. Police themselves reinforce this conception by denying that decisions are involved in their work or that they have informal standards for making their decisions.

Full enforcement of criminal law, however, is far from possible because of numerous limitations and circumstances. First, a few *procedural* restrictions limit the enforcement of some laws. Second, *interpretational* latitude, resulting primarily from ambiguous wording in many statutes, permits much discretion on what constitutes a criminal offense. Third, *technical* matters confound law enforcement, such as limited police time, personnel, and equipment for detecting and investigating crime. Fourth, *organizational* norms of local police departments provide guides for both the enforcement and nonenforcement of criminal law. Fifth, *ideological* orientations or values of policemen provide a basis for selective law enforcement. Sixth, *societal* pressures prevent full enforcement of some criminal laws. These pressures are a lack of correspondence between criminal statutes and current norms, failure of victims and the public to report offenses, and the harmful social consequences that might follow enforcement of some criminal laws. Whatever the reasons, law enforcement is a matter of decision-making, of discretion.

Most people continue to have little idea about the extent of discretionary decisions in law enforcement and little knowledge of the ways in which discretion operates. Police discretion rarely comes to the average citizen's attention. Only when we find ourselves in an encounter with the police do we realize how important police discretion is for us. Solutions such as these are currently being suggested:

> The first step is to elevate police discretion from the sub-rosa position it now occupies; the role of police as decision-makers must be expressly recognized. Then, as has been found possible with respect to other administrative agencies, the areas in which discretion properly may be exercised must be delimited, principles to govern its exercise must be established, and effective means of control must be discovered.[18]

It is unlikely, however, that any solutions to the problem will be possible as long as the police are an agency apart from the community in which law enforcement takes place. But no matter what solutions are proposed and implemented, we must immediately recognize in learning to understand law enforcement that discretion does exist and that it is basic to law enforcement in America. At a crucial stage in the legal process persons are defined as criminal because police act in some ways rather than in others. Law enforcement is discretionary.

Law Enforcement in the Community

The Police Force

As traditionally conceived and currently practiced, the primary function of the police is to operate as a permanent presence in the community; they are employed to impose force or the threat of force in solving the problems that arise in the community's everyday life. Their concrete activities may be diverse, but the objective is singular. Bittner writes,

> Whatever the substance of the task at hand, whether it involves protection against an undesired imposition, caring for those who cannot care for themselves, attempting to solve a crime, helping to save a life, abating a nuisance, or settling an explosive dispute, police intervention means above all making use of the capacity and authority to overpower resistance to an attempted solution in the native habitat of the problem.[19]

The police enter situations that require solutions that are "non-negotiably coercible."

Because of their conventional role in American society, natural forces isolate the police from other members of the community.[20] By definition, police activity involves intruding upon the citizen's affairs, usually restricting one's freedom. Also, it is natural to separate from your life those who are charged with detecting and arresting members of the community. This response is reinforced by the fear and mistrust aroused by the police following experience with them. The police, in addition, have come to represent by their role and their behavior the forces of sanction and punishment.

The organization and procedure of police work itself isolates the police. The requirements of patrol, investigation, surveillance, and the like clearly separate the police from the public. Furthermore, most of their operating policies are beyond public scrutiny; they are secretive and known only to the police themselves. Isolation from the community is inevitable, because of what is conventionally expected of the police in American society.

Maintaining Order

We must, nevertheless, understand police activity in a context larger than law enforcement. Although the general purpose is to maintain a particular kind of domestic order, the day-to-day police activities in the community are quite varied. We may not go so far as to argue, as some have, that the police are "peace officers," unless this means preserving domestic order for the benefit of dominant classes in the community.[21] Yet it is true that the objectives of the police are not always accomplished by making an arrest. Indeed, in many situations other methods may be more appropriate for keeping order in the community.

Maintaining order often involves giving support to some members of the community while denying it to others, controlling one member but lending support to another. Many disputes are handled by police intervention, which has been documented in a study of the calls received at a metropolitan police department.[22] Nearly half were requests for assistance of some kind. The calls for support were about personal problems: requests for health services (such as ambulance escorts, investigation of accidents, suicide attempts), problems with children (complaints about trespassing or destructive behavior), and the problems of incapacitated persons. Other calls were requests for assistance in personal disputes and quarrels, violence or protection from potential violence, and requests for assistance about missing persons and behavior of youths. The policeman performs many actions that are not directly related to enforcement of the law but with other aspects of order in the community.

Community Variations

The kind and quantity of law enforcement varies among communities and from one area to another within communities. One of the most important reasons for these variations is found in the varying *expectations* of law enforcement in different kinds of communities. First, communities differ in the kinds of behavior that community members and the police think should receive criminal sanctions. The correspondence between the criminal law and what is actually condemned may vary too. Within one community, or part of it, arrest of a violent spouse may be expected, though such an arrest would be entirely inappropriate elsewhere. Second, communities differ in their norms on seeking assistance from the police. One community may prescribe that complaints be made to the police, another may restrict the citizen's use of the police. Third, community attitudes toward the police affect both the use of the police by community members and the way in which police respond to situations in which law-breaking may be involved.

Perhaps the most significant characteristic affecting law enforcement is the community's homogeneity in cultural values, social class, race, and occupation. A homogeneous community has fairly well-defined expectations on appropriate community behavior, and its police will operate more consistently according to those shared expectations.

In a heterogeneous community, the police must operate by departmental procedures more than by community expectations. The police in a homogeneous community may detect more law violations, but they handle the cases informally rather than by the formality of an arrest. Furthermore, in a homogeneous community, violators of the law may be referred back to the community for disposition rather than to the legal process. Invoking the law may be the only means of maintaining order in the heterogeneous community. Thus, in the homogeneous community a wide scope of law-violating behavior is handled informally by the police, and in the heterogeneous community criminal sanctions are more readily applied to the same behaviors to accomplish the same objectives.

The relationship between community homogeneity and law enforcement is found in a study of how juvenile cases were handled by police in four communities in the Pittsburgh area.[23] The researcher investigated how police differentially selected juvenile offenders for court appearance, finding clear differences in the rates of juvenile arrests and court referrals in the four kinds of communities. The large industrial community ("Steel City") had a juvenile arrest rate of 37.3 per 1,000 juvenile population, compared to 12.4 in the residential and commercial community ("Trade City"), 34.8 in the small industrial community ("Mill Town"), and 49.7 in the well-to-do residential community ("Manor Heights"). Further an-

alyzing police records and interviewing police, Goldman confirmed the community differentials.

Goldman found several patterns in the way juvenile offenders were handled in the four communities, apparently a function of the relations between the police and the community. In general, the police in each community tried to reflect what they considered to be the community's attitudes toward delinquency. He summarized the differentials in arrests as follows:

(1) Where there exists an objective, impersonal relation between the police and the public, court referral rates will be high and there will be little discrimination with respect to seriousness of offense, race, and sex of the offender; (2) Where there exists a personal face-to-face relation between the police and the public, there will be more discriminations with respect to court referral of an arrested juvenile.[24]

The research thus showed that law enforcement is affected by the specific role of the police in the community, and that the relationship between the community and the police explains some of the differences in law enforcement from one community to another.

Law enforcement in rural areas seems to be especially influenced by the community's expectations and the role of law enforcement in the community. A study of the county sheriff's social role describes law enforcement in a rural area.[25] In "Star County," in southern Illinois, the sheriff was permitted (or expected) to use a great amount of discretion in law enforcement. His primary function was to conserve the peace, and peace was not always best preserved by making an arrest. The rule of thumb in enforcement was public safety. We may conclude that a community organized on informal relations resorts to official sanctions only when other means are exhausted or for some reason are inappropriate. In rural communities, whenever possible, informal controls are used in place of law enforcement; discretion is at a maximum.

In the final analysis, however, no matter what the community is like, the primary objective of the police is simply to maintain order in the community. Police behavior must therefore be understood as part of the conflict in most communities.[26] The police usually define as criminal, by arrest and criminal charges, those who threaten class arrangements in the community, thereby containing conflict — at the expense, of course, of the subordinate classes.

Organization

Bureaucratic-Military Structure

The most significant thing about law enforcement is the strongly bureaucratic and military organization of the police. American police departments, structured like quasi-military institutions, give community law enforcement its special character. The military model is especially appropriate to law enforcement's purpose:

> Both institutions are instruments of force and for both institutions the occasions for using force are unpredictably distributed. Thus, the personnel in each must be kept in a highly disciplined state of alert preparedness. The formalism that characterizes military organization, the insistence on rules and regulations, on spit and polish, on obedience to superiors, and so on, constitute a permanent rehearsal for "the real thing."[27]

The mission is warlike and the organization is structured for that purpose.

The system is built on subordination and a chain of command.[28] Modernized metropolitan police departments also are organized according to a centralized command system, with the communications center as the principal source of structure. That is, each police department is divided into a number of units. Each has its specialized occupational role, and all are necessary because of the variety of cases dealt with by the police (Figure 10.1).

The functional divisions of police departments follow the kinds of activities they handle: (1) traffic patrol and other patrol of structural disorder, enforcing regulations that do not entail moral turpitude in those who break the law; (2) street patrol (including radio cars), especially in downtown areas, to control individual offenses in public places; (3) investi-

gative work, generally involving complaints; (4) undercover work, sometimes using fraud to get inside situations otherwise protected by privacy; and (5) quasi-military action, in which the problem is to apply coercion to control public riot.[29] The differentiated structure within police departments means that the criminal law is selectively enforced according to the organization and the normative expectations of the separate units within the police department. Each division develops and perpetuates its unique system of law enforcement.

Police Organization

The "effectiveness" of the police in enforcing the law has much to do with the way in which the departments are organized.[30] In a study of a nonprofessionalized police department in an east-coast city and a professionalized police department in a west-coast city, James Q. Wilson found that the nonprofessionalized department's members had no strong sense of urgency about police work and produced low rates of official actions on offenders.[31] In the professionalized department, however, infractions of the law were more likely to be detected and offenders were more likely to be arrested, producing a higher crime rate.

How much difference police organization and procedure can make in the rate of reported crime shows too in the yearly change of crime rates within cities. The annual fluctuations sometimes are an obvious result of changes in law-enforcement policy. Policy changes do occur within police departments in such matters as recording crime. During organizational change in the New York City Police Department in 1966, it was decided to change the procedure of recording crime statistics. The newly appointed chief inspector suggested that under the old system a great number of offenses either went unrecorded or were "downgraded" in the official reports. He estimated that roughly 60 per cent of the complaints involving burglary had been officially recorded in the previous year as lesser crimes, such as petty larceny, or had been given a noncriminal label, such as lost property. "To insure factual recording of crime statistics," the inspector ordered that "there should be no discretion with regard to reporting a crime and no am-

Figure 10.1   One Form of a Well-organized Municipal Police Department

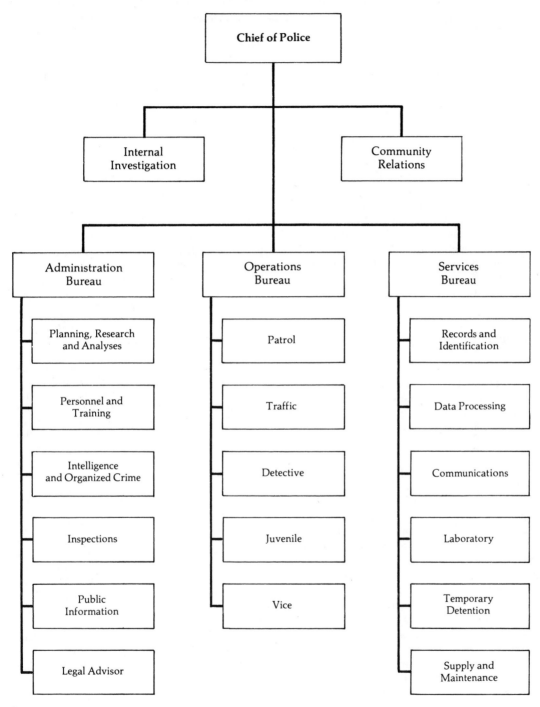

Source: President's Commission on Law Enforcement and Administration of Justice, *Task Force Report: The Police* (Washington, D.C.: U.S. Government Printing Office, 1967), pp. 46–48.

biguity with regard to categorizing a crime."[32] Needless to say, the burglary rate for the following year climbed. The new organizational policy affected the imposing and recording of criminal definitions.

A very obvious effect of changed organizational policy influencing the rate of crime is the rate at which traffic tickets are issued by the police. The rate for moving violations in eight cities was studied and it was found that they varied greatly.[33] The researcher concluded that the variations were caused by the policies of the police departments and not the characteristics of the communities. Departments with high rates of traffic offenses had specialized policies for traffic-law enforcement. Pressure applied by the department administrator also increased the issuing of traffic tickets. Departments with high rates of traffic violation include in their policies the quota system of law enforcement. Such departmental policies can determine the rate of crime.

Occupational Ideology

Developing an Ideology

Carrying out their special mandate in American society has led police to develop their private occupational ideology. They have built an occupational culture with their own assumptions about everyday life and use it as a base for their strategies and tactics.[34] Much of their behavior is understandable when we know the job's context.

The police learn to behave appropriately according to this ideology. During his training, the recruit gradually adopts an outlook on his work and justifications for the procedures and methods he uses in the line of "duty." Socialization of police recruits into the occupation is also affected by their backgrounds. A researcher studied policemen training for the New York City Police Department and found that police candidates are drawn primarily from the lower middle class.[35] The recruits considered their new source of employment to be an upward step, but at the same time were convinced that police work, in relation to other occupations, was not assigned high prestige by the general population. Because of similar socioeconomic status and career expectations, the recruits adapted similarly to their training, eventually displaying a common lack of ability to handle enforcement situations impersonally. They also shared the belief, which grew stronger during their training, that the police lack the basic legal authority to effectively carry out their work.

When he completes academy training and is assigned to a local precinct, the police rookie is called upon to face the challenge of actual duty. Arthur Niederhoffer observes: "His reputation is made in the next few weeks and will shadow him for the rest of his police career: no matter where or when he is transferred, a phone call will precede his arrival, reporting the evaluation that was made of his handling of his first few important cases."[36] The new patrolman's principal challenge is the dilemma of choosing between the professional ideal of police work learned in the academy and the precinct's pragmatic approach. The "lock-them-up" philosophy of the precinct contradicts the professional orientation toward police work learned in the academy.

> In the case of the young policeman the choice between professionalism and pragmatism is apt to depend largely on the circumstances of the case. It is, for example, no great feat for a policeman working in an upper-class neighborhood to protect the rights of his white clientele. It is much more difficult in a lower-class community. In a slum area the professional ethic loses most of the time; the civil rights of lower-class individuals do not count as much as the necessity to accomplish a staggering amount of police work as expeditiously as possible. Shifting from idealism to pragmatism, the newcomer to a lower-class precinct house enters a new reference group whose members are a little contemptuous of all the Academy represents.[37]

It becomes obvious to the new policeman that every law on the book cannot be enforced and that the laws are, in fact, to be enforced with much discretion according to the norms of his department and neighborhood.

The occupational ideology learned by the policeman is formed by two characteristics of his day-to-day work: danger and authority.

DOCUMENT

LAW ENFORCEMENT CODE OF ETHICS

As a Law Enforcement Officer, my fundamental duty is to serve mankind; to safeguard lives and property; to protect the innocent against deception, the weak against oppression or intimidation, and the peaceful against violence or disorder; and to respect the Constitutional rights of all men to liberty, equality and justice.

I will keep my private life unsullied as an example to all; maintain courageous calm in the face of danger, scorn, or ridicule; develop self-restraint; and be constantly mindful of the welfare of others. Honest in thought and deed in both my personal and official life, I will be exemplary in obeying the laws of the land and the regulations of my department. Whatever I see or hear of a confidential nature or that is confided to me in my official capacity will be kept ever secret unless revelation is necessary in the performance of my duty.

I will never act officiously or permit personal feelings, prejudices, animosities or friendships to influence my decisions. With no compromise for crime and with relentless prosecution of criminals, I will enforce the law courteously and appropriately without fear or favor, malice or ill will, never employing unnecessary force or violence and never accepting gratuities.

I recognize the badge of my office as a symbol of public faith, and I accept it as a public trust to be held so long as I am true to the ethics of the police service. I will constantly strive to achieve these objectives and ideals, dedicating myself before God to my chosen profession . . . law enforcement.

Source: From *The Patrol Operation* (Washington, D.C.: International Association of Chiefs of Police, 1970), p. 4.

Jerome Skolnick suggests that these lead to the policeman's "working personality":

The element of danger seems to make the policeman especially attentive to signs indicating a potential for violence and lawbreaking. As a result, the policeman is generally a "suspicious" person. Furthermore, the character of the policeman's work makes him less desirable as a friend, since norms of friendship implicate others in his work. Accordingly, the element of danger isolates the policeman socially from that segment of the citizenry which he regards as symbolically dangerous and also from the conventional citizenry with whom he identifies.

The element of authority reinforces the element of danger in isolating the policeman. Typically, the policeman is required to enforce laws representing puritanical morality, such as those prohibiting drunkenness, and also laws regulating the flow of public activity, such as traffic laws. In these situations the policeman directs the citizenry, whose typical response denies recognition of his authority, and stresses his obligation to danger. The kind of man who responds well to danger, however, does not normally subscribe to codes of puritanical morality. As a result, the policeman is unusually liable to the charge of hypocrisy. That the whole civilian world is an audience for the policeman further promotes police isolation and, in consequence, solidarity. Finally, danger undermines the judicious use of authority.[38]

The combination of danger and authority in police work frustrates any possibility of procedural regularity in law enforcement.

Socialization and experience within the occupation develop other personal attributes. In a study of the New York City Police Department, it was found that many policemen after appointment to the force become cynical. "When they succumb, they lose faith in people, society, and eventually in themselves. In their Hobbesian view the world becomes a jungle in which crime, corruption, and brutality are normal features of the terrain."[39] Cynicism is part of the occupational ideology, learned during socialization into the occupation, and an authoritarian personality usually follows during his police career. "The police occupational system is geared to manufacture the 'take charge guy,' and it succeeds in doing so with outstanding efficiency. It is the police system, not the personality of the candidate, that is the more powerful determinant of behavior and ideology."[40]

Police Abuse

Their ideology ultimately affects the way in which police define persons as criminal. Although their activities are governed officially by procedural law, their real behavior conforms to their occupational code. The policeman sees the exclusionary rule not as guaranteeing greater protection of the citizen's freedom, but unnecessarily complicating the task of detecting and apprehending criminals.[41] Many practices of the police are opposed to the guarantee of due process. Actual police practices are minimally affected by legalistic considerations:

> When he (the policeman) sees a black girl and a white serviceman enter a hotel together, he assumes an act of prostitution is in the offing. To him, these are not constitutionally protected citizens, but predictable actors whose misbehavior he usually judges correctly. Sometimes, to be sure, he may be in error. The probabilities, however, are so strong, he feels, that his judgment is rarely going to be wrong.[42]

For the policeman, "due process of law is, therefore, not merely a set of constitutional guarantees for the defendant, but also a set of working conditions which, under increasingly liberal opinions by the courts, are likewise becoming increasingly arduous."[43]

Because of their special role in society, police have particular kinds of occupational values. As part of the occupational structure, these provide the rationale for using harsh and often illegal methods.[44] With some justification, the police believe that the public supports their use of such methods, because it has traditionally given them an implicit directive to use violence and other expedient methods to accomplish their goals. Police brutality finds much support in a public ideology that grants authority to state sovereignty.

The police continue to carry out their mandate, resorting to violence and brutality as part of their occupational activity. That they use brutality should surprise no one, because their mandate is coercing the population; they manage violence for the state. Paul Chevigny studied some abuses by the police in New York City, and says that "the one truly iron and inflexible rule we can adduce from the cases is that any person who defies the police risks the imposition of legal sanctions, commencing with a summons, on up to the use of firearms."[45] He continues, "The police may arrest *anyone* who challenges them (as they define the challenge), but they are more likely to further abuse anyone who is poor, or who belongs to an outcast group."[46] But the real problem, the author says, is that the police often provoke citizens to violence or disorderly conduct in order to make an arrest. Such provocation then allows the police to continue abusing the citizen.

The worst abuse, Chevigny observes, is manhandling power, when the police not only assault people but arrest them also.

> If the police simply hit a man and let him go, there would be an abuse of the authority conferred by the uniform and the stick, but not the compound abuse of hitting a man and then dragging him to court on criminal charges, really a more serious injury than a blow. One's head heals up, after all, but a criminal record never goes away. There is no more embittering experience in the legal system than to be abused by the police and then to be tried and convicted on false evidence.[47]

The policeman is likely to get in trouble if he lets an abused person go free; therefore he makes an arrest to cover the abuse, concealing his own violence.

With their private code of conduct, and

complicity by the courts in accepting the criminal charges, the police continue to practice violence, arrest, and cover charges. And as long as the public accepts this situation, the abuses will go on, because the police institution is generally accepted by the public, and law enforcement is thought the most appropriate way to handle problems.

Encounter between Police and Citizens

The Encounter

With class interests and police organization complicating matters, making an arrest is made even more involved by social relations and personal perceptions. That which is defined as criminal is not so much behavior obviously violating a specific criminal law as it is a definition of circumstances in the encounter between interacting parties in a concrete situation. Few cases of law enforcement show clear evidence that a specific person is the "criminal." Usually it is only in the totality of the encounter that a decision is made to apply the criminal label to a person.

The encounter can take place only when the police have been mobilized. They usually are mobilized when private citizens act, rather than by police initiative. The police may be mobilized in several ways:

Police departments refer to incidents or complaints that originate by mobilizing police units through the communications center as *"calls-for-service," "dispatches,"* or *"runs,"* the first term referring to the citizen's call or complaint and the latter terms to the fact that a mobile unit is radio-dispatched to take the complaint. A request for police action made by a citizen personally appearing at the police station is referred to as a *"station complaint"* or a *"citizen station mobilization."* All incidents arising in a field setting are commonly referred to as *"on-view"* incidents, but a distinction can be made among them. A direct, in-the-field, citizen request for police action, usually by flagging a patrol car or a call to an officer on the beat, is sometimes referred to as a *"field complaint"* or a *"citizen field mobilization."* When an officer initiates contact and reports on an incident that occurs in his presence, it is referred to as an *"on-view"* mobilization. Any law violation occurring in an officer's presence that leads to an arrest with the officer as complainant is an *"on-view arrest."*[48]

It was found in a study of 5,360 mobilization situations in Boston, Chicago, and Washington, D.C., that 81 per cent of the mobilizations were dispatches, 14 per cent were on-views, and the remaining 5 per cent were citizen field mobilization. Most important, nearly three-quarters of the mobilizations consisted of some kind of police-citizen interaction.[49] More often than not, then, the police are involved in criminal defining situations because citizens report offenses.

The encounter between police and citizens in a situation potentially definable as criminal involves a number of social roles. Beyond the policeman, we can see eight citizen's roles: complainant, member of complainant group, offender, member of offender group, victim, member of victim group, informant, and bystander.

A *complainant* is a person who wants police action in response to what he sees as an "offense" of some kind; e.g., a man whose car has been stolen or a woman who complains about a noisy party is a complainant. A *member of a complainant group* is a person who supports or stands with the central complainant. An *offender* is either a person who is seen or treated as a possible violator of the law or as a person who is not fulfilling role obligations or expectations that the complainant regards as "legal." The first kind of offender is represented by a person accused of a larceny, the second by a man whose wife thinks he has been negligent in fulfilling his obligations as husband or head of the household. A *member of an offender group* is a person who supports or stands with the offender. A citizen is called a *victim* who needs or requests help or a service from the police in a situation that does not involve an "offense" or possible criminal violation of any kind, e.g., a sick or accidentally injured person. A *member of a victim group* is a person who supports or is behaviorally concerned about a victim. The *informant* is a participant who gives information relative to the nature of any situation or incident but who does not support or stand with any of the more involved participants; he is, however, more than a mere guide or person who gives information only about the location of a situation. The *bystander* is nothing more than an onlooker.[50]

These roles may lead to a criminal arrest.

The most important social roles in the situations that may become defined as criminal are those of the policeman, the suspect, and the victim. The *victim*, when a crime is created, is not just the object of an offense, but may be the only person able to report the offense to the police so that an arrest can be made. In the studies for the President's Commission on Law Enforcement and Administration of Justice it was discovered that in only about half the cases of victimization did the victim report the offense to the police.[51] The tendency to report or not to report varied, of course, according to the type of offense and the victim's characteristics, but victims had several reasons for not reporting (Table 10.1). The most common was a resigned belief that the police could not do anything about the incident, would not catch the offender, or would not want to be bothered. Many other nonreporting victims believed that the incident was not a police matter. These victims either did not want the offender to be known to the police or thought that the incident was a private affair. Other victims simply did not want to get involved with the police, to take the time or the trouble to report the offense. Still others were afraid of possible reprisal by the offender and his friends or some other kind of loss. Finally, some did not notify the police because they were uncertain about what ought to be done. It is not always clear that a criminal offense has been committed or what procedure is proper for reporting an offense. For all these reasons, many possible criminal defining situations do not come to the attention of the police.

The ultimate encounter that may lead to a criminal definition is between the *policeman* and the *suspect*. The possible encounter is guided by a conflict between opposing interests: (1) those of a person who wants to carry out some behaviors (some of which may conceivably violate the criminal law), and (2) those of the policeman who wants to prevent

criminal violations and apprehend criminals. These opposing interests lead both parties to develop strategies, according to what one party expects of the other.[52] Each attempts to predict the other's behavior, at the same time trying to reduce the opponent's ability to predict his own moves.

Yet it is the policeman who has the ability to officially define a crime: in the encounter between the police and the citizen a social reality is being constructed. The policeman is creating his own order.

> Whenever the police intervene in a situation, whether it be in response to a citizen request or on their own volition, they have at their disposal a wide range of alternative modes of action ranging from simply issuing orders or giving warnings through the making of arrests. In engaging in any or all of these activities, the police possess the sole official monopoly over the use of physical force, to the point of taking a human life. Through any one or a combination of these means the police may and do make in behavior a reality of the order they anticipate.[53]

Making an arrest, creating a crime, is constructing a reality that the policeman has already anticipated.

Making the Arrest

Once the encounter has taken place, the conflicting interests of the policeman and the suspect continue to be important in the relationship. The question they now confront is how that encounter will be conducted. During this confrontation the policeman decides whether or not to impose a criminal definition by the act of arrest.

Threat of arrest is a means of conducting the encounter. But the bargaining is one-sided, with the policeman having the power and possessing the ultimate weapon:

> The ability to claim a given identity in an interaction involves . . . bargaining. But, as in many bargaining relations, the power is not equally distributed in police-citizen encounters. The police have one mechanism that can alter the negotiations over status claims — the arrest. By placing a citizen under arrest, the officer shifts the interaction from police-civilian to police-suspect. Arrest

Table 10.1   Crime Reports to the Police: Victims' Most Important Reason for Not Notifying Police[a] (NORC Survey; in Percentages)

Crimes	Percentage of cases in which police not notified	Reasons for not notifying police				
		Felt it was private matter or did not want to harm offender	Police could not be effective or would not want to be bothered	Did not want to take time	Too confused or did not know how to report	Fear of reprisal
Robbery	35%	27%	45%	9%	18%	0%
Aggravated assault	35	50	25	4	8	13
Simple assault	54	50	35	4	4	7
Burglary	42	30	63	4	2	2
Larceny ($50 and over)	40	23	62	7	7	0
Larceny (under $50)	63	31	58	7	3	(c)
Auto theft	11	[b]20	[b]60	[b]0	[b]0	[b]20
Malicious mischief	62	23	68	5	2	2
Consumer fraud	90	50	40	0	10	0
Other fraud (bad checks, swindling, etc.)	74	41	35	16	8	0
Sex offenses (other than forcible rape)	49	40	50	0	5	5
Family crimes (desertion, non-support, etc.)	50	65	17	10	0	7

[a] Willful homicide, forcible rape, and a few other crimes had too few cases to be statistically useful, and they are therefore excluded.
[b] There were only 5 instances in which auto theft was not reported.
[c] Less than 0.5%.
Source: President's Commission on Law Enforcement and Administration of Justice, *The Challenge of Crime in a Free Society* (Washington, D.C.: U.S. Government Printing Office, 1967), p. 22.

gives the police officer much greater protection of his role identity at the same time it strips certain identities held by the citizen.[54]

Many factors beyond the principal reason for the encounter between the policeman and the suspect enter into the decision to arrest. The policeman, using a *probabilistic* model of law enforcement, looks for personal characteristics that may indicate criminal behavior. The outward appearance and demeanor of the suspect obviously interest him in a possible arrest situation. A study of the disposition of juvenile cases showed that the decision on whether or not to bring a boy to the station — and the decision made at the station — "were based largely on cues from which the officer inferred the youth's character."[55] The cues included

group affiliation, age, race, grooming, and dress. Members of known delinquent gangs, older boys, blacks, and youths with well-oiled hair, black jackets, and soiled denims or jeans, usually received the more serious dispositions.

But the most important cue the police used in handling juveniles was demeanor. The patrolmen themselves stated that was the major determinant in 50 to 60 per cent of the cases they processed. Youths perceived as uncooperative were more likely to be dealt with severely than those who seemed cooperative. The researchers reached this conclusion:

The cues used by police to assess demeanor were fairly simple. Juveniles who were contrite about their infractions, respectful to officers, and fearful of the sanctions that might be employed against them tended to be viewed by patrolmen as basically law-abiding or at least "salvageable." For these youths it was usually assumed that informal or formal reprimand would suffice to guarantee their future conformity. In contrast, youthful offenders who were fractious, obdurate, or who appeared nonchalant in their encounters with patrolmen were likely to be viewed as "would-be tough guys" or "punks" who fully deserved the most severe sanction: arrest.[56]

The policeman, then, uses symbols and behavioral cues in applying criminal definitions. He has an image of the kind of person who is a "troublemaker" or is likely to be a lawbreaker. When the suspect lives up to this expectation, he increases the possibility of his own arrest. And the attitude the person assumes in his relationship with the policeman does affect the outcome of the encounter. Those who behave antagonistically toward the police are more likely to be treated in a hostile, authoritarian, or belittling manner by the police than are other citizens.[57] The encounter between police and citizen is, indeed, a crucial moment of interaction and assessment. Both parties are involved in jockeying for their personal fates. The encounter may create a crime.

Offense Situations and Selective Law Enforcement

The police and the citizen encounter each other in a specific offense situation, the outcome of which is affected not only by their interactions, perceptions, and reactions, but also by the setting. The situations may vary in such matters as the racial context, police and community objectives in enforcing the laws, and the kind of offense. Law is selectively enforced according to these variations and the person's characteristics. Law enforcement is unevenly distributed in the social structure.

Racial Context of Arrest

The police, we know from many studies, have long had differential policies toward race and minority status.[58] They are more likely to arrest blacks and Third-World people on slight evidence compared with the amount they require for arresting whites. These two groups have also been exposed more than others to the misuse of police power. Police attitudes and policies on race were described by a police captain some time ago in a southern town, when he told a writer: "In this town there are three classes of homicide. If a nigger kills a white man, that's murder. If a white man kills a nigger, that's justifiable homicide. If a nigger kills a nigger, that's one less nigger."[59]

Official police statistics reveal that blacks are arrested between three and four times more often than whites.[60] Although blacks comprise about one-ninth of the population, they account for more than a quarter of the persons arrested for all offenses. Being black entails a greater risk of arrest than does the status of being white. The different arrest rates do not mean, however, that blacks may be involved more than whites in law-violating behavior, but that in similar situations blacks are more likely than whites to be apprehended.

This selective enforcement is partly caused by prejudices of individual policemen.[61] But blacks also tend to fit the stereotype that police have of the criminal.[62] Using their cues, a probabilistic model of law violation, and their experience, the police are more likely to arrest the black than the white in a similar offense situation; how often they use a racial image of the offender came out in a survey of police officers in Philadelphia: 75 per cent of them overestimated the percentage of arrests involving blacks made in the districts to which they were assigned.[63] With a conception of events and offenders like this one, difference in law enforcement according to race is inevitable.

Community Objectives

To accomplish objectives that may be known only to the police and some community members, an arrest may be made, possibly solving a problem that seemingly could not be resolved in any other way. A policeman might arrest a person who ordinarily would not be arrested to maintain respect for the police system.

A police patrol stopped a car that had been traveling at 39 m.p.h. in a 30 m.p.h. zone. They decided prior to leaving the squad car that they would only issue a warning. When the deputies approached, the driver said in a sarcastic tone, "What in hell have I done now?" Because of his belligerent attitude the driver was placed under arrest.[64]

Another kind of arrest for extralegal objectives is made to preserve an image of full enforcement. It is most often used when an offense not usually handled by arrest comes to public attention:

The police were aware of the operation of a private card game in which there was no house "cut." Since this operation therefore qualified as mere social gambling, no action was taken against the offenders. However, the operators of the game made no attempt to conceal the operation, and it was soon apparent to the general public that the police must be aware of it. Realizing this, the police arrested the gamblers.[65]

Once an offense is widely publicized, an arrest becomes imminent. Sometimes an arrest is intended to detain or punish someone suspected of other criminal activity:

The police learned of a minor property theft. As the victim was not interested in prosecution, the police, in accord with their usual policy, decided not to arrest. However, when they learned that the offender was known to the police department as a "bad actor," and that the police had been unsuccessful in obtaining his conviction for other, more serious offenses, they arrested him.[66]

An arrest may also follow a minor offense when the police think a suspect is responsible for a relatively serious offense, but they need more time to gather evidence to successfully prosecute the case.

Officers had reasonable grounds to believe that a particular man was responsible for a recent homicide. However, desiring an opportunity to conduct a prolonged in-custody investigation, they arrested him on a vagrancy charge. He was then convicted for vagrancy, and the murder investigation was continued while he served his sentence.[67]

Offenders may be arrested too if other alternatives are lacking. The drunk may be arrested to protect him from the cold, because he has injured himself, or because he is likely to become a criminal victim; he will probably be released the next morning.[68]

Arrest charges often used to accomplish a multitude of extralegal objectives are those of vagrancy and disorderly conduct. Not usually made to enforce the laws, they are intended to banish unwanted persons, prevent and control other offenses, and clear public areas.[69] Police departments may even conduct drives during the year, in the name of enforcing the vagrancy and disorderly statutes, to get "undesirables" out of town.

Public Morals and Enforcement

Some forms of private conduct become the business of the police. Criminal laws created primarily for reprobation are enforced (or not enforced) with a great amount of discretion, occasionally, and only in specific circumstances. In the appropriate situations the police are expected to enforce public morals by arresting private citizens.

In general the police are not called upon to enforce laws that regulate private conduct. Although some laws are based on moral behavior, they are not usually enforced as long as the conduct is not harmful to those involved and the participating parties consent to the behavior. Enforcement is likely however, when personal violence erupts and also when conduct becomes defined by the community as a public nuisance. Solicitation by homosexuals and prostitutes in public places may bring the police into action to enforce laws on homosexuality and prostitution.[70]

Because the behavior of homosexuals in public is likely to be offensive to a large segment of the community, numerous complaints may be registered with the police. The police are then responsible not so much for fully enforcing the law but ensuring a public order that satisfies the sensibilities of some community members: the police provide the community with an inoffensive environment.

Prostitutes are usually arrested for purposes other than prosecution. Those who are arrested, however, are the ones who come to public attention, the street walkers rather than the call girls. Prostitution may be condoned in the community, so long as it does not recruit our wives and daughters, but community members do not like to be reminded of the behavior. The police are required, therefore, to crack down on the girls who publicly solicit for their favors. And the police may get information about other criminals by arresting prostitutes.[71] Most of the time, though, such arrests are meant simply to harass the prostitutes. The latter may then work out strategies that are less obvious and offensive to the public.

Enforcing Dormant Laws

A great many of our criminal laws were created to support values that have since ceased to be important. Although the laws have remained on the books, they have in essence become dormant. On occasion, however, these laws are enforced for brief periods, most often for purposes other than those intended in the original legal formulations. The sporadic enforcement of dormant laws is the ultimate use of discretion in law enforcement.

Sunday closing laws are one of the best examples of a sporadically enforced dormant law. These laws, enacted early in the history of our states, usually have been enforced by local authorities; that, is according to particularistic objectives.

Within communities, too, Sunday laws, when enforced, have been enforced for diverse reasons. In New York City sporadic attempts to enforce the law have been guided by different objectives. Several times in this century alone organized efforts have been put on to enforce the law on Sunday closing of business establishments, each for different reasons.[72]

In 1924 police actions on Sunday closing rose 77 per cent in New York City over the previous year. The sudden enforcement policy was caused by a group known as the Lord's Day Alliance, which crusaded to get it enforced primarily on religious grounds. In the following year the arrest rate for being open on Sunday declined to its regular low level. Then in 1938 another campaign was launched in the Flatbush section of Brooklyn by the Flatbush Chamber of Commerce. Local busi-

nessmen were exercising their civic interest in keeping a law-abiding image for the community.

In 1954 in the Bedford-Stuyvesant area of Brooklyn increased enforcement of the Sunday law was prompted by a campaign for better working conditions by a union, the American Federation of Retail Kosher Butchers, trying to abolish forced work on Sunday by management. In the next year, this time on Manhattan's West Side, police responded to pressures by unions, which were organizing the car wash industry there. The police reacted by acting upon any business establishment that was open on Sunday. One of the last police crackdowns on Sunday openings in New York was in August 1962 in the upper Broadway area. Behind the drive, which lasted one week, was an attempt by the large chain-store supermarkets to have the small neighborhood stores closed on Sundays. Selective law enforcement had become a way of accomplishing objectives quite apart from law enforcement itself.

Political Protest

One other kind of selective law enforcement is the police reaction to political protest. The police then are sometimes used by those who hold power to resolve conflicts in their own favor. Law enforcement here consists of selectively applying criminal definitions to those who protest against the established government in ways the government thinks illegitimate and threatening to its existence; this behavior may, consequently, be defined as criminal.

Political protest almost by definition is a threat and danger to a government. The police become involved not only for the express purpose of maintaining peace, but also to preserve the society's status quo. The police do as much to punish the protesters as to keep order. Police intimidation and brutality have been claimed in many instances of political protest, as in the "race riots," in which much of the violence may have been either prompted or initiated by the police.[73] In many other protests and demonstrations almost the only violence is that which the police inflicted on the participants. The only illegalities may be those committed by the police themselves.[74] But the police impose criminal definitions, and are not likely to be the ones defined as criminals.

The federal government, especially, has resorted to the police to protect its own interests. In the name of national security, laws have been created and enforced to protect the government from threats it perceived. The scare about communism in this century got thousands arrested under laws especially enacted or conveniently enforceable for that purpose.[75]

The selective police reaction to political protest was brought to public attention during the 1968 Democratic Convention in Chicago. In that week in August, the Chicago police, arresting 668 demonstrators, were said to have committed numerous violent acts against them. A report of the events, sponsored by the National Commission on the Causes and Prevention of Violence, concluded that the police response to the demonstrators was unrestrained and indiscriminate.

Whether violence has been used by the police, harassment has been attempted, or arrests have been made, the police have been used to protect and help preserve the state and its interests.

The Police-Community Relationship

Police Manpower and Professionalization

In recent years, in response to events, a number of changes have been made in law enforcement. Among the proposals that have been advanced, and initiated with the support of the federal government, are those meant to strengthen and make more effective the traditional police role. Instead of examining the law-enforcement institution, proponents of these measures wish to increase the ability of the police to perform their order-maintaining and crime-prevention functions in the community.

Programs are under way to improve the organization of police departments, increase their training, recruitment, and size, professionalize them, improve their deployment, and enhance their public image. With such recommendations, the President's Commission on Law Enforcement and Administration of Justice made this statement about improving the police "in a free society":

Widespread improvement in the strength and caliber of police manpower, supported by a radical revision of personnel practices, are the basic essentials for achieving more effective and fairer law enforcement. Educational requirements should be raised to college levels and training programs improved. Recruitment and promotion should be modernized to reflect education, personality, and assessment of performance. The traditional, monolithic personnel structure must be broken up into three entry levels of varying responsibility and with different personnel requirements, and lateral entry into advanced positions encouraged.

The need is urgent for the police to improve relations with the poor, minority groups, and juveniles. The establishment of strong community relations programs, review of all procedures in light of their effect on community relations, recruitment of minority group members, and strengthening of community confidence in supervision and discipline, all aim at making the police more effective in high-crime areas. Increased effectiveness also requires that law enforcement improve its facilities and techniques of management — particularly that it utilize manpower more efficiently, modernize communications and records, and formulate more explicit policy guidelines governing areas of police discretion. The pooling of services and functions by police forces in each metropolitan area can improve efficiency and effectiveness.[76]

The problem was perceived as a technical one that could be solved by money combined with manipulation of the public by community relations.

For some reformers the necessary change is definitely in "police manpower." Although improving police-community relations is important, mainly for gaining information about "the character and habits" of the people in the community, the most important problem is that of "improving the way in which the police perform their critical function — patrolling to prevent crime, preserve order, and enforce laws."[77] This improvement, of course, is time-consuming and costly, but the battle can be won by "deploying" large numbers of police in the community.

VIEWPOINT_____

DEVELOPMENT OF POLICE-COMMUNITY RELATIONS

Although it is difficult to determine the origins of police-community relations, it is clear that the idea was being expressed by the early decades of the twentieth century. Perhaps, because of concern with the public image of law enforcement, "public relations" was the initial problem addressed. Policies and training were modified in the hopes of exerting a one-way influence upon the public view of the police. The massive urban migration of blacks, accelerated by two World Wars, prompted a specific concern with "race relations." By World War II, many departments trained policemen in race relations.

By the early 1950's, regional conferences and training seminars in community relations were created. The 1954 Supreme Court decision in Brown v. the Board of Education inspired additional law enforcement race relations efforts. By the mid- and late 1950's, a few departments went beyond training to the development of formal organizational subunits specializing in the problems of relations with the community. For example, St. Louis developed a program in the mid-1950's which served as a prototype. Even these modest developments were not well received by some. One knowledgeable national official reported to the authors that the Justice Department wished to promote the idea of police-community relations in the early 1960's. Although they were willing to finance research and development in the area, they were not willing to have the finished products of these projects associated with the Justice Department. In many police departments, the issue was too sensitive. Thus, by the early 1960's, some departments had developed community relations programs, and there were influential national organizations ready to promote the concept. However, the prospect for rapid adoption of such programs in most departments was poor. The time for the concept of police-community relations had not come; however, it soon did come.

The late 1960's have witnessed expansion of existing programs and rapid adoption of new community relations programs. While a number of factors are involved in the rapid improvement of the fortunes of the police-community relations idea, the most important factor has been the series of urban civil disturbances in the period 1965 through 1968. The civil disturbances presented massive demands for police departments. It became clear that the capabilities of even the best equipped and best staffed departments would be challenged by these heavy demands. The sensitivity of the issues involved and the intense public response to these disturbances made brute force an undesirable and unsuccessful tactic on the part of police departments. While the departments we studied made efforts to organize, equip, and train themselves for actual civil disturbance response, they clearly preferred not to make those responses at all. Also, police personnel themselves were intimately involved in many of the incidents which triggered the initial outbreak of civil disturbances. The difficulty of these problems and the uncertainty involved with these threats made noncoercive approaches to the problem seem attractive. These factors, the facilitation of federal funding, and the catalyst of public pressure combined to promote the rapid spread of police-community relations programs from 1965 to 1970.

Source: From Gary A. Kreps and Jack M. Weller, "The Police-Community Relations Movement: Conciliatory Responses to Violence," *American Behavioral Scientist,* 16 (January-February, 1973), pp. 404–406.

VIEWPOINT (Continued)

Rapid growth occurred in all the areas associated with police-community relations. Changes in existing training programs were among the easiest and least expensive ways to affect police-community relations problems. Thus, the addition of recruit and in-service community relations training was among the fastest spreading innovations associated with the movement. Much of the material presented as community relations training was novel, and police training officers often searched outside regular police information channels for instructors and information. The use of nonpolice sources such as local universities, community service organizations, and minority group organizations was common. Some of these nonpolice organizations not only supplied instructors and information, but were also involved in the actual development of training programs.

In addition to general training programs, community relations subunits were also developed. In a 1967 survey of 75 larger departments, about 37% had formal community relations subunits (National Center on Police and Community Relations, 1967). A larger 1970 survey showed proportional increases in formal community relations programs and specialized subunits. For example, 100% of cities over 500,000 and 96% of cities between 250,000 and 500,000, 72% of cities between 100,000 and 250,000, and 63% of cities between 50,000 and 100,000 had formal programs. Of the cities with formal programs, 71% had specialized community relations subunits (International City Management Association, 1970). While these programs clearly emphasized race relations, there was considerable variation in organizational location, size, objectives, and effectiveness. Some units came into existence only after a major racial conflict. Others were clearly the result of diffusion of the ideas independent of actual civil disturbance experience. Expansion was particularly apparent in departments from larger cities.

More liberal proposals on the police go beyond the manpower problem to "professionalizing" the police. These proposals begin with the notion that the police must develop a professional attitude toward their work. Efficient enforcement of the law is not the sole end of the police function, but a respect for "the rule of law" is essential. An argument for developing a *legal* professionalism among police is presented by Jerome Skolnick:

The needed philosophy of professionalism must rest on a set of values conveying the idea that the police are as much an institution dedicated to the achievement of legality in society as they are an official social organization designed to control misconduct through the invocation of punitive sanctions. The problem of police in a democratic society is not merely a matter of obtaining newer police cars, a higher order of technical equipment or of recruiting men who have to their credit more years of education. What must occur is a significant alteration in the ideology of police, so that police "professionalization" rests on the values of a democratic legal order, rather than on technological proficiency.[78]

The police, some argue, should be guided by "civility." A civil relationship between police and the public is needed, involving a feeling for the interests of others. Albert Reiss thus writes, after documenting the prevalence of police malpractice and illegality:

So far as civil relations between the police and the public are concerned, the following conditions must prevail: (1) that citizens be civil in their relations with one another, including the police; (2) that citizens grant legitimacy to police authority and respect their legal intervention in the affairs of men;

(3) that the police be accountable to civil authority and the citizen protected from police tyranny.[79]

The community member then must grant legitimacy to the police, and show deference to police authority.

Added to civility, especially among citizens in their relationships with the police, is the notion that the police should be "accountable" to the citizens. This "civic accountability," however, is controlled by the state and the police, not by the people of the community. And it is the "responsibility of the government," of which the police are a part, "to insure that its servants behave in a civil fashion."[80]

Finally, as the police become "professionalized," we will have to respect what they do and grant them a great deal of self-regulation as a profession. We are back to expecting misconduct, but this time the police are acting as professionals. With some negative reasoning, Bittner writes:

> It must be said, however, that the true professionalization of police work, in and of itself, is no weapon against sloth and corruption, no more than in the case of medicine, the ministry, law, teaching, and social work. That is, the professionalization of police work still leaves open the matter of its control. But if we are not willing to settle for having physicians who are merely honest, and who would frankly admit that in curing diseases and dealing with patients they have to rely entirely on "playing by ear," it is difficult to see why we would devote all our energies to trying to make the police honest without any concern whatever for whether or not they know, in a technical sense, how to do what they are supposed to do.[81]

Again, the police role is accepted; what we need is a more efficient police force. Bittner concludes: "But it is not good manners that I expect. Instead, I should like, in my dealings with policemen, to be able to perceive them as qualified to do the serious and important work I know they have to do."[82]

The Police-Community Relations Movement

Following the racial disorders in the sixties, police officials and government leaders insti-

tuted "police-community relations" programs, trying to restore order to communities, to improve the public's image of the police, and to improve the effectiveness of the police. New measures of coercive control were devised and implemented, with new equipment and increased manpower, and police departments adopted other means of manipulation as well.

Faced with the political sensitivity of applying stringent control measures to large numbers of a disaffected minority and the sheer tactical difficulty of meeting the immense demands of civil disturbances, police also developed more conciliatory responses. Most of these noncoercive responses to the threat of civil disturbances are lumped under the label "police-community relations programs."[83]

Although these efforts were being considered and sporadically practiced before, major programs have been created only in the last decade, especially in the larger cities across the country (Figure 10.2). All the programs have the intention of shaping public opinion about the police; "community relations" is a synonym for public relations. Furthermore:

> While there are wide differences from program to program and even from time to time in individual departments, programs do have certain elements in common. Generally they attempt to develop new relationships and new interaction with segments of the community that police identify as potential adversaries in civil disturbances. Also, there are certain common patterns in the means to be used to pursue these goals. Community relations programs depend on nonviolent, noncoercive, and communicative strategies of influence.

Thus, some aspects of community relations programs are aimed at the environment of the police. These efforts include establishing relationships with traditional minority interest groups, with newer militant interest groups, and with minority people in general. Other aspects of police community relations efforts are internal to police organizations, being directed to the departments. These include, for example, community relations training efforts, specialized positions within the police depart-

Figure 10.2   Police Departments Having a Police-Community Relations Program, 1970

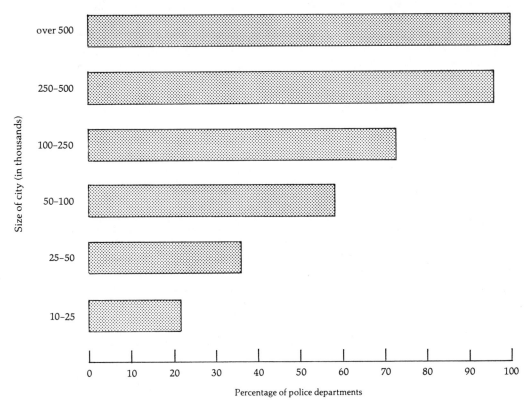

Source: Advisory Commission on Intergovernmental Relations, *State-Local Relations in the Criminal Justice System* (Washington, D.C.: U.S. Government Printing Office, 1971), p. 267. (Data gathered by the International City Management Association.)

ment responsible for community relations, and special efforts to recruit minority policemen.[84]

There are now several approaches to police-community relations. One is a police-community relations unit attached to the local police department. Police personnel trained in community relations administer the policies and programs, according to the department's needs.

The idea of a Community Relations Unit can scarcely be considered new. Such units have for a long time been features of most large, urban police departments. They are usually staffed by police officers of diverse ethnic backgrounds who, as part of their official duties, seek out and respond to civic groups to explain the police department's operations. In certain instances the unit

may make itself available to citizens for complaints and suggestions regarding law enforcement procedures, with the implication that these complaints and suggestions might help alter unpopular police practices. What often remains unclear is precisely how the unit does or might go about correcting practices in a police department of which it is only a small part. Consequently the chief objection to it is that it is too weak and isolated within the department to serve as a real channel for responsive communication between the community and the police or that it is patent window dressing behind which police practices remain unchanged.[85]

Another approach is the community-wide citizens' group, sometimes in combination with police officials. These "civilian review boards," as they are called, deal mainly with citizen complaints of malpractice by the police. Agencies such as a municipal ombudsman office or third-party organizations such as a civil liberties union are similar to such boards. The general problem with these programs is that they are far removed from the citizenry's day-to-day life, giving community members little recourse for grievances, to say nothing about any real control over the policing their communities get.

Still another approach to police-community relations involves massive programs of education — or indoctrination — of community members. These programs are based on the liberal notion that knowledge and information — combined of course with "dialogue" — will reconcile differences and conflicts. The President's Crime Commission, an obvious partisan, writes about these public education programs:

> Citizens who distrust the police will not easily be converted by information programs they consider to come from a tainted source. However, even for these groups, long-term education based upon honest and free dialogue between the police and the public can have an effect. Indeed, this is one of the basic goals of the citizen advisory committees.
>
> On the other hand, citizens who are neutral or supportive can benefit from increased understanding of the complicated problems and tasks of the police. Informational programs can also generate support for more personnel, salary increases, sufficient equipment, and other resources to improve the efficiency of police work. It can help the cooperative citizen to avoid becoming a victim of crime and show him how to work more effectively with the police. And, to the extent that the police department is genuinely working at improved community relations, dissemination of this information to the press and other media does have a positive effect on community relations.[86]

Without changing any social conditions or the economic structure, it is assumed that community education programs can make community members understanding of and respectful toward the police. As with all the other approaches, the purpose is to make the police more efficient in maintaining order in the community.

Community Control

There is an alternative to solving the police-community problem by police professionalization and increased manpower, or by police-community relations. It is community control over the police. This is more than community representation or community participation in police policies and practices; it is community determination of how it is to be policed. Community control is still heavily debated, but some recognized successes have been made in various realms of community life.[87] Few people today deny the potential of community control.

The principle behind community control of the police is community self-government. The police now in American communities can be thought of as an occupying force. In some cities they are even required to live outside the neighborhoods they police. And in few communities are the police actually created by the residents of these communities. Instead, they are created and managed by governments outside the community. Any true relationship between the community and the police must therefore begin with the police being an integral part of the community, which necessarily involves community control of the police.

At the beginning of the seventies a number of communities began to consider and propose plans that involve some form of community control over the police. Berkeley, California, voted on a community control amendment that would have set up separate police forces in the communities within the city, with the police being controlled by the respective communities.[88] Although the amendment failed, two years later other amendments were passed giving community members control over several important parts of policing in the city.

There are, of course, several approaches to community control. Arthur I. Waskow, of the Institute for Policy Studies, describes three:

> There are at least three major possible directions in which to go to achieve the kind of change in police forces that seems necessary to restore democratic, civilian control over the police:
>
> 1. Formal restructuring of metropolitan

DOCUMENT

THE PRESIDENT'S CRIME COMMISSION ON
COMMUNITY RELATIONS PROGRAMS

Citizen hostility toward the police is every bit as disruptive of peace and order, of course, as police indifference to or mistreatment of citizens. It is so obvious as almost to be a truism that ghetto residents will not obtain the police protection they badly want and need until policemen feel that their presence is welcome and that their problems are understood. However, in the effort to achieve this state of affairs, the duty of taking the initiative clearly devolves on the police, both because they are organized and disciplined and because they are public servants sworn to protect every part of the community. It is an urgent duty. Social tensions are growing and crime rates are mounting. Police agencies cannot preserve the public peace and control crime unless the public participates more fully than it now does in law enforcement. Bad community feeling does more than create tensions and engender actions against the police that in turn may embitter policemen and trigger irrational responses from them. It stimulates crime.

The Commission believes that a police-community relations program is one of the most important functions of any police department in a community with a substantial minority population. It believes further that such programs must be organized and administered in accordance with certain principles:

A community-relations program is not a *public*-relations program to "sell the police image" to the people. It is not a set of expedients whose purpose is to tranquilize for a time an angry neighborhood by, for example, suddenly promoting a few Negro officers in the wake of a racial disturbance. It is a long-range, full-scale effort to acquaint the police and the community with each other's problems and to stimulate action aimed at solving those problems.

Community relations are not the exclusive business of specialized units, but the business of an entire department from the chief down. Community relations are not exclusively a matter of special programs, but a matter that touches on all aspects of police work. They must play a part in the selection, training, deployment, and promotion of personnel; in the execution of field procedures; in staff policymaking and planning; in the enforcement of departmental discipline; and in the handling of citizens' complaints.

The needs of good community relations and of effective law enforcement will not necessarily be identical at all times. For example, restricting the way field interrogations are carried out could lead, in the short run, to apprehending fewer criminals; imposing harsh penalites on officers who verbally abuse minority-group citizens could temporarily depress departmental morale. Moreover, professionalization of the police has meant, to a considerable extent, improving efficiency by such methods as decreasing the number of officers on foot patrol, reducing the number of precinct stations and insisting that patrol officers spend more time on law enforcement duties and less on maintaining relations with citizens on the street. A result of this has been a lessening of the informal contacts between policemen and citizens. Conflicts of this sort are not easy to resolve, but the attempt must be made. While immediate law enforcement con-

---

Source: From President's Commission on Law Enforcement and Administration of Justice, *The Challenge of Crime in a Free Society* (Washington, D.C.: U.S. Government Printing Office, 1967), p. 100.

DOCUMENT (Continued)_____

siderations may take precedence, it should be remembered that sound community relations are, in the long run, essential to effective law enforcement.

Improving community relations involves not only instituting programs and changing procedures and practices, but re-examining fundamental attitudes. The police will have to learn to listen patiently and understandingly to people who are openly critical of them or hostile to them, since those people are precisely the ones with whom relations need to be improved. Quite evidently, it is not easy for a man who was brought up to obey the law and to respect law enforcement officers to maintain his poise and equanimity when he is denounced, sneered at, or threatened. However, policemen must do just that if police-citizen relationships on the street are to become person-to-person encounters rather than the black-versus-white, oppressed-versus-oppressor confrontations they too often are.

The police must adapt themselves to the rapid changes in patterns of behavior that are taking place in America. This is a time when traditional ideas and institutions are being challenged with increasing insistence. The poor want an equal opportunity to earn a share of America's wealth. Minority groups want a final end put to the discrimination they have been subjected to for centuries. Young people, the fastest growing segment of the population, have more freedom than they ever have had. The police must be willing and able to deal understandingly and constructively with these often unsettling, even threatening, changes.

---

police departments into federations of neighborhood police forces, with control of each neighborhood force in the hands of neighborhood people through election of commissions.

2. Creation of countervailing organizations (in effect, "trade unions" of those policed) responsible to a real political base, able to hear grievances and force change.

3. Transformation of the police "profession" and role so as to end the isolation of policemen from the rest of the community, and thus to establish de facto community control by chiefly informal means.

The neighborhood control approach could be institutionalized by election of neighborhood or precinct police commissions which would (1) appoint high precinct officers (perhaps with approval of metropolitan headquarters, the mayor or a civil service commission); (2) approve the assignment in the precinct of new policemen and be able to require transfers out; (3) discipline officers, perhaps with the concurrence of a city-wide appeal board; and (4) set basic policy on law enforcement priorities in the neighborhood.[89]

Waskow suggests that many combinations of the models are possible, and that these models can be used in different ways in a strategy for achieving community control.

Obviously, what political strategy is developed in achieving community control over police depends heavily on which model one intends to pursue, and which end result within them one hopes to achieve. Let us assume, however, that a decision is made to pursue a combination of Models I and III — which together seem to offer the fullest control over a police force to those in the neighborhood — by transforming both the formal lines of command and the informal processes to converge on the community.

With that goal in view, it would make sense to strive immediately to set up Model II. Such a countervailing "community union to police the police" could then become not simply a grievance-processing organization, but also a continuous pressure group for the adoption of a Model I/III arrangement *in the form of a present version of what the future Model I/III control would look like.* Imagine an open-ended community group that anyone in a given police precinct could join, the directors of which would be periodically elected, and that would be funded by neighborhood "dues" and, perhaps, matching foundation grants. Such a strong community union to police the police could (1) itself put peacekeepers on the street — unarmed, distinctively uniformed, oriented to conflict resolution rather than enforcing the law, including women, young dropouts and clergymen; (2) itself patrol the police, taking evidence of bad behavior and offering to settle problems instead of the police; (3) hear and investigate and judge complaints; (4) mobilize political pressure for the transfer of bad policemen, bad precinct commanders and others; and (5) keep up constant pressure for the transfer of power over the neighborhood police to the neighborhood itself. It must be clear that such a community union to police the police would be a focus of intense political conflict, including great hostility and possibly physical danger from the police. But if the groundwork in organizing community support for a Model I/III arrangement had been well done, the very intensity of political conflict over a strong Model II might persuade the city to allow Model I/III to be established. In any case, it is hard to see how democratic civilian control over a staff of armed men who are widely believed to hold a monopoly over legitimate violence and who are well organized in a separate subculture and a strong political force can be re-established without intense political conflict.[90]

Those who suggest police professionalization and increased manpower dismiss the community control movement because they are afraid that the local arrangement, "by organizing the police on a local community basis, leaves the citizen more vulnerable to a local police tyranny, since the state's right and

opportunity to intervene is limited."[91] The state, though, already intervenes to establish its own tyranny when *it* controls the police. They also suggest that community control of the police will undermine the "rule of law."

> One of the more difficult problems in policing is the development of policy that is consistent with the democratic ideology of maintaining respect for the rule of law. The law requires universality in its application, but community standards often hold it should be otherwise. Whenever citizens are subject to widely varying standards in the application of any law, they lose respect for it and for the rule of law. Local control of police policy and practice, therefore, runs the risk of undermining the rule of law.[92]

And lurking in the background is the fear that local control of the police will thwart the development of a "professional police cadre."

Opponents of community control fear too that once the movement catches on, every community will want to control its own police. And then what would happen in periods of "civil disorder"?

> If any one neighborhood obtains control over its police, all other neighborhoods will be able to make similar demands. In a period of civil disorder, the prospects for peace are not likely to be enhanced by ·balkanizing the city, equipping each area with its own police force, and letting the disputants, thus armed, settle their differences as best they can.[93]

The idea of community control of the police, a police force controlled by the people, is controversial and implies a vastly different kind of society. To bring about that control is to start working toward a new American society.

11

Judicial Administration

Administration of criminal law, in American legal ideology, is the same as "administration of *justice*." Whenever the system tries to administer the law in keeping with an ideal such as impartiality, all assume that justice has been obtained. But the legal idea of justice does not take in the societal context within which the law is administered, and a critical understanding of social reality requires a standard beyond our current juridical concept of justice.[1]

Nevertheless we will recognize the conventional notion and will examine how the law is administered once people have been arrested. Their fate is then in the hands of the judicial system and its related bureaucracies. Decisions about the accused's condition are made at many places in the judicial process (Figure 11.1). The officials' decisions limit the alternatives for decisions that come later in the proceedings.

Politics and Justice

Politics and the Judicial System

How is justice, in the legal sense, administered in the United States? Though many believe that criminal law is "above politics," it is by its very nature political. The judicial system exists in the first place to maintain order for the state; whenever decisions are made within the system — and that is what the judiciary is for — politics necessarily is involved. Criminal law is administered by and for the state.

The courts are an essential part of the political structure. The kinds of criminal cases they handle are influenced by local as well as national politics. The prosecuting attorney is an elected official and often the key figure in the local political machine; he determines, according to his discretion, which law is being violated. His actions result in getting the suspects released or indicted. If they are indicted, the prosecutor decides on the charge. Later, the fate of the accused depends upon the judge's discretion; he too is an appointed or locally elected official. Two political scientists describe how the local political system and the administration of criminal laws are specifically related:

> Thus, elected officials sensitive to the political process charge, prosecute, convict,

Figure 11.1   A General View of the Criminal Justice System

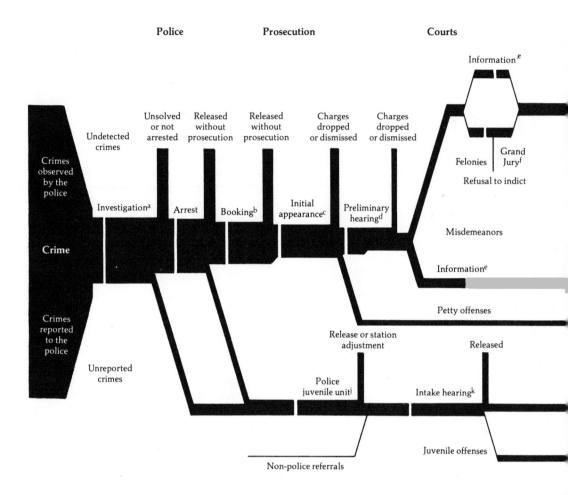

a May continue until trial.

b Administrative record of arrest. First step at which temporary release on bail may be available.

c Before magistrate, commissioner, or justice of peace. Formal notice of charge, advice of rights.   Bail set. Summary trials for petty offenses usually conducted here without further processing.

d Preliminary testing of evidence against defendant. Charge may be reduced.   No separate preliminary hearing for misdemeanors in some systems.

e Charge filed by prosecutor on basis of information submitted by police or citizens. Alternative to grand jury indictment; often used in felonies, almost always in misdemeanors.

f Reviews whether government evidence sufficient to justify trial. Some states have no grand jury system; others seldom use it.

Source: President's Commission on Law Enforcement and Administration of Justice, *The Challenge of Crime in a Free Society* (Washington, D.C.: U.S. Government Printing Office, 1967), pp. 8-9.

Corrections

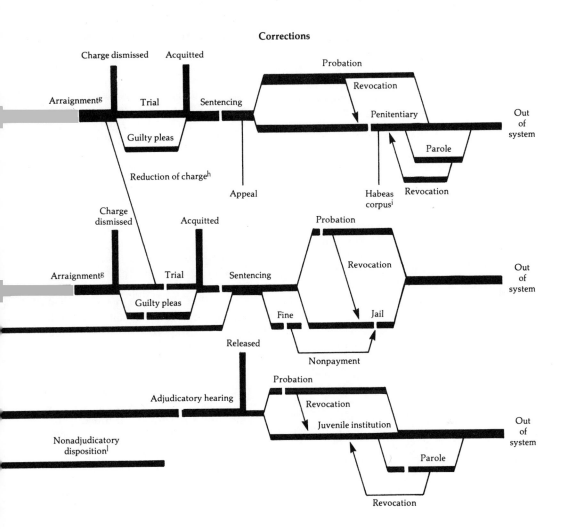

g Appearance for plea; defendant elects trial by judge or jury (if available); counsel for indigent usually appointed here in felonies. Often not at all in other cases.

h Charge may be reduced at any time prior to trial in return for plea of guilty or for other reasons.

i Challenge on constitutional grounds to legality of detention. May be sought at any point in process.

j Police often hold informal hearings, dismiss or adjust many cases without further processing.

k Probation officer decides desirability of further court action.

l Welfare agency, social services, counseling, medical care, etc., for cases where adjudicatory handling not needed.

and sentence criminal defendants. This means that such decisions are made in response to cues from the political structure; thereby the political system provides channels by which local claims and local interests can influence judicial outcomes. In this way, the judiciary helps create the conditions necessary for the re-election of court officials or for their frequent promotion to higher offices in the state or nation. In short, criminal prosecutions provide opportunities for the political system to affect judicial decisions and for the judicial process to provide favors which nourish political organizations.[2]

Much of the politics in local criminal justice is shaped by the American two-party system. Political leadership is dispersed among the political parties, which are spread throughout the society, and local politics is influenced by party considerations. Party leaders use the judiciary as a source of patronage. Elected judges usually owe their office to favors rendered to a political party. Specific party interests inevitably enter public policy, including decisions on criminal matters. Because courts are the arena in which the conflicting claims of diverse groups are presented and resolved, control over them is desired by the dominant economic class.

Within the judiciary system, the dominant groups have ways of gaining access to those who make decisions: (1) influencing selection of judges, (2) influencing content of decisions, and (3) maximizing or minimizing effects of decisions as they are implemented.[3] Such methods enable dominant groups to have criminal statutes interpreted in their favor. The administration of criminal law is mostly selective interpretations of the law favoring some interests and negating others. Under the adversary system of justice, compromise is rare: someone wins, someone else loses. And since the legal system is an institution of the dominant class, the administration of justice naturally favors that class.

Discretion in the Judicial Process

Whenever political decisions are made, discretion necessarily occurs, and judicial decision-making means exercising discretion. Within

the judicial proceedings different types of political decisions are made at each stage. Once a case is admitted to the judicial system, after an arrest, decisions are made about the suspect's fate. Some cases may be removed entirely from the system by the decision reached during the first judicial appearance, but others move sequentially from one stage to another before going out of the system. At each stage, the decision reached by some officials limits the alternatives for decisions in the subsequent stages.

After the arrest the suspect is usually brought before a court official, the magistrate, to determine the nature of the case. A preliminary hearing may follow to establish "probable cause," and a decision is also made on detaining the suspect, and setting the bail, if any. Between the first judicial appearance and the indictment, the prosecution decides what charges to press or whether to press charges at all. Once formal charges are made, pretrial proceedings are established during the arraignment. Decisions are reached on the time of trial, use of the plea, challenge of the formal charge, the kind of evidence, and the defendant's mental or physical capacity. If a trial takes place, rather than a settlement by guilty plea proceedings, decisions are made by judge and jury in the courtroom. Arguing their cases, the prosecuting attorney and the lawyer for the defense make innumerable strategic decisions. The decision to convict the accused and to impose a sentence are the consequences of the decisions made from the moment at which the arrest was made.

The convicted person's fate is still somewhat problematic, however, in that an appellate review may alter previous decisions. But the convicted person will probably have to continue within the judicial system until officials make decisions on his release. From the time the suspect enters the judicial process, decisions by others determine whether or not he will be defined as criminal.

The boundaries of discretion, as used by the police or in the administration of criminal law, are not clearly defined.[4] Obviously judicial decisions are made, not uniformly, but according to endless extralegal factors, including the age, race, and social class of the offenders.

Judicial systems themselves, with their great variety, are a major source for the variation in judicial decision-making. The United States has fifty-two separate court jurisdictions in the fifty states, the District of Columbia, and the federal government.[5] The state jurisdictions have several forms of courts, known as "police" courts, "special sessions" courts, and "quarter" courts. Some deal with minor criminal violations of local laws and ordinances and others with more serious offenses. They have specialized functions but cause much confusion by their overlapping jurisdictions.

The federal judicial system also has several types of courts with diverse activities and functions. And the federal circuit courts are divided according to geographical areas. All this complexity and diversity in the judiciary guarantees variations in judicial decision-making. The criminal law cannot be uniformly administered, but has to involve local discretion.

Judicial discretion shows most obviously in the handling of cases of persons from minority groups. Blacks are generally convicted with less evidence and sentenced to more severe punishments than whites. In a study of 821 homicides in several counties of North Carolina between 1930 and 1940, it was found that the fewest indictments were made when whites killed blacks and the highest proportion when blacks killed whites.[6] The courts seemed to consider the slaying of a white by a black as almost prima facie evidence of guilt, but the murder of a black by a white appeared to require mitigating circumstances such as provocation.

Haywood Burns wrote that the law in America has been used against minorities "to make sure that these inferior beings stayed in their place — whatever that might be at the moment."[7] Laws have excluded Indians, Orientals, and blacks from their lands, from participation in politics, and from basic human rights. In spite of Supreme Court decisions and civil-rights legislation, racism continues to operate in the American legal system, keeping some groups subordinate. Justice for blacks is still different from that for whites; racism in American law survives "institutionally" as a product of caste and class subordination.[8]

Yet, discretion works unseen by the public. Partly by design, the public is shielded from the system's workings by the highly formal and technical language of the law. It is also organized in ways that prevent us from observing its day-to-day operations. The criminal court, in particular, has an organization and an operation outside of public scrutiny and beyond legal considerations. Abraham Blumberg, a lawyer-sociologist who has gotten behind the "purple curtain" of justice, writes:

> The court, unlike most other formal organizations, functions as a genuinely "closed community" in that it successfully conceals the true nature of its routine operations from the view of outsiders — and sometimes even from some of the participants themselves. It socializes its members and participants toward compliance with specific objectives which are not part of the official goals of justice and due process.[9]

The bureaucratic complexity that enshrouds the judicial system makes it difficult for the citizen to see political bias and institutionalized discrimination at work, allowing the myth of justice to prevail.

The Political Trial

The politics of justice comes to the surface in the criminal trial. The courtroom trial can be used to eliminate political foes who are a threat to the regime.[10] The wielders of state power use the courts to maintain their domination. Although this country has always had political trials, the response of the government to the challenges of the last decade has increased the number of political trials. Indeed, all trials today are political in one way or another.

The United States has a rich history of political trials. Dramatic trials for such offenses against the state as treason have been rare, but the courts have been used for political purposes, from the trials during the country's founding years to the recent cases involving civil rights, war resistance, demonstrations, and conspiracy. Reviewing some of these trials, Leon Friedman dispels the myth that trials by the state are not political: "In short, the concept of a politically insulated prosecutor, a neutral court and jury and a

VIEWPOINT

JUDICIAL DISCRETION AND LEGALITY: THE RESPONSE OF A LAW PROFESSOR

The dominance of discretionary processes in key criminal administration decisions is not an accidental phenomenon. Rather, the prevalence of discretion is closely related to the overextension of the criminal sanction, in terms of the kinds of cases handled and the severity with which condemned individuals are treated. Discretion tends to be found at points of overambition, where the disparity between public expectations and official capacity is most notable. Officials tend to respond to the undue harshness of punishments provided by the law by seeking discretion to avoid the imposition of that harshness in most cases. Yet, ironically, it is when the system is particularly severe that discretion may be most abusive and the temptation to act unjustly becomes greatest. When the system is severe, discretionary decision-making becomes unacceptable because it reposes excessive authority in the hands of an often unsupervised individual official. In such a situation the advantages of legal rules and process become exaggerated.

Working alone, traditional procedural reforms, such as judicialization and the provision of counsel, cannot adequately control the exercise of discretion. Instead they merely displace the occasion for official discretion to another setting and complicate the process. A common result is increased severity as officials try to discourage defendants from invoking the complex formal process by placing a high tariff, in the form of severity, on those who do so unsuccessfully.

There are unexploited opportunities to bring the question of official discretion into a more acceptable context by dealing directly with the overbreadth of the system in operation, thereby moderating the prominence of discretionary decision-making. Some of these opportunities are procedural. They include a more conscious legislative and administrative grading of standards and procedures in terms of the severity and intrusiveness of the decision that may result. An effort might be made to structure the choices open to the official so that he is motivated to select less intrusive alternatives. A related procedural suggestion emphasizes the function of decision rules in establishing the official's action in cases of doubt. By structuring both formal and informal decision rules to favor the less severe options available, the presumption of innocence can be given concrete meaning and the opportunity for the imposition of severity would be reduced.

Discretionary decision-making is strongly associated with official bureaucracy, and efforts to deal with it must take into account the organizational structures that have spawned it. The possibilities here are less clearly delineated, although power over agency budgets would appear crucial to any substantial change.

At some point the problems cease to be technical and become political. The root of the danger of excessive severity and the key to its resolution lie in the place the criminal justice system occupies in the perceptions and anxieties of people. There are few opportunities to deal directly with these fears and fantasies. What the legal community can do is work to limit the potential of the criminal law for harm and its tendency to outgrow its capacity for good. The specific approaches suggested are designed to aim directly at this overambition while encouraging the continued development of the affirmative functions of punishment and social condemnation.

Source: From Arthur Rosett, "Discretion, Severity and Legality in Criminal Justice," _Southern California Law Review,_ 46 (1972), pp. 49–50.

normal trial is more an ideal than a reality, and it ceases to exist entirely when political out-groups and vociferous dissenters are brought into the judicial system."[11]

Several recent trials have drawn to public attention the politicality of the courts, especially the war resisters, the Black Panthers, and the conspiracy cases.[12] In fact, in the Chicago conspiracy trial, the defendants explicitly attempted to show how the court was being political, refusing to observe the traditional decorum of the courtroom. The severe contempt charges that followed the trial indicated the court's reaction to the defendants' political use of the trial. Friedman said: "It is total hypocrisy to attack the Chicago defendants for bringing politics into their proceeding: it was politics that brought *them* to the court room. To accuse them of tainting the trial with extraneous political considerations is to swallow the government's whitewash."[13] Courts are not "above the battle," but can be active participants, indeed instigators, of politics in administering criminal law.

In recent years the state has created a judicial structure explicitly designed to deal with threats to itself. Modern criminal justice has a complex of judicial weapons for securing domestic order: conspiracy charges, preventive detention, grand jury proceedings, mass prosecutions, and the like.[14] These tactics do not usually result in a successful prosecution, and often are judged to be unconstitutional, but the government is able to repress threatening thoughts and actions.

Prosecution and Nontrial Adjudication

Pretrial Proceedings

For the public, the focal point of judicial administration consists of the court trial, where the fate of the accused is decided by twelve of his peers. Not only is this conception incorrect about the *way* in which people are convicted, but it is misleading in implying that adjudication consists *only* of the decision by judge or jury to convict or acquit. As we have seen, several judicial stages precede a trial. But it is significant that in these pretrial proceedings most criminal cases never reach the criminal trial stage. The decision to impose a criminal

definition is usually made in the *pretrial* proceedings by *nontrial* adjudication.

Upon arrest, or after a summons or on-the-spot citation is issued, the suspect is supposed to be brought promptly before a magistrate, who reads the warrant to him.[15] If the offense is a minor one, triable by the magistrate, a summary trial may be held immediately. If the offense is more serious, not triable by the magistrate, the purpose of the initial appearance is more limited. The suspect will be given the opportunity of having a preliminary hearing to determine if there is sufficient evidence to justify being held for possible trial. If he waives a preliminary hearing, he is then bound over to a court of trial jurisdiction.

The principal function of the first judicial appearance is not, however, to determine whether the evidence is sufficient for trial. Neither the prosecuting attorney nor the defense lawyer is yet ready to determine whether probable cause exists. The first appearance is meant mainly to provide for the defendant's release, pending further judicial proceedings. Release itself is a constitutional right, but the bail procedure of temporarily forfeiting money for freedom has resulted in a number of unjust practices. Ideally the only criterion for determining the amount of bail money is to make it enough to ensure that the defendant will reappear. In practice, however, the bail system discriminates against those who cannot afford to pay the bail fee, feeds a shady bail-bond business, and promotes questionable judicial procedures in setting bail.[16] Recent alternatives to the bail system, such as pretrial parole, are eliminating the deficiencies of bail, at the same time providing for both the constitutional release of the defendants and assurance of their return for subsequent judicial processing.[17]

In some jurisdictions the suspect is arraigned immediately after being booked at the police station, thus bypassing the appearance before a magistrate. Whether arraignment is the first judicial appearance or a later one, it consists of an appearance before a judge of the trial court. There the judge reads the charge to the defendant and informs him of his right to counsel. The initial charge is based upon either the "information" or the "indictment," depending upon the procedures used in the jurisdiction. Some jurisdictions rely on a grand jury

**Table 11.1 Guilty Plea Convictions in Several States
(1964 Statistics unless Otherwise Indicated)**

State	Total convictions	Guilty pleas	
		Number	Percentage
California (1965)	30,840	22,817	74.0%
Connecticut	1,596	1,494	93.9
District of Columbia (yr. end. June 30, 1964)	1,115	817	73.3
Hawaii	393	360	91.5
Illinois	5,591	4,768	85.2
Kansas	3,025	2,727	90.2
Massachusetts (1963)	7,790	6,642	85.2
Minnesota (1965)	1,567	1,437	91.7
New York	17,249	16,464	95.5
U.S. District Courts	29,170	26,273	90.2
Average			87.0

Source: President's Commission on Law Enforcement and Administration of Justice, *Task Force Report: The Courts* (Washington, D.C.: U.S. Government Printing Office, 1967), p. 9.

to return an indictment for felony cases and charges for misdemeanors use information filed by the prosecuting attorney.

Whichever procedure is used for reaching a charge, the judge then asks the defendant to plead to the charge, and he may plead guilty, not guilty, or may stand mute. With the judge's permission, he may also have the option of pleading *nolo contendere*, the same as a plea of guilty except that it cannot be used as an admission in subsequent civil suits. If the defendant pleads guilty, the judge will ordinarily enter a judgment of conviction, postponing the sentence until a presentence investigation can be made by the probation department. If the defendant stands mute, the judge will enter a plea of not guilty, and a trial will follow. If the plea is not guilty, the judge asks whether the defendant desires a jury trial or whether he prefers to be tried by the judge without a jury. A plea of not guilty places the burden on the state to prove every element of the offense beyond a reasonable doubt.

Plea Bargaining

The trial, important as it is in administering justice, is about the least common method of convicting and acquitting defendants. Roughly 90 per cent of criminal convictions are based on guilty pleas that are adjudicated without a trial.[18] It is hard to estimate how many cases are disposed of by guilty pleas, however, because of such matters as variations in use from one jurisdiction to another, fluctuations from time to time, and variations according to the kinds of crime being tabulated. The statistics in Table 11.1 show how often these are used in the general trial jurisdictions in several states.

The American judicial system has come to depend on the guilty plea. If all or even most criminal cases were to receive a trial upon a plea of not guilty, the courts simply could not handle the case load. There are not enough, and conceivably could never be enough, judges, prosecutors, and defense attorneys.

The judicial necessity of guilty pleas has given rise to the practice commonly known as "plea bargaining." A substantial portion of guilty pleas result from negotiations between the prosecutor and defense lawyer or between the prosecutor and the defendant. The negotiated plea lightens the case load and accomplishes other objectives.

VIEWPOINT_____

IDEOLOGY AND RATIONALISM IN THE CRIMINAL COURT

The official goals of an organization are not difficult to determine in most instances. They are stated in corporate charters, advertising slogans, or prefaces to annual reports, or even on company or agency stationery. In the case of Metropolitan Court, as with certain other public agencies, they are engraved on the building façades:

Equal and Exact Justice to All Men of Whatever State or Persuasion

Good Faith Is the Foundation of Justice

The Only True Principle of Humanity Is Justice

Justice Is Denied No One

Impartiality Is the Life of Justice as Justice Is of Good Government

Every Place Is Safe to Him Who Lives in Justice

Only the Just Man Enjoys Peace of Mind

Where Law Ends There Tyranny Begins

One need not have a sophisticated knowledge of the historical roots of these mottoes to discern the goals of the organization or the presumed values underlying them.

It is commonly assumed that the basis for due process and rule of law in Western jurisprudence rests on the Magna Carta of 1215. But their real origin is in the Old and New Testaments, and in a social era whose life style has little resemblance or relevance to modern mass societies. Somehow we assume that our values, including due process, have maintained their relative order of importance regardless of the passage of time and the shift in Western society from an emphasis on kinship and status relations to the impersonal, secular, rational modes and instruments of social organization. Lawyers and judges still speak, perhaps naively, of "immutable principles" when they talk about justice and due process. When virtually every other aspect of human existence has been touched and modified by mass society and its precursors of secularism and rationalism, they find it difficult to recognize that their universe of discourse has also been affected.

The official goals of the criminal court, based on ancient values, remain; due process, justice, and rule of law are necessary ideologies. But concerns of secularism and rationality, based on modern values of efficiency, maximum production, and career enhancement, have deflected and perhaps displaced those goals. So there is also a new angle of vision more harmoniously in accord with the rationalization of justice. These perspectives are organizationally geared through bureaucratic discipline to mesh with the new goals. The impersonal relations inherent in this kind of social structure produce accusers and accused possessed of a self which is ideal for organizational purposes — one which is vulnerable to manipulation and capable of manipulating others.

Source: From Abraham S. Blumberg, *Criminal Justice* (Chicago: Quadrangle Books, 1967), pp. 76–78.

VIEWPOINT_____

CONSTITUTIONALITY/UNCONSTITUTIONALITY
OF PLEA BARGAINING

Plea bargaining nullifies constitutional guarantees for a substantial number of criminal defendants, yet it is a key element of the existing criminal justice bureaucracy. The conflict between administrative economy and constitutional values is intense. The Constitution guarantees the primacy of the individual in the criminal process; the fifth and sixth amendments embody the basic protections to be afforded all criminal defendants. Efficiency, on the other hand, is simply the general interest of the state in achieving its goals. This diffuse interest is not usually recognized as a justification for undermining constitutional protections. Perhaps elimination of plea bargaining would require so drastic a reallocation of resources that the basic social order would be seriously threatened. But to accept such a justification would be to admit that the fifth and sixth amendment guarantees have proved unworkable. Abolition of constitutional protections should come only through full and open public debate, not through the unsupervised practices of prosecutors, defense counsel, and judges.

The elimination of plea bargaining will obviously place the existing criminal justice system under severe stress, and no court is capable of fully restructuring the system in response to the change. But legislatures also have an obligation to seek out other means of mitigating the conflict between administrative efficiency and fundamental rights, means which will withstand constitutional scrutiny. Thus, society might allocate more resources to the criminal process. It might choose to penalize many fewer forms of individual behavior. By appropriate reduction of penalties, the right to jury trial might be bypassed for many offenses. Indeed, a system which depended less on incarceration and more on parole and similar programs might prove more effective as well as less expensive.

Well aware of the need for legislative response to a judicial decision that invalidates plea bargaining, judges have avoided analyzing the constitutionality of the practice. The bar, which has actively participated in plea bargaining, has attempted to dress it in procedural niceties and has manufactured weak or faulty justifications for it. But neither the lack of an assured legislative response nor the bar's substantial involvement in the practice should affect the legal profession's evaluation of it. Lawyers and judges more than other citizens are under an obligation to maintain the criminal process in conformity with the Constitution. To restore the defendant's fundamental trial rights to their traditional preeminence, plea bargaining should be declared unconstitutional.

Source: From "Plea Bargaining," *Harvard Law Review,* 83 (April 1970), pp. 1410–1411.

As the term implies, plea negotiation involves an exchange of concessions and advantages between the state and the accused. The defendant who pleads guilty is treated less severely than he would be if he were convicted of the maximum charge and assessed the most severe penalty. At the same time, he waives his right to trial, thereby losing his chance, no matter how slight, for outright acquittal. The state, at the relatively small cost of charge reduction leniency, gains the numerous administrative advantages of the guilty plea over a long, costly, and always uncertain trial. In this way the negotiated plea in a real sense answers two important objectives of criminal justice administration: the individualization of justice and the maintenance of the guilty plea system.[19]

The negotiated guilty plea is thus a compromise conviction reached by the state and the accused for the benefit of both.

Having studied this informal conviction process, Donald J. Newman reported that plea bargaining occurred in more than half the felony cases studied.[20] The accused, directly or through an attorney, offered to plead guilty providing the charge was reduced in kind or degree, or exchanged for a specific type or length of sentence. The subsequent conviction agreements followed several patterns according to the types of bargains:

1. *Bargain Concerning the Charge.* A plea of guilty was entered by the offenders in exchange for a reduction of the charge from the one alleged in the complaint. This ordinarily occurred in cases where the offense in question carried statutory degrees of severity such as homicide, assault, and sex offenses. This type was mentioned as a major issue in 20 percent of the cases in which bargaining occurred. The majority of offenders in these instances were represented by lawyers.

2. *Bargain Concerning the Sentence.* A plea of guilty was entered by the offenders in exchange for a promise of leniency in sentencing. The most commonly accepted consideration was a promise that the offender would be placed on probation, although a less-than-maximum prison term was the basis in certain instances. All offenses except murder, serious assault, and robbery were represented in this type of bargaining process. This was by far the most frequent consideration given in exchange for guilty pleas, occurring in almost half (45.5 percent) of the cases in which any bargaining occurred. Again, most of these offenders were represented by attorneys.

3. *Bargain for Concurrent Charges.* This type of informal process occurred chiefly among offenders pleading without counsel. These men exchanged guilty pleas for the concurrent pressing of multiple charges, generally numerous counts of the same offense or related violations such as breaking and entering and larceny. This method, of course, has much the same effect as pleading for consideration in the sentence. The offender with concurrent convictions, however, may not be serving a reduced sentence; he is merely serving one sentence for many crimes. Altogether, concurrent convictions were reported by 21.8 percent of the men who were convicted by informal methods.

4. *Bargain for Dropped Charges.* This variation occurred in about an eighth of the cases who reported bargaining. It involved an agreement on the part of the prosecution not to press formally one or more charges against the offender if he in turn pleaded guilty to (usually) the major offense. The offenses dropped were extraneous law violations contained in, or accompanying, the offense alleged in the complaint, such as auto theft accompanying armed robbery and violation of probation where a new crime had been committed. This informal method, like bargaining for concurrent charges, was reported chiefly by offenders without lawyers. It occurred in 12.6 percent of cases in which bargaining was claimed.[21]

Although most of the remainder of the sample pleaded guilty without considerations, in many of these cases the attorneys probably bargained, or attempted to bargain, without successfully achieving a compromise on conviction.

The plea bargaining system, always controversial, is under severe attack. Recently the National Advisory Commission on Criminal Justice Standards called for totally abolishing plea bargaining by 1978. Their proposal is based on the argument that "sentences should depend not on whether the defendant has saved the state the expense of a trial but, instead, on what is needed to rehabilitate him."[22] The courts continue to protect the plea bargaining system. The Supreme Court recently ruled in *Brady* v. *U.S.* that the pressures of plea bargaining do not in themselves violate the privilege against self-incrimination. This decision was followed by *North Carolina* v. *Alford,* in which the Supreme Court ruled that a person accused of a crime should be permitted to plead guilty to a lesser offense and avoid the possibility that a jury might impose a stiffer sentence, even if the defendant insists that he or she is innocent.

Prosecution and Negotiation in the Court

How the defendant will be prosecuted is decided by the agents in the court system. The charges that will be brought against the defendant, and how they will be negotiated, are determined mostly beyond the accused's reach. His fate is decided somewhere within the interactions and relationships the judiciary has already built before this defendant ever becomes a problem for the court.

The framework for negotiation can be characterized as an "exchange system," in which linkages bind the actors in the judicial business of making decisions. In a marketlike setting, judicial decisions are made following exchanges between legal agents. The decision to prosecute, as described in a study of the Office of the Prosecuting Attorney in King County (Seattle), is characterized as one in which the prosecutor exercises discretionary powers "within the network of exchange relationships."[23]

Curbing the flow of cases through the court is vital in the decision to prosecute. The prosecutor, in making decisions, is aware of the needs and expectations of others in the court system. As in the King County court:

Within the limits imposed by law and the demands of the system, the prosecutor is able to regulate the flow of cases to the court. He may control the length of time between accusation and trial; hence he may hold cases until he has the evidence which will convict. Alternatively, he may seek repeated adjournment and continuances until the public's interest dies; problems such as witnesses becoming unavailable and similar difficulties make his request for dismissal of prosecution more justifiable. Further, he may determine the type of court to receive the case and the judge who will hear it. Many misdemeanors covered by state law are also violations of a city ordinance. It is a common practice for the prosecutor to send a misdemeanor case to the city prosecutor for processing in the municipal court when it is believed that a conviction may

not be secured in justice court. As a deputy said, "If there is no case — send it over to the city court. Things are speedier, less formal, over there."[24]

The prosecutor regulating court cases is at the same time considering the interests of all involved in administering criminal law, including his own political interests and the needs of the judicial system in general.

The interactions and perceptions of the prosecutor and the defense, in particular, are critical in negotiating a guilty plea. David Sudnow observes that the prosecutor (district attorney) and the defense (public defender) develop during their interactions a common position on altering charges.[25] The negotiators are not able to arrange a suitable reduction in charge by referring to a statutory definition of an offense, because the penal code does not give enough guidance for deciding how the offender's conduct and the legal category correspond. In a charge of burglary, the prosecutor and defense negotiate about a class of "burglaries," which Sudnow calls *normal burglaries*. A burglary charge can be reduced to a charge of petty theft because the negotiators are able to see the reduction as reasonable and consistent with the kinds of behaviors normally associated with that charge. Sudnow describes this bargain:

The method of reduction involves, as a general feature, the fact that the particular case in question is scrutinized to decide its membership in a class of similar cases. But *the penal code does not provide the reference for deciding the correspondence between the instant event and the general case; that is, it does not define the classes of offense types.* To decide, for purposes of finding a suitable reduction, if the instant case involves a "burglary," reference is not made to the statutory definition of "burglary." To decide what the situationally included offenses are in the instant case, the instant case is not analyzed as a *statutorily* referable course of action; rather, reference is made to a *non-statutorily* conceived class "burglary" and offenses that are typically situationally included in it, taken as a class of behavioral events. Stated again: in searching an instant case to decide what to *reduce it to,* there is no analysis of the statutorily referable elements of the instant case; instead, its membership in a class of events, the features of which cannot be described by the penal code, must be decided.[26]

During their interaction and repeated negotiations, then, the prosecutor and defense develop unstated guides for reducing original charges to lesser charges.

The reasons for plea bargaining between the prosecutor and the accused or his defense are more immediate than individualizing justice and maintaining the judicial system.[27] The charge is often reduced because the prosecutor realizes his evidence is insufficient for conviction at a trial. Reduction may be necessary too because of the reluctance of complainants, victims, or witnesses to testify. The prosecutor at other times may suggest reducing the charge because he believes that the judge or jury is unlikely to convict the defendant. Judges themselves may favor charge reduction to avoid imposing the mandatory sentence (either maximum or minimum) associated with the original charge. A parole sentence may be possible only if the original charge is reduced to a lesser charge. Whatever the bargaining agreement, though, the judge may acquit the defendant for a number of reasons that grow out of an interest in individualized justice and judicial maintenance. Acquittals are made because (1) the conduct is regarded as a minor violation, (2) the offender is thought unaccountable for his or her behavior, (3) the conduct is considered normal for the defendant's subculture, (4) the conduct is a matter of private morality, (5) specialized treatment may look more appropriate than punishment, (6) restitution is otherwise made to the victim, and (7) the judge disagrees with the purpose of the law or with the law-enforcement effort.[28]

Whether the judge convicts according to the plea negotiated by the prosecutor and defense or acquits the defendant, he obviously has a personal interest in the outcome of each case. Technically the judge is not supposed to enter into the bargaining, but by subtle cues and not-so-subtle demands, the judge influences the negotiation of pleas. The advantages of plea negotiation for the judge are mentioned in a study of "Metropolitan Court":

According to the ideology of the law, the judge is required to be not only impartial but active in seeking out and preserving the rights of all offenders. Nevertheless, he also has a vested interest in a high rate of negotiated pleas. He shares the prosecutor's earnest desire to avoid the time-consuming, expensive, unpredictable snares and pitfalls of an adversary trial. He sees an impossible backlog of cases, with their mounting delays, as possible public evidence of his "inefficiency" and failure. The defendant's plea of guilty enables the judge to engage in a social-psychological fantasy — the accused becomes an already repentant individual who has "learned his lesson" and deserves lenient treatment. Indeed, as previously indicated, many judges give a less severe sentence to a defendant who has negotiated a plea than to one who has been convicted of the same offense after a trial.[29]

No matter what the reason for negotiating a guilty plea is, for the prosecutor's interest or that of the defense, the judge, or the judicial system in general, the resulting conviction is a criminal definition. Guilty plea negotiation ultimately creates a crime.

Negotiated justice makes the judicial system possible, for without it the criminal justice system would collapse from its burden. The American legal system and what it serves benefit by processing cases as speedily as possible through the criminal justice system. Getting defendants to plead guilty to lesser charges eliminates the time and expense of further judicial processing, especially avoiding costly and time-consuming criminal trials.

The criminal justice system, despite this short-cut, is in crisis. The backlog in criminal cases is mounting. People are recognizing too that defendants are waiting months, often in jail, to have their cases processed.[30] Officials are frantically proposing "sweeping changes" in the administration of criminal justice, including day-and-night court sessions, overhauled bail policies, more judges, and making the courts more efficient.[31] All are an attempt to make criminal justice more rational, to create an efficiently managed criminal justice system. The problem is seen as administrative — with enough planning and engineering, the "administrative chaos" will be corrected and justice will be achieved. The survival of a legal system preserving the established order is at stake.

These reform measures are being applied to deal with the heavy case loads in the courts, and plea bargaining by itself seems incapable of handling the increased loads. Furthermore, plea negotiation is being questioned, with proposals that it at least be regularized and subjected to procedural rules. David Sternberg, examining the consequences of the radical-criminal trials of the late sixties and early seventies, suggests that the old plea-bargaining system may be in jeopardy. Defendants and their lawyers may be less willing in the future to bargain for justice. Writing about the radicalization of criminal trials, he observes:

> I believe that these trials, interacting with rebellions in the houses of detention and prisons during the same period, have permanently affected the political consciousness of large numbers of present (and future) "clients" in various stages of the administration of justice. Although it is blurred by the complicating variable of race consciousness in our society, it seems to me that the political element is substantial enough to allow one to refer, in Marxist-Leninist terms, to an acceleration of *class* consciousness among these clients, and to some progress toward a "class-for-itself." The emerging solidarity and power of that class-for-itself, catalyzed by the radical-criminal trials, may drastically reshape the ground rules and outcomes of criminal proceedings during the 1970s. There is already fragmentary but suggestive and significant evidence to support its contention.[32]

Although defendants using radical strategies could disrupt the bureaucratic functioning of the courts, it is possible that the courts might make some administrative concessions, allowing a new kind of bargaining that would reduce the selection of defendants for indictments, be more lenient in bail procedures, and give better "deals" for the defendants. Another breed of reforms could be instituted to deal with defendants in more formal and insidious ways. Instead of processing defendants through the formal judicial system, accused persons might be "treated" and "corrected"

outside the court. This appears to be the direction that criminal justice in the United States is taking.

The Criminal Lawyer in the Adversary System

The Adversary System

The system for administering criminal justice in the United States has still another pillar holding it up: the adversary principle. The adversary system has the opposing parties — the state and the accused — engage in a public battle. The game is right versus wrong; one side must be entirely correct and the other all wrong. One side wins when the judgment is in its favor. Rules and procedures guide the battle throughout.[33]

The adversary system and criminal justice are bureaucratically organized in distinct legal work roles with specified duties and obligations. Each position has its own definition and another relating it to the others. Expectations of performance regulate the occupational behavior of those who occupy the work roles, the principal ones being the prosecutor, the defense attorney, and the judge. Each, in his separate way, is engaged in work that results in defining people and behaviors as criminal.

The judge acts on evidence and arguments presented by the prosecuting and the defense attorneys. He finds the defendant guilty or innocent, sometimes by referring to a jury's decision, and then imposes a sentence. The prosecutor's role is more critical in the early judicial stages. As the representative of the state, he has the authority to determine whether an alleged offender should be charged and the authority to obtain a conviction by negotiation. He has the responsibility of presenting the state's case in court, that is, of prosecuting the accused. His skill as a trial lawyer is important in convicting the defendant. The prosecutor also affects the arrest practices of the police, the volume of cases in the courts, and the number of offenders referred to the correctional system.

According to the adversary principle of justice, the lawyer for the defense is also engaged in a battle against the other agents of the court. The defendant's lawyer represents the accused in opposition to the court's interests. In reality, however, the adversary principle does not work in that way. Instead, the criminal lawyer shares in the system of criminal justice with the prosecutor and the other representatives of the court. The accused person finds that his or her interests are being overshadowed by the needs of the criminal justice system. Everyone in the court, except the defendant, sees himself as a colleague, not an adversary. The social reality in the judicial process, contrary to the legal ideology, is based on cooperation rather than adversary relationships. The fate of the defendant, who remains on the outside except when assisting in plea negotiation, is decided within this social reality.

Legal Representation of the Accused

The right of the accused to be represented by legal counsel has been ensured in the Sixth Amendment to the Constitution, and is essential to the adversary system of criminal justice. An individual forced to answer to a criminal charge needs assistance from one who understands the legal system and who will protect the defendant's legal rights. The defendant is not likely to understand the legal system, mainly because of its planned obscurity. For the judicial system to be effective and efficient, counsel for the defendant is necessary. An adversary system of justice depends too upon vigorous challenges to the state's accusations.

When and how to ensure or provide legal counsel for the accused has been the vital issue in the adversary system. Procedures that were inspired in part by rulings of state supreme courts and the United States Supreme Court entitle or require defendants to have legal counsel from the moment of arrest. The Supreme Court decision in the Gault case expanded the jurisdictional rights of counsel to include juvenile delinquency proceedings.

Several schemes provide defendants with legal counsel.[34] The types of legal representation include (1) court-appointed counsel, as in the legal-aid system, (2) the public-defender system, whereby the state provides permanent lawyers to defend the accused, and (3) lawyer-reference plans, in which private or public agency lawyers are made known to defendants.

The availability of these and other forms of legal representation varies from one jurisdiction to another. Most important for the conviction process, the outcome of cases can depend on the kind of legal counsel the defendant receives.[35]

That criminal justice is differently administered according to social class is at least vaguely realized by most persons. Because the poor are accused of criminal behavior more often than members of other classes, their dependence upon legal service is total. However, legal services are most inadequate for the class that needs legal assistance most. The poor are least likely to use lawyers; when they do they usually have access only to the least competent ones, and the legal counsel with which they are provided is generally of limited character. Surveys from several states indicate that about two out of three lower-class families have never employed a lawyer, compared with about one out of three upper-class families.[36] The few private attorneys available to the poor, because of the insecurity of their practice, are likely to succumb to temptations to exploit clients.[37]

To supplement private legal representation, special agencies and procedures, such as legal-aid societies and the public-defender system, have extended legal services to the poor. Nevertheless, it appears that indigents are not provided with adequate legal services, and the result is higher rates of conviction and severer sentences for the poor.

With respect to the representation of criminal defendants, there is considerable evidence to suggest that neither the assigned counsel nor public defender system as now constituted is capable of providing adequate service to the indigent accused. A large proportion of poor defendants (particularly in misdemeanor cases) are not represented at all. Moreover, when counsel is provided he frequently has neither the resources, the skill nor the incentive to defend his client effectively; and he usually enters the case too late to make any real difference in the outcome. Indeed, the generally higher rate of guilty pleas and prison sentences among defendants represented by assigned counsel or the public defender suggest that these attorneys may actually undermine their clients' position.[38]

Justice in the United States, even with the legalities supplied by due process, seems mostly to be for the classes that are able to dominate and control the social, economic, and political institutions.

Career Patterns in Criminal Law

Lawyers who represent criminal defendants privately usually are engaged in a specialized type of legal practice. They also have distinctive career patterns. Both tendencies affect their way of handling criminal cases.

More than half the lawyers practicing in cities in the United States are self-employed. The other half are either employed in firms or as lawyers in corporations, governmental legal departments, and legal-aid societies.[39] The individual practitioner (or "solo" lawyer) differs sharply from those engaged in the other types of legal practice. It was found in a comparison of individual practitioners and firm lawyers in Detroit that solo lawyers more often came from minority, religious-ethnic, entrepreneurial, and working-class homes, and had inferior educations and chaotic work histories.[40] They also restrict their practices to residual matters that the large law firms have not pre-empted. Their practice, as found in Chicago, includes these matters:

(1) matters not large enough or remunerative enough for the large firms to handle — most general work for small to medium-sized businesses and corporations, the smaller real estate transactions (for individuals or small businesses), and estate matters for middle-income families; (2) the undesirable cases, the dirty work, those areas of practice that have associated with them an aura of influencing and fixing and that involve arrangements with clients and others that are felt by the large firms to be professionally damaging. The latter category includes local tax, municipal, personal injury, divorce, and criminal matters.[41]

The lawyers who privately handle the criminal cases of lower- and working-class defendants usually are individual practitioners. They are also likely to be engaged in a diversified legal practice in which criminal cases are only an occasional affair. Their practice of law generally is built on the local police court or the traffic court and is ethnic- and neighborhood-oriented. This solo lawyer in Chicago shows how diverse legal matters are related for the individual practitioner:

I handle some small criminal cases. This year I had one case, an indictment in felony court, a bench trial. The rest would be either police court — up to the preliminary hearing, getting charges reduced to misdemeanors, and so on — assault and battery, domestic problems, mostly drunks and disorderlies, assaults, etc. Neighborhood stuff. So many domestic relations cases come out of the police court; after representing them in the police court, you get them dismissed for divorce.[42]

The individual practitioners who do specialize must maintain regular sources of case referral. They depend on close relationships with bondsmen, policemen, and community leaders for their business. The competition for criminal cases among solo lawyers who specialize in criminal law produces a legal practice that is based more on sharp business practices than pursuing criminal justice.

The difference between lawyers with criminal practices and those with civil practices is documented in a study of lawyers in five cities, comparing criminal lawyers and civil lawyers on such characteristics as social origins, choice of legal career, preparation for law, adjustment to legal practice, and the reasons for entering their field of legal practice.[43] The criminal lawyers had relatively low socioeconomic backgrounds, less professional training, had difficulty getting established, were solo practitioners engaged in an entrepreneurial career, and were not especially satisfied with criminal practice.

Using the characteristics of the criminal lawyers, the study distinguished between two types of criminal-law careers. In the first type,

the attorney did not choose to enter criminal law, but rather he accepted criminal cases as they came his way in the process of establishing a practice or as a supplement to a meager practice in civil law. From the standpoint of the legal profession, these lawyers are among the least successful, and accordingly one may judge their morale to be correspondingly low. The second type of criminal lawyer is one who often chose this field, but in any case he enjoys the drama and thrill of those accused of crime. He may achieve considerable success; lacking this, he is compensated by his intense absorption in the work.[44]

Only about a quarter of the criminal lawyers can be placed in the second type of criminal law career. Of course, some criminal lawyers do not fit into either of the two types, including the successful ones who do not have a welfare orientation and those who strongly identify with the welfare of their clients but whose careers may be described as failures. Most practitioners of criminal law can be described as either those who have failed to establish a successful practice and therefore accept criminal cases as a way of enlarging a legal practice, or those who relish the excitement in criminal work and feel that their practice secures some justice for the accused.

The public-defender lawyer's career presents its own problems. In a study of lawyers in the Public Defender Office in California's Alameda County (which includes Oakland and Berkeley), Anthony Platt and Randi Pollock found rather disheartening career patterns among the public defenders. Most recruits regarded the public defender office as a place to develop technical skills and professional values. Very few stayed longer than two and a half years, usually leaving with a feeling of being "burned out" and often embittered by the experience. They leave the public defender office to pursue a more lucrative private practice with predominantly middle-class clients. Platt and Pollock conclude their analysis:

> They come to justify their role as mediators between the poor and the courts, resigned to seeking occasional loopholes in the system, softening its more explicitly repressive features, and attempting to rescue the victims of blatant injustices. But even this makeshift effort to link everyday work with liberal humanitarianism proves inadequate, since most Assistants are regarded with resentment, ingratitude or indifference by

their clients. When they leave PDO [Public Defender Office], they have become cynical and embittered, alienated from politics, and preoccupied with problems of survival and success in the legal marketplace.[45]

Behavior and Ethics of Criminal Lawyers

All lawyers are subject to the normative controls of their occupation. Among those controls are (1) standards that proscribe behavior considered unethical by society in general, such as cheating, bribery, and stealing; (2) standards dealing with professional problems, such as relations among colleagues, methods of obtaining business, and conflicts of interest. Lawyers differ in the extent to which they conform to these standards. Ultimately the legal assistance the client receives is influenced by the behavior and ethics of the lawyer who handles the case.

In a study on the ethical conduct of New York City bar members, it was found that characteristics of the practice influence violation of professional standards.[46] Because of the instability in their practice, lawyers with low-status clients are subject to far more temptations, opportunities, and client pressure to violate professional ethics than are lawyers with high-status clients. Another influence on their ethical conduct is the court setting in which they work and the constraints provided by their work group. Conformity to professional norms and ethics thus depends greatly on where the lawyer is within the structure of the legal profession.

For the lawyer in criminal practice, professional norms cover several areas: "(1) confidentiality of the attorney-client relationship; (2) affective or emotional neutrality with respect to the merits of the case, while at the same time service in the interests of the client; and (3) participation in procedures in which a professional as opposed to a personal relationship is maintained with other participants — the police, the bondsman, the prosecutor and the judge."[47] The defense lawyer's behavior is especially complicated by the fact that he is confronted with conflicting claims. Because of his legal role, the defense attorney must act as a mediator between the client and judicial agents. His professional conduct, therefore, is related to the way in which he manages the conflicting claims imposed by the adversary system of justice.

Most defendants handled by criminal lawyers are guilty of some offense. Because of a precarious position, the defendant is subject to much manipulation by the attorney, and the case is guided by the lawyer's personal interests. Finally, the lawyer's handling of the defendant's case is affected by the court's bureaucratic structure: "In the sense that the lawyer in the criminal court serves as a double agent, serving higher organizational rather than professional ends, he may be deemed to be engaged in bureaucratic rather than private practice."[48] In this way, criminal law practice is actually bureaucratic practice, because the lawyer and his client are enmeshed in the authority and discipline of the judicial system. Strategies and decisions affecting the application of criminal definitions are made within the boundaries established by the adversary system of justice.

The Criminal Trial

The Trial Stage

The accused may eventually be adjudicated in a criminal trial. When negotiation between the legal agents has failed to bring the defendant to plead guilty, or the defendant pleads not guilty without any attempt at bargaining, a criminal trial will provide the setting for the remaining parts in the drama of imposing a criminal definition. The criminal trial constructs the reality of the case; it is not strictly an exercise in finding the truth, but is a product of politics and discretion.

Variations do change the trial's proceedings, but it generally follows these eight steps.[49] The arraignment and plea may be followed by: (1) selection of the jury, (2) opening statements by the prosecutor and the defense, (3) presentation of evidence by the state and the defense, (4) prosecutor's and defense's arguments to the jury, (5) prosecutor's rebuttal, (6) judge's instructions on the law, (7) rendering of the jury verdict, and (8) imposition of a sentence.

All these steps are of course not included in every trial. It may be decided that the defendant will be tried before a judge or panel of judges, rather than by a jury. Motions for change in procedure may be entered during the trial. Decisions may be made on waiving statements, evidence, and testimony. The defense may move for a new trial or to hold immediate judgment. Following the sentence, the case may be appealed to a higher court, or if the defense charges denial of due process there may be further litigation. In other words, the final conviction depends on many more decisions and actions once the defendant reaches the trial stage.

Extralegal Factors

In the popular mind the criminal trial is a symbol for justice in America. This notion depends on another — that justice is rationally dispensed, that all who are involved in the judicial process (lawyers, defendants, witnesses, jurors, judges) — rest their statements, arguments, and judgments on facts, according to the rules of law. All parties supposedly are pursuing the "truth" about the case. But human actions and the organizational constraints imposed by the judicial system itself make the reality harsher. The criminal trial may be most profitably analyzed as a system of human actions that entails perceptions and behaviors like those in any social situation. Those involved in the trial are acting according to their own past, their present perspectives, and their future expectations, and their actions are adjusted according to the behavior of others.

> In a sense the courtroom may be viewed as a microcosm of the larger social world in which human beings exist, act, and interact. That the action reconstructed in court and the action-process of reconstruction are meaningful and purposive, that they involve subjective as well as objective meanings, and that they significantly hinge on human goals, purposes and motives becomes at once apparent. If some juridical writers envisage a mere mechanical application of formalized law, the participants in the ordinary court trial of a criminal case are involved in more mundane practices.[50]

The combativeness in the criminal trial ensures that judicial actions will be social and extralegal rather than logical deductions from abstract principles. As a substitute for private brawls, the modern criminal trial places parties in opposing camps. The adversary system of justice promotes a "fight" method rather than a "truth" method of trying cases.[51]

In other words, the criminal trial constructs a reality — a social reality. Objective facts are not gathered in a criminal trial, but decisions are reached on "evidence" that is meaningful to the interacting and conflicting participants. Subjectivity enters into arguments by the attorneys, testimony by the witnesses, deliberations by jurors, and the judge's actions. All the actors in the drama react subjectively to the actions of all others. The decisions reached during the trial, including the one that ultimately defines the defendant as a convicted criminal, are made by people as social beings. That is to say, though the criminal trial is not an exercise in fact finding and logical deduction, it is a product of human action. Could anything else be expected?

Yet, the fate of the accused is being decided here. Factors totally unrelated to the formal legal system are determining the defendant's future. Not least of these factors is the way in which the accused person presents himself or herself in the courtroom. The participants there judge not only the alleged offense of the accused but his or her demeanor in the courtroom. Studying the courtroom ceremonies, Robert M. Emerson describes the kind of performance expected of the juvenile defendant:

A totally consistent performance is required, and this demands that the repentant delinquent convey a properly deferential and remorseful attitude by his demeanor. Deferential demeanor, expressing appreciation and respect toward both the court and the violated norm, constitutes a basic expectation in the courtroom ceremony. In this way, posture and expression should conform to the solemn and serious definition of the occasion. It is expected that the child maintain a formal, rigid, and controlled posture, both in entering the courtroom and in sitting through the course of the hearing. Facial expression must be carefully controlled in order to show worry and concern or at last serious interest in the unfolding scene. Similarly, any talking or comment

must be addressed to the whole court and show respect for the officials involved.[52]

To be judged one must enter into degrading and humiliating ceremonies. No matter what the outcome, the ordeal is part of the message that the court conveys.

Testimony and Witnesses

Testimony by all types of witnesses is used by both the prosecution and the defense to argue the merits of their positions. The defense attorney has to decide whether or not it is strategically wise to put the defendant on the stand as a witness in his own behalf; the decision is usually based on speculation about how the jury will react to the defendant's performance. The defense will be reluctant to place a defendant with a prior criminal record on the witness stand.[53] Though procedurally a previous conviction should not be considered as evidence of guilt on another charge, the defendant with a previous conviction is especially vulnerable to probing by the prosecuting attorney.

Both the prosecution and defense will utilize any witness who may favorably shape the opinions of the judge and jury members. Such witnesses, however, often end up in an insecure position.[54] In spite of procedures to guarantee his protection, the witness is subject to pressures from the public, the press, and personal contacts. He may later suffer repercussions from his testimony. The witness is most dramatically subjected to harassment during the opposition's cross-examination in the courtroom. Little wonder that the "facts" provided by witnesses are selective and subjective.

One kind of testimony that may be used in adjudicating the accused is that of the "experts." Criminal procedure today relies especially on the psychiatrist's testimony. Most states provide for preliminary observation of defendants suspected of mental disorders. If a judge decides to accept evidence provided by a psychiatrist, the accused may be declared incompetent to stand trial and then be committed indefinitely to a mental hospital.

During the criminal trial, the psychiatrist, in responding to the M'Naghten test of insanity, is asked to judge the responsibility and, in essence, the guilt or innocence of the defendant.[55] In jurisdictions that have rules of the Durham type, the psychiatrist may describe the mental state of the defendant entirely in psychiatric language, deciding if the "unlawful act was the product of mental disease or mental defect." The psychiatrist's part in the criminal trial is crucial because of the information he can supposedly provide about the defendant's legal responsibility.

The psychiatrist's power in the criminal trial, because of his questionable practice, has been deeply criticized in recent years. A person charged with a criminal offense may be denied the right to trial because of the pretrial psychiatric examination — psychiatrists are putting people away without the guarantee of a trial. And the "putting away" may be inspired by adversaries who do not want the would-be defendant around.

Thomas S. Szasz describes the case of a filling station operator in Syracuse, New York, who had been pressed by real estate developers to sell his property so that a shopping center could be built on the site.[56] When agents of the developers attempted to erect a sign on the property, the enraged operator fired warning shots from a rifle into the air. He was arrested but was never brought to trial. On the prosecuting attorney's recommendation, the operator was ordered to undergo psychiatric examination to determine his fitness to stand trial. He was held incapable and was committed to a state mental hospital. Still in a hospital after ten years, he had already served more time than he would have spent in prison had he been tried and convicted. Whether we criticize or support the use of psychiatric evidence, the defendant's fate may be directly affected by the "experts'" testimony.

Now that the dangers in psychiatric testimony and the problems in the insanity defense are recognized, some changes have been proposed. In a federal case, Judge David L. Bazelon (who earlier ruled on Durham) wrote this opinion:

It may be that psychiatry and the other social and behavioral sciences cannot provide sufficient data relevant to a determination of criminal responsibility no matter what our rules of evidence are. If so, we may be forced to eliminate the insanity defense altogether.[57]

In place of the insanity defense all technical formulations would be scrapped and the jury would be instructed simply to consider whether the defendant can "justly be held responsible for his act." The moral issue would be considered by the jury instead of being left in the hands of the expert witness.

Proposed legislation would prevent a defendant from pleading not guilty by reason of insanity as long as the prosecution can establish that all the elements of crime are present.[58] The defendant's mental state would come up only if the condition was so serious that the prosecution could not prove criminal intent at the time of the crime. Not much will be changed by these proposals, however. Witnesses probably will continue to testify, as they have for more than a century, about the defendant's state of mind. "The battlefield may shift from the issue of right versus wrong to the equally troublesome issue of intent, but the jurors will hear testimony not substantially different from what they hear today."[59]

Trial by Jury

Trial by a jury is the cornerstone of American criminal justice. In practice, about 80 per cent of the world's criminal jury trials are held in the United States today.[60] Yet the jury trial is the mode of conviction for only a small fraction of criminal prosecutions in this country. Of the cases that are tried, nearly half are tried without a jury. Only about one in seven felony prosecutions ends in a trial by jury.

The relatively small use of the jury trial for criminal conviction is accounted for by (1) legal restrictions on the right of trial by jury, (2) decision by the prosecution and defense to settle by guilty plea conviction, and (3) choice by the defendant to be tried before a judge without a jury.[61] Although the Sixth Amendment to the Constitution guarantees the right to trial by jury, the states specify the kinds of offenses that will be tried in that way. A trial may be denied for such minor offenses as traffic violations, disorderly conduct, petty gambling, public drunkenness, and prostitution.

Where not otherwise stipulated by state laws, trial by jury is a choice that is left open to the defendant. Whether to be prosecuted without a trial or to be tried with the waiver of a jury, depends on the strategy worked out by the defendant and the legal actors. The decision to avoid a jury trial varies according to the offense and local custom. About 90 per cent of forgeries but only about 30 per cent of murders are prosecuted by guilty pleas. When trials are used for murder, the jury is waived only about 15 per cent of the time, whereas for forgery the jury is waived about 50 per cent of the time. Local variations in the waiver of jury are conspicuous. In Wisconsin, the jury is waived in about three-fourths of criminal cases; in Utah in only about 5 per cent of the cases.[62]

Although the jury trial is not used as much as we might think, its influence on American criminal justice is deep. The trial is a control on the judicial administration of cases that are not tried by a jury.

It has become something of a commonplace to read the statistics on the impact of guilty pleas and jury waivers as gravely reducing the significance of the jury and transferring its power largely to the prosecuting attorney in the bargaining over guilty pleas. But we saw at every stage of this informal process of pre-trial dispositions that decisions are in part informed by expectations of what the jury will do. Thus, the jury is not controlling merely the immediate case before it, but the host of cases not before it which are destined to be disposed of by the pre-trial process. The jury thus controls not only the formal resolution of controversies in the criminal case, but also the informal resolution of cases that never reach the trial stage. In a sense the jury, like the visible cap of an iceberg, exposes but a fraction of its true volume.[63]

Once it has been decided to try the defendant before a jury, many social factors enter into the way in which the jury arrives at a decision on the defendant's guilt or innocence. The prosecutor and defense are well aware that jurors' backgrounds and personal characteristics influence their way of responding to the evidence and arguments presented in the trial. In selecting the jury, during the *voir dire* (competence) examination, the attorneys try to choose jurors who will make decisions favorable to the respective sides of the case. For each attorney, a trial may be won or lost during the jury's empaneling. The composition of the jury is important in determining the kind of definition that will be imposed on the defendant.

Defendants are supposedly tried by a representative body of the citizenry, but social and economic biases are built into the methods by which jurors are selected, and the lower occupational groups are systematically excluded from juries in the United States.[64] This unrepresentative character affects the way in which juries deliberate and arrive at decisions about the defendant's innocence or guilt.

The sources of bias in jury deliberation have been commented on in several studies of jury behavior. A study of mock jury deliberations revealed that foremen are usually selected according to their social position in the community.[65] Proprietors were selected three and a half times more often than laborers, and only a fifth as many women were made foremen as would be expected by chance. Foremen are particularly important in jury deliberation because they can change the opinion of the individual jurors according to their own views.[66]

The social status and sex of the individual jurors appear to be related to how much they participate in jury deliberations and influence the jury's overall decision. Studies of mock juries show that men and people of higher social status, not women and people of lower social status, have higher participation rates and greater influence in jury deliberations.[67] Men of the upper occupational groups act more in jury deliberation than any other type of juror. Women and people in the lower occupational groups, on the other hand, when they do participate, usually react to the contributions of the others.

Jurors also differ according to the kinds of things they focus on during the deliberation. In another mock jury study, it turned out that jurors spend about half their time exchanging experiences and opinions either directly or indirectly related to the trial. About a quarter of the time is spent on procedural matters, about 15 per cent is spent on reviewing the facts in the case, and about 8 per cent on the court instructions.[68] The more educated give relatively more emphasis to procedure and instructions; the less educated emphasize testimony, personal and daily life experiences, and opinions based on the trial rather than on procedure and instruction. The same researcher found that in insanity trials lower-class jurors are more likely to favor the defendant. Women jurors, on the other hand, are more sympathetic toward the defendant than men, but are likely to qualify their verdict according to the offense.[69]

In the end, the verdict reached by the jury may not be the same as the one the trial judge would have rendered. The difference between verdicts of juries and judges has been extensively researched.[70] One study investigated and analyzed 3,576 actual jury verdicts and the matching hypothetical verdicts of the judges involved in the cases. The major finding was that the judge and jury *agreed* in 75.4 per cent of the trials. More specifically, the judges and juries agreed to acquit in 13.4 per cent of the cases and to convict in 62.0 per cent. In the trials in which the judges and juries disagreed, the disagreement was predominantly in one direction: the jury was more likely than the judge to acquit. The jury acquitted when the judge would have convicted in 16.9 per cent of the cases. But the jury convicted when the judge would have acquitted in 2.2 per cent of the cases. That is, the juries were more lenient than the judges in 16.9 per cent of the cases and less lenient than the judges in 2.2 per cent of the cases. Practically speaking, then, when the defense decides to bring the case before a jury, the defendant fares better 14.7 per cent of the time than he would have in a bench trial. The defense strategy in choosing the type of trial, in other words, has an important part in determining the probability of a criminal conviction.

Judicial Sentencing

The Sentencing Procedure

After the defendant is convicted, a decision is made on the sanction that will be attached to the newly ascribed status of "criminal." The specification of the sanction, which is known as *sentencing,* involves manipulations and discretions of many people. In some jurisdictions the type and length of sentence are determined by the jury; in others sentencing is the responsibility of an administrative board; but in most jurisdictions in the United States the judge assigns the sentence.[71]

Even when sentencing is the judge's province, other people participate in the decision. Many states provide for a presentence investigation of the convicted defendant. The decision to proceed with such an investigation depends on the defense attorney's discretion and also on maneuvers by the prosecutor and the judge. The presentence investigation is then made by the probation department attached to the court. The report, which covers the defendant's personal and social background, criminal record, and mental and physical condition, includes the probation department's recommendations for sentencing. With the report and recommendations in hand, the judge imposes a sentence. But as shown in a study of the relation between presentence reports and dispositions, most judges sentence according to the recommendations by the probation department.[72] Although the final sentencing decision may belong to the judge, the decisions of others are crucial in the actual disposition.

The sentence imposed by the judge must fall within the limits provided by the penal law. The codes of penal law contain an elaborate classification of crimes with penalties graded according to seriousness of the crime.[73] Within the boundaries of penal law, however, judges may exercise a great deal of discretion in deciding upon a sentence. A range of alternative sentences and lengths of sentences are available to the judge for any crime.

Legal innovations, especially the indeterminate sentence and probation, have increased the discretionary possibilities of sentencing. The movement toward individualizing treatment has provided both a rationale and justifi-

Table 11.2   Average Sentences, in Months, by Selected Offense and
Judicial Circuit, of Federal Prisoners Received from the Courts
into Federal Prisons (Fiscal Year Ended June 30, 1972)

Judicial circuit	Narcotics laws	Forgery	Robbery	All offenses
1st Circuit (Me., Mass., N.H., R.I., P.R.)	68.0	19.7	133.5	52.5
2nd Circuit (Conn., N.Y.)	58.8	30.4	114.7	44.3
3rd Circuit (Del., N.J., Penna., V.I.)	77.4	27.3	128.3	67.7
4th Circuit (Md., N.C., S.C., Va., W. Va.)	77.0	36.4	158.8	57.3
5th Circuit (Ala., Fla., Ga., La., Miss., Tex.)	74.8	36.7	144.0	41.3
6th Circuit (Kent., Mich., Ohio, Tenn.)	54.0	39.3	134.4	52.8
7th Circuit (Ill., Ind., Wis.)	75.6	38.2	114.4	50.4
8th Circuit (Ark., Iowa, Minn., Mo., Neb., N.D., S.D.)	103.3	36.6	155.8	52.4
9th Circuit (Alaska, Ariz., Calif., Hawaii, Idaho, Mont., Nev., Ore., Wash., Guam)	70.8	42.9	131.1	40.5
10th Circuit (Colo., Kansas, N.M., Okla., Utah, Wyo.)	85.7	56.5	134.9	54.3
Circuit totals	69.7	37.3	134.6	46.8

Source: U.S. Department of Justice, Federal Bureau of Prisons, *Statistical Report, Fiscal Years 1971 and 1972* (Washington, D.C., 1973), pp. 96–101.

cation for using discretion in sentencing convicted offenders.

Sentencing Practices

Most sentencing decisions are made within the framework provided by the law, including the nature of the crime and the offender's prior criminal record.[74] Nevertheless, within the law decisions can be affected by many social and extralegal considerations. The criminal sanctions that are ultimately imposed on the convicted defendant are influenced by such extralegal factors as the personalities of the judges who assign the sentences, the norms that regulate sentencing, the judiciary's social organization, the attorney's activities, the responses and cues provided by the defendant, and the socioeconomic and racial characteristics of the defendant.

That sentencing practices of judges vary is

Table 11.3   Individual Probation Officer Recommendations for Probation and Imprisonment, Northern District of California, September 1964 to February 1967 (Unpublished San Francisco Project Data)

Probation officer	Number of recommen-dations	Number of probation recommen-dations	Number of prison recommen-dations	Percentage of probation recommen-dations
1	55	40	15	72.7%
2	39	25	14	64.1
3	46	21	25	45.7
4	57	35	22	61.4
5	16	14	2	87.5
6	20	13	7	65.0
7	55	22	33	40.0
8	38	22	16	57.9
9	22	17	5	77.3
10	58	46	12	79.3
11	59	32	27	54.2
12	57	35	22	61.4
13	54	42	12	77.8
14	36	17	19	47.2
15	56	34	22	60.7
16	46	31	15	67.4
17	60	43	17	71.7
18	18	16	2	88.9
19	42	24	18	57.1

Source: Robert M. Carter and Leslie T. Wilkins, "Some Factors in Sentencing Policy," *Journal of Criminal Law, Criminology and Police Science,* 58 (December 1967), p. 512.

easy to illustrate with sentencing statistics. A study of sentences assigned in nearly 7,500 criminal cases handled by six judges over a ten-year period in a New Jersey county reported that the judges differed considerably in the frequency, length, and types of sentences they assigned to convicted offenders.[75] The diversity was even more evident when the sentences were analyzed according to the type of crime.

An explanation for these varied practices may be found in the judges' backgrounds and attitudes. We see some indication of how background and attitude affect judges' decisions in research on the judicial decisions of state and federal supreme court judges.[76] Each judge was given a decision score representing the proportion of times he favored

the defense. Judges who were more defendant-minded were likely to be Democrats rather than Republicans, not members of the American Bar Association, not former prosecutors, Catholics rather than Protestants, and relatively liberal as measured by off-the-bench attitudes. Because of such attributes, then, judges often make particular kinds of decisions.

The decisions also vary geographically. Ecological variations in sentencing statistics seem to indicate that the sentencing behavior of judges is normatively regulated and that the normative patterns differ from one region to another. Table 11.2 (page 219) shows average sentences assigned to those convicted of federal crimes and committed to federal institutions. As the table shows, the average sen-

Table 11.4   Average Sentences of Court Commitments to Federal Prisons, by Race and Offense (Fiscal Year Ended June 30, 1972)

	Average sentences (in months)	
Offenses in which nonwhites have longer average sentences than whites	Whites	Nonwhites
Assault	51.1	81.2
Burglary	41.8	43.1
Drug laws	51.9	73.5
Embezzlement	26.9	31.0
Escape	20.1	46.0
Forgery	34.1	40.1
Immigration	10.4	14.0
Income tax	14.2	30.7
Juvenile delinquency	35.0	36.1
Selective Service acts	29.3	38.6
Offenses in which whites have longer average sentences than nonwhites		
Counterfeiting	45.3	44.0
Extortion	56.0	51.4
Firearms	44.9	37.8
Fraud	34.5	33.0
Kidnaping	248.8	219.0
Larceny	39.5	33.3
Liquor laws	20.4	14.8
National security laws	66.9	24.0
Robbery	138.3	130.3
Securities	45.9	44.9
Average sentence for all offenses	43.3	58.7

Source: U.S. Department of Justice, Federal Bureau of Prisons, *Statistical Report, Fiscal Years 1971 and 1972* (Washington, D.C.), pp. 60–61.

tences differ considerably from one federal court district to another. Judges are influenced by local sentencing customs and local bureaucratic considerations in sentencing those who violate federal laws. For the convicted offender, the sentence received depends greatly on the sentencing patterns of the jurisdiction in which the case is tried and sentenced.

That the fate of the convicted person is in the hands of legal agents, in addition to the judge, is illustrated in a study of the recommendations made by probation officers to judges.[77] The researchers observed wide differ-

ences in the recommendations the probation officers gave as to whether the convicted person should be granted probation or sentenced to prison. The extreme is shown in Table 11.3: one probation officer recommended probation for 88.9 per cent of his cases and another made that recommendation in only 40 per cent of the cases. The researchers then suggest that variations in probation recommendations are produced by the background of the officer and his training and vocational experience. As probation officers gain experience they decrease their recommendations for probation.

Again, the sanction received by the criminal is based on the discretion of others.

Discretion in sentencing takes place, of course, with an awareness of the offender. It is often the offender's characteristics, not the offense, which determines the sentence the person will receive, as we see in the sentences given to blacks and Third-World people. Sentencing statistics indicate that such persons are committed to prison longer than are whites for the same offenses. In Table 11.4 (page 221) are the average sentences of persons committed to federal prisons. Nonwhites receive, on the average, longer sentences than whites. Whites have an average sentence (for all offenses) of 43.3 months, but nonwhites have received an average sentence of 58.7. Nevertheless, the variations differ according to the offense; for some types of crimes nonwhites receive longer sentences than whites; conversely, whites receive longer sentences than nonwhites for some other types of crimes. No matter how you look at it, sentencing is administered differentially according to race and minority status.

In another study of prison sentences, as assigned by juries in regions of Texas, it was also found that the sentences varied in length according to the offender's race.[78] Even when nonracial factors were controlled in the analysis, blacks received longer sentences than whites. The amount of the differences also varied from one region to another in Texas, indicating local biases at work in the administration of criminal justice.

The racial and class bias of criminal justice in sentencing, as in the other stages of the legal process, continues to be supported in criminological investigations. One researcher found recently that for juveniles, even when the seriousness of the offense is held constant, blacks are more likely than whites to receive a more serious disposition from the courts.[79] It was found in the same research that lower-class delinquents are less likely to be put on probation and more likely to be institutionalized than delinquents from other classes. No matter what the offense, lower-class juveniles receive more severe dispositions than middle-class juveniles.[80]

Such studies tell us that, for juveniles or adults, justice is administered according to the characteristics of those who are judged as being criminals. To be of the lower class, black, or of the Third World, with little education, and without the "proper respect" for the law, or some combination of these, increases the likelihood that you will be processed in the criminal justice system — and more severely than others in the society. That criminal justice is dispensed in terms of the ·dominant order in the United States is the conclusion of our analysis. Criminal justice is, in fact, a device for preserving that order.

12
Custody and Punishment

Those who threaten the state and class interests are controlled by means of the criminal law. Criminal sanctions are applied to those who are defined as criminal. The official definition of crime thus anticipates the official response, and that which makes for the definition and behavior of crime also produces the policies of crime control.

A criminal sanction can be imposed on *any* citizen. The sanction's primary purpose is to warn the people that a transgression against the rules of order will lead to punishment or deprivation of some kind. Imposing the criminal sanction for an adjudicated offense is the state's retaliation against those who fail to abide by its dictates. That sanction, including its administration, is the state's final step in preserving order.

Custody and Punishment in the Prisons

Punishment has been justified by motives ranging from retribution, to reformation, to deterrence. Those who insist on retribution assume that offenders must "pay" for their crimes. Believers in reformation suggest that the individual must be changed to prevent future transgressions. And deterrence is pursued to discourage potential offenders.[1] The motives differ, but the general intentions of punishment are the same: to preserve the legal order.

Punishment to preserve order traditionally has been accomplished by physically confining offenders to an institution. Even when rehabilitation has been attempted, it has usually been done within the punitive custodial setting. Custody has not been mitigated by efforts at rehabilitation. Confinement is punishment, but rehabilitation is also part of punishment.

Confining offenders to an institution as a way of dealing with crime began in a particular historical context in the United States. After the American Revolution, the officials of the state became greatly worked up about protecting and preserving the new order. The asylum, including the penitentiary, was an attempt by the leaders in the Jacksonian period to promote stability in the republic, eradicating any conduct that threatened the new nation.

Legislators, philanthropists, and local officials, as well as students of poverty, crime,
and insanity were convinced that the nation
faced unprecedented dangers and unprecedented opportunities. The asylum, they believed, could restore a necessary social
balance to the new republic, and at the same
time eliminate long-standing problems. At
once nervous and enthusiastic, distressed
and optimistic, they set about constructing
and arranging institutions.[2]

The penitentiary would rehabilitate offenders
and at the same time set an example of right
action for the rest of society.

The movement to confine offenders to institutions spread rapidly in the first part of the
eighteenth century. Two systems of prison
organization eventually competed as models
for the whole country. In the "separate" system, as practiced in Pittsburgh and Philadelphia, prisoners were placed in solitary confinement. They could then reflect upon their
crimes and gain insight for their own reformation. The "congregate" system, as practiced at
Auburn, New York, emphasized common
activities rather than separate confinement.
The first model stressed the possibilities of
personal conversion; the second, external discipline and forced rehabilitation. Gradually the
Auburn system became the model for nearly
all maximum-security prisons in the United
States.

Custody in American prisons today is essentially the same as it was at an earlier time.
The prisons may have more programs of treatment, but the prisoner's daily life is one of
routine and regimentation, all strictly controlled.[3] The military style of command colors
all prison life. In organization as well as in
architecture the prison represents obedience
and order, a model for the whole society.

A large proportion of the country's population is imprisoned at any one time. As shown
in Table 12.1, nearly 200,000 persons were
confined to state and federal prisons in 1970.
Add the penal institutions for juveniles (including reformatories) to this estimate of the
prison population, and the total grows to about
350,000 persons. The rate of imprisonment for
adult offenders (per 100,000 civilian popula-

tion) has remained fairly constant for three
decades. Nearly one adult out of every thousand people in the United States is held in
state and federal prisons.

Then add to the people in state and federal
prisons the many confined to local jails. A
survey of the 97,500 city and county jails
found that about 161,000 persons are incar-
cerated at a time in these institutions.[4] Further,
it was found that more than half of these inmates have not been convicted of a crime.
They are confined to local jails while awaiting
either arraignment or trial. Jails can be used
for detaining people before a trial and to confine others convicted of misdemeanors. Jail
sentences usually do not exceed one year, but
in some jails prisoners are held for at least
five years. Thus, combining the jail and prison
figures, about one out of every 370 adults is
confined to a penal institution in the United
States.

Prisons in this country are used mainly for
those who commit a select group of crimes,
primarily burglary, robbery, and assault. This
means in effect that prisons are institutions of
custody and punishment disproportionately
filled with persons of the lower class, the poor,
and the uneducated. Here the statistics are
compared and summarized:

Forty-one percent of the general labor force
falls into white-collar employment categories (clerical and sales, managers and
owners, and professional and technical
workers), compared to only 14 percent of
the prison population. At the other extreme,
43 percent of the prisoners are manual
or service workers, compared to only 17
percent of the total labor force. The same
pattern is found for education: 55 percent
of the prisoners have an elementary school
education or less, compared to only 34 percent of the general population; 45 percent
of the general population are high school
graduates compared to only 18 percent of
the prison population.[5]

Yet, more crime causing economic and social
loss to the country and society is committed
by middle- and upper-class persons, but these
crimes do not often result in prison sentences.
One consequence of imprisoning lower-class

Table 12.1   Sentenced Prisoners Present at End of Year in State and Federal
Institutions, for the United States, 1939–1970

Year	Number			Rate per 100,000 of the estimated civilian population of the U.S.		
	All insti-tutions	Federal insti-tutions	State insti-tutions	All insti-tutions	Federal insti-tutions	State insti-tutions
1970	196,429	20,038	176,391	96.7	9.8	86.8
1969	196,007	19,623	176,384	97.6	9.7	87.8
1968	187,914	19,703	168,211	94.3	9.9	84.3
1967	194,896	19,579	175,317	99.1	10.0	89.2
1966	199,654	19,245	180,409	102.7	9.9	92.8
1965	210,895	21,040	189,855	109.5	10.9	98.6
1964	214,336	21,709	192,627	112.6	11.4	101.2
1963	217,283	23,128	194,155	115.7	12.3	103.4
1962	218,830	23,944	194,886	118.3	12.9	105.3
1961	220,149	23,696	196,453	120.8	13.0	107.8
1960	212,953	23,218	189,735	118.6	12.9	105.7
1959	207,446	22,492	184,954	117.7	12.8	104.9
1958	205,493	21,549	183,944	118.8	12.5	106.3
1957	195,256	20,420	174,836	114.9	12.0	102.9
1956	189,421	20,134	169,287	113.5	12.1	101.4
1955	185,780	20,088	165,692	113.4	12.3	101.1
1954	182,848	20,003	162,845	113.8	12.4	101.3
1953	173,547	19,363	154,184	110.2	12.3	97.9
1952	168,200	18,014	150,186	108.8	11.6	97.1
1951	165,640	17,395	148,245	108.9	11.4	97.4
1950	166,123	17,134	148,989	110.3	11.4	98.9
1949	163,749	16,868	146,881	110.0	11.3	98.6
1948	155,977	16,328	139,649	106.6	11.2	95.4
1947	151,304	17,146	134,158	105.2	11.9	93.3
1946	140,079	17,622	122,457	99.7	12.5	87.2
1945	133,649	18,638	115,011	100.5	14.0	86.5
1944	132,456	18,139	114,317	104.2	14.3	89.9
1943	137,220	16,113	121,107	108.0	12.7	95.3
1942	150,384	16,623	133,761	116.4	12.9	103.5
1941	165,439	18,465	146,974	126.0	14.1	112.0
1940	173,706	19,260	154,446	132.0	14.6	117.3
1939	179,818	19,730	160,088	137.1	15.0	122.0

Source: Bureau of Prisons, United States Department of Justice, "Prisoners in State and Federal Institutions for Adult Felons," *National Prisoner Statistics Bulletin*, No. 47 (April 1972), p. 2.

people is that a very large number of prisoners are blacks. It is estimated that one out of every 26 black men between the ages of 25 and 34 is either in jail or prison on a specified day, compared to one out of every 163 white men in the same age group.[6] During any year one out of every three to four black men in their early twenties spends some time in prison, jail, on parole, or on probation:

By the time a black man in America is twenty-five years of age (perhaps even earlier) he has in all probability had some serious encounter with the criminal justice system, and there is a good chance he has spent some time behind bars. For most whites, especially affluent whites, the criminal justice system is an abstraction. Except in rare instances, it does not directly impinge on their lives. For young blacks, the repressive arm of the law — arrest, probation, jail, prison — is an immediate reality.[7]

Custody and punishment are indeed a reality for a good share of the American people.

Social Organization in the Prison

Once prisons are populated with inmates, the primary task is custody, providing for their secure maintenance.

The prison wall, that line between the pure and the impure, has all the emotional overtones of a woman's maidenhead. One escape from the maximum security prison is sufficient to arouse public opinion to a fever pitch and an organization which stands or falls on a single case moves with understandable caution. The officials, in short, know on which side their bread is buttered. Their continued employment is tied up with the successful performance of custody and if society is not sure of the priority to be attached to the tasks assigned the prison, the overriding importance of custody is perfectly clear to the officials.[8]

The prison's internal order is maintained by strictly controlling inmates and regimenting all functions and personnel within the prison. The prison, as a "system of total power," is an organization unto itself, which is supposed to be unaffected by external events and in which social control is paramount.[9] A distinct castelike division is maintained between those who rule and those who are ruled.

Operating the prison requires several, often contradictory, internal hierarchic organizations.

The structure of prisons provides for three principal hierarchies — devoted to *keeping, using,* and *serving* inmates — but not for the integration of their divergent purposes. The separate organizations concerned with keeping and with serving inmates, for ex-

ample, are not merely overlapping, but have entirely different and partly contradictory purposes.[10]

Each type of organization, in turn, promotes a particular kind of relationship between the staff and the inmates and a specific pattern of authority, communication, and decision-making. The people most affected by these divergent organizations are, of course, the inmates. Differences in handling their affairs are caused mostly by the organizational problems inherent in the prison.

We can best understand how the prison is administered if we recognize the pressures exerted by groups trying to achieve conflicting objectives. These "correctional interest groups" determine the ways in which prison policy is established and administered.[11] Some of these operate within the prison, such as the groups that make up the staff (administrative staff, custodians, professional workers) and the inmate population. Interest groups at work outside the prison include welfare agencies, educational groups, religious organizations, legal agents, and leaders of political parties. The numerous inconsistencies and contradictions in prisons are caused by these groups. The unique organization that is the prison is made by these converging, competing groups, which define their interests according to the ways in which prisons are operated.

Custody as an objective creates its own form of communication and decision-making within the prison. In an authoritarian way, the administrators impose a social order on the inmates, with its conditions maintained by a rigid system of communication. A massive body of regulations is passed from above to those below. Decision-making occurs at the top of the administrative structure and is communicated through well-defined channels of authority. At the bottom of the chain of command, among the inmates, decision-making is kept at a minimum: "Inmates are officially permitted to make only those types of decisions which prior study by administrators has shown to be of no danger to community safety."[12]

The custodial regime presents the inmate with personally demeaning and frustrating requirements. Being used to achieving goals, the prisoner finds it next to impossible to realize any within the prison, and is deprived too of basic liberties, goods and services, heterosexual relationships, and autonomy.[13] Imprisonment is painful. The physical deprivations are overwhelming, and having all the everyday freedoms withdrawn is also an attack against the foundations of one's sense of being.

The pains of imprisonment cannot be removed by the inmate, but only mitigated:

> Unable to escape either physically or psychologically, lacking the cohesion to carry through an insurrection that is bound to fail in any case, and bereft of faith in peaceful innovation, the inmate population might seem to have no recourse but the simple endurance of the pains of imprisonment. But if the rigors of confinement cannot be completely removed, they can at least be mitigated by the patterns of social interaction established among the inmates themselves. In this apparently simple fact lies the key to our understanding of the prisoner's world.[14]

This social world is an uneasy solution to the rigors of penal custody.

The inmate society is composed of related social roles, structured by an ideology, the inmate code: (1) Do not interfere with the interests of other inmates; (2) Refrain from arguments and quarrels with fellow inmates; (3) Do not exploit or take advantage of one another; (4) Maintain integrity in the face of privation; and (5) Do not side with the custodial authorities.[15] Inmate society orders and classifies inmates by their orientations to the maxims of the code in prison argot. The *rat* is an inmate who violates the norm proscribing betrayal of a fellow inmate, the *merchant* exploits fellow inmates by manipulation, and the *tough* quarrels with other prisoners. The *square John* or *center man* makes the mistake of allying with officials. The role that most nearly fulfills the norms of the inmate code is that of the *right guy*, the *real con*, or the *real man*. But all the social roles are important for understanding this society, for they establish patterns of social interaction among inmates.[16] Only this interaction, within a society created by the inmates, can make the rigors of imprisonment bearable.

Prisoners conform to the inmate culture and oppose the expectations of the prison staff differently. An early study observed that most inmates gradually assimilate the prison culture, which has been called "prisonization," suggesting that inmates increase their commitment to the prison culture with the *length* of time they serve in the prison.[17] It was found more recently that conformity to expectations of the prison staff also depends on the length of time *remaining* to be served.[18] Wheeler showed that inmates follow an adaptive, U-shaped pattern of conformity. In the early and late phases of incarceration they conform to staff expectations, whereas those in the middle phase deviate from such expectations. Further research by others has specified these relationships: the temporal effect of the inmate code on administrative expectations varies according to the inmate's social characteristics, the type of crime he committed, the experiences he had before imprisonment, and his social role in the inmate society.[19] Also evidence shows that inmates in a prison designed primarily for custody are less likely to become committed to prison objectives than those in a treatment-oriented prison.[20] All these findings indicate how much the social organization of custody affects the administration of penal and correctional policy.

A final part of the prison's social organization is the relationship between inmates and the prison staff. Although it has an inmate system and an administrative system, prison organization also contains an informal system of inmate-staff relationships. Both inmates and staff find it necessary to establish patterns of interaction to secure their separate interests. Successful operation of the inmate society requires some cooperation from the staff. Likewise, the staff can achieve its interests only with the inmates' cooperation. In a sense, a "corruption of authority" appears among the members of the staff.[21] The guard, under pressure to maintain a smoothly running cell block, ignores breaches of prison rules in return for manageable conduct. The informal inmate-staff system is a response to the problem of maintaining control in a custodial institution. Informal patterns, not specified in prison regulations, are essential for administering penal and correctional policy within the confines of custody, and for the inmates' survival.

Probation and Parole

The state maintains control over convicted offenders in other ways as well. The offender is supervised outside the prison as well as inside, and may be sentenced to a period of supervision. Satisfactory completion of this probationary period depends on the offender's "good behavior" and on conforming to the stipulated conditions of probation. The other form of state supervision is parole, whereby prisoners are released from confinement in an institution to supervision by a parole officer. Removing the status of "criminal" from the convicted offender depends in the end on the actions and recommendations of the state's officials.

Supervising Probation

Probation is a relatively new form of social and legal control. During the last twenty-five years, it has been used increasingly in sentencing offenders. Although there are no national statistics on probation, probably about 40 per cent of adjudicated offenders are placed on probation, with wide variations in the use of probation from one jurisdiction to another.

Probation is usually thought of as a correctional reform measure, obscuring its punitive intentions and consequences. Nevertheless,

> implicit in probation supervision are numerous opportunities for punishment. With his awesome authority over the probationer, the probation officer may in various ways restrict his liberty. It is easily argued that restriction of liberty amounts to punishment. The probation officer, in the name of rehabilitation and under the banner of standard conditions of probation, can demand that the probationer not live in or frequent certain areas, that he not engage in certain employment, and that he refrain from a number of interpersonal associations.[22]

Probation officers work within the broader framework of the judicial system, carrying out a legal and punitive role, making decisions from the beginning of cases to their completion. The probation officer, in other words, is very much like a prosecutor in the court.[23] The adjudication of criminal cases is influenced by the decisions and recommendations made by probation officers during hearings or trials. The sentence that the judge imposes is directly shaped by the interests of the court's probation department.

The probation system is "involved in a transitional period of organizational conflict as a consequence of moving from a politically oriented to a professionally career-oriented service."[24] More officers with a "professional" orientation are being drawn from the field of social work. These more recent workers contrast with the older, politically oriented officers. The newer professional workers are liberal in ideology, recognizing the diversity of human personality, but the older workers, drawing ideological support from a conservative, middle-class philosophy of life, act as paternal counselors to the offender. The professional officers, trained in the casework approach, believe in promoting the community's welfare by changing the offender, and the politically oriented officers, relying on their common sense and experience, try to protect the community from the offender.

Probation, therefore, is beset by a conflict between the different types of officers and a struggle for the control of probation agencies; the probation officers' decisions are affected by these organizational problems. Because of several incompatible obligations in their occupation, officers have difficulty in making consistent and satisfactory decisions. Officers trained in social work find that their skills have not equipped them to deal with authoritative demands, and demonstrate a great deal of disagreement and confusion about the proper way of supervising cases.[25] Many regard some of the surveillance and enforcement activities as inappropriate responsibilities. Officers without training in social work, on the other hand, discover that they lack the knowledge and ability to understand the offenders they are supervising. Most probation officers, whatever their occupational direction, experience some kind of conflict in their work.

Aside from the officers' personal inconveniences, the people ultimately affected by the organization of probation are those on probation. The divergent approaches to probation work directly affect the ways in which probationers are handled. "Competing philosophies and working principles within the agency result in the inconsistent handling of cases and produce frustrations on the part of the workers which, in turn, affect the counseling and disposition of problem cases."[26] Like the offenders throughout the processing of their cases, the officers' fate is decided as much by the problems and actions of others as by their own volitions.

Maintaining surveillance over the offender, the probation officer makes crucial decisions about the probationer's behavior. Probation can be successfully completed only when the terms stipulated in the sentence have been met to the officer's satisfaction — or to that of any other legal agents who may come in contact with the probationer. If the probationer should be suspected of violating the terms of probation, his or her probationary status can be revoked. The officer then recommends whether or not probation should be revoked. In many jurisdictions the decision is made during a judicial hearing.[27] At that time the probation officer can testify that the probationer has violated probation and can also offer an appropriate course of action. Officers differ on the kinds of decisions they make in revocation proceedings.[28] The differences in recommendations are related to the personal characteristics of the officers, extenuating circumstances in the cases, the role relationships of the officers and offenders, and the involvement of other legal agents in the cases. Again, decisions that directly determine the offender's future are made by others, and are influenced by social and political considerations.

Supervising Parole

The major form of release from prison is parole. Nearly 70 per cent of the inmates released from state and federal prisons are discharged by parole or some form of mandatory supervision.[29] In principle, a parole is the conditional release of an offender who has served a portion of his or her sentence in a penal or correctional institution. The parole decision is made by the members of a parole board. Such boards may be staffed by personnel of an institution or by members of a statewide board of parole. In some jurisdictions the parole boards have the authority to administer parole as well as to grant it.[30]

The wide range of discretion in paroling offenders is made obvious by reviewing the statistics on parole releases from state prisons. As shown in Table 12.2, differences in the use of parole by the states are vast. At the extremes, 100 per cent of the releases from New Hampshire and Washington were by parole, but only 7 per cent of those from Wyoming were by parole. The variations are caused by differences in both state penal laws and the organization and administration of parole within the states.

The person most obviously affected by variations in parole practice is the offender. His or her future is settled by the decisions made by others. And as the President's Commission on Law Enforcement and Administration of Justice argued, the decisions are not made adequately and fairly:

> Except for sentencing, no decision in the criminal process has more impact on the convicted offender than the parole decision, which determines how much of his maximum sentence a prisoner must serve. This again is an invisible administrative decision that is seldom open to attack or subject to review. It is made by parole board members who are often political appointees. Many are skilled and conscientious, but they generally are able to spend no more than a few minutes on a case. Parole decisions that are made in haste and on the basis of insufficient information, in the absence of parole machinery that can provide good supervision, are necessarily imperfect decisions. And since there is virtually no appeal from them, they can be made arbitrarily or discriminatorily.[31]

Decisions to release prisoners on parole are not usually made according to the offender's interests. Though much descriptive and predictive information is available on prospective parolees, decisions are often made intuitively.

**Table 12.2　Prisoners Released on Parole from State Prisons, 1970
(Includes Conditional Releases under Mandatory Supervision)**

Region and state	Total releases	Percentage released on parole	Region and state	Total releases	Percentage released on parole
Northeast			Virginia	1,695	44.6
Maine	539	76.4	West Virginia	375	86.4
New Hampshire	142	100.0	North Carolina	2,333	62.4
Vermont	48	70.8	South Carolina	1,571	25.9
Massachusetts	1,052	71.9	Georgia	2,014	42.4
Rhode Island	—	—	Florida	3,682	55.1
Connecticut	1,293	68.5	Kentucky	1,581	56.4
New York	6,685	84.5	Tennessee	1,620	59.2
New Jersey	3,722	86.3	Alabama	2,345	46.6
Pennsylvania	3,308	72.3	Mississippi	651	62.3
			Arkansas	—	—
North Central			Louisiana	1,769	48.1
Ohio	4,147	95.8	Oklahoma	1,653	74.2
Indiana	1,086	82.8	Texas	5,464	37.7
Illinois	3,588	80.4			
Michigan	4,551	84.5	**West**		
Wisconsin	1,472	93.7	Montana	394	78.6
Minnesota	—	—	Idaho	174	85.6
Iowa	729	55.0	Wyoming	141	7.0
Missouri	1,771	43.1	Colorado	1,216	91.9
North Dakota	138	60.8	New Mexico	511	75.6
South Dakota	241	31.9	Arizona	804	55.9
Nebraska	611	63.1	Utah	230	96.5
Kansas	984	99.4	Nevada	280	58.9
			Washington	1,407	99.4
South			Oregon	967	46.4
Delaware	1,543	8.2	California	8,819	96.5
Maryland	—	—	Hawaii	120	77.5
Dist. of Columbia	538	47.9			
			United States total	80,043	70.1

Source: Bureau of Prisons, United States Department of Justice, "Prisoners in State and Federal Institutions for Adult Felons," *National Prisoner Statistics Bulletin,* No. 47 (April 1972), pp. 22–23.

Parole boards also develop their own informal procedures for processing cases.[32] Parole decisions are often based on such characteristics as the original length of sentence rather than the individualities in the case. Inmates, when they are paroled, are likely to be released according to decisions made early in the prisoner's incarceration, not his prognosis for a successful parole. Such procedures, combined with the kind of people on parole boards and the haste with which decisions must be reached, are the basis for the decision to parole prisoners.

Once parole has been granted, its satisfactory completion depends on variations in its regulation and supervision. Nationally, the average parole period for offenders is 29 months.

Regionally the variations are wide: 31 months in the East and Northeast, 20 months in the Midwest and plains states, 28 months in the border South, 37 months in the South, and 24 months in the West.[33] State averages for the parole period range from less than 12 months to more than 84 months.

Parole is administered according to many factors. Parole supervision is influenced, in particular, by the relationship between the parolee and the parole officer. One of the officer's principal duties is to observe the parolee's behavior, especially to determine if he is violating the conditions of parole or any other regulations and laws.[34] Such parole conditions generally forbid unauthorized association with anyone who has a criminal record, and seek to control behavior in drinking, employment, and mobility. Parolees usually must obtain permission to change their residence, to travel to another area, to marry, or to purchase specific items.

The parolee is expected to fulfill a number of expectations, but the status of being a parolee does not correspond to the realities of being a convicted offender. The discrepancies between the legal expectations imposed on parolees and their own situation are described by John Irwin in his study of released felons:

This status has for its underpinnings several premises which are often not shared by many deviants and ex-deviants. Two of these premises are self-evident axioms: (1) society, i.e., the existing political organization and government agencies, the laws and the government institutions, are both necessary and "good" per se; and (2) this society, especially the existing political organization and government agencies, has the right to imprison some of its members for acts which it has outlawed, to deny the ex-prisoner full citizen rights, and to impose special restrictions upon him. Furthermore, the conditions are underpinned by the belief that to be a worthy member of the society and, therefore, to be allowed to remain a free person, the ex-felon must live according to a puritanical code of conduct — he must work steadily ("steady employment is an essential for anyone's satisfactory adjustment in life"), not drink to excess ("it is conceded that total abstinence from the use

of alcohol would benefit most parolees"), not use narcotics or dangerous drugs, not associate with persons of "bad" reputation, and conduct himself as a "good citizen."[35]

These prescriptions and proscriptions are derived from the pragmatic consideration of controlling the parolee. The released offenders' view of things is likely to be quite different from that which underlies their official status.

Parolees often do not share the belief in the "goodness" of society or the existing social organizations, agencies, and persons filling positions in these organizations. Some deviants believe that conventional society, conventional people, legitimate businessmen, and public organizations are corrupt. Often they believe that the laws and the workings of the public agencies are part of a power struggle where the big and powerful are protecting what they have from the small and weak. . . . They, the deviants or ex-deviants, do not feel that the conventional society, the dominant society, the government agencies, are "right". . . .

Parolees (that is, the criminal parolees) have other definitions of good and proper conduct. Even those who have resolved to live a conventional life — resolved to "straighten up their hand" and to "make it" in terms of a conventional life — are in disagreement with the conditions of parole and tend to believe that it is all right to break many of the rules. From their viewpoint, the only restrictions the agency should impose are on extreme criminal behavior.[36]

In practice the parole officer uses broad discretion in supervising the parolee. Ultimately the decisions made during the interaction between the officer and the parolee determine when, whether, and how parole will be completed. These decisions are shaped by the difficult role the parole officer is expected to perform.[37] He is expected to supervise and assist the parolee and, at the same time, to protect the community from the ex-prisoner. He must fulfill the authoritarian function of representing the state, but must simultaneously try to "rehabilitate" the offender. As a middleman, or one who plays the "stranger," the parole officer must elicit the parolee's participation and that of the community's members in integrating the parolee into community life. The parole officer's job is both a handicap and a resource in accomplishing these diverse tasks.

The dual considerations of protecting the public and helping the parolee have inspired different types of performance by parole officers, oriented in various degrees to these demands.[38] Some parole officers emphasize both control and assistance (the "paternal" officers), and others pay little attention to either (the "passive" officers). Others emphasize assistance but not control (the "welfare" officers). Finally, some emphasize control but not assistance (the "punitive" officers). Each officer has a different way of perceiving and evaluating parolees. The offender's fate is determined by the type of parole officer assigned to handle the case. Organizational needs as well as the broader interests of the social order shape the lives of those controlled by the American system of justice.

Capital Punishment

Several administrative means are used for releasing inmates from the prison. The original sentence may be modified by the executive in the form of pardon, commutation, or amnesty. Others are released on parole or simply by expiration of their sentences. An expiration date may be fixed by the legislature or, with an indeterminate sentence, an administrative board decides upon the date of release within the minimum and maximum limits set by the court.

The final and fatal solution removing the prisoner is either execution or death from other causes while in prison. Some prison deaths are caused by mistreatment or murder of inmates. Other deaths are carried out by the state as capital punishment. Death is the most consequential aspect of the legal system.

Administering Capital Punishment

That death, as a legal sentence, is subject to human discretion seems absurd. But the death sentence is a provision of law and is an administrative action, so that discretion operates in the legal decision to execute convicted offenders. To begin with, the decision to make

capital punishment a sentencing alternative is variable. At the end of 1970, capital punishment was legally provided for in all but nine jurisdictions.[39] Among these, the number and types of crimes that are subject to the death penalty differ. States differ too in stipulating whether the death penalty is mandatory upon conviction.[40] Alabama provides capital punishment for sixteen offenses, making it mandatory for assault by a person serving a life sentence. California has provisions for six capital crimes, with the mandatory sentence for train wrecking, assault by a lifer, perjury, and treason. Most of the states with capital punishment specify murder and kidnaping as capital offenses. Rape and treason are subject to the death penalty in about half. Others cover scattered offenses such as robbery, arson, dueling, illegal use of explosives, attempt on the life of the executive, and lynching. Most of the variations result from differences in regional and local customs. Although death may be a private affair, lives are taken legally by the wills and actions of others.

The extent of discretion possible in administering capital punishment is obvious from statistics on executions. The number of executions has been decreasing through the years. Between 1900 and 1966 there were about 7,126 executions in the United States.[41] But since 1930, when statistics began to be systematically compiled, executions have declined from an annual average of 167 during the thirties to 21 each year between 1960 and 1970.[42] Though 1935 had 199 executions, there were 15 in 1964, 7 in 1965, 2 in 1967, and none in 1970. Even with the decrease in executions, at the end of 1970, 524 persons were under sentence waiting death in state and federal prisons.

There have always been regional variations in executions. As shown in Table 12.3, approximately 60 per cent of the executions between 1930 and 1970 occurred in the South. Of the executions between 1930 and 1970, 2,306 were in the southern states, 608 in the northeastern states, 509 in the western states, and 403 in the north central states. These regional variations are also evident according to executions for *types* of offense. Of the 455 executions for rape, 443 took place in the South. Less than 1 per cent of the executions in the northeastern region were for rape, whereas rape accounted for 15 per cent in the southern region.

Execution patterns also prevail in the *race* of execution victims. Review of the execution statistics for the years 1930–1970, in Table 12.3, shows that the majority of those executed, 2,066, were blacks, compared to 1,751 whites. For rape, in particular, far more of those executed, 89 per cent, were blacks. These figures indicate that capital punishment is highly discriminatory. Although the disproportional percentage of blacks executed, compared to the proportion of blacks in the general population, reflects lower-class and racial involvement in violence, this disproportion *also* indicates the greater willingness of jurisdictions to apply the death penalty to blacks than to whites convicted of similar crimes. Lower-class persons from the discriminated-against racial and ethnic groups have a greater risk of being executed than their counterparts in crime.

The discriminatory character of execution operates at several stages before the final execution. Not only are blacks and lower-class persons more likely than others to be convicted for committing similar crimes, but they are more likely to be given a death sentence than some alternative sentence. Further, once blacks and lower-class persons are placed on death row, their sentences are less likely to be commuted.

The officials responsible for commuting execution sentences have grave discretionary powers. The authority and procedures for granting clemency vary considerably from one jurisdiction to another. They can be classified generally as:

(1) a board alone; (2) a board alone, with the governor sitting as a member; (3), a board alone, the governor sitting as a member with grant, conditional on his being in the majority; (4) the governor, empowered to act only if a board makes a favorable recommendation (governor can overrule, denying commutation); (5) the governor with the advice and consent of an executive council, an elected body. Under the Federal Constitution the President alone has the power to abrogate a death sentence, derived from the power to grant reprieves and pardons.[43]

These pardoning authorities, in turn, hold differing philosophies about their responsibilities and use various criteria in making their decisions: the nature of the crime, the character of the trial, the mental and physical condition of the offender, and rehabilitation possibilities.[44] But also important in their decisions are such extralegal considerations as the publicity surrounding the case, political pressures, precedents in other cases, and personal views on capital punishment. Once a person is placed in death row, life depends on the problems of others and on the state's actions.

The selective factors affecting commutation and execution have been documented in research. The records for capital offenders in North Carolina showed that, of those committed to North Carolina's death row since 1909, the sentences of whites were commuted more often than the sentence of blacks. Sixty-two per cent of the blacks committed to death row were executed, compared to 43.8 per cent of the whites waiting for execution. Also, inmates who went to their death had less education and more menial jobs than those who were granted clemency.[45]

Of condemned inmates executed in Pennsylvania since 1914, significantly more blacks than whites were executed.[46] After finding that specific characteristics distinguished the executed inmates from those who had their execution orders commuted, such as the kind of counsel received during the trial, the researchers established that the offender's race was most important. It was concluded that blacks "have not received equal consideration for commutation of the death penalty."[47] Subsequent research continues to confirm the discriminatory character of capital punishment. When executions are carried out, blacks are executed more often than whites, for lesser offenses, at younger ages, and more often without appeals and commutation of the death penalty.[48]

The Death Penalty

Despite the moral questions raised about administering capital punishment, arguments for

Table 12.3 Prisoners Executed in the United States, by Offense, Race, and State, 1930–1970

Region and State	All offenses				Murder				Rape				Other offenses		
	Total	White	Negro	Other	Total	White	Negro	Other	Total	White	Negro	Other	Total	White	Negro
Northeast	608	424	177	7	606	422	177	7	—	—	—	—	2	2	—
New Hampshire	1	1	—	—	1	1	—	—	—	—	—	—	—	—	—
Vermont	4	4	—	—	4	4	—	—	—	—	—	—	—	—	—
Massachusetts	27	25	2	—	27	25	2	—	—	—	—	—	—	—	—
Rhode Island	—	—	—	—	—	—	—	—	—	—	—	—	—	—	—
Connecticut	21	18	3	—	21	18	3	—	—	—	—	—	—	—	—
New York	329	234	90	5	327	232	90	5	—	—	—	—	2	2	—
New Jersey	74	47	25	2	74	47	25	2	—	—	—	—	—	—	—
Pennsylvania	152	95	57	—	152	95	57	—	—	—	—	—	—	—	—
North Central	403	257	144	2	393	254	137	2	10	3	7	—	—	—	—
Ohio	172	104	67	1	172	104	67	1	—	—	—	—	—	—	—
Indiana	41	31	10	—	41	31	10	—	—	—	—	—	—	—	—
Illinois	90	59	31	—	90	59	31	—	—	—	—	—	—	—	—
Iowa	18	18	—	—	18	18	—	—	—	—	—	—	—	—	—
Missouri	62	29	33	—	52	26	26	—	10	3	7	—	—	—	—
North Dakota	1	1	—	—	1	1	—	—	—	—	—	—	—	—	—
South Dakota	1	1	—	—	1	1	—	—	—	—	—	—	—	—	—
Nebraska	4	3	—	1	4	3	—	1	—	—	—	—	—	—	—
Kansas	15	12	3	—	15	12	3	—	—	—	—	—	—	—	—
South	2,306	637	1,659	10	1,824	585	1,231	8	443	43	398	2	39	9	30
Delaware	12	5	7	—	8	4	4	—	4	1	3	—	—	—	—
Maryland	68	13	55	—	44	7	37	—	24	6	18	—	—	—	—
Dist. of Columbia	40	3	37	—	37	3	34	—	3	—	3	—	—	—	—
Virginia	92	17	75	—	71	17	54	—	21	—	21	—	—	—	—
West Virginia	40	31	9	—	36	28	8	—	1	—	1	—	3	3	—
North Carolina	263	59	199	5	207	55	149	3	47	4	41	2	9	—	9
South Carolina	162	35	127	—	120	30	90	—	42	5	37	—	—	—	—
Georgia	366	68	298	—	299	65	234	—	61	3	58	—	6	—	6

Region and State	All offenses				Murder				Rape				Other offenses		
	Total	White	Negro	Other	Total	White	Negro	Other	Total	White	Negro	Other	Total	White	Negro
Florida	170	57	113	—	133	55	78	—	36	1	35	—	1	1	1
Kentucky	103	51	52	—	88	47	41	—	10	1	9	—	5	3	2
Tennessee	93	27	66	—	66	22	44	—	27	5	22	—	—	—	—
Alabama	135	28	107	—	106	26	80	—	22	2	20	—	7	—	7
Mississippi	154	30	124	—	130	30	100	—	21	—	21	—	3	—	3
Arkansas	118	27	90	1	99	25	73	1	19	2	17	—	—	—	—
Louisiana	133	30	103	—	116	30	86	—	17	—	17	—	—	—	—
Oklahoma	60	42	15	3	54	40	11	3	4	—	4	—	2	2	—
Texas	297	114	182	1	210	101	108	1	84	13	71	—	3	—	3
West	509	405	83	21	496	393	82	21	—	—	—	—	13	12	1
Montana	6	4	2	—	6	4	2	—	—	—	—	—	—	—	—
Idaho	3	3	—	—	3	3	—	—	—	—	—	—	—	—	—
Wyoming	7	6	1	—	7	6	1	—	—	—	—	—	—	—	—
Colorado	47	41	5	1	47	41	5	1	—	—	—	—	—	—	—
New Mexico	8	6	2	—	8	6	2	—	—	—	—	—	—	—	—
Arizona	38	28	10	—	38	28	10	—	—	—	—	—	—	—	—
Utah	13	13	—	—	13	13	—	—	—	—	—	—	—	—	—
Nevada	29	27	2	—	29	27	2	—	—	—	—	—	—	—	—
Washington	47	40	5	2	46	39	5	2	—	—	—	—	1	1	—
Oregon	19	16	3	—	19	16	3	—	—	—	—	—	—	—	—
California	292	221	53	18	280	210	52	18	—	—	—	—	12	11	1
State total	3,826	1,723	2,063	40	3,319	1,654	1,627	38	453	46	405	2	54	23	31
Federal	33	28	3	2	15	10	3	2	2	2	—	—	16	16	—
United States total	3,859	1,751	2,066	42	3,334	1,664	1,630	40	455	48	405	2	70	39	31
Percentage	100.00	...	...	...	86.4	...	...	...	11.8	...	...	...	1.8	...	...

Source: Bureau of Prisons, United States Department of Justice, "Capital Punishment, 1930–1970," National Prisoner Statistics Bulletin, No. 46 (August 1971), pp. 12–13.

retaining statutory provisions for the death penalty are still advanced: (1) the death penalty as a deterrent to crime, (2) the certainty of punishment when the death penalty is prescribed, and (3) the financial economy of capital punishment. On the first argument, most evidence indicates that capital punishment does not act as a deterrent. Observations and researches have demonstrated, first, that murder rates have remained constant despite trends away from capital punishment; second, that where one state has abolished capital punishment and another has not, the murder rate is no higher in the abolition state than in the retention state; and, third, that the possible consequences are not considered by the murderer at the time of the offense.[49]

The second major argument favoring capital punishment, the certainty of being punished, is negated by the fact that the death penalty is seldom imposed. Witnesses are less willing to testify and juries are less willing to convict when the penalty can be death.[50] The third argument, about the financial economy of the death penalty, is refuted by the per capita cost for execution, which is higher than that for imprisonment.[51] Trials of capital cases are more costly and time-consuming than trials for other cases, and maintenance costs for inmates in death row are higher than for inmates in the rest of the prison. Thus capital punishment does not perform the functions claimed by its most vociferous advocates.

Nevertheless, the issue continues to be debated. Its legal status is more confused and uncertain than ever. In 1972 the Supreme Court in *Furman* v. *Georgia* ruled that the death penalty as carried out in the United States "constitutes cruel and unusual punishment in violation of the Eighth and Fourteenth Amendments."[52] The court was so badly split, however, that all nine judges wrote separate opinions. The decision did not eliminate capital punishment but limited the discretionary manner in which it is imposed. The consequence is a campaign in many states to enact new capital punishment laws.[53]

Public opinion continues to be divided on capital punishment. Aside from the moral need for eliminating the death penalty, the evidence shows that capital punishment is not a deterrent to crime, yet a president can proclaim to the public that "contrary to the social theorists, I am convinced the death penalty can be an effective deterrent."[54] The final outcome on the legality of the death penalty will depend upon which set of ideas dominates, inevitably being determined by the needs of maintaining the advanced capitalist state. Although capital punishment may be "an archaic custom of primitive origin," it still holds its spell over the "civilized" state.

If an intelligent visitor from some other planet were to stray to North America, he would observe, here and there very rarely, a small group of persons assembled in a secluded room who, as representatives of an all-powerful sovereign state, were solemnly participating in deliberately and artfully taking the life of a human being. Ignorant of our customs, he might conclude that he was witnessing a sacred rite somehow suggesting a human sacrifice. And seeing our great universities and scientific laboratories, our mental hospitals and clinics, our many charitable institutions, and the multitude of churches dedicated to the worship of an executed Savior, he might well wonder about the strange and paradoxical workings of the human mind.[55]

The Politics of Custody and Punishment

The first legal action against the person is imposing the label "criminal" on the offender. Once that is attached, control is established, possibly for a lifetime, and the legal restrictions are never completely removed. Upon conviction for a crime an offender automatically loses rights and privileges held out to the citizenry. Unless these civil rights are restored by some formal procedure upon release from the legal system, they may be permanently forfeited. In addition, the offender's criminal record will be with him for the rest of his life.

Convicted persons are subject to numerous disabilities and disqualifications quite apart from the sanction imposed in the sentence.[56] A number of civil rights that others possess by citizenship are lost by those convicted of felonies and some misdemeanors. Most state statutes and constitutions provide for deprivation of some rights upon criminal conviction. Some states provide for the blanket loss or suspension of civil rights, including the right to vote, to hold public office, to sue, to enter into contracts, to inherit property, to testify, and to serve as a juror. Where statutes provide for restoring rights, it is often unclear which rights are restored and which disabilities and disqualifications remain. Also, the length of time for which rights are to be forfeited may depend on the sentence. The law is complex and confusing in such matters.

Along with their loss of civil rights, convicted persons are usually prohibited from participating in other activities. They may be barred from obtaining professional, occupational, and business licenses, or from other kinds of employment. The procedures for restoring such privileges are not always clear. The statutes usually restore only specific rights, leaving other privileges to the discretion of regulatory agencies. In spite of legal efforts to remove the definition of "criminal" from the convicted person, and regardless of the provisions for restoring rights and privileges, the effects of a criminal conviction are likely to be felt forever.

In a prison's lawlessness the politics of custody and punishment is most dramatically displayed. The prison, as a microcosm of society, is an order unto itself. Screened from public visibility and control, it develops its own rules and fosters its own order of lawlessness.

There is almost nothing the prison cannot do, and does not do to inmates, including keeping them beyond the expiration dates of their sentences (via procedures declaring them dangerous or mentally ill). It can and does transfer them far from their families; limit and restrict their visitors; censor what they read, what they may write; decide whom they may associate with inside, what medicine or other medical care they will or will not receive, what education they may or may not have, whether they will be totally locked up, for weeks, months, occasionally even years, or enjoy limited physical freedom. Inmates' personal property may be misplaced and destroyed, incoming and outgoing letters sometimes not delivered, and, in the extreme, prisoners may be starved, brutalized and killed.[57]

The prison's social organization maintains the political goals of imprisonment, keeping prisoners powerless. By its own lawlessness, by "classification" and segregation, by administering dehumanizing schemes of confinement, prison officials can establish the maximum forms of security. In fact, prison administrators must keep inmates as unorganized among themselves as possible, to prevent them from joining forces.

To this end, psychological solitary confinement is substituted, to the fullest extent possible, for physical isolation. This permits inmates to work and to participate in prescribed activities, but it minimizes the danger of violence, revolt or riot. To facilitate the state of unorganization or anomie, administrators always admonish inmates to "do your own time," and consistently, officially distribute rewards such as parole and good-time allowances to inmates who remain isolated from other prisoners.[58]

By attempting to maintain powerlessness among prisoners, the traditional authority structure promotes the political objectives of the custody and punishment establishment.

13

Treatment and Corrections

The modern trend toward corrections continues the objectives of punishment. Correctional reform, however, involves controlling crime and criminals by means of modern scientific knowledge and professional management. The state's business is to maintain domestic peace; and correction is to treat or "rehabilitate" anyone who threatens public order. Prisons are to be made into therapeutic centers, where offenders will be scientifically managed and perhaps changed, and at last reintegrated into society. Following the correctional model, eventually most offenders may be dealt with outside the prison, in the "community," with the whole society as a therapeutic environment.

Institutional Treatment

The correctional movement of this century has counted on the prison serving as a center for rehabilitating offenders as well as confining and punishing them. The offenders find themselves subjected to both the punishment of custody and the punishment of treatment. Institutional treatment is not incompatible with punishment.

The rehabilitation ideal has spawned many repressive practices under the name of liberal reform and individualized treatment. Because the modern prison's purpose is to rehabilitate the offender, people are kept in prison until authorities or professional workers think that they have been successfully rehabilitated. This reasoning has brought about the indeterminate sentence, which coerces the inmate into adjusting to the needs and interests of the institution's custodians and professionals; otherwise release from the institution will not be forthcoming. Furthermore, the treatment model is pursued either without examining important theoretical assumptions or according to dangerous practices by sometimes well-intentioned people.[1] Instead of dealing with society's chronic problems, treatment policies are designed for the victims of the social and economic conditions beyond the individual's control.

In spite of the influence that the rehabilitation ideal has on correctional policy, treatment programs in the prison are quite primitive.

241

Treatment rhetoric is common, but the business of confinement still dominates the modern prison. Jessica Mitford observed:

> In prison parlance, "treatment" is an umbrella term meaning diagnosis, classification, various forms of therapy, punishment as deemed necessary, and prognosis, or the prediction of the malfeasant's future behavior: will/won't he err again? While the Corrections crowd everywhere talk a good line of "treatment" — phrases like "inadequate personalities," "borderline sociopaths," "weak superegos" come trippingly off the tongue of the latter-day prison warden, having long since replaced the sin-stained souls and fallen men or women with whom his predecessor had to cope — very few prison systems have actually done much about implementing it in practice. Nationwide, only 5 percent of the prison budget goes for services labeled "rehabilitation," and in many states there is not even the pretense of making "therapy" available to the adult offender.[2]

Nevertheless, inmates are supposed to be reformed during their prison experience. Prisoners are expected to be changed in the course of confinement.

Any efforts at treating the offender within the prison are affected by its social organization, especially by the relationship of staff members to one another, the relationships of inmates, and the interaction between staff members and inmates. The staff in charge of treatment is faced with the problem of getting the inmates' respect while they are being required by other staff members to obey elaborate regulations. The regulations themselves are restrictive, and their violation results in penalties and even harsher restrictions. The therapeutic staff must maintain the restrictions while simultaneously offering treatment to the inmates. Furthermore, the therapeutic staff's attempts to administer treatment conflict with some of the custodial staff objectives.[3] Some of the specific techniques of the two staffs are contradictory. The therapeutic and custodial staffs see each other's daily activities as working at cross-purposes.

Custodial workers are concerned with maintaining control and this concern is reflected

in their priorities of action in a given situation as well as in the considerations they express in planning and supervising inmates' activities. On the other hand, treatment personnel tend to be concerned with mitigating the psychological or interpersonal problems of inmates. Conflict engendered by these different priorities is exacerbated because custodial and treatment workers, by virtue of their different responsibilities, are also frequently confronted in a different manner by inmates. These workers thus develop different conceptions of the inmates and each staff group becomes convinced of the correctness of its view and derides that of the other.[4]

The relationships that the inmates develop among themselves also determine how treatment programs will work. The inmate system shapes the way in which treatment is administered. The inmates' willingness to participate in treatment programs is influenced by their involvement in the inmate system: those committed to the inmate system are less likely to participate in treatment programs.[5]

How well a treatment program can be administered in an institution setting likewise varies according to the prison's ideology and structure. Although all prisons are punitive, and physical confinement produces social and psychological deprivations, prisons differ somewhat in their way of balancing punitive and treatment goals. A few prisons are primarily arranged for rehabilitating the inmates; others are devoted mostly to punitive custody.

We have much evidence that the prison's ideology and structure influence the administration of institutional treatment programs. In one study, the organization of six institutions for male delinquents was examined.[6] The institutions differed in their emphasis on punishment and treatment. The findings showed that the treatment-oriented institutions varied systematically from the custodial ones in distribution of power, departmental structure, role definition, organizational conflict, and systems of social control. Staff attitudes toward inmates also differed in the two types of institution. All these influenced the effectiveness of treatment. Other research has shown that in treatment-oriented institutions inmates are more positive toward the prison goals and inmate leaders often choose to serve as coordinators and interpreters for administrative policies.[7]

Many treatment "techniques" have been designed and administered to change criminals into noncriminals. The punitive-oriented prisons have relied on clinical techniques, working with individual inmates in some form of counseling or psychotherapy. Treatment-oriented prisons, though, have used a group-relations principle, trying to change the inmates' attitudes and behavior by manipulating social relationships.[8]

But how effective is institutional treatment? According to Clinard, "Prisons are highly successful as a means of incapacitating persons for a period of time, but their success in deterring them from becoming recidivists or repeaters is much less."[9] Imprisonment as a means of rehabilitation seems to have very slight success. More than half the people received into state and federal prisons and reformatories have had experience with institutional rehabilitation. Some prisons, though, may be more effective in rehabilitation than previously indicated. An analysis of several follow-up studies of inmates released from prison concludes that reimprisonment rates actually vary between 20 and 40 per cent for some correctional systems.[10] Also, it is argued, the offender's criminal career is reversed during prison experience and at least 90 per cent of the inmates released from the federal prison system seek legitimate careers for a month or more after they leave prison.[11]

Some of the variations in reimprisonment rates can be accounted for by the ways in which treatment programs are implemented, and by the structure of the inmate populations, the selective use of probation, and the policies of the parole officers.[12] Some researchers have strongly suggested that some types of prisoners are better risks for rehabilitation than others. Treatment methods used with one type of inmate could be less effective with others.[13] More recently, an elaborate typology of criminal careers has been proposed, along with treatment strategies for each type.[14] Group therapy or milieu forms of therapy are recommended for semiprofessional property offenders, drug addicts, joyriders, aggressive rapists, and other types. Intensive psychiatric treatment is suggested for nonviolent sex offenders, incest cases, male homosexuals, violent sex offenders, and psychopathic assaultists. Minimal treatment is recommended for statutory rapists and for "one-time loser" property or personal offenders. The implication is that inmate recidivism rates would be lowered if treatment programs were related to the offenders' special needs.

Another reason for our inconclusive evidence on recidivism is the lack of systematic postrelease information and reliable follow-up studies of inmates, in part because of underdeveloped rehabilitation theories. Correctional workers also have not been trained in the skills necessary for evaluative research. But more important, those who administer institutional treatment have vested interests in specific kinds of programs. A negative evaluation of a program might mean personal loss for those associated with it.

Precise research on the "success" of either general programs of crime control or more specific methods of correction furnishes information which is the basis for public esteem and professional reputation, as well as information about the correctional technique being evaluated. These two are very different. Personal and organizational needs supplement the societal needs being met by administration and utilization of various correctional techniques. For example, by utilizing or advocating use of particular techniques in correctional work, a person may secure employment and income, good professional reputation, prestige as an intellectual or scholarly authority, the power stemming from being the champion of a popular ideology, and many other personal rewards. An agency organized around administration of a technique may fill such needs for dozens, even hundreds, of employees, and may itself have more general, organizational needs for survival. Hence, evaluative research results which would show that the technique is ineffective and would, thereby, seriously threaten the agency or the personnel must be avoided if possible.[15]

Ignoring the varying effectiveness of institutional treatment, we are left with a question:

Why do some inmates *not* return to prison? The usual answer is that those who do not return have been rehabilitated *because of* specific treatment they have received in prison. But perhaps some do not return to prison *in spite of* institutional treatment. Some ex-prisoners may not return because of circumstances they encounter upon their release. This is the basis of the argument that most of those who return to prison have not been able to find legitimate opportunities during the first crucial weeks after their release.[16] Those who remain outside of prison most often find it is no longer necessary to engage in criminally defined activity or are able to avoid criminal definitions in some other way. If that is true, the prison is almost useless as a rehabilitative agency, serving instead as a holding device while the inmate ages and society changes. Time itself can create new circumstances for the offender. And there is the added possibility that the prisons radicalize the inmate. Emerging revolutionary activity among prisoners can change the collective lives of the oppressed.

Juvenile Delinquency Programs in the Community

Much of the effort devoted to dealing with juvenile delinquency has taken place within the community setting, focusing not on individuals, but on groups or circumstances beyond individuals. When individuals are considered, they are dealt with according to their social environment. These programs, therefore, are usually located within the community or neighborhood. Such programs are administered according to the scope and comprehensiveness of environmental change.

One of the first community-centered juvenile delinquency programs, and the most limited in scope, was the Cambridge-Somerville Youth Study.[17] In the late thirties in that area of Boston, 325 boys under twelve years of age were selected to receive preventive treatment. A matched group of the same size was selected as a control. Several community agencies cooperated in counseling, guidance for the family, medical and academic assistance, and recreational activities. The control group was given

none of these services. At the end of the experimental period, in 1945, the two groups were compared for their contact with legal authorities. To the chagrin of the many involved, the offense records of the two groups were similar; 27.7 per cent of the treatment group members had appeared in court for offenses, compared to 26.1 per cent of the control group. Still later, in 1956, a follow-up study traced the adult lives of the two groups.[18] As many treated boys as control boys had been convicted of crimes in later years. The number of crimes committed was also similar for the two groups. The study indicated that behavior cannot be altered by limited change in social conditions.

A step beyond the casework approach are the programs that involve participant work with *street-corner groups*. Such efforts are sometimes referred to as "detached worker" programs, meaning that a social worker is detached from the local agency and assigned to make contact with gangs in the community, with the objective of changing the members' attitudes and behavior.

One of the earliest projects of this kind was conducted in New York City.[19] From 1947 to 1950, trained workers were attached to several street gangs in central Harlem. They tried, with some reported success, to redirect the gangs' activity from fighting, stealing, sex offenses, and marijuana smoking to organized athletics, block parties, movie programs, camping trips, and the like. This approach was expanded by the New York City Youth Board to include work with gangs in several of the city's high-delinquency areas.[20] A more recent but similar project was the YMCA-sponsored program in Chicago, which has produced much research.[21]

The results of gang-work programs in Los Angeles have recently been reported.[22] The program, led by Malcolm Klein, was based on the assumptions that gangs have little "natural" cohesion and the cohesion they do have is produced by "external" sources. Delinquency then is increased with more gang cohesion. The program was meant to reduce the gang's cohesion, but it was concluded disappointingly.

A somewhat broader project operated in Boston from 1954 to 1957.[23] Attempting to reduce juvenile offenses in a lower-class area, the

Boston Delinquency Project included efforts to better coordinate community agencies and improve the family system. But the primary objective was shifting the values of street-corner groups from law-violating behavior to law-abiding behavior. Project field workers established and maintained contact with 400 youths who were members of some 21 corner groups. The evaluative results were mixed. Apparently the project had a negligible effect on the law-violating behavior of the gang members.[24] Nevertheless, it was successful in other ways; it did confront issues of community organization.

Instituting these programs within a city usually creates or brings to the surface conflict among city agencies. A post-mortem on the prevention project in Boston documented the conflicts in administering the project.[25] About a dozen public and private organizational groups were interested in the city's handling of crime and delinquency. The principal public agencies were the municipal government, the recreation department, the police department, the courts, the public schools, and the state youth corrections division. The major private groups were medical and psychiatric clinics, social-work agencies, churches, universities, and special cause groups, such as ethnic associations and crime-prevention societies. Each group had its own philosophy on etiology of delinquency, appropriate disposition of the delinquent, organization and procedures for prevention, and qualifications for personnel in delinquency programs. Conflicts both *between* and *within* the agencies diminished coordination and blocked efforts to administer the city's prevention program. The agencies acted as special interest groups to have their vested interests satisfied. Prevention programs often have a major (unstated) objective: satisfying the interests of those who administer the programs.

But some juvenile delinquency programs do include reorganizing and developing the whole community. Such programs treat delinquent behavior as a reflection of the social and cultural milieu; to bring about change in behavior patterns the workers understand that the entire community's structure must be altered. A basic procedure for implementing these pro-grams is encouraging the people in the community to lead and participate. Instead of outsiders imposing their will and techniques on the inhabitants, the residents themselves determine or help determine the changes that are to be made in their community. Success for these programs does not necessarily mean reducing delinquent activity. Behavior patterns may eventually be changed. But in the meantime, improvements in the residents' lives and the community's social climate are much more important.

The Chicago Area Project, beginning in about 1930, is the best known of these programs in community development.[26] It began in three slum areas in Chicago and expanded to other parts of the city. Under the direction of Clifford R. Shaw, the Area Project was based on sociological assumptions about human behavior and community organization, specifically that people support and participate only in enterprises in which they have a meaningful role. The first phase of the project required knowledge about the area and its population. Local residents were encouraged to become the developers and administrators of the programs. Then residents developed services and organizations to meet the community's welfare needs. The project's aim and methods are summarized here:

(1) It emphasizes the development of a program for the neighborhood as a whole. (2) It seeks to stress the autonomy of the local residents in helping to plan, support, and operate constructive programs which they may regard as their own. (3) It attaches special significance to the training and utilization of community leaders. (4) It confines the efforts of its professional staff, in large part, to consultation and planning with responsible neighborhood leaders who assume major roles in the actual development of the program. (5) It seeks to encourage the local residents to utilize to the maximum all churches, societies, clubs, and other existing institutions and agencies, and to coordinate these in a unified neighborhood program. (6) Its activities are regarded primarily as devices for enlisting the active participation of local residents in a constructive community enterprise, for creating and crystallizing neighborhood sentiment on behalf of the welfare of the children and the

social and physical improvement of the community as a whole. (7) It places particular emphasis upon the importance of a continuous, objective evaluation of its effectiveness as a device for reducing delinquency, through constructive modification of the pattern of community life.[27]

From all evaluations of the Area Project, it is evident that residents of low-income areas have been able to organize themselves to promote their own communal interests.[28] Also, though precise measurement is not possible, apparently delinquent and criminal activity has been reduced by such efforts in community development.[29]

For some time Saul Alinsky argued that the problem of crime and delinquency is part of a larger program of institutional reorganization.[30] His program was not aimed specifically at crime and delinquency, but toward eradicating unemployment, disease, inadequate housing, demoralization, and other aspects of social deterioration. He advocated forming "people's organizations" in the community. His program, variously known as Back of the Yards Project, People's Organization, and Industrial Areas Foundation, differs from the Chicago Area Project in several important ways:

First, the membership is wider; each local organization, such as a church, a union, an industry, a club, is represented. Second, the primary purpose is the development of groups composed of persons who are interested in their own welfare and are organized for political action to improve their welfare. Third, the ultimate aim is the development of a nation-wide federation of people's organizations, involving millions of people; through such a federation powerful political influence could be exerted.[31]

It is putting political power into the people's hands that makes this program more radical than most others. Because government officials must approve programs and appropriate funds, most such programs have remained proposals.

Through the years, then, these programs have gradually evolved into ideas based on community development, institutional reorganization, and political involvement. The culmination of some of these ideas is Mobilization for Youth, a project in a 67-block area on the Lower East Side of New York City. Beginning in the early sixties, Mobilization for Youth was founded on the theoretical proposition that obstacles to economic and social betterment are chiefly responsible for crime and delinquency among low-income groups.[32] The objectives of the project were "(1) to increase the employability of youths from low-income families, (2) to improve and make more accessible training and work preparation facilities, (3) to help young people achieve employment goals equal to their capacities, (4) to increase employment opportunities for the area's youth, and (5) to help minority group youngsters overcome discrimination in hiring."[33]

Fairly orthodox remedies were designed to implement job training and work projects for the unemployed youth and young adults. Specific programs included a youth job center, an urban youth service corps, on-the-job training, reading clinics, preschool education, and guidance counselors. But the rest of the project, the community action portion, has been devoted to more unorthodox procedures. Among these are a staff of lawyers for welfare clients, a housing unit that collects data on landlord violations, and a group of organizers who advise and assist the poor to collectively change their lives.

Mobilization for Youth is distinguished from many other programs because it organizes the poor for social protest and human betterment. The project's main hope is to "organize the unaffiliated — to overturn the status quo and replace it with a higher level of stability, without delinquents, alcoholism or drug addiction."[34] This political aspect got the project into trouble with government officials. The FBI investigated those who have engaged in organized action; newspapers charged the project with subversion; its files were confiscated; and federal and local funds were questioned and altered. To provide the poor with services and assistance from above has been the traditional way of doing things; it is regarded as subversive when the poor attempt to change the social pattern of their poverty.

Fear of the more radical aspects of Mobilization for Youth is also imbedded in the potential of a widespread movement among the poor.

If a movement of welfare recipients should, in fact, take form and gather strength, the ghetto and the slum will have yielded up a new political force. And it is conceivable that such a force could eventually be turned to the objective of procuring federal legislation for new programs of income redistribution (such as a guaranteed minimum income) to replace a welfare system that perpetuates poverty while it strips men of their fundamental rights as citizens.[35]

Indeed, programs within the community, when in the hands of community members, have wide and significant implications for social change in the United States.

Community-based Corrections

Recent developments in institutional treatment have involved modifying the custodial setting in which treatment is administered. Among these are work-release programs outside the prison, halfway houses where offenders receive residential treatment while they also work or attend school, and community treatment centers.[36]

These developments respond to growing pessimism about the possibilities of institutional treatment. Even some prison reformers realize that prisons are failing to rehabilitate inmates and that for most offenders treatment cannot be successful in an institution. This is the argument:

During the past many years there has been considerable evidence justifying the increasing disillusionment with the rehabilitative and treatment effectiveness of traditional correctional institutions. It has become glaringly evident that such institutions have been designed primarily to meet the societal objectives of restraint and containment, rather than the stated concerns with treatment and rehabilitation. Indeed not only are correctional institutions generally ineffective in regard to attaining their rehabilitative objectives (which objectives they cannot be expected to meet without considerable efforts in and by the larger community), but the deleterious and destructive effects of such incarceration appear further to add to the problems of correctional clients.[37]

Efforts have grown in recent years to develop "community-based" treatment and correctional programs for adult offenders. Even the Bureau of Prisons, always a strong defender of the prison system, is formulating and implementing these programs. The notion of dealing with adult offenders in the community was given strong support by a director of the Bureau of Prisons in a congressional hearing:

We in corrections know that offenders can change — can be reintegrated into the community — if provided the proper assistance, support and supervision. The focus of this effort is, of course, the community-based programs. We must continue and expand these programs and develop new ones of promise. All of us at every level of government, in public and private agencies, must share in this work.

Two of the major goals of the Federal Bureau of Prisons are: to increase the program alternatives for offenders who do not require traditional institution confinement, and expand community involvement in correctional programs and goals.

In achieving the first goal, we will attempt to minimize the corrosive effects of imprisonment, lessen the offenders' alienation from society and reduce the economic costs of the taxpayer.

We must achieve the second goal because only with the successful reintegration of the ex-offender into the community will we have fulfilled our mission — the correction of the offender.

With the help of agencies such as yours and the skilled and dedicated work of each of you, I am confident we in corrections will achieve our goals and accomplish our mission.[38]

In the movement away from complete confinement toward treatment in the community, however, the notion of "community-based" corrections has become a catch-all for assorted experiments and practices.

Thus, almost any correctional program conducted outside the walls of traditional juvenile and adult correctional institutions has been lumped into this category. For example, probation, parole, halfway houses, noninstitutionalized boarding arrangements (such as foster and group homes), and even small institutions or residential facilities located in the community, have been included under the description "community-based correctional programs." Indeed, the impression is often obtained that the very fact of labeling or designating a program as "community-based" is supposed to connote that the effort is "innovative," "enlightened," and "progressive."[39]

In addition to the traditional programs of probation and parole, usually supervised within the community, states are establishing community treatment programs of some kind. More than half the states already have instituted community-based correctional programs.[40] Many prisoners released from federal prisons are being sent to community treatment centers before they are released from the federal system. The Bureau of Prisons operates fourteen community-center programs, and the federal prison system has contracts with at least sixty other facilities for supervising federal parolees in the community. A parolee may have to reside or participate in these programs as a condition of release. The Bureau of Prisons plans to expand this form of "treatment," increasing the size and number of community-based centers.

Other community-based programs consist of noninstitutional boarding arrangements such as foster care, small-group homes, and semi-institutional cottage living. There are also community programs with forestry work and outdoor camps, nonresidential work or group-therapy programs, and a number of day-care programs. Applied to juveniles, community treatment is essentially preventive — intervention in gang activity or treatment of "predelinquents."[41] Some of these programs provide an alternative to legal processing in the criminal justice system.

All the community-based programs, however, are administered by the authorities — local, state, or federal officials. These are not community programs controlled by the people who are subjected to the treatment procedures. By definition, correctional programs — in the institution or in the community — are the property of the state that originally defines the

behavior as criminal; community-based treatment consists of "intensive intervention in lieu of institutionalization."[42] One type of control is substituted for another and the citizen's life is still to be supervised, controlled, and manipulated. The purpose is usually to "integrate" the person into the community, not to change the community or the society in which the person found that crime was an appropriate solution.

The "success" of community-based corrections is still being evaluated and debated; it will depend on the standards used to evaluate the programs. Almost by definition, corrections in the community may be the proper alternative to institutionalization. One criminologist writes:

In summary, from the standpoints of assessment, control, and assistance, but primarily through more timely and relevant assistance, community corrections for adults provide vast advances from traditional jailing or imprisonment. As has been indicated, these methods of graduating and deferring decision on confinement have numerous implications for the entire criminal justice system, beginning at arrest and pretrial processing. All of these implications can be consolidated well by the general maxim: never set apart from the community, any more than can possibly be avoided, those whom you wish some day to bring safely back into the community.[43]

From another point of view, the success of community-based corrections depends on the program's ability to handle a large number of cases in an economically feasible way; a "cost-benefit" analysis may be used to judge their merit.

Until alternatives to institutionalization are demonstrated to be more effective than imprisonment in preventing further crime, a major rationale for the use of community programs will be that correctional costs can be considerably reduced by handling in the community setting a large number of those offenders normally institutionalized. Experimental/demonstration projects in intensive intervention have shown that for a large number of institution candidates incarceration is clearly unnecessary. Thus, if society is still determined, in the light of this evidence, to keep these offenders in prisons and training schools, it must be willing to pay the price. The central question becomes: are the goals of punishment and custodial control worth the high costs of constructing institutions, and maintaining the inmate in the institution, as well as the observed and the still unknown personal and social costs incurred through exposing individuals to the institutional experience.[44]

Returns on funds invested is becoming a standard by which programs of punishment, correction, and control are being evaluated and compared. This is an economic determination of criminal justice.

In the movement from putting people in institutions to handling corrections in the community, the emphasis remains on finding solutions to crime in the offender's makeup and behavior. Until we seek solutions in the social, economic, and political organization of the society, we will find no real success in handling the problem of crime.

From Treatment to Behavior Modification

Treatment programs, administered in institutions or in the community, have not produced the results desired by many authorities and professionals. Recidivism remains high and reaction by prisoners, often in a political form, is growing. Even more repressive techniques are being developed and applied to control any who disrupt the social order.

Some of these techniques, applied randomly in the prison system, are therapy conditioning, electronic surveillance, controlling emotions with drugs, and electrical and chemical stimulation. These are more subtle and insidious than old-fashioned imprisonment and rehabilitation, but have been tried by only a few institutions.

Some aspects of behavior control technology are sufficiently established to be usefully incorporated by existing criminal justice and correction systems. Psychotherapy, mood-changing drugs, and some conditioning methods are suitable alternative or adjunctive rehabilitation procedures for a variety of offenses. They are appropriate

alternative penalties for offenses where imprisonment is not necessary for the protection of society, so that probationary, voluntary correctives are in order. Precedents exist in the mandatory counseling or treatment required by some domestic and juvenile courts and the "safety classes" required of some traffic offenders. For offenses requiring mandatory restraints, these methods are useful adjuncts which may reduce length of incarceration and/or recidivism.[45]

A few social scientists, with support from the federal government, are now involved in developing "coercive behavior modification techniques" for controlling and manipulating those who threaten the social order. The techniques for treating and handling offenders range from operant and classical conditioning to aversion suppression and electronic monitoring. Ralph Schwitzgebel, one of the leading researchers and advocates of these forms of social engineering, observes: "Regardless of orientation, the basic underlying theory usually involves carefully specified changes in the environment of the person whose behavior is to be changed."[46] Scientific behavior modification is systematic and total, not limited to the "nontransferable" techniques of individual therapist or change agent.

Scientific knowledge is being applied to the legal order, separated from morality but providing the way to a stable social order. "A science of behavior must be developed on the model of an input-output system, with adaptation to the environment as a key component."[47] The behaviorist, with "environmental design," would control information and experiences for the rest of us. "A successful crime control model must deal with behavior before the crime occurs, must deal directly with criminal behavior, and must deal with environmental design, rather than the individual offender."[48]

Behavior Control Technology

Already the technology for changing and controlling human behavior exists. Some techniques are currently being applied or are in the experimental stage. Among these are behavioral methods using computers and electronics.

In the very near future, a computer technology will make possible alternatives to imprisonment. The development of systems for telemetering information from sensors implanted in or on the body will soon make possible the observation and control of human behavior without actual physical contact. Through such telemetric devices, it will be possible to maintain twenty-four-hour-a-day surveillance over the subject and to intervene electronically or physically to influence and control selected behavior. It will thus be possible to exercise control over human behavior and from a distance without physical contact.[49]

For several years scientists have been experimenting with electronic surveillance and control equipment. Schwitzgebel has devised and patented devices that can track, monitor, and modify offenders twenty-four hours a day.[50] One device, called the Behavior Transmitter-Reinforcer is carried on the offender's belt; another is locked to his wrist. These contain batteries and transmitters that automatically send radio signals between the subject and the control station. The equipment can track the wearer's location, and also transmit information about his activities, communicating with him and modifying his behavior directly by reward and punishment.

Other experimental behavior control devices are placed *inside* the offender, operating as internal radio-telemetry devices, with tiny transmitters that are swallowed or implanted in the body.[51] They measure and transmit gastrointestinal pressure, body temperature, blood pressure, heart rate, and oxygen levels. The telemetric control systems not only monitor the activity of individual offenders, but they would let the state supervise a much larger number of offenders. The advantages, we are told, are many:

The envisioned system of telemetric control while offering many possible advantages to offenders over present penal measures also has several possible benefits for society. Society, through such systems, exercises control over behavior it defines as deviant, thus insuring its own protection. The offender, by returning to the community, can help support his dependents and share in the overall tax burden. The offender is also in a better position to make meaningful

restitution. Because the control system works on conditioning principles, the offender is habituated into non-deviant behavior patterns — thus perhaps decreasing the probability of recidivism and, once the initial cost of development is absorbed, a telemetric control system might provide substantial economic advantage compared to rather costly correctional programs. All in all, the development of such a system could prove tremendously beneficial for society.[52]

By an extension of this philosophy, the whole community could be tracked and controlled, and the entire society could become a prison.

Some offenders are also being controlled by drugs. "Drug therapy" is one of the most common methods of dealing with "difficult" prisoners.[53] Such prisons or "correctional facilities" as Vacaville in California, Patuxent in Maryland, and the Illinois Security Hospital have been using powerful drugs such as Thorazine and Prolixin for many years. These are depressants used to pacify inmates. The effects can linger for weeks, altering the thoughts and emotions of the subjects.

An even more powerful drug, said to have been used in the California prison system, is Acetine, which slows the heart, causes respiratory arrest, and makes the subjects feel as if they are dying. The drug is used in "aversion therapy," a *Clockwork Orange* technique whereby the inmate is reminded of past misdeeds, associating his negative experience with the drug with these actions. Failure to respond favorably brings more of the drug, increasing the sensations of suffocation and drowning, producing the sensation of death.

A more drastic form of experimental behavior control involves electrically stimulating the brain by psychosurgery. Replacing massive lobotomy as a solution to behavioral problems, psychosurgery is the ultimate means of physiologically controlling human behavior.[54] In a number of prisons and hospitals, inmates are being subjected to these modern techniques; wires are implanted and electrodes are attached to the brain. With the electrodes the surgeon can destroy brain cells selectively and gradually while testing the conscious patient's intellectual and emotional reactions. Psychosurgeons can stimulate areas of the brain to create reactions in the patient. Researchers have devised computerized methods of mind control; by connecting the electrodes to a computer program, subjects exhibit the proper sensations and behavior. Remote mind control is a possible future for those who defy the established order.

Behavior Modification

For a decade federal and state departments of corrections have been trying to develop ways of modifying the behavior of prisoners who threaten the order and discipline of the prison. Furthermore, "the growing political consciousness of prisoners and their increased resistance to the inhumanity of prison has provided a special impetus to prison officials to establish special facilities for 'aggressive, manipulative, prisoners' who are 'resistive to authority.' "[55]

The principles began to be worked out in a conference of prison administrators held in Washington, D.C., in 1962, called by the director of the Federal Bureau of Prisons. The primary subject of this meeting was applying newly developed brainwashing techniques to the rehabilitation of prisoners. At the conference Edgar H. Schein, professor at the Massachusetts Institute of Technology, explained how the North Korean brainwashing techniques used on American prisoners of war could be applied to convicts in prisons in the United States. In a speech entitled "Man Against Man," Schein stated:

In order to produce marked change of behavior and/or attitudes, it is necessary to weaken, undermine, or remove the supports to the old patterns of behavior and old attitudes. Because most of the supports are the face-to-face confirmation of present behavior which are provided by those with whom close emotional ties exist, it is often necessary to break these emotional ties. This can be done by removing the individual physically and preventing any communication with those he cares about, or by proving to him that those whom he respects are not worthy of it, and indeed, should actively be mistrusted. If at the same time, the total environment inflexibly provides rewards and punishments only in terms of the new behavior to be obtained, and provides new

human contacts around which to build up relationships, it is highly likely that the desired new behavior and attitudes will be learned.[56]

In his presentation Dr. Schein identified several tactics used in brainwashing that would be appropriate for modifying prisoners' behavior. A listing of these tactics has since been referred to by prisoner groups as the Manifesto of Dehumanization:

1. Physical removal of prisoners to areas sufficiently isolated to effectively break or seriously weaken close emotional ties.
2. Segregation of all natural leaders.
3. Use of cooperative prisoners as leaders.
4. Prohibition of group activities not in line with brainwashing objectives.
5. Spying on the prisoners and reporting back private material.
6. Tricking men into written statements which are then shown to others.
7. Exploitation of opportunists and informers.
8. Convincing the prisoners that they can trust no one.
9. Treating those who are willing to collaborate in far more lenient ways than those who are not.
10. Punishing those who show uncooperative attitudes.
11. Systematic withholding of mail.
12. Preventing contact with anyone unsympathetic to the method of treatment and regimen of the captive populace.
13. Building a group conviction among the prisoners that they have been abandoned by and totally isolated from their social order.
14. Disorganization of all group standards among the prisoners.
15. Undermining of all emotional supports.
16. Preventing prisoners from writing home or to friends in the community regarding the conditions of their confinement.
17. Making available and permitting access to only those publications and books that contain materials which are neutral to or supportive of the desired new attitudes.
18. Placing individuals into new and ambiguous situations for which the standards are kept deliberately unclear and then putting pressure on them to conform to what is

desired in order to win favor and a reprieve from the pressure.

19. Placing individuals whose will power has been severely weakened or eroded into a living situation with several others who are more advanced in their thought-reform and whose job it is to further the undermining of the individual's emotional supports which was begun by isolating him from family and friends.

20. Using techniques of character invalidation, e.g., humiliations, revilements, shouting to induce feelings of guilt, fear and suggestibility, coupled with sleeplessness, an exacting prison regimen and periodic interrogational interviews.

21. Meeting all insincere attempts to comply with cellmates' pressures with renewed hostility.

22. Repeated pointing out to prisoner by cellmates of where he was in the past, or is in the present, not even living up to his own standards or values.

23. Rewarding of submission and subservience to the attitudes encompassing the brainwashing objective with a lifting of pressure and acceptance as a human being.

24. Providing social and emotional supports which reinforce the new attitudes.[57]

The director of the Bureau of Prisons closed the conference by telling the assembled group of correctional officials:

> We are a group that can do a lot of experimenting and research and we can change our methods, our environments, and perhaps come up with something more specific.
>
> What I am hoping is that the audience here will believe that we here in Washington are anxious to have you understand these things. Do things on your own — undertake a little experiment with what you can do with some of the sociopathic individuals.[58]

The experimental ventures suggested by the director of the Bureau of Prisons soon began to be implemented. The program was instituted at Marion Federal Prison in Illinois, with the objective of determining how effective brainwashing techniques could be in dealing with prisoners who are "agitators," suspected militants, writ-writers, and general troublemakers in the prison. Under the direction of

Dr. Martin Groder, the prison psychiatrist, the first step involved severing the inmates' ties with their family and friends, moving the inmates to an isolated location until they agreed to participate in Groder's program. As described in a report prepared by the Federal Prisoners' Coalition at Marion, inmates who succumb are moved to new living quarters where they are confronted by members of the "prisoner thought-reform" team and subjected to intense group pressures. As the report notes:

> His emotional, behavioral, and psychic characteristics are studied by the staff and prisoner paraprofessionals to detect vulnerable points of entry to stage attack-sessions around. During these sessions, on a progressively intensified basis, he is shouted at, his fears played on, his sensitivities ridiculed, and concentrated efforts made to make him feel guilty for real or imagined characteristics or conduct. . . . Every effort is made to heighten his suggestibility and weaken his character structure so that his emotional responses and thought-flow will be brought under group and staff control as totally as possible.[59]

Another behavior modification program, initiated at the Federal Facility, Springfield, Missouri, is called START (Special Treatment and Rehabilitative Training). It has this purpose: "to provide care, custody, and correction of the long term adult offender in a setting separated from this home institution" and "to develop behavioral and attitudinal changes in offenders who have not adjusted satisfactorily to institutional settings."[60] This program extends the one designed at Marion, providing an experimental model for future "correctional facilities" and behavior modification programs.

These programs in themselves can be called criminal. The Federal Prisoner Coalition says: "Factors of the START Program, with respect to classification of humans for compulsory participation in medical experiments, violate clearly stated World Court laws about conditions in which a civilized government can engage, and this in such a way as to constitute commission and conspiracy to commit crimes against Humanity. These comprise violations in every respect similar to those charges against the people of Germany at the conclusion of

World War II during the Nuremberg Trials."[61] As the crimes of corrections continue, any prisoner is subject to these programs. The objective is to pacify those who disrupt the prison.

The newest institution to employ and further develop the techniques of behavior modification is the Federal Center for Correctional Research at Butner, North Carolina. Costing about 14 million, it is designed as a federal experimental center, under the direction of warden-psychiatrist Martin Groder. In addition to its own staff and facilities, it will utilize the expertise, services, and research facilities of the three universities within twenty miles of the center: Duke University, University of North Carolina at Chapel Hill, and North Carolina State University. The center is to be composed of several units, a Mental Health Center, a Behavior Modification Unit, and a Training and Conference Center.[62] The programs probably will be changed as they are implemented. They will have to change because of the restriction on funds from the Law Enforcement Assistance Administration for use in behavior modification. Nevertheless, Butner is to serve as the most "forward-looking" institution dedicated to further developing new forms of behavioral control.

Judging from past attempts at corrections, however, combined with the increasing consciousness of prisoners, behavior modification cannot ultimately be accomplished. Prisoners will be found not cooperating with the new "treatment" programs, no matter how scientific and insidious the programs are. "They will actively resist these attempts to strip them of their humanity and their consciousness that it is society's ills rather than their own individual psychological problems, which perpetrate their plight."[63]

Diversion from the Criminal Justice System

The two trends in corrections seem contradictory: (1) processing and manipulating offenders in the legal system and (2) diverting offenders from the criminal process. In both theory and practice, the two are related. The objective of both responses is to control in some way those who disrupt the established order. They may even be combined, as in the civil processing of offenders into compulsory commitment and treatment. Where the two responses are compatible we may understand the recent trend toward diverting cases from the criminal justice system.

Correctional reformers have argued for some time that offenders may be more appropriately dealt with by means other than the criminal process — that there are more effective responses than those of the criminal law.

> The American system has a general tendency to rely too heavily on the law and legal process for the solution of pressing social problems. In particular, the arbitrary assignment to the criminal law and its processes of a variety of human conduct and conditions has come to be regarded as a problem of "overcriminalization."[64]

That is the reason for the recent attempts to find correctional alternatives outside the legal process.

People have always been diverted naturally from the formal criminal justice system in the United States. Legal officials, particularly the police and prosecutors, exercise discretion at various stages in the legal system, dismissing or transferring cases anywhere during their processing. Diversion is an especially acute issue today because the judicial system cannot handle the volume of cases. The current emphasis is on the "diversion of certain offenders before court processing."[65]

Hundreds of new diversion programs are being undertaken, but "because of the fragmentation of the criminal justice operations among counties, cities, states, and the federal system, it is impossible to make even a rough quantitative assessment of the extent to which offenders are being diverted out of the system."[66] Correctional reformers and many legal officials are committed to some form of diversion from the criminal process; many of them feel that diversion is an "enlightened" approach to the problem of crime.

> In effect, diversion seeks to offer the offender a set of social controls in lieu of the criminal justice system, our most drastic

and overpowering form of social control. The assumption is that many who violate criminal laws are people whose lives will always be difficult and who need continuing support and that supervision and supplemental services may be more promising than the combination of a stigma and a cage. Diversion with its gentler, less debilitating controls, may offer the best hope of developing in such people a lasting capacity to deal with a complex and difficult society.[67]

Those who are threats to the society, nevertheless, are to be controlled, even "humanely" controlled, treated, and changed — reintegrated into the established order.

The most basic form of diversion is eliminating some categories of offenders from the legal code, bypassing the legal system at the very beginning. Legal scholars are suggesting that some criminal laws in the United States should be repealed. This "decriminalization," it is argued, should begin by eliminating the laws that serve moralistic interests. This is characteristic of the discussions and conclusions that are being offered:

> The first principle of our cure for crime is this: we must strip off the moralistic excrescences on our criminal justice system so that it may concentrate on the essential. The prime function of the criminal law is to protect our persons and our property; these purposes are now engulfed in a mass of other distracting, inefficiently performed legislative duties. When the criminal law invades the spheres of private morality and social welfare, it exceeds its proper limits at the cost of neglecting its primary tasks. The unwarranted extension is expensive, ineffective, and criminogenic.[68]

The more specific proposals include the partial or complete repeal of criminal laws that regulate drunkenness, drug use, gambling, disorderly conduct, vagrancy, abortion, adultery, prostitution, and homosexuality.[69]

The arguments for decriminalization are many. They say that the law should stay out of moral questions and that "overcriminalization" results in practices that make the law less rational and efficient. The case, in summary form, is presented by Sanford H. Kadish:

Excessive reliance upon the criminal law to perform tasks for which it is ill-suited has created acute problems for the administration of criminal justice. The use of criminal law to enforce morals, to provide social services, and to avoid legal restraints on law enforcement, to take just three examples, has tended both to be inefficient and to produce grave handicaps for enforcement of the criminal law against genuinely threatening conduct. In the case of morals offenses, it has served to reduce the criminal law's essential claim to legitimacy by inducing offensive and degrading police conduct, particularly against the poor and the subcultural, and by generating cynicism and indifference to the criminal law. It has also fostered organized criminality and has produced, possibly, more crime than it has suppressed. Used as an alternative to social services, it has diverted enormous law-enforcement resources from protecting the public against serious crime. Finally, its use to circumvent restrictions on police conduct has undermined the principle of legality and exposed the law to plausible charges of hypocrisy.[70]

By decriminalizing some of the law, the remaining laws, which regulate the public order, can be more effectively enforced. In the meantime, so the argument goes, the citizenry will gain respect for law and order.

The problem with these proposals is that law cannot be simply stripped of its moral judgments: all law is basically moral. A moral position is taken whenever any human conduct is limited and controlled. The decision to regulate some conduct, to the exclusion of other behavior, is an action to construct and protect a particular kind of social order. Some people, usually those in power, always determine what behaviors are harmful to the society. Even when individuals harm themselves, it may be argued, the whole society is morally harmed.[71] Legal reform, therefore, always involves the dominance of one morality over another.

A logical consequence of decriminalization in the United States is substituting civil sanctions and processing for the controls formerly applied by the legal system. An alternative to criminalization is the *civil* commitment of offenders. By channels other than the criminal procedures, those defined as drug addicts, chronic drunkenness offenders, sexual psychopaths, and juvenile delinquents are confined to institutions (such as hospitals) and forced to submit to treatment programs. Several contemporary beliefs support this form of civil intervention, although its consequences can be as dangerous as those of the criminal process:

(1) that offenders should be treated instead of punished; (2) that some conditions — alcoholism, addiction — are not criminal but manifestations of illness; (3) that some persons, because of their condition — youth, mental illness — should be given special consideration or dealt with less severely; and (4) the belief that the State has a right and obligation to intervene where the individual or society is endangered. The quasi-criminal "civil" measures (civil commitment, juvenile court procedure, or compulsory treatment of the noncrime enforced by the prospect of penal processing for a crime) come into operation to satisfy the requirements of these beliefs. The supposed diversion of persons to civil processing whose condition or behavior is held noncriminal

appears to be an attempt to have it both ways: the individual, not being criminal, is not subject to penal sanction *but*, for the protection of all concerned, he may be subjected to similar measures classified as nonpenal.[72]

The compulsory commitment and treatment of persons are in reality not much different whether carried out in a prison or a hospital. The "medical model" of dealing with those who threaten the social order offers little real alternative for someone considered deviant or "sick." Indeed, the laws on civil commitment and compulsory treatment are even more constitutionally defective than some criminal laws. These defects are "(1) that due process in these proceedings is inadequate, (2) that treatment — the rationale of the proceeding — is not provided, (3) that the statutes are unconstitutionally vague, and (4) that they permit action by the State against an individual exceeding the police powers of the State."[73] For the person subjected to civil procedures, the consequences go beyond these constitutional issues and can last a lifetime.

THE POLITICAL
ECONOMY OF CRIME

"GROUP ONE: VOICE PRINTS OF YOUR FATHER'S VOICE. TWO: VOICE PRINTS OF THE MAN WE HAVE TO FIND!"

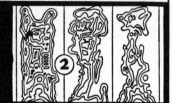

YOU MADE THE VOICE PRINTS POSSIBLE, HOMER, BY LENDING US YOUR WIRETAP CASSETTES.

"I DO ALL THIS FOR TRAINING, EXPERIMENTATION, RESEARCH. WITH THIS I COULD PICK UP DAD'S CONVERSATION."

HEAR ME?

YEAH.

"HIS PHONE LINE COMES THROUGH THE WALL AND ALONG MY FLOOR. THIS IS THE WIRETAP SETUP."

I RECORDED HIS DIAL CLICKS, THEN PLAYED THE TAPES BACK SLOW AND COUNTED THE CLICKS.

I KNEW EVERY NUMBER HE CALLED.

SO YOU WANT TO BE A SUPER COP.

NOT YOUR KIND OF SUPER COP —BUT A SUPER PROFESSIONAL SPY.

REMEMBER, WE'RE TRYING TO BREAK A RING OF SABOTEURS THAT WERE USING YOUR FATHER.

IT'S RIGHT DOWN YOUR ALLEY, SON.

MOTHER SENT THESE.

YOU'RE LOOKING FOR A PROBLEM TO FIT THAT "BRAIN."

I'M FULL OF TRICKS. I'M A GENIUS.

ALL RIGHT, WHAT ELSE DO YOU KNOW? WE CAN GO FAR TOGETHER.

JUST WHAT IS YOUR MASTER PLAN?

CHESTER GOULD

14
Social
Reaction to
Crime

The public reacts to the social reality of crime and in turn produces conceptions of crime. On the one hand, people react in specific ways to criminally defined activity, to the enforcement and administration of the law, and to the treatment given the offender. If crime had no social reality, there would be no reaction to it. On the other hand, the reactions to crime shape a social reality for it. As people react to crime, they develop patterns for their future responses.

Social Reactions

Personal responses to crime are often spontaneous, but reaction to it always takes place in a social and cultural context. That is to say, the social reaction is socially structured and is patterned according to a system of norms. All societies have *reactive* norms that prescribe the reactions appropriate for particular situations and specify how and by whom the reactions are to be administered.[1] For many human activities both *legal* and *extralegal* reactions are prescribed. The violation of a criminal law is accompanied by appropriate formal sanctions, which are, in turn, administered through procedures established by law. The same violation is likewise subject to extralegal sanctions, including such public reactions as stigmatizing the offender and denying employment.[2] Moreover, social reactions are normatively patterned according to such contingencies as the type of offense, the offender's personal and social characteristics, the social location of the offense, and the degree to which it violates other social norms. All these affect the manner and the regularity with which reactions (both legal and extralegal) will be practiced. Thus, social reactions, like all other forms of behavior, are to be understood according to their social patterning and cultural regulation.

The reactive norms in any society may vary from one group to another. Extralegal prescriptions, in particular, vary throughout a population according to such social characteristics as the age, sex, ethnicity, religion, and social class of the reactors.[3] Among the legal reactions are specific prescriptions in the criminal codes of the political units. But the legal codes provide alternative reactions for any offense. Because of the latitude the prescriptions cover, the patterns of legal reaction differ in each kind of criminal case in the types of sanctions utilized and the consistency with which the reactions are imposed and administered. Social reactions, whether legal or extralegal, are not socially monolithic in either their cultural prescription or their actual patterning. Variations in social reactions are to be sought and explained as reflecting society's organization.

For the individual, responses to crime are influenced by *knowledge* about crime and *perceptions* about what it means. People's attitudes toward criminal behavior, law enforcement, and the handling of offenders are affected by the kinds and amounts of knowledge they have about these matters and about the existence and substance of laws in the society.[4] Reaction to all that is associated with crime initially rests upon knowledge about crime, and perception of the crime phenomenon underlies any social reaction to crime. How you perceive crime gives you a framework for understanding and subsequently reacting to crime.

> Attitudes to crime and criminals then, vary, not so much in terms of the intrinsic nature of the criminal act, but in terms of the likelihood of the act being an established part of the observer's own social world. Crime is in the last analysis what the other person does. What I do, if it is against the law, is susceptible to redefinition through rationalization. Even if the observer is unlikely to commit the particular crime in question, his attitude to it will be conditioned by a degree of modification which may result in either a lenient tolerance or a punitive rejection, depending upon how far the crime threatens the observer, or the group to which they all belong.[5]

Perception precedes a response of any kind.

Today's social reactions must be considered within a cultural framework developed *historically*. With this in mind, it has been suggested that the Puritan image of deviation is still reflected in many of our modern reactions to crime.[6] For the Puritans in Massachusetts Bay Colony, crime was an act against the symmetry and orderliness of nature itself. The criminal, in keeping with the Puritans' theo-

logical doctrine, was relegated to the permanent misfits who were predestined to oppose the social order by engaging in unacceptable activities. The Puritans developed a "deployment pattern" toward crime and deviance:

> To characterize the New England deployment pattern in a word, we may say (1) that the Puritans saw deviant behavior as the special property of a particular class of people who were more or less frozen into deviant attitudes; and (2) that they generally thought it best to handle the problem by locking these people into fairly permanent deviant roles. Puritan theories of human development began with the assumption that men do not change a great deal as they mature or are exposed to different life experiences, and in this sense the settlers of the Bay had little faith in the promise that men might "reform" or overcome any pronounced deviant leanings. A person's character, like his social estate, is fixed by the preordained pattern of human history, and if he should somehow indicate by his surly manners and delinquent ways that he is not a very promising candidate for conversion, the community was not apt to waste many of its energies trying to change him or mend his character. In a very real sense, he belonged to a deviant "class" and was not expected to improve upon that condition.[7]

The Puritan heritage is still very much a part of our public and legal reaction to crime. Our image of the criminal is framed by belief in irreversible human nature. Strengthened by positivistic assumptions in our criminology, in our social reactions we place the criminal in a special class.

> Now, as then, we leave few return routes open to people who try to resume a normal social life after a period of time spent on the community's boundaries, because most of us feel that anyone who skids off into the more severe forms of aberrant expression is displaying a serious defect of character, a deep blemish which cannot easily be erased. We may learn to think of such people as "sick" rather than "reprobate," but a single logic governs both of these labels, for they imply that nothing less than an important change of heart, a spiritual conversion or a clinical cure, can eliminate that inner seed which leads one to behave in a deviant fashion.[8]

DOCUMENT

NATIONAL POLL

What Are the Main Reasons Why People Become Criminals?

	Total[a]	Negro	White
Parents too lax	59%	35%	63%
Environments are bad	16	19	16
Poverty	16	25	14
Unemployment	12	21	11
Lack of education	12	18	11
Young people have no morals	12	9	12
Alcohol	10	18	9
Drugs — narcotics	10	9	10
Broken homes	9	7	10
Not enough recreation for young	9	8	10
For kicks	9	13	8
People have too much, spoiled	7	4	8
Too many on welfare	7	13	6
Lack of religion	7	8	7
Courts too lenient — don't prevent crimes	5	1	5
Time of unrest	4	5	4
Kids see violence on TV	4	2	4
Mentally ill	3	1	3
Too many restrictions on police	3	—	3
Other	8	7	8
Not sure	3	5	3

[a] Figures add to more than 100 per cent as some respondents gave more than one answer.
Source: From Louis Harris and Associates, *The Public Looks at Crime and Corrections* (Washington, D.C.: Joint Commission on Correctional Manpower and Training, 1968), p. 5.

Diffusing the Ideology of Crime

Once a society has a general criminal ideology, conceptions of crime are diffused throughout the population. The *diffusion* of these conceptions simultaneously involves *constructing* conceptions of crime among individuals and groups, which is accomplished in a number of ways. All the means that facilitate construction of conceptions, however, are mediated by the social context of diffusion and by the interpersonal relations associated with adopting the conceptions of crime.

Among the most important agents in diffusing the conceptions of crime are the media of mass communication. Crime coverage in the newspapers, television, and movies affects our estimate about frequency of crime as well as the interpretations we attach to crime. Research has shown that newspapers present a special reality for crime. In one study, it was found that the amount of crime news in each of four Colorado newspapers varied independently of the amount of crime in the state as reflected by crime statistics.[9] Persons were then asked, in a public opinion poll, to estimate the amount of crime in the state. The results indicated that public opinion about crime reflected trends in the amount of crime news rather than the actual crime rates. Coverage of crime in the newspapers created a conceptual reality meaningful to the public in spite of any other social reality of crime.

The style and content in much of the media

present a continual preoccupation with crime. For the many who find this sort of coverage to their liking, the real world is a selective one, a crime-centered one. Not only is their attention focused on crime, but its sensational and adventuresome aspects are portrayed. The routineness in most crimes is neglected. Coverage of crime in the mass media, therefore, is selective and also distorts the everyday world of crime. Such is the stuff from which reality worlds are constructed for much of the population.

The effects caused by this kind of coverage in the mass media have inspired much speculation and research.[10] Many educators, social observers, and parents have worried about the effects that depiction of crime and violence in the media might have. As the mass media presents it, crime affects the recipient's attitudes and behavior. Sometimes people are "tried" by the press before their cases are decided in a court of law.[11] But the relationship between exposure to media and the attitudes and behaviors of persons is important in that public conceptions of crime are created in part by its images in the mass media. Also, this relationship must be examined along with social context and interpersonal relations, which are mediating forces.

Recent research on mass communications confirms that the possible effects of the mass media are mediated by interpersonal networks of communication and by such contextual matters as integration in social groups and membership in various kinds of groups.[12] Personal social contacts influence one's interpretation of the media's contents. Moreover, mass communication, working through mediators, reinforces our conceptions. The social effect of exposure to mass media, therefore, influences the portrayal of crime in mass communication.

Exposure to such images affects individuals differently according to their experiences and their present associations. People involved in criminally defined activity are more likely to be influenced by crime portrayals than those not so involved.[13] More subtly, however, exposure to crime in the mass media may not be significantly effective until a personal problem or a social condition presents itself. Exposure in the past may furnish a future alternative for action.

Certainly we can argue convincingly that mass communications are socially mediated. Nevertheless, there would be nothing to mediate if an image did not appear in the mass media in the first place. Mass communications *do* make a difference. My argument, reinterpreting the thesis on the effects of the mass media, is that a specific kind of crime coverage in the media provides the source for building criminal conceptions. A conception of crime is presented in the mass media; that conception, diffused throughout the society, becomes the basis for the public's view of reality. Not only is a symbolic environment created within the society, but personal actions take their reference from that environment. Indeed, the construction of a conceptual reality is also the creation of a social reality of actions and events.

The media presentations about crime, whether as fiction or reality, are ultimately based on a general acceptance of the prevailing social and economic order.[14] And on such a basis the portrayals of crime and crime-fighting inevitably adhere to the legal system and the need to control crime. Crime as we see it in the media is a threat to the American Way of Life, and the state's right to intervene in controlling crime is presented as the only legitimate reality. This is the ideology presented by officials when they appear in the media and this is the message in the fictional accounts of crime and the law. The ideology and the reality they communicate maintain the established order.

Social Types in the World of Crime

All the nuances of crime cannot be exactly communicated. In communication, images must be simplified, sharpened, and reduced to their essentials. To make conceptions of crime easier to diffuse, *stereotypes* of crime and criminals are created. Offenders are grouped by the public into such categories as the thief, the burglar, the robber, the sex offender, and the murderer, furnishing the boundaries for the public's view of crime.

With these stereotypes, people construct their conceptual realities of crime, and the criminal becomes a *social type*.[15] As a social type, "the criminal" can be understood by the observer as one who has attributes believed to characterize a class of people. The criminal, as socially typed, is a construct incorporating a description of what such people are like, why they act as they do, and how they should act in the future. All that is associated with crime can be categorized by the public.

We have some systematic evidence on public stereotyping of criminals. In a series of pilot studies the extent and nature of stereotyped images of deviants were investigated.[16] The researcher found, first, public stereotypes for such deviant categories as homosexuals, drug addicts, prostitutes, murderers, and juvenile delinquents. It was then determined that people also consistently portray each type of deviant in a specific way. Homosexuals were likely to be described as sexually abnormal, perverted, mentally ill, and maladjusted, whereas marijuana smokers were characterized as persons looking for kicks, escapists, insecure, lacking self-control, and frustrated. It was concluded that "discernible stereotypes of at least several kinds of deviants do exist in our society and that there is a fair amount of agreement on the content of these stereotypes."[17] Imputed deviance, including deviance that may also be criminally defined, is publicly stereotyped. These stereotypes of human behavior are structured and patterned in society.

The category "criminal" has its own stereotyped characteristics. According to public conception, the criminal is a social type. The principal model for the type is the *villain*, who is feared, hated, and ridiculed. The criminal is generally the "bad guy" in popular conception. Criminals are the enemies of law and order (desperadoes, rebels, flouters, rogues, troublemakers), villainous strangers (intruders, suspicious isolates, monsters), disloyal and underhanded types (renegades, traitors, deceivers, sneak-attackers, chiselers, shirkers, corrupters), or are among the miscellaneous social undesirables (vagrants, derelicts, convicts, outcasts).[18] Such villains are with us in popular conception, nominally as criminals, covering a multitude of sins.

But the criminal as a social type incorporates more than the image of villain. He may also be cast as *hero*. Notorious outlaws are an example:

Billy the Kid did not make a good villain because he was blonde, blue-eyed, well built, and rather handsome; women fell for him. He was brave and a square shooter. Such discrepancies in the character of a bad man made him resemble others (Robin Hood, Don Juan, François Villon, Pancho Villa), who perhaps should have been villains but were not.[19]

The villainous criminal is often a popular favorite of heroic proportions.

A major reason for the ambiguity between villainous and heroic criminal conceptions is that they support similar value themes. Both types depend upon aggressiveness, cleverness, and the ability to "outdo" others in some way.

Not only in fiction but in real life confusion between good guys and bad guys occurs. Since Edwin H. Sutherland's epochal studies, Americans have gotten rather used to the idea that a whitecollar criminal looks very like an honest businessman. Expense account chiseling, kickbacks, payoffs, tax evasion, even a little fraud or larceny, may be all in a day's work. If the old distinction between honesty and dishonesty has become blurred, no less has the quaint notion that "crime does not pay" (if you want to get a laugh from an audience, just smile when you say this). When the Brinks Express robbers were caught a few years back, a housewife remarked, "I was kind of sad. It seemed a shame, when they had only a few days to go before the statute of limitations would have let them keep all that money." A strange kind of casting is occurring today — good guys do not have to live up to codes, bad guys do not have to be caught and punished (especially if they look enough like good guys); it may be that the distinction is ceasing to be important.[20]

With a bit more humor, Mark Twain observed the same American tendency to respect that which is also regarded as criminal:

And he grew up and married and raised a large family, and brained them all with an ax one night, and got wealthy by all manner of cheating and rascality; and now he is the infernalest wickedest scoundrel in his native village, and is universally respected, and belongs to the legislature.[21]

The ambiguous reaction to crime can be traced in part to the tradition of the *romantic outlaw*. Tales of the maverick who defied the law are everywhere.

Even today annual celebrations are devoted to Jesse James at Northfield, Minnesota (because he happened to ride through and rob a bank there), and to Wild Bill Hickok at Deadwood, South Dakota. Were a proposal made to abolish the outlaw tradition, there would probably be a storm of protest from movie-makers, writers, and the public. Crooks like John Dillinger, the "Yellow Kid" Weil, and Al Capone, get wrapped in glamor, even outlaws from other countries, such as Pancho Villa, who, in spite of train robberies and murders, became as much of a celebrity in America as Buffalo Bill; reporters stayed with his staff to tell of the women he kidnapped or how he ordered a thousand-dollar bathtub from a firm in Chicago.[22]

Certainly the romantic outlaw is more than villain. He is also something else — "too good to be a villain, too bad to be a hero, too serious to be a mere clown, too interesting to forget."[23]

Perhaps some criminals capture the modern imagination as *antiheroes*, representing the attempt to make it outside the system. Inevitable failure gives charisma to the antihero's noble attempt. And, along the way, such a criminal is likely to assist those who are made to fail in other ways because of the system. Woody Guthrie had Pretty Boy Floyd singing in Shawnee, Oklahoma:

> You say that I'm an outlaw
> You say that I'm a thief
> Here's a Christmas dinner
> For the families on relief

Then adding:

> Now as through this world I ramble
> I see lots of funny men
> Some will rob you with a six gun
> And some with a fountain pen.
>   But as through your life you roam
>   You won't never see an outlaw
>   Drive a family from their home.[24]*

Criminals are not the only social types that fill the public world of crime. Also included are the types associated with criminals. Policemen, lawyers, and detectives have become socially typed in all the forms of communication. The detective, in particular, has had a great deal of characterizing in the mystery novel. Edgar Allan Poe, interested in unraveling puzzles by reasoning, wrote a number of stories in which the detective had the dominant role. In 1852 Charles Dickens introduced readers of *Bleak House* to a Scotland Yard detective, Inspector Bucket. But it was not until Arthur Conan Doyle introduced Sherlock Holmes to the public in "A Study in Scarlet" in the 1880s that the detective story became a public favorite. He was not only a "consulting detective," but a cultured gentleman who transcended the law with his own code of right and wrong. In the world of Holmes the business of upholding the right fell upon the shoulders of private men rather than public officials.[25] Holmes was always, morally and scientifically, beyond the reach of Inspector Lestrade of Scotland Yard.

The crime-fighting heroes of today display virtues for another age, and are more likely to be found in suspense and science fiction stories than in detective stories.[26] The "private eye," such as Dashiell Hammett's Sam Spade or Raymond Chandler's Philip Marlowe, is a tough guy, cynical, hard-boiled, and hard-drinking, at war with criminals in his *own* way, often outside the law. Mickey Spillane's Mike Hammer killed numerous innocent people in his pursuits against crime. But perhaps James Bond of Ian Fleming's novels best presents the modern figure in a world of crime. As a secret agent, Bond is licensed to kill, and with great finesse. He is talented also as a lover, a sportsman (who cheats), and a connoisseur of fashionable luxuries. Ian Fleming symbolizes something that appeals to many men.

What he offers his readers is the beguiling modern dream of a life of total self-sufficiency and sophisticated self-indulgence. Solitary, composed, self-assured, acting with ritualistic deliberation and meeting his trials single-handedly and resourcefully, Bond is an existential deep-sea diver. In his casual moments (enjoying a good meal or an evening with a lovely woman) he projects the satisfaction of feeling cool and superior; at critical times he demonstrates the capacity of the lone individual to pull through unaided. His only use for society is as a hospital, where he can recoup his strength for the next plunge into the void.[27]

Images such as these have been presented to a wide audience by television and the movies as well as by fictional literature. Detective heroes have been portrayed in leading roles as "smarter than the cops, craftier than the crooks, too quick to be caught and domesticated by the classiest doll."[28] And we have been presented with the shadowy figure of Perry Mason, a lawyer who behaves like a private detective in preparing his cases. The list need not be extended; the world of crime is readily before us for the taking. The world of fiction is also the world of reality. Fiction is fact when it is believed and taken as the object of action. When criminals and their counterparts are characterized in a particular way, they are already becoming social types that find their fulfillment in society. Social reality begins in the imagination.

Periodic Investigations

Sporadically, the public is made dramatically aware of the crime problem. The alarm fluctuates from one period to another, each providing in a new "crime wave."[29] How and why are these waves manufactured? The answer can be found in part in the interests that have something to gain from constructing a reality that includes an aroused fear and anxiety about crime.

Concerted efforts to increase public concern about crime are often managed by appointing committees to investigate what someone feels is the current crime problem. Crusades on crime have been organized explicitly to promote a criminal conception. Realities of crime are shaped by such periodic investigations of crime.

Many crime commissions have been organized in communities in the last fifty years to investigate that which some leaders saw as the local crime problem. In 1920, civic groups in Cleveland (headed by the Cleveland Bar Asso-

ciation) commissioned a survey of crime. The report concentrated on the machinery of criminal justice.[30] At about the same time the Chicago Crime Commission was established in response to a sensational case in which a four-man gang killed two armed guards carrying a factory payroll. The Chicago Crime Commission exists to this day, looking into crime and criminal justice. Other cities, both in the past and recently, have established commissions to investigate aspects of the crime problem.[31]

New York has been the setting for innumerable criminal investigations. One of the earliest organizations was the Society for the Prevention of Crime, started in 1878; it brewed a religious fervor under its leader, the Reverend Charles Henry Parkhurst. In the twenties, when a crime wave was the principal topic of conversation, the society engaged the public by sponsoring an essay contest on how best to reduce crime. Professor Franklin H. Giddings and a panel of prominent citizens awarded the first prize of $2,500 to a former police captain and the second prize of $500 to a police detective. The proposals to curb crime included a criticism of the police commissioner, a recommendation that parole be eliminated, and the suggestion that the heads of prisoners be shaved and that they wear striped uniforms.

Committees and citizens' groups then concentrated on specific forms of crime and deviance in New York, especially prostitution and organized crime. Criminal justice in the city received attention in the thirties when the Appellate Court appointed the Seabury Commission. Quite a lot of graft and corruption in the city government were exposed, but city officials, as could be expected, denounced and then ignored the investigation. Characteristically, Mayor Jimmy Walker responded by condemning those who called for further investigations as "slanderers of the fair name of the City we love."[32]

State as well as local crime commissions have been established to investigate the crime problem. In 1925 the Missouri Bar Association called a meeting of civic and business leaders to enlist their support for a statewide crime survey. Research covered law enforcement, prosecution, penal sanctions, and corrections.[33] Although recommendations on the criminal justice system were made, few were implemented. The proposals, if they had been instituted, would have destroyed the political machines in the metropolitan areas. Corrupt and inefficient criminal "justice" systems, as well as crime, are not terribly serious when the interests of those who hold political power are at stake.

Similar commissions, with similar results, completed their tasks in other states during this period.[34] The conclusion we can draw from all these efforts is that crime commissions have been appointed primarily for political reasons. Politicians would like to give their constituents the idea that something is being done about crime. But when the commissions' recommendations go against the politicians' interests, legislation is more likely to be restricted to controlling "the criminal" than to reforming the criminal justice system. Yet, everyone can be happy with the results of a criminal investigation. Civic, business, and professional groups have been active; the researchers have carried out their study; politicians have fought crime without upsetting the political apparatus; and nothing has changed. All has been accomplished by appointing a crime commission.[35]

Until recent times, the major experiment with a crime investigation on the national level was the Wickersham Commission, formally titled the National Commission on Law Observation and Enforcement. Chaired by former United States Attorney General George W. Wickersham, it was established by an act of Congress in 1929. From the beginning, it fulfilled a campaign promise by Herbert Hoover to conduct a thorough inquiry into the enforcement of the prohibition laws.

Things had been going rather badly for the prohibition laws — they seemed to be unenforceable, and the lack of enforcement was making a mockery of the American legal system. In response, the commission, with a large staff of researchers, assistants, and writers, completed an impressive report that ran to fifteen volumes.[36] The material extended beyond enforcing prohibition laws to the causes of crime, crime among the foreign born, child offenders, criminal statistics, the costs of crime, criminal courts, deportation, criminal procedure, and penal institutions.

The commission's recommendations on its primary subject, enforcing prohibition laws, were confusing and contradictory, indicating its desire to satisfy opposing interests. The federal government could rest with the satisfaction that it found no recommendations for repealing the prohibition laws, but the public was told that the laws were unenforceable. Prohibition soon ended nevertheless, out of its own exhaustion.

Today it is commonplace to condemn the Wickersham Commission as ineffectual and to bemoan the lack of significant legislation and reform resulting from its work. Its immediate significance, though, was considerable, for it provided a forum for the clashing political, intellectual, and philosophical positions on crime and justice in America. That was no mean accomplishment, because such conflicts usually remain blurred and disguised from public view.

Crime commissions of the past left no lasting results because of factors that are now changing. The more recent commissions are closely tied to the society's power structure and have large technical staffs, representing the most respected institutions. Organized along bureaucratic lines, they have some permanence and continuity, and a possibility for implementing their proposals. Their activities are also made known to most of the public. Through mass communication, we are all being presented with the image that crime is a national problem. The whole population is alerted to a social reality of crime that is being constructed by government-appointed commissions.

The President's Crime Commission

On March 9, 1966, Lyndon Johnson told the nation:

> The problems of crime bring us together. Even as we join in common action, we know there can be no instant victory. Ancient evils do not yield to easy conquest. We cannot limit our efforts to enemies we can see. We must, with equal resolve, seek out new knowledge, new techniques, and new understanding.[37]

Johnson's resolve in the "war on crime" had been confirmed less than a year before (July

23, 1965) in signing an executive order that established the President's Commission on Law Enforcement and Administration of Justice.

The President's Crime Commission was composed of 19 commissioners, 63 staff members, 175 consultants, and hundreds of advisors. During the investigation, it called three national conferences, conducted five national surveys, held hundreds of meetings, and interviewed tens of thousands. A number of publications came from the commission and its staff. Several task force reports were made on specific subjects and field surveys reported the research findings. The investigation is summarized in the volume *The Challenge of Crime in a Free Society*.[38] The general report also contains the commission's recommendations — more than 200 specific proposals.

The appointment of the commission was an expedient political move.[39] During the presidential campaign of the previous year, Barry Goldwater had campaigned on the theme of "lawlessness." Although he lost the election, the theme became ingrained in the public's reality of crime. President Johnson, recognizing the fears upon which the theme of "lawlessness" played, reacted by organizing something very American: a commission that would identify a broad evil, a thorough study of that problem, and proposals that would offend no one. A "war on crime" would also divert the public's attention from a nasty and unpopular war abroad to a common evil at home.

The commission was composed of "men and women of distinction," most of them ignorant of the problem they were supposed to analyze. All the commissioners, however, had a vested interest in analyzing the crime problem. In typical consensus style, the commission was a careful balance of recognized constituencies: members from the law-enforcement establishment, lawyers, judges, the mayor of New York, a publisher, a university president, a couple of law professors, a civil-rights leader, a woman attorney, and the President of the League of Women Voters. Although the group covered a range of opinion about crime, the report was noncontroversial and clearly within the bounds of the established political and legal order.

The commission's recommendations reflect the "liberal" thinking of the time, and are related to its conclusion that crime can be reduced by "vigorously" pursuing these objectives:

First, society must seek to prevent crime before it happens by assuring all Americans a stake in the benefits and responsibilities of American life, by strengthening law enforcement, and by reducing criminal opportunities.

Second, society's aim of reducing crime would be better served if the system of criminal justice developed a far broader range of techniques with which to deal with individual offenders.

Third, the system of criminal justice must eliminate existing injustices if it is to achieve its ideals and win the respect and cooperation of all citizens.

Fourth, the system of criminal justice must attract more people and better people — police, prosecutors, judges, defense attorneys, probation and parole officers, and corrections officials with more knowledge, expertise, initiative, and integrity.

Fifth, there must be much more operational and basic research into the problems of crime and criminal administration, by those within and without the system of criminal justice.

Sixth, the police, courts, and correctional agencies must be given substantially greater amounts of money if they are to improve their ability to control crime.

Seventh, individual citizens, civic and business organizations, religious institutions, and all levels of government must take responsibility for planning and implementing the changes that must be made in the criminal justice system if crime is to be reduced.[40]

By spending enough energy and money, the commission reasoned, crime can be abolished without significantly altering American institutions.

Certainly the President's Crime Commission did not suggest major changes in the legal system. It expected the causes of crime to be found in the nature of individuals ("criminals") and in social conditions. That criminal law is itself the "cause" of crime was not considered. No assessment was offered for using the criminal law as a sanction for human behavior.[41] The criminal law as a force in defining and perpetuating crime was not conceived of as part of the crime problem's reality. Crime is not that which the law defines as criminal, but an evil that exists in spite of the law. Such evil, according to the President's Commission, can be eradicated in an ultimate victory over crime.

The President's Crime Commission has thus provided us with a particular conception of the reality of crime. The war on crime has become a political weapon to accomplish the objectives of those in positions of power. Moreover, the criminal reality that is being constructed for us is resulting in a reality of events. Our state of mind is leading to a particular kind of social order. Its implications are beginning to be fully realized today in the United States.

Public Attitudes about Crime

Although crime has been a public concern at other times in American history, it gets unprecedented attention today, and continues unabated — officially and publicly. During the sixties it became the major public issue.

The sharp rise in public attention has two kinds of explanation.[42] First, it is an irrational response by the public to the rapid social changes that have supposedly taken place in the past decade. The second explanation suggests that the public's reaction to crime is justified by the increase in the crime rate. The establishment of the President's Crime Commission in 1965 was justified by these kinds of explanations. And the Crime Commission studied the public's attitude:

> A chief reason that this Commission was organized was that there is widespread public anxiety about crime. In one sense, this entire report is an effort to focus that anxiety on the central problem of crime and criminal justice. A necessary part of that effort has been to study as carefully as possible the anxiety itself.[43]

The President's Crime Commission and the resulting omnibus crime bill were also justified — officially — by the public's uneasiness.

The President's Crime Commission, indeed, found that the public sees crime as one of the most serious domestic problems.[44] In a national survey conducted for the commission by the National Opinion Research Center (NORC),

citizens were asked to choose, from a list of six major domestic problems facing the nation, the one to which they had been paying the most attention recently. Crime was the second most frequently selected problem; only race relations was picked by more people. Most thought crime in their own community was getting worse. By 1972, however, when another national poll asked "What do you regard as your community's worst problem?" crime had become the number one problem.[45]

The *fear* of crime, the commission found, is greatest over personal safety and the theft of private property. Most intense is the fear of being accosted by a stranger on the street or that a stranger will break into the home and attack the person. Although these are the crimes that occur least frequently, fear about them significantly affects people's lives. The commission reported the following:

> Perhaps the most revealing findings on the impact of fear of crime on people's lives were the changes people reported in their regular habits of life. In the high-crime districts surveyed in Boston and Chicago, for example, five out of every eight respondents reported changes in their habits because of fear of crime, some as many as four or five major changes. Forty-three percent reported they stayed off the streets at night altogether. Another 21 percent said they always used cars or taxis at night. Thirty-five percent said they would not talk to strangers any more.[46]

By 1972 the fear of crime had climbed even higher. According to a Gallup poll, 41 per cent of a national sample are afraid to walk at night in their neighborhoods.[47] Nearly six out of ten women interviewed, 58 per cent, said they were afraid to go out alone at night — an increase of 14 per cent from the answer to a similar question asked in 1968. And when all persons interviewed were asked what factor they believe is behind the high crime rate, the greatest portion listed "Laws are too lenient/ penalties not stiff enough." The next most frequent responses were "Drugs/drug addiction," and "Lack of supervision by parents."

Most people today, according to the polls, depend on the police and related agencies for controlling crime, which shows up in the public's generally positive attitude toward the

DOCUMENT_____

THE GALLUP POLL: CRIME IS RATED WORST URBAN PROBLEM

Evidence that fear of crime has pervaded all levels of U.S. society is found in the latest Gallup survey, which shows crime and the crime-related problem of drugs — topping the list of concerns of residents of cities and communities of all sizes across the nation.

In addition, half of all persons interviewed (51 per cent) think there is more crime in the areas where they live than there was a year ago, while only 10 per cent say less. Twenty-seven per cent see little change and 12 per cent do not express an opinion.

A comparison of current survey findings with those recorded in a survey taken a year ago, in early 1972, shows increasing pessimism. At that time, a considerably smaller proportion of citizens (35 per cent) than today said crime was on the increase.

Increased use of drugs and leniency on the part of courts are named most often as reasons explaining the increase in crime. Other reasons named relatively often are that there are too few police to handle the situation, population growth, and the high mobility of people today. Mentioned somewhat less frequently are poor parental guidance, lack of recreational opportunities, and unemployment.

Despite the U.S. Supreme Court's ruling of last year which, in effect, struck down the death penalty, public support for capital punishment is currently at the highest point in nearly two decades.

In a survey conducted in December, a majority of 57 per cent of adults, 18 and older, said they favor the death penalty for persons convicted of murder. This percentage represents an increase in support since March 1972, when 50 per cent favored the death penalty.

The current survey also shows that 21 per cent of Americans, 18 and older, have suffered one or more of the following crimes during the last seven months: breaking and entering, mugging or assault, robbery or burglary, vandalism, or auto theft.

In the case of some of these crimes, however, as many as half of the victims did not report the incident.

The current survey is based on personal interviews with 1,504 adults, 18 and older, in more than 300 localities across the nation, interviewed during the period December 8–11. Following are the questions and results:

What Do You Regard as Your Community's (Your City's) Worst Problem?
(Views of Residents of Cities of 500,000 and Over)

Crime	21%	Poor housing/slums	4%
Transportation/traffic	11	Education and related needs	4
Drugs	10	Sanitation	3
Juvenile delinquency	6	Racial problems	3
High taxes	6	Unemployment	3
Community services	5	Other problems	23
Pollution: air/water	4	No opinion	14
			117%

Total adds to more than 100 per cent since some persons named more than one problem.

Source: From George Gallup, "Crime Is Rated Worst Urban Problem," *The Washington Post,* January 16, 1973, p. A3.

DOCUMENT (Continued)_____

Is There More Crime in This Area than There Was a Year Ago, or Less?

	More %	Less %	Same %	No opinion %
National	51	10	27	12
Men	47	11	31	11
Women	54	9	24	13
Whites	51	9	28	12
Non-whites	48	22	18	12
East	48	8	29	15
Mideast	48	11	31	10
South	54	11	23	12
West	55	8	26	11
Center city areas	60	9	19	12
Suburban areas	50	9	28	12
Smaller communities/rural	45	10	32	13

All persons in the survey who said there is more crime in their communities now than a year ago (51 per cent) were then asked this question:

How Do You Account for This?

Increased use of drugs	13%
Courts too lenient	11
Not enough police	7
Population growth/mobility	7
Poor parental influence	5
Unemployment	3
Lack of recreational facilities	3
Other reasons	15
	64%

Total exceeds 51 per cent (total who said crime has increased) since some persons gave more than one reason.

To determine attitudes toward the courts, this question was asked:

In General, Do You Think the Courts in This Area Deal Too Harshly or Not Harshly Enough with Criminals?

Not harshly enough	74%
About right	13
Too harshly	5
No opinion	8
	100%

police. A Gallup poll in 1967 showed that 77 per cent of the public had a "great deal" of respect for the police, 17 per cent had "some" respect, and only 4 per cent had "hardly any" respect.[48] The national survey in 1965 by the NORC showed that 67 per cent of those interviewed thought the police were doing a good to excellent job of enforcing the law.[49] The findings, however, are qualified by the income, race, and sex of the respondents. It was found in the NORC study that upper income groups are consistently more favorable in their evaluation of the police, that blacks at all income levels have fairly strong negative attitudes toward the police, and that black women are more critical than black men of the job the police are doing. Furthermore, although blacks more than whites feel that the police are not "respectful" to them, persons of both races and sexes feel that the police are not sufficiently respectful.

In spite of the criticism, the public generally relies on the police to control crime, and along with this acceptance (and mandate) it is willing to permit the police to have much freedom in their efforts to control crime. A majority (73 per cent) of those interviewed in Washington, D.C., agreed that the police have the right to act tough when deemed necessary.[50] More than half (56 per cent) thought that police dogs should be used more. In the national survey, 52 per cent of the respondents believed the police should have more power, and 42 per cent believed that police should risk arresting an innocent person rather than risk missing an offender.[51] Yet, the surveys found interest in protecting the individual's civil rights in enforcing the law.

Attitudes about court actions show too that the public believes responsive measures, rather than changes in social conditions, are the most effective way to control crime. A 1973 Gallup survey found that 74 per cent of adults believe that the courts do not deal harshly enough with criminals.[52] Only 5 per cent said the courts in their area deal "too harshly" with criminals, and 13 per cent agreed that treatment by the courts is "about right." Further evidence that the public wants to crack down on crime shows in another poll in which 58 per cent of the respondents agreed that it was a good idea to give a double sentence to anyone who commits a crime with a gun.[53] And 71 per cent of the respondents believed that it is a good idea to deny parole to a person convicted of crime a second time.

Surveys continue to show a pattern of attitudes on punishing specific offenses. In a national survey conducted in 1967, the public was asked the best way of dealing with an adult convicted of a specific crime.[54] The alternative sentences, from a list of seven crimes ranging from embezzlement to murder, were probation, a short prison sentence with parole, or a long prison sentence. Probation found little favor with the public. Considering each of the crimes, only about a quarter of the respondents felt that probation was an appropriate sentence. Only for prostitution, judged more harshly by women than men, did as much as 26 per cent of the public feel probation should be used. A further breakdown by education showed an increasingly severe attitude as the amount of education decreased. That is, those with less than a high school education were the most willing to have someone sent to prison.[55]

A similar pattern appears in a national survey with questions on prisons and corrections.[56] More than half the adults polled felt that the prison system was doing a good job in helping to deal with the problem of crime. (The more education the participant had, the less likely he was to give the prison a positive rating.) But though the majority of the respondents believed in the prison's worth as a form of punishment, an even larger proportion (72 per cent) felt that rehabilitation should be the main emphasis within the prison. The respondents showed little interest (only 20 per cent) in using parole more often to release inmates from prison.

Another consideration in public attitudes toward the control of crime is the death penalty. Changes in attitude toward capital punishment are among the most sensitive indicators of shifts in the public's feelings about crime control. There has been a gradual shift from a punitive reaction to one that is less oriented to punishment. Since 1953 Gallup has been polling the American public on capital punishment, asking: "Are you in favor of the death penalty for persons convicted of murder?"[57] In the 1953 survey, 68 per cent of the

DOCUMENT

NATIONAL POLL OF PUBLIC ATTITUDES TOWARD CRIME CONTROL

How Would You Rate the Job Law Enforcement Officials Are Doing?

	Total adults	Region				Size of place				Race		Total teen-agers
		East	Midwest	South	West	Metro-politan	Suburbs	Town	Rural	Negro	White	
Local officials												
Positive	68%	68%	70%	65%	69%	69%	71%	69%	62%	57%	70%	58%
Negative	32	32	30	35	31	31	29	31	38	43	30	42
(Not sure)	(6)	(6)	(4)	(6)	(7)	(5)	(4)	(7)	(7)	(10)	(5)	(3)
State officials												
Positive	72	71	75	67	74	74	73	74	65	58	74	77
Negative	28	29	25	33	26	26	27	26	35	42	26	23
(Not sure)	(14)	(16)	(13)	(13)	(16)	(21)	(12)	(11)	(10)	(26)	(13)	(9)
Federal officials												
Positive	72	69	72	69	75	70	74	73	66	69	72	72
Negative	28	31	28	31	25	30	26	27	34	31	28	28
(Not sure)	(19)	(16)	(18)	(21)	(21)	(20)	(16)	(17)	(22)	(25)	(18)	(14)

How Have Courts Dealt with Criminals?

	Total adults	Education			Region				Race		Total teen-agers
		8th grade	High school	College	East	Mid-west	South	West	Negro	White	
Too lenient	49%	46%	47%	56%	53%	48%	39%	59%	26%	52%	26%
Too severe	1	1	1	1	2	a	1	1	6	a	3
Some too lenient, some too severe	15	15	16	11	14	18	14	12	26	13	17
Fair	29	30	30	28	25	28	37	26	28	30	49
(Not sure)	(6)	(8)	(6)	(4)	(6)	(6)	(9)	(2)	(14)	(5)	(5)

a Less than 1 per cent.

What Kind of a Job Has the Prison System Done in Helping to Deal with the Problem of Crime?

	Total adults	Education			Race		Total teen-agers
		8th grade	High school	College	Negro	White	
Positive	51%	60%	52%	39%	51%	51%	55%
Negative	49	40	48	61	49	49	45
(Not sure)	(14)	(18)	(13)	(10)	(21)	(13)	(7)

How Successful Have Prisons and Other Correctional Systems Been in Rehabilitating Criminals?

	Total adults	Education			Race		Total teen-agers
		8th grade	High school	College	Negro	White	
Very successful	5%	9%	4%	2%	6%	5%	7%
Somewhat successful	49	45	54	41	38	50	53
Slightly successful	41	41	39	48	42	42	32
Not at all successful	5	5	3	9	14	3	8
(Not sure)	(13)	(24)	(10)	(9)	(22)	(11)	(8)

Source: From Louis Harris and Associates, *The Public Looks at Crime and Corrections* (Washington, D.C.: Joint Commission on Correctional Manpower and Training, 1968), pp. 6–8.

VIEWPOINT_____

CRIME, DELINQUENCY, AND YOU

THE PROBLEM

On any given day, thousands of Americans will be the victims of crime. Their homes will be burglarized, their cars stolen, their property vandalized and, too often, some will be the victims of violence.

This is the fate of Americans in the suburbs, in big cities, on fashionable avenues, and in the slums. Crime is present everywhere and it is growing daily.

Citizens are understandably fearful. People hesitate to go to a park after nightfall. Women venture on lonely streets with apprehension. Store owners have seen their places of business burglarized again and again.

Youngsters from affluent suburbs as well as the core city frequently tangle with the police. Delinquency knows no boundaries.

ACTION IS NEEDED

The problem will surely grow — as it has each year — if something is not done. People search for an answer and ask, "What can the individual citizen do"?

Officials have stated that the police, the courts and the correctional agencies, acting alone, cannot control the problem. Crime and delinquency *can* be reduced when each citizen recognizes that it is his problem, too, and when he becomes personally involved in the struggle. In fact, it is maintained that the *only* answer to reducing crime significantly is *vigorous citizen action*.

The citizen can and must do his share in halting the growth of crime if we are to preserve our American way of life.

HERE'S WHAT YOU CAN DO

1. Let's Start with the Youngsters. Do the schools in your community have an anti-delinquency program — one which spells out what delinquency is and its consequences can be? Call your Junior High School or High School principal and find out.

The school is critically important in preventing delinquency now and forming good citizens for the future. NCCD's widely-endorsed "You and the Law" program is used in civics and social studies classes throughout the country. Write for a free copy. *Ask your principal or your school board to establish an anti-delinquency program in your school.*

Children sometimes need help. Teachers can spot children headed for trouble — even in the earliest grades. Does your school system have trained social workers available to help parents or teachers deal with a behavior problem? Skilled help given early can prevent delinquency. *Ask your superintendent to make social work assistance available when needed.*

2. Personal Conduct Is Important. Private citizens must cooperate with the law. If you see a crime, report it promptly. Likelihood of discovery and conviction is a deterrent to delinquency and crime.

If you are called for jury duty, serve willingly. It is a priceless democratic privilege.

If you are asked to testify in court, do so, even if it is an inconvenience. You would want a witness, too, if it were your case.

_____

Source: From "Crime, Delinquency and You," a pamphlet, produced in cooperation with the Kemper Insurance Company (Hackensack, N.J.: National Council on Crime and Delinquency, n.d.).

VIEWPOINT (Continued)_____

In brief, support our system of justice. It can't work well without your co-operation.

Protect yourself! Don't make it easy for the burglar. Simple, sensible steps can be taken to safeguard your home, your apartment, your car. All too often, the unthinking homeowner contributes to crime through careless practices. *For good advice, request NCCD's free leaflet on "How to Protect Your Home."*

Do you unwittingly break the law? Don't gamble illegally. A seemingly innocent illegal two-dollar bet of a 50¢ policy ticket is the lifeblood of the organized crime syndicate. Gambling profits finance other forms of organized crime. *You can cripple the syndicate by not gambling illegally. You can cripple law enforcement, government and society itself by patronizing illegal gambling.*

3. A Well-run Community Is Your Best Insurance. Demand modern police protection, effective courts, and correctional services. Your community's crime control system must be well trained, well equipped, and well paid. It must be free from politics. The voter and tax-payer can achieve this. Do not vote into office politicians who have visible links with crime. *Exercise vigilance over your elected officials through non-partisan community-oriented groups.*

Most Americans belong to one or more organizations — Kiwanis, Rotary, PTA's, Chambers of Commerce, Women's Clubs, etc. Such organizations can and do undertake specific projects aimed at community betterment. They can help local crime control efforts. *Use your community organizations to combat crime.*

WHAT CAN YOUR ORGANIZATION DO?

The range of possibilities for organized citizen action is very wide. Here are just a few of the possibilities:

Is there an institution in your community — a detention home, jail, city or county penitentiary or farm? Often inmates are handicapped by illiteracy and this prevents them from getting and holding down worthwhile jobs after release. *Ask your organization to undertake a literacy project.*

Almost any civic organization can help by opening up job opportunities for released offenders and parolees. A civic group can induce local industry to provide special in-plant training for the youth and young offender who lacks good work habits and has limited job skills. *Ask your court-connected probation department for advice on specific help needed.*

Is your police department one of many which have established reserve or volunteer programs? Such programs free police to serve in prevention and detection work. Volunteers aid the police in rescue work, traffic control, crowd control (parades), clerical functions, interpreters and many other non-dangerous but useful assignments. *Ask your police department how members of your organization can help them.*

Youngsters who drop out of school often become delinquent. Can your organization establish a tutoring and guidance program to prevent youngsters in early grades from becoming educationally retarded and frustrated — help keep them in school until they are graduated. This is worthy work. *Call the superintendent of school for information on how your group can serve.*

Many a young boy or girl who has had a grim and neglected childhood winds up in court. At some point, they may need the morale building friendship of kindly adults. Your organization doubtless has some members who can supply the warm friendship that a neglected or delinquent youngster needs. *Call the*

VIEWPOINT (Continued)_____

*chief probation officer at your local Family or Juvenile Court for information on
how you or your organization can help.*

*There are other possibilities for organizational efforts to control crime. Write
NCCD for information on these and additional projects.*

The National Council on Crime and Delinquency is the only national voluntary,
non-profit organization which combines professional expertise and citizen action
to foster better crime-control programs.

Established in 1907, NCCD provides consultation and guidance to federal, state
and local governments. It sponsors much-needed research. Its citizen-action
councils in 18 states are active, well-directed forces for crime reduction whose
success has been widely acclaimed. Thousands of Americans are now participating
in NCCD programs.

The problem of fighting crime, however, is awesomely large and difficult. We
urge you to help NCCD by contributing to and supporting its programs. . . .

---

sample favored the death penalty; by 1960
the proportion had shifted to 51 per cent; by
1965 it had decreased to 45 per cent; by 1966,
42 per cent were for it and 47 per cent against
it.

But then, a reversal in this trend appeared.
A Gallup survey in March 1972 found 50 per
cent in favor and 41 per cent against the death
penalty. And the trend picked up even greater
speed: by the end of 1972, 57 per cent approved of executions, with only 32 per cent
against them.[58] A breakdown of the figures
shows that most people in small towns and in
big cities, under 30 years of age and over,
college-educated and not, all support the death
penalty. The exception to this trend: nonwhites are against the death penalty, with 53
per cent against it.

There is no need to continue citing these
polls and surveys of public attitudes toward
crime and crime control, but these findings do
have to be placed in context with the official
ideology of crime control.[59] The correspondence between public opinion and official
policies is striking. Rather than follow the traditional assumption that official policy reflects
public opinion, I suggest that officials use
public opinion for their own advantage and
that, at the same time, they and others in
power manipulate public opinion to suit the

policies they are establishing. Certainly if public opinion could be freed from official interests, we might find quite different ways of
dealing with social problems. It is to be expected that public opinion and official ideology
are now the same. A critical public intelligence
would spell a different attitude and approach
toward crime and criminal justice.

In other words, public opinion about crime
is conventionally thought to be a major force
in determining criminal policy. But with power
and economics as they are in America, the
opposite is closer to the truth. It is criminal
policy and official ideology that shape public
opinion about crime. And that also means
public opinion is shaped by government officials and powerful people in government and
outside of it. Public attitudes about law and
order are influenced greatly by the statements
and actions of the president, the attorney general, the director of the FBI, the administrator
of the Law Enforcement Assistance Administration (LEAA), executives of large corporations, congressmen, local officials, lawyers of
the American Bar Association, members of
government commissions, and so on. The
public, because of the support the political
system demands, is ready to follow the words
and deeds of government officials and successful professional and business men. Whenever

"responsible" leaders utter words and formulate policies, we are expected to follow. Such is the force of modern government and such is the way in which public opinion is formed.

The Politics of Reality

Conceptions of crime are important because of their consequences, but the conceptions most critical in creating a social reality of crime are those held by the people who impose their views and actions on others in the name of the whole society. The social reality of crime is constructed mainly from the criminal ideology held by the politically, economically, and socially dominant class, whose interests are protected by a particular reality of crime. This is the politics of reality.

The ideology of crime has its own consequences. It gives us a perspective as to what is regarded as crime, how crime should be controlled, how criminals should be punished and treated, and how the population is to conduct itself in an environment with crime and criminals. All these issues are resolved in political actions. As thoughts become deeds, a social reality is constructed.

But the most significant consequence of these conceptions is that they create crime; without that idea, crime would not exist as a phenomenon. It follows that the more people think about crime, the greater is the probability that definitions of crime will be formulated and applied. The concept of crime is continually reified according to the powerful interests.

So it is that crime is billed today as "a threat to the American way of life."[60] We are all told to join the struggle. "What can the individual citizen do?"

There is no end. The ideology and the consequential events go on making the social reality of crime very much a part of the modern world. In constructing this reality, some of the most important problems of modern times are being played out.

15

A Political Economy of Crime

Crime in the United States rests ultimately on a materialistic, objective base. The law that defines behavior as criminal serves the social, economic, and political order, and is used by the state and those who control it to preserve the capitalist system. The underclass, in turn, is defined as criminal as it attempts to survive under that system's oppression, and is continually in revolt against it.

The political economy of crime, beginning with the economics of crime and moving to a radical analysis of that economy, is our final step toward theoretically understanding crime in American society. This critical theory provides us with a perspective for further analyzing crime in this country.

From Economics to Political Economy

The newest theoretical perspective in criminology is used to examine crime as an economic phenomenon. With it, economists are formulating their own explanations of crime and making suggestions for solving the crime problem. An economic analysis of crime using orthodox economics is assured acceptance because it provides for preserving the established order:

> Until very recently, economists generally ignored the field of crime and law enforcement. They now contend, however, that their explanation of criminal behavior is superior to psychological or sociological explanations. The implications of this development for criminologists are profound. For the past generation, economic analyses and predictions on a wide variety of issues have been extremely useful to government policymakers. Furthermore, of all the social scientists, the economists have been most successful in selling the idea that they are the most scientific: their methods of model-building, their adaptations of mathematical and statistical analyses, and their procedures for hypothesis-testing more closely approximate those of the physical sciences, and where they do not, economists design analytic and predictive techniques that facilitate our understanding of how society works and of how government policies should be changed to achieve specific goals. As a result, economic researchers have al-

ways been able to obtain a very large share of foundation grants and government research money.

Academic economists are beginning to swarm into the field of criminology. Their publications and studies on this subject are growing. . . . This means that in the next few years economic studies dealing with criminology will receive a great deal of attention both because of their volume and their novel approach to the field and because many professional criminologists will feel compelled to refute or elaborate on these explanations.[1]

Although the orthodox economic analysis of crime is likely to predominate, it is rivaled by a radical economics of crime. We will look at each form of analysis before presenting a critical theory on the political economy of crime.

Orthodox Economic Analysis of Crime

The orthodox approach begins with the assumption that criminal behavior, like any economic activity, is rational:

A person commits an offense if the expected utility to him exceeds the utility he could get by using his time and other resources at other activities. Some persons become "criminals," therefore, not because their basic motivation differs from that of other persons, but because their benefits and costs differ.[2]

This form of economic analysis also suggests that participation in crime varies directly with its net benefits and inversely with the attractiveness of legitimate activity. Crime is treated as a cost-benefit calculation.

The orthodox economic analysis of crime is directed toward explaining crime with the primary goal of preventing it. Such analyses promise to furnish the knowledge necessary for policies for optimally controlling crime.

By using methods such as cost-benefit analysis, systems analysis, and program budgeting, economists are striving to develop criteria for an improved allocation of resources in law enforcement. For research purposes the economists assume that all divisions of the criminal justice system have one goal: the protection of society. All other presumed goals, such as deterrence, rehabilitation, prevention, punishment, and the law itself, are treated as alternative programs implemented to achieve that goal.[3]

This is the science that will serve the modern capitalist state.

A Radical Economic Analysis

Radical analysis begins with quite different and opposing assumptions. David M. Gordon writes about it:

It presumes, first of all, that the basic structure of social and economic institutions in any society fundamentally shapes the behavior of individuals in that society and, therefore, that one cannot in fact understand the behavior of individuals in a society like the United States without first understanding the structures and biases of the basic "system-defining" institutions in this country. It argues, furthermore, that the "social relations of production" in capitalist societies help define an economic class structure and that one cannot therefore adequately understand the behavior of individuals unless one first examines the structure of institutionally determined opportunities to which members of the respective economic classes are more or less confined. The analysis depends, at another level, on the radical theory of the State, according to which radicals hypothesize that the activities of the State in capitalist societies serve primarily to benefit members of the capitalist class — either directly, by bestowing disproportionate benefits upon them, or indirectly, by helping preserve and solidify the structure of class inequalities upon which capitalists so thoroughly depend. The radical analysis expects, finally, that various social problems in capitalist societies, although they may not have been created by capitalists, cannot easily be solved within the context of capitalist institutions because their solution would tend to disrupt the functioning of the capitalist machine. If the disruptive potential of solutions to such problems therefore inclines the State to postpone solution, one can expect to solve those problems only by changing the power relationships in society so that the State is forced to serve other interests than those of the capitalist class.[4]

VIEWPOINT_____

AN ORTHODOX ECONOMIC ANALYSIS OF CRIME

Adam Smith, Jeremy Bentham, Beccaria-Bonesana, Karl Marx, and William Bonger wrote about economics and crime, but their observations have been largely ignored by recent generations of economists. Before 1968, some academic criminologists in North America and England adapted economic techniques to the study of criminology. This was also true of some civil servants working within various branches of the criminal justice system. But the current interest in the economic approach to criminology began in 1968 with the publication of a major article by Gary S. Becker in the *Journal of Political Economy*.[1] Since then, the stage has been set for a vigorous academic dialogue with far-reaching policy implications. . . .

Becker states that "a useful theory of criminal behavior can dispense with special theories of anomie, psychological inadequacies, or inheritance of special traits and simply extend the economist's usual analysis of choice" and that "the general criterion of social loss is shown to incorporate as special cases, valid under special assumptions, the criteria of vengeance, deterrence, compensation, and rehabilitation that historically have figured so prominently in practice and criminological literature."[2]

Becker is saying that for a broad range of criminals everything we have been told — that they are sick, abnormal, deviant, or deprived — is wrong. Criminals are relatively simple, normal people like the rest of us, and any attempt to treat them as abnormal or deviant or to "rehabilitate" them is doomed to fail.

Traditional explanations of criminality have applied the concepts of depravity, insanity, deviance, abnormality, and deprivation. Economists maintain that criminals are rational and normally calculating people maximizing their preferences subject to given constraints. This is a psychological explanation that economists prefer over nearly all other explanations of criminal behavior.

Economists use the term *opportunity cost* to refer to whatever it is that must be sacrificed to acquire something else. The opportunity cost of war is peace; of the constraints of marriage, the freedoms of being single; of the earnings in one career, the earnings in another; of choosing legally obtained income, obtaining illegal income. In accordance with this reasoning, a heroin addict is no more abnormal or deviant than a nicotine addict. Through a historical accident, the act of possessing heroin has been declared criminal while the act of possessing the dangerous drug nicotine has r ⌐+ The nature of the addictions is not so very different, in that, given our present knowledge, the heroin user is no less rational than the nicotine user. The law has simply driven up the price for the heroin addict's article of consumption, and, as a result, has often forced the addict to resort to illegitimate earnings. Change the law and the behavior of many heroin users would become similar to that of many nicotine addicts. They court death in different ways but otherwise lead normal lives — giving lectures, driving trucks, raising children, running governments — obliviously smoking or shooting away. . . .

To avoid complications, I will restrict the discussion to various forms of theft.

Source: From Richard F. Sullivan, "The Economics of Crime: An Introduction to the Literature," *Crime and Delinquency,* 19 (April 1973), pp. 139–144.

[1] Gary S. Becker, "Crime and Punishment: An Economic Approach," *Journal of Political Economy,* March–April 1968, pp. 169–217.

[2] Becker, supra note 1.

VIEWPOINT (Continued)_____

According to the economic explanation of criminality, the individual calculates (1) all his practical opportunities of earning legitimate income, (2) the amounts of income offered by these opportunities, (3) the amounts of income offered by various illegal methods, (4) the probability of being arrested if he acts illegally, and (5) the probable punishment should he be caught. After making these calculations, he chooses the act or occupation with the highest discounted return. To arrive at a discounted return he must include among his cost calculations the *future costs* of going to prison if he is apprehended. It is in this sense that the criminal is understood to be a normal, rational, calculating individual.

Parents, police, probation and parole officers, and judges are always saying, "If you keep it up, you will end up in jail (or in jail again)." Economists believe that this kind of admonition is irrelevant. The individual knows perfectly well that he will probably end up in jail, but he still reasons that he will be better off than were he to go "straight." He has already calculated the costs and benefits. If he is not caught or sent to jail, so much the better. But even if he pays the cost of a stretch in jail, he is still ahead of the game — according to his own calculations. His calculations are not assumed to be accurate: he may overestimate the income to be received or he may underestimate the costs — just as many graduate students in recent years overestimated the material benefits of graduate study.

The "amateur" criminal who overestimates the pay-off from a certain job or underestimates the probability of being apprehended and thus the cost to himself may be considered "irrational" and short-sighted. Many of the individuals who come through our court systems can be characterized this way. But their miscalculations are no more irrational than those of the consumer who gets too much in debt, the worker who does not save in anticipation of layoffs, the man who squanders a week's pay on a whim, or the businessman who goes bankrupt. In all of these cases, there has been a miscalculation in the discounting of future costs. The basic economic assumption does not maintain that people do not make mistakes but rather that they do their best given their reading of present and future possibilities and given their resources.

Since criminals calculate costs and benefits, the economist concludes that we must increase the cost to them by increasing the probability that they will be caught or by increasing the punishment if they are caught. Most of the evidence so far — if it can be called evidence — seems to indicate that criminals are more responsive to the probability of apprehension than to the extent of the punishment. This is not encouraging since it is highly doubtful that the proportion of solved crimes will dramatically increase given our scarce resources, the state of technology in the field of criminology, and the constraints of the law. . . .

Academic criminologists and practitioners have initiated a strong movement for prison reform. The economic view should reinforce drastic reform of prison-education programs, and it should argue for a social insurance system that would guarantee reimbursement for any financial loss incurred by hiring an ex-convict. This would be a minimal guarantee and there could be many variations on such a scheme.

The economist believes that the criminal is a rational human being making rational choices according to his constraints, opportunities, and preferences. To alter his calculations we must change his opportunities, increase his opportunity costs, and teach him to discount the future more realistically. Consequently, any

VIEWPOINT (Continued)_____

"rehabilitative" program that assumes the criminal is abnormal, deviant, inadequate, irrational, or characterized by anomie is doomed to failure.

   The economist takes tastes and preferences for granted and assumes that an
individual maximizes satisfaction subject to constraints of wealth given his reading
of his opportunities. The non-economist might assert that it is not enough to
change an individual's opportunity costs or to teach him to read or discount his
future costs more realistically; his "tastes" or "preferences" must be changed by
effective programs of "rehabilitation" or "punishment.". . .

We can consider crime in American society
by examining its economic functions in the
capitalist system, as suggested by Karl Marx.[5]
Although Marx never systematically examined
crime, he suggested the ways in which crime
in capitalist countries maintains class relations.
Marx argued: "Crime takes off the labour
market a portion of the excess population,
diminishes competition among workers, and
to a certain extent stops wages from falling
below the minimum, while the war against
crime absorbs another part of the same population."[6] The criminal is therefore a "counter-
weight," balancing the capitalist structure.

   More specifically, the criminal produces
legitimate occupations and work activities in
the society. Marx continues:

The criminal produces the whole apparatus
of the police and criminal justice, detectives,
judges, executioners, juries, etc., and all
these different professions, which constitute
so many categories of the social division of
labour, develop diverse abilities of the human spirit, create new needs and new ways
of satisfying them.[7]

Crime's economic functions are readily apparent in our economy. A great deal of capital,
to begin with, is kept in circulation because of
crime. In 1965, the President's Crime Commission estimated its economic effect at $21 billion
a year. As for the crimes themselves, the
Crime Commission estimated that about $200
million is embezzled from organizations each
year; $1.3 billion is taken by shoplifting; about
$82 million by forgery; income tax evasion is

as high as $40 billion; and more than $600
million is transferred each year by robbery,
burglary, and larceny.[8]

   On top of these figures, we must add the
vast amount of money spent annually on crime
prevention and control. The Crime Commission estimated for the year 1965 that more
than $4 billion of public money would be spent
for law enforcement and the administration of
justice (local, state, and federal) — $2.8 billion
for the police, $782 million for judicial ad-
ministration, and $1 billion for corrections.[9]
Even *before* the war on crime, it was a big and
flourishing business.

   Since the mid-sixties the economic impact of
crime has escalated. By 1970 the Economic
Unit of the business magazine *U.S. News &
World Report* estimated that the "annual
crime burden" on the nation was $51.1 billion
(Figure 15.1). They placed law enforcement
and criminal justice costs at $8.6 billion and
private crime-fighting costs at $5.5 billion.
The magazine characterized the economics of
crime as follows: "Now emerging is a full
accounting of the price that Americans are
paying each year to support one of the nation's
fastest-growing industries."[10]

   The "manpower aspects" of the economics
of crime are obvious in the expenditures for
crime control personnel. A study of these
figures showed that local police departments
increased from 319,000 police employees in
1966 to 365,000 in 1969.[11] If the current trends
of employment continue, it is projected that
by 1975, local police departments will be
employing 560,000 people, including policemen, detectives, and civilian personnel. Ex-

Figure 15.1   Estimates of Economic Impact of Crime per Year (in Billions of Dollars)

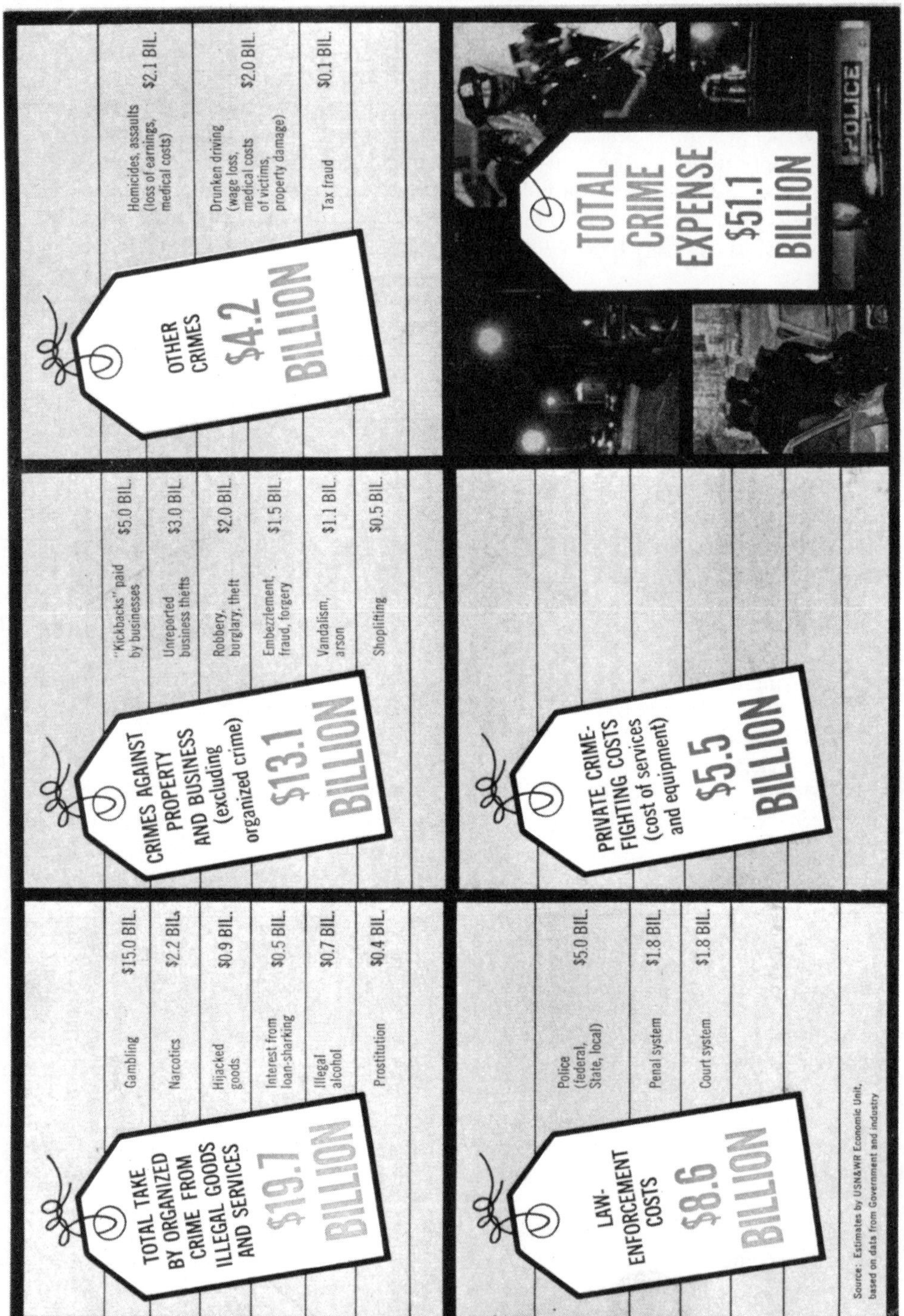

TOTAL TAKE BY ORGANIZED CRIME FROM ILLEGAL GOODS AND SERVICES **$19.7 BILLION**	
Gambling	$15.0 BIL.
Narcotics	$2.2 BIL.
Hijacked goods	$0.9 BIL.
Interest from loan-sharking	$0.5 BIL.
Illegal alcohol	$0.7 BIL.
Prostitution	$0.4 BIL.

CRIMES AGAINST PROPERTY AND BUSINESS (excluding organized crime) **$13.1 BILLION**	
"Kickbacks" paid by businesses	$5.0 BIL.
Unreported business thefts	$3.0 BIL.
Robbery, burglary, theft	$2.0 BIL.
Embezzlement, fraud, forgery	$15 BIL.
Vandalism, arson	$1.1 BIL.
Shoplifting	$0.5 BIL.

OTHER CRIMES **$4.2 BILLION**	
Homicides, assaults (loss of earnings, medical costs)	$2.1 BIL.
Drunken driving (wage loss, medical costs of victims, property damage)	$2.0 BIL.
Tax fraud	$0.1 BIL.

LAW-ENFORCEMENT COSTS **$8.6 BILLION**	
Police (federal, State, local)	$5.0 BIL.
Penal system	$1.8 BIL.
Court system	$1.8 BIL.

PRIVATE CRIME-FIGHTING COSTS (cost of services and equipment) **$5.5 BILLION**	

TOTAL CRIME EXPENSE $51.1 BILLION

Source: Estimates by USN&WR Economic Unit, based on data from Government and industry.

Source: Reprinted from *U.S. News & World Report,* October 26, 1970. Copyright © 1970, U.S. News & /World Report, Inc.

penditures for the police departments will be about $7 billion a year. Moreover:

> The largest percentage growth and the bulk of the increase in police department employment is projected to take place outside the large cities, in the suburbs and, to a lesser extent, in the small towns and rural areas. These areas will develop full-time, modern police forces to deal with the new problems created by juvenile delinquency, drug use, organized crime, and traffic congestion.[12]

And that is not all: millions of people are employed in judicial administration and corrections, involving billions of dollars in salaries. For the year 1969, 137,000 persons were employed in the correctional fields alone, costing more than $1 billion.[13] And behind much of this expenditure, certainly shaping future trends, is the great increase in federal support for state and local crime control. Nearly $600 million was provided in federal aid to state and local governments in 1973. Crime is, indeed, a national problem.

All these manpower figures omit the hundreds of thousands of Americans who balance the labor market by remaining confined in prisons, jails, workhouses, reformatories, training schools, and halfway houses. Many of these people find economic security in such confinement, which has an additional function — lowering the nation's unemployment rate. Their confinement provides employment, as well, for the thousands of people who work to keep them confined, from the legislator to the policeman, the lawyer to the guard, the judge to the social worker and staff psychiatrist. We can be certain also that of the 5 million major property crimes (not to mention fraud, embezzlement, commercialized vice, gambling, drug sales, and so on), many are providing economic support for those who commit the offenses. It is not at all facetious to argue that in an economic way crime does pay for millions of Americans. And in the end the American capitalist system reaps the rewards of crime. As Marx suggested, crime in a capitalist society must be understood according to its productivity for that society.

In our radical analysis of crime's political economy, we begin to understand crime in American society, and to see that a complete resolution of the crime problem would require the drastic reconstruction of society.

A Critical Theory

We are now ready for our critical theory. The state, contrary to conventional wisdom, is the instrument of the ruling class. Law is the state's coercive weapon, with which it maintains the social and economic order. Criminal law, in particular, is established and enforced to secure domestic order. We understand crime in society as part of the capitalist state's political reality and that of its dominant class.

In developing this critical theory of crime, we must consider these topics: (1) crime and the dominant class, (2) crime control in the capitalist state, and (3) demystifying criminal law. Our objective is a critical understanding of the modern legal order.[14]

Crime and the Dominant Class

According to conventional wisdom, the state exists to maintain stability in civil society. Law, accordingly, is a body of rules established by consensus among those who are governed, or rather by the "representatives" of the governed. Such a notion of the state and its law misrepresents reality, but it serves those who benefit from it — those who govern.

An alternative position gets to the deeper meaning. Contrary to the accepted idea, the state is created by the class of society that has the power to impose its will on the rest of society. The state is thus a real, but falsely presented, political organization, established by those who desire to protect their material basis and have the power (because of those material means) to maintain the state. The law in capitalist society gives political recognition to powerful private interests, and is created to secure these interests. Contrary to conventional belief, law is a tool of the ruling class providing the mechanism for forcefully (and sometimes violently) controlling the rest of the population. In the battle, the agents of the law (police, prosecutors, judges) are the military force protecting domestic order. And the legal system prevents the rest of the people from becoming powerful. The rates of crime

VIEWPOINT_____

CONCENTRATION OF WEALTH AND POWER IN AMERICA

In 1965 there were some 340,000 industrial corporations in the United States. The biggest 500 of these, amounting to .15% of the total, had 60.2% of the industrial sales and 71% of the industrial profits. In 1969 the biggest 200 controlled well over 60% of the industrial assets. The biggest 100 industrials, only .03% of the total number, had nearly 40% of the industrial sales. More than 68% of the workers in the 340,000 industrial corporations worked for the biggest 500 in 1968.

A similar state of affairs existed in other branches of the economy. The 50 biggest merchandising chains had a net increase of over a billion dollars in 1966; 62.5% of that net income went to the ten largest chains. The three biggest commercial banks owned one-eighth of the assets of the some 13,000 banks in the country. There were 1,718 life insurance companies in the country with total assets of $167 billion. The ten biggest of these held $94 billion, or 56½% of the life insurance assets. Even more striking, the two biggest, Prudential and Metropolitan Life, owned 36% of the life insurance assets. American Tel & Tel owned 84% of the telephones in the country, while General Telephone, its "competition," owned 50% of the remainder.

While the telephone industry — like auto, steel, oil and some others — has for some time been highly monopolized, the recent period has seen a sharp increase in mergers in other sectors of the economy. The food, textiles, retail trade, aircraft and electronics industries are increasingly being controlled by two or three corporations. Just since 1965 we have seen: (1) Consolidation Coal, itself the biggest amalgamation of coal mines, taken over by Continental Oil; (2) Douglas Aircraft, maker of the DC-8, merged with McDonnell Aviation; (3) Atlantic Refining combined with Richfield Oil and then merging with Sinclair Oil; (4) Sunshine Biscuits acquired by American Tobacco; (5) North American Aviation merge with Rockwell Standard; (6) Signal Oil & Gas taking over Mack Trucks; (7) Gulf & Western Industries digesting Consolidated Cigar, then E. W. Bliss & Co., and finally Universal-American; (8) Container Corporation of America bought by Montgomery Ward; (9) Kern County Land merge with Tenneco Oil Co.; (10) Sunray DX Oil by Sun Oil; (11) Peabody Coal by Kennecott Copper; (12) Hooker Chemical by Occidental Petroleum; (13) Crucible Steel by Colt Industries; (14) General Precision by Singer; (15) Westinghouse Air Brake by American Standard.

These are just some recent highlights of a general trend. When billion dollar outfits like Douglas Aircraft are being gobbled up, thousands of smaller fish are also going under. In fact, while from 1948–1957 there were 4,303 mergers, in 1967 alone there were 1,496 mergers; 607 of those companies taken over were worth $50 million or more. Twelve companies, each worth over $250 million were gobbled up in 1968. In the first three months of 1969, 43 large manufacturing firms worth $45.5 billion were taken over.

While monopolization in each industry has increased, most of the large corporations, unable and unwilling to take on the giants in their own industry, use their surplus capital to move into other industries where monopolization is not yet complete. This forces an increased rate of monopolization in those few sectors of the economy where some competition still prevailed. Almost all of the big industrial corporations now have interests in a wide variety of industries. Some, like

Source: From Richard Pelton, "Who Really Rules America?" *Progressive Labor* (February 1970), pp. 16–17.

VIEWPOINT (Continued) _____

Litton Industries or Gulf & Western, are called conglomerates because of their extreme diversification.

An example of the latter is the Dallas-based Ling-Temco-Vought. Organized only in 1953, it has, with the backing of big money (Rockefeller) from the East, become one of the 100 largest industrials. It started as Ling Electronics; when in the late nineteen-fifties it fell under the sway of Eastern money, it began a campaign of rapidly gobbling up other electronics companies; more than 10 were taken over from 1957–1960. In 1960 it entered the aircraft industry by merging first Temco Aircraft, then Chance-Vought. Then in rapid succession, refrigeration, chemical, pharmaceutical, mobil communications and missile companies were bought up. In 1967 Wilson & Co., itself a conglomerate of meat, pharmaceutical and sporting goods equipment, was taken over. Then Goldschmit Chemicals was taken. In 1968 the company bought out Greatamerica, giving Ling-Temco-Vought control of Braniff International Airways, National Car Rentals, a big California bank and three insurance companies. It sold the bank and with that money bought control of Jones & Laughlin Steel, the sixth largest manufacturer of basic steel. Thus by the company's 16th birthday, it occupied an important monopoly position in the meat, aerospace, electronics, wire and cable, sporting goods, airline, pharmaceutical, car rentals and steel industries.

The Penn-Central Railroad, the largest in the nation, is another example. Formed by a merger of the biggest and the fourth biggest railroads, it operates directly 27,000 miles of track. But that's not all; it also operates under lease 39 other railroads, including such major ones as the New Haven Railroad, the Pittsburg Lake Erie Railroad, the Lehigh Valley Line, the Wabash Line, etc. But even that's not the end of it. The Penn-Central owns securities (effective control) in 90 other railroads. Outside the railroad field, the company owns Buckeye Pipe Line Co., the Biltmore, Barclay, Roosevelt, Commodore and Waldorf-Astoria Hotels in New York City, 20 acres of Park Avenue real estate in downtown New York and is acquiring Kayser-Roth Co., the garment monopoly that owns 119 garment sweatshops in the U.S., Canada, Puerto Rico and Italy.

General Telephone, the "independent phone company," has 30 subsidiary companies in the U.S.; it also controls the phone companies in Quebec, British Columbia and the Dominican Republic. It also owns Sylvania Electronics with its 57 plants and Automatic Electric Co. General Telephone operates plants in Canada, Italy, Belgium, Brazil, Argentina, Mexico and Germany.

Ford, the seventh largest industrial, makes 23% of the cars and 30% of the trucks in North America; its Philco division makes everything from missiles to home appliances. It has divisions that make all kinds of parts for motor vehicles, all kinds of tractors and farm equipment. Overseas its subsidiary in Germany, Ford-Werke A.G., is the third largest. With assembly and manufacturing plants in Canada, Great Britain, Germany, Brazil, Argentina, Mexico, Australia, South Africa, New Zealand, Malaysia, Finland, the Netherlands and elsewhere, more than 400,000 of the world's workers work for Ford.

Chase-Manhattan Bank, the second largest, has 142 branches in the New York area. It owns Banco del Commerce with 120 branches in Columbia and Panama, Banco Continental with 42 branches in Peru, Banco Atlantida with 24 branches in Honduras, Nederlandische Crediet with 66 branches in the Netherlands and major banks in Brazil, Venezuela, Belgium, Austria, West Indies and Ireland. Chase-Manhattan controls the Standard Bank Group, which with 1,100 branches dominates finance in Kenya, Malawi, Tanzania, Uganda, Zambia, South Africa, Rho-

VIEWPOINT (Continued)‗‗‗‗‗‗‗‗‗‗‗‗‗‗‗‗‗‗‗‗‗‗‗‗‗‗‗‗‗

desia, Nigeria, Ghana and eight other African countries. But this is just the tip of the iceberg of Chase-Manhattan's power. Its huge financial resources allow it to control and influence many of the other biggest monopolies and imperialist concerns in the U.S. and abroad.

---

in any state show how much the dominant class, by its machinery of criminal law, must coerce the rest of the population, preventing any threats to its ability to rule and possess. Criminal law as a coercive means in establishing domestic order for the government is a basic assumption in a radical critique of crime.

That American society can best be understood by its class structure violates conventional knowledge. It still comes as a surprise to many citizens that 1 per cent of the population owns 40 per cent of the nation's wealth, indicating that the liberal perspective dominates. The liberal assumption of a pluralistic American economy — with corporations as just one kind of interest group among many others — is negated, however, by the evidence that the major portion of the wealth and nearly all the power in American society are concentrated in a few large corporations. Furthermore, those who benefit from this economy make up a small, cohesive group of persons related in their power, wealth, and corporate connections. The pluralistic conception also ignores all the manifestations of the alliance between business and government. From the evidence, we can see that government and business are inseparable.

A critique of the American political economy begins then with the assumption that life in the United States is determined by the capitalist mode of production. And because it is a capitalist society, a class division separates those who rule from those who are ruled. Miliband writes about this class structure:

> The economic and political life of capitalist societies is *primarily* determined by the relationship, born of the capitalist mode of production, between these two classes — the class which on the one hand owns and controls, and the working class on the other. Here are still the social forces whose con-

frontation most powerfully shapes the social climate and the political system of advanced capitalism. In fact, the political process in these societies is mainly *about* the confrontation of these forces, and is intended to sanction the terms of the relationship between them.[15]

There are other classes, such as professionals, small businessmen, office workers, and cultural workmen, and some of them are either within or cut across the two major classes, but it is the division between the leading class and the subordinate class that establishes the political, economic, and social ways of life in capitalist society.

American society is governed according to interests of the leading class. Pluralists may suggest that we cannot ignore the diverse and conflicting interests among groups in the upper class, but they ignore the fact that members of that class work within a common framework in formulating public policy. Superficially, groups within the dominant class may differ on some issues. But they share many interests, and they can entirely exclude members of the other classes from the political process. Unlike pluralist theory, radical theory recognizes that the basic interests, in spite of concrete differences, place the elite in a distinct ruling class.

The radical critique also helps us get at the objective interests outside the consciousness of the individuals who compose them, and we can suggest normative evaluations of these interests. Pluralists, on the other hand, are bound by the subjective interests of individuals.[16] The critical perspective allows us to understand the actual and potential interests of classes.

Threats to American economic security abroad are dealt with militarily; an arsenal manned by armed forces is ready to attack any foe that attempts (as in a revolution) to upset the foreign markets of American capitalism.[17] The history of American foreign relations has been dominated by the corporate interests, securing American hegemony throughout as much of the world as possible.[18] And the criminal law is used at home by those who govern to maintain domestic order.

From this critical perspective, then, crime is worthy of the greatest consideration. To understand crime radically is to understand how the American empire was made and how it works.

Crime Control in the Capitalist State

Once we see that the legal system serves not society as a whole, but the interests at the top of society, we have begun to reach a critical understanding of criminal law in capitalist society. But this class is not in direct control of the legal system; it must operate through the state, to which we will turn to further understand what the legal order is and how it operates. The state defends the leading interests, and crime control is its major device.

Criminologists and legal scholars generally neglect the state as a subject for their inquiry. Failing to distinguish between civil society and that society's political organization, they ignore the major fact that civil society is secured politically by the state and that a dominant economic class can use the state to advance its own interests. Or when the state is admitted into a criminological or legal analysis, it is usually conceived as an impartial agency devoted to balancing and reconciling the diverse interests of competing groups in the society. This view, I am arguing, not only obscures the underlying reality of advanced capitalist society, but is basically wrong about the legal order.

We need several basic observations in our critical analysis of crime control in the capitalist state. First, we must understand the state and its complexity. Second, we need to know how the dominant economic class relates to the state, that is, how it becomes a ruling class and how the state governs in relation to it. Third, we must observe how the state develops in a capitalist economy.

"The state," Miliband writes, is not a thing that exists as such. "What 'the state' stands for is a number of particular institutions which, together, constitute its reality, and which interact as parts of what may be called the state system."[19] He observes that the state, or state system, is made up of these elements: (1) the government, (2) the administration, (3) the military and the police, (4) the judiciary, and (5) the units of subcentral government. The administration of the state is composed of a large variety of bureaucratic bodies and departments, managing the economic, cultural, and other activities in which the state is involved. The directly coercive forces of the state, at home and abroad, are handled by the police and the military. They form that branch of the state whose job is the "management of violence." The judiciary is an integral part of the state, supposedly independent of the government, which affects the exercise of state power. Finally, the various units of subcentral government are the extension of the central government. They are the administrative devices for centralized power, although some units may exercise power on their own over the lives of the populations they govern.[20]

In these institutions state power lies and is wielded by the persons who occupy the leading positions within each institution. Most important, these people are the *state elite*, as distinct from those who wield power outside of state institutions.[21] Some holders of state power, members of the state elite, may also be the agents of private economic power. But when members of private economic power are not members of the state elite, how are they able to rule the state? Somehow the interests of the dominant economic class must be translated into the governing process, to make it a true ruling class.

Miliband observes the essential relationship between the dominant economic class and the process of governing:

> What the evidence conclusively suggests is that in terms of social origin, education and class situation, the men who have manned *all* command positions in the state system have largely, and in many cases overwhelmingly, been drawn from the world of business and property, or from the professional middle classes. Here as in every other field, men and women born into the subordinate classes, which form of course the vast majority of the population, have

fared very poorly — and not only, it must be stressed, in those parts of the state system, such as administration, the military and the judiciary, which depend on appointment, but also in those parts of it which are exposed or which appear to be exposed to the vagaries of universal suffrage and the fortunes of competitive politics. In an epoch when so much is made of democracy, equality, social mobility, classlessness and the rest, it has remained a basic fact of life in advanced capitalist countries that the vast majority of men and women in these countries has been governed, represented, administered, judged, and commanded in war by people drawn from other, economically and socially superior and relatively distant classes.[22]

Looking back through history, we find that the capitalist state is the natural product of a society divided by economic classes. Only when a division of labor appeared, based on the exploiting of one class by another, and when the communal society broke up, was there a need for the state. The newly dominant class created the state as a means for coercing the rest of the population into economic and political submission. That the American state was called "democratic" does not lessen its actual purpose.

As Engels observed in his study of the state's origins, some societies have had no notion of state power. Only with a specific kind of economic development, with economic divisions, did the state become necessary. The new stage of development, Engels observes, called for the creation of the state.

Only one thing was wanting: an institution which not only secured the newly acquired riches of individuals against the communistic traditions of the gentile order, which not only sanctified the private property formerly so little valued, and declared this sanctification to be the highest purpose of all human society; but an institution which set the seal of general social recognition on each new method of acquiring property and thus amassing wealth at continually increasing speed; an institution which perpetuated, not only this growing cleavage of society into classes, but also the right of the possessing class to exploit the non-pos-

sessing, and the rule of the former over the latter.

And this institution came. The *state* was invented.[23]

The state did not appear as a third party in the conflict between classes, but arose to protect and promote the interests of the dominant economic class, which owns and controls the means of production. The state continues as a device for holding down the exploited class, the class that labors, for the benefit of the dominant class. Modern civilization, as epitomized by capitalist societies, is thus founded on the exploitation of one class by another. The state secures this arrangement, because the state is in the hands of that dominant economic ruling class.

And law became the ultimate means by which the state secures the interests of the governing class. Laws institutionalize and legitimize property relations. A legal system, a public force, is established:

This public force exists in every state: it consists not merely of armed men, but also of material appendages, prisons and coercive institutions of all kinds, of which gentile society knew nothing. It may be very insignificant, practically negligible, in societies with still undeveloped class antagonisms and living in remote areas, as at times and in places in the United States of America. But it becomes stronger in proportion as the class antagonisms within the state become sharper and as adjoining states grow larger and more populous.[24]

It is through the legal system, then, that the state explicitly and forcefully protects the interests of the capitalist class. Crime control becomes the coercive means of checking threats to its economic arrangements. The state defines its welfare according to the general well-being of the capitalist economy. Crime control in the capitalist state is the concrete means by which it protects its interests.

Demystifying Criminal Law

The purpose of a critical understanding of crime control is to expose the meaning of criminal law in capitalist society. The false reality by which we live, which serves the established system, must be understood. To demystify law in America is the goal of a critical theory of criminal law.

My critical discussion of criminal law can be summarized in these assertions:

1. *American society is based on an advanced capitalist economy.*

2. *The state is organized to serve the interests of the dominant economic class, the capitalist ruling class.*

3. *Criminal law is an instrument that the state and dominant ruling class use to maintain and perpetuate the social and economic order.*

4. *Crime control in capitalist society is accomplished by institutions and agencies established and administered by a governmental elite, representing dominant ruling class interests, to establish domestic order.*

5. *The contradictions of advanced capitalism — the disjunction between existence and essence — requires that the subordinate classes remain oppressed by whatever means necessary, especially by the legal system's coercion and violence.*

6. *Only with the collapse of capitalist society, based on socialist principles, will there be a solution to the crime problem.*

Thus criminal law in America can be critically understood as preserving the social and economic order. Criminal law is used by the state and the ruling class to secure the survival of the capitalist system. And as capitalist society is further threatened, criminal law is increasingly used in the attempt to maintain domestic order. The underclass, which must remain oppressed for the dominant class to triumph, will continue to be the object of criminal law as the dominant class seeks to perpetuate itself. To remove the oppression, to eliminate the need for further revolt, would necessarily mean the end of that class and its capitalist economy.

Criminal law continues to secure the colonial status of the oppressed in the social and economic order of the United States. The events of the last few years relating to crime, including both "disruption" and repression, can be understood as a crisis in the American system. The dominant class, by its control of the state, resorts to a worldwide counterrevolution.

A counterinsurgency program is carried out by the CIA abroad and the FBI; LEAA, and local police at home.

Crime and the criminal law can be understood only as they reflect this crisis.

By posing on the national level the central issues of the international conflict, by linking the international struggle for self-determination with the internal quest for social equality and social control, the crisis of democracy increasingly presents itself as the revolutionary crisis of the epoch. The movement for the sovereignty of the people within the imperial nation coincides with the struggle for self-determination in the international sphere. Just as domestically the demand for domestic power is a demand to overthrow the corporate ruling class and to make the productive apparatus responsive to social needs, so internationally the precondition of democratic sovereignty and inter-state coexistence is the dissolution of the government of the international corporations and financial institutions which have expropriated the sovereignty of nations in order to appropriate the wealth of the world.[25]

The consequences are revolutionary. Never before has our understanding of crime been so crucial. Never before has our understanding been so closely related to the way in which we must live our lives. To think critically and radically today is to be revolutionary. To do otherwise is to concede to oppression.

Conclusion

For the criminologist, the implications of a critical theory explaining the political economy of crime are far-reaching. Everything we have done in criminology and the sociology of law has to be redone; we will have to uncover all the orthodox assumptions we have held about crime and crime control in the United States. Both theoretically and empirically, we must reconsider everything that has preceded us. But more important, new problems are now before us. As we develop a critical imagination, we are thinking about things that have never appeared to us. Where will a critical theory of crime lead? It will take us to places where no one has been. In thought and in action, we are entering new realms of life, imagination, and human possibility.

16

Crime Control and the Future of American Society

Crime and control over it reflect our political, economic, and social system. If we understand crime in the United States, we can see some of the important forces at work in America today.

Our advanced capitalist society is challenged by opposing forces within itself, and it must deal with these somehow. Crime control is repression, legal repression; it is the state's response to one of capitalism's crises.

Crime programs in recent years have been primarily meant to control crime. Many have been a part of the reform programs dealing with other problems in the society, and all are directed at ensuring survival for the existing order.

The prospects for our future suggested by our critical understanding of crime are colored by the opposing forces in modern capitalism. The system, even with reforms, must respond to growing challenges by designing and administering still more repression. This kind of control does little but increase state authoritarianism. The alternative to this future is liberation of the capitalist state, achieving a more human society, a socialist one. The forces that will determine our future are at work in the United States.[1]

Science and Technology in the Control of Crime

Modern repression at its worst is realized in some techniques that go with rationalized crime control. The legal order, itself a rationalized form of regulation, demands the latest technology. Science has been called upon to serve the state's interest in crime control. And with science on its side, the legal order can be the most repressive (and rational) that any society has known.

We may be experiencing the "Americanization of 1984," a police state built by science and modern techniques of control.

The enactment of this police state — less conspicuous yet far more threatening than one dominated by the military — is a scientific enterprise. Its low-profiled selective repression is based on surveillance, fear, intimidation, and information control, rather than on the massive deployment of police.

DOCUMENT

ORIGINS OF THE WAR ON CRIME

Crime, Its Prevalence, and Measures of Prevention

TO THE CONGRESS OF THE UNITED STATES:

Crime has become a malignant enemy in America's midst.

Since 1940 the crime rate in this country has doubled. It has increased five times as fast as our population since 1958.

In dollars the cost of crime runs to tens of billions annually. The human costs are simply not measurable.

The problems run deep and will not yield to quick and easy answers. We must identify and eliminate the causes of criminal activity whether they lie in the environment around us or deep in the nature of individual men. This is a major purpose of all we are doing in combating poverty and improving education, health, welfare, housing, and recreation.

All these are vital, but they are not enough. Crime will not wait while we pull it up by the roots. *We must arrest and reverse the trend toward lawlessness.*

This active combat against crime calls for a fair and efficient system of law enforcement to deal with those who break our laws. It means giving new priority to the methods and institutions of law enforcement —

> *to our police,* who are our frontline, both offensive and defensive, in the fight against crime. There is a great need not only for improved training of policemen but for all people to learn about, to understand, and to assist the policeman in his work;

> *to our courts,* traditionally the symbol and guardian of our cherished freedoms. Local criminal courts are so overloaded that their functioning is impeded and their effectiveness weakened. More courts and judges is one answer, but every possibility of improvement must be explored; and

> *to our correctional agencies.* We cannot tolerate an endless, self-defeating cycle of imprisonment, release, and reimprisonment which fails to alter undesirable attitudes and behavior. We must find ways to help the first offender avoid a continuing career of crime.

No right is more elemental to our society than the right to personal security and no right needs more urgent protection.

Our streets must be safe. Our homes and places of business must be secure. Experience and wisdom dictate that one of the most legitimate functions of government is the preservation of law and order.

Our system rejects the concept of a national police force. The protection responsibilities lie primarily with State and local governments.

That is right and proper.

Yet, crime is no longer merely a local problem. Every city, every State is troubled by the same hard statistical — and human — facts. The extent and seriousness of the problem have made it of great national concern.

Crime is as old as history. It is hardly new to America. But in our increasingly

Source: From "Message from the President of the United States Relative to Comments on Crime, Its Prevalence, and Measures of Prevention," March 8, 1965, 89th Congress, 1st Session, House of Representatives, Document No. 103.

DOCUMENT (Continued)_____

mobile, urban society, crime problems are not only greater, they are immensely more complex.

We have not stood idly by in the face of these problems. Many cities and States, as well as the Federal Government, have developed new programs reflecting their growing concern.

Yet the crime rate continues to increase.

The time has come *now*, to check that growth, to contain its spread, and to reduce its toll of lives and property.

I believe the way to do so is to give new recognition to the fact that crime *is* a national problem and to intensify our crime prevention and crime fighting *at all levels of government.*

An underlying drive facilitating development of a police state is the historical governmental trend toward centralization. Information-gathering is merely one more example of the federal government's tendency to centralize and coordinate state and local activities. The implications of information concentrated in Washington are clear: Senator Charles Mathias, commenting in 1967 on the government's 3.1 billion records about individual citizens, suggested that "if knowledge is power, this encyclopedic knowledge gives government the raw materials of tyranny."

Technological advances have facilitated the drive to increased concentration of information and power. Computers and Vietnam-perfected hardware applied on the home front are smothering the road to 1984.[2]

The move to apply the latest in science and technology to crime control was made in the mid-sixties by the President's Commission on Law Enforcement and Administration of Justice. This application was probably inevitable because of the tendency to rationalize all systems of management and control. Yet the President's Crime Commission, staffed by scientists, justified and presented scientific crime control to the public. The commission's recommendations were soon made concrete and instituted by the newly created crime control agencies. Science and technology keep today's control systems advanced and make them insidious. The modern state has the most advanced system for maintaining domestic order, that is, for perpetuating itself.

The President's Crime Commission included in its coverage of the crime problem a special task force report on *Science and Technology.* The project was funded by the Office of Law Enforcement Assistance of the Justice Department, which was also responsible for its staff and organization. The actual work was conducted by the Institute for Defense Analyses (of the Department of Defense). The project was directed by Dr. Alfred Blumstein, a staff member of the institute. The complete study appears in the task force report, and the recommendations and arguments of the task force are included in the commission's final report, *The Challenge of Crime in a Free Society.*   .

The message that the task force's research and analysis came up with is that: (1) crime control must become more scientific, (2) it must utilize the kind of science and technology that already serves the military, and (3) the federal government must institute and support such a program. The chapter on "Science and Technology" in the commission's final report begins:

The scientific and technological revolution that has so radically changed most of American society during the past few decades has had surprisingly little impact upon the criminal justice system. In an age when many executives in government and industry, faced with decision-making problems, ask the scientific and technical community for independent suggestions on possible alternatives and for objective analyses of possible consequences of their actions, the public officials responsible for establishing and administering the criminal law — the legislators, police, prosecutors, lawyers, judges, and corrections officials — have almost no communication with the scientific and technical community.[3]

That a science and a technology, a military one, is available for crime control is the good news presented in the opening lines of the task force's own report:

> The natural sciences and technology have long helped the police to solve specific crimes. Scientists and engineers have had very little impact, however, on the overall operations of the criminal justice system and its principal components: police, courts, and corrections. More than 200,000 scientists and engineers have applied themselves to solving military problems and hundreds of thousands more to innovation in other areas of modern life, but only a handful are working to control the crimes that injure or frighten millions of Americans each year. Yet, the two communities have much to offer each other: science and technology is a valuable source of knowledge and techniques for combating crime; the criminal justice system represents a vast area of challenging problems.[4]

The task force lists the kind of equipment and tactics that should be used in the war on crime:

> In the traditional view, science and technology primarily means new equipment. And modern technology can, indeed, provide a vast array of devices beyond those now in general use to improve the operations of criminal justice agencies, particularly in helping the police deter crime and apprehend criminals. Some of the more important possibilities are:
>
> Electronic computers for processing the enormous quantities of needed data.
>
> Police radio networks connecting officers and neighboring departments.
>
> Inexpensive, light two-way portable radios for every patrolman.
>
> Computers for processing fingerprints.
>
> Instruments for identifying criminals by their voice, photographs, hair, blood, body chemistry, etc.
>
> Devices for automatic and continual reporting of all police car locations.
>
> Helicopters for airborne police patrol.
>
> Inexpensive, reliable burglar and robbery alarms.
>
> Nonlethal weapons to subdue dangerous criminals without inflicting permanent harm.
>
> Perimeter surveillance devices for prisons.
>
> Automatic transcription devices for courtroom testimony.
>
> Many of these devices are now in existence, some as prototypes and some available commercially. Others still require basic development but are at least technically feasible and worthy of further exploration.[5]

The similarities between military operations and domestic crime control are made clear, and the Crime Commission is advised to pursue the militarization:

> Crime control, being largely a social problem, may appear to be outside the realm of the scientists' skills. Indeed, many aspects of the problem do fall outside their scope. The experience of science in the military, however, suggests that a fruitful collaboration can be established between criminal justice officials on one hand and engineers, physicists, economists, and social and behavioral scientists on the other. In military research organizations these different professions, working with military officers in inter-disciplinary teams, have attacked defense problems in new ways and have provided insights that were new even to those with long military experience. Similar developments appear possible in criminal justice.[6]

Military operations abroad and crime control at home have become one — in objective and technique.

The remainder of the Science and Technology Task Force report is devoted, in great detail, to "the applications of science and technology to the problems of crime, and especially to improving the criminal justice system." The task force director, Alfred Blumstein, appeared before John McClellan's Senate Subcommittee on Criminal Laws and Procedures, making the same recommendations to the committee that was creating the Omnibus Crime bill. Blumstein suggested reinforcing Senator McClellan's initial intentions, that the federal government must play the crucial role in mounting the new form of crime control:

> It may very well be that the application of science and technology to criminal justice has been retarded so long as a result of the fragmentation of the criminal justice system. We have over 40,000 separate police agencies, and several thousand court systems and correctional systems. Only a handful of these are large enough and rich enough to undertake major research or equipment development projects on their own. There is little incentive for them to do so, since that would probably be an inefficient investment of resources for any one of them. Although the results would benefit all, the innovator alone would have to bear the high cost. Even if the individual agencies independently conducted their own projects, we would probably see many of them pursuing identical questions not knowing of the work and results of the other. Furthermore, there would be little incentive for an individual agency to disseminate the results of its work to other agencies that might be able to use them.
>
> This is a typical situation in which it is appropriate for the Federal Government to take a leading and coordinating role. The Federal Government could provide the risk capital to conduct the research or to develop the new technology at a cost that would be small by Federal standards but would swamp the budget of any individual criminal justice agency.
>
> It could also assure that a coordinated and mutually supporting program is developed, and it could foster the implementation of the results. Without such a major Federal involvement, it appears unlikely that there can be significant innovation in the operation of the criminal justice system. And all recent trends in crime rates, arrest rates, and recidivism rates indicate that what we are doing today is inadequate to cope with the crime problem.[7]

This federally sponsored program, Blumstein continued, would:

> Undertake basic research into the causes of crime and into the consequences of actions taken to control it.
>
> Provide for the development of equipment that could be widely used by criminal justice agencies throughout the country.
>
> Create a coordinated program whose parts would complement and build upon each other.
>
> Assure that the results of the program are made available in a form that would be usable by criminal justice agencies throughout the Nation.
>
> Provide technical assistance and guidance to State and local agencies in planning and implementing their programs and to the Federal Government in administering its subsidy program.[8]

The government responded, making history, a history that continues to shape our lives.

The War on Crime

The war on crime has been launched. The military strategy toward domestic disorder now prevails. LEAA began by creating and sponsoring counterinsurgency and military-like projects for the home front. States, upon receiving block grants, have distributed their funds to local agencies to develop a broad range of anticrime programs. A total of 643 "Discretionary Grant" projects were supported by LEAA in 1970, and more than $340 million was allocated for the projects, which, we are told, will enable state and local units of government to "improve their criminal justice systems."[9]

In just a few years LEAA has been able to change criminal justice in the United States. One author, reviewing the projects since 1968, tells some of the ways in which criminal justice has been affected.

Civil Disorder Assistance

The sweeping arrest of 894 students (out of a total enrollment of 2,500) at all-black Mississippi Valley State College, thereby breaking a peaceful campus-wide strike. The *Washington Post* noted that LEAA's action "marked the beginning of one of the Nixon Administration's potentially most volatile policies — federal 'technical assistance' in local suppression of 'campus disorders.'" The crime in this "disorder" was "obstructing a public road on a campus." Police action was made possible by a LEAA grant of $288,405 to the Mississippi State Commission for "developing plans and procedures for coping with civil disorders (riot control and natural disaster) and organized crime."

The deaths of four people in the disorders in Baton Rouge, Louisiana, were underwritten in part by LEAA grants, one of which was for $48,708 on June 25, 1970, and called for the creation of a "special trouble shooting squad." Another was for $31,942 on November 30, 1970, for "police technical assistance for prevention and control of civil disorders." A special squad made up of city police, sheriffs, and parish county police, equipped with submachine guns and M-16's with bayonets, sealed off the streets where a Black Muslim rally was being held. Soon afterward the shooting began.

LEAA has to date supplied $750,000 to the cities of San Diego and Miami to develop joint defenses against potential demonstrations at the conventions this summer.

Weapon Stockpiling

LEAA is arming the police to the teeth. For $16,464 LEAA bought the tank used by Louisiana police to storm a New Orleans Black Panther headquarters September 10, 1970. The same tank, classified by LEAA bureaucrats as a "command and control vehicle," had been used earlier against demonstrating black students.

Clandestine Surveillance

A LEAA grant in Delaware financed mobile surveillance units hidden in civilian rental trucks. The grant provided for operators dressed in the uniforms of dry-cleaner delivery men, salesmen, public utilities workers, and others, "making it possible to be in a neighborhood without being obvious." The trucks are to be equipped with infrared cameras and video equipment for taking pictures night or day of "suspicious persons."

In Tampa, Florida a LEAA-sponsored surveillance system costing $150,000 will use computers to control a network of videotape cameras and alarms placed in "convenient" grocery stores and overlooking shopping center parking lots. Operators will monitor the cameras constantly, using their zoom lenses for close-ups of any "suspicious activity."

In San Jose, California; Hoboken, New Jersey; and Mount Vernon, New York; TV cameras are placed throughout the cities' business areas, flashing their images back to the local police headquarters where they are monitored for "suspicious" goings on. The Mt. Vernon equipment, which cost LEAA $47,000, is capable of discerning a man-sized object in extreme darkness more than a half-mile away.

Data Gathering

LEAA has sponsored the construction of statewide data banks on "actual or *potential* troublemakers." In Oklahoma, for example, a $29,453 grant enabled the National Guard to compile dossiers on six thousand individuals, only one-third of them Oklahomans. The ACLU and Oklahoma Civil Liberties Union have filed suit in federal court maintaining the dossiers are used to "harass and intimidate." One of the lawyers, Stephen Jones, has evidence that some Oklahomans have been blacklisted as a result of the dossiers. "A number of Negroes and whites who have taken part in peace rallies or racial demonstrations," he told the *New York Times*, began "having trouble finding jobs or getting into college."

A $46,000 appropriation has been made to the New Haven, Connecticut, Police Department for an "exploration of law enforcement utilization of the 1970 Census Bureau Data." The police can use the census data, which will be stored in IBM computers, during "civil disorders" to obtain vital background information (age, schooling, occupation) on the residents of the area.[10]

In addition to financing state and local programs, LEAA is sponsoring a massive project aimed at developing a national intelligence network. Started as a $45 million LEAA pilot project called SEARCH (Systems for Electronic Analysis and Retrieval of Criminal Histories), it has grown into a computerized "criminal justice information center," operated by the FBI. The information includes not only official records, such as an individual's arrest record (regardless of the eventual disposition of the case), but information compiled from other sources as well. The computerized intelligence system will contain information derived from informants, wiretaps, employers, and the like.[11]

The intelligence-gathering network functions through separate computer centers set up by each state. All records, criminal and otherwise, will be stored and then transmitted to the FBI for filing in the National Crime Information Center (NCIC).

All 50 states will be able to "talk" to each other through the FBI master computer. In addition, every major municipal police department in the country will be hooked into the network, either with its own computer or a less expensive teletype operation. There are already 135 local and state police agencies that are using or will soon be using the memory links to the FBI. Before long, 75 per cent of the nation's police agencies will be plugged in, and by 1975 the figure should rise to 95 per cent.[12]

Each locality decides how much and what kind of information to feed into its computer; and all the information, regardless of its validity or legality, is pumped into the national computer in Washington.

By the time the intelligence system is in full operation (in 1975) law-enforcement agents will have instant access to information on any person they regard as "suspicious." The state will have a system that will enable government agents to control domestic order. In the name of combating crime, the state is now able to obtain information on as many people as it wants to and make it instantly available for use against them. This new anticrime technology, in the form of a computerized data bank, has threatening implications, even from a constitutional standpoint.

The new technology has made it literally impossible for a man to start again in our society. It has removed the quality of mercy from our institutions by making it impossible to forget, to understand, to tolerate. . . . The undisputed and unlimited possession of the resources to build and operate data banks on individuals, and to make decisions about people with the aid of computers and electronic data systems, is fast securing to

executive branch officials a political power which the authors of the Constitution never meant any one group of men to have over all others.[13]

The modern criminal justice system, aided by science and technology, may indeed be the state's ultimate political instrument.

Further weaponry for the war on crime is being developed rapidly. The technology for domestic security has lagged behind that for scientific warfare abroad, but the deficiency is being corrected.

Up until recently the standard arsenal for the patrolman was the sidearm and nightstick. Occasionally a labor strike was met with riot guns and gas bombs. Today's rapid expansion in the variety of the police arsenal illustrates the rapid expansion of domestic counterinsurgency planning. Today's police can employ a number of different gas dispensing devices, from shotguns to helicopters; carry individual two-way radios; fire machine guns on the practice range and high-powered rifles from moving aircraft; wear helmets and body armor; carry MACE in their belts; engage in mock confrontations; as well as use computers to sort out large quantities of information in seconds. Recently, for instance, the Pentagon announced plans to provide $20 million worth of riot control equipment to the National Guard — including face shields, batons, protective vests, shotguns, floodlights, public address systems, radios and tear gas.[14]

Aided by the federal government, mainly by grants from LEAA, the local police department has a stockpile of the latest weapons for maintaining domestic order. The federal government's role in modern crime control is summarized by Blumstein:

Think of where military technology would be if each battalion commander were responsible for his own research and development. A national agency was needed to represent the combined interests of police departments across the nation. The creation of the Law Enforcement Assistance Administration, and especially its research and development arm, the National Institute of Law Enforcement and Criminal Justice, was an important step in that direction.[15]

If it ever decides the time is right, the government can now launch a full-scale war against
its own people. Scientifically and technologi-
cally the state has been made ready.

Crime Control in the United States

Crime control today is a natural outgrowth of
a political and economic system, the advanced
capitalist society. For that kind of society to
continue, any threats from the people must be
repressed or in some way controlled; the society's contradiction is that a system which
violates human sensibilities in turn calls for
resistance and rebellion by the population. And
the more often these threats come, whether in
outright political acts or in behaviors that
otherwise violate the society's rules, the more
the state must bring its repressive devices to
bear on the people. If the state fails to respond,
changes would undoubtedly spell the end of
its political economy. Today in America we are
witnessing repression in a society that refuses
to use its resources to solve its own problems;
to protect the system from its own victims, a
war on crime is being waged.

The crime-control programs of the last ten
years have been constructed with the idea of
"reform," a way of adjusting the established
system so that it will survive according to its
own terms. Many of these programs have been
an integral part of others that were built to
confront poverty, racial inequality, and campus
disorders. Under the guise of working toward
"new frontiers" and "the great society," they
have been instituted to preserve social and
economic arrangements. At the same time,
measures have been developed to prevent and
control resistance to the reforms or to threats
that suggest changes going beyond the reforms. The state activates the option that must
accompany reform, namely repression. Reform
and repression are not alternatives but are
complementary:

> However, as reform reveals itself in-
> capable of subduing pressure and protest,
> so does the emphasis shift towards repres-
> sion, coercion, police power, law and order,
> the struggle against subversion, etc. Faced
> as they are with intractable problems, those

who control the levers of power find it increasingly necessary further to erode those
features of "bourgeois democracy" through
which popular pressure is exercised. The
power of representative institutions must
be further reduced and the executive more
effectively insulated against them. The independence of trade unions must be whit-
tled away, and trade union rights, notably
the right to strike, must be further surrounded by new and more stringent inhi-
bitions. The state must arm itself with more
extensive and more efficient means of repression, seek to define more stringently
the area of "legitimate" dissent and opposition, and strike fear in those who seek to
go beyond it.[16]

Repression is cumulative. Further repression
can only arouse protest, and further protest
necessitates more repression by the state. Then
a new kind of control transforms crime control
into a larger system of state authoritarianism.

> This transition need not assume a dra-
> matic character, or require a violent change
> in institutions. Neither its progression nor
> its end result need be identical with the
> Fascism of the inter-war years. It is indeed
> most unlikely to assume the latter's par-
> ticular forms, because of the discredit which
> has not ceased to be attached to them, and
> of the loathing which Fascism has not
> ceased to evoke. In fact, the usage of Fas-
> cism as a reference point tends dangerously
> to obscure the less extreme alternatives to
> it, which do not require the wholesale dis-
> mantling of all democratic institutions, the
> total subversion of all liberties, nor cer-
> tainly the abandonment of a democratic
> rhetoric. It is easily possible to conceive
> of forms of conservative authoritarianism
> which would not be "Fascist," in the old
> sense, which would be claimed to be "demo-
> cratic" precisely because they were not
> "Fascist," and whose establishment would
> be defended as in the best interests of "de-
> mocracy" itself. Nor is all this a distant
> projection into an improbable future: it de-
> scribes a process which is already in train,
> and which is also, in the condition of ad-
> vanced capitalism, more likely to be ac-
> centuated than reversed. The gradual transi-
> tion of capitalism into socialism may be a
> myth: but the gradual transition of "bour-
> geois democracy" into more or less pro-
> nounced forms of authoritarianism is not.[17]

That we are entering a new kind of America, or rather a modern version of the old one, seems evident from our study of crime control. The state, supporting advanced capitalism, an economic system that cannot respond to human needs and still exist, must remake itself. The modern state, with its ruling class, maintains its control over internal challenges by developing and institutionalizing the instruments of science and technology. This new style of fascism is a complex of modernized control mechanisms. It is a pervasive, insidious form of control, indeed, a managed society. As Bertram Gross has described this new order, "A managed society rules by a faceless and widely dispersed complex of warfare-welfare-industrial-communications-police bureaucracies caught up in developing a new-style empire based on a technocratic ideology, a culture of alienation, multiple scapegoats, and competing control networks."[18] Not only will the economy be managed, but the whole society will be managed by the modern state.

The police component of the new state involves (and we are presently experiencing it) a network of law-enforcement systems decentralized geographically yet guided by federal agencies. "It will include the Attorney General's office, the FBI, the CIA, the military intelligence agencies, federal-aid crime agencies, and new computer-based dossier facilities tied in with the Internal Revenue Service, the Census Bureau, and credit-rating offices."[19] This central complex will, of course, be integrated into an expanding welfare system that itself helps control the population. We will be bound, finally, by a communications network:

In toto, the warfare-welfare-industrial-communication-police complex would be the supermodern fascist form of what has hitherto been described as "oligopolistic state capitalism." Its products would be: (1) increasingly differentiated armaments (including more outer-space and under-sea instruments of destruction) that in the name of defense and security would contribute to world insecurity; (2) increasingly specialized medical, education, housing, and welfare programs that would have a declining relation to health, learning, community, or social justice; (3) industrial products to serve warfare-welfare purposes and provide consumer incentives for acceptance of the system; (4) communication services that would serve as instruments for the manipulation, surveillance, and suppression — or prettifying — of information on domestic and foreign terrorism; and (5) police activities designed to cope with the new "crime" of opposing the system, probably enlisting organized crime in the effort.[20]

Is there an alternative to this future? Certainly the liberal reform solutions are not the answer; they lead only to further repression and open the way for the neofascist state. Only a vision that goes beyond reform of the capitalist system can provide us with a humane existence and a world free of the authoritarian state. Crime control in modern America is a crucial indication of the world that could come to be under present images and theories of society and human nature. Only with a critical philosophy of our present condition can we suggest a way out of our possible future.

Notes

1 The Study of Crime

1. Richard Quinney, "There's a Lot of Folks Grateful to the Lone Ranger: With Some Notes on the Rise and Fall of American Criminology," *The Insurgent Sociologist*, 4 (Fall 1973), pp. 56–64.
2. A more extensive discussion of the development of criminology is found in my book *The Problem of Crime* (New York: Dodd, Mead, 1970), Chapter 3.
3. Cesare Beccaria, *Essay on Crime and Punishment*, 1st American ed. (New York: Stephen Gould, 1809); Jeremy Bentham, *An Introduction to the Principles of Morals and Legislation*, corrected ed. (Oxford: Clarendon Press, 1823); Coleman Phillipson, *Three Criminal Law Reformers: Beccaria, Bentham, Romilly* (London: J. M. Dent, 1923).
4. Willem A. Bonger, *Introduction to Criminology*, trans. Emil Van Loo (London: Methuen, 1936). Also see C. Berneldo de Quirós, *Modern Theories of Criminality*, trans. Alfonso de Salvio (Boston: Little, Brown, 1911).
5. Yale Levin and Alfred R. Lindesmith, "English Ecology and Criminology of the Past Century," *Journal of Criminal Law, Criminology and Police Science*, 27 (March-April 1937), pp. 801–816.
6. T. S. Simey and M. B. Simey, *Charles Booth, Social Scientist* (London: Oxford University Press, 1960), p. 4.
7. Floyd N. House, *The Development of Sociology* (New York: McGraw-Hill, 1936), pp. 331–337.
8. Ellen Elizabeth Guillot, *Social Factors in Crime: As Explained by American Writers of the Civil War and Post Civil War Period*, published Ph.D dissertation (Philadelphia: University of Pennsylvania, 1943), p. 172.
9. Quoted in Charles Goring, *The English Convict: A Statistical Study* (London: His Majesty's Stationery Office, 1913), p. 13.
10. Quoted in Quirós, *Modern Theories of Criminality*, p. 16.
11. George B. Vold, *Theoretical Criminology* (New York: Oxford University Press, 1958), pp. 35–36.
12. Arthur MacDonald, *Criminology* (New York: Funk and Wagnalls, 1892); August Draehms, *The Criminal, His Personnel and Environment: A Scientific Study* (New York: Macmillan, 1900); Philip A. Parson, *Crime and the Criminal* (New York: Alfred A. Knopf, 1926).
13. E. A. Hooton, *The American Criminal: An Anthropological Study* (Cambridge: Harvard University Press, 1939); William H. Sheldon, *Varieties of Delinquent Youth* (New York: Harper and Brothers, 1949); Sheldon and Eleanor Glueck, *Physique and Delinquency* (New York: Harper, 1956).

14. Goring, *The English Convict*, p. 18.
15. Henry Goddard, *Human Efficiency and Levels of Intelligence* (Princeton: Princeton University Press, 1920); Carl Murchison, *Criminal Intelligence* (Worcester, Mass.: Clark University Press, 1926); Simon H. Tulchin, *Intelligence and Crime* (Chicago: University of Chicago Press, 1939).
16. See Michael Hakeem, "A Critique of the Psychiatric Approach to Crime and Correction," *Law and Contemporary Problems*, 23 (Autumn 1958), pp. 650–682.
17. Frances A. Kellor, *Experimental Sociology* (New York: Macmillan, 1901), pp. ix–x.
18. Arthur C. Hall, *Crime and Its Relation to Social Progress* (New York: Columbia University Press, 1902), p. xi.
19. Robert E. Park. ed., *The City* (Chicago: University of Chicago Press, 1925).
20. Frederick M. Thrasher, *The Gang* (Chicago: University of Chicago Press, 1927).
21. Clifford R. Shaw, *Delinquency Areas*, with Frederick M. Zorbaugh, Henry D. McKay, and Leonard S. Cottrell (Chicago: University of Chicago Press, 1929).
22. Edwin H. Sutherland, *Principles of Criminology*, 4th ed. (Philadelphia: J. B. Lippincott, 1947), pp. 6–7.
23. Robert K. Merton, "Social Structure and Anomie," *American Sociological Review*, 3 (October 1938), pp. 672–682.
24. Thorsten Sellin, *Culture Conflict and Crime* (New York: Social Science Research Council, 1938).
25. See, for example, Austin T. Turk, *Criminality and Legal Order* (Chicago: Rand McNally, 1969); Robert L. Burgess and Ronald L. Akers, "A Differential Association-Reinforcement Theory of Criminal Behavior," *Social Problems*, 14 (Fall 1966), pp. 128–147; Melvin L. De Fleur and Richard Quinney, "A Reformulation of Sutherland's Differential Association Theory and a Strategy for Empirical Verification," *Journal of Research in Crime and Delinquency*, 3 (January 1966), pp. 1–22; Daniel Glaser, "Criminality Theories and Behavioral Images," *American Journal of Sociology*, 61 (March 1956), pp. 433–444; Walter C. Reckless, Simon Dinitz, and Barbara Kay, "The Self Component in Potential Delinquency," *American Sociological Review*, 22 (October 1957), pp. 566–570; Marshall B. Clinard, ed., *Anomie and Deviant Behavior* (New York: Free Press, 1964); Albert K. Cohen, *Delinquent Boys* (New York: Free Press, 1955); Richard A. Cloward and Lloyd E. Ohlin, *Delinquency and Opportunity* (New York: Free Press, 1960).
26. For example, see Abraham S. Blumberg, *Criminal Justice* (Chicago: Quadrangle Books, 1967); Marshall B. Clinard and Richard Quinney, *Criminal Behavior Systems: A Typology*, 2nd ed. (New York: Holt, Rinehart and Winston, 1973); Donald R. Cressey, *Theft of the Nation* (New York: Harper and Row, 1969); Don C. Gibbons, *Changing the Lawbreaker* (Englewood Cliffs, N.J.: Prentice-Hall, 1965); Daniel Glaser, *The Effectiveness of a Prison and Parole System* (Indianapolis: Bobbs-Merrill, 1964); Edwin M. Lemert, *Human Deviance, Social Problems, and Social Control* (Englewood Cliffs, N.J.: Prentice-Hall, 1964); Arthur Niederhoffer, *Behind the Shield* (Garden City: Doubleday, 1967); Richard Quinney, ed., *Crime and Justice in Society* (Boston: Little, Brown, 1969); Jerome H. Skolnick, *Justice Without Trial* (New York: Wiley, 1966).
27. Edwin H. Sutherland and Donald R. Cressey, *Criminology*, 8th ed. (Philadelphia: J. B. Lippincott, 1970), pp. 61–70. Also see Donald R. Taft and Ralph W. England, Jr., *Criminology*, 4th ed. (New York: Macmillan, 1964), pp. 70–74.
28. The following discussion is adapted from my book *Critique of Legal Order: Crime Control in Capitalist Society* (Boston: Little, Brown, 1974), pp. 2–15.
29. See A. R. Louch, *Explanation and Human Action* (Berkeley: University of California Press, 1969).
30. See John H. Schaar, "Legitimacy in the Modern State," in Philip Green and Sanford Levinson, eds., *Power and the Community: Dissenting Essays in Political Science* (New York: Vintage Books, 1970), especially pp. 303–308.
31. See C. Ray Jeffery, "The Structure of American Criminological Thinking," *Journal of Criminal Law, Criminology and Police Science*, 46 (January 1956), pp. 658–672.
32. Alfred Schutz, "Concept and Theory Formation in the Social Sciences," in Maurice Nathanson, ed., *Philosophy of the Social Sciences* (New York: Random House, 1963), p. 242.
33. See Alfred Schutz, *The Problem of Social Reality: Collected Papers, I* (The Hague: Martinus Nijhoff, 1962); and Peter L. Berger and Thomas Luckmann, *The Social Construction of Reality* (Garden City, N.Y.: Doubleday, 1966).
34. Richard Lichtman, "Symbolic Interactionism and Social Reality: Some Marxist Queries," *Berkeley Journal of Sociology*, 15 (1970–71), pp. 75–94.
35. Howard S. Becker, *Outsiders: Studies in the Sociology of Deviance* (New York: Free Press, 1963).
36. See Quentin Lauer, *Phenomenology: Its Genesis and Prospect* (New York: Harper Torchbooks, 1965), pp. 1–2; Pierre Thévanaz, *What Is Phenomenology?* James M. Edie, ed. (Chi-

cago: Quadrangle Books, 1962), pp. 42–43.

37. This distinction is found in Immanuel Kant, *Critique of Pure Reason*, trans. Norman Kemp Smith (New York: Macmillan, 1929).

38. Martin Heidegger, *Discourse on Thinking*, trans. John M. Anderson and E. Hans Freund (New York: Harper & Row, 1966), p. 53.

39. Ibid.

40. See Richard M. Zaner, *The Way of Phenomenology: Criticism as a Philosophical Discipline* (New York: Pegasus, 1970), especially pp. 112–113, 117, 196, and 203.

41. Alan F. Blum, "Theorizing," in Jack D. Douglas, ed., *Understanding Everyday Life: Toward the Reconstruction of Sociological Knowledge* (Chicago: Aldine, 1970), p. 305.

42. See Jurgen Habermas, *Knowledge and Human Interests*, trans. Jeremy J. Shapiro (Boston: Beacon Press, 1971), pp. 301–317.

43. Hannah Arendt, "Thinking and Moral Considerations," *Social Research*, 38 (Autumn 1971), pp. 417–446.

44. Ibid., p. 424.

45. Herbert Marcuse, *One-Dimensional Man* (Boston: Beacon Press, 1964), p. 9.

46. Herbert Marcuse, *Reason and Revolution* (Boston: Beacon Press, 1960), especially pp. vii–xiv and 3–29.

47. Anthony Platt, "The Triumph of Benevolence: The Origins of the Juvenile Justice System in the United States, in Richard Quinney, ed., *Criminal Justice in America: A Critical Understanding* (Boston: Little, Brown, 1974), pp. 356–389.

48. See Herman and Julia Schwendinger, "Defenders of Order or Guardians of Human Rights?" *Issues in Criminology*, 5 (Summer 1970), pp. 123–157; Clayton A. Hartjen, "Legalism and Humanism: A Reply to the Schwendingers," *Issues in Criminology*, 7 (Winter 1972), pp. 59–69; Gene Grabiner, "The Limits of Three Perspectives on Crime: 'Value-Free Science,' 'Objective Law,' and State 'Morality,'" *Issues in Criminology*, 8 (Spring 1973), pp. 35–48.

2 Criminal Statistics and Crime Rates

1. The following is a revision and expansion of my discussion of criminal statistics in *The Problem of Crime* (New York: Dodd, Mead, 1970), pp. 108–123.

2. Sources of criminal statistics are discussed in, among other places, Ronald H. Beattie, "Sources of Statistics on Crime and Correction," *Journal of the American Statistical Association*, 54 (September 1959), pp. 582–592; Walter A. Lunden, *Facts on Crimes and Criminals* (Ames, Iowa: The Art Press, 1961);

James A. McCafferty, "Prisoner Statistics — National and State," *Proceedings of the American Statistical Association* (1960), pp. 25–33; Edward B. McConnell, "Judicial Criminal Statistics," *National Probation and Parole Association Journal*, 3 (July 1957), pp. 250–262; Edward E. Schwartz, "Statistics of Juvenile Delinquency in the United States," *Annals of the American Academy of Political and Social Science*, 261 (January 1949), pp. 9–20.

3. Thorsten Sellin, "The Measurement of Criminality in Geographic Areas," *Proceedings of the American Philosophical Society*, 97 (April 1953), p. 163.

4. Louis N. Robinson, "History of Criminal Statistics, 1908–1933," *Journal of Criminal Law, Criminology and Police Science*, 24 (May-June 1933), p. 126. Also see C. E. Gehlke, "Development of Criminal Statistics in the Past Century," *Proceedings of the American Prison Association* (1931), pp. 176–190.

5. These and other surveys are discussed in Virgil Peterson, *Crime Commissions in the United States* (Chicago: Chicago Crime Commission, 1945).

6. Ronald H. Beattie, "Problems of Criminal Statistics in the United States," *Journal of Criminal Law, Criminology and Police Science*, 46 (July-August 1955), p. 178.

7. Edwin H. Sutherland and Donald R. Cressey, *Criminology*, 8th ed. (Philadelphia: J. B. Lippincott, 1970), p. 25.

8. See, for example, Peter P. Lejins, "Uniform Crime Reports," *Michigan Law Review*, 64 (April 1966), pp. 1011–1030; David J. Pittman and W. F. Handy, "Uniform Crime Reporting: Suggested Improvements," *Sociology and Social Research*, 46 (January 1962), pp. 135–143; Sophia M. Robison, "A Critical View of the Uniform Crime Reports," *Michigan Law Review*, 64 (April 1966), pp. 1031–1054; Thorsten Sellin, "The Uniform Criminal Statistics Act," *Journal of Criminal Law, Criminology and Police Science*, 40 (March-April 1950), pp. 679–700; Leslie T. Wilkins, "New Thinking in Criminal Statistics," *Journal of Criminal Law, Criminology and Police Science*, 56 (September 1965), pp. 277–284; Marvin E. Wolfgang, "Uniform Crime Reports: A Critical Appraisal," *University of Pennsylvania Law Review*, 111 (April 1963), pp. 708–738.

9. Ronald H. Beattie, "Criminal Statistics in the United States — 1960," *Journal of Criminal Law, Criminology and Police Science*, 51 (May-June 1960), pp. 49–65.

10. Thorsten Sellin, "The Basis of a Crime Index," *Journal of Criminal Law, Criminology and Police Science*, 22 (September-October 1931), p. 346.

11. C. C. Van Vechten, "Differential Criminal

Case Mortality in Selected Jurisdictions," *American Sociological Review*, 7 (December 1942), pp. 833–839.

12. Based on Marshall B. Clinard, *Sociology of Deviant Behavior*, rev. ed. (New York: Holt, Rinehart and Winston, 1963), pp. 20–21; and Thorsten Sellin, *Research Memorandum on Crime and the Depression* (New York: Social Science Research Council, 1936), pp. 69–70.

13. Sophia M. Robison, *Can Delinquency Be Measured?* (New York: Columbia University Press, 1936).

14. Fred J. Murphy, Mary M. Shirley, and Helen L. Witmer, "The Incidence of Hidden Delinquency," *American Journal of Orthopsychiatry*, 16 (October 1946), pp. 686–696.

15. Austin L. Porterfield, *Youth in Trouble* (Fort Worth, Texas: Leo Potishman Foundation, 1946).

16. James F. Short, Jr., and F. Ivan Nye, "Extent of Unrecorded Juvenile Delinquency: Tentative Conclusions," *Journal of Criminal Law, Criminology and Police Science*, 49 (November-December 1958), pp. 296–302.

17. Among the studies are Ronald L. Akers, "Socio-Economic Status and Delinquent Behavior: A Retest," *Journal of Research in Crime and Delinquency*, 1 (January 1964), pp. 38–46; John P. Clark and Eugene P. Wenninger, "Socio-Economic Class and Areas as Correlates of Illegal Behavior among Juveniles," *American Sociological Review*, 27 (December 1962), pp. 826–834; Robert A. Dentler and Lawrence J. Monroe, "Social Correlates of Early Adolescent Theft," *American Sociological Review*, 26 (October 1961), pp. 733–743; Maynard L. Erickson and Lamar T. Empey, "Court Records, Undetected Delinquency and Decision-Making," *Journal of Criminal Law, Criminology and Police Science*, 54 (December 1963), pp. 456–469; F. Ivan Nye and James F. Short, Jr., "Socioeconomic Status and Delinquent Behavior," *American Journal of Sociology*, 63 (January 1958), pp. 381–389; Albert J. Reiss and Albert Lewis Rhodes, "The Distribution of Juvenile Delinquency in the Social Class Structure," *American Sociological Review*, 26 (October 1961), pp. 720–732; Harwin L. Voss, "Socio-Economic Status and Reported Delinquent Behavior," *Social Problems*, 13 (Winter 1966), pp. 314–324. Studies of self-reported delinquency are summarized in Robert H. Hardt and George E. Bodine, *Development of Self-Report Instruments in Delinquency Research: A Conference Report* (Syracuse, N.Y.: Syracuse University Youth Development Center, 1965).

18. James S. Wallerstein and Clement J. Wyle, "Our Law-Abiding Law-Breakers," *Probation*, 25 (April 1947), pp. 107–112.

19. Harry Manuel Schulman, "The Measurement of Crime in the United States," *Journal of Criminal Law, Criminology and Police Science*, 57 (December 1966), pp. 485–486.

20. President's Commission on Law Enforcement and Administration of Justice, *The Challenge of Crime in a Free Society* (Washington, D.C.: U.S. Government Printing Office, 1967), p. 21. For an analysis of the research, see Albert D. Biderman, "Surveys of Population Samples for Estimating Crime Incidence," *Annals of the American Academy of Political and Social Science*, 374 (November 1967), pp. 16–33.

21. *Ibid.*, p. 21.

22. See, for example, John C. Ball, Alan Ross, and Alice Simpson, "Incidence and Estimated Prevalence of Recorded Delinquency in a Metropolitan Area," *American Sociological Review*, 29 (February 1964), pp. 90–93; E. Jackson Baur, "The Trend of Juvenile Offenses in the Netherlands and the United States," *Journal of Criminal Law, Criminology and Police Science*, 55 (September 1964), pp. 359–369; Joseph W. Eaton and Kenneth Polk, *Measuring Delinquency* (Pittsburgh: University of Pittsburgh Press, 1961); Thomas P. Monahan, "On the Incidence of Delinquency," *Social Forces*, 39 (October 1960), pp. 66–72; Austin L. Porterfield, "A Decade of Serious Crimes in the United States: Some Trends and Hypotheses," *American Sociological Review*, 13 (February 1948), pp. 44–54; Thorsten Sellin, "Crime," *American Journal of Sociology*, 47 (May 1942), pp. 898–906; Thorsten Sellin, "Crime and Delinquency in the United States: An Overview," *Annals of the American Academy of Political and Social Science*, 339 (January 1962), pp. 11–23; Harry Willbach, "The Trend of Crime in New York City," *Journal of Criminal Law, Criminology and Police Science*, 29 (May-June 1938), pp. 62–75.

23. Such an approach to criminal statistics is suggested in John I. Kitsuse and Aaron V. Cicourel, "A Note on the Uses of Official Statistics," *Social Problems*, 11 (Fall 1963), pp. 131–139; Donald J. Newman, "The Effect of Accommodations in Justice Administration on Criminal Statistics," *Sociology and Social Research*, 46 (January 1962), pp. 144–155; Stanton Wheeler, "Criminal Statistics: A Reformulation of the Problem," *Journal of Criminal Law, Criminology and Police Science*, 58 (September 1967), pp. 317–324.

24. Donald R. Cressey, "The State of Criminal Statistics," *National Probation and Parole Association Journal*, 3 (July 1957), pp. 240–241. A similar view is presented in Albert D. Biderman and Albert J. Reiss, Jr., "On Exploring the 'Dark Figure' of Crime," *Annals of the American Academy of Political and Social Science*, 374 (November 1967), pp. 1–15.

25. Quoted in Fred J. Cook, "There's Always a Crime Wave — How Bad's This One?" *The New York Times Magazine*, October 6, 1968,

p. 38. The quotations from the other presidential candidates are also in Cook's article.

26. Quoted in Albert J. Reiss, "Crime, Law and Order as Election Issues," *Trans-action*, 5 (October 1968), p. 3.

27. *The New York Times*, April 27, 1973, p. 1.

3 Sociology of Criminal Law

1. Eugen Ehrlich, *The Fundamental Principles of the Sociology of the Law*, trans. W. Moll (Cambridge: Harvard University Press, 1936).

2. E. A. Ross, *Social Control* (New York: Macmillan, 1922), p. 106 (originally published in 1901).

3. Lester F. Ward, *Applied Sociology* (Boston: Ginn, 1906), p. 339.

4. Albion W. Small, *General Sociology* (Chicago: University of Chicago Press, 1925).

5. The relationship between early American sociologists and the development of Pound's sociological jurisprudence is discussed in Gilbert Geis, "Sociology and Jurisprudence: Admixture of Lore and Law," *Kentucky Law Journal*, 52 (Winter 1964), pp. 267–293. Also see Edwin M. Schur, *Law and Society* (New York: Random House, 1968), pp. 17–50.

6. Roscoe Pound, *Social Control Through Law* (New Haven: Yale University Press, 1942), p. 18. Earlier statements by Pound are found in Roscoe Pound, *An Introduction to the Philosophy of Law* (New Haven: Yale University Press, 1922); Roscoe Pound, *Outline of Lectures on Jurisprudence* (Cambridge: Harvard University Press, 1928).

7. Wolfgang Friedmann, *Law in a Changing Society* (Harmondsworth, Eng.: Penguin Books, 1964), p. 143.

8. Pound, *An Introduction to the Philosophy of Law*, pp. 98–99.

9. Carl A. Auerbach, "Law and Social Change in the United States," *UCLA Law Review*, 6 (July 1959), pp. 516–532. Similarly, see Julius Stone, *The Province and Function of Law* (Cambridge: Harvard University Press, 1950), Part III; Julius Stone, *Social Dimensions of Law and Justice* (Stanford: Stanford University Press, 1966), chaps. 4–8.

10. Roscoe Pound, "A Survey of Social Interests," *Harvard Law Review*, 57 (October 1943), p. 39.

11. George Lee Haskins, *Law and Authority in Early Massachusetts* (New York: Macmillan, 1960), p. 226.

12. Pound, "A Survey of Social Interests," pp. 1–2.

13. Jerome Michael and Mortimer J. Adler, *Crime, Law and Social Science* (New York: Harcourt, Brace, 1933).

14. Ibid., p. 5.

15. Ibid., p. 2.

16. Paul W. Tappan, *Crime, Justice and Correction* (New York: McGraw-Hill, 1960), p. 10.

17. Paul W. Tappan, "Who Is the Criminal?" *American Sociological Review*, 12 (February 1947), p. 100.

18. C. Ray Jeffery, "The Structure of American Criminological Thinking," *Journal of Criminal Law, Criminology and Police Science*, 46 (January-February, 1956), pp. 658–672.

19. Ibid., p. 672.

20. George C. Vold, *Theoretical Criminology* (New York: Oxford University Press, 1958), pp. v–vi. For recent discussions of these dual problems, behavior and definition, see David J. Bordua, "Recent Trends: Deviant Behavior and Social Control," *Annals of the American Academy of Political and Social Science*, 369 (January 1967), pp. 149—163; Jack P. Gibbs, "Conceptions of Deviant Behavior: the Old and the New," *Pacific Sociological Review*, 9 (Spring 1966), pp. 9–14; Ronald L. Akers, "Problems in the Sociology of Deviance: Social Definitions and Behavior," *Social Forces*, 46 (June 1968), pp. 455–465.

21. Austin T. Turk, "Prospects for Theories of Criminal Behavior," *Journal of Criminal Law, Criminology and Police Science*, 55 (December 1964), pp. 454–461.

22. Richard Quinney, "Crime in Political Perspective," *American Behavioral Scientist*, 8 (December 1964), pp. 19–22. This perspective is utilized and developed in Stuart L. Hills, *Crime, Power, and Morality: The Criminal-Law Process in the United States* (Scranton, Pa.: Chandler, 1971).

23. See Gilbert Geis, "Sociology, Criminology, and Criminal Law," *Social Problems*, 7 (Summer 1959), pp. 40–47.

24. Richard D. Schwartz, "From the Editor," *Law and Society Review*, 1 (November 1966), p. 6.

25. For a critique of this research, see Elliott Currie, "Sociology of Law: the Unasked Questions," *Yale Law Journal*, 81 (November 1971), pp. 134–147. The positivistic position is defended in Donald J. Black, "The Boundaries of Legal Sociology," *Yale Law Journal*, 81 (May 1972), pp. 1086–1100.

26. Norval Morris and Gordon Hawkins, *The Honest Politician's Guide to Crime Control* (Chicago: University of Chicago Press, 1970); Herbert L. Packer, *The Limits of the Criminal Sanction* (Stanford: Stanford University Press, 1968).

27. An excellent critique on some of this research is found in Nanette J. Davis, "Labeling Theory in Deviance Research: A Critique and Reformulation," *Sociological Quarterly*, 13 (Autumn 1972), pp. 447–474; Alvin W. Gouldner, "The Sociologist as Partisan: Sociology and the Welfare State," *The American Sociologist*, 3 (May 1968), pp. 103–116; Alex-

ander Liazos, "The Poverty of the Sociology of Deviance: Nuts, Sluts, and Perverts," *Social Problems*, 20 (Summer 1972), pp. 103–120; Alex Thio, "Class Bias in the Sociology of Deviance," *The American Sociologist*, 8 (February 1973), pp. 1–12.

28. Philip Selznick, "The Sociology of Law," in Robert K. Merton, Leonard Broom, and Leonard S. Cottrell, Jr., eds., *Sociology Today* (New York: Basic Books, 1959), p. 126.

29. This is a revision of my theory on the social reality of crime as originally presented in Richard Quinney, *The Social Reality of Crime* (Boston: Little, Brown, 1970), pp. 15–25.

30. Richard Quinney, "Crime Control in Capitalist Society: A Critical Philosophy of Legal Order," *Issues in Criminology*, 8 (Spring 1973), pp. 75–99.

31. Considerable support for this proposition is found in William J. Chambliss and Robert B. Seidman, *Law, Order, and Power* (Reading, Mass.: Addison-Wesley, 1971). Also see George Rusche and Otto Kirchheimer, *Punishment and Social Structure* (New York: Columbia University Press, 1939).

32. Vold, *Theoretical Criminology*, p. 202. Also see Irving Louis Horowitz and Martin Liebowitz, "Social Deviance and Political Marginality: Toward a Redefinition of the Relation Between Sociology and Politics," *Social Problems*, 15 (Winter 1968), pp. 280–296.

33. See Michael Banton, *The Policeman and the Community* (London: Tavistock, 1964); Egon Bittner, "The Police on Skid-Row: A Study of Peace Keeping," *American Sociological Review*, 32 (October 1967), pp. 699–715; John P. Clark, "Isolation of the Police: A Comparison of the British and American Situations," *Journal of Criminal Law, Criminology and Police Science*, 56 (September 1965), pp. 307–319; Nathan Goldman, *The Differential Selection of Juvenile Offenders for Court Appearance* (New York: National Council on Crime and Delinquency, 1963); James Q. Wilson, *Varieties of Police Behavior: The Management of Law and Order in Eight Communities* (Cambridge: Harvard University Press, 1968).

34. Abraham S. Blumberg, *Criminal Justice* (Chicago: Quadrangle Books, 1967); David J. Bordua and Albert J. Reiss, Jr., "Command, Control and Charisma: Reflections on Police Bureaucracy," *American Journal of Sociology*, 72 (July 1966), pp. 68–76; Aaron V. Cicourel, *The Social Organization of Juvenile Justice* (New York: John Wiley, 1968); Arthur Niederhoffer, *Behind the Shield: The Police in Urban Society* (Garden City, N.Y.: Doubleday, 1967); Jerome H. Skolnick, *Justice Without Trial* (New York: John Wiley, 1966); Arthur L. Stinchcombe, "Institutions of Privacy in the Determination of Police Administrative

Practice," *American Journal of Sociology*, 69 (September 1963), pp. 150–160; David Sudnow, "Normal Crimes: Sociological Features of the Penal Code in a Public Defender Office," *Social Problems*, 12 (Winter 1965), pp. 255–276; William A. Westley, "Violence and the Police," *American Journal of Sociology*, 59 (July 1953), pp. 34–41; Arthur Lewis Wood, *Criminal Lawyer* (New Haven: College & University Press, 1967).

35. Austin T. Turk, "Conflict and Criminality," *American Sociological Review*, 31 (June 1966), p. 34. For research on evaluation of suspects by policemen, see Irving Piliavin and Scott Briar, "Police Encounters with Juveniles," *American Journal of Sociology*, 70 (September 1964), pp. 206–214.

36. Assumed within the theory on the social reality of crime is Sutherland's theory of differential association. See Edwin H. Sutherland, *Principles of Criminology*, 4th ed. (Philadelphia: J. B. Lippincott, 1947). An analysis of the differential association theory is found in Melvin L. De Fleur and Richard Quinney, "A Reformulation of Sutherland's Differential Association Theory and a Strategy for Empirical Verification," *Journal of Research in Crime and Delinquency*, 3 (January 1966), pp. 1–22.

37. On the operant nature of criminally defined behavior, see Robert L. Burgess and Ronald L. Akers, "A Differential Association-Reinforcement Theory of Criminal Behavior," *Social Problems*, 14 (Fall 1966), pp. 128–147; C. Ray Jeffery, "Criminal Behavior and Learning Theory," *Journal of Criminal Law, Criminology and Police Science*, 56 (September 1965), pp. 294–300.

38. A discussion of the part the person plays in manipulating the deviant-defining situation is found in Judith Lorber, "Deviance as Performance: The Case of Illness," *Social Problems*, 14 (Winter 1967), pp. 302–310.

39. Edwin M. Lemert, *Human Deviance, Social Problems, and Social Control* (Englewood Cliffs, N.J.: Prentice-Hall, 1964), pp. 40–64; Edwin M. Lemert, *Social Pathology* (New York: McGraw-Hill, 1951), pp. 3–98. A related and earlier discussion is in Frank Tannenbaum, *Crime and the Community* (New York: Columbia University Press, 1938), pp. 3–81.

40. See Peter L. Berger and Thomas Luckmann, *The Social Construction of Reality* (Garden City, N.Y.: Doubleday, 1966). Relevant research on the dissemination of information is discussed in Everett M. Rogers, *Diffusion of Innovations* (New York: The Free Press, 1962).

41. See Alexander L. Clark and Jack P. Gibbs, "Social Control: A Reformulation," *Social Problems*, 12 (Spring 1965), pp. 398–415; Thomas E. Dow, Jr., "The Role of Identifica-

tion in Conditioning Public Attitude Toward the Offender," *Journal of Criminal Law, Criminology and Police Science,* 58 (March 1967), pp. 75–79; William P. Lentz, "Social Status and Attitudes Toward Delinquency Control," *Journal of Research in Crime and Delinquency,* 3 (July 1966), pp. 147–154; Jennie McIntyre, "Public Attitudes Toward Crime and Law Enforcement," *Annals of the American Academy of Political and Social Science,* 374 (November 1967), pp. 34–46; Anastassios D. Mylonas and Walter C. Reckless, "Prisoners' Attitudes Toward Law and Legal Institutions," *Journal of Criminal Law, Criminology and Police Science,* 54 (December 1963), pp. 479–484; Elizabeth A. Rooney and Don C. Gibbons, "Social Reactions to 'Crimes Without Victims,'" *Social Problems,* 13 (Spring 1966), pp. 400–410.

42. President's Commission on Law Enforcement and Administration of Justice, *The Challenge of Crime in a Free Society* (Washington, D.C.: United States Government Printing Office, 1967).

4 Legal Order and Crime Control

1. Ralph Miliband, *The State in Capitalist Society* (New York: Basic Books, 1969), p. 1.
2. Karl Marx, *Selected Writings in Sociology and Social Psychology,* trans. T. B. Bottomore (New York: McGraw-Hill, 1964), pp. 222–223.
3. Stanley Diamond, "The Rule of Law Versus the Order of Custom," *Social Research,* 38 (Spring 1971), p. 47.
4. Ibid., pp. 65–68. This is also observed in Frederick Engels, *The Origin of the Family, Private Property, and the State* (New York: International Publishers, 1942).
5. Ibid., p. 71.
6. George M. Calhoun, *The Growth of Criminal Law in Ancient Greece* (Berkeley: University of California Press, 1927).
7. Ibid., p. 52.
8. George Novack, *Democracy and Revolution* (New York: Pathfinder Press, 1971), p. 32.
9. Hans Julius Wolff, *Roman Law: An Historical Introduction* (Norman, Okla.: University of Oklahoma Press, 1951), pp. 54–61. Also Barry Nicholas, *An Introduction to Roman Law* (Oxford: Oxford University Press, 1962), pp. 208–209.
10. Wolfgang Kunkel, *An Introduction to Roman Legal History and Constitutional History* (Oxford: Oxford University Press, 1966), p. 61.
11. Erich S. Gruen, *Roman Politics and the Criminal Courts, 149–78 B.C.* (Cambridge: Harvard University Press, 1968).
12. C. Ray Jeffery, "The Development of Crime in Early English Society," *Journal of Criminal Law, Criminology and Police Science,* 47 (March-April, 1957), pp. 647–666.
13. See F. L. Attenborough, ed., *The Laws of the English Kings* (Cambridge: Cambridge University Press, 1922).
14. G. O. Sayles, *Medieval Foundation of England* (London: Methuen, 1966), chap. 21. Also John W. Jeudwine, *Tort, Crime and Police in Medieval Britain* (London: Williams and Norgate, 1917), especially chaps. 7 and 8.
15. Jerome Hall, *Theft, Law and Society,* 2nd ed. Indianapolis, Ind.: Bobbs-Merrill, 1952).
16. Ibid., p. 10.
17. Ibid., p. 19.
18. Ibid., p. 31.
19. Ibid., p. 33.
20. Roscoe Pound, "The Development of American Law and Its Deviation from English Law," *Law Quarterly Review,* 67 (January 1951), pp. 49–66.
21. Julius Goebel, Jr., "King's Law and Local Custom in Seventeenth Century New England," *Columbia Law Review,* 31 (March 1931), pp. 416–448.
22. See Edwin C. Surrency, "Revision of Colonial Laws," *American Journal of Legal History,* 9 (July 1965), pp. 189–202; Elizabeth Caspar Brown, *British Statutes in American Law, 1776–1836* (Ann Arbor: University of Michigan Law School, 1964).
23. See Carl J. Friedrich, "Rights, Liberties, Freedoms: A Reappraisal," *American Political Science Review,* 57 (December 1963), pp. 841–854; Roscoe Pound, *The Formative Era of American Law* (Boston: Little, Brown, 1938).
24. Perry Miller, *The Life of the Mind: From the Revolution to the Civil War* (New York: Harcourt, Brace and World, 1965), pp. 99–265.
25. W. Stitt Robinson, "The Legal Status of the Indian in Colonial Virginia," *Virginia Magazine of History and Biography,* 61 (July 1953), pp. 247–259.
26. Quoted in Glenn Shirley, *Law West of Fort Smith: Frontier Justice in the Indian Territory, 1834–1896* (New York: Collier Books, 1961), p. 146.
27. Ibid., p. 180. Further material on frontier law is found in Lawrence M. Friedman, *A History of American Law* (New York: Simon and Schuster, 1973).
28. For one of the few studies of law in the mining territory, see Charles Howard Shinn, *Mining Camps: A Study in American Frontier Government* (New York: Harper and Row, 1965), originally published 1884.
29. The remainder of this chapter is adapted from my book, *Critique of Legal Order: Crime Control in Capitalist Society* (Boston: Little, Brown, 1974), pp. 99–119.
30. "Crime, Its Prevalence, and Measures of Prevention," Message from the President of the

United States, House of Representatives, 89th Congress, March 8, 1965, Document No. 103.

31. "Omnibus Crime Control and Safe Streets Act," Public Law 90-351, *United States Statutes at Large*, 1968, vol. 82 (Washington, D.C.: U.S. Government Printing Office, 1969), pp. 197–198.

32. See Richard Harris, *The Fear of Crime* (New York: Praeger, 1969).

33. "Controlling Crime Through More Effective Law Enforcement," *Hearings* Before the Subcommittee on Criminal Law and Procedures of the Committee on the Judiciary, United States Senate, 90th Congress (Washington, D.C.: U.S. Government Printing Office, 1967), p. 1.

34. See Herbert L. Packer, "Nixon's Crime Program and What It Means," *The New York Review of Books*, 15 (October 22, 1970), pp. 26–37.

35. *The New York Times*, July 24, 1970, p. 1. See District of Columbia Committee, "Anti-Crime Proposals," *Hearings* Before the Select Committee on Crime, U.S. House of Representatives, 91st Congress (Washington, D.C.: U.S. Government Printing Office, 1970).

36. "Organized Crime Control," *Hearings* Before the Subcommittee on Criminal Laws and Procedures of the Committee on the Judiciary, United States Senate, 91st Congress (Washington, D.C.: U.S. Government Printing Office, 1970).

37. *Congressional Record*, Vol. 16, Part 2, 91st Congress, January 28, 1970 (Washington, D.C.: U.S. Government Printing Office, 1970), p. 1690.

38. See Joseph C. Goulden, "Tooling Up for Repression: The Cops Hit the Jackpot," *The Nation*, 211 (November 23, 1970), pp. 520–533.

39. Law Enforcement Assistance Administration, *Grants and Contracts Awarded Under the Law Enforcement Assistance Act of 1965*, Fiscal 1966–1968 (Washington, D.C.: U.S. Government Printing Office, 1968), p. 1.

40. *Third Annual Report of the Law Enforcement Assistance Administration*, Fiscal Year 1971 (Washington, D.C.: U.S. Government Printing Office, 1972), p. ii.

41. Law Enforcement Assistance Administration, *A Program for a Safer, More Just America* (Washington, D.C.: U.S. Government Printing Office, 1970), p. 3.

42. Law Enforcement Assistance Administration, *Safe Streets: The LEAA Program at Work* (Washington, D.C.: U.S. Government Printing Office, 1971), p. i.

43. *Third Annual Report of the Law Enforcement Assistance Administration*, p. iii. Also see the *LEAA Newsletter*, 1 (July 1971), pp. 1–6.

44. See "Crime Program Held Inefficient," *The New York Times*, April 11, 1972, p. 14.

45. Quoted in the *LEAA Newsletter*, 2 (November 1971), p. 8.

46. For some of the FBI's history, see Fred J. Cook, *The FBI Nobody Knows* (New York: Macmillan, 1964).

47. Hank Messick, *John Edgar Hoover* (New York: David McKay, 1972); Ralph de Toledano, *J. Edgar Hoover: The Man and His Times* (New Rochelle, N.Y.: Arlington House, 1973); Pat Watters and Stephen Gillers, eds., *Investigating the FBI* (New York: Doubleday, 1973).

48. Tom Wicker, "A Gross Invasion," *The New York Times*, December 19, 1971, p. E 11.

49. Quoted in the *NCCD Newsletter*, 50 (May-June 1971), p. 15.

50. Ben A. Franklin, "Federal Computers Amass Files on Suspect Citizens," *The New York Times*, June 28, 1970, p. 42. On the Army's surveillance of the population, see *The New York Times*, January 18, 1971, p. 1; September 7, 1971, p. 39. Also "Army Surveillance of Civilians: A Documentary Analysis," Subcommittee on Constitutional Rights, Committee on the Judiciary, United States Senate, 92nd Congress, 2nd Session (Washington, D.C.: U.S. Government Printing Office, 1972).

51. Quoted in Richard Harris, *Justice: The Crisis of Law, Order, and Freedom in America* (New York: E. P. Dutton, 1970), p. 186.

52. Ibid. Also see John T. Elliff, *Crime, Dissent, and the Attorney General: The Justice Department in the 1960's* (Beverly Hills, Calif.: Sage Publications, 1971).

53. On this trial and other political trials, see *Trials of the Resistance* (New York: Vintage Books, 1970).

54. Frank J. Donner and Eugene Cerruti, "The Grand Jury Network: How the Nixon Administration Has Secretly Perverted a Traditional Safeguard of Individual Rights," *The Nation*, 214 (January 3, 1972), p. 5.

55. Ibid.

5 Criminal Laws in America

1. See Perry Miller, *The New England Mind: The Seventeenth Century* (New York: Macmillan, 1939).

2. George Lee Haskins, *Law and Authority in Early Massachusetts* (New York: Macmillan, 1960), p. 44.

3. Quoted in Richard B. Morris, *Studies in the History of American Law*, 2nd ed. (New York: Joseph M. Mitchell, 1959), p. 35.

4. Haskins, *Law and Authority in Early Massachusetts*, pp. 44–45.

5. See Kai T. Erikson, *Wayward Puritans: A Study in the Sociology of Deviance* (New York: John Wiley, 1966), pp. 54–64. Also see Edwin Powers, *Crime and Punishment in Early Massachusetts* (Boston: Beacon Press, 1966).

6. Quoted in Haskins, *Law and Authority in Early Massachusetts*, p. 145.

7. Ibid., p. 146.

8. Ibid., pp. 146–147.

9. Ibid., p. 225.

10. David J. Rothman, *The Discovery of the Asylum* (Boston: Little, Brown, 1971), especially pp. 57–78.

11. William E. Nelson, "Emerging Notions of Modern Criminal Law in the Revolutionary Era: An Historical Perspective," *New York University Law Review*, 42 (May 1967), p. 463. Also see Roger Lane, "Crime and Criminal Statistics in Nineteenth-Century Massachusetts," *Journal of Social History*, 2 (Winter 1968), pp. 156–163.

12. See Otto Kirchheimer, *Political Justice: The Use of Legal Procedure for Political Ends* (Princeton: Princeton University Press, 1961).

13. Paul B. Horton and Gerald R. Leslie, *The Sociology of Social Problems*, 3rd ed. (New York: Appleton-Century-Crofts, 1965), pp. 632–633.

14. This is the thesis found in Lawrence Henry Gipson, *The Coming of the Revolution, 1763–1775* (New York: Harper and Row, 1954). Also see George Adrian Washburne, *Imperial Control of the Administration of Justice in the Thirteen Colonies, 1684–1776* (New York: Columbia University Press, 1923).

15. Harold L. Nelson, "Seditious Libel in Colonial America," *American Journal of Legal History*, 3 (April 1959), pp. 160–172; and Frederick S. Siebert, *Freedom of the Press in England, 1476–1776* (Urbana: University of Illinois Press, 1952).

16. Leonard W. Levy, *Freedom of Speech and Press in Early American History: Legacy of Suppression* (New York: Harper and Row, 1963); James Morton Smith, "The Sedition Law, Free Speech, and the American Political Process," *William and Mary Quarterly*, 9 (October 1952), pp. 497–511.

17. Herbert L. Packer, "Offenses Against the State," *Annals of the American Academy of Political and Social Science*, 339 (January 1962), pp. 77–89.

18. Bradley Chapin, *The American Law of Treason: Revolutionary and National Origins* (Seattle: University of Washington Press, 1964); J. Willard Hurst, "Treason in the United States," *Harvard Law Review*, 58 (December 1944), pp. 226–272; 58 (February 1945), pp. 395–444; and 58 (July 1945), pp. 806–857.

19. Claude H. Van Tyne, *The Loyalists in the American Revolution* (New York: Macmillan, 1902), especially appendix C.

20. Walter Gellhorn, "A General View," in Walter Gellhorn, ed., *The States and Subversion* (Ithaca: Cornell University Press, 1952), p. 359.

21. Herbert H. Hyman, "England and America: Climates of Tolerance and Intolerance," in Daniel Bell, ed., *The Radical Right* (Garden City, N.Y.: Doubleday, 1963), chap. 12.

22. Norman Redlich and Kenneth R. Feinberg, "Individual Conscience and the Selective Conscientious Objector: The Right Not to Kill," *New York University Law Review*, 44 (November 1969), pp. 875–900.

23. Quoted in Peter and Deborah Babcox and Bob Abel, eds., *The Conspiracy* (New York: Dell, 1969), pp. 28–29.

24. B. L. Ingraham and Kazuhiko Tokoro, "Political Crime in the United States and Japan: A Comparative Study," *Issues in Criminology*, 4 (Spring 1969), pp. 145–170.

25. Hans B. Thorelli, *The Federal Antitrust Policy: Origination of an American Tradition* (Baltimore: Johns Hopkins Press, 1955), pp. 9–53.

26. Ibid., pp. 54–163.

27. Quoted in Arthur P. Dudden, "Men Against Monopoly: The Prelude to Trust-Busting," *Journal of the History of Ideas*, 18 (October 1957), p. 593.

28. Quoted in Samuel Eliot Morison and Henry Steele Commager, *The Growth of the American Republic*, vol. 2 (New York: Oxford University Press, 1950), p. 143.

29. Wolfgang Friedmann, *Law in a Changing Society* (Harmondsworth, Eng.: Penguin Books, 1964), p. 161.

30. Quoted in Morison and Commager, *The Growth of the American Republic*, vol. 2, p. 391.

31. Gabriel Kolko, *The Triumph of Conservatism: A Reinterpretation of American History, 1900–1916* (New York: Free Press, 1963), p. 2.

32. Ibid., p. 278.

33. Morison and Commager, *The Growth of the American Republic*, vol. 2, p. 630.

34. A natural history of the social problem of food adulteration is found in Donald J. Newman, "A Study of the Criminal Nature of Pure Food Law Violations," unpublished M.A. thesis, University of Wisconsin, 1952.

35. Morton Mintz, *The Therapeutic Nightmare: A Report on Prescription Drugs, the Men Who Take Them, and the Agency That Controls Them* (Boston: Houghton Mifflin, 1965), p. 41.

36. For these and later laws, see Stephen Wilson, *Food and Drug Regulation* (Washington, D.C.: American Council of Public Affairs, 1942).

37. Arthur Kallet and F. J. Schlink, *100,000,000 Guinea Pigs* (New York: Vanguard Press, 1933); Ruth deForest Lamb, *American Chamber of Horrors* (New York: Farrar and Rinehart, 1936).

38. From Mintz, *The Therapeutic Nightmare*, pp. 45–46.

39. Thomas W. Christopher and Charles W. Dunn, *Special Federal Food and Drug Laws* (New York: Commerce Clearing House, 1954).

40. David H. Vernon and Franklin M. Depew, *General State Food and Drug Laws* (New York: Commerce Clearing House, 1955). For a study on how occupational laws are formulated according to the interests of the occupations, pharmacy included, see Ronald L. Akers, "The Professional Association and the Legal Regulation of Practice," *Law and Society Review*, 2 (May 1968), pp. 463–482.

41. U.S. Congress, Senate, Subcommittee of the Committee on the Judiciary, *Hearings Before the Subcommittee on Antitrust and Monopoly*, 86th Congress, 1st and 2nd Sessions, Parts 14–22, 1959–1960; U.S. Congress, Senate, Subcommittee of the Committee on the Judiciary, *Report of the Committee on the Judiciary*, "Antitrust and Monopoly Activities, 1960," Report No. 167, 87th Congress, 1st Session, 1961; U.S. Congress, Senate, Subcommittee of the Committee on the Judiciary, *Report of the Committee on the Judiciary*, "Administered Prices: Drugs," Report No. 448, 87th Congress, 1st Session, 1961.

42. James S. Turner, *The Chemical Feast* (New York: Grossman, 1970), p. 209.

43. Ibid., p. 81.

44. Ibid., p. 43.

45. Ronald L. Akers, "The Professional Association and the Legal Regulation of Practice," *Law and Society Review*, 2 (May 1968), p. 465.

46. Ibid., p. 467.

47. Ibid., p. 476. Also see Ronald L. Akers, "Professional Organization, Political Power, and Occupational Laws," unpublished Ph.D. dissertation, University of Kentucky, 1966.

48. Howard R. and Martha E. Lewis, *The Medical Offenders* (New York: Simon and Schuster, 1970), p. 21.

49. Ibid., p. 24. For related research on disbarment of lawyers, see Kenneth J. Reichstein, "Ambulance Chasing: A Case Study of Deviation and Control within the Legal Profession," *Social Problems*, 13 (Summer 1965), pp. 3–17.

50. Lewis, *The Medical Offenders*, pp. 312–320.

51. For a history of Sunday law, see Abram H. Lewis, *A Critical History of Sunday Legislation from 321 to 1888 A.D.* (New York: D. Appleton, 1888); and George E. Harris, *A Treatise on Sunday Laws* (Rochester, N.Y.: Lawyers' Cooperative, 1892).

52. Sunday laws in America are discussed in Alvin W. Johnson, "Sunday Legislation," *Kentucky Law Journal*, 23 (November 1934), pp. 131–166; and Warren L. Johns, *Dateline Sunday: U.S.A.: The Story of Three Centuries of Sunday-Law Battles in America* (New York: Taplinger, 1967).

53. Eugene P. Chell, "Sunday Blue Laws: An Analysis of Their Position in Our Society," *Rutgers Law Review*, 12 (Spring 1958), p. 520.

54. Chell, "Sunday Blue Laws," pp. 511–512.

55. McGowan v. Maryland, in 366 United States Reports (October term, 1960), p. 421.

56. McGowan v. Maryland, pp. 451–452.

57. McGowan v. Maryland, p. 435.

58. See Alan H. Swanson, "Sexual Psychopath Statutes: Summary and Analysis," *Journal of Criminal Law, Criminology and Police Science*, 51 (July-August, 1960), pp. 215–235.

59. Habitual offender laws are discussed in Paul W. Tappan, "Habitual Offender Laws in the United States," *Federal Probation*, 13 (March 1949), pp. 28–31.

60. Edwin H. Sutherland, "The Diffusion of Sexual Psychopath Laws," *American Journal of Sociology*, 56 (September 1950), pp. 142–148.

61. Ibid., p. 145.

62. Edwin H. Sutherland, "The Sexual Psychopath Laws," *Journal of Criminal Law, Criminology and Police Science*, 40 (January-February, 1950), pp. 543–554.

63. Paul W. Tappan, "Sex Offender Laws and Their Administration," *Federal Probation*, 14 (September 1950), p. 33.

64. Ibid., p. 33.

65. Ibid., p. 34.

66. See Morris Ploscowe, "Sex Offenses: The American Legal Context," *Law and Contemporary Problems*, 25 (Spring 1960), pp. 217–225; Also, Gerhard O. W. Mueller, *Legal Regulation of Sexual Conduct* (Dobbs Ferry, N.Y.: Oceana, 1961).

67. Morris Ploscowe, *Sex and the Law* (Englewood Cliffs, N.J.: Prentice-Hall, 1951), pp. 136–164.

68. Philip Alexander Bruce, *Social Life in Old Virginia* (New York: Capricorn Books, 1965), p. 45 (originally published in 1910).

69. Henry H. Foster, Jr., "The 'Comstock Load' — Obscenity and the Law," *Journal of Criminal Law, Criminology and Police Science*, 48 (September-October, 1957), pp. 245–258.

70. *The Report of the Commission on Obscenity and Pornography* (New York: Bantam Books, 1970).

71. *The New York Times*, October 25, 1970, p. 71.

72. The Wolfenden Report, *Report of the Committee on Homosexual Offenses and Prostitution* (New York: Stein and Day, 1963), pp. 143–144.

73. Pamela A. Roby, "Politics and Criminal Law: Revision of the New York State Penal Law on Prostitution," *Social Problems*, 17 (Summer 1969), pp. 83–109.

74. See Martin Hoffman, *The Gay World* (New York: Basic Books, 1968), pp. 77–97.

75. See Edwin M. Schur, *Crimes Without Victims* (Englewood Cliffs, N.J.: Prentice-Hall, 1965), pp. 11–66.

76. An excellent coverage of the abortion controversy is presented in Daniel Callahan, *Abortion: Law, Choice and Morality* (New York: Macmillan, 1970).

77. *The New York Times*, January 23, 1973, p. 1.

78. These offenses are discussed in Irwin Deutscher, "The Petty Offender: A Sociological Alien," *Journal of Criminal Law, Criminology and Police Science,* 44 (January-February, 1954), pp. 592–595; David J. Pittman and C. Wayne Gordon, *Revolving Door* (New York: Free Press of Glencoe, 1958); and Earl Rubington, "The Chronic Drunkenness Offender," *Annals of the American Academy of Political and Social Science,* 315 (January 1958), pp. 65–72.

79. Andrew Sinclair, *Era of Excess: A Social History of the Prohibition Movement* (New York: Harper and Row, 1964).

80. Ibid., p. 105.

81. Ibid., p. 170.

82. Ibid., pp. 5–6. Laws, such as that on Prohibition, are discussed as responses to the lack of consensus on norms in Joseph R. Gusfield, "Moral Passage: The Symbolic Process in Public Designations of Deviance," *Social Problems,* 15 (Fall 1967), pp. 175–188.

83. Forrest W. Lacey, "Vagrancy and Other Crimes of Personal Condition," *Harvard Law Review,* 66 (May 1953), p. 1203. Also see Caleb Foote, "Vagrancy-Type Law and Its Administration," *University of Pennsylvania Law Review,* 104 (March 1956), pp. 603–650.

84. William J. Chambliss, "A Sociological Analysis of the Law of Vagrancy," *Social Problems,* 12 (Summer 1964), pp. 67–77. Also George Rusche and Otto Kirchheimer, *Punishment and Social Structure* (New York: Columbia University Press, 1939), pp. 32–41.

85. Chambliss, "A Sociological Analysis of the Law of Vagrancy," p. 69.

86. Ibid., p. 76.

87. Arthur H. Sherry, "Vagrants, Rogues, and Vagabonds – Old Concepts in Need of Revision," *California Law Review,* 48 (October 1960), p. 567.

88. *The New York Times,* July 8, 1967, pp. 1 and 9.

89. Troy Duster, *The Legislation of Morality: Laws, Drugs, and Moral Judgment* (New York: Free Press, 1970), pp. 3–28.

90. Alfred R. Lindesmith, *The Addict and the Law* (Bloomington: Indiana University Press, 1965), chap. 1.

91. See Alfred R. Lindesmith, "Federal Law and Drug Addiction," *Social Problems,* 7 (Summer 1959), pp. 48–57; Howard S. Becker, *Outsiders: Studies in the Sociology of Deviance* (New York: Free Press, 1963), pp. 135–146; Donald T. Dickson, "Bureaucracy and Morality: An Organizational Perspective on a Moral Crusade," *Social Problems,* 16 (Fall 1968), pp. 143–156.

92. Alfred R. Lindesmith, "The British System of Narcotics Control," *Law and Contemporary Problems,* 22 (Winter 1957), pp. 138–154; Edwin M. Schur, *Narcotic Addiction in Britain*

and America: The Impact of Public Policy (Bloomington: Indiana University Press, 1962).

93. Lindesmith, *The Addict and the Law,* p. 270. Legalization of marijuana use has recently been recommended by the National Commission on Marijuana and Drug Abuse, *Marihuana: A Signal of Misunderstanding* (Washington, D.C.: U.S. Government Printing Office, 1972).

94. *The New York Times,* June 18, 1971, p. 1.

6 Sociology of Criminal Behavior

1. Ralf Dahrendorf, *Class and Class Conflict in Industrial Society* (Stanford: Stanford University Press, 1959), especially pp. 161–162.

2. Hans Gerth and C. Wright Mills, *Character and Social Structure* (New York: Harcourt, Brace, 1963), especially pp. 192–273; C. Wright Mills, *The Power Elite* (New York: Oxford University Press, 1956).

3. See, for example, Paul A. Baran and Paul M. Sweezy, *Monopoly Capitalism: An Essay on the American Economic and Social Order* New York: Monthly Review Press, 1966).

4. Edwin H. Sutherland, *Principles of Criminology,* 3rd ed. (Philadelphia: Lippincott, 1939).

5. Donald R. Cressey, "Epidemiological and Individual Conduct: A Case from Criminology," *Pacific Sociological Review,* 3 (Fall 1960), p. 55.

6. Richard A. Cloward and Lloyd E. Ohlin, *Delinquency and Opportunity: A Theory of Delinquent Gangs* (New York: Free Press of Glencoe, 1960), p. 148.

7. For the variations in arrest statistics according to such characteristics as sex and race, see Federal Bureau of Investigation, *Uniform Crime Reports — 1972* (Washington, D.C.: United States Government Printing Office, 1973), pp. 124–133.

8. Ibid., p. 128.

9. Ibid., p. 129. For rates in a particular city, see Victor Eisner, *The Delinquency Label: The Epidemiology of Juvenile Delinquency* (New York: Random House, 1969).

10. James F. Short, Jr., and F. Ivan Nye, "Extent of Unrecorded Juvenile Delinquency: Tentative Conclusions," *Journal of Criminal Law, Criminology and Police Science,* 49 (November-December, 1958), pp. 296–302.

11. James S. Wallerstein and Clement J. Wyle, "Our Law-Abiding Law Breakers," *Probation,* 25, (April 1947), pp. 107–112.

12. See Herbert A. Bloch and Arthur Niederhoffer, *The Gang: A Study of Adolescent Behavior* (New York: Philosophical Library, 1958).

13. Paul Goodman, *Growing up Absurd* (New York: Random House, 1960).

14. See Erik H. Erikson, *Childhood and Society* (New York: W. W. Norton, 1950); Edgar Z.

Friedenberg, *The Vanishing Adolescent* (New York: Dell, 1962).

15. Delinquency in relation to sex roles is discussed in Ruth Morris, "Female Delinquency and Relational Problems," *Social Forces*, 43 (December 1964), pp. 82–89; Albert J. Reiss, Jr., "Sex Offenses: The Marginal Status of the Adolescent," *Law and Contemporary Problems*, 25 (Spring 1960), pp. 309–334; John C. Ball and Nell Logan, "Early Sexual Behavior of Lower-Class Delinquent Girls," *Journal of Criminal Law, Criminology and Police Science*, 51 (July-August, 1960), pp. 209–214. For excellent critiques of research on the criminality of women, see Dorie Klein, "The Etiology of Female Crime: A Review of the Literature," *Issues in Criminology*, 8 (Fall 1973), pp. 3–30; and Dale Hoffman Bustamante, "The Nature of Female Criminality," *Issues in Criminology*, 8 (Fall 1973), pp. 117–136.

16. W. Lloyd Warner and Paul S. Lunt, *The Social Life of a Modern Community* (New Haven: Yale University Press, 1941). Similarly, see August B. Hollingshead, *Elmtown's Youth* (New York: John Wiley, 1949).

17. F. Ivan Nye, James F. Short, Jr., and Virgil J. Olson, "Socio-economic Status and Delinquent Behavior," *American Journal of Sociology*, 63 (January 1958), pp. 381–389. For related findings, see Ronald L. Akers, "Socio-Economic Status and Delinquent Behavior: A Retest," *Journal of Research in Crime and Delinquency*, 1 (January 1964), pp. 38–46; Robert A. Bentler and Lawrence J. Monroe, "Social Correlates of Early Adolescent Theft," *American Sociological Review*, 26 (October 1961), pp. 733–743.

18. Walter B. Miller, "Lower Class Culture as a Generating Milieu of Gang Delinquency," *Journal of Social Issues*, 14 (November 3, 1958), pp. 5–19.

19. Albert K. Cohen, *Delinquent Boys: The Culture of the Gang* (New York: Free Press of Glencoe, 1955).

20. Critiques of the theory of the "delinquent subculture" are found in David J. Bordua, "Delinquent Subcultures: Sociological Interpretations of Gang Delinquency," *Annals of the American Academy of Political and Social Science*, 338 (November 1961), pp. 119–136; John I. Kitsuse and David C. Dietrick, "Delinquent Boys: A Critique," *American Sociological Review*, 24 (April 1959), pp. 208–215; Lamar Empey, "Delinquency Theory and Recent Research," *Journal of Research in Crime and Delinquency*, 4 (January 1967), pp. 28–42.

21. David Matza and Gresham M. Sykes, "Juvenile Delinquency and Subterranean Values," *American Sociological Review*, 26 (October 1961), pp. 712–719. Also see Ralph W. England, Jr., "A Theory of Middle Class Juvenile Delinquency," *Journal of Criminal Law,*

Criminology and Police Science, 50 (March-April, 1960), pp. 535–540; Harold L. Myerhoff and Barbara G. Myerhoff, "Field Observations of Middle Class 'Groups,'" *Social Forces*, 42 (March 1942), pp. 328–336.

22. Gresham M. Sykes and David Matza, "Techniques of Neutralization: A Theory of Delinquency," *American Sociological Review*, 22 (December 1957), pp. 664–670.

23. See Marvin E. Wolfgang, *Crime and Race: Conceptions and Misconceptions* (New York: Institute of Human Relations, 1964), pp. 31–35.

24. Federal Bureau of Investigation, *Uniform Crime Reports — 1972*, p. 131. For rate differences between racial groups according to self-report delinquency measures, see Leroy C. Gould, "Who Defines Delinquency: A Comparison of Self-Reported and Officially Reported Indices of Delinquency in Three Racial Groups," *Social Problems*, 16 (Winter 1969), pp. 325–336.

25. For a discussion of these rates, see Donald R. Cressey, "Crime," in Robert K. Merton and Robert A. Nisbet, eds., *Contemporary Social Problems*, 2nd ed. (New York: Harcourt, Brace and World, 1966), pp. 153–155.

26. C. C. Van Vechten, "The Criminality of the Foreign-Born," *Journal of Criminal Law, Criminology and Police Science*, 32 (July-August, 1941), pp. 139–147.

27. See Guy B. Johnson, "The Negro and Crime," *Annals of the American Academy of Political and Social Science*, 271 (September 1941), pp. 93–104; Earl R. Moses, "Differentials in Crime Rates Between Negroes and Whites Based on Comparisons of Four Socio-Economically Equated Areas," *American Sociological Review*, 12 (August 1947), pp. 411–420. Documentation that the excess of black arrests rates over white arrest rates results from greater concentration of blacks in the lower class and their higher rate of unemployment is contained in Edward Green, "Race, Social Status, and Criminal Arrest," *American Sociological Review*, 35 (June 1970), pp. 476–490.

28. For research and theoretical development, see John M. Martin, Joseph P. Fitzpatrick, and Robert E. Gould, *The Analysis of Delinquent Behavior: A Structural Approach* (New York: Random House, 1968).

29. Critiques of the ecological approach in criminology can be found in Terrence Morris, *The Criminal Area* (London: Routledge & Kegan Paul, 1958); Judith A. Wilks, "Ecological Correlates of Crime and Delinquency," in President's Commission on Law Enforcement and Administration of Justice, *Crime and Its Impact — An Assessment* (Washington, D.C.: U.S. Government Printing Office, 1967), pp. 138–156. Much of the research on the ecology

of crime is contained in Harwin L. Voss and David M. Petersen, eds., *Ecology of Crime and Delinquency* (New York: Appleton-Century-Crofts, 1971).

30. Stuart Lottier, "Distribution of Criminal Offenses in Sectional Regions," *Journal of Criminal Law, Criminology and Police Science*, 29 (September-October, 1938), pp. 329–344.

31. Lyle W. Shannon, "The Spatial Distribution of Criminal Offenses by States," *Journal of Criminal Law, Criminology and Police Science*, 45 (September-October, 1954), pp. 264–274.

32. Federal Bureau of Investigation, *Uniform Crime Reports — 1972*, pp. 62–67.

33. See Walter C. Reckless, *The Crime Problem*, 3rd ed. (New York: Appleton-Century-Crofts, 1961), pp. 69–70.

34. See Wilks, "Ecological Correlates of Crime and Delinquency," pp. 150–151.

35. See Federal Bureau of Investigation, *Crime in the United States — 1971*, pp. 116–117.

36. Marshall B. Clinard, "The Process of Urbanization and Criminal Behavior," *American Journal of Sociology*, 48 (September 1942), pp. 202–213; William P. Lentz, "Rural and Urban Differentials in Juvenile Delinquency," *Journal of Criminal Law, Criminology and Police Science*, 47 (September-October, 1956), pp. 331–339; Theodore N. Ferdinand, "The Offense Patterns and Family Structures of Urban, Village, and Rural Delinquency," *Journal of Criminal Law, Criminology and Police Science*, 55 (March 1964), pp. 86–93; John P. Clark and Eugene P. Wenninger, "Socio-Economic Class and Area as Correlates of Illegal Behavior Among Juveniles," *American Sociological Review*, 27 (December 1962), pp. 826–834; Richard Quinney, "Structural Characteristics, Population Areas, and Crime Rates in the United States," *Journal of Criminal Law, Criminology and Police Science*, 57 (March 1966), pp. 45–52.

37. Clifford R. Shaw and Henry D. McKay, *Delinquent Areas* (Chicago: University of Chicago Press, 1929); Clifford R. Shaw and Henry D. McKay, *Juvenile Delinquency and Urban Areas* (Chicago: University of Chicago Press, 1942).

38. Bernard Lander, *Toward an Understanding of Juvenile Delinquency* (New York: Columbia University Press, 1954).

39. Charles V. Willie and Anita Gershenovitz, "Juvenile Delinquency in Racially Mixed Areas," *American Sociological Review*, 29 (October 1964), pp. 740–744; David J. Bordua, "Juvenile Delinquency and Anomie," *Social Problems*, 6 (Winter, 1958–1959), pp. 230–238; Ronald J. Chilton, "Continuity in Delinquency Area Research: A Comparison of Studies for Baltimore, Detroit and Indianapolis," *American Sociological Review*, 29 (February 1964), pp. 71–83. Some of this research is analyzed

in Gerald T. Slatin, "Ecological Analysis of Delinquency: Aggregation Effects," *American Sociological Review*, 34 (December 1969), pp. 894–907.

40. Calvin F. Schmid, "Urban Crime Areas: Part II," *American Sociological Review*, 25 (October 1960), pp. 655–678; Kenneth Polk, "Juvenile Delinquency and Social Areas," *Social Problems*, 5 (Winter, 1957–1958), pp. 214–217; Richard Quinney, "Crime, Delinquency and Social Areas," *Journal of Research in Crime and Delinquency*, 1 (July 1964), pp. 149–154.

41. Frederick M. Thrasher, *The Gang* (Chicago: University of Chicago Press, 1927). Also see William F. Whyte, *Street Corner Society* (Chicago: University of Chicago Press, 1943).

42. Lewis Yablonsky, *The Violent Gang* (New York: Free Press of Glencoe, 1962); Harold W. Pfantz, "Near-Group Theory and Collective Behavior: A Critical Reformulation," *Social Problems*, 9 (Fall 1961), pp. 167–174.

43. Solomon Kobrin, "The Conflict of Values in Delinquency Areas," *American Sociological Review*, 16 (October 1951), pp. 653–661.

44. Cloward and Ohlin, *Delinquency and Opportunity*, pp. 161–186.

45. For further empirical works to support this position, see Irving Spergel, *Racketville, Slumtown, Haulburg: An Exploratory Study of Delinquent Subcultures* (Chicago: University of Chicago Press, 1964); Irving Spergel, "Male Young Adult Criminality, Deviant Values, and Differential Opportunities in Two Lower Class Negro Neighborhoods," *Social Problems*, 10 (Winter 1963), pp. 237–250; Albert J. Reiss, Jr., and Albert Lewis Rhodes, "The Distribution of Juvenile Delinquency in the Social Class Structure," *American Sociological Review*, 26 (October 1961), pp. 720–732. For an example of cross-cultural variations, see Lois B. De Fleur, "Ecological Variables in the Cross-Cultural Study of Delinquency," *Social Forces*, 45 (June 1967), pp. 556–570.

46. Sarah L. Boggs, "Urban Crime Patterns," *American Sociological Review*, 39 (December 1965), pp. 899–908.

47. For essentially this view of social psychology, see Peter Berger, *Invitation to Sociology: A Humanistic Perspective* (New York: Doubleday, 1963), chap. 6; Max Mark, "What Image of Man for Political Science?" *Western Political Quarterly*, 15 (December 1962), pp. 593–604; Dennis Wrong, "The Oversocialized Conception of Man in Modern Sociology," *American Sociological Review*, 26 (April 1961), pp. 183–193.

48. Tamotsu Shibutani, *Society and Personality: An Interactionist Approach to Social Psychology* (Englewood Cliffs, N.J.: Prentice-Hall, 1961), especially pp. 60, 91–94, 276–278. Also see S. F. Nadel, "Social Control and Self-Regulation," *Social Forces*, 31 (March 1953), pp.

265–273; Erving Goffman, *Asylums* (New York: Doubleday, 1961), pp. 318–320.

49. Richard A. Schermerhorn, "Man the Unfinished," *Sociological Quarterly*, 4 (Winter 1963), pp. 5–17; Gordon W. Allport, *Becoming: Basic Considerations for a Psychology of Personality* (New Haven: Yale University Press, 1955); Julian Huxley, *New Bottles for New Wines* (New York: Harper, 1957); John Lofland, *Deviance and Identity* (Englewood Cliffs, N.J.: Prentice-Hall, 1969).

50. Florian Znaniecki, *Social Actions* (New York: Farrar and Rinehart, 1936); Robert M. MacIver, *Social Causation* (Boston: Ginn, 1942); S. F. Nadel, *Foundations of Social Anthropology* (New York: Free Press, 1951); Talcott Parsons, *The Structure of Social Action* (New York: Free Press, 1949); Howard Becker, *Through Values to Social Interpretation* (Durham, N.C.: Duke University Press, 1950).

51. Max Weber, *The Theory of Social and Economic Organization*, trans. A. M. Henderson and Talcott Parsons (New York: Free Press, 1964), p. 88.

52. Alfred Schutz, *The Problem of Social Reality: Collected Papers I* (The Hague: Martinus Nijhoff, 1962), p. 53.

53. See Peter L. Berger and Thomas Luckmann, *The Social Construction of Reality* (Garden City, N.Y.: Doubleday, 1966).

54. Karl Marx, *The Eighteenth Brumaire of Louis Bonaparte* (New York: International Publishers, 1964).

55. See R. D. Laing and D. G. Cooper, *Reason and Violence: A Decade of Sartre's Philosophy, 1950–1960* (New York: Random House, 1971), pp. 49–51; Antonio Gramsci, *Selections from the Prison Notebooks*, edited and translated by Quintin Hoare and Geoffrey Nowell Smith (New York: International Publishers, 1972).

56. This "naturalistic" notion of social action is developed in David Matza, *Becoming Deviant* (Englewood Cliffs, N.J.: Prentice-Hall, 1969), pp. 3–14.

57. George H. Mead, *Mind, Self, and Society* (Chicago: University of Chicago Press, 1934); Herbert Blumer, "Sociological Implications of the Thought of George Herbert Mead," *American Journal of Sociology*, 71 (March 1966), pp. 535–544.

58. Shibutani, *Society and Personality: An Interactionist Approach to Social Psychology*, pp. 224–225.

59. Helen M. Lynd, *On Shame and the Search for Identity* (New York: Harcourt, Brace and World, 1958), p. 13.

60. On delinquency, for example, see Albert K. Cohen, *Delinquent Boys* (New York: Free Press of Glencoe, 1955); Harold W. Pfantz, "Near-Group Theory and Collective Behavior: A Critical Reformulation," *Social Problems*, 9 (Fall 1961), pp. 167–194; John P. Clark and Eugene P. Wenninger, "Goal Orientations and Illegal Behavior Among Juveniles," *Social Forces*, 42 (October 1963), pp. 49–59; Delbert S. Elliott, "Delinquency and Perceived Opportunity," *Sociological Inquiry*, 32 (Spring 1962), pp. 216–227; Judson R. Landis and Frank R. Scarpitti, "Perceptions Regarding Value Orientation and Legitimate Opportunity: Delinquents and Non-Delinquents," *Social Forces*, 44 (September 1965), pp. 83–91; Gerald Maxwell, "Adolescent Powerlessness and Delinquent Behavior," *Social Problems*, 14 (Summer 1966), pp. 35–47.

61. Irving Louis Horowitz and Martin Liebowitz, "Social Deviance and Political Marginality: Toward a Redefinition of the Relation Between Sociology and Politics," *Social Problems*, 15 (Winter 1968), pp. 280–296; Richard Quinney, "A Conception of Man and Society for Criminology," *Sociological Quarterly*, 6 (Spring 1965), pp. 119–127.

62. Walter C. Reckless, Simon Dinitz, and Ellen Murray, "Self-concept as an Insulator Against Delinquency," *American Sociological Review*, 21 (December 1956), p. 745.

63. Walter C. Reckless, Simon Dinitz, and Barbara Kay, "The Self Component in Potential Delinquency and Potential Non-Delinquency," *American Sociological Review*, 22 (October 1957), pp. 566–570.

64. Frank R. Scarpitti, Ellen Murray, Simon Dinitz, and Walter C. Reckless, "The 'Good' Boy in a High Delinquency Area: Four Years Later," *American Sociological Review*, 25 (August 1960), pp. 555–558; Simon Dinitz, Frank R. Scarpitti, and Walter C. Reckless, "Delinquency Vulnerability: A Cross Group and Longitudinal Analysis," *American Sociological Review*, 27 (August 1962), pp. 515–517.

65. Walter C. Reckless and Simon Dinitz, "Pioneering with Self-Concept as a Vulnerability Factor in Delinquency," *Journal of Criminal Law, Criminology and Police Science*, 58 (December 1967), pp. 515–523.

66. Reckless has formulated his ideas and research into a "containment theory," in Walter C. Reckless, *The Crime Problem*, 4th ed. (New York: Appleton-Century-Crofts, 1967), pp. 469–483. Other research on self-conceptions of offenders includes Leon F. Fanin and Marshall B. Clinard, "Differences in the Conception of Self as a Male Among Lower and Middle Class Delinquents," *Social Problems*, 13 (Fall 1965), pp. 205–214; John W. Kinch, "Self-Conceptions of Types of Delinquents," *Sociological Inquiry*, 32 (Spring 1962), pp. 228–234; James F. Short, Jr., and Fred L. Strodtbeck, *Group Process and Gang Delinquency* (Chicago: University of Chicago Press, 1965), pp. 140–184.

67. See Michael Schwartz and Sandra S. Tangri,

"A Note on Self-Concept as an Insulator Against Delinquency," *American Sociological Review*, 30 (December 1965), pp. 922–926; Sandra S. Tangri and Michael Schwartz, "Delinquency Research and the Self-Concept Variable," *Journal of Criminal Law, Criminology and Police Science*, 58 (June 1967), pp. 182–190. A theory of socialization and self is formulated in James C. Hacker, "A Developmental Theory of Delinquency," *Canadian Review of Sociology and Anthropology*, 8 (May 1971), pp. 61–75.

68. Hadley Cantril, *The Politics of Despair* (New York: Basic Books, 1958), p. 17.

69. See, for example, Tamotsu Shibutani, "Reference Groups as Perspectives," *American Journal of Sociology*, 60 (May 1955), pp. 562–569; Ralph H. Turner, "Role Taking, Role Standpoint, and Reference Group Behavior," *American Journal of Sociology*, 61 (January 1956), pp. 316–328.

70. Edwin H. Sutherland, *Principles of Criminology*, 4th ed. (Philadelphia: J. B. Lippincott, 1947), pp. 1–9.

71. See Melvin L. De Fleur and Richard Quinney, "A Reformulation of Sutherland's Differential Association Theory and a Strategy for Empirical Verification," *Journal of Research in Crime and Delinquency*, 3 (January 1966), pp. 1–22.

72. See Albert J. Reiss, Jr., and A. Lewis Rhodes, "An Empirical Test of Differential Association Theory," *Journal of Research in Crime and Delinquency*, 1 (January 1964), pp. 5–18; James F. Short, Jr., "Differential Association and Delinquency," *Social Problems*, 4 (January 1957), pp. 233–239; James F. Short, Jr., "Differential Association as a Hypothesis: Problems of Empirical Testing," *Social Problems*, 8 (Summer 1960), pp. 14–25; Harwin L. Voss, "Differential Association and Reported Delinquent Behavior: A Replication," *Social Problems*, 12 (Summer 1964), pp. 78–85.

73. This strategy for empirical verification is proposed in De Fleur and Quinney, "A Reformulation of Sutherland's Differential Association Theory and a Strategy for Empirical Verification," pp. 17–21. For related discussions, see S. Kirson Weinberg, "Personality and Method in the Differential Association Theory: Comments on 'A Reformulation of Sutherland's Differential Association Theory and a Strategy for Empirical Verification,'" *Journal of Research in Crime and Delinquency*, 3 (July 1966), pp. 165–172; Allen E. Liska, "Interpreting the Causal Structure of Differential Association Theory," *Social Problems*, 16 (Spring 1969), pp. 485–492.

74. Daniel Glaser, "Criminality Theories and Behavioral Images," *American Journal of Sociology*, 61 (March 1956), pp. 433–444.

75. Ibid., p. 440. Empirical support for the theory of differential identification is found in Victor Matthews, "Differential Identification: An Empirical Note," *Social Problems*, 15 (Winter 1968), pp. 376–383.

76. C. R. Jeffery, "Criminal Behavior and Learning Theory," *Journal of Criminal Law, Criminology and Police Science*, 56 (September 1965), p. 300.

77. Robert L. Burgess and Ronald L. Akers, "A Differential Association-Reinforcement Theory of Criminal Behavior," *Social Problems*, 14 (Fall 1966), pp. 128–147. The theory subsequently has been applied to a wide range of deviant behaviors in Ronald L. Akers, *Deviant Behavior: A Social Learning Approach* (Belmont, Calif.: Wadsworth, 1973).

78. Howard S. Becker, "Notes on the Concept of Commitment," *American Journal of Sociology*, 66 (July 1960), pp. 32–40.

79. Scott Briar and Irving Piliavin, "Delinquency, Situational Inducements, and Commitment to Conformity," *Social Problems*, 13 (Summer 1965), p. 39.

80. Related research is found in Gary F. Jensen, " 'Crime Doesn't Pay': Correlates of a Shared Misunderstanding," *Social Problems*, 17 (Fall 1969), pp. 189–201; Gary F. Jensen, "Delinquency and Adolescent Self-Conceptions: A Study of the Personal Relevance of Infraction," *Social Problems*, 20 (Summer 1972), pp. 84–103; John R. Stratton, "Differential Identification and Attitudes Toward the Law," *Social Forces*, 46 (December 1967), pp. 256–262.

81. David Matza, *Delinquency and Drift* (New York: John Wiley, 1964), especially pp. 27–30. For related research, see Michael J. Hindelang, "The Commitment of Delinquents to Their Misdeeds: Do Delinquents Drift?" *Social Problems*, 17 (Spring 1970), pp. 502–509.

82. Gresham M. Sykes and David Matza, "Techniques of Neutralization: A Theory of Delinquency," *American Sociological Review*, 22 (December 1957), pp. 644–670.

83. Travis Hirschi, *Causes of Delinquency* (Berkeley: University of California Press, 1969), pp. 16–34.

84. See Edwin M. Lemert, *Social Pathology* (New York: McGraw-Hill, 1951), pp. 54–72; Alexander L. Clark and Jack P. Gibbs, "Social Control: A Reformulation," *Social Problems*, 12 (Spring 1965), pp. 398–415.

85. Frank Tannenbaum, *Crime and the Community* (New York: Columbia University Press, 1938), pp. 17–18.

86. Cesare Lombroso, *Crime: Its Causes and Remedies* (Boston: Little, Brown, 1911). Also see E. A. Hooton, *Crime and the Man* (Cambridge: Harvard University Press, 1937). For more recent research and interpretation, see Raymond J. Corsini, "Appearance and Criminality," *American Journal of Sociology*, 65 (July 1959), pp. 49–51.

87. Hans von Hentig, "Redhead and Outlaw," *Journal of Criminal Law, Criminology and Police Science*, 38 (May-June, 1947), pp. 1–6.

88. William H. Sheldon, *Varieties of Delinquent Youth: An Introduction to Constitutional Psychiatry* (New York: Harper & Row, 1949). Also see Sheldon and Eleanor T. Glueck, *Physique and Delinquency* (New York: Harper & Row, 1956). The controversy over the XYY chromosomal constitution in relation to crime, especially the excessive body height attributed to people who have it, may be similarly resolved. On the evidence, see *Report on the XYY Chromosomal Abnormality* (Chevy Chase, Maryland: National Institute of Mental Health, Center for Studies of Crime and Delinquency, 1970). A critical discussion is found in Theodore Sarbin and Jeffrey Miller, "Demonism Revisited: The XYY Chromosomal Anomaly," *Issues in Criminology*, 5 (Summer 1970), pp. 195–208.

89. Edwin M. Lemert, *Human Deviance, Social Problems, and Social Control* (Englewood Cliffs, N.J.: Prentice-Hall, 1967), pp. 40–41.

90. See Edwin M. Schur, *Crimes Without Victims* (Englewood Cliffs, N.J.: Prentice-Hall, 1965), pp. 5–7.

7 Conventional Crime in American Society

1. For a detailed typology of criminal behavior, from which some of the discussion in the next three chapters is drawn, see Marshall B. Clinard and Richard Quinney, *Criminal Behavior Systems: A Typology*, 2nd ed. (New York: Holt, Rinehart and Winston, 1973).

2. See David M. Gordon, "Capitalism, Class, and Crime in America," *Crime and Delinquency*, 19 (April 1973), pp. 174–177. Also Ian Taylor, Paul Walton, and Jock Young, *The New Criminology* (London: Routledge and Kegan Paul, 1973), pp. 209–221.

3. Richard Maxwell Brown, "Historical Patterns of Violence in America," in *Violence in America: Historical and Comparative Perspectives*, A Report to the National Commission on the Causes and Prevention of Violence, prepared by H. D. Graham and Ted R. Gurr (New York: Bantam Books, 1969), pp. 45–84.

4. Susan Griffin, "Rape: The All-American Crime," *Ramparts*, 10 (September 1971), p. 34. Research on rape is found in Menachem Amir, *Patterns in Forcible Rape* (Chicago: University of Chicago Press, 1971).

5. Sheldon Hackney, "Southern Violence," in *Violence in America*, p. 524.

6. *Firearms and Violence in American Life*, A Staff Report to the National Commission on the Causes and Prevention of Violence, prepared by George D. Newton and Franklin E. Zimring (Washington, D.C.: U.S. Government Printing Office, 1969).

7. Ibid., pp. 69–74.

8. Marvin E. Wolfgang, *Patterns in Criminal Homicide* (Philadelphia: University of Pennsylvania Press, 1958).

9. Ibid., p. 252.

10. National Commission on the Causes and Prevention of Violence, *To Establish Justice, to Insure Domestic Tranquility* (Washington, D.C.: U.S. Government Printing Office, 1969), pp. 25–26.

11. President's Commission on Law Enforcement and Administration of Justice, *The Challenge of Crime in a Free Society* (Washington, D.C.: U.S. Government Printing Office, 1967), p. 18.

12. *Crimes of Violence*, vol. 11, A Staff Report Submitted to the National Commission on the Causes and Prevention of Violence, codirectors Donald J. Mulvihill and Melvin M. Tumin (Washington, D.C.: U.S. Government Printing Office, 1969), pp. 216–219.

13. Ibid., p. 210.

14. Alex Pokorny, "A Comparison of Homicides in Two Cities," *Journal of Criminal Law, Criminology and Police Science*, 56 (December 1965), pp. 479–487.

15. Harwin L. Voss and John R. Hepburn, "Patterns in Criminal Homicide in Chicago," *Journal of Criminal Law, Criminology, and Police Science*, 5 (December 1968), p. 502.

16. *Crimes of Violence*, vol. 11, p. 209.

17. Edwin M. Lemert, "An Isolation of Closure Theory of Naive Check Forgery," *Journal of Criminal Law, Criminology and Police Science*, 44 (October 1953), p. 298.

18. Mary Owen Cameron, *The Booster and the Switch: Department Store Shoplifting* (New York: Free Press, 1964), p. xii.

19. William E. Wattenberg and James Balistrieri, "Automobile Theft: A 'Favored-Group' Delinquency," *American Journal of Sociology*, 57 (May 1952), pp. 575–579.

20. Bertram Spiller, "Delinquency and Middle Class Goals," *Journal of Criminal Law, Criminology and Police Science*, 56 (December 1965), pp. 463–478.

21. Gresham M. Sykes and David Matza, "Techniques of Neutralization: A Theory of Delinquency," *American Sociological Review*, 22 (December 1957), pp. 664–670; David Matza and Gresham M. Sykes, "Juvenile Delinquency and Subterranean Values," *American Sociological Review*, 26 (October 1961), pp. 712–719. David Matza, *Delinquency and Drift* (New York: John Wiley, 1964).

22. President's Commission on Law Enforcement and Administration of Justice, *The Challenge of Crime in a Free Society* (Washington, D.C.:

U.S. Government Printing Office, 1967), p. 35. Italics added.

23. Federal Bureau of Investigation, *Uniform Crime Reports — 1972* (Washington, D.C.: U.S. Government Printing Office, 1973), p. 128.

24. André Normandeau, "Violence and Robbery: A Case Study," *Acta Criminologica*, 5 (1972), p. 77.

25. John E. Conklin, *Robbery and the Criminal Justice System* (Philadelphia: J. B. Lippincott, 1972), pp. 103–105.

26. Normandeau, "Violence and Robbery," p. 83.

27. A similar estimate is made in Russell R. Dynes, Alfred C. Clarke, Simon Dinitz, and Iwao Ishino, *Social Problems: Dissensus and Deviation in an Industrial Society* (New York: Oxford University Press, 1964), p. 543.

28. Don C. Gibbons, *Changing the Lawbreaker: The Treatment of Delinquents and Criminals* (Englewood Cliffs, N.J.: Prentice-Hall, 1965), p. 105.

29. Walter C. Reckless, *The Crime Problem*, 3rd ed. (New York: Appleton-Century-Crofts, 1961), p. 164.

30. Edwin M. Lemert, *Social Pathology* (New York: McGraw-Hill, 1951), pp. 323–324.

31. Joseph R. Weil and W. T. Brannon, *"Yellow Kid" Weil* (Chicago: Ziff-Davis, 1948), p. 293.

32. Edwin H. Sutherland, *The Professional Thief* (Chicago: University of Chicago Press, 1937), pp. 197–228.

33. David W. Maurer, *The Big Con* (New York: Signet Books, 1962); David W. Maurer, *Whiz Mob* (New Haven: College and University Press, 1964).

34. Bruce Jackson, *A Thief's Primer* (New York: Macmillan, 1969), p. 23.

35. Cameron, *The Booster and the Snitch*, pp. 40–45.

36. Edwin M. Lemert, "The Behavior of the Systematic Check Forger," *Social Problems*, 6 (Fall 1958), p. 143.

37. Werner J. Einstadter, "The Social Organization of Armed Robbery," *Social Problems*, 17 (Summer 1969), pp. 67–68. For research on professional burglary, see Neal Shover, "The Social Organization of Burglary," *Social Problems*, 20 (Spring 1973), pp. 499–514.

38. See Harry King, *Bag Man: A Professional Thief's Journey*, Bill Chambliss, ed. (New York: Harper & Row, 1972), especially pp. 97–108. Also Edwin H. Schur, "Sociological Analysis of Confidence Swindling," *Journal of Criminal Law, Criminology and Police Science*, 48 (September-October, 1957), pp. 296–304.

39. President's Commission on Law Enforcement and Administration of Justice, *Crime and Its Impact — An Assessment* (Washington, D.C.: U.S. Government Printing Office, 1967), pp. 98–99.

40. Women Endorsing Decriminalization, "Prostitution: A Non-Victim Crime?" *Issues in Criminology*, 8 (Fall 1973), pp. 137–138.

41. John C. Pollard, "Some Comments on Nonnarcotic Drug Abuse," paper presented at the Nonnarcotic Drug Institute, Southern Illinois University, Edwardsville, Ill., June 1967. Also see Carl D. Chambers and Leon Brill, "Some Considerations for the Treatment of Non-Narcotic Drug Abusers," in Leon Brill and Louis Lieberman, eds., *The Treatment of Drug Addiction and Drug Abuse* (Boston: Little, Brown, 1970).

42. Hugh Parry, "Tranquilizer Users," *Wayfarers Magazine*, February 1969. Also see Henry L. Lennard, Leon J. Epstein, Arnold Bernstein, and Donald C. Ransom, *Mystification and Drug Misuse: Hazards in Using Psychoactive Drugs* (San Francisco: Jossey-Bass, 1971).

43. Edwin H. Lemert, *Social Pathology*, p. 246.

44. See Abraham S. Blumberg, "The Politics of Deviance: The Case of Drugs," *Journal of Drug Issues*, 3 (Spring 1973), pp. 105–114.

45. Allen Ginsberg, "Abbie Hoffman — Political Poet," *Berkeley Barb*, October 5–11, 1973, p. 5.

46. See James H. Bryan, "Apprenticeships in Prostitution," *Social Problems*, 12 (Winter 1965), pp. 287–296; Norman R. Jackman, Richard O'Toole, and Gilbert Geis, "The Self-Image of the Prostitute," *Sociological Quarterly*, 4 (Spring 1963), pp. 150–161.

47. For a general discussion of prostitution today see T. C. Esselstyn, "Prostitution in the United States," *The Annals*, 376 (March 1968), pp. 123–135.

48. Maurice Leznoff and William Westley, "The Homosexual Community," *Social Problems*, 3 (1956), p. 263.

49. Donald W. Cory, *The Homosexual in America* (New York: Greenberg, 1951), p. 90. Also see D. J. Mercer, *They Walk in the Shadow* (New York: Comet Press, 1959).

50. See Gordon Westwood, *Society and the Homosexual* (New York: E. P. Dutton, 1953), chaps. 19–21.

51. Michael Schofield, *Sociological Aspects of Homosexuality: A Comparative Study of Three Types of Homosexuals* (Boston: Little, Brown, 1965), p. 183.

52. See Barry Dank, "Coming Out in the Gay World," *Psychiatry*, 34 (May 1971), pp. 180–197.

53. Alfred R. Lindesmith and John H. Gagnon, "Anomie and Drug Addiction," in Marshall B. Clinard, ed., *Anomie and Deviant Behavior: A Discussion and Critique* (New York: Free Press, Macmillan, 1964), p. 170; and Charles Winick, "Physician Narcotic Addicts," *Social Problems*, 9 (Fall 1961), pp. 174–186.

54. For a discussion of drug use in a college setting, see James T. Carey, *The College Drug*

Scene (Englewood Cliffs, N.J.: Prentice-Hall, 1968).

55. Erich Goode, "Multiple Drug Use Among Marijuana Smokers," *Social Problems*, 17 (Summer 1969), p. 54.

56. Seymour Fiddle, "The Addict Culture and Movement into and out of Hospitals," in Senate Committee on the Judiciary, Subcommittee to Investigate Juvenile Delinquency, *Hearings*, Pt. 13, New York City, September 20–21 (Washington, D.C.: U.S. Government Printing Office, 1963), p. 3156.

57. This argument is presented in Richard Quinney, "Introduction," in Nicholas M. Regush, *The Drug Addiction Business* (New York: Dial Press, 1971), pp. ix–xiii.

58. For a more detailed discussion of victimization, see Richard Quinney, "Who is the Victim?" *Criminology*, 10 (November 1972), pp. 314–323.

59. R. M. Perkins, *Criminal Law* (Brooklyn, N.Y.: Foundation Press, 1957), p. 5.

60. President's Commission on Law Enforcement and Administration of Justice, *The Challenge of Crime in a Free Society*, p. 80.

8   Crimes of Business in the American Economy

1. Robert Blauner, *Alienation and Freedom* (Chicago: University of Chicago Press, 1964), chap. 1.

2. Karl Marx, *Early Writings*, trans. and ed. by T. B. Bottomore (New York: McGraw-Hill, 1963), pp. 122–123.

3. Donald N. M. Horning, "Blue-Collar Theft: Conceptions of Property, Attitudes Toward Pilfering, and Work Group Norms in a Modern Industrial Plant," in Erwin O. Smigel and H. Laurence Ross, eds., *Crimes Against Bureaucracy* (New York: Van Nostrand Reinhold, 1970), pp. 46–64.

4. André Gorz, *Strategy for Labor: A Radical Proposal*, trans. Martin A. Nicolaus and Victoria Ortiz (Boston: Beacon Press, 1964), pp. 57–58.

5. Donald R. Cressey, "The Respectable Criminal," *Transaction*, 3 (March-April, 1965).

6. *The New York Times*, September 22, 1970, p. 1.

7. William N. Leonard and Marvin Glenn Weber, "Automakers and Dealers: A Study of Criminogenic Market Forces," *Law and Society Review*, 4 (February 1970), p. 411.

8. Edwin M. Schur, *Our Criminal Society: The Social and Legal Sources of Crime in America* (Englewood Cliffs, N.J.: Prentice-Hall, 1969), pp. 185–186.

9. Donald R. Cressey, *Other People's Money* (New York: Free Press, 1953).

10. Marshall B. Clinard, *The Black Market: A Study of White Collar Crime* (New York: Holt, Rinehart and Winston, 1952), p. 295.

11. Frank E. Hartung, "A Study in Law and Social Differentiation, as Exemplified in Violations of the Emergency Price Control Act in the Detroit Wholesale Meat Industry," unpublished Ph.D. dissertation, University of Michigan, 1949, p. 221; and Richard Quinney, "Retail Pharmacy as a Marginal Occupation: A Study of Prescription Violation," unpublished Ph.D. dissertation, University of Wisconsin, 1962, p. 261.

12. Edwin H. Sutherland, "White-Collar Criminality," *American Sociological Review*, 5 (February 1940), pp. 1–12.

13. Clinard, *The Black Market*. Also see the selections in Gilbert Geis, ed., *White-Collar Criminal: The Offender in Business and the Professions* (New York: Atherton Press, 1968).

14. Richard Quinney, "Occupational Structure and Criminal Behavior: Prescription Violation by Retail Pharmacists," *Social Problems*, 11 (Fall 1963), pp. 179–185.

15. Daniel R. Fusfeld, "The Rise of the Corporate State in America," *Journal of Economic Issues*, 6 (March 1972), p. 1. Also see Paul A. Baran and Paul M. Sweezy, *Monopoly Capitalism: An Essay on the American Economic and Social Order* (New York: Monthly Review Press, 1966); Frank Pearce, "Crime, Corporations and the American Social Order," in Ian Taylor and Laurie Taylor, eds., *Politics and Deviance* (Harmondsworth, Eng.: Penguin Books, 1973), pp. 13–41.

16. Gus Hall, *Ecology: Can We Survive Under Capitalism?* (New York: International Publishers, 1972), p. 7.

17. Ibid., p. 34.

18. Schur, *Our Criminal Society*, p. 168.

19. *The New York Times*, May 26, 1966, p. 1.

20. Morton Mintz, "There's No Bloody Place Like Home," *The Progressive*, 34 (September 1970), pp. 22–24.

21. Gilbert Geis, "The Heavy Electrical Equipment Antitrust Cases of 1961," in Marshall B. Clinard and Richard Quinney, *Criminal Behavior Systems: A Typology* (New York: Holt, Rinehart and Winston, 1967), p. 144.

22. Ibid., pp. 150–151.

23. Ibid., p. 143.

24. James S. Turner, *The Chemical Feast* (New York: Grossman Publishers, 1970), pp. 82–106.

25. A definition given by the New York Joint Legislative Committee on Crime, as quoted in Hank Messick and Burt Goldblatt, *The Mobs and the Mafia* (New York: Thomas Y. Crowell, 1972), p. ix.

26. Donald R. Cressey, *Criminal Organization* (New York: Harper & Row, 1972), pp. 1–17.

27. See Hank Messick, *Lansky* (New York: G. P. Putnam's Sons, 1971); Messick and Goldblatt, *The Mobs and the Mafia*, pp. 181–204.

28. George B. Vold, *Theoretical Criminology* (New York: Oxford University Press, 1958), p. 240.
29. President's Commission on Law Enforcement and Administration of Justice, *The Challenge of Crime in a Free Society* (Washington, D.C.: U.S. Government Printing Office, 1967), p. 189.
30. Ibid.
31. U.S. Senate Special Committee to Investigate Organized Crime in Interstate Commerce, *Third Interim Report*, 2nd Session, 81st Congress, 1950 (Washington, D.C.: U.S. Government Printing Office, 1950), p. 171. Also see Estes Kefauver, *Crime in America* (New York: Greenwood Press, 1951).
32. Donald R. Cressey, *Theft of the Nation: The Structure and Operations of Organized Crime in America* (New York: Harper & Row, 1969), pp. 99–107.
33. Ibid., pp. 241–242.
34. See Solomon Kobrin, "The Conflict of Values in Delinquency Areas," *American Sociological Review*, 16 (October 1951), pp. 653–661; Irving Spergel, *Racketville, Slumtown, Haulburg: An Exploratory Study of Delinquent Subcultures* (Chicago: University of Chicago Press, 1964).
35. See Virgil W. Peterson, "The Career of a Syndicate Boss," *Crime and Delinquency*, 8 (October 1962), pp. 339–354.
36. Cressey, *Theft of the Nation*, p. 171.
37. Ibid., pp. 186–187.
38. As presented in Marshall B. Clinard and Richard Quinney, *Criminal Behavior Systems: A Typology*, 2nd ed. (New York: Holt, Rinehart and Winston, 1973).

9   Crime in the American State

1. For documentation on crimes by the government, see Jethro K. Lieberman, *How the Government Breaks the Law* (New York: Stein and Day, 1972); Theodore L. Becker and Vernon G. Murry, eds., *Government Lawlessness in America* (New York: Oxford University Press, 1971).
2. Richard Halloran, "Army Spied on 18,000 Civilians in Two-Year Operation," *The New York Times*, January 18, 1971, pp. 1 and 22.
3. The documentation is extensive. See, for example, the reports of the various congressional committees, such as the hearings conducted by the Senate Subcommittee on Constitutional Rights and the hearings of the Senate Watergate Committee. Also see the daily coverage by *The New York Times*.
4. See Marshall B. Clinard and Richard Quinney, *Criminal Behavior Systems: A Typology*, 2nd ed. (New York: Holt, Rinehart and Winston, 1973), pp. 154–186.
5. Homer Bigart, "Berrigan Case: A Strategy that Failed," *The New York Times*, April 9, 1972, p. E2; John Kifner, "Court in Chicago Frees 5 in 1968 Convention Case," *The New York Times*, November 23, 1972; "Ellsberg Case: Defendants Freed, Government Convicted," *The New York Times*, May 13, 1973, p. E1; John Kifner, "Eight Acquitted in Gainesville of G.O.P. Convention Plot," *The New York Times*, September 1, 1973, p. 1.
6. David Burnham, "Misconduct Laid to 27% of Police in Three Cities' Slums," *The New York Times*, July 5, 1968, p. 1.
7. Fred J. Cook, "How Deep Are the Police in Heroin Traffic?" *The New York Times*, April 25, 1971, p. E3; Andrew H. Malcolm, "Violent Drug Raids Against the Innocent Found Widespread," *The New York Times*, June 25, 1973, p. 1; Ralph Blumenthal, "Officer in Albany Says Fellow Police Joined in Thievery," *The New York Times*, September 21, 1973, p. 1; Ralph Blumenthal, "Brothel Boss Tells of Albany Bribes," *The New York Times*, September 25, 1973, p. 39.
8. *The Knapp Commission Report on Police Corruption* (New York: George Braziller, 1972).
9. Paul Chevigny, *Police Power: Police Abuses in New York City* (New York: Random House, 1969), pp. 136–146.
10. William A. Westley, "Violence and the Police," *American Journal of Sociology*, 59 (July 1953), p. 35.
11. Ellwyn R. Stoddard, "The Informal 'Code' of Police Deviancy: A Group Approach to 'Blue-Coat Crime,'" *Journal of Criminal Law, Criminology and Police Science*, 59 (June 1968), p. 212. Also see Barbara Raffel Price, "Police Corruption: Analysis," *Criminology*, 10 (August 1972), pp. 161–176.
12. Jerome H. Skolnick, *Justice Without Trial: Law Enforcement in Democratic Society* (New York: John Wiley, 1966), p. 202.
13. See Donald J. Black and Albert J. Reiss, Jr., "Patterns of Behavior in Police and Citizen Transactions," in the President's Commission on Law Enforcement and Administration of Justice, *Studies in Crime and Law Enforcement in Major Metropolitan Areas*, vol. 2, Field Surveys III (Washington, D.C.: U.S. Government Printing Office, 1967), pp. 132–139.
14. The Walker Report to the National Commission on the Causes and Prevention of Violence, *Rights in Conflict* (New York: Bantam Books, 1968), p. 1.
15. Jerome H. Skolnick, *The Politics of Protest* (New York: Ballantine Books, 1969). Also see Rodney Stark, *Police Riots* (Belmont, Calif.: Wadsworth, 1972).
16. Paul L. Montgomery, "Crisis in Prisons Termed Worst Mayor Has Faced," *The New York Times*, October 15, 1970, p. 1.
17. Quoted in Jack Newfield, "The Law is an

Outlaw," *The Village Voice*, December 17, 1970, p. 1.

18. John Kifner, "Jury Indicts 25 in Kent Disorder; Guard is Cleared," *The New York Times*, October 17, 1970, p. 1.

19. *Attica*, The Official Report of the New York State Special Commission on Attica (New York: Bantam Books, 1972).

20. Citizens Research and Investigation Committee and Louis E. Tackwood, *The Glass House Tapes* (New York: Avon Books, 1973), p. 259.

21. Paul Jacobs, "Informers, the Enemy Within," *Ramparts*, 12 (August-September, 1973), pp. 53–54.

22. Other cases of provocation against the Black Panthers are presented in Paul Chevigny, *Cops and Rebels: A Study of Provocation* (New York: Random House, 1972). On the sociological implications of provocation, see Gary T. Marx, "Thoughts on a Neglected Category of Social Movement Participant: The Agent Provocateur and Informant," *American Journal of Sociology*, forthcoming.

23. Citizens Research and Investigation Committee and Louis E. Tackwood, *The Glass House Tapes*, p. 42.

24. Ibid., p. 173.

25. Telford Taylor, *Nuremberg and Vietnam: An American Tragedy* (Chicago: Quadrangle Books, 1970), pp. 19–41.

26. Nuremberg Principle VI, clause b. The full text can be found in *The Nation*, January 26, 1970, p. 78.

27. Anthony A. D'Amato, Harvey L. Gould, and Larry D. Woods, "War Crimes and Vietnam: The 'Nuremberg Defence' and the Military Service Resister," *California Law Review*, 57 (November 1969), p. 1058.

28. U.S. Department of the Army, *The Law of Land Warfare*, Field Manual No. 27-10, 1956. On the applicability of the international law of warfare to an undeclared war in Vietnam, the Manual clearly states: "As the customary law of war applies to cases of international armed conflict and to the forcible occupation of enemy territory generally as well as to declared war in its strict sense, a declaration of war is not an essential condition of the application of this body of law. Similarly, treaties relating to 'war' may become operative notwithstanding the absence of a formal declaration of war."

29. Stuart Hampshire, "Russell, Radicalism, and Reason," *New York Review of Books*, 15 (October 8, 1970), p. 3. Also see Noam Chomsky, *American Power and the New Mandarins* (New York: Vintage Books, 1969).

30. Richard A. Falk, "War Crimes and Individual Responsibility: A Legal Memorandum," *Transaction*, 7 (January 1970), pp. 33–34.

31. Ibid., p. 34.

32. Quoted in Edward S. Herman, *Atrocities in Vietnam: Myths and Realities* (Philadelphia: Pilgrim Press, 1970), pp. 43–45.

33. Herman, *Atrocities in Vietnam*, pp. 54–60.

34. D'Amato, Gould, and Woods, "War Crimes and Vietnam," pp. 1081–1082.

35. John Gerassi, *North Vietnam: A Documentary* (Indianapolis: Bobbs-Merrill, 1968).

36. Gabriel Kolko in Erwin Knoll and Judith Nies McFadden, eds., *War Crimes and the American Conscience* (New York: Holt, Rinehart and Winston, 1970), p. 57.

37. D'Amato, Gould, and Woods, "War Crimes and Vietnam," p. 1075.

38. For some of the sources of documentation, see ibid., pp. 1077–1081.

39. Arthur W. Galston in Knoll and McFadden, eds., *War Crimes and the American Conscience*, p. 69.

40. D'Amato, Gould, and Woods, "War Crimes and Vietnam," pp. 1091–1093.

41. Taylor, *Nuremberg and Vietnam*, pp. 96–97.

42. See *The New York Times*, December 20, 1970, p. 8.

43. Falk, "War Crimes and Individual Responsibility," p. 39.

44. Taylor, *Nuremberg and Vietnam*, pp. 154–207. Also *The New York Times*, January 9, 1971, p. 3.

45. Richard A. Falk, in *The New York Times Book Review*, December 27, 1970, p. 14.

46. Peter Maas, *The Valachi Papers* (New York: G. P. Putnam's Sons, 1968), p. 274. Quoted in Stuart L. Hills, *Crime, Power, and Morality: The Criminal-Law Process in the United States* (Scranton, Pa.: Chandler, 1971), p. 121.

47. Hills, *Crime, Power, and Morality*, pp. 121–122.

48. Ibid., p. 123.

49. John A. Gardiner, *The Politics of Corruption: Organized Crime in an American City* (New York: Russell Sage Foundation, 1970), pp. 22–23.

50. William J. Chambliss, "Vice, Corruption, Bureaucracy, and Power," *Wisconsin Law Review*, 1971 (No. 4, 1971), pp. 1172–1173.

51. See Anthony Ripley, "After the Defiance, Guilt and Resignation," *The New York Times*, October 14, 1973, p. E2.

52. "How Agnew Bartered His Office to Keep from Going to Prison," *The New York Times*, October 23, 1973, p. 1.

53. Hank Messick, *John Edgar Hoover* (New York: David McKay, 1972), pp. 172–176.

54. Ibid., pp. 190–191.

55. Ibid., p. 254.

56. On the Watergate events, see J. Anthony Lukas, "The Story So Far," *The New York Times Magazine*, July 22, 1973, pp. 1–41. Also *Watergate: Chronology of a Crisis* (Washington, D.C.: Congressional Quarterly, 1973).

57. Kirkpatrick Sale, "The World Behind Watergate," *The New York Review of Books*, 20 (May 3, 1973), p. 14.

58. Ibid., p. 15.

59. *Congressional Quarterly Almanac*, 1972, vol. 28 (Washington, D.C.: Congressional Quarterly Inc., 1972), p. 91.

60. L. Fletcher Prouty, "Watergate and the World of the CIA," *Ramparts*, 12 (October 1973), p. 50.

61. Much of the evidence is summarized in Mae Brussell, "Why Was Martha Mitchell Kidnapped?" *The Realist*, No. 93 (August 1972), pp. 1, 27–47.

62. Jeff Gerth, "Nixon and the Mafia," *SunDance*, 1 (November-December, 1972), p. 32. Also see Hank Messick, *Lansky* (New York: Berkley Medallion Books, 1973); Lucian K. Truscott IV, "The Rebozo Connection," *The Village Voice*, 18 (August 30, 1973), pp. 1, 24–34; "Nixon and Organized Crime," *NACLA's Latin America & Empire Report*, 6 (October 1972), pp. 3–17.

10   Police in the Community

1. Allan Silver, "The Demand for Order in Civil Society: A Review of Some Themes in the History of Urban Crime, Police, and Riot," in David J. Bordua, ed., *The Police: Six Sociological Essays* (New York: John Wiley, 1967), p. 3.

2. Ibid., p. 14.

3. See Leon Radzinowicz, *A History of English Criminal Law and Its Administration from 1750* (London: Stevens, 1956), vols. 2 and 3; Alwyn Solmes, *The English Policeman 1871–1935* (London: George Allen & Unwin, 1935); William Alfred Morris, *The Medieval English Sheriff to 1300* (Manchester, Eng.: University Press, 1927).

4. J. L. Lymon, "The Metropolitan Police Act of 1829: An Analysis of Certain Events Influencing the Passage and Character of the Metropolitan Police Act in England," *Journal of Criminal Law, Criminology and Police Science*, 55 (March 1964), pp. 141–154.

5. Cyrus Harreld Karreker, *The Seventeenth-Century Sheriff: A Comparative Study of the Sheriff in England and Chesapeake Colonies* (Chapel Hill: University of North Carolina Press, 1930); Julius Goebel and T. Raymond Naughton, *Law Enforcement in Colonial New York* (New York: Commonwealth Fund, 1944).

6. Roger Lane, *Policing the City: Boston, 1822–1885* (Cambridge: Harvard University Press, 1967), p. 26.

7. Evelyn L. Parks, "From Constabulary to Police Society: Implications for Social Control," *Catalyst* (Summer 1970), p. 80.

8. Evelyn L. Parks summarizes the rise of the police in response to the needs of the city's class structure in ibid., pp. 81–82.

9. Bruce Smith, *Police Systems in the United States*, 2nd rev. ed. (New York: Harper, 1960).

10. Rita W. Cooley, "The Office of United States Marshal," *Western Political Quarterly*, 12 (March 1959), pp. 123–140.

11. Jack J. Preiss and Howard J. Ehrlich, *An Examination of Role Theory: The Case of the State Police* (Lincoln: University of Nebraska Press, 1966).

12. J. P. Shalloo, *Private Police: With Special Reference to Pennsylvania* (Philadelphia: American Academy of Political and Social Science, Monograph No. 1, 1933).

13. James S. Kakalik and Sorrel Wildhorn, *The Private Police Industry: Its Nature and Extent*, vol. II (Washington, D.C.: Law Enforcement Assistance Administration, 1972).

14. Supreme Court decisions on law enforcement are discussed by, among others, Richard C. Donnelly, "Police Authority and Practices," *Annals of the American Academy of Political and Social Science*, 339 (January 1962), pp. 90–110; David Robinson, Jr., "Massiah, Escobedo, and Rationales for the Exclusions of Confessions," *Journal of Criminal Law, Criminology and Police Science*, 56 (December 1965), pp. 412–431; Bernard Weisberg, "Police Interrogation of Arrested Persons: A Skeptical View," *Journal of Criminal Law, Criminology and Police Science*, 52 (May-June, 1961), pp. 21–46; "A Symposium on the Supreme Court and the Police: 1966," *Journal of Criminal Law, Criminology and Police Science*, 57 (September 1966), pp. 237–311. On the regulation of private police, see *The Law and Private Police*, vol. IV (Washington, D.C.; Law Enforcement Assistance Administration, 1972).

15. Albert J. Reiss, Jr., and Donald J. Black, "Interrogation and the Criminal Process," *Annals of the American Academy of Political and Social Science*, 374 (November 1967), pp. 47–57. Also see Neal A. Milner, *The Court and Local Law Enforcement* (Beverly Hills, Calif.: Sage Publications, 1970); Edwin M. Driver, "Confessions and the Social Psychology of Coercion," *Harvard Law Review*, 82 (November 1968), pp. 42–61.

16. Egon Bittner, *The Functions of the Police in Modern Society* (Chevy Chase, Maryland: National Institute of Mental Health, 1970), pp. 28–29.

17. Joseph Goldstein, "Police Discretion Not to Invoke the Criminal Process: Low Visibility Decisions in the Administration of Justice," *Yale Law Journal*, 69 (March 1960), pp. 543–594; Sanford H. Kadish, "Legal Norm and Discretion in the Police and Sentencing Processes," *Harvard Law Review*, 75 (March

1962), pp. 904–931; Edward L. Barrett, Jr., "Police Practices and the Law — From Arrest to Release of Charge," *California Law Review*, 50 (March 1962), pp. 11–55.

18. Wayne R. LaFave, "The Police and Nonenforcement of the Law," *Wisconsin Law Review*, 1962 (January-March, 1962), p. 239.

19. Bittner, *The Functions of the Police*, p. 40.

20. John P. Clark, "Isolation of the Police: A Comparison of the British and American Situations," *Journal of Criminal Law, Criminology and Police Science*, 56 (September 1965), pp. 307–319.

21. See Michael Banton, *The Policeman in the Community* (London: Tavistock, 1964). Also Egon Bittner, "The Police on Skid-Row: A Study of Peace Keeping," *American Sociological Review*, 2 (October 1967), pp. 699–715.

22. Elaine Cumming, Ian Cumming, and Laura Edell, "Policeman as Philosopher, Guide and Friend," *Social Problems*, 12 (Winter 1965), pp. 276–286.

23. Nathan Goldman, *The Differential Selection of Juvenile Offenders for Court Appearance* (New York: National Council on Crime and Delinquency, 1963).

24. Ibid., p. 129.

25. T. C. Esselstyn, "The Social Role of the County Sheriff," *Journal of Criminal Law, Criminology and Police Science*, 44 (July-August, 1953), pp. 177–184.

26. John F. Galliher, "Explanations of Police Behavior: A Critical Review and Analysis," *Sociological Quarterly*, 12 (Summer 1971), pp. 308–318.

27. Bittner, *The Functions of the Police*, p. 53.

28. David J. Bordua and Albert J. Reiss, Jr., "Command, Control and Charisma: Reflections on Police Bureaucracy," *American Journal of Sociology*, 72 (July 1966), pp. 68–76.

29. Arthur L. Stinchcombe, "Institutions of Privacy in the Determination of Police Administrative Practice," *American Journal of Sociology*, 69 (September 1963), pp. 158–159.

30. Robert Edward Mitchell, "Organization as a Key to Police Effectiveness," *Crime and Delinquency*, 12 (October 1966), pp. 344–353.

31. James Q. Wilson, "The Police and the Delinquent in Two Cities," in Stanton Wheeler, ed., *Controlling Delinquents* (New York: John Wiley, 1968), pp. 9–30.

32. *The New York Times*, March 15, 1966, pp. 1 and 26.

33. James Q. Wilson, *Varieties of Police Behavior* (Cambridge: Harvard University Press, 1968), pp. 95–99. Other studies of traffic law enforcement are found in John A. Gardiner, "Police Enforcement of Traffic Laws: A Comparative Analysis," in James Q. Wilson, ed., *City Politics and Public Policy* (New York: John Wiley, 1968), pp. 151–172; David M. Petersen, "In-

formal Norms and Public Practice: the Traffic Ticket Quota System," *Sociology and Social Research*, 55 (April 1971), pp. 354–362.

34. Peter K. Manning, "The Police: Mandate, Strategies, and Appearances," in Jack D. Douglas, ed., *Crime and Justice in American Society* (Indianapolis: Bobbs-Merrill, 1971), pp. 149–193.

35. John H. McNamara, "Uncertainties in Police Work: the Relevance of Police Recruits' Backgrounds and Training," in David J. Bordua, ed., *The Police: Six Sociological Essays* (New York: John Wiley, 1967), pp. 163–252.

36. Arthur Niederhoffer, *Behind the Shield: The Police in Urban Society* (Garden City, N.Y.: Doubleday, 1967), p. 52.

37. Ibid., p. 54.

38. Jerome H. Skolnick, *Justice Without Trial: Law Enforcement in Democratic Society* (New York: John Wiley, 1966), p. 44.

39. Niederhoffer, *Behind the Shield*, p. 9.

40. Ibid., p. 151.

41. Skolnick, *Justice Without Trial*, pp. 211–219.

42. Ibid., p. 202.

43. Ibid., p. 202.

44. Albert J. Reiss, Jr., "Police Brutality — Answers to Key Questions," *Transaction*, 5 (July-August, 1968), pp. 10–19; Ellwyn R. Stoddard, "The Informal 'Code' of Police Deviancy: A Group Approach to 'Blue-Coat Crime'," *Journal of Criminal Law, Criminology and Police Science*, 59 (June 1968), pp. 201–213; David Burnham, "Police Violence: A Changing Pattern," *The New York Times*, July 7, 1968, pp. 1 and 34.

45. Paul Chevigny, *Police Power: Police Abuses in New York City* (New York: Random House, 1969), p. 136.

46. Ibid. Further documentation of police misconduct and illegal behavior is found in Ed Cray, *The Enemy in the Streets: Police Malpractice in America* (New York: Anchor Books, 1972); Albert J. Reiss, Jr., *The Police and the Public* (New Haven: Yale University Press, 1971); and William A. Westley, *Violence and the Police: A Sociological Study of Law, Custom, and Morality* (Cambridge: MIT Press, 1970).

47. Ibid., p. 141.

48. Donald J. Black and Albert J. Reiss, Jr., "Patterns of Behavior in Police and Citizen Transactions," in the President's Commission on Law Enforcement and Administration of Justice, *Studies in Crime and Law Enforcement in Major Metropolitan Areas*, vol. 2, Field Surveys III (Washington, D.C.: U.S. Government Printing Office, 1967), pp. 4–5.

49. Ibid., p. 17.

50. Ibid., pp. 53–54.

51. Philip H. Ennis, *Criminal Victimization in the United States: A Report of a National Survey*, President's Commission on Law Enforcement

and Administration of Justice, Field Surveys II (Washington, D.C.: U.S. Government Printing Office, 1967), pp. 41–51.

52. The game-like conception of police-suspect relationships is found in Dean R. Smith, "Random Patrol: An Application of Game Theory to Police Problems," *Journal of Criminal Law, Criminology and Police Science*, 53 (June 1962), pp. 258–263.

53. Clayton A. Hartjen, "Police-Citizen Encounters: Social Order in Interpersonal Interaction," *Criminology*, 10 (May 1972), p. 70.

54. James R. Hudson, "Police-Citizen Encounters that Lead to Citizen Complaints," *Social Problems*, 18 (Fall 1970), p. 190.

55. Irving Piliavin and Scott Briar, "Police Encounters with Juveniles," *American Journal of Sociology*, 70 (September 1964), p. 210.

56. Piliavin and Briar, "Police Encounters with Juveniles," pp. 210–211.

57. Black and Reiss, "Patterns of Behavior in Police and Citizen Transactions," pp. 33–37. Other research findings are reported in Donald J. Black and Albert J. Reiss, Jr., "Police Control of Juveniles," *American Sociological Review*, 35 (February 1970), pp. 63–77; Donald J. Black, "Production of Crime Rates," *American Sociological Review*, 35 (August 1970), pp. 733–748.

58. See Guy B. Johnson, "The Negro and Crime," *Annals of the American Academy of Political and Social Science*, 271 (September 1941), pp. 93–104; and more recently, Theodore N. Ferdinand and Elmer G. Luchterhand, "Inter-City Youth, the Police, the Juvenile Court, and Justice," *Social Problems*, 17 (Spring 1970), pp. 510–527.

59. Cited in Banton, *The Policeman in the Community*, p. 173.

60. See the discussion on Negro crime rates in Marvin E. Wolfgang, *Crime and Race: Conceptions and Misconceptions* (New York: Institute of Human Relations Press, 1964).

61. For documentation of anti-Negro attitudes among police, according to race of police and racial composition of the police precinct, see Black and Reiss, "Patterns of Behavior in Police and Citizen Transactions," pp. 132–139.

62. Piliavin and Briar, "Police Encounters with Juveniles," pp. 212–213.

63. William M. Kephart, *Racial Factors and Urban Law Enforcement* (Philadelphia: University of Pennsylvania Press, 1957), pp. 88–93.

64. See Wayne R. LaFave, *Arrest: The Decision to Take a Suspect Into Custody* (Boston: Little, Brown, 1965), p. 146.

65. Ibid., p. 147.

66. Ibid., p. 149.

67. Ibid., p. 151.

68. Ibid., pp. 439–449.

69. Caleb Foote, "Vagrancy-Type Law and Its Administration," *University of Pennsylvania Law Review*, 104. (March 1956), pp. 603–650.

70. LaFave, *Arrest*, pp. 465–470.

71. Skolnick, *Justice Without Trial*, pp. 96–109.

72. The following information was obtained from the records of the New York City Police Department.

73. Allen D. Grimshaw, "Actions of Police and the Military in American Race Riots," *Phylon*, 24 (Fall 1963), pp. 271–289.

74. See Joseph C. Mouledoux, "Political Crime and the Negro Revolution," in Marshall B. Clinard and Richard Quinney, *Criminal Behavior Systems: A Typology* (New York: Holt, Rinehart and Winston, 1967), pp. 217–231.

75. Robert K. Murray, *Red Scare: A Study of National Hysteria, 1919–1920* (Minneapolis: University of Minnesota Press, 1965); William Preston, Jr., *Aliens and Dissenters: Federal Suppression of Radicals, 1903–1933* (Cambridge: Harvard University Press, 1963).

76. President's Commission on Law Enforcement and Administration of Justice, *The Challenge of Crime in a Free Society* (Washington, D.C.: U.S. Government Printing Office, 1967), pp. 294–295.

77. James Q. Wilson, "The Police in the Ghetto," in Robert F. Steadman, ed., *The Police and the Community* (Baltimore: Johns Hopkins University Press, 1972), p. 80.

78. Skolnick, *Justice Without Trial*, pp. 238–239. Other aspects of professionalization are discussed in Susan O. White, "A Perspective on Police Professionalism," *Law and Society Review*, 7 (Fall 1972), pp. 61–85.

79. Reiss, *The Police and the Public*, pp. 174–175.

80. Ibid., p. 221.

81. Bittner, *The Functions of the Police*, p. 61.

82. Ibid., p. 121.

83. Gary Kreps and Jack M. Weller, "The Police-Community Relations Movement: Conciliatory Responses to Violence," *American Behavioral Scientist*, 16 (January/February, 1973), p. 402.

84. Ibid., p. 403.

85. William C. Berleman, "Police and Minority Groups: The Improvement of Community Relations," *Crime and Delinquency*, 18 (April 1972), pp. 162–163.

86. President's Commission on Law Enforcement and Administration of Justice, *Task Force Report: The Police* (Washington, D.C.: U.S. Government Printing Office, 1967), p. 159.

87. See, for example, Saul D. Alinsky, *Reveille for Radicals* (New York: Random House, 1969); Alan A. Altshuler, *Community Control* (New York: Pegasus, 1970); Stanley Aronowitz, "The Dialectics of Community Control," *Social Policy*, 1 (May/June, 1970), pp. 47–51; Frank Riessman and Alan Gartner, "Community Control and Radical Social Change," *Social Policy*, 1 (May/June, 1970), pp. 52–55.

88. See *To Stop a Police State: The Case for Community Control of Police* (Berkeley: The Red Family, n.d.).

89. Arthur I. Waskow, "Community Control of the Police," *Transaction*, 7 (December 1969), p. 4.

90. Ibid., p. 7.

91. Reiss, *The Police and the Public*, p. 186.

92. Ibid., p. 208.

93. Wilson, "The Police in the Ghetto," p. 88.

11 Judicial Administration

1. Allen W. Wood, "The Marxian Critique of Justice," *Philosophy and Public Affairs*, 1 Spring 1972), pp. 244–282.

2. Herbert Jacob and Kenneth Vines, "The Role of the Judiciary in American State Politics," in Glendon Schubert, ed., *Judicial Decision-Making* (New York: Free Press of Glencoe, 1963), p. 250. Specific studies are found in James R. Klonoski and Robert I. Mendelsohn, eds., *The Politics of Local Justice* (Boston: Little, Brown, 1970).

3. Jack Peltason, *Federal Courts in the Political Process* (New York: Doubleday, 1955), p. 29.

4. For a critique, see Kenneth Culp Davis, *Discretionary Justice: A Preliminary Inquiry* (Urbana: University of Illinois Press, 1971).

5. See Herbert Jacob, *Justice in America: Courts, Lawyers, and the Judicial Process* (Boston: Little, Brown, 1965), pp. 131–148.

6. Harold Garfinkel, "Research Note on Inter- and Intra-Racial Homicides," *Social Forces*, 27 (May 1949), pp. 369–381. Also see Thorsten Sellin, "Race Prejudice in the Administration of Justice," *American Journal of Sociology*, 41 (September 1935), pp. 212–217.

7. Haywood Burns, "Racism in American Law," in Robert Lefcourt, ed., *Law Against the People: Essays to Demystify Law, Order and the Courts* (New York: Random House, 1971), p. 41.

8. Ibid., p. 54. Also see Sara Blackburn, ed., *White Justice: Black Experience Today in America's Courtrooms* (New York: Harper & Row, 1971).

9. Abraham S. Blumberg, *Criminal Justice* (Chicago: Quadrangle Books, 1967), p. 70. For related research, see Maureen Mileski, "Courtroom Encounters: An Observation Study of a Lower Criminal Court," *Law and Society Review*, 5 (May 1971), pp. 473–538. Observations on the juvenile court's social organization are found in Aaron V. Cicourel, *The Social Organization of Juvenile Justice* (New York: John Wiley, 1968).

10. Otto Kirchheimer, *Political Justice: The Use of Legal Procedure for Political Ends* (Princeton: Princeton University Press, 1961), p. 46.

11. Leon Friedman, "Political Power and Legal Legitimacy: A Short History of Political Trials," *The Antioch Review*, 30 (Summer 1970), p. 167.

12. See *Trials of the Resistance* (New York: New York Review, 1970); Jason Epstein, *The Great Conspiracy Trial: An Essay on Law, Liberty and the Constitution* (New York: Random House, 1970).

13. Friedman, "Political Power and Legal Legitimacy," pp. 167–168.

14. See Richard Harris, *Justice: The Crisis of Law, Order, and Freedom in America* (New York: E. P. Dutton, 1970).

15. Frank W. Miller and Frank J. Remington, "Procedures Before Trial," *Annals of the American Academy of Political and Social Science*, 339 (January 1962), pp. 111–124.

16. Caleb Foote, "The Bail System and Equal Justice," *Federal Probation*, 23 (September 1959), pp. 43–48; Frederic Suffet, "Bail Setting: A Study of Courtroom Interaction," *Crime and Delinquency*, 12 (October 1966), pp. 318–331; Ronald Goldfarb, *Ransom: A Critique of the American Bail System* (New York: Harper & Row, 1965).

17. Charles E. Ares, Anne Rankin, and Herbert Sturz, "The Manhattan Bail Project: An Interim Report on the Use of Pre-Trial Parole," *New York University Law Review*, 38 (January 1963), pp. 67–95.

18. See Donald J. Newman, *Conviction: The Determination of Guilt or Innocence Without Trial* (Boston: Little, Brown, 1966), pp. 3–4.

19. Ibid., p. 77.

20. Donald J. Newman, "Pleading Guilty for Considerations: A Study of Bargain Justice," *Journal of Criminal Law, Criminology and Police Science*, 46 (March-April, 1956), pp. 780–790.

21. Ibid., p. 787.

22. *The New York Times*, January 20, 1973, p. 32.

23. George F. Cole, "The Decision to Prosecute," *Law and Society Review*, 4 (February 1970), p. 342.

24. Ibid., p. 338.

25. David Sudnow, "Normal Crimes: Sociological Features of the Penal Code in a Public Defender Office," *Social Problems*, 12 (Winter 1965), pp. 255–276.

26. Ibid., pp. 258–259.

27. Newman, *Conviction*, pp. 67–75, 105–130, 177–187.

28. Ibid., pp. 152–172, 188–196.

29. Blumberg, *Criminal Justice*, p. 65.

30. John B. Jennings, *The Flow of Arrested Adult Defendants through the Manhattan Criminal Court in 1968 and 1969* (New York: New York City Rand Institute, 1971), pp. 8–14.

31. On proposals for New York State and New York City, see *The New York Times*, October 11, 1970, p. 1; October 18, 1970, p. 1; March

14, 1971, p. 1; April 30, 1971, p. 1; July 30, 1972, p. 1.

32. David Sternberg, "The New Radical-Criminal Trials: A Step Toward a Class-for-Itself in the American Proletariat?" *Science and Society*, 36 (Fall 1972), p. 295.

33. See Jerome H. Skolnick, "Social Control in the Adversary System," *Journal of Conflict Resolution*, 11 (March 1967), pp. 52–70.

34. Albert P. Blaustein and Charles O. Porter, *The American Lawyer: A Summary of the Survey of the Legal Profession* (Chicago: University of Chicago Press, 1954), pp. 64–96.

35. Differences in the outcomes of criminal cases according to type of legal representation are reported in Lee Silverstein, *Defense of the Poor in Criminal Cases* (Chicago: American Bar Foundation, 1965); Dallin H. Oaks and Warren Lehman, "Lawyers for the Poor," *Transaction*, 4 (July-August, 1967), pp. 25–29; Laura Banfield and C. David Anderson, "Continuances in the Cook County Criminal Courts," *University of Chicago Law Review*, 35 (Winter 1968), pp. 259–316. Differences in juvenile cases are reported in Edwin M. Lemert, "Legislating Change in the Juvenile Court," *Wisconsin Law Review* (Spring 1967), pp. 421–448.

36. Jerome E. Carlin and Jon Howard, "Legal Representation and Class Justice," *UCLA Law Review*, 12 (January 1965), pp. 382–383.

37. Jerome E. Carlin, *Lawyers' Ethics: A Survey of the New York City Bar* (New York: Russell Sage Foundation, 1966), pp. 71–73.

38. Jerome E. Carlin, Jon Howard, and Sheldon L. Messinger, "Civil Justice and the Poor: Issues for Sociological Research," *Law and Society Review*, 1 (November 1966), p. 56.

39. 1958 Supplement to *Lawyers in the United States: Distribution and Income* (Chicago: American Bar Foundation, 1959), pp. 54–55.

40. Jack Ladinsky, "Careers of Lawyers, Law Practice, and Legal Institutions," *American Sociological Review*, 28 (February 1963), pp. 47–54.

41. Jerome E. Carlin, *Lawyers on Their Own: A Study of Individual Practitioners in Chicago* (New Brunswick, N.J.: Rutgers University Press, 1962), pp. 17–18.

42. Ibid., pp. 105–106.

43. Arthur Lewis Wood, *Criminal Lawyer* (New Haven: College & University Press, 1967), pp. 34–67.

44. Ibid., p. 238.

45. Anthony Platt and Randi Pollock, "Channeling Lawyers: The Careers of Public Defenders," *Issues in Criminology*, 9 (Spring 1974), p. 27.

46. Carlin, *Lawyers' Ethics*, pp. 165–182.

47. Wood, *Criminal Lawyer*, p. 93.

48. Abraham S. Blumberg, "The Practice of Law as Confidence Game: Organizational Cooptation of a Profession," *Law and Society Review*, 1 (June 1967), pp. 15–39.

49. Robert E. Knowlton, "The Trial of Offenders," *Annals of the American Academy of Political and Social Science*, 339 (January 1962), pp. 125–141.

50. Edwin M. Schur, "Scientific Method and the Criminal-Trial Decision," *Social Research*, 25 (Summer 1958), p. 178.

51. Jerome Frank, *Courts on Trial: Myth and Reality in American Justice* (Princeton: Princeton University Press, 1950), pp. 80–102.

52. Robert M. Emerson, *Judging Delinquents: Context and Process in Juvenile Court* (Chicago: Aldine, 1969), p. 192.

53. Arnold S. Trebach, *The Rationing of Justice* (New Brunswick, N.J.: Rutgers University Press, 1964), pp. 172–173.

54. See Rudolph E. Morris, "Witness Performance Under Stress: A Sociological Approach," *Journal of Social Issues*, 13 (November 2, 1957), pp. 17–22; Israel Gerver, "The Social Psychology of Witness Behavior with Special Reference to Criminal Courts," *Journal of Social Issues*, 13 (November 2, 1957), pp. 23–29.

55. Seymour L. Halleck, "A Critique of Current Psychiatric Roles in the Legal Process," *Wisconsin Law Review* (Spring 1966), pp. 379–401. Also see Abraham S. Goldstein, *The Insanity Defense* (New Haven: Yale University Press, 1967).

56. Thomas S. Szasz, *Psychiatric Justice* (New York: Macmillan, 1965), pp. 85–143.

57. *The Washington Post*, April 13, 1971, p. 1.

58. *The New York Times*, March 19, 1973, p. 1.

59. Alan M. Dershowitz, "The Real Issue is 'Free Will,'" *The New York Times*, March 25, 1973, p. E6.

60. Harry Kalven, Jr., and Hans Zeisel, *The American Jury* (Boston: Little, Brown, 1966), p. 13. A survey of research on juries is found in Howard S. Erlanger, "Jury Research in America: Its Past and Future," *Law and Society Review*, 4 (February 1970), pp. 345–370.

61. Ibid., pp. 14–17.

62. Ibid., pp. 19–30.

63. Ibid., pp. 31–32.

64. W. S. Robinson, "Bias, Probability, and Trial by Jury," *American Sociological Review*, 15 (February 1950), pp. 73–78.

65. Fred L. Strodtbeck, Rita M. James, and Charles Hawkins, "Social Status in Jury Deliberations," *American Sociological Review*, 22 (December 1957), pp. 713–719.

66. William Bevan, Robert S. Albert, Pierre R. Loiseaux, Peter N. Mayfield, and George Wright, "Jury Behavior as a Function of the Prestige of the Foreman and the Nature of His Leadership," *Journal of Public Law*, 7 (Fall 1958), pp. 419–449.

67. Strodtbeck, James, and Hawkins, "Social Status in Jury Deliberations," pp. 713–719; also see Fred L. Strodtbeck and Richard D. Mann, "Sex Role Differentiation in Jury Deliberations," *Sociometry*, 19 (March 1956), pp. 3–11.

68. Rita M. James, "Status and Competence of Jurors," *American Journal of Sociology*, 64 (May 1959), pp. 536–570.

69. Rita James Simon, *The Jury and the Defense of Insanity* (Boston: Little, Brown, 1967), pp. 98–119.

70. Kalven and Zeisel, *The American Jury*, especially pp. 55–65.

71. See Paul W. Tappan, "Sentencing Under the Model Penal Code," *Law and Contemporary Problems*, 23 (Summer 1958), pp. 528–543.

72. Robert M. Carter and Leslie T. Wilkins, "Some Factors in Sentencing Policy," *Journal of Criminal Law, Criminology and Police Science*, 58 (December 1967), pp. 503–514. Also see Robert M. Carter, "The Presentence Report and the Decision-Making Process," *Journal of Research in Crime and Delinquency*, 4 (July 1967), pp. 203–211; Trebach, *The Rationing of Justice*, pp. 178–187.

73. On the statutory framework for sentencing, see the President's Commission on Law Enforcement and Administration of Justice, *Task Force Report: The Courts* (Washington, D.C.: U.S. Government Printing Office, 1967), pp. 14–18.

74. Edward Green, *Judicial Attitudes in Sentencing* (London: Macmillan, 1961).

75. Frederick J. Gaudet, "The Difference Between Judges in Granting Sentences of Probation," *Temple Law Quarterly*, 19 (April 1946), pp. 471–484; Frederick J. Gaudet, "Individual Differences in Sentencing Tendencies of Judges," *Archives of Psychology*, 32 (1938); Frederick J. Gaudet, G. S. Harris, and C. W. St. John, "Individual Differences in Penitentiary Sentences Given by Different Judges," *Journal of Applied Psychology*, 8 (October 1934), pp. 675–680.

76. Stuart S. Nagel, "Judicial Backgrounds and Criminal Cases," *Journal of Criminal Law, Criminology and Police Science*, 53 (September 1962), pp. 333–339.

77. Carter and Wilkins, "Some Factors in Sentencing Policy," pp. 512–513.

78. Terence P. Thornberry, "Race, Socioeconomic Status and Sentencing in the Juvenile Justice System," *Journal of Criminal Law and Criminology*, 64 (March 1973), pp. 90–98.

79. Ibid., pp. 95–98.

80. Also see Theodore G. Chiricos, Phillip D. Jackson, and Gordon P. Waldo, "Inequality in the Imposition of a Criminal Label," *Social Problems*, 19 (Spring 1972), pp. 553–572; Frank R. Scarpitti and Richard M. Stephenson, "Juvenile Court Dispositions: Factors in the Decision-Making Process," *Crime and Delinquency*, 17 (April 1971), pp. 142–151.

12   Custody and Punishment

1. American Friends Service Committee, *Struggle for Justice: A Report on Crime and Punishment in America* (New York: Hill & Wang, 1971), p. 22.

2. David J. Rothman, *The Discovery of Asylum: Social Order and Disorder in the New Republic* (Boston: Little, Brown, 1971), p. xviii.

3. See Lawrence E. Hazelrigg, ed., *Prison Within Society* (New York: Doubleday, 1968).

4. Jack Rosenthal, "Jail Census Finds 52% Not Convicted," *The New York Times*, January 7, 1971, p. 1.

5. Erik Olin Wright, *The Politics of Punishment: A Critical Analysis of Prisons in America* (New York: Harper & Row, 1973), p. 26.

6. Ibid., pp. 31–32.

7. Ibid., pp. 33–34.

8. Gresham M. Sykes, *The Society of Captives: A Study of a Maximum Security Prison* (New York: Atheneum, 1965), p. 18.

9. See Erving Goffman, "On the Characteristics of Total Institutions," in Donald R. Cressey, ed., *The Prison: Studies in Institutional Organization and Change* (New York: Holt, Rinehart and Winston, 1961), pp. 15–106; Sykes, *The Society of Captives*, pp. 40–62.

10. Donald R. Cressey, "Limitations on Organization of Treatment in the Modern Prison," in Richard A. Cloward et al., *Theoretical Studies in Social Organization of the Prison* (New York: Social Science Research Council, 1960), pp. 79–80.

11. Lloyd E. Ohlin, "Conflicting Interests in Correction Objectives," in Cloward et al., *Theoretical Studies in Social Organization of the Prison*, pp. 111–129.

12. Donald R. Cressy, "Prison Organizations," in James G. March, ed., *Handbook of Organizations* (Chicago: Rand McNally, 1965), p. 1044. Also see Richard McCleary, "Communication Patterns as Bases of Systems of Authority and Power," in Cloward et al., *Theoretical Studies in Social Organization of the Prison*, pp. 49–77.

13. Sykes, *The Society of Captives*, pp. 63–83.

14. Ibid., p. 82.

15. Gresham M. Sykes and Sheldon L. Messinger, "The Inmate Social System," in Cloward et al., *Theoretical Studies in Social Organization of the Prison*, pp. 5–9.

16. Sykes, *The Society of Captives*, pp. 84–108. For an excellent study of inmate roles in a women's prison, see Esther Heffernan, *Making It in Prison: The Square, the Cool, and the Life* (New York: John Wiley, 1972).

17. Donald Clemmer, *The Prison Community* (New York: Rinehart, 1940), pp. 294–320.

18. Stanton Wheeler, "Socialization in Correctional Communities," *American Sociological Review*, 26 (October 1961), pp. 697–712.

19. See, in particular, Peter G. Garabedian, "Social Roles and Processes of Socialization in the Prison Community," *Social Problems*, 11 (Fall 1963), pp. 139–152; Daniel Glaser, *The Effectiveness of a Prison and Parole System* (Indianapolis: Bobbs-Merrill, 1964), pp. 548–583; Charles Wellford, "Factors Associated with Adoption of the Inmate Code: A Study of Normative Socialization," *Journal of Criminal Law, Criminology and Police Science*, 58 (June 1967), pp. 197–203; Charles W. Thomas, "Prisonization or Resocialization? A Study of External Factors Associated with the Impact of Imprisonment," *Journal of Research in Crime and Delinquency*, 10 (January 1973), pp. 13–21.

20. David Street, "The Inmate Group in Custodial and Treatment Settings," *American Sociological Review*, 30 (February 1965), pp. 40–55.

21. Gresham M. Sykes, "The Corruption of Authority and Rehabilitation," *Social Forces*, 34 (March 1956), pp. 257–262.

22. Eugene Czajkoski, "Exposing the Quasi-Judicial Role of the Probation Officer," *Federal Probation*, 37 (September 1973), p. 13.

23. Ibid., p. 11.

24. Lloyd E. Ohlin, *Sociology and the Field of Corrections* (New York: Russell Sage Foundation, 1956), p. 45.

25. See Lloyd E. Ohlin, Herman Piven, and Donnell M. Pappenfort, "Major Dilemmas of the Social Worker in Probation and Parole," *National Probation and Parole Journal*, 11 (July 1956), pp. 211–225; Dale E. Van Lanengham, Merlin Taber, and Rita Dimants, "How Adult Probation Officers View Their Job Responsibilities," *Crime and Delinquency*, 12 (April 1966), pp. 97–108; Seymour Z. Gross, "Biographical Characteristics of Juvenile Probation Officers," *Crime and Delinquency*, 12 (April 1966), pp. 109–116.

26. Ohlin, *Sociology and the Field of Corrections*, p. 47.

27. Ronald B. Sklar, "Law and Practice in Probation and Parole Revocation Hearings," *Journal of Criminal Law, Criminology and Police Science*, 55 (June 1964), pp. 175–198.

28. John P. Reed and Charles E. King, "Factors in the Decision-Making of North Carolina Probation Officers," *Journal of Research in Crime and Delinquency*, 3 (July 1966), pp. 120–128.

29. Bureau of Prisons, U.S. Department of Justice, "Prisoners in State and Federal Institutions for Adult Felons," *National Prisoner Statistics Bulletin*, No. 47 (April 1972), p. 6.

30. Information on parole boards, and recent trends in decision-making, is contained in Vincent O'Leary and Joan Nuffield, "A National Survey of Parole Decision-Making," *Crime and Delinquency*, 19 (July 1973), pp. 378–393.

31. President's Commission on Law Enforcement and Administration of Justice, *The Challenge of Crime in a Free Society* (Washington, D.C.: U.S. Government Printing Office, 1967), p. 12.

32. Some information on parole-board decisions is found in Don M. Gottfredson and Kelley B. Ballard, Jr., "Differences in Decisions Associated with Decision Makers," *Journal of Research in Crime and Delinquency*, 3 (July 1966), pp. 112–119.

33. President's Commission on Law Enforcement and Administration of Justice, *Task Force Report: Corrections* (Washington, D.C.: U.S. Government Printing Office, 1967), p. 187.

34. Considerable research has been done on the violation of parole and parole prediction, primarily on the parolee's characteristics and behavior. See, for example, Dean V. Babst, Don M. Gottfredson, and Kelley B. Ballard, Jr., "Comparison of Multiple Regression and Configural Analysis Techniques for Developing Base Expectancy Tables," *Journal of Research in Crime and Delinquency*, 5 (January 1968), pp. 72–80; Daniel Glaser, "A Reconsideration of Some Parole Prediction Factors," *American Sociological Review*, 19 (June 1954), pp. 335–341; Lloyd E. Ohlin, *Selection for Parole: A Manual of Parole Prediction* (New York: Russell Sage Foundation, 1951); Jerome H. Skolnick, "Toward a Developmental Theory of Parole," *American Sociological Review*, 25 (August 1960), pp. 542–549. For a discussion of some of the problems and issues in parole prediction, see Charles W. Dean and Thomas J. Duggan, "Problems in Parole Prediction: A Historical Analysis," *Social Problems*, 15 (Spring 1968), pp. 450–459.

35. John Irwin, *The Felon* (Englewood Cliffs, N.J.: Prentice-Hall, 1970), pp. 155–156.

36. Ibid., pp. 156–157.

37. Elmer H. Johnson, "The Parole Supervisor in the Role of Stranger," *Journal of Criminal Law, Criminology and Police Science*, 50 (May-June, 1969), pp. 38–43. Research on role conflicts in the organization of parole is found in Paul Takagi, "Administrative and Professional Conflicts in Modern Corrections," *Journal of Criminal Law and Criminology*, 64 (September 1973), pp. 313–319; Paul Takagi and James Robison, "The Parole Violator: An Organizational Report," *Journal of Research in Crime and Delinquency*, 6 (January 1969), pp. 78–86; Rodney Kingsnorth, "Decision-Making in a Parole Bureaucracy," *Journal of Research in Crime and Delinquency*, 6 (July 1969), pp. 210–218.

38. Glaser, *The Effectiveness of a Prison and Parole System*, pp. 429–442. Further research on

parole-officer orientations toward parole decisions is reported in Richard Dembo, "Orientation and Activities of the Parole Officer," *Criminology*, 10 (August 1972), pp. 193–215.

39. Bureau of Prisons, United States Department of Justice, "Capital Punishment, 1930–1970," *National Prisoner Statistics Bulletin*, No. 46 (August 1971), p. 2.

40. See Robert H. Finkel, "A Survey of Capital Offenses," in Thorsten Sellin, ed., *Capital Punishment* (New York, Harper & Row, 1967), pp. 22–31; Leonard D. Savitz, "Capital Crimes as Defined in American Statutory Law," *Journal of Criminal Law, Criminology and Police Science*, 46 (September-October, 1955), pp. 355–363.

41. Hugo Adam Bedua, "Introduction: The Laws, the Crimes, and the Executions," in Hugo Adam Bedua, ed., *The Death Penalty in America* (Garden City, N.Y.: Doubleday, 1964), p. 35.

42. Bureau of Prisons, "Capital Punishment, 1930–1970," p. 8.

43. Solie M. Ringold, "The Dynamics of Executive Clemency," in Sellin, ed., *Capital Punishment*, p. 227.

44. See Elkan Abramowitz and David Paget, "Executive Clemency in Capital Cases," *New York University Law Review*, 39 (January 1964), pp. 136–189.

45. Elmer H. Johnson, "Selective Factors in Capital Punishment," *Social Forces*, 36 (December 1957), pp. 165–169.

46. Marvin E. Wolfgang, Arlene Kelly, and Hans C. Nolde, "Comparison of the Executed and the Commuted Among Admissions to Death Row," *Journal of Criminal Law, Criminology and Police Science*, 53 (September 1962), pp. 301–311.

47. Ibid., p. 311.

48. William J. Bowers, *Executions in America: Discrimination and Deterrence and an Inventory of 5,769 State-Imposed Executions* (Lexington, Mass.: Lexington Books, 1974); Marvin E. Wolfgang and Marc Riedel, "Race, Judicial Discretion, and the Death Penalty," *Annals of the American Academy of Political and Social Science*, 407 (May 1973), pp. 119–133.

49. See Hans Mattick, *The Unexamined Death* (Chicago: World Correctional Center for Community and Social Concerns, 1972). Also Frank E. Hartung, "Trends in the Use of Capital Punishment," *Annals of the American Academy of Political and Social Science*, 284 (November 1952), pp. 8–19; Leonard D. Savitz, "A Study in Capital Punishment," *Journal of Criminal Law, Criminology and Police Science*, 49 (December 1958), pp. 338–341; Karl F. Schuessler, "The Deterrent Influence of the Death Penalty," *Annals of the American Academy of Political and Social Science*, 284

(November 1952), pp. 54–62; Thorsten Sellin, "Capital Punishment," *Federal Probation*, 15 (September 1961), pp. 3–11; Thorsten Sellin, *The Death Penalty* (Philadelphia: American Law Institute, 1959).

50. Herbert B. Ehrmann, "The Death Penalty and the Administration of Justice," *Annals of the American Academy of Political and Social Science*, 284 (November 1952), pp. 73–84.

51. See Edwin H. Sutherland and Donald R. Cressey, *Criminology*, 8th ed. (Philadelphia: Lippincott, 1970), pp. 335–336.

52. 408 U.S. 238 (1972).

53. "Capital Punishment After Furman," *Journal of Criminal Law and Criminology*, 64 (September 1973), pp. 281–289.

54. Warren Weaver, Jr., "President Asks Law to Restore Death Penalty," *The New York Times*, March 11, 1973, p. 1.

55. Thorsten Sellin, "The Inevitable End of Capital Punishment," in Sellin, ed., *Capital Punishment*, p. 253.

56. See President's Commission on Law Enforcement and Administration of Justice, *Task Force Report: Corrections*, pp. 82–92; Mirjan R. Damaska, "Adverse Legal Consequences of Conviction and Their Removal: A Comparative Study," *Journal of Criminal Law, Criminology and Police Science*, 59 (September 1968), pp. 347–360, and 59 (December 1968), pp. 542–568.

57. David F. Greenberg and Fay Stender, "The Prison as a Lawless Agency," *Buffalo Law Review*, 21 (Spring 1972), p. 806.

58. Donald R. Cressey, in the foreword to Donald Clemmer, *The Prison Community* (New York: Holt, Rinehart and Winston, 1958), p. ix.

13   Treatment and Corrections

1. American Friends Service Committee, *Struggle for Justice: A Report on Crime and Punishment in America* (New York: Hill & Wang, 1971), pp. 34–47; Francis A. Allen, "Criminal Justice, Legal Values and the Rehabilitative Ideal," *Journal of Criminal Law, Criminology and Police Science*, 50 (September-October, 1959), pp. 226–232; Robert Martinson, "The Age of Treatment: Some Implications of the Custody-Treatment Dimension," *Issues in Criminology*, 2 (Fall 1966), pp. 275–293. For a discussion about infringement on constitutional and civil rights of prisoners who are made to participate in therapy programs, see David Sternberg, "Legal Frontiers in Prison Group Psychotherapy," *Journal of Criminal Law, Criminology and Police Science*, 56 (December 1965), pp. 446–449.

2. Jessica Mitford, *Kind and Usual Punishment: The Prison Business* (New York: Alfred A. Knopf, 1973), p. 97.

3. See Gene G. Kassebaum, David A. Ward, Daniel M. Wilner, and Will C. Kennedy, "Job Related Differences in Staff Attitudes Toward Treatment in a Women's Prison," *Pacific Sociological Review*, 5 (Fall 1962), pp. 83–88; Joseph C. Mouledoux, "Organizational Goals and Structural Change: A Study of the Organization of a Prison System," *Social Forces*, 41 (March 1963), pp. 283–290; George H. Weber, "Conflicts Between Professional and Non-Professional Personnel in Institutional Delinquency Treatment," *Journal of Criminal Law, Criminology and Police Science*, 48 (June 1957), pp. 26–43; Stanton Wheeler, "Role Conflict in Correctional Communities," in Donald R. Cressey, ed., *The Prison: Studies in Institutional Organization and Change* (New York: Holt, Rinehart and Winston, 1961), pp. 229–259; Mayer N. Zald, "Power Balance and Staff Conflict in Correctional Institutions," *Administrative Science Quarterly*, 7 (June 1962), pp. 22–49.

4. Irving Piliavin, "The Reduction of Custodian-Professional Conflict in Correctional Institutions," *Crime and Delinquency*, 12 (April 1966), pp. 125–134.

5. See Daniel Glaser and John R. Stratton, "Measuring Inmate Change in Prison," in Cressey, ed., *The Prison*, pp. 381–392; Clarence Schrag, "A Preliminary Criminal Typology," *Pacific Sociological Review*, 4 (Spring 1961), pp. 11–16; Charles R. Tittle and Drollene P. Tittle, "Structural Handicaps to Therapeutic Participation: A Case Study," *Social Problems*, 13 (Summer 1965), pp. 75–82.

6. David Street, Robert D. Vinter, and Charles Perrow, *Organization for Treatment* (New York: Free Press, 1966). Also see Mayer N. Zald, "Organization Control Structures in Five Correctional Institutions," *American Journal of Sociology*, 68 (November 1962), pp. 335–345.

7. Bernard B. Berk, "Organizational Goals and Inmate Organization," *American Journal of Sociology*, 71 (March 1966), pp. 522–534. Also see David Street, "The Inmate Group in Custodial and Treatment Settings," *American Sociological Review*, 30 (February 1956), pp. 40–55; Richard M. Stephenson and Frank R. Scarpitti, "Argot in a Therapeutic Correctional Milieu," *Social Problems*, 15 (Winter 1968), pp. 384–395.

8. The theoretical background of the "group-relations principle" is discussed in Donald R. Cressey, "Social Psychological Foundations for Using Criminals in the Rehabilitation of Criminals," *Journal of Research in Crime and Delinquency*, 2 (July 1965), pp. 49–59. For a discussion of specific programs, see Lloyd W. McCorkle, "Group Therapy in the Treatment of Offenders," *Federal Probation*, 16 (December 1952), pp. 22–27; Lloyd W. McCorkle and

Richard Korn, "Resocialization Within Walls," *Annals of the American Academy of Political and Social Science*, 293 (May 1954), pp. 88–98. For an evaluation of group therapy programs, see Karl A. Slarkeu, "Group Treatment of Juvenile and Adult Offenders in Correctional Institutions," *Journal of Research in Crime and Delinquency*, 10 (January 1973), pp. 87–100.

9. Marshall B. Clinard, *Sociology of Deviant Behavior*, 3rd ed. (New York: Holt, Rinehart and Winston, 1968), p. 792.

10. Daniel Glaser, *The Effectiveness of a Prison and Parole System* (Indianapolis: Bobbs-Merrill, 1964), pp. 13–35.

11. Ibid., pp. 475–487.

12. Ibid., pp. 13–35.

13. George B. Vold, *Theoretical Criminology* (New York: Oxford University Press, 1958), pp. 296–304.

14. Don C. Gibbons, *Changing the Lawbreaker: The Treatment of Delinquents and Criminals* (Englewood Cliffs, N.J.: Prentice-Hall, 1965), pp. 228–282. Also see Daniel Glaser, *Adult Crime and Social Policy* (Englewood Cliffs, N.J.: Prentice-Hall, 1972), pp. 27–66.

15. Donald R. Cressey, "The Nature and Effectiveness of Correctional Techniques," *Law and Contemporary Problems*, 23 (Autumn 1958), p. 758.

16. Glaser, *The Effectiveness of a Prison and Parole System*, pp. 487–496.

17. Edwin Powers and Helen L. Witmer, *An Experiment in the Prevention of Delinquency — the Cambridge-Somerville Youth Study* (New York: Columbia University Press, 1951).

18. Joan and William McCord, "A Follow-up Report on the Cambridge-Somerville Youth Study," *Annals of the American Academy of Political and Social Science*, 322 (March 1959), pp. 89–96.

19. Paul L. Crawford, Daniel I. Malamud, and James R. Dumpson, *Working with Teen-Age Gangs* (New York: Welfare Council of New York City, 1950).

20. New York City Youth Board, *Reaching the Fighting Gang* (New York: New York City Youth Board, 1960).

21. James F. Short, Jr., and Fred L. Strodtbeck, *Group Process and Gang Delinquency* (Chicago: University of Chicago Press, 1965). For a description and analysis of other juvenile delinquency projects, see John R. Stratton and Robert M. Terry, eds., *Prevention of Delinquency: Problems and Programs* (New York: Macmillan, 1968). A residential treatment facility within a community is described in Lamar T. Empey and Jerome Rabow, "The Provo Experiment in Delinquency Rehabilitation," *American Sociological Review*, 26 (October 1961), pp. 679–695.

22. Malcolm W. Klein, *Street Gangs and Street*

Workers (Englewood Cliffs, N.J.: Prentice-Hall, 1971).

23. Walter B. Miller, "Preventive Work with Street-Corner Groups: Boston Delinquency Project," *Annals of the American Academy of Political and Social Science*, 322 (March 1959), pp. 97–106.

24. Walter B. Miller, "The Impact of a 'Total-Community Delinquency Control Project,'" *Social Problems*, 10 (Fall 1962), pp. 168–191.

25. Walter B. Miller, "Inter-Institutional Conflict as a Major Impediment to Delinquency Prevention," *Human Organization*, 17 (Fall 1958), pp. 20–23. Further documentation on the groups involved in delinquency prevention is found in Robert M. MacIver, *The Prevention and Control of Delinquency* (New York: Atherton Press, 1966). Conflict between agencies in a New York community, in relation to drug programs, is described in Clayton A. Hartjen and Richard Quinney, "Social Reality of the Drug Problem: New York's Lower East Side," *Human Organization*, 30 (Winter 1971), pp. 381–391.

26. Solomon Kobrin, "The Chicago Area Project —A 25-Year Assessment," *Annals of the American Academy of Political and Social Science*, 322 (March 1959), pp. 12–29.

27. Clifford R. Shaw and Jesse A. Jacobs, "The Chicago Area Project: An Experimental Community Program for Prevention of Delinquency in Chicago" (Chicago: Institute for Juvenile Research, undated). Quoted in Clinard, *Sociology of Deviant Behavior*, p. 738.

28. Kobrin, "The Chicago Area Project — A 25-Year Assessment"; Anthony Sorrentino, "The Chicago Area Project After 25 Years," *Federal Probation*, 23 (June 1959), pp. 40–45; Helen L. Witmer and Edith Tufts, *The Effectiveness of Delinquency Prevention Programs*, U.S. Children's Bureau Publication No. 350 (Washington, D.C.: U.S. Government Printing Office, 1954), pp. 11–17.

29. The community development approach has since been expanded and applied in the Delhi Project, by Marshall B. Clinard, *Slums and Community Development: Experiments in Self-Help* (New York: Free Press, 1966).

30. Saul D. Alinsky, *Reveille for Radicals* (Chicago: University of Chicago Press, 1946).

31. Edwin H. Sutherland and Donald R. Cressey, *Principles of Criminology*, 7th ed. (Philadelphia: J. B. Lippincott, 1967), p. 697.

32. Richard A. Cloward and Lloyd E. Ohlin, *Delinquency and Opportunity: A Theory of Delinquent Gangs* (New York: Free Press, 1960).

33. *Action on the Lower East Side*, Program Report: July, 1962–January, 1964 (New York: Mobilization for Youth, 1964).

34. Quoted in Murray Kempton, "When You Mobilize the Poor," *The New Republic* (December 5, 1964), p. 12.

35. Richard A. Cloward and Richard M. Elman, "Advocacy in the Ghetto," *Transaction*, 4 (December 1966), p. 33. Also see Richard A. Cloward and Frances Fox Piven, "The Weight of the Poor: A Strategy to End Poverty," *The Nation* (May 2, 1966), pp. 510–517.

36. See, for example, Oliver J. Keller, Jr., and Benedict S. Alper, *Halfway Houses: Community-Centered Correction and Treatment* (Lexington, Mass.: Lexington Books, 1970); President's Commission on Law Enforcement and Administration of Justice, *Task Force Report: Corrections* (Washington, D.C.: U.S. Government Printing Office, 1967), pp. 38–44; Roberta Rovner-Preczenik, *The First Decade of Experience: A Synthesis of Manpower R & D Projects in Criminal Justice and Corrections, 1963–1973* (Cambridge, Mass.: Criminal Justice Research, 1973).

37. Saleem A. Shah, foreword to Marguerite Q. Warren, *Correctional Treatment in Community Settings: A Report of Current Research* (Rockville, Md.: National Institute of Mental Health, 1972), p. iii.

38. "Future Role of the U.S. Bureau of Prisons," *Hearings* before the Subcommittee on National Penitentiaries of the Committee on the Judiciary, United States Senate, 92nd Congress (Washington, D.C.: U.S. Government Printing Office, 1971). The President's Commission on Law Enforcement and Administration of Justice strongly recommended community-based corrections as an alternative to imprisonment — see Elmer K. Nelson, Jr., "Community-Based Correctional Treatment: Rationale and Problems," *Annals of the American Academy of Political and Social Science*, 374 (November 1967), pp. 82–91.

39. Shah, foreword to Warren, *Correctional Treatment in Community Settings*, p. iii.

40. Bertram S. Griggs and Gary R. McCune, "Community-Based Correctional Programs: A Survey and Analysis," *Federal Probation*, 36 (June 1972), pp. 7–13.

41. Some of the specific programs are described in *Community Based Correctional Programs: Models and Practices* (Rockville, Md.: National Institute of Mental Health, 1971).

42. Ibid., p. 3.

43. Daniel Glaser, "Correction of Adult Offenders in the Community," in Lloyd E. Ohlin, ed., *Prisoners in America* (Englewood Cliffs, N.J.: Prentice-Hall, 1973), p. 116.

44. *Community Based Correctional Programs*, pp. 33–34.

45. Perry London, "Behavior Control," in *Crimes of Violence*, vol. 12, A Staff Report Submitted to the National Commission on the Causes and Prevention of Violence, Donald J. Mulvi-

hill and Melvin M. Tumin, Co-Directors (Washington, D.C.: U.S. Government Printing Office, 1969), p. 1374.

46. Ralph K. Schwitzgebel, *Development and Legal Regulation of Coercive Behavior Modification Techniques with Offenders* (Rockville, Md.: National Institute of Mental Health, 1971), p. 5.

47. C. Ray Jeffery, *Crime Prevention Through Environmental Design* (Beverly Hills, Calif.: Sage Publications, 1971), p. 276.

48. Ibid., p. 278.

49. Barton L. Ingraham and Gerald W. Smith, "The Use of Electronics in the Observation and Control of Human Behavior and Its Possible Use in Rehabilitation and Parole," *Issues in Criminology*, 7 (Fall 1972), p. 35.

50. Ralph K. Schwitzgebel, "Development of an Electronic Rehabilitation System for Parolees," *Law and Computer Technology*, 2 (1969), pp. 9–12; Ralph K. Schwitzgebel, "Behavioral Supervision System with Wrist Carried Transceiver," United States Patent Office, Washington, D.C., No. 3, 478, 344, November 11, 1969.

51. R. S. Mackay, "Radiotelemetering from Within the Body," *Science*, 134 (1961), p. 1196.

52. Ingraham and Smith, "The Use of Electronics in the Observation and Control of Human Behavior and Its Possible Use in Rehabilitation and Parole," p. 43.

53. See Mitford, *Kind and Usual Punishment*, pp. 95–137. Further documentation is cited in Chicago Peoples Law Office, "Check Out Your Mind: Behavior Modification, Experimentation and Control in Prison," *Chicago Connections Newsletter*, Supplement No. 1, n.d., p. 4.

54. See Lee Edson, "The Psyche and the Surgeon," *The New York Times Magazine*, (September 30, 1973), pp. 14ff.; Chicago Peoples Law Office, "Check Out Your Mind," pp. 4–5.

55. Chicago Peoples Law Office, "Check Out Your Mind," p. 1. Some of my discussion follows this source.

56. Edgar H. Schein, "Man Against Man: Brainwashing," *Correctional Psychiatry and Journal of Social Therapy*, 8 (No. 2, 1962), pp. 91–92.

57. Quoted from Federal Prisoner's Coalition, "The Mind Police," *Penal Digest International*, 2 (August 1972), pp. 4–5; "Manifesto of Dehumanization: Neo-Nazism," *Penal Digest International*, 2 (August 1972), pp. 8–10.

58. Quoted in Chicago Peoples Law Office, "Check Out Your Mind," p. 1.

59. Quoted in Mitford, *Kind and Usual Punishment*, p. 123.

60. "Operations Memorandum," Bureau of Prisons, Washington, D.C., October 25, 1972.

61. "Federal Coalition Protects Bureau's New START Program," *Prisoners' Digest International*, 2 (January 1973), p. 3.

62. Chicago Peoples Law Office, "Check Out Your Mind," p. 3.

63. Ibid., p. 4.

64. *Diversion from the Criminal Justice System* (Rockville, Md.: National Institute of Mental Health, 1971), p. 3.

65. Ibid., p. 1.

66. Elizabeth W. Vorenberg and James Vorenberg, "Early Diversion from the Criminal Justice System: Practice in Search of a Theory," in Ohlin, ed., *Prisoners in America*, p. 154.

67. Ibid., p. 183.

68. Norval Morris and Gordon Hawkins, *The Honest Politician's Guide to Crime Control* (Chicago: University of Chicago Press, 1970), p. 2.

69. See, for example, Edwin H. Schur, *Crimes Without Victims: Deviant Behavior and Public Policy* (Englewood Cliffs, N.J.: Prentice-Hall, 1965).

70. Sanford H. Kadish, "The Crisis of Overcriminalization," *Annals of the American Academy of Political and Social Science*, 374 (November 1967), p. 157. Also see Herbert L. Packer, *The Limits of the Criminal Sanction* (Stanford, Calif.: Stanford University Press, 1968). The effect of legalization (and decriminalization) is analyzed in Austin T. Turk, *Legal Sanctioning and Social Control* (Rockville, Md.: National Institute of Mental Health, 1972).

71. This issue is considered in Gilbert Geis, *Not the Law's Business? An Examination of Homosexuality, Abortion, Prostitution, Narcotics and Gambling in the United States* (Rockville, Md.: National Institute of Mental Health, 1972).

72. *Diversion from the Criminal Justice System*, p. 8. For a critique of some of the civil procedures, see Thomas S. Szasz, *Law, Liberty and Psychiatry: An Inquiry into the Social Uses of Mental Health Practices* (New York: Macmillan, 1963).

73. *Civil Commitment of Special Categories of Offenders* (Rockville, Md.: National Institute of Mental Health, 1971), p. 11.

14   Social Reaction to Crime

1. See Alexander L. Clark and Jack P. Gibbs, "Social Control: A Reformulation," *Social Problems*, 12 (Spring 1965), pp. 402–406; Jack P. Gibbs, "Sanctions," *Social Problems*, 14 (Fall 1966), pp. 152–154.

2. See Richard D. Schwartz and Jerome H. Skolnick, "Two Studies of Legal Stigma," *Social Problems*, 10 (Fall 1962), pp. 133–142.

3. On varied social reactions toward homosexuals, see John I. Kitsuse, "Societal Reaction to Deviant Behavior: Problems of Theory and

Method," *Social Problems*, 9 (Winter 1962), p. 256.

4. Torgny T. Segerstedt, "A Research into the General Sense of Justice," *Theoria*, 15 (1949), pp. 323–338; Frederick Beutel, *Some Potentialities of Experimental Jurisprudence as a New Branch of Social Science* (Lincoln: University of Nebraska Press, 1957).

5. Terence Morris, "The Social Toleration of Crime," in Hugh J. Klare, ed., *Changing Concepts of Crime and Its Treatment* (Oxford: Pergamon Press, 1966), pp. 33–34.

6. Kai T. Erikson, *Wayward Puritans: A Study in the Sociology of Deviance* (New York: John Wiley, 1966).

7. Ibid., pp. 196–197.

8. Ibid., pp. 204–205.

9. F. J. Davis, "Crime News in Colorado Newspapers," *American Journal of Sociology*, 57 (January 1952), pp. 325–330.

10. Much of the research is reviewed in Joseph T. Klapper, *The Effects of Mass Communications* (New York: Free Press of Glencoe, 1960), pp. 135–165.

11. See Alfred Friendly and Ronald L. Goldfarb, *Crime and Publicity: The Impact of News on the Administration of Justice* (New York: Vintage Books, 1968).

12. See Elihu Katz, "The Two-Step Flow of Communication: An Up-to-Date Report of an Hypothesis," *Public Opinion Quarterly*, 21 (Spring 1957), pp. 61–78; John W. Riley, Jr., and Mathilda White Riley, "Mass Communications and the Social System," in Robert K. Merton, Leonard Broom, and Leonard S. Cottrell, Jr., eds., *Sociology Today* (New York: Basic Books, 1959), pp. 537–578; Everett M. Rogers, *Diffusion of Innovations* (New York: Free Press of Glencoe, 1962), pp. 57–75, 208–253.

13. Herbert Blumer and Philip Hauser, *Movies, Delinquency, and Crime* (New York: Macmillan, 1933).

14. See Richard Quinney, *Critique of Legal Order: Crime Control in Capitalist Society* (Boston: Little, Brown, 1974), pp. 155–162.

15. The concept of social type is from Orrin E. Klapp, *Heroes, Villains, and Fools* (Englewood Cliffs, N.J.: Prentice-Hall, 1962), pp. 1–24.

16. J. L. Simmons, "Public Stereotypes of Deviants," *Social Problems*, 13 (Fall 1965), pp. 223–232.

17. Ibid., p. 229. Research on reactions to the *appearance* of deviants is reported in Darrell J. Steffensmeier and Robert M. Terry, "Deviance and Respectability: An Observational Study of Reactions to Shoplifting," *Social Forces*, 51 (June 1973), pp. 417–426.

18. Klapp, *Heroes, Villains, and Fools*, pp. 50–67.

19. Ibid., p. 50.

20. Ibid., pp. 145–146. Also see Nathan Hare,

"The Ambivalent Public and Crime," *Crime and Delinquency*, 9 (April 1963), pp. 145–151.

21. "Story of the Bad Little Boy," in *The Complete Short Stories of Mark Twain*, Charles Neider, ed. (New York: Bantam Books, 1957), pp. 8–9.

22. Klapp, *Heroes, Villains, and Fools*, p. 146.

23. Ibid., p. 147.

24. "Pretty Boy Floyd," *American Folksong, Woody Guthrie*, Moses Asch, ed. (New York: Oak Publications, 1961), p. 27.

25. See Martin Maloney, "A Grammar of Assassination," *Etc.*, 11 (Winter 1954), pp. 83–95.

26. See Christopher Hibbert, *The Roots of Evil: A Social History of Crime and Punishment* (Harmondsworth, Eng.: Penguin Books, 1966), pp. 302–314.

27. Albert Goldman, "Elegant Narcissist," *The New York Times Book Review*, December 11, 1966, p. 36, a review of John Pearson, *The Life of Ian Fleming* (New York: McGraw-Hill, 1966). Also see Lycurgus M. Starkey, Jr., *James Bond's World Values* (Nashville, Tenn.: Abingdon Press, 1966).

28. Quoted in Hibbert, *The Roots of Evil*, p. 311 (originally from *Time*, October 1959). Also see Melvin L. De Fleur, "Occupational Roles as Portrayed on Television," *Public Opinion Quarterly*, 28 (Spring 1964), pp. 57–74.

29. See Yale Kamisar, "When the Cops Were Not 'Handcuffed,'" *The New York Times Magazine*, November 7, 1965, p. 34.

30. Roscoe Pound and Felix Frankfurter, eds., *Criminal Justice in Cleveland* (Cleveland: The Cleveland Foundation, 1922).

31. See Ralph G. Murdy, *Crime Commission Handbook* (Baltimore: Criminal Justice Commission, 1965), pp. 12–35. Also E. Connor, "Crime Commissions and Criminal Procedure in the United States since 1920," *Journal of Criminal Law, Criminology and Police Science*, 21 (May 1930), pp. 129–144; Allen Eaton, *A Bibliography of Social Surveys* (New York: Russell Sage Foundation, 1930); A. F. Kuhlman, ed., *A Guide to Material on Crime and Criminal Justice* (New York: H. W. Wilson, 1929); Virgil Peterson, *Crime Commissions in the United States* (Chicago: Chicago Crime Commission, 1945).

32. William B. Northrop, *The Insolence of Office — the Story of the Seabury Investigations* (New York: G. P. Putnam's Sons, 1932), p. 54.

33. Missouri Association for Criminal Justice, *The Missouri Crime Survey* (New York: Macmillan, 1926).

34. Illinois Association for Criminal Justice, *The Illinois Crime Survey* (Chicago: Illinois Association for Criminal Justice, 1929); Wayne Morris and Ronald H. Beattie, *Survey of the Administration of Justice* (Eugene: University of Oregon Press, 1932).

35. On the political nature of government commissions, see Anthony Platt, "The Politics of Riot Commissions, 1917–1970," in Anthony Platt, ed., *The Politics of Riot Commissions* (New York: Macmillan, 1971), pp. 3–43.

36. See especially National Commission on Law Observance and Enforcement, *Report on the Enforcement of the Prohibition Laws of the United States* (Washington, D.C.: U.S. Government Printing Office, 1931).

37. President Lyndon B. Johnson, Message to the Congress, March 9, 1966.

38. President's Commission on Law Enforcement and Administration of Justice, *The Challenge of Crime in a Free Society* (Washington, D.C.: U.S. Government Printing Office, 1967).

39. See Isidor Silver, "Crime and Punishment," *Commentary*, 45 (March 1968), pp. 68–73; Isidor Silver, "Introduction," *The Challenge of Crime in a Free Society* (New York: Avon, 1968), pp. 17–36.

40. President's Commission on Law Enforcement and Administration of Justice, *The Challenge of Crime in a Free Society*, p. vi.

41. Herbert L. Packer, "Copping Out," *New York Review of Books*, 9 (October 12, 1967), pp. 17–20.

42. Frank F. Furstenberg, Jr., "Public Reaction to Crime in the Streets," *The American Scholar*, 40 (Autumn 1971), pp. 601–602.

43. President's Commission on Law Enforcement and Administration of Justice, *The Challenge of Crime in a Free Society*, p. 49.

44. See President's Commission on Law Enforcement and Administration of Justice, "Public Attitudes Toward Crime and Law Enforcement," *Crime and Its Impact — An Assessment* (Washington, D.C.: U.S. Government Printing Office, 1967), pp. 85–95.

45. *The Washington Post*, January 16, 1973, p. A3.

46. President's Commission on Law Enforcement and Administration of Justice, *Crime and Its Impact — An Assessment*, p. 88.

47. *The New York Times*, April 23, 1972, p. 23.

48. George Gallup, "U.S. Public Gives Police Big Vote of Confidence," *The Gallup Report* (Princeton, N.J.: American Institute of Public Opinion, August 30, 1967).

49. Phillip H. Ennis, *Criminal Victimization in the United States: A Report of a National Survey*, President's Commission on Law Enforcement and Administration of Justice, Field Surveys II (Washington, D.C.: U.S. Government Printing Office, 1967), pp. 52–72. Also see Phillip H. Ennis, "Crime, Victims, and the Police," *Transaction*, 4 (June 1967), pp. 36–44.

50. Albert D. Biderman, Louise A. Johnson, Jennie McIntyre, and Adrianne Weis, *Report on a Pilot Study in the District of Columbia on Victimization and Attitudes Toward Law Enforcement*, President's Commission on Law Enforcement and Administration of Justice, Field Surveys I (Washington, D.C.: U.S. Government Printing Office, 1967), pp. 144–149.

51. Ennis, *Criminal Victimization in the United States*, pp. 58–60.

52. *The Washington Post*, January 16, 1973, p. A3.

53. *The New York Times*, February 16, 1969, p. 47.

54. Louis Harris and Associates, *The Public Looks at Crime and Corrections* (Washington, D.C.: Joint Commission on Correctional Manpower and Training, 1968), pp. 11–12.

55. Research on public attitudes toward crime control is found in John E. Conklin, "Criminal Environment and Support for the Law," *Law and Society Review*, 5 (November 1971), pp. 247–265; Sarah L. Boggs, "Formal and Informal Crime Control: An Exploratory Study of Urban, Suburban, and Rural Orientations," *Sociological Quarterly*, 12 (Summer 1971), pp. 319–327; Jennie McIntyre, "Public Attitudes Toward Crime and Law Enforcement," *Annals of the American Academy of Political and Social Science*, 374 (November 1967), pp. 41–44; Don C. Gibbons, "Crime and Punishment: A Study in Social Attitudes," *Social Forces*, 47 (June 1969), pp. 391–397.

56. Ibid., pp. 7–9.

57. George Gallup, "Opposition to the Death Penalty Continues to Mount," *The Gallup Poll* (Princeton, N.J.: American Institute of Public Opinion, July 1, 1966).

58. *The New York Times*, November 26, 1972, p. E3.

59. This is argued in Quinney, *Critique of Legal Order*, pp. 154–155.

60. "Crime Control Projects for Citizens and Their Organizations" (New York: National Council on Crime and Delinquency, 1968), p. 4.

15   A Political Economy of Crime

1. Richard F. Sullivan, "The Economics of Crime: An Introduction to the Literature," *Crime and Delinquency*, 19 (April 1973), p. 139.

2. Gary S. Becker, "Crime and Punishment: An Economic Approach," *Journal of Political Economy*, 76 (March-April 1968), p. 176.

3. Sullivan, "The Economics of Crime: An Introduction to the Literature," p. 138. The orthodox economics is applied to crime prevention in Llad Phillips and Harold L. Votey, Jr., "An Economic Analysis of the Deterrent Effect of Law Enforcement on Criminal Activity," *Journal of Criminal Law, Criminology and Police Science*, 63 (September 1972), pp. 330–342.

4. David M. Gordon, "Capitalism, Class, and Crime in America," *Crime and Delinquency*, 19 (April 1973), p. 173.

5. Willem Bonger, the Belgian sociologist, is often credited with applying a Marxist analysis to crime, emphasizing the relation of economic privation to criminal behavior. Although providing a beginning, Bonger greatly simplified and misconceived the Marxian dialectic in an economic analysis of crime. See Willem Bonger, *Criminality and Economic Conditions*, abridged with an introduction by Austin T. Turk (Bloomington, Ind.: Indiana University Press, 1969).

6. Karl Marx, *Selected Writings in Sociology and Social Philosophy*, trans. by T. B. Bottomore (New York: McGraw-Hill, 1956), p. 159.

7. Ibid., pp. 158–159.

8. President's Commission on Law Enforcement and Administration of Justice, *Crime and Its Impact — An Assessment* (Washington, D.C.: U.S. Government Printing Office, 1967), pp. 43–53.

9. Ibid., pp. 54–55.

10. *U.S. News & World Report*, October 26, 1970, p. 30.

11. Morris Cobern, "Some Aspects of the Criminal Justice System," *Crime and Delinquency*, 19 (April 1973), p. 189.

12. Ibid., p. 192.

13. Ibid., pp. 196–197.

14. This theory was originally presented in Richard Quinney, "Crime Control in Capitalist Society: A Critical Philosophy of Legal Order," *Issues in Criminology*, 8 (Spring 1973), pp. 75–99. The theory is developed, with supporting research, in my book *Critique of Legal Order: Crime Control in Capitalist Society* (Boston: Little, Brown, 1974).

15. Ralph Miliband, *The State in Capitalist Society* (New York: Basic Books, 1969), p. 16. For a discussion of the need for further historical, class analysis of Miliband's theory, see Isaac Balbus, "Ruling Elite Theory vs. Marxist Class Analysis," *Monthly Review*, 23 (May 1971), pp. 36–46.

16. Isaac D. Balbus, "The Concept of Interest in Pluralist and Marxian Analysis," *Politics and Society*, 1 (February 1971), pp. 151–177.

17. David Horowitz, *Empire and Revolution: A Radical Interpretation of Contemporary History* (New York: Random House, 1969).

18. William Appleman Williams, *The Roots of the Modern American Empire* (New York: Random House, 1969).

19. Miliband, *The State in Capitalist Society*, p. 49.

20. Ibid., pp. 49–55.

21. Ibid., p. 54.

22. Ibid., pp. 66–67.

23. Frederick Engels, *The Origin of the Family, Private Property, and the State* (New York: International Publishers, 1942), p. 97.

24. Ibid., p. 156.

25. Horowitz, *Empire and Revolution*, pp. 257–258.

16   Crime Control and the Future of American Society

1. Portions of this chapter are adapted from my book *Critique of Legal Order: Crime Control in Capitalist Society* (Boston: Little, Brown, 1974), pp. 119–135, 187–188, 192, 195–196.

2. Jeff Gerth, "The Americanization of 1984," *SunDance*, 1 (April-May 1972), pp. 64–65.

3. President's Commission on Law Enforcement and Administration of Justice, *The Challenge of Crime in a Free Society* (Washington, D.C.: U.S. Government Printing Office, 1967), p. 245.

4. *Science and Technology*, Task Force Report of the President's Commission on Law Enforcement and Administration of Justice, Prepared by the Institute for Defense Analyses (Washington, D.C.: U.S. Government Printing Office, 1967), p. 1.

5. Ibid.

6. Ibid., p. 2.

7. "Controlling Crime Through More Effective Law Enforcement," *Hearings* Before the Subcommittee on Criminal Laws and Procedures of the Committee on the Judiciary, United States Senate, 90th Congress (Washington, D.C.: U.S. Government Printing Office, 1967), pp. 1070–1071.

8. Ibid., p. 1071.

9. *LEAA*, 3rd Annual Report of the Law Enforcement Assistance Administration, Fiscal Year 1971 (Washington, D.C.: U.S. Government Printing Office, 1972), pp. 269–377.

10. Gerth, "The Americanization of 1984," p. 59.

11. See Joseph C. Goulden, "Tooling Up for Repression: The Cops Hit the Jackpot," *The Nation*, 211 (November 23, 1970), pp. 520–533; and Gerth, "The Americanization of 1984," pp. 60–61. Also see Lawyers' Committee for Civil Rights Under Law, *Law and Disorder III: State and Federal Performance Under Title I of the Omnibus Crime Control and Safe Streets Act of 1968* (Washington, D.C., 1973).

12. Michael Sorkin, "The FBI's Big Brother Computer," *The Washington Monthly*, 4 (September 1972), p. 24.

13. Senator Sam J. Ervin, Jr., as quoted in Goulden, "Tooling Up for Repression," p. 528. Also see "Federal Data Banks, Computers and the Bill of Rights," *Hearings* Before the Subcommittee on Constitutional Rights of the Committee on the Judiciary, Part I, United States Senate, 92nd Congress (Washington, D.C.: U.S. Government Printing Office, 1971).

14. Vince Pinto, "Weapons for the Homefront," in National Action/Research on the Military-Industrial Complex, *Police on the Homefront* (Philadelphia: American Friends Service Committee, 1971), p. 74.

15. Alfred Blumstein, "Science and Technology for Law Enforcement: Prospects and Problems," *The Police Chief*, 36 (December 1969), p. 61.

16. Ralph Miliband, *The State in Capitalist Society* (New York: Basic Books, 1969), pp. 271–272.

17. Ibid., p. 272.

18. Bertram Gross, "Friendly Fascism, A Model for America," *Social Policy*, 1 (November-December 1970), p. 46.

19. Ibid., p. 47.

20. Ibid., p. 48.

Index to Names

Index to Subjects